The Composition of Everyday Life

A Guide to Writing | CONCISE | Sixth Edition

John Mauk
Miami University

John Metz
Kent State University
at Geauga

CENGAGE

Australia • Brazil • Mexico • Singapore • United Kingdom • United States

***The Composition of Everyday Life:
A Guide to Writing,*** **Concise
Sixth Edition
John Mauk, John Metz**

Product Manager: Laura Ross

Senior Content Developer: Kathy
Sands-Boehmer

Product Assistant: Shelby Nathanson

Senior Marketing Manager: Kina Lara

Content Project Manager:
Fola Orekoya

Manufacturing Planner:
Betsy Donaghey

IP Analyst: Ann Hoffman

IP Project Manager: Betsy Hathaway

Production Service/Compositor:
MPS Limited

Senior Art Director: Marissa Falco

Text Designer: Deborah Dutton

Cover Designer: Deborah Dutton

Cover Image: shaineast/
Shutterstock.com

For product information and technology assistance, contact us at
Cengage Customer & Sales Support, 1-800-354-9706.

For permission to use material from this text or product, submit
all requests online at **www.cengage.com/permissions.**
Further permissions questions can be emailed to
permissionrequest@cengage.com.

Library of Congress Control Number: 2017942693

Student Edition:
ISBN: 978-1-337-55608-8

Loose-leaf Edition:
ISBN: 978-1-337-55609-5

Cengage
20 Channel Center Street
Boston, MA 02210
USA

Cengage is a leading provider of customized learning
solutions with employees residing in nearly 40 different
countries and sales in more than 125 countries around
the world. Find your local representative at
www.cengage.com.

Cengage products are represented in Canada
by Nelson Education, Ltd.

To learn more about Cengage platforms and services, visit
www.cengage.com.

To register or access your online learning solution
or purchase materials for your course, visit
www.cengagebrain.com.

Printed in Mexico
Print Number: 04   Print Year: 2018

Brief Contents

MINDTAP
From Cengage
Online Chapter

MINDTAP
From Cengage
Online Chapter

Contents

Chapter 4 Observing   92

Chapter 5 Analyzing Concepts   122

Chapter 10 Evaluating   298

INTRODUCTION   299

READINGS   301

INVENTION   317

Chapter 11 Searching for Causes   332

INTRODUCTION   333

READINGS   335

Chapter 12   Proposing Solutions   364

Chapter 19 Vitalizing Sentences   552

MINDTAP
From Cengage
Online Chapter

Chapter 20 Anthology: Everyday Rhetoric

Remembering Who You Were
"A Beat Education" *Leonard Kress*
"The Grapes of Mrs. Rath " *Steve Mockensturm*
Explaining Relationships
"What the Honey Meant " *Cindy Bosley*
"Dog-Tied " *David Hawes*
Observing
"Onward, Gamers, Onward!" *Royce Flores*
"The Farm on the Hill" *Evan Proudfoot*
Analyzing Concepts
"Why We No Longer Use the "H" Word" *Dan Wilkins*
"This Is What a Feminist Looks Like" *Barack Obama*

∴∴ MINDTAP
From Cengage
Online Chapter

Chapter 21: Rhetorical Handbook

Using *The Composition of Everyday Life* as a Thematic Reader

Here we suggest how readings from different chapters might be grouped together thematically. As you explore a subject (education and learning, for example), you might focus on a particular rhetorical aim (such as evaluating or proposing a solution). Or you might explore a subject area without an aim in mind, eventually discovering a specific topic and rhetorical aim.

EDUCATION AND LEARNING

Are students customers? What is the practical value of studying great works of literature? Is school too easy? The following essays explore the complexity of education and learning. Through reading, writing, and discussion, you might explore and come to think differently about education and its role in people's lives. You might discover an important point about education by exploring a memory, a relationship, an observation, a concept, and so on.

"Living Like Weasels," *Annie Dillard* (4)

"The Default Setting: An Analysis of David Foster Wallace," *Adrienne Carr* (6)

"Entitlement Education," *Daniel Bruno* (9)

"Have It Your Way: Consumerism Invades Education," *Simon Benlow* (9)

"The Power of Failure: J.K. Rowling's 2008 Harvard Commencement Speech," *Liz Winhover* (9)

"Is Google Making Us Stupid?" *Nicholas Carr* (11)

"Infomania," *Manoush Zomorodi* (12)

"Your Kids Bored at School? Tell Them to Get Over It," *Laura Hanby Hudgens* (12)

"The Grapes of Mrs. Rath," *Steve Mockensturm* (20)

"A Beat Education," *Leonard Kress* (20)

"Internet Addiction," *Greg Beato* (20)

"Not Homeschooling? What's Your Excuse?" *Tricia Smith Vaughan* (20)

JUSTICE AND EQUALITY

A quick survey of the readings about justice and equality suggests a range of areas: immigration, Native American rights, body type, the mentally and physically challenged, wildlife, and so on. These readings can help you identify and explain a relationship, analyze a concept (such as "justice" or "equality"), respond to an argument, identify a cause, propose a solution, and so on. What is justice, and how might exploring the concept of justice in today's world be of value? What revelatory idea about justice and equality might you discover and share with others?

"How I Lost the Junior Miss Pageant," *Cindy Bosley* (2)

"Americans and the Land," *John Steinbeck* (3)

"Cruelty, Civility, and Other Weighty Matters," *Ann Marie Paulin* (8)

"Important and Flawed," *Kareem Abdul-Jabbar* (10)

"*Star Trek:* Where No Man Has Gone Before," *Jaren Provo* (10)

"Why Are Millennials Weak?" *Quinn Greenwell* (11)

"Unemployed, and Working Hard," Simon Wykoff (13)

"Why We No Longer Use the 'H' Word," *Dan Wilkins* (20)

"This Is What a Feminist Looks Like," *Barack Obama* (20)

"Crimes Against Humanity," *Ward Churchill* (20)

"Not Homeschooling? What's Your Excuse?" *Tricia Smith Vaughan* (20)

"An Apology to Future Generations," *Simon Benlow* (20)

ENVIRONMENT AND ANIMALS

These readings, which offer different ways of looking at the environment and animals, encourage you to explore ideas beyond conventional beliefs. What is your relationship to the land? To the air? To the animals? How might you think differently about that relationship? And what might be the consequence of your new way of thinking?

"Americans and the Land," *John Steinbeck* (3)

"Living Like Weasels," *Annie Dillard* (4)

"The Front Porch," *Chester McCovey* (4)

"Why 'Natural' Doesn't Mean Anything Anymore," *Michael Pollan* (5)

"The Dog Delusion," *April Pedersen* (8)

"Hive Talkin': The Buzz around Town about Bees," *Teresa Scollon* (8)

"Dog-Tied," *David Hawes* (20)

"The Farm on the Hill," *Evan Proudfoot* (20)

"Trees Please," *Michael Rust* (20)

"An Apology to Future Generations," *Simon Benlow* (20)

CONSUMERISM AND ECONOMY

Several readings in this book suggest some fundamental questions about consumerism: What and how do you consume? And what, if anything, do you produce by consuming? As with other subjects in *The Composition of Everyday Life,* you might spend an entire semester exploring this area, or you might explore it for just one assignment. It could be of great value to spend a semester exploring just one question: What does it mean to be a consumer?

"Selling Manure," *Bonnie Jo Campbell* (2)

"Mugged," *Jim Crockett* (3)

"To Fish and Be Fished: A Tinder-fied Game of Love," *Kellie Coppola* (3)

"The Front Porch," *Chester McCovey* (4)

"Why 'Natural' Doesn't Mean Anything Anymore," *Michael Pollan* (5)

"The Real, the Bad, and the Ugly, " *Cassie Heidecker* (5)

"Rise of the Image Culture: Re-Imagining the American Dream," *Elizabeth Thoman* (7)

"Have It Your Way: Consumerism Invades Education," *Simon Benlow* (9)

"Is Google Making Us Stupid?" *Nicholas Carr* (11)

"Why We Binge Watch Television," *Kevin Fallon* (11)

"Build the Wall," *Ed Bell* (13)

"American Consumerism," *Jamie Bentley* (20)

"An Apology to Future Generations," *Simon Benlow* (20)

AMERICA

These readings deal with America and being American. They allow you to explore the relationship between yourself and your country. (International students may find this subject to be especially interesting as they bring a unique perspective to the topic.) To what degree do the two—individual and country—influence each other? You can make observations, evaluate, identify causes, propose solutions, and so on. And, you can explore how America communicates with and influences you.

"Americans and the Land," *John Steinbeck* (3)

"Rise of the Image Culture: Re-Imagining the American Dream," *Elizabeth Thoman* (7)

"Talibanned," *Benjamin Busch* (10)

"Build the Wall," *Ed Bell* (13)

"The Grapes of Mrs. Rath," *Steve Mockensturm* (20)

"Cartoons 'n Comics: Communication to the Quick," *Joy Clough* (20)

"Protests with the Mostest: The Art of Opposition with Protest Signs," *Deanna Krokos* (20)

"Crimes Against Humanity," *Ward Churchill* (20)

"Military Fraud: The Myth of Automatic Virtue," *Steve Gillman* (20)

"American Consumerism," *Jamie Bentley* (20)

"Reverence for Food," *Rachel Schofield* (20)

"Not Homeschooling? What's Your Excuse?" *Tricia Smith Vaughan* (20)

"An Apology to Future Generations," *Simon Benlow* (20)

SELF

Readings in this book encourage you to explore your own life in a way you have perhaps not done before. These readings about self go beyond expressive writing. They encourage you to connect with others, even though—or perhaps *especially when*—you are looking inward at yourself. You can explore how these readings, your own writing, and focused discussion with others helps you to see differently—to learn something about yourself and connect it to the world around you.

"Selling Manure," *Bonnie Jo Campbell* (2)

"How I Lost the Junior Miss Pageant," *Cindy Bosley* (2)

"Thrill of Victory . . . The Agony of Parents," *Jennifer Schwind-Pawlak* (2)

"Mugged," *Jim Crockett* (3)

"Black Like I Thought I Was," *Erin Aubry Kaplan* (5)

"Cruelty, Civility, and Other Weighty Matters," *Ann Marie Paulin* (8)

"Celibate Passion," *Kathleen Norris* (13)

"What the Honey Meant," *Cindy Bosley* (20)

"This Is What a Feminist Looks Like," *Barack Obama* (20)

"American Consumerism," *Jamie Bentley* (20)

OTHERS (COMMUNITY)

Can we look at ourselves without looking at our community? Both subjects (self and others) explore relationships between an individual and his or her surroundings. What is community? How is community created? These readings will help you to explore what we commonly call *community,* to consider how it works, and to examine your place in it. An entire writing course might be an exploration of one very important question: What is the relationship between community and communication?

"The Front Porch," *Chester McCovey* (4)

"Cruelty, Civility, and Other Weighty Matters," *Ann Marie Paulin* (8)

"Hive Talkin': The Buzz around Town about Bees," *Teresa Scollon* (8)

"Different Jobs," *Dana Stewart* (12)

"Build the Wall," *Ed Bell* (13)

"Unemployed, and Working Hard," *Simon Wykoff* (13)

"The Farm on the Hill," *Evan Proudfoot* (20)

"Technology, Movement, and Sound," *Ed Bell* (20)

"An Apology to Future Generations," *Simon Benlow* (20)

LANGUAGE AND CULTURE

What is the relationship between language and culture? For example, how does the way that a group of people communicates affect their shared values, beliefs, customs, attitudes, and practices—and vice versa? (How, for example, does what a group values about education influence the way that group uses, and thinks about, language?) These readings and others will help you step back and explore the relationship between words, ideas, and actions. Through exploration of this subject, you might discover that your college writing class is something more than you had originally imagined it to be.

"The Real, the Bad, and the Ugly," *Cassie Heidecker* (5)

"Why 'Natural' Doesn't Mean Anything Anymore," *Michael Pollan* (5)

"The Default Setting: An Analysis of David Foster Wallace," *Adrienne Carr* (6)

"Politics and Audience: *The New York Times'* Appeal to Undecided Voters," Alison Block (6)

"Rise of the Image Culture: Re-Imagining the American Dream," *Elizabeth Thoman* (7)

"An Imperfect Reality," *Rebecca Hollingsworth* (7)

"Look on My Works: *Breaking Bad*'s Final Season Trailer," *Nick Fendinger* (7)

"The Power of Failure: J.K. Rowling's 2008 Harvard Commencement Speech*" Liz Winhover* (9)

"Why Are Millennials Weak?" *Quinn Greenwell* (11)

"Unemployed, and Working Hard," *Simon Wykoff* (13)

"Why We No Longer Use the 'H' Word," *Dan Wilkins* (20)

"This Is What a Feminist Looks Like," *Barack Obama* (20)

"Protests with the Mostest: The Art of Opposition with Protest Signs," *Deanna Krokos* (20)

"Cartoons 'n Comics: Communication to the Quick," *Joy Clough* (20)

"Crimes against Humanity," *Ward Churchill* (20)

GENDER AND IDENTITY

What does it mean to be male or female? How does gender affect our identities? What influence can we have on issues of gender and identity? This group of readings can be used in combination with other reading groups—from America or pop culture, for example. Instead of exploring just gender and identity, you might narrow your focus to readings that relate to gender and identity *and* pop culture.

"Selling Manure," *Bonnie Jo Campbell* (2)

"How I Lost the Junior Miss Pageant," *Cindy Bosley* (2)

"The Thrill of Victory . . . The Agony of Parents," *Jennifer Schwind-Pawlak* (2)

"To Fish and Be Fished: A Tinder-fied Game of Love," *Kellie Coppola* (3)

"Cruelty, Civility, and Other Weighty Matters," *Ann Marie Paulin* (8)

"Important and Flawed," *Kareem Abdul-Jabbar* (10)

"*Star Trek:* Where No Man Has Gone Before," *Jaren Provo* (10)

"Celibate Passion," *Kathleen Norris* (13)

"This Is What a Feminist Looks Like," *Barack Obama* (20)

"Are Female Long-Distance Runners More Prone to Suicidal Depression?" *Emily de la Bruyere* (20)

PARENTS AND FAMILY

What role do our parents play in our lives? Such a question might be explored endlessly with interesting results for both writer and readers. You might spend an entire semester exploring issues about parents and family. Such a simple subject area can prove to be far more complicated—and interesting—than you first imagined. What might be the value of thinking analytically and finding public resonance regarding the subject of parents and family?

"Selling Manure," *Bonnie Jo Campbell* (2)

"How I Lost the Junior Miss Pageant," *Cindy Bosley* (2)

"The Thrill of Victory . . . The Agony of Parents," *Jennifer Schwind-Pawlak* (2)

"The Front Porch," *Chester McCovey* (4)

"Black Like I Thought I Was," *Erin Aubry Kaplan* (5)

"The Dog Delusion," *April Pedersen* (8)

"Cruelty, Civility, and Other Weighty Matters," *Ann Marie Paulin* (8)

"Unemployed, and Working Hard," *Simon Wykoff* (13)

"What the Honey Meant," *Cindy Bosley* (20)

"American Consumerism," *Jamie Bentley* (20)

"An Apology to Future Generations," *Simon Benlow* (20)

POPULAR CULTURE

What is the relationship between an individual and his or her popular culture? In what ways are we products of our own pop culture? From beauty pageants to theme parks, these readings allow you to consider the world that surrounds you from a fresh perspective. You can explore the *why* of your own behavior, considering how you and others are influenced by pressures of which you are both very aware and barely aware.

"How I Lost the Junior Miss Pageant," *Cindy Bosley* (2)

"Tinder, You, Me," *Kellie Coppola* (3)

"The Front Porch," *Chester McCovey* (4)

"Why 'Natural' Doesn't Mean Anything Anymore," *Michael Pollan* (5)

"The Default Setting: An Analysis of David Foster Wallace," *Adrienne Carr* (6)

"Politics and Audience: *The New York Times'* Appeal to Undecided Voters," *Alison Block* (6)

"Rise of the Image Culture: Re-Imagining the American Dream," *Elizabeth Thoman* (7)

TECHNOLOGY

We cannot overlook technology. How does it influence the way we live? Through reading, writing, and discussion, you can explore beyond your initial thoughts and perceptions to consider the complex relationship in today's world between an individual and technology—or between one individual and another *because of technology*. What idea about technology might you discover and share with others, helping them to think or act differently?

Note to Instructors

Like most college writing instructors, we see English composition as a vital component of an academic career. Without a transformative composition experience, many college students will struggle, fumble, or worse. And beyond the college classroom, we see writing instruction as intimately connected to students' everyday lives. We believe that composition courses are not only preparation for more academic work but also a genuine study of one's own rhetorical situations. More specifically, we assume that student writing should do two things:

1. It should emerge from the discursive entanglements of students' everyday lives. Student writing is often stiffened by the popular-but-distant topics of the day: gun control, abortion, cloning, cell phone use, and so on. Of course, for some students, these topics intersect with everyday life, but for the vast majority, they are glorified encyclopedic preformulations. They offer no possibility for new connections, no possibility for radical rethinking, no hope for discovery, and no exigence whatsoever. They are dead. Therefore, we hope to offer a pedagogy that genuinely guides students into the tensions, cracks, and unseen notches of their own lives. Perhaps, then, they will see that this whole enterprise is worthy of the immense intellectual energy it requires.

2. It should prompt students to invent ideas. We believe the only reason to write an essay is to generate a better way of thinking about a topic. In professional academic work, essays are not written to prove grammatical prowess or syntactic proficiency, but to share an important new insight, to contribute to an ongoing conversation, to reveal an otherwise hidden position or viewpoint. In a composition course, it should be no different. And it's been our experience that classroom engagement increases dramatically when students understand this rhetorical mission.

Over the editions of this book, we've been asked: Why such focus on invention? What led us to place invention at the center of the pedagogy? Initially, this focus came from understanding our own students—from witnessing how they struggle, succeed, and fail. We asked ourselves some basic questions: What do we value but fail to teach explicitly? What do other writing instructors value and assess? What are the gaps between proficient high school writing and proficient college writing? What we discovered was a type of hidden curriculum. Instructors want revelation, discovery, depth, rigor, and intellectual richness. But such qualities are not taught explicitly and consistently at the high school level. Students entering college often lack the discursive tools for generating the richness and complexity that college composition instructors hope to see. Our conclusion: Students need specific guidance in developing that complexity.

As we looked closely at our students, we noticed that successful writers tend to:

- Start thinking about their topics and their own responses early on
- Turn ideas and positions around—investigating intellectual possibilities
- Rethink based on the values, assumptions, and claims of others
- Address and even envelop opposing ideas

In short, successful writers invent. They do what the classical rhetoricians taught: use language to explore what's possible.

Contrarily, unsuccessful writers skip invention. Their relationship with language is at best tentative—at worst, antagonistic. And they often carry some counterproductive notions about thinking and writing: ideas emerge fully formed from an individual's head; good writers do not struggle or rethink; the only way to develop an idea is by adding facts; an essay is good if it's properly arranged and grammatically correct. Such assumptions work against writers—even more than their unfamiliarity with grammatical conventions. Before they even begin a course or an assignment, these quiet notions stymie many students' foray into an intensive writerly experience.

With *The Composition of Everyday Life*, we hope to vitalize students' assumptions about writing, and to dramatize a simple but crucial point: Language is not merely a conduit for expression but a tool for developing ideas. We hope that students imagine writing as an act of public exploration, a process of inventing and sharing what can be thought, what can be said, what can be known. This book, then, is grounded in and driven by a set of principles that we've deemed *invention pedagogy*. It emerges not only from our understanding of students but also from the pre-Socratic Greek sophists—those folks who invented rhetoric (and the practice of democracy). The broader goal is to help students to develop increasingly sophisticated ideas. More specific goals are related to chapter sections:

Point of Contact sections encourage students to slow down and notice the nuances of life around them while considering possibilities for writing topics. The questions pull students away from stiff and distant topics and toward the real entanglements of their own lives.

Analysis sections help students develop meaning and significance while prompting them to explore their topics with questions and dialogic activities.

Public Resonance sections draw attention to the rhetorical situation—to the assumptions, values, and beliefs of others. Writers are prompted to explore what others believe and how the particular writing project can influence common belief.

Thesis sections in each invention chapter help students to hone their ideas to a fine edge. Each section contains prompts, sample thesis statements, common thesis problems, and "Evolution of a Thesis" subsection, which illustrates the gradual development of an idea.

Rhetorical Tools sections explain the support strategies that are most applicable and appropriate to the writing situation. The sections teach students that all rhetorical tools (such as narration, argumentative appeals, allusions, and so on) can be applied according to the writer's particular needs.

Revision sections suggest ways to work back through essay drafts, applying even more invention strategies. Each section also features chapter-specific questions for peer reviewers.

Reflection sections ask students to articulate ideas about how their essays work. These prompts get students writing about writing, dealing metacognitively with the particular intellectual maneuvers required/prompted in that chapter. Many of the "Reflection" sections also invite students to go "Beyond the Essay"—to take their ideas from the chapter and recast them in some other format: a poster, a cartoon, and so on.

As they work through the sections, students may feel their ideas getting more complex, even unwieldy. That's okay. In fact, if we are doing our jobs well, our students' thinking will likely get messier. But if we walk through the entire intellectual journey (that is, an assignment) with them, students may see their ideas regain focus. They may see assignments as intellectual pathways.

As all writers know, good ideas require intellectual grappling, occasional cognitive slippage, and plenty of revision. We think students at this point in history, in these economic and cultural times, must learn how to grapple and rethink. We cannot assume that such critical and nuanced skills will seep into student consciousness—that some lucky students will "pick up on" the most crucial discursive moves. If writing instructors value rigorous (*inventive, rich, deep, intensive, analytical, critical*) thinking, and if we reward it with a grade, then we owe students the tools for making it happen. We cannot simply provide interesting samples and expect them to extract the epistemology. If we value invention, we must teach students how to explore, how to unpack their initial thoughts, and how to persist beyond the commonplace.

A quick glance at the economy, labor relationships, world politics, and demographic shifts portends a new kind of literacy: people will need intellectual agility; they will have to think around topics, beyond themselves, beyond their initial assumptions, to simply get along in a fast-changing cultural landscape. Having an opinion and writing it neatly in five coherent paragraphs will be its own kind of illiteracy. Those who can only say what they think will get left behind. Those who can invent new intellectual postures for themselves and others will thrive.

NEW TO THIS EDITION

New Reading Selections: Fifteen new and diverse readings illustrate the rhetorical tools essential to inventive writing. The latest additions include widely celebrated writers such as Michael Pollan and Annie Dillard as well as some high-profile figures such as Kareem Abdul-Jabbar and Barack

Obama. In keeping with previous editions, this edition includes new student writing—vibrant analytical essays that show real students developing highly sophisticated and revelatory ideas.

Refined Invention Sections: As with each edition, the Invention sections in Chapters 2–13 have been refined to maximize students' engagement with the driving elements of the pedagogy: the Invention Questions. This time around, chapter sections guide students to the most (intellectually) energizing questions—those designed to move thinking forward.

Streamlined Chapter 1: Inventing Ideas: Because students in composition courses should get writing as quickly as possible, Chapter 1 has been streamlined. It focuses on the most critical elements, those necessary to help students' writing become more inventive, more connected to their everyday lives, and more resonant with the world around them.

Chapter Objectives: Each chapter now begins with specific learning objectives so teachers can better determine how the material will align with their curriculum.

Latest MLA Guidelines and Updated Research Papers: Chapter 16: Integrating and Documenting Sources includes the updated documentation guidelines put forth in the eighth edition of the *MLA Handbook* (2016). It also features revised and updated student essays in MLA and APA style.

KEY FEATURES

Emphasis on Invention: Unlike any other writing guide, *The Composition of Everyday Life* offers thirteen invention chapters, guiding students to be inventive thinkers and writers. In addition, "Point of Contact" sections encourage students to slow down and notice the nuances of life around them while considering possibilities for writing topics.

Step-by-step Invention Instruction: Included in each invention chapter, "Point of Contact" sections will help students discover a topic from everyday life. "Analysis" will launch them beyond initial thoughts and help explore the topic. "Public Resonance" will help students extend the topic outward, to make the topic relevant to a community of readers. "Thesis" will help you focus students' thinking and develop a revelatory point. "Rhetorical Tools" will help students support their point with a variety of common strategies.

Thorough Revision and Editing Coverage: "Peer Review" activities specific to each chapter as well as "Public Resonance" sections illustrate that writing is public in nature, and help students shape their writing for their audience. Adding an intensive editing step to the invention process, the new Chapter 19: Vitalizing Sentences explains and illustrates particular strategies for pruning, weeding, trimming, and giving life to students' writing.

Beyond the "Final" Draft: Prompting students into some theorizing about their own language and intellectual moves, the "Reflection" sections can help students transfer to other writing situations what they have learned while writing a single essay. These activities can also help students identify areas for revision toward a course portfolio.

Attractive Design in a Concise Package: *The Composition of Everyday Life* still offers the clean and elegant design students and instructors value, but the look and feel are lighter and more approachable.

INSTRUCTOR RESOURCES

MindTap® English for Mauk/Metz, *The Composition of Everyday Life, 6th edition* is the digital learning solution that powers students from memorization to mastery. It gives you complete control of your course—to provide engaging content, to challenge every individual, and to build their confidence. Empower students to accelerate their progress with MindTap. MindTap: Powered by You.

MindTap gives you complete ownership of your content and learning experience. Customize the interactive assignments, emphasize the most important topics, and add your own material or notes in the E-book.

- Interactive activities on grammar and mechanics promote application to student writing.

- An easy-to-use paper management system helps prevent plagiarism and allows for electronic submission, grading, and peer review.

- A vast database of scholarly sources with video tutorials and examples supports every step of the research process.

- A collection of vetted, curated student writing samples in various modes and documentation styles to use as flexible instructional tools.

- Professional tutoring guides students from rough drafts to polished writing.

- Visual analytics track student progress and engagement.

- Seamless integration into your campus learning management system keeps all your course materials in one place.

MindTap® English comes equipped with the diagnostic-guided JUST IN TIME PLUS learning module for foundational concepts and embedded course support. The module features scaffolded video tutorials, instructional text content, and auto-graded activities designed to address each student's specific needs for practice and support to succeed in college-level composition courses.

The Resources for Teaching folder provides support materials to facilitate an efficient course setup process focused around your instructional goals: The MindTap Planning Guide offers an inventory of MindTap activities correlated to common planning objectives, so that you can quickly determine what you need. The MindTap Syllabus offers an example of how these activities could be incorporated into a 16-week course schedule. The Instructor's Manual provides suggestions for additional activities and assignments.

MindTap® English for Mauk/Metz, *The Composition of Everyday Life, 6th edition* also includes the following book-specific features:

- Auto-graded quizzes for select readings in Chapters 2–13 provide quick comprehension checks to keep students on track.

- Rhetorical Handbook offers comprehensive coverage of grammar, punctuation, style, and usage. Available online only in MindTap.

MindTap for The Composition of Everyday Life
The MindTap version includes twenty-one chapters of E-book content—rhetoric, research guide, reader, and handbook and tools and resources to take advantage of digital affordances.
It can be paired with these print products:

The Composition of Everyday Life: A Guide to Writing, Brief Sixth Edition
The brief version of *The Composition of Everyday Life* includes twenty chapters, including the rhetoric, research guide and reader.

The Composition of Everyday Life: A Guide to Writing, Concise Sixth Edition
The concise version of *The Composition of Everyday Life* includes nineteen chapters, including the rhetoric and research guide.

Instructor's Manual
The instructor's manual for the sixth edition of *The Composition of Everyday Life* has been revised. Teaching tips, syllabus planning, and lesson organization are all included.

WPA Outcomes Correlation Guide
"Using *The Composition of Everyday Life: A Guide to Writing* to Meet WPA Outcomes" is a guide that clearly specifies the ways *The Composition of Everyday Life* supports the primary outcomes of the Council of Writing Program Administrators' (WPA) Outcomes Statement for First-Year Composition. It is included in the frontmatter of the book and also in the Resources for Teaching folder in MindTap.

Acknowledgments

A textbook is a big invention workshop, and we are fortunate to have extremely savvy collaborators. We offer our humble gratitude: to our development editor, Kathy Sands-Boehmer, for her ongoing support and good eyes; to Laura Ross for reinforcing the company's commitment to our work; to Rebecca Donahue for overseeing production; to Richard Camp for checking the style and soundness of every assertion; to Edward Dionne for deftly steering us through production; to the marketing crew at Cengage, who keep their radar on these editions; to Ann Hoffman and Betsy Hathaway for managing rights and permissions; and as always, to the intensive sales folks throughout the country who give arms and legs to our books.

Thanks also to our students and colleagues who graciously stumble along with us in our efforts to transcend what is and to invent what could be. Thanks to our families and friends for enduring yet another edition.

Any textbook project requires hearty professionals who give up their time and energy to help steer the pedagogy in valuable directions. We relied heavily on the insights of our reviewers and were often humbled at their prowess. We are indebted to the following teachers, theorists, rhetoricians, and scholars:

Carmen Amavizca, *Pima Community College*

Goretti Benca, *SUNY Ulster*

Susan Burris, *Owens Community College*

Richard Compean, *City College of San Francisco*

Denise Cosper, *Ferris State University*

Deborah M. Coulter-Harris, *University of Toledo*

Brianne Di Bacco, *University of Southern Indiana*

Suzanne Disheroon, *Cedar Valley College*

Kathleen Duguay, *East Stroudsberg University*

Leslie Jane Harrelson, *Dalton State College*

Sally Heymann, *Collin College*

Amanda Huber, *University of Detroit Mercy*

Anna Ingram, *Northeast Texas Community College*

Darlene Johnston, *Ohio Northern University*

Kim Lacey, *Saginaw Valley State University*

Amy Lerman, *Mesa Community College*

Melissa Lewis, *Davenport University*

Deborah Miller-Zournas, *Stark State College*

Arthur Orme, *Mott Community College*

Katherine Parr, *University of Illinois at Chicago*

Rosalie Petrouske, *Lansing Community College*

Jennifer Randall, *Dalton State University*

Garth Sabo, *Michigan State University*

Andrew Scott, *Ball State University*

Amy Shinabarger, *Arizona State University, Polytechnic Campus*

Henry Smiley, *Central Baptist College*

Suzanne Smith, *University of Toledo*, Ellen Sorg, *Owens Community College*

Maria Straton, *Ball State University*, Marie Trevino, *Lansing Community College*

Dale Uhlmann, *Stark State College of Technology;* and Lorna Valentine, *Diablo Valley College.*

Using *The Composition of Everyday Life: A Guide to Writing* to Meet WPA Outcomes (v3.0)

An Instructor's Guide

By Goretti Vianney-Benca
SUNY Ulster

Table of Contents

Using *The Composition of Everyday Life* to Meet WPA Outcomes (v3.0)

When the Council of Writing Program Administrators (WPA) first began discussing an outcomes statement for first-year writing, the goal was to help collegiate writing programs outline national expectations for students who have completed a first-year composition course. In addition to being a standard for assessment, it also outlined a set of common objectives to establish professional accountability for collegiate writing courses across the country. The five WPA outcomes draw attention to "common knowledge, skills, and attitudes" that are representative for students completing first-year composition courses.

The purpose of this instructor's manual is to highlight how *The Composition of Everyday Life* addresses these outcomes both in content and approach and to serve as a guide for instructors who are incorporating the WPA outcomes into their day-to-day teaching, assignment design, and course assessment practices. Different parts of the book speak to the outcomes in a unique way, lending flexibility to instructors using the book as an assessment tool.

WPA Outcomes	*The Composition of Everyday Life*
➤ Rhetorical Knowledge	✓ Chapters 1–13, 20
➤ Critical Thinking, Reading, and Writing	✓ Chapters 1–13, 14–15, 17, 20
➤ Processes	✓ Chapters 2–13, and 17–19
➤ Knowledge of Conventions	✓ Chapters 14–17, and 21 (online only)

The information that follows details the WPA outcomes and identifies assignments, readings, and class activities in *The Composition of Everyday Life* that may help you meet primary course goals. Lastly, it's worth noting that many of these outcomes overlap in effective writing assignments. So although suggestions are often linked to specific outcomes, they do not exist independently of any single outcome and are often appropriate for overall assessment of the WPA outcomes.

For a full copy of the WPA statement, visit: http://wpacouncil.org/positions/outcomes .html. The most current "WPA Outcomes Statement for First-Year Composition (v3.0)" was adopted on July 17, 2014.

The WPA and *The Composition of Everyday Life* Approach: A Quick-Start Guide

Suggestions for Assessing Rhetorical Knowledge

From the start, *The Composition of Everyday Life* sets the stage for a conversation about rhetoric that investigates why people write and how writers respond to this call based on the rhetorical situation.

Rhetorical Knowledge	*The Composition of Everyday Life*
By the end of first-year composition, students should • Learn and use key rhetorical concepts through analyzing and composing a variety of texts. • Gain experience reading and composing in several genres to understand how genre conventions shape and are shaped by readers' and writers' practices and purposes. • Develop facility in responding to a variety of situations and contexts calling for purposeful shifts in voice, tone, level of formality, design, medium, and/or structure. • Understand a variety of technologies to address a range of audiences. • Match the capacities of different environments (e.g., print and electronic) to varying rhetorical situations.	**Chapter 1:** ✓ In *CEL, invention* is more than finding a topic; it involves committing to an idea, exploring it in depth, and discovering its worth or resonance. Chapter 1 discusses how ideas come about, how they emerge from language, how they thicken and deepen through questioning and dialogue. It gives students the most direct and crucial element of *rhetorical knowledge*: an understanding that language is generative, that it makes ideas. ✓ Chapter 1 also emphasizes the importance of understanding the values and expectations of an *academic audience*, that is, the prevailing attitudes that instructors and peers bring to their writing. **Chapter 2–13:** ✓ Chapters 2–12 each focus on a different *purpose or aim of communication*—to narrate, explain, observe, analyze, argue, evaluate, and more. Students read professional and student selections that exemplify these different purposes and are asked to identify the rhetorical moves made by each writer. "Invention" sections then guide students through the process of creating compositions that exemplify these various purposes.

✓ The "Invention" sections of Chapter 2–13 include several components that focus on *key rhetorical concepts*:

- "Analysis"—encourages students to explore a topic with questions and dialogic activities. These sections also often include explanation of rhetorical concepts that students need to understand in order to effectively analyze.
- "Public Resonance"—invites students to consider their rhetorical situation, to analyze how people think about a topic, and discover a topic's worth or resonance
- "Rhetorical Tools"—reviews common strategies that students can use in their compositions. These sections teach students that all rhetorical tools (such as narration, argumentative appeals, allusions, and so on) can be applied according to the writer's particular needs.

✓ In a couple chapters, the "Invention" sections also include a spotlight on how to write in specific *genres*—the literacy narrative in Chapter 2, and an ethnography in Chapter 4.

✓ Each chapter ends with a "Beyond the Essay" assignment that invites students *to use and compose in various media and genres*—create a cover image for an essay, a conceptual map, a video briefing, and more.

Chapter 20:

✓ This "Anthology" chapter includes a broad variety of essays. These additional readings are framed by introductions and questions, so that students can read them critically and closely.

Individual Assessment: At the beginning of the term, challenge the students' basic rhetorical knowledge by assigning the students to find, read, and bring in to class an academic journal article (or you could provide one for the students). You can limit the scope to the theme of your course or to the students' majors. Ask the students to write a short summary of the article focusing on how the author's point of view is being conveyed. Ask the students to record whether or not the essay was effective in influencing their understanding of the topic and why/why not. This can be submitted to the instructor for feedback, shared with the rest of the class, or shared in small groups. By asking students to choose a piece of writing and to analyze the rhetorical situation, you will begin pushing them to work closely with a text to understand a writer's purpose and audience. Return to this assignment throughout the semester, adding new genres and different types of texts to the discussion. As a final project, ask students to write a rhetorical analysis essay. Students could use the Reflection section in Chapter 6 (page 185) as a guide. A sample prompt for a rhetorical analysis essay follows:

> After you've completed the final draft of your essay project, please develop a brief but intensive rhetorical analysis. In a two-page essay, describe the rhetorical moves in your argument: various support strategies, counterarguments, concessions, etc. The goal is not to re-argue your point or sum up your essay, but to describe the machinery of argument, to analyze its rhetoric.

Course Level Assessment: At the end of the term, students should showcase their work from throughout the semester in a portfolio; this can be an e-portfolio or a physical collection of their work. Ask students to write a letter introducing their portfolios and the work they've completed in various genres. The letter should craft an argument that addresses the objectives set forth in the Rhetorical Knowledge outcome, as well as reflect on what they have learned about composing for different purposes and in various genres. Students should use examples from their portfolios as evidence.

Suggestions for Assessing Critical Thinking, Reading, and Composing

Critical Thinking, Reading, and Writing	The Composition of Everyday Life
By the end of first-year composition, students should • Use composing and reading for inquiry, learning, critical thinking, and communicating in various rhetorical contexts.	**All Chapters:** ✓ If there is one point made most consistently in *CEL*, it is that *writing is a mode of thinking and learning.* From the first page to the last, *CEL* explains and models how specific, learnable, and deliberate discursive acts make ideas.

▪ Read a diverse range of texts, attending especially to relationships between assertion and evidence, to patterns of organization, to the interplay between verbal and nonverbal elements, and how these features function for different audiences and situations.	**Chapters 2–13:** ✓ Each of these chapters contains one auto-graded reading comprehension quiz in the MindTap program. **Chapters 2–13, 20:** ✓ The extensive "Invention" sections, the many professional and student readings and models, and the questions that accompany the readings in Chapters 2–13 all consistently emphasize the idea that *writing is an act of inquiry.* CEL helps students see that they can make their ideas more sophisticated by asking key questions, reflecting on their own claims, and inspecting their own language.
▪ Locate and evaluate (for credibility, sufficiency, accuracy, timeliness, bias, and so on) primary and secondary research materials, including journal articles and essays, books, scholarly and professionally established and maintained databases or archives, and informal electronic networks and Internet sources.	✓ In Chapters 2–13, "Reflection" sections encourage students to think about their own work and composing processes. These prompts get students writing about writing and practicing metacognition, with a focus on the intellectual maneuvers discussed in the chapter.
▪ Use strategies—such as interpretations, synthesis, response, critique, and design/redesign—to compose texts that integrate the writer's ideas with those from appropriate sources.	✓ In Chapters 2–13, the "Rhetorical Tools" discussion reviews key strategies that students can use to integrate others' ideas with their own. ✓ Students have opportunities to read selections that model various rhetorical purposes and genres in Chapters 2–13 and 20. These professional and student selections each include an introductory headnote and questions ("Writing Strategies," "Exploring Ideas," and "Ideas for Writing") that call attention to the development of ideas and the rhetorical moves in each selection.

	Chapters 14–15, 17:
	✓ Chapters 14 and 15 cover finding primary and secondary sources and then working to synthesize those sources, evaluate them, and integrate them appropriately through paragraph, summary, or quotation. Chapter 15 includes two sample essays that model the strategies of synthesis and source evaluation. ✓ Chapter 17 also addresses integrating outside sources into a composition, and ways to engage with other's ideas by counterarguing.

Individual Assessment: Ask small groups of students to research, design, and implement a PowerPoint presentation introducing a rhetorical tool (such as an appeal, allusion, or a form of evidence). This collaborative learning exercise combines critical thinking, reading, and writing skills, as well as various methods for research and presentation, allowing students to effectively communicate course knowledge to a peer audience.

Course Level Assessment: At the end of the term, assign a research paper that presents a particular position on a topic. This project asks students to find outside examples. Or, you can make this an in-class essay with pre-chosen texts. This final assignment builds on the critical thinking, reading, and writing skills demonstrated in the individual presentations and assesses the retention and translation of genre knowledge past an individual assignment.

Suggestions for Assessing Processes

The Composition of Everyday Life calls on students to analyze writing as a collaborative and reflective process that requires initiative, social responsibility, and an awareness of differing perspectives.

Processes	*The Composition of Everyday Life*
By the end of first-year composition, students should ▪ Develop a writing project through multiple drafts.	**Chapters 2–13, 17–19:** ✓ Each of the main project chapters (2–13) guides students through a thorough but recursive process—one in which they are encouraged and shown how to build ideas with their own language. The "Analysis,"

▪ Develop flexible strategies for reading, drafting, reviewing, collaborating, revising, rewriting, rereading, and editing.	with their own language. The "Analysis," "Public Resonance," "Thesis," and "Rhetorical Tools" sections especially help students to ask vital questions about their thinking—and to keep generating throughout the process, even all the way to final editing and polishing.
▪ Use composing processes and tools as a means to discover and reconsider ideas.	✓ Chapters 2–13 teach students dialogic knowledge making. "Invention Workshop" prompts invite students to enlist the help of others *throughout the composing process*—not simply at the end of the process when ideas tend to already be solidified.
▪ Experience the collaborative and social aspects of writing processes.	
▪ Learn to give and act on productive feedback to works in progress.	✓ Chapters 2–13 also end with a "Revision" section that guides students through specific self-assessment and peer review. Questions are focused on the specific rhetorical nuances and possibilities associated with that chapter.
▪ Adapt composing processes for a variety of technological modalities.	✓ "Reflection" assignments in Chapters 2–13 get students writing about writing and practicing metacognition.
▪ Reflect on the development of composing practices and how those practices influence their work.	✓ The chapters on writer's voice, vitality, and organizational strategies (Chapters 17–19) show students specific academic conventions. These chapters always present strategies as decisions that writers can make and continue the point established in the first chapter: that each decision impacts both the writer and readers' relationship with the ideas.

Individual Assessment: Implement regular oral and written reflections throughout the writing process and at the end of each writing assignment. Use the "Reflection" prompts at the end of Chapters 2 through 13 (example: Chapter 3, page 90) to have students assess the writing process and the roles they played with their teacher and peers throughout the review. Reflections can be completed as in-class writing, discussion, or formal writing assignments.

Course Level Assessment: Use writing portfolios to track process and assess progress in your writing class. Students should complete written "Reflection" assignments after each project. At the end of the course, ask students to use their drafts, projects, and reflections to write a piece of commentary examining the writing process throughout the term. Students can comment on any or all parts of the process, from invention to reflection, and should use their individual writing projects and reflections for research and development.

Suggestions for Assessing Knowledge of Conventions

Knowledge of Conventions	The Composition of Everyday Life
By the end of first-year composition, students should • Develop knowledge of linguistic structures, including grammar, punctuation, and spelling, through practice in composing and revising. • Understand why genre conventions for structure, paragraphing, tone, and mechanics vary. • Gain experience negotiating variations in genre conventions. • Learn common formats and/or design features for different kinds of texts.	**Chapters 14–16:** ✓ These chapters teach *information literacy*—not simply the acts of summary, quotation, paraphrase, documentation, and so on, but also the intellectual work behind each of these acts. ✓ Chapter 16 addresses the ethical use of others' words and ideas and offers strategies for avoiding plagiarism. The chapter also provides instruction and models for how to cite and use sources in accordance with MLA and APA style conventions. **Chapter 17, "Organizing Ideas":** ✓ Chapter 17 addresses integrating outside sources into a composition, ways to engage with other's ideas by counterarguing, separating problems and solutions, developing effective introductions and conclusions, and more. This chapter consistently makes the point that conventions of format and structure are alive, brimming with possibility, and contingent on the project and situation.
• Explore the concepts of intellectual property (such as fair use and copyright) that motivate documentation conventions. • Practice applying citation conventions systematically in their own work.	**Chapter 21, "Rhetorical Handbook":** ✓ This handbook chapter is available only online in MindTap for *The Composition of Everyday Life*. The chapter begins with a review of basic grammatical elements, and then moves through the conventions of standard academic English—as applied to words, sentences, and paragraphs.

Individual Assessment: Conduct a writing workshop that puts the knowledge of conventions in the hands of the students. As a class, read the "Revision" and "Peer Review" sections of Chapters 2–13 (e.g., Chapter 3, pages 88–90). Discuss the "Peer Review" questions at the end of each of these chapters as a class, and use your personal course emphases on writing conventions and documentation to guide the discussion. From there, ask students to complete a peer workshop in pairs, using the "Peer Review" questions to assess their partner's work.

Course Level Assessment: As a final project in conventions, ask students to apply the questions at the end of Chapter 18, "Developing Voice" (pages 550–551), to a paper or project (or portfolio) they have composed.

Adopting WPA Outcomes for Assessing Your First-Year Writing Course

The Big Picture: An Overview of Outcomes-Based Assessment in Your Course

1. Determine what you want to assess: Assessing writing is a difficult task worthy of many arguments in the composition world; however, using the WPA outcomes makes the instructor's job a bit clearer. In adopting the WPA outcomes for first-year composition, you are starting with a general idea of the knowledge that students should have when exiting your first-year writing course. Although writing can be a subjective discipline, the WPA agrees that there is specific knowledge students *should* be working toward, and in an outcomes-based education, this knowledge is assessable. With that in mind, outcomes such as rhetorical knowledge and processes move from abstract ideas to concrete objectives that can be evaluated using writing assignments from *The Composition of Everyday Life*.

2. Write and establish course objectives: These objectives will probably be a combination of the WPA outcomes with your specific program and course goals. Think about what skills or knowledge of writing your school's population of students *should* have when they leave your course. How is this knowledge similar to or different from the five WPA outcomes? Where do they overlap? Where are there conflicts? How might you compromise to work with the WPA outcomes? Writing course objectives is not an easy task; however, the clearer you can be with what you want to accomplish, the easier it will be to use *The Composition of the Everyday* to meet those expectations.

3. Design assignment sequences: After you have determined course objectives, think about how you might achieve those objectives. What needs to happen in and out of class for you to reach these goals? Start with the larger writing projects first and work backward. Working backward will ensure that you've covered all material for the assignment. For example, have the students just write an essay—this can be done as homework or as an in-class assignment—without worrying about the essay being completely polished. Then, work through the appropriate chapter backward, moving from "Reflection," to "Revision," to "Rhetorical Tools," to "Thesis," to "Public Resonance," to "Analysis," and finally to "Point of Contact." By reversing the process, the students will be able to break down the writing process to further develop ideas and their ability to convey ideas more effectively. This kind of reverse process could also be used if you are assigning a "Beyond the Essay" project.

Taking Action: Using Outcomes as Pedagogy for Lesson Plans

Now that you've established the big-picture goals, you can create lesson plans based on your outcomes-based pedagogy.

Working with Students

When dealing with assessment, it is easy to get caught up in the outcomes and objectives, but it is important not to forget who this assessment directly affects: the students. Explaining the course objectives at the start of the semester, and frequently returning to these goals, will help students comprehend how each assignment works to further their knowledge in the course. Students often misinterpret writing assessment as one teacher's subjective grade on a finished paper. However, putting an emphasis on the WPA outcomes as an education in writing that students should develop and acquire throughout the first year will help to diffuse the misconception that students need to write assignments "for the instructor" because "each instructor grades differently." Adopting a clear set of objectives based on the WPA outcomes and showing how *The Composition of Everyday Life* can help students develop this knowledge is one way to turn that subjective point of view into a more tangible and objective evaluation process.

Sample Student Assignment Handout

One way in which to effectively convey outcomes to students is to translate your weekly lesson plans into detailed assignment sequences that explain the course objectives and tasks for each writing project. This is illustrated in the following model.

English 110: Intro to Writing

Week One: An Introduction to the Writing Process

Objective: To gain an understanding that students should

- develop a writing project through multiple drafts.
- develop flexible strategies for reading, revising, drafting, reviewing, collaborating, revising, rewriting, rereading, and editing.
- use composing processes and tools as a means to discover and reconsider ideas.
- experience the collaborative and social aspects of writing processes.
- learn to give and act on productive feedback to works in progress.
- reflect on the development of composing practices and how those practices influence their work.

(Continued)

English 110: Intro to Writing (*Continued*)

Day 1: Students should arrive to class already having read Chapter 1. Discuss what an "essay" is as a class based on the reading in Chapter 1. Provide students with an example of an academic journal article. Do the "Activity" on page 6 as a class. Continue working with this same article and discuss the article using the prompts in the "Readings" section of Chapter 2, page 27. Homework: Complete the "Exploring Ideas" section on pages 29–30 in Chapter 2. Students should come to the next class with the completed assignment and be prepared to share their writing with a small group of peers, and students should be ready to continue working with this piece to develop it into a longer writing sample. Students should also read Chapter 2.

Day 2: As students arrive to class, resume the same groups from the previous class meeting. Students will share their writing sample to the rest of the group. Using the prompts in Chapter 2's "Ideas for Writing" (page 30), students will begin to revise writing samples. This will take up the entire class period. Homework: Students should revise their writing sample for submission and grading the next class meeting. Drafts and notes should be included in the final submission for review. This further emphasizes the importance of working through the writing process.

Day 3: In Chapter 2, using the readings as samples or models, students choose a topic for their next essay. Instructor will guide the students through the prompts, but students are to come up with their own topics. Remember that as you move through the remaining sections of the chapter, writing throughout the process is essential; a notebook must be kept so that all drafts and notes can be reviewed as part of the assessment process. Before the class is dismissed, peer review partners will be assigned. Homework: Draft essay.

Daily Exercises from *The Composition of Everyday Life* That Work with WPA Outcomes

WPA Outcomes	*The Composition of Everyday Life*
Rhetorical Knowledge	✓ Reading selections in Chapters 2–13 and 20, and accompanying questions ✓ Activities and short assignments in "Public Resonance," "Analysis," and "Rhetorical Tools" sections in Chapters 2–13 ✓ "Beyond the Essay" assignments in Chapters 2–13

Critical Thinking, Reading, and Writing	✓ Reading selections in Chapters 2–13 and 20, and accompanying headnotes and questions ✓ Activities and questions in "Rhetorical Tools" and "Reflection" sections in Chapters 2–13. ✓ Activities and assignments in Chapters 14, 15, and 17
Processes	✓ Extensive "Invention" process sections in Chapters 2–13, including "Point of Contact," "Analysis," "Public Resonance," "Thesis," "Revision," and "Reflection" discussions and activities. ✓ "Invention Workshops" in Chapters 2–13 ✓ Chapters 17–19
Knowledge of Conventions	✓ Activities and assignments in Chapters 14–16. ✓ Chapter 17 ✓ Activities in Chapter 21: Rhetorical Handbook (available online only in MindTap for CEL)

Sample Lesson Plan: Introduction to Argument Writing

- WPA Outcomes for Assessment: Processes and Rhetorical Knowledge
- Outcomes-based Course Objective: Writing is a process requiring multiple drafts, research, and collaborative critiques to communicate a message to an audience.
- Task: Making Arguments, *The Composition of Everyday Life*, Chapter 8

	Objectives	Tasks from *The Composition of Everyday Life*
Week One	✓ Knowledge and conventions of the rhetorical mode ✓ Working draft of the project	**Read:** Chapter 8, Making Arguments, Introduction, page 223; April Pedersen, "The Dog Delusion," page 225; Ann Marie Paulin, "Cruelty, Civility, and Other Weighty Matters," page 230; Teresa Scollon, "Hive Talkin': The Buzz around Town about Bees," page 240 **Discuss:** "Writing Strategies" and "Exploring Ideas" after each of the readings in the chapter **Write:** Choose one of the "Ideas for Writing" after each of the readings in the chapter **Homework:** Choose a topic and begin drafting topic for argument essay

Week Two	✔ Further exploration of rhetorical mode ✔ Awareness of writing processes ✔ Revision methods	**Read:** Chapter 8, "Making Arguments," Invention, page 245; "Point of Contact," page 245; "Analysis," page 247; "Public Resonance," page 249; "Thesis," page 251; "Rhetorical Tools," 254; "Reflection," page 264 **Discuss:** Application of the "Rhetorical Tools" and organizational strategies to students' drafts **Write:** Revise drafts **Homework:** Revise drafts
Week Three	✔ Revised assignment ✔ Peer review ✔ Knowledge of genre in a new context	**Read:** Chapter 8, "Making Arguments," "Invention Workshop," page 259; "Revision," page 263; "Reflection," page 264; "Beyond the Essay," page 264 **Discuss:** Peer review of drafts **Write:** Revise drafts **Homework:** Revise drafts for submission for grading

Evaluating Multiple Genres

The Composition of Everyday Life connects academic writing with real-life situations and topics in which students will need strong and effective written communication skills. Yet, with such varied forms of writing, the question of evaluation often looms in the classroom, as both students and teachers try to negotiate how to grade items from personal exploratory essays to more formal research-based argument essays with the same set of guidelines. Translating the WPA outcomes into a rubric for evaluation is one way to tackle this issue. Instead of grading each assigned genre only by its conventions and mechanics, instructors can construct a rubric that assesses all written projects on the same composition plane. Depending on course and assignment design, rubrics can be focused and personalized to meet instructor goals, while still addressing the WPA outcomes—and also assessing the independent genre projects.

Single Outcome Rubric

Rhetorical Knowledge Rubric	*excellent*	*above average*	*meets standards*	*insufficient*
Attention to Audience				
Responds to Rhetorical Situation				
Knowledge of Genre Conventions				
Appropriate Use of Language and Tone				

Multiple Outcomes Rubric

Grading Rubric for Argument Writing Assignment	Comments
Rhetorical Knowledge: demonstrates a rhetorical awareness through audience appeal, writing persona, genre knowledge, and context	
Critical Thinking, Reading, and Writing: uses research for communicating, synthesizing ideas, and integrating multiple perspectives	
Processes: demonstrates evidence of critique and large-scale revision through a peer-review and self-evaluation process	
Knowledge of Conventions: employs a knowledge of genre conventions, formal mechanics, and style	

E-Portfolios, WPA Outcomes, and *The Composition of Everyday Life*

Electronic portfolios are an increasingly popular method of assessing student work not only for single courses but also for long-term measurements over a student's educational career. Likewise, for a two-semester course or a multi-course assessment program, e-portfolios can be useful for collecting data and tracking the progress of groups and individuals. Using e-portfolios in coordination with the WPA outcomes and *The Composition of Everyday Life* will require the same representative sample of student writing that would accompany a print portfolio. The difference and perks of e-portfolios come in the convenience and organization of the various assignments (no more large stacks of folders to carry) and also in the critical connections that students can make, linking texts and peer commentary to revisions and reflections via the functions of electronic folders.

E-portfolios allow students to easily retain writing projects from all steps in the writing process to access them for later analysis and assessment. The writing assignments in *The Composition of Everyday Life* begin with invention and lead students through multiple drafts and critiques to an eventual writing reflection at the end of the chapter. In addition to a representative sample of writing, students could also include a reflective letter, revised writing assignments, a case study of a single writing assignment, peer commentary, or commentary on collaborative learning. *The Composition of Everyday Life's* approach to analyzing rhetorical situations creates an easy platform for this type of assessment because it forces students to locate and evaluate their own writing in the same way they've been reading and critiquing the work of their peers all semester. Asking students to design and complete a written analysis of the e-portfolio to show knowledge of (a) rhetoric, (b) critical thinking, reading, and writing, (c) processes, and (d) conventions requires the same critical approach used in the "Peer Review" and "Reflection" sections of Chapters 2 through 13. This culminating assignment applies all of the elements that have been introduced throughout the course and emphasizes the importance of the composing process while allowing students to showcase their work. In addition, e-portfolios raise student awareness of the idea that a "finished" draft does not mean the writing is done. When asked to compile a portfolio, the writing is reborn, revisited, and redefined through the organization and rewriting involved in the e-portfolio project. Suddenly the documents become part of a public and professional presentation of their writing identity.

The Composition
of Everyday Life

1

Inventing Ideas

Chapter Objectives

This chapter will help you to:

- Use writing as a means of inquiry.
- Apply invention questions and collaborate with others to develop increasingly sophisticated ideas.
- Seek out layers of meaning, significance, tension, and complexity in a range of topics.
- Identify opportunities for discovery and revision in your own writing.
- Evaluate sources of information.
- Integrate a range of sources into your own writing.
- Develop increasingly focused claims.
- Apply support strategies most appropriate for the text, situation, and audience.
- Use a range of media to communicate sophisticated ideas.
- Experiment with voice, organization, and syntax to enhance persuasiveness and vitality of your writing.
- Apply common revision and editing strategies to intensify your writing.

"Writing is not simply a one-way flow of information from the brain to the hand. Quite the opposite . . ."

INTRODUCTION

Thousands of students across the country are required to take introductory college writing courses. These courses are nearly universal requirements, and it seems reasonable to ask: Why? What's the purpose of these courses, and more specifically, what's the purpose of writing? How does writing well relate to engineering, nursing, photography, business management, or aviation? Why do business and governmental leaders throughout the country want all students to take more, not less, writing? If students will not be writing essays in their jobs, why should they write essays in college?

When asked such questions, people tend to respond that writing is important for two reasons: because it helps to *express* thoughts and *communicate* ideas. However, they often forget a third point. Beyond expression and communication, there is another, perhaps far more powerful, reason: Writing is an invention tool. It helps us to generate new ideas and add dimension to the ideas we already have. Writing is not merely the performance or expression of something we know or believe. It's also an *act of inventing, developing, and reinventing what can be known.*

Writing is not simply a one-way flow of information from the brain to the hand. Quite the opposite: It actually produces new ideas, changes everyday life, and vitalizes the thinking of writers, readers, and the people who interact with them both. These are the reasons that writing is a nearly universal requirement in college. And it is not simply because our culture needs better communicators, but because we will always need better ideas and better ways of thinking about the situations we face every day.

Have you ever asked yourself where ideas come from? Do they pop out of thin air? Do they come from divine beings whispering in our ears? Do they come from lab experiments? From someone's heart? Another organ? Most scholars who wrestle with such questions believe that ideas come from language, that people build, refine, pull apart, and rebuild ideas with words. And although we can use words silently in our heads, the act of writing dramatizes and amps up the whole idea-making process. In other words, writing is like an idea calculator. It allows us to put ideas "out there" on a page or a screen and then process them—adding, subtracting, multiplying, and dividing. Writing allows us to put an idea into a formula, add exponents, and radicalize. It allows us to keep several abstractions floating around at once, to link thoughts, to collapse them, to evaluate them, and even to cancel them out. Granted, some people can do these operations to some degree just by using language inside their heads. But the act of writing greatly increases almost everyone's ability to process ideas.

At the individual level, inside one's own head, writing is the act of developing a better relationship with ideas. When we develop a point in writing, we get distance from it and see it in front of us. Like a painter, a writer cannot simply hold his or her ideas in the mind. They must be drawn out, in language. Then the writer can add color, shading, sky, ground, background—or redraw from a different perspective.

At the social level, writing can be an invitation, a convergence of many minds. In fact, in academia, writing is seen as a tool for creating social and institutional momentum: for directing people's energies, for guiding policies, for urging on new and better enterprises. Writing changes the way people act, spend, vote, teach, think, and hope—which means this is all pretty serious and heavy business.

ASKING QUESTIONS

One of the most powerful ways to invent ideas is to ask questions. For instance, let's explore a basic concept such as *freedom*. We might ask, *What is it?* First, we might write out some initial thoughts:

What is freedom?
Freedom is the ability to do whatever one wants. It's the feeling we get when we know that we can do whatever we want.

But can we go further? What else can be known or thought about freedom? Let's apply more questions, the kinds of questions you'll encounter in Chapters 2 through 13:

What particular behaviors are associated with freedom?
Politically speaking, voting, protesting, speaking one's mind, worshipping whatever or whomever one desires—or not worshipping at all. Personally, free people do what they want whenever they want. They make their own choices: what they want to buy or drive or eat, how they want to spend their time, where they want to go, what they want to read, whom they want to love or marry.

What responsibilities come with freedom?
Maybe none. If people are free, they do what they want and let others clean up the mess or worry about the consequences. That sounds somehow wrong or bad, but that's what true freedom is. There's no impending rule that says one must do something or think something. Put this way, freedom—true freedom—might be pretty messy. People would get away with murder. Literally.

What hidden role does freedom play in people's lives?
Most people are always trying to get free—from work, duty, homework, etc. They want to be "done" with the things other people assign to them. They want Saturday afternoon—when no one is saying, "Be here and do this." And politically (again), people throughout the world are dying for it. They stand in front of tanks, blow up government buildings, or pack their families onto wagons and trudge for hundreds of miles so they can experience freedom. So those are the obvious ways freedom works. But "a hidden role"? Is freedom hidden? Do we hide it from ourselves? Why would we do that? Don't we want it? I think most Americans spend their time in some kind of duty—work, school, both. When they're not working under someone else's guidelines, they look to fill up the freedom time. They schedule it. I wonder if people know what to do with freedom . . . with time not gobbled up by duty. Skateboard? Listen to music? Read? Watch TV? Is that what freedom is? What about retirement? Isn't that supposed to be total freedom? If so, why do people get lonely? Why do senior citizens want something to do? Why do they volunteer? (They're always the ones at polling locations, libraries, bake sales, etc.) Maybe people want to be given things to do. Maybe they want to be a part of something. Beyond having the right to speak, marry, vote, work, and travel at will, people want to feel commissioned—to be of some good use. And in some way, that's the opposite of freedom. People yearn for freedom but suffer when they experience it in the extreme.

These questions—Invention Questions—help to launch our thinking. They help the writer uncover hidden layers of a seemingly simple concept. The writer discovers a potentially negative quality of freedom—that unmitigated freedom could be ugly. After the third question, the writer gets past the obvious, taken-for-granted layer and digs up some interesting ideas.

Obvious Layer: Freedom is about escaping duty.

Deeper Layer: Escaping all duty comes with a price.

This process is invention. Asking questions and writing responses makes writers go from an obvious idea (*Freedom is doing whatever one wants*) to something less obvious (*Freedom is the sometimes spiritually hollow lack of duty*). And in academic writing, readers are hoping for something less obvious. The goal isn't to state what most people, or even some people, already think. Rather, it is to bring hidden layers to the surface.

This is no easy task. The process requires endurance—a willingness and ability to continue thinking through intellectual walls and past the easy answers. In other words, inventive writers do not imagine having answers stored up inside their heads. Instead, they imagine the questions as highways, backroads, alleys, and off-road trails. Offering a quick answer to an Invention Question is like starting out on a cross-country trip and stopping at the first rest area—and never leaving.

Imagine these excerpts about freedom as part of a larger exploration that involved more writing and thinking. Much of that invention work (not shown here) stalled out, went in new directions, hit dead ends, started up again, and eventually *through persistence* led to discoveries. Writers should not expect a few sentences or paragraphs to automatically create a new idea. It might take a few paragraphs or pages to work through their initial thinking, then more paragraphs or pages to break through the wall to less obvious, more insightful ideas.

ACTIVITY

With a small group, take a concept (such as education, individuality, authority, crime, or art) and try to dig up something new—some hidden layer or less obvious quality, something that others in your class may not imagine. Use the following questions:

- What is it?

- What particular behaviors are associated with it?

- What responsibilities come with it?

- What hidden role does it play in people's lives?

RE-INVENTING EDUCATION

Some may ask, *Why go through all this work? Why not just write a draft of the first idea that comes to our heads? Why twist and turn the ideas and potentially get confused?* The answers lie in the broader goals of education and of writing courses. In the twentieth century, public education in the United States emphasized getting things in the right order. It was the age of factory thinking. In writing classrooms, students wrote essays to demonstrate their mastery of a format. But such thinking, assignments, and assumptions about good work are fading into history.

The world is changing at an exponential pace. The information students learn today becomes outdated more quickly than before, and graduates' jobs and careers will change more often and markedly throughout their lives. Many students will have jobs that don't even exist today, in industries or services that are not currently imagined. In this shifting professional life, workers, leaders, employees, and employers who can invent new ways of thinking will thrive. Good thinkers will be in high demand!

While students who can invent ideas will thrive in their academic and professional lives, we must stress that invention is difficult work. The act of writing is an intellectual struggle to shape thoughts and make connections that seem, at first, *impossible*. Good writers do not look for the easy topics, and they understand that valuable ideas do not jump out at them. Instead, they must seek out these ideas. Because the human brain is not a *linear* machine producing thoughts in a simple straight line, writers know their ideas must be formed then re-formed. In that process, they turn frustration into inquiry and find insights in moments of uncertainty.

And we should note that invention does not belong only to academic and professional life. It is a vital practice in everyday life. An inventive thinker asks probing questions that explore possibilities, not just for a college writing assignment but for life's inevitabilities:

- How can I calm my mother-in-law's anger about my religious views?

- Why does my roommate think I'm against her?

- How do we get out of this constant battle with the neighbor's teenage kids?

- Which candidate will really change the economy for the better?

What we call *invention* was not created for schoolwork, essay assignments, or business. It was conceived 2,400 years ago by the ancient Greeks as a tool for analyzing and debating everyday issues. Invention was the first part of a bigger practice called *rhetoric*—the study or art of persuasion. The Greeks had the radical notion that common people, not just holy or military leaders, could think for themselves and make policies best suited for their own affairs. In other words, the Greeks invented what we now call democracy. And when they started to solve problems and debate issues publicly, some people realized that successful thinkers and speakers employed certain moves; they weren't just the loudest talkers or the most charming personalities. It didn't take them long to realize that good thinking was about inventing new insights, not simply rephrasing a common opinion in fancy words. Good thinkers could ask hard questions. They could use language to show complexity and possibility. It was soon obvious to the Greeks that everyday life in a democracy requires good, *inventive* thinking.

READING FOR RHETORIC

If your situation is like that of nearly every other college student, instructors will ask you to read essays that have little or no obvious connection to your life. You may be interested in football, and your college English instructor may assign an essay about the punk movement in Europe or vineyards in Washington. Why? Why should urban students read about agricultural practices, rivers, or forests? Why should rural students read about the streets of Chicago, the Manhattan subway, or the opera? Why should twenty-year-olds read about the role of the World War II generation in shaping the suburbs? Is it because instructors want students to get specific information on those topics? Probably not. Reading assignments in college English courses are often connected to a larger academic goal: to broaden students' perspectives.

Most readers ask themselves questions, and two questions seem to arise consistently:

Do I like this essay?

Can I relate to this information?

But those questions can limit readers. If they're the *only* questions available, they put readers at a big disadvantage by limiting what they can learn. Most instructors want students to think about topics from different angles, and to examine life outside of their own spheres. In other words, instructors hope that students gain some *intellectual agility*—the ability to move from position to position without tremendous difficulty, to imagine a realm of experience and perspective beyond their own biases and reflexes.

If readers have some other questions in mind, some other reasons to continue (besides liking something or relating to it), they might discover something and gain intellectual agility. Imagine, for instance, how the following questions might take a reader somewhere more valuable than the two preceding questions:

How does this essay prompt me to think?

What new idea does it offer?

What new connections does it make?

Why am I resisting the point? Why do I agree with the point?

Where is this essay taking me? How far will it go?

With such questions swirling in their heads, good readers are more apt to push onward through foreign ideas, to examine new assumptions, to carry away something significant.

Good readers do more than read. They read and monitor their own thinking as they move through the text, and they allow themselves to go further than their personal likes or ability to relate. They tolerate (and maybe even bask in) intellectual discomfort. They consider ideas and assumptions that might seem foreign, weird, abstract, or provocative.

So the purpose of reading in college goes beyond the two most common questions readers may ask themselves. In an academic setting, we do not read merely to relate or associate with the information. We read to rethink issues, to discover positions we had not previously imagined, to revise common perceptions. And to fulfill such goals, we must expect to work through ideas, even struggle at times. Most importantly, we must expect to be surprised, to have our tidy mental rooms messed up occasionally. Reading in academia means being intellectually adventurous and expecting something new or radically different.

Another goal of reading assignments involves the *rhetorical* layer: Behind the obvious content of an essay, there lurks a complex set of *rhetorical tools*—strategies that persuade readers to accept the writer's ideas. Even though an essay may be about pollution, cats, childhood obesity, or any other topic, it has another dimension, a rhetorical dimension. You might think of this as the machinery of the essay, the stuff that makes it go. And most often, that rhetorical dimension is the reason instructors assign particular essays. It's not the "information" that instructors want students to focus on, but the way information is dealt with (analyzed, revised, dramatized, and radicalized). For example, in Chapter 4, Annie Dillard's essay "Living Like Weasels" focuses on her surprise encounter with a weasel. The essay is widely read in college writing courses but not because instructors love small rodents or because people who teach writing love nature. It must have some other appeal. It must be up to something other than celebrating the mighty weasel. And that something must be important to college writing—and to higher education. What is that something?

The answer lies in Dillard's rhetorical prowess: her ability to persuade readers to think differently, to yank readers' attention away from the mundane aspects of everyday life and conventional ways of thinking:

> I would like to learn, or remember, how to live. I come to Hollins Pond not so much to learn how to live as, frankly, to forget about it. That is, I don't think I can learn from a wild animal how to live in particular—shall I suck warm blood, hold my tail high, walk with my footprints precisely over the prints of my hand?—but I might learn something of mindlessness, something of the purity of living in the physical senses and the dignity of living without bias or motive.

It wouldn't matter if the essay were about weasels, house flies, or moths. What's important are Dillard's strategies for nudging readers to think—to re-see themselves, their lives, their biases, and their prejudices. So when you get to the Dillard essay, don't be fooled. *It ain't about the weasel.*

ACTIVITY

When we see only the obvious content (or information) of an essay and miss the rhetorical dimension, we miss the most transferable and usable part. It is like going for a drive and seeing only the windshield of your car; like seeing a movie and remembering only the names of the actors; like walking through a town and seeing only the street signs. To illustrate your understanding of this point, generate another analogy and share it with the class. *When we see only the obvious content of the essay and miss the rhetorical dimension, it's like ____.*

The rhetorical dimension of an essay is the layer of strategies that prompt readers to accept its ideas. When we read an essay, we get not only the information but also the set of intellectual moves and rhetorical strategies the writer employs. We can learn from and use these strategies in our own writing. In the following passage from "How I Lost the Junior Miss Pageant" (Chapter 2), Cindy Bosley makes a sophisticated rhetorical move. She focuses on her own misunderstanding or naiveté, but then quickly pulls reader outward and focuses on the town of her childhood—a hard-knuckled town that seemed out of sync with the idea of beauty contests:

> Clearly, I lacked the save-the-whales-and-rainforest civic-mindedness required not only of Miss America, but of Junior Miss America, too. Even, although one wouldn't think it, in Ottumwa, Iowa, where my mother would go on to work in a bathtub factory, and then a glue factory, and then an electrical connectors factory (the factory worker's version of upward mobility), and finally, a watch factory where they shipped and received not just watches but cocaine in our town that at that time had more FBI agents in it than railroad engineers. And even in this town where my sister would go to work the kill floor of the pork plant where, for fun, the workers shot inspection dye at each other and threatened each other's throats with hack-knives. And even in this town where my cousin, age 13, would bring a bomb to seventh grade for show-and-tell, and get caught and evacuated, and be given community service to do because the public-school-as-terrorist-ground phenomenon hadn't yet been born.

Bosley's passage holds some valuable lessons for writers. At the grammatical level, she takes significant risks (such as some intentional sentence fragments) that parallel some of the essay's insights. At the rhetorical level, she lines up particular details about her hometown. These details are intensely specific and even gruesome, and more importantly, they add up to a feeling about the place, about Bosley's childhood, which was completely at odds with the notion of a beauty contest.

If we remove specific content (information about beauty contests, pork plants, and bombs for show-and-tell), what do we have left? We have some rhetorical moves that we can transport to other topics:

- Personal testimony works if the details are riveting.

- Grotesque details can be highly engaging, even necessary.

- If the details are specific enough and lined up together, they can add up to an undeniable conclusion about a place or an event.

- As writers, we're allowed to wonder ourselves.

In an essay from Chapter 4: Observing, Chester McCovey contrasts the past and the present. Like Bosley, he does not simply say that something happened. He imagines how it happened and what it means:

> My grandparents' garages were small, just enough for one car and a few tools—not much of a garage for today's homeowner. In those days the garage kept a car and a small lawnmower, some rakes, and so on. The garage today must keep much more. One can see, then, how the exchange occurred. Like an old-fashioned trade in baseball, gone is the home team's beloved front porch, replaced by a big, new garage. Of course the trade is much more interesting than that. And a look at how it occurred enlightens us a little about the world in which we live. More importantly, it tells us not so much about how life is now but about how it came to be. And, I would argue, it shows us the way in which things will continue to change.

After making the simple contrast between the past and present, McCovey offers an analogy (a comparison to trading in baseball). And then he suggests some hidden complexity—some "interesting" dynamics going on behind the shift from porch to garage. (He later deals with these dynamics in the essay.) For both Bosley and McCovey, meaning lies beyond the facts of the case. The writer must probe behind the physical things and events.

In his essay "Americans and the Land" (Chapter 3), John Steinbeck describes how early Americans ravaged the continent, and he laments that modern Americans carry on those early traditions. In the following passage, he notes how carefully scientists work to avoid polluting outer space:

> Since the river-polluters and the air-poisoners are not criminal or even bad people, we must presume that they are heirs to the early conviction that sky and water are unowned and that they are limitless. In the light of our practices here at home it is very interesting to me to read of the care taken with the carriers of our probes into space, to make utterly sure that they are free of pollution of any kind. We would not think of doing to the moon what we do every day to our own dear country.

Steinbeck reveals the absurdity of common practice—a standard yet critical move for writers. His point is not simply "don't pollute," a common sentiment. Instead, he shows the blindness and hypocrisy of polluting one's own country. He references one behavior (being careful not to pollute the moon, where no one lives) and juxtaposes it to a common behavior (openly poisoning our land, where all humans live). From this passage, we might carry away a single powerful question: What act do we allow or even defend in one situation that we forbid in another?

Good reading leads to good writing. If we keep our radar on and look at the content *and* the rhetorical dimension of essays, we are more apt to see the moves, questions, and strategies that can be used for any topic.

HOW TO USE *THE COMPOSITION* OF EVERYDAY LIFE

This book is about discovering and developing ideas through reading, inventing, and writing. Each of the Invention chapters (2 through 13) begins with three sample essays that illustrate key rhetorical moves. The Invention sections following the sample essays constitute the majority of each chapter.

Sample Essays

The essays in this book were written for fellow scientists, philosophers, economists, business leaders, politicians, family members, students, and public citizens. They show the real writing that is done in the public sphere—how professionals in all walks of life talk to their colleagues and to the public. Despite their individual discipline or career field, the writers develop ideas that impact the world around them.

Chapters include essays by professional writers (whose writing was published prior to this textbook), commissioned writers (who used the chapter to develop an essay), and student writers (who used an earlier version of the textbook to create a successful project). Although the writing techniques and personal styles differ, these qualities are constant: valuable insights, well-supported ideas, and engaging voices.

To help you read these essays closely, each is followed by Writing Strategies and Exploring Ideas questions. Also, each chapter features an *annotated* essay with comments and analysis in the margins. These annotations show a reader stopping at certain places, noticing particular claims and strategies, and speaking back to ideas.

Writing Topics

The Composition of Everyday Life offers several possibilities for inventing and developing writing topics. You can (1) read the essays in a designated chapter and then use the Ideas for Writing after one or more of the essays; (2) use the Point of Contact section, which will help generate topics from everyday life; or (3) read several content-related essays, according to the thematic table of contents at the front of the book, and then develop topics that emerge from the readings. For all three options, the Invention section of each chapter can be used to develop writing projects.

As you consider your own writing projects, imagine that topics are not prepackaged issues, as though writers simply choose something they like and start drafting. Instead, imagine topics as ideas that emerge slowly through an invention process. If you imagine topics as something to *develop,* rather than something to *choose,* your intellectual experience and writing will be more intense.

INVENTION

"Invention is the mother of necessities."

—Marshall McLuhan

Invention is the process of discovering some new idea and developing that idea through focused exploration. It is often associated with one particular activity: coming up with an idea to write about. However, invention is a complex activity that extends beyond finding a topic. It involves committing to an idea, exploring it in depth, and discovering its worth.

When writers take the time to explore topics, they discover something worth sharing, something that is not already floating around in everyone's minds. In short, invention means the difference between powerful, engaging writing that introduces new ideas, and dull, lifeless writing that offers nothing but a writer's attempt to fulfill an assignment.

Because invention is the most difficult but most crucial part of academic writing, each chapter devotes several sections to it. The following sections appear in each chapter and are designed to help you invent:

- **Point of Contact** will help you discover a topic from everyday life.

- **Analysis** will launch you beyond initial thoughts and help you explore the topic.

- **Public Resonance** will help you extend the topic outward, to make the topic relevant to a community of readers.

- **Thesis** will help you focus your thinking and develop a revelatory point.

- **Rhetorical Tools** will help you support your point with a variety of common strategies.

The Invention Questions, marked by arrows, are not meant to be answered directly in a final essay. Instead, they are meant to help generate ideas before writing a draft.

Invention Workshops

In Chapters 2 through 13, you will see Invention Workshops—prompts to enlist the help of others in the development of your projects. Rather than answer the Invention Questions alone, you can gather in a small group and take turns explaining your topic to others. The whole group then can explore your topic by focusing on a single question or set of questions.

Invention Workshops can be the most powerful element in a composition course. If all parties are invested in the struggle to focus and vitalize ideas, the process can dramatically improve the thinking and writing for each project. But be mindful of the process. If approached uncritically or lackadaisically, workshops can decrease energy and deflate ideas. For example, in the first four workshop transcriptions that follow, the ideas get derailed. One of the participants shuts down the thinking or diffuses it somehow. But in the fifth workshop, the participants take Linda's topic to a compelling place. By following the ideas put forward, they build to a new insight:

Workshop 1

LINDA: What is the significance of a tattoo?
MARCUS: The significance is just whatever people think it is.

Workshop 2

LINDA: What is the significance of a tattoo?
DIANA: Well, it depends on the actual tattoo, doesn't it? A flower has a different significance than a skull.
LINDA: Maybe. But why do people get any tattoos?
DIANA: They just want to. Everybody has their own reasons.

Workshop 3

LINDA: What is the significance of a tattoo?
JACK: What do you mean?
LINDA: What do tattoos mean? What's the *meaning* behind inscribing ink permanently onto the skin?
JACK: My cousin has this huge tattoo on his back.

Workshop 4

LINDA: What is the significance of a tattoo?
MARCUS: What do you mean, "significance"?
LINDA: You know, what's the fundamental meaning of a tattoo? What's the *meaning* behind inscribing ink permanently onto the skin?
DIANA: I think it's gross, myself. I mean, don't get me wrong, people can do whatever they want with their own bodies, but it's really disgusting to me.

Workshop 5

LINDA: What is the significance of a tattoo?
MARCUS: What do you mean, "significance"?

LINDA: You know, what's the fundamental meaning of a tattoo? What's the *meaning* behind inscribing ink permanently onto the skin?

DIANA: Well, when people get a tattoo, they're doing something permanent to themselves—or at least they assume they are.

MARCUS: They're making a statement of some kind.

DIANA: A statement that has permanence.

JACK: Yeah, that's gotta mean something. People must want to have something about themselves, on themselves, that is not going to go away. It must feel . . . sorta . . . important, ritualistic, big, you know . . .

LINDA: So, people long for permanence. That's interesting. And a tattoo is a little (maybe tiny) way of establishing that . . . on their own bodies.

MARCUS: It's also something that is totally personal. I mean, you can have a tattoo of anything, and it's all your own.

DIANA: Yeah, that's why people get tattoos of their loved ones' names.

JACK: My brother has a tattoo of his old girlfriend's name.

DIANA: Yeah, my dad has a tattoo of some kind that doesn't really mean anything, and he won't even tell us what it's from. He got it when he was a teenager.

LINDA: OK. But what do those examples show? Tattoos are still there, but the people's lives go on.

MARCUS: Well, life is change. You can't escape change.

LINDA: And tattoos are a way of resisting change? A way of marking the present on one's body—storing it, keeping it with you.

MARCUS: Right! That's the significance.

Point of Contact

The Point of Contact section in each chapter invites the writers to slow down, to stop, to notice common and not-so-common aspects of life. The point of contact refers to a writer's moment of awareness where the writer's vision collides with issues, events, situations, behaviors, and other people. The idea is that writing begins with a discovery—a realization about something that might otherwise go unnoticed.

As you go through the Point of Contact sections, you will notice lists of questions designed to generate possibilities for writing. Think of the questions as exploration tools that raise points of interest for writing. The lists are by no means exhaustive; they are examples of what can be asked. Follow up (in peer groups or alone) to generate more questions. (And if you are outside of an academic setting, borrow a family member or friend to help invent.)

Analysis

We are all familiar with analysis. We participate in it constantly. We see auto mechanics analyze our cars to discover the cause of the knocking sound. We see our doctors analyze conditions to understand why we feel sick. Such analysis is a process of discovering why and/or how something occurs. But analysis also involves discovering meaning. Writers are not content to simply see a person, situation, or object. They explore the significance, imagining what ideas a thing *might* suggest. For instance, a writer sees an empty storefront in a strip mall and imagines that it suggests corporate irresponsibility or a declining economic system or the end of an era when businesses lasted for years before leaving a community. When analyzed, the storefront has potential meaning, and that analysis, as explained in the next section, can make a topic relevant to a broader community.

The Invention Questions in each Analysis section help you reveal the complexities of your topic. (For example, see the questions and responses about *freedom* on pages 5–6.) The goal is to generate an idea that is distinct, surprising . . . even weird.

Public Resonance

Perhaps the most important feature of writing is that it matters to a reader. This may sound obvious, but topics are not intrinsically relevant to people's lives. They need to be made relevant. They need to be expressed in a way that involves readers. Consider capital punishment: It is not, in itself, a relevant topic to the average college student, or even the average American citizen. Most people have not had a personal experience with the death penalty, but many people still have much to say about it because capital punishment has been made relevant. Human rights activists, civil liberties groups, and religious groups have spoken or written the relevance of capital punishment into being. They have made the life of a death row inmate in Texas relevant to a suburban schoolteacher in Minnesota or a biology major at UCLA.

Good writers can make an issue resonate with their readers' feelings, thoughts, and situations. They can transform a bad day at the office into an important efficiency issue for all workers. Or they can make a seemingly distant event, like the destruction of rain forests or the death of a prison inmate, real and immediate. They make a connection between two things: (1) what they see, know, do, believe, and feel; and (2) how that matters to other people. It may not matter to *every* other person, but generally, it *resonates* with the public. It engages the members of a community who, like the writer, are able to look beyond themselves (the "me") and into the public arena (the "we").

The assumption behind public resonance is that we are deeply connected to others in our communities, and even beyond those communities. Our identities are bound to a complex system of relationships that extend into different realms of social life. We are tied by economic, social, institutional, political, familial, religious, and physiological connections. We share laws, fears, dreams, and hopes. And when writers tap into those connections, when they make topics part of that large social network, they achieve public resonance.

Consider the Public Resonance sections as analysis. In these sections, we're not simply analyzing the topic; we're analyzing how people tend to think about the topic.

Analysis: Focuses on the topic itself.

Public Resonance: Focuses on how people think.

In other words, writers should consider the values, assumptions, beliefs, and opinions that people have about the topic in question. Only then can they understand what to emphasize, what to minimize, what to insist upon, what to dramatize. Generally, writers can do this without extensive research. The following questions (taken from Chapter 5: Analyzing Concepts) might help us discover some important layers to freedom:

Is the concept generally agreed upon?
Not really. People in the United States talk about freedom, but there are many disputes about it. Should people have the freedom to burn the flag, marry the person they love, get an abortion, own a machine gun or two, stockpile hand grenades, stage a protest at a funeral, or hold the majority of a company's stock and be the CEO at the same time? The answers to such questions are wrapped up with one's political beliefs.

What is the possible connection between the topic and some public concern?
People are deeply concerned about not simply their own freedom but also other people's freedom. In the 2004 election, millions of people voted to make sure that other people didn't have the freedom to marry whom they want. In this sense, personal freedom is a kind of misnomer. It's not personal at all. An individual's freedom in the United States depends entirely on what everyone else thinks! I'm only free as far as others allow me to be.

Here, we're beginning to explore how complex freedom gets when it's analyzed against a backdrop of human affairs. This is the spirit of the Public Resonance sections throughout this book. The goal is to seek out the most resonant layers of the topic—the most powerful way the topic embeds itself into the deep structure of public life. This is no easy task. Often, the most resonant layer is the most hidden. For example, we can easily discover how freedom comes up in everyday life in songs, anthems, and public documents, but it's more difficult to discover how freedom works in public thinking, beneath those songs and anthems.

Thesis
A thesis statement is more than a one-sentence summary of an essay. It represents an essay's most pointed and dense idea, the one that gives everything else in the essay purpose. Whether the essay is observing, arguing, or problem solving, thesis statements focus both writer and reader on some new insight.

Throughout the chapters, we make a distinction between flat and revelatory thesis statements—between statements that announce an obvious opinion and those that provoke a new way of thinking. Revelatory statements contribute something; they prompt readers to imagine topics differently; they pose alternative notions, reveal hidden sides:

Flat statements: obvious, plain

Revelatory statements: provocative, insightful, contributive

For example, in the following sentences, the first statement is flat, a simple announcement of common thinking. But the follow-up sentences dig up something new. The last three statements are ripe for a powerful essay on an otherwise typical topic:

Cell phones can make people behave rudely.

Cell phones enable people to perform their social lives for an audience.

Cell phones reinforce the quiet notion that everyone is starring in his or her own reality show.

Cell phone calls crowd out time for the most important dialogue in life—the one in our own heads.

Creating revelatory statements is not magic. In fact, language drives the process. When writers replace words with other words in a sentence, they replace patterns of thinking. The revelatory statements about cell phones were created by trading out the main verb in the original sentence. The writer removed *can make* and started dropping in other verbs: *enable, reinforce, crowd out.* These verbs made the writer think differently: What acts or attitudes do cell phones enable? What ideas, behaviors, or assumptions do cell phones reinforce? What voices do cell phones crowd out?

Thesis statements do not emerge out of thin air. They come from an intensive evolution in which writers develop ideas with hard questions, focused dialogue, and reflective writing. Each chapter of *The Composition of Everyday Life* includes a Thesis section with prompts, sample thesis statements, and common thesis problems. Each section also shows the Evolution of a Thesis, the gradual development of one writer's idea. The section comes after the Analysis and Public Resonance sections to allow writers the opportunity to think through their topics and imagine a range of possible positions before committing to a particular statement.

Rhetorical Tools

A rhetorical tool is a persuasion technique, a strategy for making people believe or accept an idea. Throughout the book, we refer to the rhetorical strategies writers use to develop their ideas and convince others to accept their positions. These rhetorical tools come in many forms:

Narration is the act of storytelling. Stories are often used to persuade people, to help them appreciate the value of an idea.

Description involves giving specific details to readers. Sensory details (sounds, smells, sights, tastes, touches) prompt readers to experience a topic and so accept the ideas that the writer offers.

Illustration is the graphic depiction of an idea. Although illustration certainly suggests pictures and charts, it can also be accomplished with words.

Allusions are references to some bit of public knowledge such as a historical event, a news event, a popular culture icon, or a literary text.

Scenarios are hypothetical situations.

Testimony is an eyewitness account of a particular scene or situation.

These tools can be used for any topic, and writers apply them according to their specific needs. For example, allusions function in many writing situations. Imagine that we're developing an analytical essay about freedom. We might allude to various moments in history: the Revolutionary War, the Emancipation Proclamation, women's suffrage, Woodstock, the Patriot Act, gay marriage, marijuana legalization, and so on. Writers can reference—or allude to—these well-known situations to make meaning about the idea of freedom.

The Rhetorical Tools section in each chapter explains the strategies that are most appropriate to that writing situation. However, no strategy is exclusive to any particular kind of writing. (The tools depend on the task at hand—the purpose, the audience, the topic.) In Chapter 8: Making Arguments, the rhetorical tools become a bit more complicated. They involve *appeals, counterarguments,* and *concessions.* The latter chapters of the book (starting with Chapter 8) involve argumentative rhetorical tools; however, those introduced earlier in the book (such as narration and allusion) can also apply to argumentative writing. As you move through the book, your collection of rhetorical tools will grow.

Revision and Peer Review

Revision is about reapproaching ideas. Academic writers constantly rethink their original ideas. To some degree, revision is fused into every act of the writing process. Writers are constantly asking questions: "Is this the best way to do this? Is there a better way to engage my readers?" Writers also benefit from a holistic rereading of their work: a process that involves first stepping away from the text for a period of time, and then reexamining everything (the main ideas, the supporting points, the organization, and even the voice). Rethinking everything might sound intimidating. But revision is where writers finally have a grasp on the whole, where they can make the ideas cohere, tighten, and come to life.

Each chapter provides a variety of revision prompts. They appear throughout the Invention sections and invite you to stop, refocus on the ideas you've created, and investigate the value and complexity of those ideas with the hope that everything can be more intense, more focused, more engaging. So that writers can share their projects with others and receive focused and helpful feedback, each chapter also includes a final Revision section with Peer Review questions.

Reflection

We often need time and distance from daily events before we understand them. As our brains and bodies rush onward, we rarely have time to think about our own thinking—to get *meta-cognitive*. But when we're lying down at night, we can review the day and realize causes, effects, and nuances that we ignored in the moment. And it's often weeks, months, or years after an event that we begin to understand it.

The same goes with academic work. Often, the real intellectual benefit occurs after we are done writing. Only when we are in the fumes of the chaos, in the cerebral aftermath, do we understand what happened, what we had thought, and what we think now. For this reason, writers often reflect on and even write about their own work *after* it is completed and submitted. They look back on what they wrote, and they keep thinking. In fact, much of the work that we now call scientific discovery was written as a reflection on a previous study.

When writers look back on their writing, they can see what worked and what didn't. When they review their writing as a finished product, they can see it differently than a work in progress. They can step back and see how their rhetorical moves played out—how they worked and how they might have worked better. This kind of reflection is critical to one's development as a writer and thinker. Without a formal pause to examine their own rhetoric, writers risk jumping into the next project without developing from the previous one. Thus, each chapter of this book offers an opportunity to reflect—to look back and see your own rhetoric from the vantage point that a finished project allows.

Part II: Research

While the chapters in Part I focus on invention, the chapters in Part II focus on research—on the critical steps for engaging and integrating what other scholars have written:

Chapter 14: Finding Sources

Chapter 15: Analyzing, Synthesizing, and Evaluating Sources

Chapter 16: Integrating and Documenting Sources

These chapters can be applied to any of the writing projects in Part I. While these chapters explain practical steps for sound academic research, they also explore some important intellectual and rhetorical problems related to researching across digital landscapes. Taken together, the three chapters will help you to understand the nature of potential sources and the ways they can intensify, shift, and shape your writing projects.

Part III: Organization and Delivery

So far we've been exploring, discovering, and developing ideas about a writing topic. In Part III, we consider issues of delivery: organization, writer's voice, and sentence vitality. *The Composition of Everyday Life* offers a chapter on each:

Chapter 17: Organizing Ideas

Chapter 18: Developing Voice

Chapter 19: Vitalizing Sentences

Whether narrating an event, describing a scene, offering evidence, or making an allusion, writers can arrange rhetorical tools in many different ways. Chapter 17 (Organizing Ideas) provides strategies for presenting ideas that read like a journey: beginning with a sense of direction (an introduction), passing through various locations over different terrain (separate paragraphs), connected with road signs (transitions), and leading somewhere (a unique and valuable conclusion). The Organizing Ideas chapter suggests ways ideas might be arranged—shaped, ordered, connected.

Every writer creates a voice—the character that is projected by the language and style of the essay. Whether or not you know it, simply writing a sentence creates *voice*. Chapter 18 (Developing Voice) helps writers become aware of strategies for stylizing voice based on the audience and writing situation. Chapter 19 (Vitalizing Sentences) makes writers aware of writing habits that zap the life from an essay. This chapter shows you specific—nuts-and-bolts—strategies for writing lively and readable sentences.

A Final Note

As you work through the chapters, remember that writing is not merely a tool for expressing opinions; rather, it is a tool for making new ideas, and for adding new dimensions to old ideas. Our purpose in writing is not merely to express what we think, but to shape what can be known. We are hoping to explore intellectual possibilities. In this light, a college essay can be seen as a record of intellectual exploration—a writer's attempt and invitation to figure out something new.

INVENTING IDEAS ASSIGNMENT

Invention is the engine behind good writing. The purpose of this assignment is to experience how writing (and language) is the way we explore, discover, and develop ideas (not just convey them). For this assignment, consider yourself a creator of ideas, not the writer of an essay.

1. Choose one of the following topics:
   - high school sports or a particular high school sport
   - college or a particular aspect of college
   - art or a particular type or work of art
   - music or a particular type of music or band/artist
   - pay or the pay/salary or work conditions for a particular job
   - nature or a particular aspect of nature
   - technology or a particular type or aspect of technology
   - entertainment or a particular aspect of entertainment
   - drugs or a particular type or aspect of drugs

2. Use the following questions to explore into the complexity of the topic:
   - Specifically, how does the concept influence or change people's lives?
   - What particular emotions, behaviors, or ideas are associated with it?
   - What hidden role does it play in everyday life?
   - Are there complexities to the concept that people overlook?
   - Is it generally agreed upon?
   - Why is it important that people have an appropriate understanding of this concept?

As you respond to the questions above—

- Write out your responses in complete sentences and paragraphs. Avoid the temptation to jot down phrases, make a rough outline, or cluster ideas. *Why*? Jotting down phrases, outlining, and clustering involve identifying *topic areas*. But writing complete sentences helps you explore and fill in *the particulars* of those areas.

- Write several paragraphs in response to each question. *Why*? Your goal is to explore *beyond* the obvious, initial ideas that come to mind easily. Think of it as breaking through a wall. You begin on the left side of the wall that includes the obvious ideas, and you want to break through that wall to the right side that includes new and interesting ideas you aren't currently thinking. You want to discover or create these new and interesting ideas. If you stop writing too soon, you will have stopped on the left side of the wall, in familiar territory. You might think of it this way: Write until you have run out of things to say. And then instead of stopping because you are done, imagine that you have run into the wall. Now break through that wall. The ideas you have not yet written down are on the right side of the wall—and this is what you want to get to.

3. Review your Invention writing. What new idea or way of thinking did you discover or create? What particular statements or passages from your Invention writing express this new idea or way of thinking?

2

Remembering Who You Were

John Metz

Chapter Objectives

This chapter will help you to:

- Discover meaning and significance in an event from your past.
- Discover and explain the public resonance of a personal memory.
- Develop a focused and revelatory essay, using narration, allusions, and dialog.

"Those who fail to learn the lessons of history are doomed to repeat them."

—George Santayana

INTRODUCTION

You have probably heard this famous statement—perhaps when someone in a history class asked plaintively, "Why do we have to learn this stuff?" Santayana's point is the past is filled with situations that teach us about ourselves and ignoring the past results in blindness to the present and future. While Santayana's statement is most often applied to a collective history (e.g., American or world history), it also suggests something for the individual. In the same way that countries learn from their pasts, individuals come to new insights because of their own experiences. We learn basic *dos* and *don'ts* from experience (not to ride a bike over the icy patch in the driveway, not to talk during math class, not to indulge too much the night before an exam). But our pasts are filled with more opportunity for insight beyond simple I'll-never-do-that-again situations. A vast array of moments lurks in the past, moments that may mean far more than what we have always assumed.

Writers looking into their pasts attempt to learn something new, understand the importance of a moment, or understand the significance of a situation. They are retrieving an event or situation, uncovering a moment, and examining it from their present perspective. The hope is that writers will see more about the situation than they could have seen in the past. Imagine an adult writer looking back at a childhood baseball game: As a child, he fretted over striking out in the last inning. But as an adult, he can see how important that moment of failure was to his life, to his intellectual and spiritual growth. The present (adult) writer is able to see this because the elapsed time has allowed him emotional and intellectual distance.

Memories do not, in themselves, teach us anything. We must create the lesson. We must look back at the past with a certain perspective: one of curiosity and possibility. Although we have lived through the past, we must entirely rediscover it if we are to learn.

The chapter readings will provide insight into various writing strategies. For example, they all develop a particular insight from some personal memory. Although the main insight of an essay is often placed in the opening paragraph, the essays in this chapter might communicate this insight elsewhere. Look for this insight as you read. Then identify, as much as possible, a particular moment the insight hinges on. Also look for the public resonance of the essay—the connection between the particular memory and a shared, or public, concern.

After reading the essays, you can find a topic in one of two ways—either go to the Point of Contact section to find a topic from your everyday life, or choose one of the Ideas for Writing that follow the essays. After finding a topic, go to the Analysis section to begin developing your ideas.

Selling Manure
Bonnie Jo Campbell

Writers try to see beyond the obvious—beyond simple reflexes and common associations. As they reach beyond the usual responses to everyday life, they may discover vulgarity in nice places and beauty where others least expect it. In this essay, Bonnie Jo Campbell, a celebrated short story writer and novelist, helps readers to see value in a dirty and potentially menial job—selling manure. Obviously, such work would stink. But Campbell helps us to consider the quiet honor and honesty of the job.

Mid-May, after school was out, I found myself staring six weeks of unemployment in the face. This bothered me only until I began to envision myself reading novels in the shade of my favorite hickory tree, or making and eating entire batches of chocolate fudge, staying up late to watch black and white movies. How long had it been, I tried to recall, since I spent an entire day on my horse or in the treehouse? My mother, however, had no patience for such idleness, and she lined up myriad farm chores to occupy me—including mucking out her big horse barn. The manure was so deep in places that the horses were scraping their heads on the ceilings.

"How are we going to get rid of this stuff?" I asked.

"You're going to load it in the back of the truck," said Mom, who was conveniently under doctor's orders to refrain from activities such as scooping, lifting, and flinging. "And then we're going to sell it."

She placed ads in the *Kalamazoo Gazette* and *The Kalamazoo Shopper,* offering manure for 35 dollars a truckload. My portion for doing the physical work was a generous 20 bucks; Mom got 15 for providing the truck and the product. Right away we got calls. A surprising number of people wanted the stuff we were so anxious to get rid of.

I spent much of that unseasonably hot May and June sweating inside the barn, moving layer after layer of manure and urine-soaked straw. Periodically, Mom brought me quart jars of iced tea to keep up my spirits and electrolytes—I could tell she was even feeling a little guilty about my working so hard. I didn't tell her that, far from feeling wretched as I loaded the truck, I was feeling revived. For one thing, I was in good company. The horses and donkeys wandered through and sniffed at me; the dogs lay in holes they'd dug outside the barn door and chewed on chunks of manure; a little garter snake who lived in a hole in the dirt floor slithered in and out of the barn under the wall. And I was enjoying letting my thoughts wander. After months of sitting in class, focusing on the drone of professors and poring over books and notes, I finally had rejoined the world of the living.

Delivering the manure was a little embarrassing at first. The body of my mother's pick-up truck was rusting away and the two sides of the bed were held together with shock cords. Most of our deliveries were to west side neighborhoods, and it was problematic that construction crews had narrowed West Main to one lane in each direction. Stuck in a traffic jam, in ninety-five degree heat with a half a ton of manure in the back, we made quite a sensation. In the beginning, I put my hand over my face and hoped that I wouldn't see anyone I knew.

Within about a week, however, I began to see the absurdity of our situation as liberating. As we rattled through well-kept neighborhoods in a pickup full of stinking manure, I loosened the safety belt and hung my leg out the passenger side window, and I felt like master of all I surveyed. Perhaps this was how a prostitute felt toward a wealthy, respectable client; I might be dirty, but I have something you need.

Mom and I provided an excellent quality product at a fair price to decent folks. The people who bought our product were nice—after all, only very earthy people would order manure from the farm rather than buying it deodorized and sterilized in bags from the store. Customers often tried to help me shovel, but after I rebuffed their advances they stood back and smiled at the cascading dung. Hands on hips, eyes sparkling, they might have been fantasizing about late-summer gardens brimming with tomatoes and squash.

One man who lived just off Stadium Drive was planting a full acre of garden on land he'd rented from the utility company. After I unloaded the truck under the power lines, he took Mom and me to admire a mound across the way. "Do you know what that is?" he asked. "That's llama manure. And this pile over here, that's pig manure. And that's chicken." The pig pile was so fragrant that I figured he'd soon have trouble with his neighbors in the nearby apartment complex, but his enthusiasm was touching. I felt proud that our manure was out in the world, mingling with other manures, making things grow.

There is no vocation more honest than selling manure. Consider what most people do for a living. They go to work where they build crap, or sell crap, or move crap, or spin a line of bull over the telephone, all the while trying to convince the customer that their product is something other than crap. When I deliver a load of manure to someone's garden, the customer and I are both upfront about what we were dealing with. All I have to ask is, "Where do you want this shit?"

This experience has made me reflect on the idea of work in general. Any job is an important job, whether it is selling manure or selling insurance. People should take pride in what they do, and not assume that a low-paying job or a dirty job makes them second class citizens. And even the smelliest job has its rewards.

My darling Christopher works second shift at a paper converting plant in Parchment. "What are you doing today?" he asked me, as I walked him out to his truck. I told him I was going to spend the afternoon shoveling manure.

"Aren't we all," he said, nodding. "Aren't we all."

WRITING STRATEGIES

1. What is the main idea of Campbell's essay? And how is it something beyond the obvious?

2. Explain how detailed description works in the essay. For instance, how do the details about the barn, the dogs, and the heat figure into her main idea?

3. How does Campbell support the notion that her work was *liberating?*

4. How does Campbell create public resonance? Point to a particular passage in which Campbell makes her own experience relevant to others.

5. Explain how the customers' responses work in the essay (in ¶8 and ¶9). Focus on specific sentences or descriptions, and explain how they relate to Campbell's main idea.

EXPLORING IDEAS

1. Campbell boldly states, "There is no vocation more honest than selling manure." How is that true?

2. Campbell says that the absurdity of her situation made it liberating. How does that work? Explain how absurd predicaments free us from something—from our usual routines, from the oppression of our daily concerns.

3. In ¶7, Campbell compares herself to a prostitute. What makes that an appropriate or inappropriate comparison?

4. This essay suggests something about socioeconomic status—working-class, middle-class, and upper-class jobs. How is this essay a defense or celebration of working-class life?

IDEAS FOR WRITING

1. What experience was a little (or a lot) embarrassing at first but later became liberating? Help the reader understand how you came to feel differently about the experience. (Avoid making obvious points, such as it was no longer embarrassing because you were better at doing it.)

2. What job of yours was either very honest or very dishonest? Help the reader see the less obvious value the work had for you and for others.

If responding to one of these ideas, go to the Analysis section of this chapter to begin developing ideas for your essay.

How I Lost the Junior Miss Pageant
Cindy Bosley

Most people have never participated in a beauty pageant. But nearly everyone has experienced the angst associated with the quiet pageantry of everyday life—the constant pressure to perform well in public, to look the part of a happy, stable, well-to-do member of society. Cindy Bosley, a teacher and published poet, is brave enough to share her early attempts at dealing with this pressure. On one hand, this essay is an examination of beauty pageants and the awkward system of values and beliefs that surround them; on the other, it is an intimate look at a mother/daughter relationship defined by the social goings-on of a small city in the middle of America.

Every evening of the annual broadcast of the Miss America Pageant, I, from the age of seven or so, carefully laid out an elaborate chart so that I might also participate as an independent judge of the most important beauty contest in the world. From my viewing seat on a green striped couch in my parents' smoky living room where the carpet, a collage of white, brown, and black mixed-shag, contrasted so loudly with the cheap 70s furnishings that it threatened my attention to the television set, I sat with popcorn and soda, pen in hand, thrilled at the oncoming parade of the most beautiful women in the world.

In the hours before the show began, I'd carefully written out in ink, sometimes over and over, names of all 50 states, Washington, D.C., and Puerto Rico along the y axis of my paper. And my categories of evaluation of the contestants ribbed themselves along the x axis—beauty, poise, swimsuit, evening gown—plus categories of my own—hair, likability, teeth. Over the years, an increasingly complex system of points and penalties evolved: an extra point for being tan, a loss of points for sucking up, more points for breasts, more points for unpainted nails, fewer points for big noses, fewer points for skinny lips, an extra point for smartness, subtraction of a point for playing the piano. Who wants to hear a sonata? Dance for me, bounce your bootie.

My mother had secret hopes. Finally divorced for the second time from the same man, my father, she sat with me and gave her own running commentary about who was cute, who smiled too much, who would find a handsome husband. My mother, having always been a little to a lot overweight, excelled at swimming, and she told me much later that she chose swimming because she didn't feel fat in the water. Her sister was the cheerleader, but she was a swimmer, too heavy for a short skirt of her own, she said. My mother's secret was that she wanted the winner to be her daughter. Sitting with me on the couch at 137 North Willard Street, she already knew I wasn't tall enough or pretty enough in the way of models and movie stars to ever stand a chance, but her real fear, which I only became aware of as an older teen, was that I would always be too chubby and too backward and too different and too poor, for which she blamed herself, to win a beauty pageant. Still, there were always those surprises of the contests—Miss Utah? She was no good! Why did she win? What were those judges

---

thinking! It should have been Miss Alabama, anyone can see that. Who would have guessed Miss Utah, with that mole on her shoulder?

After my mother's never-subtle hints that if I'd just lose 20 pounds boys would like me and I might even win a beauty contest, it was my friend Bridget who wanted us to enter the Ottumwa (pronounced Uh-TUM-wuh) Junior Miss Pageant together. I secretly believed that I stood a better chance than Bridget did, though she had the right name and the right body, though she wore the right clothes and was more magazine-beautiful than I. I had *some* hope for the contest: I had *some* talents and a kind of baby-cute innocence complete with blond hair and blue eyes that I was sure the judges would find "charming and fresh." Yeah, okay, so I was already engaged to be married—so what—I was still on my way to college, and Bridget was not. And Judy was funny but had a flat face. Marcy was smart but had no breasts or hips. Carol was pretty but totally uncoordinated and her knees came together when she jumped. Desirea had enviable boobs, almost as nice as mine and probably firmer, but her chin did weird things when she smiled and her eyes were brown.

We practiced, all of us together, several times a week with a lithe woman—somebody's mom with good hair and body—getting us into form for the stage. This was the era of *Flashdance,* so we all wore our own leg warmers and torn sweatclothes and fancy headband scarves. If you were one of the north-side girls (that meant your daddy was a businessman or doctor), you had gotten your leg warmers from Marshall Field's in Chicago. If you were Bridget, your dad worked at John Deere like mine but was in management and not out in the factory threading bolts on a greasy, noisy machine, so you got your leg warmers from the mall in Des Moines. If you were me, with a factory dad who didn't even live in the same house, you got your leg warmers from Kmart down the road because Target was all the way across town and too expensive, and Wal-Mart hadn't yet been born as far as we knew. The fancy mom-lady made sure everyone had a brochure about her charm school (this is small-town Iowa, mind you, so anyone operating a charm school and modeling agency in this town was kidding themselves. But making lots of money.).

So 14 of us, nervous, jealous, ears ringing with Mirror-Mirror-on-the-Wall, met daily for two weeks prior to the pageant to go over our choreographed group fitness routine to be performed, not in swimsuits, but in short-shorts and white T-shirts, Hooters-style (also not invented yet as far as we knew), and to discuss such techniques as Vaseline along the teeth and gum lines to promote smooth smiles, lest our lips dry out and get stuck in a grin during discussions with the judges of the agonies of world hunger. We were each responsible for our own talent routines and props, and each one of us had to provide a 5×7 black-and-white photo for the spread in the town paper.

The photographs were a problem. My father did not believe in such things for girls as shoes, clothes, haircuts, college, or photographs for Junior Miss, and so there was no way he was going to give a penny for a pageant-worthy dress or a professional photographer's 10-minutes-plus-proofs. I believe my mother even humiliated herself enough to ask. This was hard for her, since he'd admitted before leaving to a five-year affair with a woman who looked surprisingly like my mother but heavier. So Mom and I tried some Polaroid headshots against the side of the house, but me dressed up in my prettiest sailor blouse couldn't counteract the hospital green of the aluminum siding. We moved up to our only other option, which was my mother's flash camera with Instamatic film, and still nothing suitable (I could have agreed on one of the Polaroid shots, but my mother knew it would knock me out of the contest for sure even before the night itself).

I don't know who she borrowed the money from or what she did to get the favor, but my mother had me down at Lee's Photography the very next afternoon, and he took one shot and offered us the one proof. Abracadabra, there was my face among all the other faces as a contestant in the Uh-TUM-wuh Junior Miss Pageant. From the layout in the paper, it looked to me, and to my flushed mother, as though I had as good a shot as any.

The contest night went quickly: my foot, couched, pinched, and Band-Aided uncomfortably in a neighbor's hand-me-down high heels, slipped (hear the auditorium's quick and loud intake of breath in horror!) as I walked forward to say my name with a strong, vibrant hello just like I'd been coached by the fancy-mom; my dress was last year's prom dress, which earned me no cool points with my peers but didn't lose me any either since I had none to subtract; I managed not to land on my bottom (as I had in every practice before the contest) in my gymnastics routine, self-choreographed with my own robot-style moves to the synthesizer-heavy tune "Electricity," by a band that was popular in Sacramento, California, in that year, 1985, but not yet in my hometown. (The cassette tape had been given to me by my Hispanic, juvenile delinquent, just-released-from-young-boy-prison-in-California ex-boyfriend Jim.)

My exercise routine went off very well in front of the crowd, and I don't think anyone could even tell that my shorts were soaking wet from having been dropped by me into the toilet just an hour before as I arranged my items for quick-change. My mother and fiancé were actually sitting together, their mutual hatred of each other squeezed like a child between them. I'd even kept myself from leaving my mother behind when, backstage after the contest as I hugged and cried in joy for the co-winners and out of desperate relief that it was over now, my mother, beside herself with embarrassment for me and disappointment for herself, and misunderstanding my tears, hissed loudly enough for the benefit of everyone, "STOP your crying, they'll think you're not a nice LOSER!"

So I had done it: I had been a contestant in the Junior Miss Pageant and my mother had the snapshots to prove it.

I'd lost the contest because I didn't yet know how to tell people what they wanted to hear. The small girl that boys secretly liked but wouldn't date doesn't win Miss America. The girl hiding in her room reading and writing poetry doesn't win Miss America. The girl playing violin despite her mother's anxiousness that other people will think she's weird doesn't win Miss America. The girl on Willard Street doesn't ever win Miss America.

But the truth is that I'd lost the contest when I told the judges, when they asked, that my most personal concern was my mother's loneliness, and if I could change anything at all, I would give her something—a man, God, anything to free her from that loneliness.

Clearly, I lacked the save-the-whales-and-rainforest civic-mindedness required not only of Miss America, but of Junior Miss America, too. Even, although one wouldn't think it, in Ottumwa, Iowa, where my mother would go on to work in a bathtub factory, and then a glue factory, and then an electrical connectors factory (the factory worker's version of upward mobility), and finally, a watch factory where they shipped and received not just watches but cocaine in our town that at that time had more FBI agents in it than railroad engineers. And even in this town where my sister would go to work the kill floor of the pork plant where, for fun, the workers shot inspection dye at each other and threatened each other's throats with hack-knives. And even in this town where my cousin, age 13, would bring a bomb to seventh grade for show-and-tell, and get caught and evacuated, and be given community service to do because the public-school-as-terrorist-ground phenomena hadn't yet been born. And even in this town where if you want to go to college, you better know someone who knows how to get you there because otherwise it's too far away and too much money and too much trouble and way, way, way beyond your own intellect and sense of self to do it alone. How scary (get married). How wasteful (get married). How expensive (get married). How strange (get married). How pretentious (get married). How escapist (get married).

If your parents are crazy and poor, and if you can't win the Junior Miss Pageant, and if it's the kind of town where you stay or they don't ever want you coming back, you get married, you move to Texas where your husband sells drugs, you hide away from the world until your self grows enough to break you out, and then you leave and you pray for your mother's loneliness and you spend your life learning to come to terms with your own, and you are smart and willful and strong, and you don't ever have to draw another chart before the pageant begins.

My mother told me later that she was just sure I would have won the Junior Miss contest if I hadn't made that awful mistake in my gymnastics routine (I don't know what mistake she was talking about—it was the least flawed part of the evening), but I knew the truth about why I'd lost, and I knew I'd lost even before the contest or the practices began. I'd lost this contest at birth, probably, to be born to my father who had a date that night, and to my mother who believed some girls—girls like me, and girls like her—had to try very hard to catch and keep a boy's attention. I'd lost the contest in borrowed shoes and an out-of-date dress. I'd lost the contest with the engagement ring on my seventeen-year-old finger. I'd lost the contest with wet shorts and too funky music. I'd lost the contest with a bargain photograph and Kmart leg warmers. I'd lost the contest with an orange Honda Express moped parked between the other girls' cars. I'd lost the contest in a falling-down green house. I'd lost the contest in the grease on my father's hands and hair and the taste of grease in his lunchbox leftovers. I'd lost the contest in my growingly cynical evaluation of Miss America as I'd gotten older—"chubby thighs touching, minus five points," "big hair, minus three points," "too small nipples, minus two," "flabby arms, minus five," and subtract and subtract and subtract. It's a contest no one should want to win. Our mothers should not have such dreams for us. Our mothers should not have such loneliness.

WRITING STRATEGIES

1. Complete the following sentence: The main idea of Bosley's essay is that _____.

2. Bosley uses details to hold the reader's interest. Select three details that got your attention and explain how they help the reader understand and accept Bosley's main idea.

3. How does Bosley make her essay matter to someone who doesn't care about pageants?

4. Describe Bosley's writer's voice. For example, would you say it is angry, comedic, intense, dark, professional, light? Come up with your own descriptive term (or terms) and explain how three sentences from the essay support your description.

5. Divide Bosley's essay into at least four parts and briefly summarize the purpose of each part.

EXPLORING IDEAS

1. What basic value or belief drives the way Bosley now thinks about pageants?

2. Explain how Bosley's point about pageants speaks to one of the following issues: competition, class, tradition, media. To what other issue does the essay speak? What point does it make about the issue?

3. Interview several people to find out how they view pageants. Record their responses, then explain what viewpoints are the most common, most unusual, and most thought provoking.

IDEAS FOR WRITING

1. Discover the significance of an experience or activity in which you participated with disappointing results.

2. Discover the significance of an experience or activity at which you exceeded your own expectations.

If responding to one of these ideas, go to the Analysis section of this chapter to begin developing ideas for your essay.

STUDENT ESSAY

STUDENT ESSAY

The Thrill of Victory . . .
The Agony of Parents
Jennifer Schwind-Pawlak

We often get caught up in the moment. As children—and as adults—we first react to situations one way, and then later make better sense of what happened. Jennifer Schwind-Pawlak, who wrote the following essay for a college writing course, explores one of these moments from her past. As you read the essay, notice how Schwind-Pawlak uses her own particular experience to tap into a more universal one. From a new perspective, allowed for by the distance of time, she finds the positive value of what appeared back then to be a negative experience. In this essay, she stands back and talks about the experience, engaging readers with key details, a mature writer's voice, and an important lesson.

Parents—one word that can strike many emotions in children when said aloud. Some children will smile and think about how silly their dad looked when he put carrot sticks up his nose that very morning, while others will cringe when they think about how their mother picked them up from school last week wearing orange polyester pants and a green shirt, oblivious to the hard work that some fellow went through to create the color wheel. My own emotional state of mind seemed to run the gamut throughout childhood. I chose to blame my parents for all of the traumatic events that unfolded but took pride in my obvious independence during the successes. One of the most heinous crimes that my parents committed was "the soccer foul." If I could have ejected them from the game of life at that point, I would have.

The relationship between parents and children. Parents commit "fouls" or "crimes."

Introduces general subject matter leading up to the main idea: parent/child dynamics.

Ironically, I was not particularly fond of soccer. Being the youngest of four children, I often chose to run around the field with friends while my brothers and sisters performed feats of soccer, the likes of which had only been seen during the World Cup. I would happily contort my fingers into chubby pretzels while singing "The Itsy Bitsy Spider" as the game's events were recounted on the drives home. Still, whether by guilt or by the need to belong, I joined the team when I became of age.

"The Thrill of Victory, The Agony of Parents," by Jennifer Schwind-Pawlak. Reprinted with permission of author.

The team that I played on was designed to turn the young and awkward into the swans of the soccer field. My father (a one-time soccer coach) explained several times that this was the time that I would learn the rules and workings of the game and that I shouldn't expect much more than that. Since it was a child's league, learning and the team experience were the focuses. Winning was a pleasant bonus but should not be achieved at the cost of the main objectives. This litany was taken and stored somewhere in the recesses of my brain. For me, however, the main objective was looking cool while running down the field chasing a spotted ball. Everything else seemed secondary.

Due to the family history, I attended every Tuesday and Thursday practice and managed to make each a social occasion while going through the motions of the game. I succeeded in understanding the game and, though not the most skilled of players, began to enjoy the half game of playing time that was required by the league for each player. Though I was far from a star player, I felt that my contribution mattered to the overall outcomes of the games, all of which had been lost to this point.

Sunday, the morning of the fifth game of the season, came with no warning. I got up, went to church with the family, then came home to suit up for the game. Upon arrival at the field, I was greeted by the coach and went to take my place along the sidelines with the rest of my team. There was a buzz of excitement that left me with the feeling that I would get when my brother would poke me with his fingertip after dragging his stocking feet across the carpet. The team that we were playing had a record identical to ours. We could win this game. I didn't care what the parents said. Winning would be a blast.

The coach kept me on the sidelines the entire first half of the game, which my pre-adolescent mind attributed to my obviously increasing skill at the game. He was saving his trump card, me, for the last half of the game. I knew this was rare, but I was sure that his reason was to bedazzle the crowd and the other team with my pure firepower on the field. The other players, except one other girl, continued to cycle in and out of the game. While I was excited because we were winning the game, I was concerned that the coach had forgotten about me. I inched, ever so slowly, toward him and started mindless conversation to let him know that I was there. He spoke to me, so I knew that he could not

Margin notes:

Develops essay through narration and description.

Details are carefully selected: father's explanation becomes key later in the essay.

Sets up the fifth game. Excitement, suspense are building.

Description of the fifth game.

We all—most of us—have not gotten to play at some point: common experience?

Three-word paragraph has dramatic effect.

She is "horrified" not to play.

Description of "the foul."

She is "horrified" and looks to her mother for help. Turns out, her mother is "horrified" too, and reacts in a way that makes things worse. What does she learn about her mother, parents, and relationships from her mother's reaction—and from her reaction to it?

Reflects on her experience—what "looking back" means.

She sees the experience differently now. Sometimes—many times—we see differently when something's happening than we do later on.

She gives possible reasons for never playing another organized sport again.

have forgotten about me. As the game was winding down, I was sure that he must have decided to put me in for the last play of the game.

The game ended.

I was horrified to realize that I had not played one moment of the first win of the season. After all of that practice and the ugly uniform, I was deemed such a poor player that I was not even good enough to play one moment of that game. How would I ever live this down at school? How would I face all of my classmates on Monday? My stomach began to churn, the way that it does when you are going down the first hill of any great roller coaster. I looked to my parents for support, which only added to the horror of that day.

Joann (the name I call my mother when she does something embarrassing) was screaming at the coach. In a voice so screeching that it rivaled fingernails on a blackboard, she told him that he was a disgraceful coach and that he should be ashamed of himself. She continued to point out the error of his ways by reminding him that I had not played at all in the game. How could she do this to me? My mother had managed to enlighten the few people that hadn't noticed on their own that I had not played at all. What was she thinking? She might as well have rented billboard space saying, "So what if Jeni sucks at soccer? The coach wouldn't let her play." My only thought was, "I don't want to go to school tomorrow!"

Looking back, I realize that it wasn't so bad the next day at school. I walked out to recess and talked about how nuts my mother was and everyone seemed to agree, sympathize, and get on with the important task of freeze tag. At that moment I wasn't sure that I would ever be able to forgive my mother for what happened that day, but, as far as I can recall, I began loving her again within the week. I am sure that she either cooked my favorite dinner, told a corny joke, or told me how much she loved me to make that lump of anger fade away.

I never went to soccer again. As a matter of fact, I never played another organized sport again. Maybe it was the fear of rejection. Maybe it was the uncertainty of my talent. Maybe I was just too busy with other things. I never really felt the urge to compete on that level after that day.

The relationship that I have with my parents has changed very much throughout the years. The polyester pants don't bother me anymore, but the carrot sticks still make me laugh. While their "soccer foul" embarrassed and angered me at the time, I understand and appreciate it now. My mother was angry *FOR* me. She was hurt *FOR* me. Through the pages of time, I can look back and see that, more often than not, I embarrassed her. She never stopped feeling for me, loving me, or protecting me. I have grown enough to realize that, though I often pointed out my parents' fouls, they scored countless goals that I didn't even notice.

She sees the experience differently now, finding meaning through reflection: Parents and children embarrass each other sometimes. This is part of the relationship. In this situation, her mother was angry/hurt FOR her.

WRITING STRATEGIES

1. Explain why Schwind-Pawlak's opening paragraph makes the reader want to continue reading.

2. Why does Schwind-Pawlak tell us that her father "explained several times that this was the time that <she> would learn the rules and workings of the game and that <she> shouldn't expect much more than that" (¶3)?

Julie Elliot/StockXchng

3. Is Schwind-Pawlak's writer's voice funny, serious, pensive, silly? Describe it in your own words and then refer to three sentences that support your decision.

4. What subject would you say Schwind-Pawlak's essay is about: parents, soccer, life, growing up, or something else? What is Schwind-Pawlak's main point about the topic?

5. What details does Schwind-Pawlak use to help the reader understand and accept her main idea?

EXPLORING IDEAS

1. In groups or on your own through writing, discuss experiences like Schwind-Pawlak's. Can you recall a similar embarrassing experience of your own? Are such experiences inevitable? What makes them valuable? What can make them harmful?

2. What activity did you have the ability, opportunity, and interest to do again, but only did once? What is it, or was it, about yourself that kept you from doing it again?

IDEAS FOR WRITING

1. What is the significance of a big game or event from your past?

2. What emotional or intellectual experience has prevented you from ever doing something again? How has the experience influenced your later decisions?

If responding to one of these ideas, go to the Analysis section of this chapter to begin developing ideas for your essay.

INVENTION

"I'm digging in the dirt/To find the places I got hurt/To open up the places I got hurt."

—"Digging in the Dirt," Peter Gabriel

Invention is not simply about finding a topic. It also involves exploring and analyzing that topic, examining your thoughts, and developing points. For a remembering essay, the process will be self-reflective. It will begin with a personal exploration, but the broader goal is to discover something that others can share. The following three sections are designed to help you through invention—to discover a particular topic, situation, or event from your past (in Point of Contact), to develop points about the topic (in Analysis), and to make it relevant to a community of readers (in Public Resonance). The Invention Questions in each section are not meant to be answered directly in your final written assignment, but using them to explore ideas will help you begin writing and keep intensive ideas flowing.

Point of Contact

You might think that nothing interesting has ever happened to you, but even if you have never won the lottery, wrestled an alligator, or been on a first date, your life is filled with thousands of situations that can reveal something to you and to your audience. Use the following questions to help find a specific situation, event, or set of events from your life.

Call or Write Someone from Your Past Ask him or her about your shared history.

- What do you remember most about our lives back then?
- What was the best part of our lives? The worst?
- How have we both changed since then? Why did we change?
- What forces, feelings, or situations kept us together?

Do Something That You Have Not Done for Many Years Go fishing, play baseball, listen to a particular song, reread a particular book. Then consider the following: How was doing the activity now different from doing it in the past?

Visit a Place from Your Past A schoolyard, a house, an apartment building, an old neighborhood, a workplace, etc.

- What memories or feelings are most prominent?
- How have my feelings about the place changed?

Jerry Zitterman/Shutterstock.com

Look through a Photo Album or Yearbook

- What do I remember thinking or feeling at the time of the photograph?
- How is that different from what I feel now looking at the photograph?

Recall an Event from Your Past Life

- **School**   Did I ever get beat up? Did I ever beat up someone else? Was I ever embarrassed by a teacher or classmate? Did I ever win or lose a big sporting event? Was I popular or unpopular? Did I fit into a particular clique (jocks, hoods, hippies, punks, nerds)? When did I come out of my shell?

- **Work**   What was my first job? Did I like or dislike it? Why did I leave? How did I get along with my peers? My boss? Did the job put me in any weird situations?

- **Social Life**   When was my first date? When did I first stay out late? Did I have a lot of friends? No friends? What situation led to my first friendship? When did I first learn about the differences between girls and boys? Was I asked to drink or try drugs? When did I first drive a car (illegally or legally)? Did I ever change my hair or image drastically?

- **Family Life**   Did I experience a sibling being born? Have I experienced a child of my own being born? Did we have a pet? Did we take any family vacations? Have I ever embarrassed my family? Has my family embarrassed me? What did we do on weekends? Did we eat dinner, watch television, or attend religious services together?

ACTIVITY

The questions above only hint at the many possible topics. In a group or alone, generate more questions until one has triggered something for you.

WRITING A LITERACY NARRATIVE

One type of remembering essay is a **literacy narrative**, which tells the story of a significant experience that contributed to your current relationship with literacy (with reading and/or writing). Because a literacy narrative is a type of remembering essay, this chapter can help you invent ideas about a moment or situation in the past and then convey them as an essay.

Point Of Contact: Begin to generate a list of possible topics by considering important literacy experiences—significant experiences and particular moments that changed your relationship with reading and writing (and ultimately with ideas). It may help to think in categories: before elementary school, elementary school, middle school, junior high, high school; summer; parents, teachers, friends, celebrities, athletes; boys; girls; good experiences, bad experiences, changes, surprises; beginnings, endings. These are not the only categories you can think about. The point is that **thinking in categories** is an invention strategy—a way for you to come up with ideas you're not currently thinking.

Analysis and Public Resonance: From your list of possibilities, choose one experience that allows you to focus on a particular moment that changed your relationship with literacy. Then use the Analysis and Public Resonance sections to explore deeper into the experience. As you respond to the Analysis and Public Resonance questions, pay attention to particular attitudes, people, places, sounds, colors, feelings, smells, and so on. You won't include all these particulars in your essay. You are noting them now because you are using writing to explore, discover, and develop ideas.

Thesis: Because your thesis will be derived from all the thinking and writing you do in response to the Analysis and Public Resonance sections, it helps to wait until after you generate ideas to make rhetorical decisions about how to convey your literacy narrative to readers. At that point, turn to the Thesis section for help focusing your ideas on one particular insight. Your thesis should make clear the significance of your literacy narrative by stating the significance in a one-sentence statement.

Delivery: The Analysis, Public Resonance, Thesis, and Rhetorical Tools sections are key to creating the raw material (the ideas) you will need *before* trying to convey ideas to readers. In addition to the information in those sections, for a literacy narrative consider the following:

- Organization—How will you arrange the narrative? Will you go chronologically from beginning to end? Will you start in the middle then fill in the details leading up to the significance? Will you start at the end and then go back to the beginning?

- Writer's Voice—Consider how your voice as a writer helps readers understand and accept your thesis.

- Vitality—Make sure you delete and combine ideas to emphasize main points and keep the story moving along. Use descriptive details to bring the narrative to life for readers, but be selective. Don't bog readers down in unnecessary details.

- Images and Design—What images (photos, drawings, diagrams, video) and document design features (spacing, font, headings) can help readers understand and accept your thesis?

- Revision—

    —Where can you combine/delete ideas for clarity, conciseness, and vitality?

    —Where can you add ideas to fill in gaps for readers?

    —If you told a story and then stated the significance at the end, how can you weave the significance throughout the story? (Avoid a closing *the-moral-of-the-story-is* paragraph.)

    —If the point (the significance) of the narrative is dull, obvious, or uninteresting, how can you narrow your focus and dig deeper to make the narrative more meaningful and interesting to readers?

Analysis

As you analyze a particular event or situation from your past, you will try to find its *significance*— why something is important for both the writer and the readers. The following Invention Questions will help you venture into possibilities that might yield insight and meaning:

> How did I change? (Who was I before and after the situation?)
> Why did the event or situation occur? What forces were at work?
> Did I realize the significance of the event at the time? Why or why not?
> What do I see now that I didn't see then? What did that younger person not understand?
> Why was the event or situation important to me?

    —Did it help me to understand myself as a man or woman?

    —Did it help me to grow intellectually? Spiritually? Socially?

    —Did it help me to see myself in a different way?

As you analyze, remember that the goal is not simply to tell a story about your past, but to discover something meaningful—something that can be shared with and valued by others. Imagine a writer, Jack, who visited his old elementary school:

What do I see now that I didn't see then?
I see that school is important, and back then I didn't.

Jack answers the question and *begins* walking the path of analysis, but his brief answer does not go far enough. It does not reveal the real complexity of his experience. He says that "school is important," but such a phrase is broad and hollow. What particular aspect of school, we might ask, is important? What specific moments or situations are valuable to a growing individual? Struggling through impossibly difficult classes? The reward of a good grade? Being prompted to read material one would otherwise ignore? Or maybe what's important is the slow and charted evolution of one's identity through various classes, teachers, friends, and hallways. Jack's answer blankets such rich possibilities, covering them up with a broad, sweeping phrase.

Another writer, Diana, goes further in her thinking:

What do I see now that I didn't see then?

When I was younger, I didn't see the big picture, how my life in school connected to anything outside of school. I went, did the work, and came home, but mostly daydreamed about the time I'd spend away from schoolwork. For me, and probably most of my friends, life was separate from schoolwork. Every day, the goal was to get it done so we could be away from it. I remember the feeling of freedom in running out the door after school or during recess, but what I was running toward was a bunch of silly games, posing, and meaningless searches for excitement. I never thought, maybe I was never taught, that learning is really what makes life worth anything, that an intellectual challenge is real excitement. When I was a teenager, I was focused on the surface—the shallow giddiness of thrills and "parties." I thought school was a drag—and I looked for every possible excuse to be bored. I actually *convinced* myself to be bored. But now that I am older, I realize that school is the only place where people actually care about your mind—where they want you to grow, imagine, and experience new ideas. These are the things that make life outside of school worth living. I see that now.

All the jobs I had after high school just wanted me to perform a certain duty. No one wanted me to explore my intellectual potential. And unfortunately, I see a lot of younger college students still thinking the way I did in high school. They moan at challenging assignments; they just want to duck out of everything. Today, a boy said to me, "Can you believe how long that reading took?" as though the goal were to get through it. What's that about? Well, I know what it's about—blindness to the big picture.

Diana's thoughts are developing as she makes specific distinctions between her present and her past understanding. In the past, she did not question her own boredom. But in the present she has distance from her old self and can see false assumptions and misplaced values.

Thinking Further

Although Diana has already analyzed further than Jack did, she should not stop yet. Through analysis she has unearthed some interesting new ideas. Now she can review her invention writing and identify her best ideas, using them not as final conclusions but as springboards into further exploration. Now she can seek out some insight that lurks even further below the surface of her previous discoveries.

For example, if Diana's goal is to share the significance of a memory, she could say that she realized *school is where people care about your mind—where they want you to grow, imagine, and experience new ideas—and that these are the things that make life outside of school worth living.* And she could illustrate her thesis by discussing how certain teachers encouraged her to grow and imagine while she scorned their encouragement. But what if Diana sought out the underlying reasons for her childhood behavior? She could quickly claim that she was a wild and typical adolescent. Or, she could think past that assumption, returning to the Invention Questions on page 44. Now that she has generated some new thinking, the same questions (and new ones that Diana comes up with on her own) can lead to even further insights. For example:

Why did the event or situation occur? What forces were at work?

Why didn't I see the big picture? Who or what is to blame? It isn't as if everybody in high school failed to take advantage of it. Many students were highly motivated. (Although even students who seemed motivated might have had misplaced priorities.) Still, had I known then what I know now, I might have worked harder and learned more, perhaps gone to a better college, and excelled in all kinds of ways. Perhaps my parents should have forced me to study harder, or helped me to better understand the importance of high school. Perhaps—probably—they didn't understand it themselves. But couldn't my teachers have gotten through to me? So many of them seemed disinterested. Others tried, but what could they do? And what about the media, pop culture, sports, the mall? All these factors competed and, in my case, won out over education.

By analyzing further, Diana is getting closer to the root of a complex issue: she is discovering that her attitude toward high school was impacted by competing factors, such as the media, pop culture, sports, and the mall. However, the writing above does not provide final answers. Diana has even more exploring to do, which might include additional invention writing, discussion with others, and secondary research.

To go further with your own thinking, focus on a key issue in your invention writing. Then return to the Invention Questions on page 44 and create probing questions on your own. Use them to reveal something deeper, more hidden, more complex, about the situation. For example:

> What other forces were at play?

> Why were they hidden from my view back then?

> What makes people blind to such forces in their lives?

In her response to the Invention Questions on page 44, Cindy Bosley hones in and finds meaning in a "small moment." Bosley's notes are exploratory. They are not simple answers to questions. Much of the language in her response does not appear in her final essay, but she is willing to explore and stretch her reasoning:

Why did the event or situation occur?

If I isolate the event or situation as the gulf between my own grasp of fun and happiness and my mother's severe disappointment and embarrassment, her concern that others would think I was not a "nice loser" in that small moment, I think it clearly speaks so much more about my mother—as though I saw her, her disappointments and worries about image and desirability in herself through me. She was no stage mother, not at all, but she must have had these fears about how people in the town looked at her, and at us, her three children, because of my father to a certain extent, but also just because she herself was a woman who'd grown up to some degree "unacceptable" in her and her family's eyes because she was heavy, or because she liked lots of boys, or because she got pregnant and married, or because she moved so far away. My mother was and is a creative, talented, vibrant woman and she worked very hard, and very successfully, sacrificing so much for herself so my sister, brother, and I could have the things that we wanted like the other kids, things that might help us break out of our own family's economic situation. Things like acrobat lessons, and cheer-leading camp, and swimming lessons, and overnight birthday parties. I have absolutely no idea how she pulled all those things off.

Bosley focuses not only on the beauty pageant but also on the layers of emotions beneath it—those tied to her mother. She discovers a fresh perspective by looking closely at the life that led up to and surrounded the pageant. And from these notes, the ideas evolve in her essay:

But the truth is that I'd lost the contest when I told the judges, when they asked, that my most personal concern was my mother's loneliness, and if I could change anything at all, I would give her something—a man, God, anything to free her from that loneliness.

Discovering the significance of the past can be tricky. The most significant events might at first seem totally normal or insignificant. For example, a single soccer game spent standing on the sidelines would seem to have no meaning, other than frustration, for the younger Schwind-Pawlak; but to the older writer looking back, the game reveals something about her relationship with her parents.

Invention Workshop

After exploring the past on your own, you might hit a wall. Here's where an invention partner can help you break through and discover a focused insight worth sharing with readers. Review your invention writing thus far, and with your invention partner(s) discuss: *What could I now tell that younger version of me?* In your discussion, explore, discover, and develop possibilities, then ask: *What hidden forces were at work? Why didn't I understand things differently back then?* Remember that the goal of this invention workshop is to reveal something new.

ACTIVITY

Record a video of an invention workshop. One group member can shoot the video while the others prompt the writer with questions, beginning with those in this (Analysis) section and then any others that emerge through the invention process. After the workshop, the writer should review the video, identifying interesting points worthy of further exploration.

Public Resonance

What you discover about your past should suggest something for the lives of your readers. Dealing with public resonance means addressing the connection between your particular memory and a public or shared issue. You may have already found public resonance. If not, closely consider your response to the following:

> What public issue is related to my memory and how?

> What does my memory reveal or show about the nature of _____? (Childhood? Teenagers? Towns? Families? Schools? Teachers? Religious institutions? Education? Parenthood? Growing up? Failing? Succeeding? Suffering? Dying? Healing?)

> Who might relate to my memory?

In this excerpt from Cindy Bosley's invention notes, she does not merely reinforce her early feelings of confusion; she discovers "the truth of" her confusion:

What public issue is related to my memory?

This isn't about my mother so much as it is about women more generally, and the images we're given through history at birth and before and never ever really break. I always felt shame after what I told the judges about wanting my mother to not have to be so lonely—how narrow of me, how far I missed the point—and yet, now I feel the truth of it, and I hope if I could go back, I'd still tell them that's the one thing I'd want to be able to change—for my mother to be able to feel beautiful and free and lovely and bright, overweight or not, advanced education or not, and with or without a man.

I remember my joy in graduate school when my friend Karen hosted a Miss America party the night of the pageant, and maybe my essay began to grow here. It was that night that I discovered I wasn't the ONLY little girl making up my own score sheets for the contest, hoping to predict who would win, and always imagining, because we thought it was the thing to wish for, that we could someday be Miss America. And all the usual stuff about women's narrow, "perfected" images in the media, Barbie dolls, fairy tales, all of it comes to bear here. There's such a feeling of shame and degradation (I don't think it is too big a word to describe it) in allowing oneself to be judged in this way, whether literally in a contest, or even just by agreeing to play, which we all do, by all the ancient rules of "fitting in," whether you're male or female. And there seems to be this desperate hole of loneliness and fear that seems anchored to it all. We often recognize it first in other people.

Although your answers to the Invention Questions may not appear word-for-word in your final writing, they should generate focused thinking that finds its way into the final draft. For example, in her notes, Bosley discovers that her situation (and her mother's loneliness) is not unique. And in the conclusion of her essay, she makes this evident by changing the personal pronoun from *I* to *our,* thereby including others in her thinking. This links her realization about pageants and mother/daughter relationships to others so that her essay is not simply about herself, but about people who grew up in similar conditions. Bosley shows us how an unusual memory can resonate with readers: the importance and meaning of the memory translates into something beyond her personal feelings.

Thesis

Like any essay, one that is based on a personal experience should have a main point or *thesis,* and that point should reveal something. Because you have already explored the significance and public resonance of your memory, you may already have a thesis. Ask yourself: *What is the most important point about this memory that should be communicated?* Then, try to express that point in one statement.

Essays sometimes state the thesis explicitly in a sentence, and sometimes they imply it. Even if you have an implied thesis, writing down the thesis now will help you develop the essay. While an *explicit* thesis is stated directly, an *implied* thesis is suggested by the details in the essay, but not directly stated. Having an implied thesis does not mean a writer can simply wander through many different ideas, though. The details throughout the essay must be focused and coherent enough to suggest a main point.

It may be tempting to offer an overly broad thesis statement about life, but more valuable statements will narrow in on a particular quality, situation, relationship, or layer of everyday life. The first broad statement in each set can be developed into more revelatory possibilities:

1. People are deeply influenced by their friends.
   - Friends develop our sense of ambition—what we want for ourselves.
   - Friends create the intellectual terrain of our past and present.
   - Friends mirror our own worldviews back to us.

2. Family is all that matters.
   - Our early struggles with brothers and sisters create the limitations we place on ourselves later in life.
   - As we grow into adulthood, our siblings keep alive the memory of our childhood selves.
   - Fathers create a sense of place, a sense of location that looms throughout our lives, even when we are spinning far out of control.

3. Teenage years are wild.

- During adolescence, the world makes sense, even though that sense is a complete illusion.

- A fourteen-year-old boy can barely contain all the energy coursing through his veins. He spends most of his time struggling to tame instincts that he cannot even name.

- Before leaving our formative years, we might glimpse the best and worst habits we have acquired from our families—if we are lucky.

So how does someone go from a broad, flat statement to a revelatory idea? Intensive analysis! More intensive analysis always (not sometimes, but *always!*) leads to more intensive and focused statements. When writers have difficulty expressing an intensive single statement, they can retool the key verbs and nouns. Notice how the more intensive and revelatory statements often avoid linking verbs (*is, am, are, was, were,* and so on). Instead, to pull the readers' mind through ideas, they rely on active verbs *(develop, create, mirror, keep, glimpse)*. Changing the verb in a sentence can prompt the writer to think differently, in more intensive ways.

ACTIVITY

Create a broad, flat sentence, something that offers very little new insight. Then, from that sentence, develop three or more intense, focused, and insightful statements. In these more insightful statements, try to reveal something that normally goes ignored or that rarely gets considered. To create more insightful statements, (1) replace broad nouns with more specific nouns; (2) replace linking verbs with active verbs. Use adventurous or unusual verbs . . . and see where your mind goes.

Evolution of a Thesis

The thesis of a remembering essay suggests the *significance of the memory.* Notice how the following statement evolves from a description of what happened to an explanation of its significance:

- I remember as a kid sitting in my grandparents' backyard listening to them and my parents tell boring family stories.

- I realize now that I learned a lot about my family history from sitting around as a kid listening to my grandparents and parents tell family stories.

- We learn important things about who we are and where we came from by listening to family stories.

- Though we might prefer not to hear them, we can better understand who we are and why by taking in family stories as children.

Common Thesis Problem: Avoiding Clichés

When it comes time to craft a focused statement, writers should avoid the temptation to flatten out their experiences into an overused phrase, or *cliché*. Clichés have a comfortable ring to them, but they rarely prompt new insight or reveal complexities. In fact, clichés often *cover up* complexities because they are applied as blanket statements to many different situations:

- You don't know what you've got until it's gone.

- Blood is thicker than water.

- What doesn't kill you only makes you stronger.

- Home is where the heart is.

Such statements may be true and worth considering, but academic writing seeks to reveal something new. Clichés are worn-out expressions. They might sound like profound statements, but when a thesis is a cliché, the main idea of the essay doesn't reveal something new. Instead, it restates an old, worn-out idea.

Revising Your Thesis

Share your thesis statement with a group of peers:

- What general words can be replaced with specific ones?

- What clichés can be replaced with intense, revelatory language?

- How can the thesis better express the significance of the memory?

- What is the most important point about this memory?

Rhetorical Tools

Even though the writing for this chapter is personal in nature, it needs to develop a point that connects to the public. As author Joan Didion said in her interview with the *Paris Review,* "Quite often you want to tell somebody your dream, your nightmare. Well, nobody wants to hear about someone else's dream, good or bad; nobody wants to walk around with it. The writer is always tricking the reader into listening to the dream." To do this, writers can use various tools.

Narration

Narration is a retelling of events, a story. As Joan Didion argues, we must do more than tell a story. We must trick readers into listening to the story and accepting its significance. The art of storytelling involves pace, or the movement of events. At important points in a narrative, the amount of detail tends to increase, and so readers slow down and experience each moment.

But good storytellers move quickly through less important events. It might be helpful to think of this strategy as it works in movies: at the climax of an adventure movie, the events slow down (we see the lead character's hand grasping for the light saber; we hear each breath of the character as she runs down the hallway and toward the open window), but during less important moments, an entire day or week can flash by in a second.

In her narrative, Jennifer Schwind-Pawlak moves quickly through unimportant events. She quickly relates the pregame events (going to church, suiting up) because they do not have a significant impact on the main idea of the essay:

> Sunday, the morning of the fifth game of the season, came with no warning. I got up, went to church with the family, then came home to suit up for the game. Upon arrival at the field, I was greeted by the coach and went to take my place along the sidelines with the rest of my team.

However, the narrative slows down (and offers more details) at important moments:

> Joann (the name I call my mother when she does something embarrassing) was screaming at the coach. In a voice so screeching that it rivaled fingernails on a blackboard, she told him that he was a disgraceful coach and that he should be ashamed of himself. She continued to point out the error of his ways by reminding him that I had not played at all in the game. How could she do this to me? My mother had managed to enlighten the few people that hadn't noticed on their own that I had not played at all. What was she thinking? She might as well have rented billboard space saying, "So what if Jeni sucks at soccer? The coach wouldn't let her play." My only thought was, "I don't want to go to school tomorrow!"

As you consider your own narrative, slow the pace when relaying events that are directly related to your main idea.

Allusions

Allusions are references to some public bit of knowledge (such as a historical event, a political situation, or a popular culture figure). An allusion can give a personal essay a more public and broader feeling. It can make the ideas and events of a personal situation relate to the readers through a shared culture. Because the allusion is shared knowledge, it communicates this broader, public feeling more quickly than a longer explanation would. This helps to keep the essay moving along. For example, Bosley's allusion to the Hooters restaurant chain ("to be performed, not in swimsuits, but in short-shorts and white T-shirts, Hooters-style . . .") quickly creates an image in the readers' mind because of the shared knowledge about the Hooters uniform. Later, when Bosley refers to "the save-the-whales-and-rainforest civic-mindedness required not only of Miss America, but of Junior Miss America, too," she quickly communicates an idea that without the allusion would take much longer to explain. Because the allusion is public knowledge, the writer connects with the readers because they feel that they, too, are *in on it*.

Dialogue

Dialogue, discussion between two or more people, can make an event or memory more real and engaging to the readers. It is most valuable when used to emphasize a main point and show something significant. Conveying general events is better left to narration. Formatting for dialogue involves several steps:

- Use quotation marks before and after the actual spoken words.
- Put end punctuation (such as a period) inside the end quotation marks.
- Indent when a new speaker begins.

Integrating a speaker's words can be accomplished in several ways:

- Use a comma between the quotation and the speaking verb (*explained, asked, said, yelled, proclaimed*, etc.).

  Louisa asked, "What are we going to do now?"

- Use a colon before the speaker's words. In this case, the narrator usually forecasts the ideas or mood of the speaker in the sentence preceding the colon.

  I was clearly agitated by her accusation: "What the heck are you talking about?"

- Work the speaker's words directly into the grammar of your sentence.

  But Louisa was convinced that our decision would "hurt us either way."

- See all of these rules operating in the following exchange:

  "Come on in," Mr. Smith said.

  "Hey, something smells great," I said as I walked into his lamp-lit living room. The small terrier looked up out of its lazy place on the sofa as Mr. Smith reached to get his wallet.

  "Yep, I've been cookin' my chili again. It's Max's favorite." He gestured at the complacent blurry-eyed dog. "So, is the price of papers still the same?"

  "Well, as far as I know, it's still $4.25 for the month." And then without considering the consequences, I asked the wrong question: "How have you been, Mr. Smith?" It took him 45 minutes to explain his "return to normal" after a long spell of stomach flu.

In this example, notice how attributive phrases (such as *he said*), which give ownership to the spoken words, are absent after the second indentation. Generally, after the dialogue pattern is established and the readers can easily tell who is speaking, attributive phrases are unnecessary.

ACTIVITY

Before drafting your essay, use writing to plan:

- Write down your thesis.

- What narrative events will you move through quickly, and what narrative events will you slow down for?

- What historical, popular, or fictional situations, events, or characters relate to your situation?

- If you are considering dialogue, how will that dialogue help show the significance of the main idea?

Revision

Revision, when you step back and analyze your own rhetorical decisions, is a necessary part of good writing, and of one's development as a writer and thinker. Writers can revise alone or with others.

Peer Review

Peer review, revising with the help of others, can be done in various ways. Your instructor may provide specific guidelines and, of course, you are free to try different approaches outside the classroom. If your instructor asks you to exchange essays with a peer or form small groups and read your essays aloud, the following advice can help you work efficiently and get results:

- Provide peer reviewers with a readable copy of your draft.

- Help focus the reviewers by writing down your carefully worded questions about your draft.

- If you read your essay aloud, don't read too fast.

- Be specific when responding. In addition to saying what you think, say why you think it.

- Be honest and encouraging. Providing only praise will not help the writer, yet phrasing your comments too negatively might be discouraging.

- Do not defend your essay, but instead view it as a work in progress. Be open to all ideas.

- Consider all comments, then make the changes you think are appropriate.

After you exchange drafts with another writer, use the following questions to guide your review:

1. How does the essay prompt you to think differently? (For instance, do you see something with more complexity, more beauty, more ugliness, or more intensity than you did before?) Explain what the essay helps you see differently. If you have a difficult time answering this question, perhaps the essay has not yet gone far enough.

2. What clichés should the writer replace with a new, revelatory idea? (Look closely. Clichés sometimes masquerade as profound thoughts.)

3. Which details best illustrate the main idea? (Which details reinforce the main idea and make you picture something specific?)

4. Which details could be added to illustrate the main idea? What particular behaviors or events could be further dramatized with details? For instance, the essay probably has a focused moment—a specific event that holds intense meaning. Could that moment use more detail?

5. Which details do not seem related to the thesis of the essay? Why not?

6. How could the writer create more public resonance?

7. Do any paragraphs lack coherence? Do they ramble or wander pointlessly through the past? Look for details that may hold meaning for the writer but don't develop the point of the essay.

8. How could the essay begin with more intensity? (For instance, if the essay begins with a broad statement such as *Children are curious creatures,* could it instead begin with a specific narrative or a more focused or surprising statement?)

9. Describe the writer's voice. Is it appropriate and consistent? Could the writer use figurative language or details that are more fitting? Where could sentence length be varied?

10. What sentences could be rewritten to create more vitality?
    - Where can the writer combine sentences with coordination?
    - Where can the writer combine with subordination?
    - What verbs can be more intense?
    - Where do basic grammatical issues (such as run-on sentences, sentence fragments, or pronoun/antecedent agreement) distract readers?

Peer Review Truisms

- **The process can make writers think differently about their own work.** Humans are great modelers. We model our behavior after others, and we make all kinds of subtle changes to our thinking when we read others' work. As modelers, peer reviewers can discover new approaches to an assignment, new writerly moves, new patterns of thinking, or new strategies for creating an engaging voice. (Reviewers can also discover qualities that they want to avoid in their own writing. They might discover some sentence or organization patterns and try to avoid them!)

- **Even the most inexperienced writer can offer valuable comments.** Some people believe that they have little to offer: "I'm not the teacher!" they'll announce. However, peer review is not about pointing out wrongs and rights. It's about reading closely and responding as a thoughtful human in a shared situation. If you can read and focus your attention, you can be a valuable reviewer. In fact, fellow students may even have more to offer one another because they're in a similar situation—faced with a similar task, experiencing the same pressures, at the same moment, in the same place.

- **Chat is the great enemy of good analysis.** Some instructors may set up sessions so that writers can converse about their drafts. Such sessions can be valuable and engaging—even intense and animated. But the danger is that they can devolve into chat sessions about the topics (or something else!). While chatting about one's topic is helpful (and can be worked into a class), a focused and intensive peer review session has its own kind of value.

- **Peer review can be the most valuable component of a writing class.** Writing in college is a social occasion. An academic essay (or any writing assignment) is an intersection of writers, instructors, and students. Peer review brings that to life. It makes the interaction of thinkers real and dramatic. When reviewers take the process seriously, it increases the value of the experience.

- **All writers need help.** Even the best of the best writers rely on the insights and assistance of others. Name a great writer from the past or the present. All of them used the ideas and thoughts of others to help shape their projects and even their sentences.

- **Done carelessly, peer review can be a terrible thing.** If peer reviewers read drafts quickly and only point to small, surface-level issues, they waste their partners' time. It is a similar waste if they read for "agreement" and "disagreement"—simply looking for passages they agree or disagree with—and then announce their approval or disapproval of certain points.

Reflection

Students develop as writers and thinkers by reflecting on an essay *after* it has been written. This involves thinking about how rhetoric was used to create and then to convey an idea. Now that you have written a remembering essay, step back and explain its rhetoric:

1. What focused insight does your essay arrive at? Is it clearly expressed in a sentence? If so, write it down. Or is it implied through the details of the essay? If so, write down the focused insight in one sentence and then explain what details convey this idea.

2. How did you discover and develop your essay's insightful point? Explain how your insight developed throughout the writing process.

3. When used effectively, narration helps readers understand a writer's insight about a topic. When used ineffectively, it can take over the essay, drowning out the insight. Explain how narration in your essay helps readers understand your insight without overshadowing it.

4. Even though your essay focuses primarily on *your* past, how does it have meaning for others? What passages from the essay connect your particular memory to a public concern?

5. The best writers work hard at saying more in fewer words. They are concise, using only the words necessary to make a point. Find a sentence in your essay that is concise, and then find one that is wordy. Rewrite the wordy sentence.

Beyond the Essay: Invention Video

1. If you recorded a video of an invention workshop for the activity on page 47, try editing that video into a four-minute (or so) movie, using video editing software such as iMovie. (If you're not familiar with editing software, work with an editing partner or team.) Your movie might end up paralleling the remembering essay, taking the same basic structure of the essay and making the same points. Or, because you shot video of some early invention work, your movie might tell a different story: you might edit the video to show how ideas evolved through discussion, eventually leading to the discovery that became the essay's thesis.

    Whether your movie parallels the remembering essay or documents the invention process, it can be a simple series of edited shots or a more complex production including titles, transitions between shots, close-ups, background music, and other effects and editing techniques. Each editing decision requires careful thought. This thought is a type of analysis that allows you to see how all the little pieces of a thing work together to create the overall message.

2. After creating your movie, describe the editing decisions you made. What was your overall purpose? What shots did you use and why? Describe the pace of your video and the effect of the pace: Did you use a lot of brief shots edited together, fewer longer ones, or a combination of both? What other video editing decisions did you make, and how did they contribute to the overall message, pace, and tone or voice of the movie?

3

Explaining Relationships

John Metz

Chapter Objectives
This chapter will help you to:

- Find meaning in the subtle, less obvious, layers of a specific relationship.
- Discover and explain the public resonance of a specific relationship.
- Develop a focused and revelatory essay supported with narration, detailed description, and figurative language.
- Use images to support and enrich your ideas.

"We no longer believe that a man, by owning a piece of America, is free to outrage it."

—John Steinbeck

INTRODUCTION

In the above quotation from "Americans and the Land," John Steinbeck characterizes the relationship between contemporary U.S. citizens and the American landscape. Earlier in his essay, he focuses on European settlers and the North American continent. Contrary to the conventional view of settlers as brave frontiersmen, Steinbeck describes them as land-mad invaders. His aim is to reveal the complexity of a relationship, to show something distinct, perhaps surprising, about the interaction between people and their environment.

John Steinbeck was a celebrated twentieth-century writer, his books translated and read throughout the world, but explaining relationships is common daily work: People on city councils explore the relationship between neighborhoods to help their cities better understand ethnic diversity; corporate executives try to understand the relationship between their own companies and their competitors; and certainly everyone is aware of the ongoing attempts by political leaders to explain the relationships between countries or regions. In a shrinking world, in which people of vastly different value systems attempt to coexist, explaining relationships is more than an exercise. It is an act of survival. To understand our place in the world, in a culture, in a family, in any system, we have to understand relationships.

One might even argue that the greatest discoveries have involved the discovery of relationships—between, for example, atomic elements, religious practices, geological events, historical figures, or heavenly bodies. Albert Einstein spent his life exploring the relationship between the impossibly small and the seemingly infinite, Carl Jung explored the relationship between the conscious and unconscious mind, Hélène Cixous explored the relationship between sexuality and language, and we might see the history of science as a series of questions about relationships: How does the sun relate to Earth? How does matter relate to energy? How do particles relate to waves? How do fish relate to mammals? How does climate relate to the atmosphere? The same goes for philosophy. From ancient civilizations to modern institutions, people have asked, for instance, how language relates to thought, how ethics relate to religion, and how the individual relates to the community.

This chapter explores relationships—among places, things, events, people, and even ideas. The readings will provide insight and necessary strategies for probing beyond the obvious layers of a relationship. For example, Jim Crockett's essay, "Mugged," makes two important discoveries: that any possible psychological "disorder" is less important than some basic human need, and that his simple coffee mug provides a form of security. Crockett's discoveries give his essay insight (a less-obvious and worthwhile point) and public resonance (a connection to the concerns of others). After reading the essays, you can begin looking for a relationship in one of two ways—go to the Point of Contact section and consider topics from everyday life, or choose one of the Ideas for Writing questions that follow the essays. After finding a topic, go to the Analysis section to begin developing your ideas.

Americans and the Land
John Steinbeck

In John Steinbeck's novels, such as *The Grapes of Wrath* and *Of Mice and Men,* the setting is a vital element. Steinbeck often draws attention to the ways in which the land influences people's lives. In this essay, from *America and Americans,* Steinbeck focuses on the American settlers' impact on the land. Notice that the land, here, is not something to simply live *on* or even *from.* Instead, it is something to live *with*—or, in the case of many early Americans, to live *against.* As with so many of his novels and stories, Steinbeck's essay invites readers to see the relationship that people cultivate with the world around them.

I have often wondered at the savagery and thoughtlessness with which our early settlers approached this rich continent. They came at it as though it were an enemy, which of course it was. They burned the forests and changed the rainfall; they swept the buffalo from the plains, blasted the streams, set fire to the grass, and ran a reckless scythe through the virgin and noble timber. Perhaps they felt that it was limitless and could never be exhausted and that a man could move on to new wonders endlessly. Certainly there are many examples to the contrary, but to a large extent the early people pillaged the country as though they hated it, as though they held it temporarily and might be driven off at any time.

This tendency toward irresponsibility persists in very many of us today; our rivers are poisoned by reckless dumping of sewage and toxic industrial wastes, the air of our cities is filthy and dangerous to breathe from the belching of uncontrolled products from combustion of coal, coke, oil, and gasoline. Our towns are girdled with wreckage and the debris of our toys—our automobiles and our packaged pleasures. Through uninhibited spraying against one enemy we have destroyed the natural balances our survival requires. All these evils can and must be overcome if America and Americans are to survive; but many of us still conduct ourselves as our ancestors did, stealing from the future for our clear and present profit.

Since the river-polluters and the air-poisoners are not criminal or even bad people, we must presume that they are heirs to the early conviction that sky and water are unowned and that they are limitless. In the light of our practices here at home it is very interesting to me to read of the care taken with the carriers of our probes into space, to make utterly sure that they are free of pollution of any kind. We would not think of doing to the moon what we do every day to our own dear country.

When the first settlers came to America and dug in on the coast, they huddled in defending villages hemmed in by the sea on one side and by endless forests on the other, by Red Indians and, most frightening, the mystery of an unknown land extending nobody knew how far. And for a time very few cared or dared to find out. Our first Americans organized themselves and lived in a state of military alertness; every community built its blockhouse for defense. By law the men went armed and were required to keep their weapons ready and available. Many of them wore armor, made here or imported; on the East Coast, they wore the cuirass and helmet, and the Spaniards on the West Coast wore both steel armor and heavy leather to turn arrows.

On the East Coast, and particularly in New England, the colonists farmed meager lands close to their communities and to safety. Every man was permanently on duty for the defense of his family and his village; even the hunting parties went into the forest in force, rather like raiders than hunters, and their subsequent quarrels with the Indians, resulting in forays and even massacres, remind us that the danger was very real. A man took his gun along when he worked the land, and the women stayed close to their thick-walled houses and listened day and night for the signal of alarm. The towns they settled were permanent, and most of them exist today with their records of Indian raids, of slaughter, of scalpings, and of punitive counter-raids. The military leader of the community became the chief authority in time of trouble, and it was a long time before danger receded and the mystery could be explored.

After a time, however, brave and forest-wise men drifted westward to hunt, to trap, and eventually to bargain for the furs which were the first precious negotiable wealth America produced for trade and export. Then trading posts were set up as centers of collection and the exploring men moved up and down the rivers and crossed the mountains, made friends for mutual profit with the Indians, learned the wilderness techniques, so that these explorer-traders soon dressed, ate, and generally acted like the indigenous people around them. Suspicion lasted a long time, and was fed by clashes sometimes amounting to full-fledged warfare; but by now these Americans attacked and defended as the Indians did.

For a goodly time the Americans were travelers, moving about the country collecting its valuables, but with little idea of permanence; their roots and their hearts were in the towns and the growing cities along the eastern edge. The few who stayed, who lived among the Indians, adopted their customs and some took Indian wives and were regarded as strange and somehow treasonable creatures. As for their half-breed children, while the tribe sometimes adopted them they were unacceptable as equals in the eastern settlements.

Then the trickle of immigrants became a stream, and the population began to move westward—not to grab and leave but to settle and live, they thought. The newcomers were of peasant stock, and they had their roots in a Europe where they had been landless, for the possession of land was the requirement and the proof of a higher social class than they had known. In America they found beautiful and boundless land for the taking—and they took it.

Galyna Andrushko/Shutterstock.com

It is little wonder that they went land-mad, because there was so much of it. They cut and burned the forests to make room for crops; they abandoned their knowledge of kindness to the land in order to maintain its usefulness. When they had cropped out a piece they moved on, raping the country like invaders. The topsoil, held by roots and freshened by leaf-fall, was left helpless to the spring freshets, stripped and eroded with the naked bones of clay and rock exposed. The destruction of the forests changed the rainfall, for the searching clouds could find no green and beckoning woods to draw them on and milk them. The merciless nineteenth century was like a hostile expedition for loot that seemed limitless. Uncountable buffalo were killed, stripped of their hides, and left to rot, a reservoir of permanent food supply eliminated. More than that, the land of the Great Plains was robbed of the manure of the herds. Then the plows went in and ripped off the protection of the buffalo grass and opened the helpless soil to quick water and slow drought and the mischievous winds that roamed through the Great Central Plains. There has always been more than enough desert in America; the new settlers, like overindulged children, created even more.

The railroads brought new hordes of land-crazy people, and the new Americans moved like locusts across the continent until the western sea put a boundary to their movements. Coal and copper and gold drew them on; they savaged the land, gold-dredged the rivers to skeletons of pebbles and debris. An aroused and fearful government made laws for the distribution of public lands—a quarter section, one hundred and sixty acres, per person—and a claim had to be proved and improved; but there were ways of getting around this, and legally. My own grandfather proved out a quarter section for himself, one for his wife, one for each of his children, and, I suspect, acreage for children he hoped and expected to have. Marginal lands, of course, suitable only for grazing, went in larger pieces. One of the largest land-holding families in California took its richest holdings by a trick: By law a man could take up all the swamp or water-covered land he wanted. The founder of this great holding mounted a scow on wheels and drove his horses over thousands of acres of the best bottom-land, then reported that he had explored it in a boat, which was true, and confirmed his title. I need not mention his name; his descendants will remember.

Another joker with a name still remembered in the West worked out a scheme copied many times in after years. Proving a quarter section required a year of residence and some kind of improvement—a fence, a shack—but once the land was proved the owner was free to sell it. This particular princely character went to the stews and skid rows of the towns and found a small army of hopeless alcoholics who lived for whisky and nothing else. He put these men on land he wanted to own, grubstaked them and kept them in cheap liquor until the acreage was proved, then went through the motions of buying it from his protégés and moved them and their one-room shacks on sled runners on to new quarter sections. Bums of strong constitution might prove out five or six homesteads for this acquisitive hero before they died of drunkenness.

It was full late when we began to realize that the continent did not stretch out to infinity; that there were limits to the indignities to which we could subject it. Engines and heavy mechanical equipment were allowing us to ravage it even more effectively than we had with fire, dynamite, and gang plows. Conservation came to us slowly, and much of it hasn't arrived yet. Having killed the whales and wiped out the sea otters and most of the beavers, the market hunters went to work on game birds; ducks and quail were decimated, and the passenger pigeon eliminated. In my youth I remember seeing a market hunter's gun, a three-gauge shotgun bolted to a frame and loaded to the muzzle with shingle nails. Aimed at a lake and the trigger pulled with a string, it slaughtered every living thing on the lake. The Pacific Coast pilchards were once the raw material for a great and continuing industry. We hunted them with aircraft far at sea until they were gone and the canneries had to be closed. In some of the valleys of the West, where the climate makes several crops a year available, which the water supply will not justify, wells were driven deeper and deeper for irrigation, so that in one great valley a million acre feet more of water was taken out than rain and melting snow could replace, and the water table went down and a few more years may give us a new desert.

The great redwood forests of the western mountains early attracted attention. These ancient trees, which once grew everywhere, now exist only where the last Ice Age did not wipe them out. And they were found to have value. The Sempervirens and the Gigantea, the two remaining species, make soft, straight-grained timber. They are easy to split into planks, shakes, fenceposts, and railroad ties, and they have a unique virtue: they resist decay, both wet and dry rot, and an inherent acid in them repels termites. The loggers went through the great groves like a barrage, toppling the trees—some of which were two thousand years old—and leaving no maidens, no seedlings or saplings on the denuded hills.

Quite a few years ago when I was living in my little town on the coast of California a stranger came in and bought a small valley where the Sempervirens redwoods grew, some of them three hundred feet high. We used to walk among these trees, and the light colored as though the great glass of the Cathedral at Chartres had strained and sanctified the sunlight. The emotion we felt in this grove was one of awe and humility and joy; and then one day it was gone, slaughtered, and the sad wreckage of boughs and broken saplings left like nonsensical spoilage of the battle-ruined countryside. And I remember that after our rage there was sadness, and when we passed the man who had done this we looked away, because we were ashamed for him.

From early times we were impressed and awed by the fantastic accidents of nature, like the Grand Canyon and Yosemite and Yellowstone Park. The Indians had revered them as holy places, visited by the gods, and all of us came to have somewhat the same feeling about them. Thus we set aside many areas of astonishment as publicly owned parks; and though this may to a certain extent have been because there was no other way to use them, as the feelings of preciousness of the things we had been destroying grew in Americans, more and more areas were set aside as national and state parks, to be looked at but not injured. Many people loved and were in awe of the redwoods; societies and individuals bought groves of these wonderful trees and presented them to the state for preservation.

No longer do we Americans want to destroy wantonly, but our new-found sources of power—to take the burden of work from our shoulders, to warm us, and cool us, and give us light, to transport us quickly, and to make the things we use and wear and eat—these power sources spew pollution on our country, so that the rivers and streams are becoming poisonous and lifeless. The birds die for the lack of food; a noxious cloud hangs over our cities that burns our lungs and reddens our eyes. Our ability to conserve has not grown with our power to create, but this slow and sullen poisoning is no longer ignored or justified. Almost daily, the pressure of outrage among Americans grows. We are no longer content to destroy our beloved country. We are slow to learn; but we learn. When a super-highway was proposed in California which would trample the redwood trees in its path, an outcry arose all over the land, so strident and fierce that the plan was put aside. And we no longer believe that a man, by owning a piece of America, is free to outrage it.

But we are an exuberant people, careless and destructive as active children. We make strong and potent tools and then have to use them to prove that they exist. Under the pressure of war we finally made the atom bomb, and for reasons which seemed justifiable at the time we dropped it on two Japanese cities—and I think we finally frightened ourselves. In such things, one must consult himself because there is no other point of reference. I did not know about the bomb, and certainly I had nothing to do with its use, but I am horrified and ashamed; and nearly everyone I know feels the same thing. And those who loudly and angrily justify Hiroshima and Nagasaki—why, they must be the most ashamed of all.

WRITING STRATEGIES

1. Focus on Steinbeck's opening paragraph. How does it function? Does it state or imply the main idea? How does it establish Steinbeck's voice? Does it invite the readers into the essay? If so, how?

2. Throughout the essay, Steinbeck describes detailed situations (anecdotes) that illustrate his point. Which of these anecdotes best supports his point about the relationship between settlers and the land?

3. In ¶10, Steinbeck describes the people that the railroad brought west as "land-crazy." He says they moved "like locusts." Identify other figurative expressions he uses to describe the people. Explain how these expressions function in the essay. How do they work with his overall point about the relationship between Americans and the land?

4. In ¶16, Steinbeck gives some examples that show contemporary Americans are, perhaps, more thoughtful about the land. How does this paragraph impact your understanding of the essay? How does it impact Steinbeck's voice?

5. In his conclusion, Steinbeck talks about shame. Explain how this passage supports his overall point about Americans' relationship with the land.

EXPLORING IDEAS

1. In several passages, Steinbeck uses the term *awe* to characterize his (and others') relationship to the natural world. What term do you think best characterizes most Americans' relationship to the natural world?

2. Imagine Steinbeck as a guest on a current political talk show. What kinds of people would call in? Who would support Steinbeck's point? Who would angrily deny it?

3. What is your relationship with the land? What everyday actions of your own have a positive impact on the land? What everyday actions of your own have a negative impact on the land?

4. How have you been taught to think about American settlers? How does Steinbeck's essay fit into or push against the history you've been taught?

IDEAS FOR WRITING

1. What is the relationship between Americans and the land today?

2. Describe your relationship with your immediate surroundings (your house, bedroom, apartment, dorm, etc.). How is it typical (or not typical) of your broader attitude concerning the relationship of humans to the land?

3. Observe the way land is used in your community. Take field notes. Discuss your observations with others, looking for ways that you might participate in Steinbeck's discussion of Americans and the land. How might you contribute to this discussion? What idea, for example, could use further explanation or clarification?

If responding to one of these ideas, go to the Analysis section of this chapter to begin developing ideas for your essay.

Mugged
Jim Crockett

MINDTAP
From Cengage
Complete the auto-graded
quiz for this reading.

Jim Crockett, a Spanish instructor, songwriter, poet, farmer, and carpenter, has been drinking coffee for fifty years. As with millions of other Americans, coffee is fused to his everyday life. In this essay, Crockett focuses on a particular part of his relationship with coffee. But the essay goes far beyond his personal rituals and habits; it reveals something about the "small behaviors we cling to" and the size and scope of those seemingly simplistic habits that create meaning and familiarity. (Portions of Crockett's invention work appear later in the chapter.)

I have been mugged. Not accosted as I walk to my parked truck across a dark lot; not waylaid by thugs in the night. But mugged, nevertheless. I have been mugged by insinuation, by the insertion into my life of a cylindrical drinking vessel: one that holds coffee. I have been mugged by a to-go cup.

The relationship, or mugging, that has developed with my coffee mug is one-sided and is, because a mug's needs are simple, an easy relationship to maintain. Oh, I rinse and wipe it out every morning, and occasionally wash it with detergent, but these are minimal maintenance requirements, ones easily met. So why, if all this object does is simply hold coffee, would I consider our relationship worthy of the time and effort spent in its exploration and explication? Why would I seek depth of meaning in a seemingly superficial attachment to such a mundane object? Maybe the very mundanity of the object, the very quotidian nature of the relationship, deepens the attachment, suggests that the relationship goes symbolically deeper, symptomatically deeper, than I think.

In exchange for its minimal upkeep, my coffee mug gives back much more than it takes. Its secure lid keeps my mustache drip-free and, therefore, my books, shirts, and papers clean. My mug is insulated so it delivers hot, delicious, organically shade-grown, fair trade coffee for a couple of hours at a time, and in so doing, helps me directly support the small coffee growers and their cooperatives around the world. It is also an environmentally friendly mug. When I buy a cup of coffee, I only buy coffee: the paper cup and insulating sleeve, both little bits of tree, remain in the store. I remain weaned from dependence upon the earth- and human-pillaging multinational coffee cartel.

Wrought in stainless steel and plastic, this bit of industrial-designer paraphernalia (it holds my drug of choice) is every cup holder's dream. Its shape, curvaceous, tapered, slim-waisted and a bit heavier on top, is designed to fit cup holders in most vehicles, while being a natural-feeling extension of the human hand; or, in my case, a necessary adjunct to, a logical appurtenance thereof. My coffee cup is in my hand a lot.

In fact, when it is not in my hand, when I misplace it momentarily, or when, like the other day, I leave it on the bumper of my truck and see a flash in the rearview mirror as my

---

mug goes airborne into the filthy slush of the winter street, I feel a twinge of separation anxiety. When I stop traffic to rescue it from the gutter after a close call with a Chevy Suburban, impatient and angry faces glare through wiper-slapped windshields to remind me that the small choices we make, the small behaviors we cling to, affect the way in which we are perceived in the world.

I worry, at times, when students and colleagues ask how much coffee I drink, or say they've never seen me without my coffee mug, that my attachment to my little friend is symptomatic of some neurosis or other, or that it indicates an obsessive/compulsive disorder. I don't, however, worry for long. Because, even though my mug is always nearby, whether on the lectern or table in front of the classroom, in the cup holder on the dashboard of my truck, on the desk where I am writing this essay, or just dangling from my hand, all it really signifies is an addiction to caffeine and the need, because I am human, for some small and securing daily grounding ritual. In an *econoculture* so far removed from its agrarian and wilderness roots, from its time-worn rituals of life, my coffee mug provides a needed, however tiny, bit of continuity in my daily doings, a small tie to place and home.

WRITING STRATEGIES

1. How does the connotation of *mugged* impact the essay? How does the idea add to Crockett's point about his own relationship with coffee?

2. Although this essay focuses primarily on Crockett's personal relationship, how does it make broader, more public, points? What passages or sentences pull readers beyond Crockett's personal situation?

3. Describe Crockett's voice. How does word choice impact the "sound" of his voice?

4. In his conclusion, Crockett characterizes the society around him as an *econoculture*. What idea is he creating with that term? How does it resonate with other passages or points in this essay?

5. What is Crockett's most compelling rhetorical move?

EXPLORING IDEAS

1. Crockett claims that humans need "some small and securing daily grounding ritual." What is a grounding ritual? Do you think it is, indeed, a fundamental human need?

2. Some sociologists, psychologists, and writers claim that the small moments in everyday life tell us the most about human behavior. Does this seem like a fair claim? In considering your own life, your own habits, is it true?

3. Why do people "cling" to their own habits?

4. To what extent does caffeine impact our present culture—or your own ability to participate in the *econoculture*?

IDEAS FOR WRITING

1. What is the most consistent daily ritual in your life? What does it reveal about your identity?

2. What common ritual do you share with millions of others?

3. Crockett says, "Maybe the very mundanity of the object, the very quotidian nature of the relationship, deepens the attachment, suggests that the relationship goes symbolically deeper, symptomatically deeper, than I think." What mundane object is symbolically, symptomatically fused to your identity?

If responding to one of these ideas, go to the Analysis section of this chapter to begin developing ideas for your essay.

John Mauk

STUDENT ESSAY

To Fish and Be Fished: A Tinder-fied Game of Love
Kellie Coppola

Human relationships are increasingly shaped—or mediated—by our reliance on technology. Thanks to advancing networks and fancy apps, everyday interactions have migrated to online environments. In the following essay, Kellie Coppola explores how a popular dating application, Tinder, has influenced the first steps of romantic involvement. She describes specific procedures in finding a personal "match" (or many matches) on Tinder, but more importantly, she digs into some culturally entrenched beliefs and fears related to choosing a potential romantic partner. Coppola is an International Studies and Professional Writing major at Miami University.

The opening relies on a common comparison between dating and fishing.

Just as humans fish for survival, we also fish for companionship, the innate need to care about another and have another care about them. And we don't just want any fish, we want THE fish. So we cast our reels—sometimes at a bar, sometimes at a singles cruise, sometimes unexpectedly—and begin the toil of catch-and-release, looking for our elusive Moby Dick amongst guppies. If love is like fishing, the world is a vast, unpredictable ocean— huge and hard to navigate, where assumptions about gender roles, attraction, and dating etiquette create waves that make it easier for some fishermen than others. Some of us find our whale; some of us will take the biggest one luck will afford; some will drop the fishing rod entirely.

The comparison gets extended to reveal a fresh way of thinking.

The comparison gets extended even further.

In 2012 technology brought us Tinder, a dating application that revolutionized the online-dating industry by taking it to a mobile phone. To extend the fishing narrative, Tinder allows you to pare down the ocean to a pond of your preferred kind of fish, and puts each fish on display for you to examine before swiping right (the equivalent of "yes, I want you"), or left (the equivalent of "no, thank you"). If both users (on either end) swipe right, conversation can be initiated, if not, nothing happens. To make an account, users simply download and open the app, upload information and up to five pictures from their Facebook profile, set their parameters for the age range, gender, distance from their location of the profiles they'd like to see, and start swiping.

The specific how-it-works information helps to show the inner workings of the relationship.

While Tinder has become popular in recent years and a catalyst for many mobile dating apps, it has certainly prompted plenty of backlash. Words like "desperate" and "creepy" get thrown around to describe Tinder users. It's also common to see "I'm willing to lie about how we met" written in Tinder profiles. But if Tinder is a dating app and plenty of romantic success stories have surfaced— people meeting their significant others, and even husbands and wives on Tinder— then why is it so problematic to have a relationship originate on Tinder? Does Tinder generate a certain type of relationship, one worthy of all the suspicion?

This acknowledges some tension surrounding the relationship.

The questions set up the focused examination to come.

HOOK, LINE, AND...

To begin answering this question, we have to look at love before Tinder. I'm talking Disney and Hallmark movies, which go like this: guy meets girl, "love at first sight", the "getting to know you" phase, they fall in love, get married, and live happily ever after. Add Valentine's Day and we've got a culture of unrealistic expectations for how a relationship should work, and, consequently, the obsession with being desired by others and the fear of being single, sad and unloved. The fear of rejection is insurmountable. Thus, meeting people and forming relationships can be terrifying and exhausting. People want their fairy tale. If a girl doesn't find her prince, she's not the princess, meaning no "Happily Ever After." Likewise, if a man isn't princely (rich, charming, and handsome), princesses won't want him and he can't have "Happily Ever After" either. The fairy tale perpetuates itself in people's hopes and fears. Any deviation from the ideal makes for many frustrated hopeless romantics.

The allusions help with public resonance: they help to characterize the broader problems with dating.

Tinder manages the frustration. It mitigates the emotional blow of rejection by reducing the first meeting to a faceless and emotionless interaction, a judgement free of consequence.[1] Tinder is a computerized platform open to everyone with a smartphone and users can start and stop the app whenever they feel like it. Compared to real-life expectations, "rejection" on this app is innocuous, which means fewer blows to our fragile, socially-crafted self-esteem. This is especially true because there isn't any direct competition: instead of experiencing all the self-loathing that comes with seeing your friends

This puts the Tinder relationship in context.

So here's what keeps the Tinder-fied relationship going: the need to protect fragile self-esteem in the dangerous world of dating.

---

[1] It is important to note that much of this analysis comes from my own experiences on Tinder; therefore, some of the assertions I make are qualified by the demographics I put on my profile and my preferences. I set my profile as a female seeking exclusively males, with an age range of 22-29, with a maximum distance of 5 miles from my location in Oxford, Ohio.

surrounded by potential romantic partners while you're standing alone, success (or failure) on Tinder is private. It also shatters two presumptions about gender roles in dating: One, either gender can seek either gender. Two, both parties have the same amount influence in the interaction. In other words, both parties have to swipe right and both parties can initiate conversation (meaning, ladies, no more external pressure to wait for the guy to come to you).

Ultimately Tinder puts all users on an emotion-free, instantaneous stream of "first impressions," and provides the opportunity for a "getting to know you" phase. While all relationships start somewhere, Tinder puts the starting point into a formulated process that guides the relationship dynamic. When a profile comes up, the user sees a huge picture. You cannot see them, smell them, touch them or hear them, so what you see is the only indication of what you might get. Ultimately, the experience, before the swipe occurs, is like looking at an object, something to be judged with total disregard of any feelings. If users aren't sure which direction to swipe, they can tap the picture to see the other user's bio tagline.[2] In theory, the tagline should serve to nudge people to swipe left or right if they have not already made their decision based on the pictures. If the picture is a hook, the tagline pulls them in or breaks if the fish wills it to. For example, some people write their name, age, hobbies, and other baseline facts. Some explain what they are allegedly looking to get: "looking for a relationship" or "looking for a good time." Or some write messages with hidden meanings as a way of finding someone with a specific commonality. While there are infinite possibilities, the tagline serves as a filter and a potential platform for setting the tone of the conversation, should both decide to swipe right.

SINKER

When I match with another user, I get a "congratulations" pop-up message as if I'd just done something worthy of celebration. Our relationship moves from person/object to person/trophy. He

---

[2]For example, "Derek" age 22 (Derek, Tinder) shows up on my screen. He's shirtless and showing off a muscular body. I might be hooked if I'm solely looking for an athletic build that likes to show off (he's flexing). If I find the alpha-male show-off type obnoxious, I might pass. If I need validation of my perception, I might scroll to see more pictures. If he's trying to put off his body as his best foot forward, he succeeds—all of his pictures are essentially different versions of the same shirtless, artificially-tanned figure. I swipe left. However, I truly have no idea what his personality is like (or if that's even him).

becomes a self-confidence boost: regardless of how successful I am with the opposite sex, he, in theory, finds my profile attractive. However, it's unsubstantiated compliment because it was a hand-crafted profile, kind of like saying "You look really nice when you're dressed up and have full makeup on." In the Tinder experience, this is an achievement; however, it is merely a gateway for initial conversation and ultimately pretty anticlimactic, especially since you can do this with minimal physical effort. The congratulations window will show his picture and invite me to either message or keep swiping. Regardless, his profile is stored for recollection and I can click on it in the my "Messages" section.

The first big problem with the relationship explained in one paragraph.

At this point, should we decide to message each other, the dynamic can change from person/trophy to person/person. Each must now assess the situation and be compelled to put words together and send them to be judged by the other. The message initiates a mirrored lead-and-follow dance. I found the uncertainty exhilarating to a small extent: every move, a swipe of the finger, a tap of the touch screen in conversation, unveils something (provided both are being honest). However, out of the 200 matches I've made in the past month, I haven't messaged any of them first. Despite the relative ease, I am still stalled from messaging first, just like I won't approach a guy in a bar. I'm not alone. This experience compelled the creation of Bumble, a dating app like Tinder in which the female has to initiate conversation. Former co-owner of Tinder, Whitney Wolfe, created this feminist app. She explains, "If you look at where we are in the current heteronormative rules surrounding dating, the unwritten rule puts the woman a peg under the man—the man feels the pressure to go first in a conversation, and the woman feels pressure to sit on her hands. I don't think there is any denying it. If we can take some of the pressure off the man and put some of that encouragement in the woman's lap, I think we are taking a step in the right direction, especially in terms of really being true to feminism. I think we are the first feminist, or first attempt at a feminist dating app" (qtd. in Yashari).

Another inventive comparison (metaphor) that helps explain the nature of the relationship.

Another, more subtle, problem with the relationship: it doesn't really change the norms of dating.

An extended quotation to show what's possible in the relationship.

But it's not only women who ignore their matches. A survey from another online dating app, Whisper, showed that "66 percent of people have matched with someone on a dating app and then never messaged them" (qtd. in Weiss). The same article points to reasons such as not feeling like coming up with something creative, or being too lazy to formulate a response. While Tinder and real-life

Rather than summarize, the conclusion characterizes the most intense problem—failure—of the Tinder relationship.

pickup situations both include some risk and judgment during initial conversation, the lack of real-time pressure on Tinder may create its own failure. Here surfaces the paradox of innovation: Tinder road the wave and even lead a revolution in relationship norms and practices, and is supposedly freeing people of gender biases and rejection. It's fair to say that Tinder creates an artificial experience where sadness from rejection is freed from the equation. But the humanity and etiquette that take place in a real-life encounter are freed as well. Ultimately, shifts in societal norms will either normalize the online dating practice or debase it for a new trial-and-error. Meanwhile, we'll all still be Ahabs searching the sea.

A return to the opening comparison—and a subtle denial of Tinder's promise.

Works Cited

Weiss, Suzannah. "Why We Swipe Right and Ignore Our Tinder Matches." *Bustle*, 10 May 2016, www.bustle.com/articles/157940-why-we-swipe-right-and-then-ignore-our-tinder-matches.

Yashari, Leora. "Meet the Tinder Co-Founder Trying to Change Online Dating Forever." *Vanity Fair*, 7 Aug. 2015, www.vanityfair.com/culture/2015/08/bumble-app-whitney-wolfe.

WRITING STRATEGIES

1. What is Coppola's thesis? (Remember that thesis statements are sometimes *implied*—suggested but not stated directly. If you believe Coppola's thesis is implied, try to characterize it in a sentence of your own.)

2. Coppola spends several passages explaining how Tinder works. How do these passages help to support her thesis?

3. Consider Coppola's introduction—specifically, the fishing analogy. What initial ideas or tensions does it establish?

4. In the final paragraphs of her essay, Coppola refers to other online dating apps. How do these references relate to her main point about Tinder? How do they serve her thesis?

5. Coppola uses two footnotes in her essay. How do they function? In other words, what is the relationship between the footnotes and her main text?

EXPLORING IDEAS

1. Coppola says, "we have a culture of unrealistic expectations" when it comes to dating. How have you witnessed or experienced unrealistic expectations?

2. Do you think Tinder and other online dating apps increase or decrease unrealistic expectations?

3. Look up the term *heteronormativity*. Beyond Whitney Wolf's characterization in ¶8, how have you witnessed or experienced heteronormative behavior?

4. Would you suggest that your child, younger sibling, or best friend try online dating? Why or why not?

5. Finish this statement: Coppola's essay isn't simply about online dating apps. It's actually about _____.

IDEAS FOR WRITING

1. What technological innovation (app, device, program, website) has become part of your intimate life? How has it influenced your self-image and/or your relationships with others?

2. What is the strangest or most risky thing you have done for the sake of romance? What does that suggest about you, romance, or your relationship?

If responding to one of these ideas, go to the Analysis section of this chapter to begin developing ideas for your essay.

INVENTION

Invention is the activity of discovering ideas, developing points, and thinking through a topic. For academic writers, it is a necessary activity, one that leads to vital and valuable ideas. In this chapter, the invention process will involve focusing on a particular relationship and exploring its possible meaning. The following sections are designed to help you through the process: specifically, to discover a topic (in Point of Contact), to develop ideas about the topic (in Analysis), to make those ideas relevant to a community of readers (in Public Resonance), to develop a focus (in Thesis), and to generate support (in Rhetorical Tools). The Invention Questions in each section are not meant to be answered directly in your final written assignment. Rather, they are meant to help you develop increasingly intense ideas for your project.

Point of Contact

When you hear the word *relationship,* you may imagine an intimate personal bond between significant others, family members, or friends. But consider the relationships that are less obvious, those that surround or define us but remain hidden by the patterns of everyday life. Imagine the intense, but also subtle, relationships that define life as we know it: between an old man and his backyard, among people in a corporate office, between a lake and a local economy, between pigeons and people in a park.

As you explore possible topics, ask yourself, "What is the nature of this relationship?" If you cannot answer the question easily, you may have a good topic—one worthy of continued thinking and writing. Use the following suggestions, questions, and images to begin exploring:

Jonas Jordan, USACE/U.S. Army

Hal Wilson/StockXchng

- **Visit a Public Place**
  —How do the people interact or depend on each other?
  —How do the people relate to their surroundings? To objects? To buildings? To nature?
  —How do the objects (buildings, tools, products, shops) relate?
  —How do people or objects influence each other?

- **Examine Your Own Relationships**
  —Consider the groups or allegiances that you claim: Are you a smoker, a cyber punk, a metal head, a gamer, a comic book fanatic?
  —What are the tensions, contradictions, or quiet associations that come along with that identity?

- **Examine a Job Site**
  —How do workers relate to their tools or equipment?
  —How must the people relate to each other? (How must they influence or depend on each other?)
  —How do workers relate to their environment?
  —How do workers relate to the public?

- **Examine Everyday Civic Bonds**
  —Between a customer and a sales clerk, a customer and a mail carrier, the public and a city police force, a politician and her constituents, or an artist and the public.

Valeria Obregon/StockXchng

John Metz

- **Imagine Human/Object Relationships**
  —Between a person and a computer, a person and a musical instrument, a person and a car; or between two objects, such as a college course and a textbook, a book and a computer, an old car and a new one, or a road and a house.

- **Examine Relationships in Your Academic Major**
  —Between the professionals in your field of study and the public (such as nurses and their patients, or business marketing professionals and potential consumers).

  —Between two things in your field of study. Students of criminal justice, for instance, can explore how one case (or one kind of case) relates to another; environmental scientists can explore the relationship between waterways and surrounding land or between trees and animal life.

  —Between your field of study and another field. Most academic disciplines and professional fields define themselves in conjunction with other fields. For instance, biology explores its relationship with ethics, computer technologies involve visual or graphic design, and political science involves religious studies.

Analysis

Analysis is the process of inspecting how or why something works, but analysis also involves discovering connections and meaning. In this chapter, analysis involves investigating all the possible ways entities relate to each other. It means going beyond the obvious relationship and exploring the hidden connections. For example, we might begin with some basic understanding of a relationship:

- Students have a relationship with education.

- Smokers have a relationship with cigarettes.

- Pet owners have a relationship with their pets.

- Athletes have a relationship with their equipment.

Inside of the broad idea, we can look for relational clusters—for more specific relationships that maintain or give meaning to the broader idea. For instance, a student has a relationship with education, but more specifically, a computer sciences student may have a relationship to technology *and* change *and* Generation Y. Or a pet owner may have many specific relationships because of her dog—say, with a certain open field, a leash law, or a neighborhood park. When we begin to see clusters of relationships within the broader idea, we get closer to revealing important connections. Use the following Invention Questions to explore deep layers of the relationship that you will explain in your essay:

> What relationships exist within the broader relationship? How do those smaller relationships drive the broader relationship?

❯ Is the broader relationship difficult? Why?

❯ What keeps it going?

❯ How does the presence of one entity (person or thing) influence the other? In what hidden or indirect ways do they influence one another?

❯ What would occur to one if the other were gone?

If you examine an intimate personal relationship, try to go beyond the initial common thoughts ("it is supportive"; "it is difficult"; "it has ups and downs"; "it is loving") and find some hidden complexity. Use the following Invention Questions to explore the complexities of a human relationship:

❯ In what ways do I communicate with this person?

❯ To what degree do I share in his or her personal crises?

❯ Do I ever feel obligated to do, think, or say something for this person?

❯ Why am I in this relationship?

❯ What kinds of disagreements arise in the relationship? Do they become sources of debate and tension, or do they fade away?

As you work through these Invention Questions, use them to develop ideas. For example, in the following excerpt, Jim Crockett's invention writing helped him discover the insights he shares in his essay. In his responses to the Invention Questions, we can see how important concepts emerge and lay the groundwork for his essay:

> **In what hidden or indirect ways do the persons or things influence one another?**
> At the outset, I'm really wondering why I need to use the same mug every day and not one of the many on the shelf that perform the same function, i.e., keep my mustache dry and drip-free while keeping coffee hot. Maybe it's because I received this mug for my birthday a few years back—received it from good friends. Maybe it's the functional good looks of the stainless steel and plastic—industrialized design good looks. Maybe it's because I have a need to carry a security object (Linus's blanket). What if I have an obsessive/compulsive disorder? What if? Does it really matter? Do I really care? Is this really a big deal? Maybe not, but it's probably worth looking into—probably worth unraveling the thread of the warm blanket (warm sweater?) of my relationship with my coffee mug.

Here, Crockett explores various layers. He raises some questions that later evolve into the essay, and he makes two important discoveries: that any possible psychological "disorder" is less important than some basic human need, and that he connects his mug with security.

Now let's look at a different topic and writer. In the following, Marcus uses the Invention Questions to explore the relationship between a police department and the surrounding community. Notice how Marcus's response to the last question (Why am I in this relationship?) takes him further into his own thinking. Although the question seems unrelated to his topic, it actually prompts him to see an essential point: *People can be in a relationship without consciously thinking about it.*

Is the relationship difficult?

Yes. My father is a police officer, and he is constantly stressed about the work. Patrolling in some neighborhoods is hard work—and dangerous. And even though many officers face dangerous situations, they are expected by people in the community to be totally passive. It's nearly impossible work.

What keeps it going?

People stay in the job for obvious reasons: They need money, they have the training, they get some satisfaction out of the job (most of them still assume that they are "protecting and serving"). But the real question is: What keeps the tension going? And that's a mixture of things: On one side, economic problems in the city create bad neighborhoods where people are desperate. On the other side, every time the news reports anything involving the police, it's going to be bad, so people learn to associate police cars and uniforms with negative feelings.

Why am I in this relationship?

Technically, I'm not in it. Or maybe I am. I am "the community." But I guess most people probably don't think they are in the relationship until they see the flashing lights behind them. That's also part of the reason that the tension keeps going. People in the community don't see themselves as part of the relationship—maybe they don't even see a relationship.

Thinking Further

How do writers identify potentially interesting ideas? Given all the possibilities, how do they decide which to pursue and which to ignore? You might consider two key strategies:

1. **Capitalize on Uncertainty.** If you are uncertain how to answer a question, or you can answer it several ways, explore further. (The uncertainty is a sign of complexity!) For example, Marcus writes, "Technically, I'm not in it. Or maybe I am." As Marcus reviews his notes, he can focus on this indefinite answer and explore the ambiguity.

2. **Look for Fresh Perspectives.** Occasionally you might see a topic differently than most other people. Because writers are looking for a new perspective, such realizations are vital. For example, when Marcus writes, "the tension keeps going" because "people in the community don't see themselves as part of the relationship," he has discovered an important idea worth pursuing further.

If writers discover some uncertainty or fresh perspective, they can then ask even more questions to pursue their thinking. For example, Marcus might explore further by asking the following questions:

"Technically, I'm not in it. Or maybe I am."

- Am I in the relationship or not? What is the nature of the relationship?
- Can I ever get out of the relationship? What would happen if I did?
- How does the relationship influence me in hidden ways? How does it influence law enforcement?

"People in the community don't see themselves as part of the relationship—maybe they don't even see a relationship."

- Why don't people in the community see the relationship? How is their not seeing helpful or harmful?

- Who does see the relationship? How do people who see the relationship act differently?

- If more people saw the relationship, would it be less difficult? Would people be influenced differently?

Invention Workshop

Meet with at least one other writer and use one of the Invention Questions (on pages 78–79) to initiate a focused discussion on your topic. Briefly explain your topic to the other writer(s), and then ask one of the Invention Questions. Try to stay focused on that question until you've reached some new insight about the relationship.

Look into the deep connections, both present and past; look at the consequences of actions; consider the effects of attitudes. And remember two key strategies: (1) Capitalize on uncertainty, and (2) look for fresh perspectives.

Sample Invention Workshop

WRITER: [Explains the Topic] I want to write about my relationship with snowboarding. I really like snowboarding. I do it all winter. It's what I do with my friends. I love the snow, the speed, and the excitement. It's expensive though, and risky.

PEER: [Applies an Invention Question] Let's use one of the Invention Questions to probe deeper: What relationships exist within the broader relationship? How do those smaller relationships drive the broader relationship?

WRITER: Well, if the broader relationship is me and snowboarding, then some smaller relationship that exists within it might be . . .

PEER: [Helps the Writer Identify Smaller Relationships] You mentioned speed and excitement and risk. Do you think speed is part of the risk? Is excitement part of the risk? Or vice versa?

WRITER: Well, I'd say both. Maybe they're all tangled together. The speed creates a kind of risk—of physical harm, I guess—and that creates excitement. The rush comes from zooming down the hill, not poking along.

PEER: [Prompts Writer to Explore Uncertainty] So the speed wouldn't be as intense if there weren't some peril involved? Are peril and intensity linked in some way?

WRITER: Probably. Well, it's not totally about the potential harm. I mean, you don't go out there looking to get hurt or fall down a mountain. It's also about the skill it takes to avoid crashing—and to go faster, to do more with your own body.

PEER: [Prompts Further Thinking] Your own body? Why's that important?

WRITER: Well, it's just you and the board—and the hill. Nothing else. You and natural forces. No computers, no monitors, no nothing. And if you move the wrong way, just a little, you feel the consequences.

PEER: And the opposite could also be said, right? That moving just the right way makes you feel something?

WRITER: Definitely. You really learn what your body's capable of—split-second decisions and reflexes.

PEER: So maybe that's how the speed figures in. It cranks up the need for your body to respond? To rely on reflexes?

WRITER: Exactly. And you don't get that anywhere else. I don't anyway. The rest of my life is about sitting, watching, pushing buttons, reading—all eyes, ears, and fingers. I need more than that.

PEER: So snowboarding makes your body wake up to itself—and in a really intense way. Okay. Here's another Invention Question. What would occur to one if the other were gone?

WRITER: Well, if I didn't have snowboarding, I don't think I'd be aware of my own reflexes. I don't know if I'd understand how my reflexes and body even work.

The writer is now digging into the relationship. From here, she could go into the Public Resonance questions and explore the issue further. For instance, the writer may examine how people need a certain degree of raw intensity—something beyond the digital, clinical, and predictable routine of everyday life. That further exploration might yield a revelatory thesis.

Public Resonance

Remember that you are not writing entirely for yourself. You are writing to explain something for others. The particular relationship you are explaining may be specific and narrow (perhaps between two people), but it may suggest something beyond the particular—something that is relevant or important to your readers. As you consider your own topic, ask the following questions:

> Does the relationship reveal something about people's strengths, weaknesses, or needs?

> Why is it important that people see the meaning of the relationship?

> Is there something unusual or usual about this relationship?

> Does this relationship show how difficult, easy, or valuable human relationships can be?

> Does this relationship show how rewarding or valuable a kind of relationship can be?

Exploring public resonance can be hard work. But the process takes writers somewhere important, even vital: to new insights. In his project, Jim Crockett discovers the bigger significance of a relationship—that his simple mug is not merely a personal habit but a representation of human habit and a basic need. He also considers how the specific relationship functions within the broader sphere of relations between humans and their economy, humans and their home, and humans and their past:

> Why is it important that people see the meaning of the relationship? We all need daily ritual in our lives in an increasingly alien world—a culture, econoculture removed from the time-worn agrarian rituals, from the ties to place and home. How much coffee do you drink anyway? The cup/mug is natural—a natural extension of the human hand, a necessary adjunct to, a logical appurtenance thereof. Small choices—these small behaviors we cling to—affect the way in which we are perceived in the world.

And in further writing, Crockett picks up on an idea that surfaces in the previous passage—the idea of ritual. He realizes that *ritual,* the term itself, has significance, meaning beyond the obvious, so he says more about it. Notice that he finds his way back to the concept, to the word, and thinks about its role in the world. In this sense, *Crockett's own language is pulling him further into ideas.* He is inventing by exploring the meaning and significance of his words:

> I'm tired of people asking how much coffee I drink. Do they really care? Caffeine or antioxidants? Whose side are you on? They should care where their coffee comes from. They should care about buying coffee in tree-killing paper cups. They should know that the small choices they make affect the world; that the smallest choices have power. !!! Ritual power—the power of small rituals. We are grounded by our rituals—in the wider world—in the econoculture—the world of corporate greed— we (individuals) have no control. My mug ritual gives me some control in the huge arena of coffee trading. My money goes to the small farmer in Chiapas (at least more of my money) not to the national cartels. The ritual grounds me and ties me to the place and affects, as well, the wider world, the world far removed from its agricultural roots, a world where wilderness is a theme park and where the agrarian rituals have been replaced with what? Maybe they haven't been replaced. Maybe just forgotten. Maybe ritual behaviors are no longer deemed important in a society driven by technology—a society enamored of subject only. Who's doing the verbing here? It doesn't matter who's the recipient, the object. That's why this matters. Maybe we should ask—maybe we should be asking: Whom or what do the small behaviors, ones we cling to, affect? How do they affect the way we are perceived in the world?

Thesis

As you focus your topic, you will also be narrowing in on a thesis statement or main idea. Like many writers, you may write your way to a thesis, or you may try to focus the idea before drafting. Either way, try developing a single statement that not only gives focus to your topic but also provides insight on that topic. Your project might do one of the following:

- **Explain the significant qualities of a particular kind of relationship.**
  —Human/dog relationships rely on so little understanding and effort from humans and so much work, agility, and determination from the dog.
  —Rock stars and their fans both rely on a sense of urgency and exclusivity.

- **Explain what is sometimes hidden in a particular kind of relationship.**
  —Beneath the obvious authority issues between teachers and students, there exists a mutual kind of awe in which each marvels at the will of the other.
  —Homeowners often forget the powerful underground struggle between plumbing and trees—until they see stems and leaves swimming in the toilet.

- **Explain the difficulties or problems of being a child, friend, parent, or significant other.**
  —Our children's birthdays are a tangle of joy and unutterable sadness that comes with knowing how time will eventually do its work and create absence.
  —College friends are surrogate families, which means they always fall short in some quiet way.

- **Explain how a particular relationship is much like something else.**
  —Presidential candidates and their potential supporters are both authors of fiction, each conjuring visions of what the other will certainly do.
  —If the surrounding neighborhood is a family, the 7-11 is like a bad in-law that has slowly been accepted.

- **Explain how a particular relationship reveals something important about a subject.**
  —The river's color beyond the city shows how water willingly carries the by-products of human endeavor.
  —The association between gun and police officer speaks of our culture's assumption about power.

Regardless of your approach, steer clear of unfocused generalizations. A narrower and more particular thesis will create a more intensive experience for both writer and readers. Notice the difference among the following:

General	Specific	More Specific
Students	Third-grade girls	The attitudes of third-grade girls
Employees	Retail sales associates	Retail sales associates' energy
Campus	The new buildings	The look of the new buildings

The more specific subjects help readers (and writers!) focus on more specific insights. They help readers and writers tune in to intricacies and intimacies. (They actually help sharpen consciousness.) If nouns (or subjects in sentences) help create focus, then verbs can help create *revelation*. A revelatory thesis statement shows something new—a commonly overlooked layer, connection, or idea. In the following statements, verbs *(depend, relies, competes)* are active and intensive. They do more than establish a relationship. They show how entities relate:

- The attitudes of third-grade girls *depend* upon the number of close friends.

- Retail sales associates' energy *relies* on the number and nature of customers.

- The flat, corporate look of the new buildings on campus *competes* with the traditional stone giants and illustrates the clash between the old academic tradition and the new corporate designs on education.

In considering the focus of your project, examine your nouns and verbs. Can the nouns be more specific? Can the verbs be more active?

Evolution of a Thesis

Writers should allow their initial ideas to become increasingly more focused and revelatory. Notice how a broad statement can become more intense and sophisticated as it becomes more focused:

- **Runners develop an intense relationship with the road.**

  Here, "intense relationship" can be defined or narrowed. It's potentially interesting, but we need to see the intensity.

- **Runners share space with humans and machines.**

  The writer can keep thinking about that space—what happens in that shared space?

- **Runners must confront the overwhelming presence of both cars and car culture when they take to the road.**

The writer has helped us to see a kind of difficulty or tension in the relationship. We're examining not only the physical presence of cars, but also some set of assumptions or attitudes related to cars.

Rhetorical Tools

The next step is to develop and support your initial ideas. Remember that potential readers already know about relationships in general. (They are certainly mired in several.) But in your essay, you have the opportunity to shed light, to go beyond ordinary thinking, and to reveal something that most people do not necessarily consider.

Using Narration

Narration, or storytelling, is appropriate for many kinds of writing. It is not simply relegated to remembering events. You might consider beginning your essay with a brief retelling of a situation regarding the relationship, or using a brief account to illustrate something about the relationship. It will be important to determine how much narration to use. For example, Kellie Coppola uses brief passages of narration to explain her interactions on Tinder. Jim Crockett uses narration only to share a brief personal experience with his mug. If you decide to use narration, make good choices: (1) Start the narrative at an appropriate place. That is, limit your story to include only relevant parts of the situation. (2) Focus on only the relevant details of the events. (3) Use consistent verb tense. (In most cases, past or present tense can work in retelling a story. However, you must be consistent throughout the narrative.) (4) At some point, make sure to explain the significance or relevance of the narrative to the readers. Refer to Chapter 2 for other valuable narrative strategies.)

Using Description

Readers like details. The more detailed the images, the more intensely readers will experience them. In this essay, you might decide to describe the people involved in the relationship— their particular postures, facial expressions, and gestures. Or you might need to detail more abstract qualities—their imaginations, their appetites, their pride, their esteem, their effect on strangers. In the following, a writer is describing the relationship between a coffee shop and the students who frequent the place. The first passage is broad and without detail:

> The coffee shop makes them feel more academic. It is more than a location to do homework and drink caffeine. It is a place where students totally surround themselves in college work.

These are valuable statements, but they remain abstract, general, and ultimately unhelpful to readers. But the ideas come to life more with details:

> The coffee shop is more than a location for doing homework. It is like a satellite campus where students and professors alike work, talk, reflect. On any given day, several tables will be pushed together while a group of students work together on a project, their papers and notebooks scattered between coffee cups and half-eaten bagels. Invariably, a professor, graduate student, or staff member from the college will sit at one of the corner tables reading a newspaper. Several students will be perched on the windowsill, their backs against the outside world as they read through textbook chapters.

You might need to describe a particular situation in detail. In that case, narration and description will work together. For instance, Steinbeck includes several situations or anecdotes in his essay that dramatize the relationship between American settlers and the land:

> Another joker with a name still remembered in the West worked out a scheme copied many times in after years. Proving a quarter section required a year of residence and some kind of improvement—a fence, a shack—but once the land was proved the owner was free to sell it. This particular princely character went to the stews and skid rows of the towns and found a small army of hopeless alcoholics who lived for whisky and nothing else. He put these men on land he wanted to own, grubstaked them and kept them in cheap liquor until the acreage was proved, then went through the motions of buying it from his protégés and moved them and their one-room shacks on sled runners on to new quarter sections. Bums of strong constitution might prove out five or six homesteads for this acquisitive hero before they died of drunkenness.

Using Figurative Language

Any explanatory essay can benefit from figurative language, which is language that goes beyond words' basic definitions and uses them to suggest imaginative connections between ideas. Figurative language does more than just make interesting comparisons. It also reveals a new dimension to the topic; it helps writers and their readers to see the topic in a new light. John Steinbeck uses simile (a comparison using *like* or *as*) to characterize the nature of the relationship between American settlers and the land:

> I have often wondered at the savagery and thoughtlessness with which our early settlers approached this rich continent. They came at it *as though it were an enemy,* which of course it was.

In his essay, Jim Crockett slides in a subtle metaphor (a comparison in which one thing is made to share the characteristics of another) that graphically describes most consumers' relationship with big coffee corporations:

> When I buy a cup of coffee, I only buy coffee: the paper cup and insulating sleeve, both little bits of tree, remain in the store. *I remain weaned from dependence* upon the earth- and human-pillaging multinational coffee cartel.

In her essay, Kellie Coppola compares dating and fishing. While this is a common comparison, Coppola extends it to find some fresh and compelling ideas:

> Just as humans fish for survival, we also fish for companionship, the innate need to care about another and have another care about them. And we don't just want any fish, we want THE fish. So we cast our reels—sometimes at a bar, sometimes at a singles cruise, sometimes unexpectedly—and begin the toil of catch-and-release, looking for our elusive Moby Dick amongst guppies. If love is like fishing, the world is a vast, unpredictable ocean— huge and hard to navigate, where assumptions about gender roles, attraction, and dating etiquette create waves that make it easier for some fishermen than others. Some of us find our whale; some of us will take the biggest one luck will afford; some will drop the fishing rod entirely.

As you consider your own topic, apply the following questions:

› What brief story will help readers to see my point about the relationship?

› What vivid details will help demonstrate the precise nature of the relationship?

› Can I compare the relationship (or the entities in the relationship) to an animal? A thing? A place? A person? What new dimension would this comparison reveal?

ACTIVITY

Before developing a draft, make a plan. It need not be highly detailed. Any rough outline can make all the difference between writerly hiccups and writerly flow. Chart out your ideas: What is your thesis? What are your main support strategies? What examples will you use? What stories will you tell? And where will you begin and end those? What comparisons will you make?

Revision

Revision is the most difficult intellectual step in writing. It requires a commitment to rethink some basics, to step back and ask if the writing does, at its most basic level, what it should. For instance, does the draft, as it stands, offer a revelatory insight about a relationship? Does it go beyond describing a relationship and, instead, offer a focused insight beyond what readers already know? Does it help readers to rethink the nature of the relationship?

Before you get a peer review, go back through the main sections of the chapter and ask some basic questions: How well does my draft explain the hidden complexities of a relationship? Does the draft connect to or involve issues or relationships beyond my personal relationship? Is the thesis sufficiently focused and revelatory? Does the draft provide details, narration, and explanation that support the thesis? Is it organized so that readers can follow the ideas? How does the voice engage readers? How does it do more than fulfill an assignment? Which sentences can be vitalized? How can the draft be woken up, turned up, or intensified?

Peer Review

Exchange drafts with at least one other writer. Before passing your draft to others, underline the thesis, or write it on the top of your essay. This way, reviewers will get traction as they read.

As a reviewer, use the following questions to guide your response:

1. Point out any phrases in the thesis that could be more specific. (See the Thesis section for more guidance.)

2. Where can the writer do more analysis and reveal more about the relationship? (Point to passages that seem most obvious to you.) As you read, look for claims that anyone could immediately offer without intensive analysis.

3. Help the writer illustrate his or her claims with details. As you read, look for broad characterizations. If you see phrases such as "influence one another" or "depend on one another," ask yourself: Could this be more specific? Can we *really* see the influence or dependence? Suggest further details to the writer. Explain what you would like to see.

4. Offer some figurative language to help characterize the relationship. After you have read the entire draft, offer your own metaphor or simile about the relationship. Make sure it is something that fits the writer's voice—something that he or she could use.

5. Are the paragraphs coherent? Do you ever get the sense that a paragraph is wandering? Mark any passages or details that seem unrelated to the point of the essay.

6. Help the writer kick-start the essay. The writer might begin with a broad statement about the relationship—or about something even broader. But the most focused statement possible often makes for a better introduction. Suggest a surprisingly focused opening statement.

7. Consider the writer's voice. Where could the writer employ a whisper or a yell (see pages 538–539) to better engage readers?

8. Point to particular sentences and phrases that could gain vitality and intensity. Use the following questions:

   • Where can the writer change *be* verbs to active verbs?

   • Look for clauses (especially those that begin with *which are, which is, that are, that is,* etc.). Suggest a strategy for boiling down the clause to a phrase.

   • Look for phrases (especially prepositional phrases that begin with *about* or *of*). Suggest a strategy for boiling down the phrase to a word.

   • Consider vitality strategies from the previous chapter:

      —Combine sentences.

      —Repeat structures.

      —Intensify verbs.

      —Help the writer avoid common grammatical errors: comma splices, sentence fragments, or lack of pronoun/antecedent agreement.

Reflection

For writers, the big insights often come after they have completed a project—after they have thought through an idea, developed an essay, revised, edited, and given it to the world beyond them. After these steps, writers should have a better sense of what they have discovered and accomplished. Look back on your essay—from invention to the final draft—and analyze its rhetoric based on the following questions:

1. How is the main insight revelatory? (How does it go beyond what people normally imagine about this kind of relationship? How might it have even taken you, as a writer, to a new intellectual place?)

2. What support strategies were the most important? If you used narrative, what made you focus on particular scenes or situations?

3. What would you say is the public resonance of the essay? How does your main insight resonate with some broader issue, idea, tension, trend, or behavior?

4. Describe your voice. If every essay has a voice, what does yours sound like? Is it sober? Formal? Lazy? Intense? Meditative? Forceful? Earnest? What particular passages best show the character of your voice?

Beyond the Essay: Images as Support

Images can function like words, sentences, and paragraphs to help readers understand a writer's main idea.

1. For your explaining relationships essay, use one to three images to help readers understand and accept your thesis. Place photographs, drawings, or other visuals within the essay to illustrate key points. Think of the images as rhetorical tools.

   Make sure the images are rhetorically and aesthetically effective. Consider, for instance, where in the essay the image should be placed; what size the image should be; how the image contributes to or detracts from the momentum of the essay; whether the image should be colorful, bold, restrained, black-and-white, and so on.

   Include a concise caption beneath each image.

2. After incorporating the images into your essay, write a separate document to explain how the images help readers understand and accept the essay's thesis. To help with your explanation, for each image think about content, framing, composition, focus, lighting, texture, and vantage point, which are discussed in Chapter 7: Analyzing Images and Videos.

4 Observing

Chapter Objectives

This chapter will help you to:

- Distinguish between a casual glance and focused observation.
- Find significance and meaning in an unscripted everyday situation.
- Develop a focused and revelatory essay about an unscripted everyday situation, using narration, allusions, and figurative language.
- Use images to express a complex idea.

"The goal here is to see something in a new way, to see beyond the casual glance."

INTRODUCTION

Observing is about discovering something unique and particular about a subject. It involves more than simple description. Careful observers go beyond the casual glance; they study their subjects and learn something by seeing them in a particular way. In some ways, then, learning how to observe involves learning how to see things and notice what is beneath the surface.

We observe our daily lives casually, watching our coworkers, friends, children, and families carrying on with life. Occasionally, we take time to study, to focus on, subjects and take in something beyond surface meanings. At those times we go beyond what something means to us and discover something outside of our expectations and biases.

Observers find the hidden meaning, the significant issues, and the important aspects of a particular subject. They point out how and why a particular subject is of interest to a broader public. We experience this kind of observing when we watch documentaries or nature specials. Writers and researchers for these programs first make general observations. Then they focus their perspective on a particular issue or subject. They analyze that issue or subject to find the most important or valuable thing to say. Throughout this process, the observing writer is always looking to discover and communicate a fresh and interesting idea.

The chapter readings will provide insight to various strategies for observing. As you read, look for how these strategies convey the hidden meaning, significant issue, or important aspect of the subject being observed and how it resonates with the lives of others. After reading the essays, you can find a topic in one of two ways: go to the Point of Contact section to find a topic from everyday life, or choose one of the Ideas for Writing that follow each essay. After you find a topic, go to the Analysis section to begin developing your observation.

Living Like Weasels
Annie Dillard

It is easy to imagine weasels as nothing more than wild animals and to see them as entirely divorced from human affairs. After all, we are civilized. Weasels live in holes and eat mice. But in this essay, Annie Dillard, a Pulitzer Prize–winning author, invites us to rethink weasels and our own everyday lives. She insists that something can be learned behind the stare of a simple animal, something essential about life's purpose. After a brief encounter with a weasel, Dillard goes beyond the first glimpse and creates important meaning for herself and others. "Living Like Weasels" first appeared in Dillard's book *Teaching a Stone to Talk* (1982).

A weasel is wild. Who knows what he thinks? He sleeps in his underground den, his tail draped over his nose. Sometimes he lives in his den for two days without leaving. Outside, he stalks rabbits, mice, muskrats, and birds, killing more bodies than he can eat warm, and often dragging the carcasses home. Obedient to instinct, he bites his prey at the neck, either splitting the jugular vein at the throat or crunching the brain at the base of the skull, and he does not let go. One naturalist refused to kill a weasel who was socketed into his hand deeply as a rattlesnake. The man could in no way pry the tiny weasel off, and he had to walk half a mile to water, the weasel dangling from his palm, and soak him off like a stubborn label.

And once, says Ernest Thompson Seton—once, a man shot an eagle out of the sky. He examined the eagle and found the dry skull of a weasel fixed by the jaws to his throat. The supposition is that the eagle had pounced on the weasel and the weasel swiveled and bit as instinct taught him, tooth to neck, and nearly won. I would like to have seen that eagle from the air a few weeks or months before he was shot: was the whole weasel still attached to his feathered throat, a fur pendant? Or did the eagle eat what he could reach, gutting the living weasel with his talons before his breast, bending his beak, cleaning the beautiful airborne bones?

I have been reading about weasels because I saw one last week. I startled a weasel who startled me, and we exchanged a long glance.

Twenty minutes from my house, through the woods by the quarry and across the highway, is Hollins Pond, a remarkable piece of shallowness, where I like to go at sunset and sit on a tree trunk. Hollins Pond is also called Murray's Pond; it covers two acres of bottomland near Tinker Creek with six inches of water and six thousand lily pads. In winter, brown-and-white steers stand in the middle of it, merely dampening their hooves; from the distant shore they look like miracle itself, complete with miracle's nonchalance. Now, in summer, the steers are gone. The water lilies have blossomed and spread to a green horizontal plane that is terra firma to plodding blackbirds, and tremulous ceiling to black leeches, crayfish, and carp.

From *Teaching a Stone to Talk* by Annie Dillard. New York: Harper Collins, 1982.

Menno Schaefer/Shutterstock.com

This is, mind you, suburbia. It is a five-minute walk in three directions to rows of houses, though none is visible here. There's a 55 mph highway at one end of the pond, and a nesting pair of wood ducks at the other. Under every bush is a muskrat hole or a beer can. The far end is an alternating series of fields and woods, fields and woods, threaded everywhere with motorcycle tracks—in whose bare clay wild turtles lay eggs.

So. I had crossed the highway, stepped over two low barbed-wire fences, and traced the motorcycle path in all gratitude through the wild rose and poison ivy of the pond's shoreline up into high grassy fields. Then I cut down through the woods to the mossy fallen tree where I sit. This tree is excellent. It makes a dry, upholstered bench at the upper, marshy end of the pond, a plush jetty raised from the thorny shore between a shallow blue body of water and a deep blue body of sky.

The sun had just set. I was relaxed on the tree trunk, ensconced in the lap of lichen, watching the lily pads at my feet tremble and part dreamily over the thrusting path of a carp. A yellow bird appeared to my right and flew behind me. It caught my eye; I swiveled around—and the next instant, inexplicably, I was looking down at a weasel, who was looking up at me.

Weasel! I'd never seen one wild before. He was ten inches long, thin as a curve, a muscled ribbon, brown as fruitwood, soft-furred, alert. His face was fierce, small and pointed as a lizard's; he would have made a good arrowhead. There was just a dot of chin, maybe two brown hairs' worth, and then the pure white fur began that spread down his underside. He had two black eyes I didn't see, any more than you see a window.

The weasel was stunned into stillness as he was emerging from beneath an enormous shaggy wild rose bush four feet away. I was stunned into stillness twisted backward on the tree trunk. Our eyes locked, and someone threw away the key.

Our look was as if two lovers, or deadly enemies, met unexpectedly on an overgrown path when each had been thinking of something else: a clearing blow to the gut. It was also a bright blow to the brain, or a sudden beating of brains, with all the charge and intimate grate of rubbed balloons. It emptied our lungs. It felled the forest, moved the fields, and drained the pond; the world dismantled and tumbled into that black hole of eyes. If you and I looked at each other that way, our skulls would split and drop to our shoulders. But we don't. We keep our skulls. So.

He disappeared. This was only last week, and already I don't remember what shattered the enchantment. I think I blinked, I think I retrieved my brain from the weasel's brain, and tried to memorize what I was seeing, and the weasel felt the yank of separation, the careening splashdown into real life and the urgent current of instinct. He vanished under the wild rose. I waited motionless, my mind suddenly full of data and my spirit with pleadings, but he didn't return.

Please do not tell me about "approach-avoidance conflicts." I tell you I've been in that weasel's brain for sixty seconds, and he was in mine. Brains are private places, muttering through unique and secret tapes—but the weasel and I both plugged into another tape simultaneously, for a sweet and shocking time. Can I help it if it was a blank?

What goes on in his brain the rest of the time? What does a weasel think about? He won't say. His journal is tracks in clay, a spray of feathers, mouse blood and bone: uncollected, unconnected, loose-leaf, and blown.

I would like to learn, or remember, how to live. I come to Hollins Pond not so much to learn how to live as, frankly, to forget about it. That is, I don't think I can learn from a wild animal how to live in particular—shall I suck warm blood, hold my tail high, walk with my footprints precisely over the prints of my hands?—but I might learn something of mindlessness, something of the purity of living in the physical senses and the dignity of living without bias or motive. The weasel lives in necessity and we live in choice, hating necessity and dying at the last ignobly in its talons. I would like to live as I should, as the weasel lives as he should. And I suspect that for me the way is like the weasel's: open to time and death painlessly, noticing everything, remembering nothing, choosing the given with a fierce and pointed will.

I missed my chance. I should have gone for the throat. I should have lunged for that streak of white under the weasel's chin and held on, held on through mud and into the wild rose, held on for a dearer life. We could live under the wild rose wild as weasels, mute and uncomprehending. I could very calmly go wild. I could live two days in the den, curled, leaning on mouse fur, sniffing bird bones, blinking, licking, breathing musk, my hair tangled in the roots of grasses. Down is a good place to go, where the mind is single. Down is out, out of your ever-loving mind and back to your careless senses. I remember muteness as a prolonged and giddy fast, where every moment is a feast of utterance received. Time and events are merely poured, unremarked, and ingested directly, like blood pulsed into my gut through a jugular vein. Could two live that way? Could two live under the wild rose, and explore by the pond, so that the smooth mind of each is as everywhere present to the other, and as received and as unchallenged, as falling snow?

We could, you know. We can live any way we want. People take vows of poverty, chastity, and obedience—even of silence—by choice. The thing is to stalk your calling in a certain skilled and supple way, to locate the most tender and live spot and plug into that pulse. This is yielding, not fighting. A weasel doesn't "attack" anything; a weasel lives as he's meant to, yielding at every moment to the perfect freedom of single necessity.

I think it would be well, and proper, and obedient, and pure, to grasp your one necessity and not let it go, to dangle from it limp wherever it takes you. Then even death, where you're going no matter how you live, cannot you part. Seize it and let it seize you up aloft even, till your eyes burn out and drop; let your musky flesh fall off in shreds, and let your very bones unhinge and scatter, loosened over fields, over fields and woods, lightly, thoughtless, from any height at all, from as high as eagles.

WRITING STRATEGIES

1. What might Dillard be trying to achieve with her introduction? Does she achieve it? Does her introduction make you want to read on? Why or why not?

2. How did you react when Dillard addressed you directly in ¶8? ("He had two black eyes I didn't see, any more than you see a window.") Were you startled? Did you know what she meant? When you write, do you sometimes speak more directly to the reader than at other times? Provide a few examples of how the writing situation influences how directly you speak to the reader.

3. Dillard describes the weasel's face as "fierce." Is this a good description? What are the characteristics of a fierce-looking face? Did her description, or word choice, help you get a better mental image of a weasel? How else might she have described the weasel?

4. What point is Dillard making in her concluding paragraph? How might she have stated her main point in a less poetic essay?

EXPLORING IDEAS

1. What is Dillard trying to accomplish in this essay?

2. What change does Dillard's essay call for? How does she ask the reader to think or live differently?

3. Dillard's experience with the weasel affected her strongly, prompting her to explore her thoughts on how she lives. What similar personal experiences have prompted you to think differently about how you, and others, live?

4. Interview others, asking them what small experiences made them think differently about their lives. Ask them to describe the experience and how it influenced their thinking.

5. Discuss your interview responses from #4 above with classmates. Which responses were most common? Which were most unusual? Which would make for the most interesting essay and why?

IDEAS FOR WRITING

1. What person, place, or thing can you describe as a way of making an interesting point?

2. Have you interacted with an animal in the way Dillard has, or in some other thought-provoking way?

If responding to one of these ideas, go to the Analysis section of this chapter to begin developing ideas for your essay.

The Front Porch
Chester McCovey

Complete the auto-graded quiz for this reading.

Chester McCovey's observing essay illustrates how one can use an observation as a point of contact and then, through analysis, explore why the observation matters. McCovey makes a simple observation: that people don't sit out on their front porches like they did when he was a kid. Then he explores and determines that the loss of the front porch equals a loss of community. Through analysis, he goes from a specific observation (about garages and porches) to a general insight (about a loss of community).

The essay begins with a personal observation and connects with the readers.

If you walk through my neighborhood, you won't see many porches, at least not the kind people sit on in the evenings. Those days are gone where I live, and likely where you live, too.

States the main observation: porch replaced by garage.

The front porch has been replaced—by the two-car garage. Both sets of my grandparents, who lived in the same small town, had big front porches, and summer visits often meant sitting on the porch, talking, and watching cars and people out walking. After a while someone might have suggested getting some ice cream. The adult conversation was often dull, sometimes painfully so for a child, but sometimes it was interesting. The everyday people a child sees in church or at the Little League field in a small town have a few years behind them, and what person who has lived a little doesn't have a story to tell—or a story to be told about them? Sometimes those stories would come out and bring to life a previously uninteresting Frank or Gretchen. Small towns are full of life's everyday dramas. A child hears and figures out many things on a place like a front porch on a thing like a warm summer night.

The front porch was a place where people used to talk (pass the time, shoot the breeze).

The writer uses personal details to develop the observation.

My grandparents' garages were small, just enough for one car and a few tools—not much of a garage for today's homeowner. In those days the garage kept a car and a small lawnmower, some rakes, and so on. The garage today must keep much more. One can see, then, how the exchange occurred. Like an old-fashioned trade in baseball, gone is the home team's beloved front porch, replaced by a big, new garage. Of course the trade is much more interesting than that. And a look at how it occurred enlightens us a little about the world in which we live. More importantly, it tells us not so much about how life is now but about how it came to be. And, I would argue, it shows us the way in which things will continue to change.

The essay moves toward analysis. Why did this happen, and what does it mean?

The shift from porch to garage tells us about the world in which we live, how it came to be, and how it will continue to change.

From Chester McCovey, "The Front Porch." Reprinted with permission of the author.

Back then, our own garage held two cars, a riding lawnmower, a push mower, bicycles, and lots of tools. We had a front porch and sat on it, but mostly just when we had company. Our house, then, represents the transition between two generations: my grandparents' generation that traveled less, received only three television stations (*sans* remote control), and didn't have air conditioning and my own generation that is more likely to be on the go (driving from one place to another) or sitting inside, on the computer or watching TV.

The writer's own childhood house illustrates the transition from porch to garage.

The front porch fell victim to its two natural enemies: the internal-combustion engine (automobiles) and electricity (air conditioning, lights, and TV). Now, instead of gathering on our front porch as our grandparents did, we are either gone somewhere thanks to our transportation or we are at home but indoors.

Main Ideas: What happened to the front porch and why: automobile and electricity. What happened because of that: we are either gone or indoors.

how life must have splashed

out of the cup

on warm summer nights

before the cool air

of electricity

urged us all to relax

in the fluttering glow

of color tv

Because of automobiles and electricity, we spend more time driving alone or watching TV than we do talking with our friends and neighbors. Is this a problem? A loss of community?

We have traded sitting on the front porch for sitting in traffic, or to be more positive about it, for sitting in our automobile as we speed along to some very important place to be. The shift from porch to garage is beautifully simple. It goes like this: I need a place to park my transportation machine (car, truck, SUV) and I don't need a large, outdoor room for sitting. The reasoning (the reality of the situation) is just as simple: There's not as much action on the sidewalk as there once was (the neighbors are indoors or driving somewhere) and I don't need to sit outdoors to stay cool on muggy nights (the air conditioning indoors takes care of that). So, a need or desire—to stay cool, to be entertained, to keep up with what's going on—is replaced not by a different need or desire but instead by a new way of meeting it.

Explanation: How/why the shift occurred.

Need or Desire—To Stay Cool

Previously met by evening breeze; now

met by air conditioning

Need or Desire—To Be Entertained

Previously met by conversation with

neighbors; now met by TV, computer,

shopping at the mall, conversation with

friends who we drive to see

Need or Desire—To Keep Up with What's Going On

Previously met by discussion with

neighbors and friends; now met through

national media (TV and Internet)

I am not saying there are no front porches. Obviously there are. And I am not saying everyone has a two-car garage instead. In my neighborhood, small garages not connected to the house still reign. But obviously, their days are numbered. The new houses sometimes look as much like a house attached to a garage as a garage attached to a house. Today's garage often dominates the house.

Finally, the careful reader is insisting that I deal with the backyard patio deck. What about *it?* When we do sit outdoors, we choose to do it out back, away from the rest of the world. This is interesting. We need a break, I would suggest, from the hustle and bustle of daily life, so we retreat to our own backyard to be left alone with our families. But that hustle and bustle is mostly the hustle and bustle of traffic, radio, television, and a few quick transactions with total strangers. Of course another reason for opting to relax in the backyard is that, as previously mentioned, there just isn't that much going on out front these days. (If there were, I wonder if we would sit on the front porch and watch it . . . *and* contribute to it.) I am arguing that we lose something very basic—very fundamental—when we lose the front porch culture.

On Sunday drives through the country, I see big new houses with big new porches. As Americans we can have it all—the house with the big front porch *and* the big garage. But I never (I am tempted to qualify this statement and say "almost never" or "rarely" but I have been thinking about it and I do mean "never")—I never see anyone out sitting on those porches. I am not prepared here to argue that we are a civilization in deep trouble because of this, though it does seem

To avoid oversimplifying, the writer qualifies the point and concedes that there are still front porches, but that their days are numbered.

Anticipates a potential concern of readers: what about the back deck?

The back deck takes us out back, away from community.

Main point: We lose something very basic—very fundamental—when we lose the front porch culture. Leaves readers to consider the cost of this change.

Sunday drives in the country bring to mind an earlier time, when people hung out on the front porch talking with neighbors.

to me appropriate that we should lament, at least a little, the loss of the front porch.

Ironically, McCovey is driving around.

Imagine: Being entertained by sitting on a porch and talking.

WRITING STRATEGIES

1. What is the essay's thesis?

2. What details help readers value the thesis and why?

3. In a paragraph, summarize McCovey's explanation of *how* the shift from porch to garage occurred and *why* it matters.

4. Why is it important that McCovey writes about the backyard patio deck? How does this paragraph help readers accept the main claim?

5. Where does McCovey use a metaphor or simile (comparing two unlike things: *The clerk was a bear* [metaphor]; *The clerk was like a bear* [simile])? Where else does he use figurative language?

EXPLORING IDEAS

1. Based on this essay, what does McCovey value? To what degree do you value the same thing?

2. In your own words, summarize McCovey's main idea. Then share your summary with several classmates who have also read the essay. Discuss your understanding of McCovey's main idea, and then reread his essay and revise your summary as necessary.

3. To further explore this issue, share your summary with people of various age groups, asking them to respond to McCovey's ideas. Describe how their views are similar to or different from McCovey's.

4. Think of a metaphor or simile of your own that might work well in this essay.

IDEAS FOR WRITING

1. Besides the move from porch to garage, what other change has taken place? How has that change impacted everyday life?

2. Observe some difference in a way of living, whether it be the result of time (your grandparents and you, for example) or location (Southern Californians and Midwesterners). Do not be afraid to generalize, as long as you do it thoughtfully and are mindful of exceptions.

If responding to one of these ideas, go to the Analysis section of this chapter to begin developing ideas for your essay.

Red Raiders Fans
Taylor Perry

"Red Raiders Fans" is an ethnography essay—a type of observing essay that focuses on a particular culture. Taylor Perry observed high school football fans over the course of three weeks, writing down observations then analyzing those observations for insight—for what it is to be an Oakville Red Raiders high school football fan. Perry acknowledged that he had preconceived ideas about the topic before and during his observation. But by remaining open to the situation and successfully putting aside those ideas, he discovers something new.

A high school football game strikes me as a rite of passage, a sort of initiation experience that one might read about in *National Geographic* or see on the History Channel. While we imagine primitive cultures dancing around fires, the elders presiding as the young boys perform acts of courage, perhaps walking across fire or ritualistically yet still realistically fighting each other, we might think how primitive they are, and how primitive we aren't. We can easily see the primitivity in their rituals, and I anticipated discovering something I already knew: that high school football is just another one of these primitive rites of passage, initiation rituals. The adults gather to watch the boys ritualistically, yet realistically too, battle each other on behalf of their communities. By doing this, they become men. A band performs. The elders who oversee all this participated in it themselves years ago. When it's over, someone wins and someone loses. There's a hero . . . and a goat. They've all proven themselves by participating. Some have achieved great status. The communities live in peace. Oakville and Harborview (both names have been changed for this essay) don't go to war. One has bragging rights, and the other has next year.

However, what I ended up observing and concluding was the way two groups of fans (a few loud ones and everyone else) interacted. Some verbal exchanges at the beginning of the third game were typical of the way the fans communicated. It was cold and windy. Fans were arriving an hour early. Forty-five minutes before the game I chose a seat across the aisle from the middle section. Red Raiders fans wore hats, gloves, heavy coats, and brought blankets. Some had hand warmers stashed inside their gloves and probably had foot and body warmers too, but if so, these were hidden from view. Red Raiders fans could be divided into three clothing groups. The largest group wore their team's color, and the same was true for each of the opposing teams' fans: team colors. Another group wore heavy hunting or work clothes, either camouflage or Carhartt brown. A third group wore other cold weather gear, in brands like North Face, Patagonia, or Columbia.

Dressed this way, fans chose their seats, some with hot dogs, pizza, soft pretzels, coffee and hot chocolate. They greeted each other before the game: "Hey, baby, where's your husband? I'll help you keep warm," a guy behind me, the back row I think, yelled to a woman heading toward her seat. Based on her response ("Now you *know* I'd rather freeze, Jerry! Michelle gonna come by after work?"), she didn't seem to take offense. Another guy from the back row yelled at someone else, "You need another blanket," not quite a question and not quite an explanation. And that fellow responded, "No, I got enough." Caught up in these greetings, I heard a woman behind me, referring to what she's wearing, say, "How stupid do I look?" I couldn't help turning around and saying, "I have to look, since you asked. You look great!" Exchanges like these seem to take the place of "Hello. How are you? Nice to see you. I am fine."

In addition to these greetings, people talked about what they did earlier in the day, what their children are up to, and I hear two men behind me reminiscing about previous football seasons. One man said, "I took a team down there twenty years ago. We played X, Y, Z (he mentioned particular schools I wasn't able to write down)." And then the discussion branched off from there and they talked about the teams, their playing styles (one man mentioned a particularly good team's Achilles heel, its lack of discipline), and some star players. A man with a blanket spoke to two women (a mother and daughter it turns out) a few rows in front of me:

"Hello, Stranger. Are you on break?"

The girl replied, "No. I graduated. I live at home now."

"I thought you were trying to get rid of her," he said to the mother.

The girl replied, "I keep coming back." And the man moved on to find a seat for the game.

This verbal behavior turned out to be interesting, though not earth-shatteringly insightful. I've been to many high school games before and this is just typical of what gets said. It was interesting to me, it turns out, because I was observing it. The act of observation made the verbal exchanges interesting. I really noticed how Red Raiders fans consistently said something besides "Hello" to say hello. Their exchanges were usually humorous. They were quick and friendly. They conveyed an acknowledgment of some aspect of the other person's life (college, spouse) and of the present situation (cold).

During Game 3, which ended in a loss for the Red Raiders, I was able to observe some contrasting cheering styles. When the announcer made the traditional pre-game announcement about fans practicing good sportsmanship, for example not harassing the referees, one of these fans yelled, "We'll be good if the officials are good," which got some laughs from the rest of the section. This fan turned out to be one of four real yellers in the top row of the section to my right (closer to the fifty yard line). It turns out these four fans—and just these four fans—were very dissatisfied throughout the game with the officiating. One woman led the crowd in front of her in a "Get that ball back, get that ball back" cheer. No one in my section cheered along. After one tackle, she and the man next to her (both dressed in Red Raiders' gear) shouted, "Horse collar! Horse collar! Don't let them horse collar tackle!" No one else around us objected to the tackle or called it an illegal horse collar tackle, though.

At one point, one of the four hollered, "Hey, wake up over there!" I heard her yell it, but didn't know what she meant until the woman sitting next to me said she was talking to our section which was more quietly watching the game, cheering for big plays, but not yelling loudly throughout the game. The Red Raiders fans in my section were at that point listening to, glancing at, talking about, and mostly trying to ignore the four loud yellers behind us and to our right, and so were the fans in front of them in the middle section, I'm pretty sure. "Hey, ref! Watch the game. You're missing a good one!" the man yelled. "Just like at Waysville Lake," one of the women yelled. "Get in the game! They can't do it on their own!" the other women yelled.

Were these yellers ruining my observation, or were they my observation? At halftime, a high school girl stood next to me in the aisle, "Mom, mom, Amy!" When she said her mom's name, she got her attention. "Want some hot chocolate?" Her mother said she did. I imagined making a joke when the girl brought her mother some hot chocolate, joking that she'd brought it for me and then passing it down to her mother. The girl never came back though. In the second half, one of the yellers yelled, "Hey, Amy! We need you over there." Amy smiled and acknowledged the yeller's comment, but she like the rest of us was watching the game more quietly, cheering for big plays and talking (what I would consider to be) more reasonably about the game.

I observed that at a high school football game, and at a Red Raiders' game in particular, most fans were pretty quiet. They cheered for their team but not maniacally. They didn't yell at the players or at the referees. They talked amongst themselves and only got loud for a touchdown, an interception, or a big hit. What surprised me, or what I observed (not sure how surprising it really was), was that most people put up with a few yellers. At one point a man in the middle section had words with the yelling man (I couldn't hear the exact exchange). Then one of the yelling women yelled, "You shut up! And you shut up!" to each of the men. No one else spoke up to try to silence the yellers and the two men went back to watching the game, one quietly and one loudly.

This behavior is probably not unique to Red Raiders fans; however, I think in some other communities (some other cultures) fans might have objected verbally to the yellers. Of course in those communities, there might just have been even more yellers. My hypothesis going into these observations was something about high school football being a rite of passage activity. I observed the dress, the food, the verbal exchanges, the seating, and I ultimately had imposed upon me an observation about several hundred people's response to four people's over-the-top yelling.

WRITING STRATEGIES

1. What is Perry's thesis? Write down one sentence, either from the essay or of your own, that expresses the essay's main insight.

2. Perry's ethnography essay could be organized differently. What paragraphs could appear elsewhere in the essay? What headings might Perry use to organize the essay? How might these changes impact the reading experience?

3. What information would you delete to preserve Perry's main idea while making the essay more concise?

4. What word would you use to describe Perry's writer's voice? Provide two passages and explain why they support your description.

5. Perry's essay includes specific observations from the Red Raiders game and knowledge from previous experiences. Identify a passage where a specific observation depends on Perry's preexisting cultural knowledge.

EXPLORING IDEAS

1. With a group of peers, discuss the following: Are fans of a particular high school sports team a culture? If so why, and why is that culture worth observing and writing about? What about fans of a college or professional team? Are they a unique culture? Why might they be worth observing?

2. Perry says the pregame verbal practices of the Red Raiders fans were interesting "it turns out, because [he] was observing them." With a group of peers, make sense of Perry's statement. Discuss it and try to discover examples in which group members found a familiar topic more interesting because they were more deliberately observing it.

IDEAS FOR WRITING

1. What non-sporting group of spectators constitutes a culture worth observing?

2. In addition to fans or spectators, what are some groups that constitute a culture?

If responding to one of these ideas, go to the Analysis section of this chapter to begin developing ideas for your essay.

INVENTION

Observation requires a good deal of analysis and planning. It goes far beyond choosing a subject and writing down details. Writers usually go through a cyclical invention process, in which they return repeatedly to their original notes to find patterns and significant points. The following sections are designed to help you through this process: discover a topic (in Point of Contact), develop particular points about the topic (in Analysis), make it relevant to a community of readers (in Public Resonance), focus your ideas (in Thesis), and develop them into an essay (in Rhetorical Tools). The Invention Questions in each section are not meant to be answered directly in your final written assignment. They are designed to help guide you through an intellectual process and generate ideas.

Point of Contact

The goal here is to see something in a new way, beyond the casual glance. You may visit places and do things you have never done before, or you may visit the usual places but with more focused attention. Use the following questions as starting points for your observation.

Observing People

Supervisor, manager, line worker, server, religious leader, teacher or professor, principal, athlete, bingo player, student. Use notes, audio and video recorders, and/or photographs to gather details about the person. You might also interview the subject. (See the section on interviews in Chapter 14.)

> In what hidden ways is the subject working with or against the surroundings?

> Does the subject reinforce or work against rules?

> How do others treat the subject (with respect, disdain, indifference, or something else)?

> If the subject is a group, how do the individuals maintain harmony or unity? How do they conflict?

> What explicit or hidden rules do they follow?

Observing a Place

Job site, family restaurant, factory, office, break room, playground, park, movie theater, shopping mall, video arcade, college hall, college club, campground, woods. Gather details about the place. In addition to obvious details, consider the less obvious:

> What subtle behavior patterns do you detect?

> Is there a hidden competition or collaboration going on?

Keith Gentry/Shutterstock.com

> What mood might the creatures (people, animals, plants) share? How do they unknowingly maintain that mood?

> Are people free to do as they please, or does something restrain them? (Do they know that something is restraining them?)

> What is the unstated, normal mode of behavior?

> Does anyone or anything break out of the norm? What are the hidden consequences?

> What is missing?

Observing an Animal

Family pet, friend's or neighborhood pet, stray cat or dog, birds, animals at a park or zoo, wild animals, farm animals. Gather basic information about the animal's behavior, but also look beyond the simple glance:

> What does it know?

> What secrets does it have?

> How does it signal its mood?

> Does it have dramatic mood changes?

> How does it get along with humans? With the world around it?

> What habits does it have?

> Is it a public or private creature?

> Does it compromise or alter its behavior to accommodate others?

Observing a Person or Event Involved in Your Major

Use the questions in this section to help gather information about a subject related to your major, but also develop more questions. By observing a particular person or event, what can you discover about the nature of your major?

ACTIVITY

Choose a category (a place, person, animal) and develop ten more questions that will help reveal something interesting about a subject.

OBSERVING A CULTURE: WRITING AN ETHNOGRAPHY ESSAY

One type of observing essay is an *ethnography* essay. *Ethnography,* from *ethno* (nation, culture, people) and *graphos* (something written down), observes the characteristics of a group of people. Although some ethnographies involve months or years of living within and observing a particular culture, we can also write an ethnography essay—a sort of mini-ethnography—based on a few weeks or days of careful observation. Because an ethnography is a type of observing essay, the Invention sections in this chapter (Analysis, Public Resonance, Thesis, and so on) will help you first invent ideas and then convey them as an essay. One essay in this chapter, "Red Raiders Fans," is an example of an ethnography essay.

Point of Contact: After reading "Red Raiders Fans," make a list of cultures you can observe—groups of people who meet at a place and time where you can observe them at least three times for more than an hour each time. It's important to be sure the group of people share an identity, instead of just happening to show up at the same place at the same time. A shared identity is based on common characteristics such as language, food, religion, fashion, dress, habits, values, beliefs, music, and so on. The purpose of your observation is to observe the practices of a culture (what members routinely say and do) and discover how the particular culture *does,* or practices, their culture. For example, "Red Raiders Fans" explains how Red Raiders fans *do* the practice of Red Raiders fans. An ethnography essay on cowboys in Wyoming would explain how cowboys in Wyoming *do* the practice of cowboys in Wyoming.

Analysis and Public Resonance: Once you decide on a culture to observe, you can use the Analysis and Public Resonance sections to record your observations and discover insights. Keep in mind that it's difficult to have insights if you allow memories and expectations to get in the way of recording what you are experiencing with your senses. Although you will have preconceived ideas, the key is to acknowledge this and continue to record your observations, letting the practices of the culture you observed influence your thinking. An ethnographer observes and records the following:

- the location, including specific descriptions of the physical environment

- verbal exchanges, including what group members routinely say and more specific exchanges among members

- how the group uses writing, if they do

- routines, including what group members do routinely; what they do every day as part of their normal experience

- rituals, including activities that are viewed as highly important or sacred

- rites of passage, including significant practices that change a member's sense of identity, social role, or status

- values and beliefs

- timelines, including what happens when

Don't let these categories or the questions limit your observations. These are just examples of the kinds of observations you can make. Remember, *recording particulars* is an invention strategy. The particulars will help you think of more ideas. And these particulars are important later because you will select *some* of them to use in your ethnography essay.

Thesis: Because you want your insight to emerge from the observations themselves, not from what you think you might observe or conclude, it's important to wait until *after* you record your observations to make rhetorical decisions about how to convey your ethnography to your readers. The Thesis section will help you focus your essay on a particular insight. Your insight can be what it means to be a member of the group; what makes someone an insider or outsider; what unifying characteristic surprised you about the group; how your preconceived idea(s) about the group changed; and so on.

Delivery: After you record your observations and discover a focused and insightful thesis, turn to the Rhetorical Tools section for help delivering your ethnography to the readers. The following guidelines can help you make effective rhetorical decisions:

- An ethnography presents your observations while focusing on a particular discovery or insight about the culture.

- Your readers will expect you to explain why you chose the subject, what happened during your observations, and what you discovered.

- Your observation should identify the group and important background (orienting) information about your observations, where/when you observed them, and your relationship to the group; then your specific observations; and your conclusions.

- While you try to be an objective observer, you can acknowledge your role as an observer and the influence of your own biases on your observations. Your ethnography essay is about the culture you observed but need not ignore your role as observer.

- Document design features such as headings, font styles, and spacing can help readers understand and accept your thesis.

- Photos or video clips can help convey your main idea.

Other parts of *The Composition of Everyday Life* will help you with your essay:

- Use the Revision questions later in the chapter to rethink a draft of your essay and make changes.

- Use Part II for help finding, analyzing, synthesizing, evaluating, integrating, and documenting information from sources.

- Use Part III for help organizing and delivering your idea.

Analysis

Details do not have their own meaning. It is up to people to *make* meaning from details. As we analyze, we move from observation notes to focused ideas, from a collection of potentially unrelated details to a set of particular points. Analysis prompts us to see patterns, connections, and paths within the particulars. The following questions can help you to make meaning out of your observation notes and look at the subject as something more than its physical characteristics.

> What is unique about the subject?

> What is ordinary about this subject? (How are its qualities common to other places, people, or animals?) What does that quality show?

> Is this subject symbolic of something? (Does it stand for some idea or ideal?)

> Does the subject seem different after the observation (more complicated, less intimidating, more human, less human, more predictable, and so on)?

> What does the subject "say" about life (about human interaction, social behavior, institutions, nature, and so on) in this place and time?

Although focusing on and gathering details may be a challenging aspect of observation, analyzing those details poses a difficulty of its own. Because a list of details offers so many options and no obvious path for making meaning, the process can be uncertain and confusing. However, it can be an intensive and valuable process. Imagine a student, Linda, who observed people at her place of work, a small factory. Her observation notes include long lists of details about the environment, the lighting, the physical actions of the workers, and their interaction with the machines and with each other. But as she begins to analyze, using one of the Invention Questions, she finds connections in those details. Notice how she goes beyond her first simplistic answer to a more complex idea:

What does the subject "say" about life (about human interaction, social behavior, institutions, nature, and so on) in this place and time?

At first, I thought that my coworkers were just miserable people at a job. They work at their individual stations, occasionally interact to communicate something about a machine part or materials, and then go to breaks—or home. But outside of that, I couldn't see anything important. But the more I looked over my notes, I realized something was going on in those small and infrequent interactions between people. While they might seem miserable and disconnected at times (maybe even most of the time), they all offer some support to one another: a small glance, a shared roll of the eyes when the supervisor inspects one person's work, the way Rob, the oldest in the shop, actually runs over to someone who needs help with something, the extra cup of coffee Bob got Maria because she didn't have time during break. All these things mean something—the underground, almost secretive, strategies to keep each other afloat in their shared situation. After I realized this, I went back over all my notes and remembered things I had not written down. The days are actually filled with these little gestures; they happen at all times: at breaks, on the way into the shop in the morning, while the machines are operating.

Linda could then develop this point in her writing. The idea may even develop into a thesis statement. This would mean that many other details (about physical structure, about the machines themselves) might be abandoned unless they have some significance for worker interaction. In this way, Linda's observation goes from a list of seemingly unrelated details to a focused idea.

ACTIVITY

Observe the activities in your classroom. As a class or in a group, discuss the possible meaning or significance of particular events, behaviors, or interactions.

Chester McCovey's invention notes explore the meaning of the garage—not simply what it does for people (store their cars) but how it works in their lives and says something about the way people live.

Is this subject symbolic of something? (Does it stand for some idea or ideal?)

It is, perhaps. These big garages are obviously a necessity for today's homeowner. I mean, most of these homes are not within walking distance of where the owner works. Many, I suspect, can only be afforded if both husband and wife work—two cars! Now, fill the garage up with all the other machinery you need to maintain the yard. The garage quite simply says "go," "drive," "automobile," "transportation." I am at home, but not for long. No doubt the cars have air conditioning, as does the house. One need never be hot (or cold). The garage has replaced the porch. You pull into the garage and go inside and stay inside the house. Then get in the air-conditioned space bubble car when you want to leave. Of course there is recreation, but recreation is getting away from life and not a part of it. Let's take a break in our day and burn some calories, not let's burn some calories in the natural course of our day. The garage symbolizes driving, moving, loss of neighborhood, community, wealth, poverty . . .

Thinking Further

In the previous paragraph, McCovey seeks out the significance of today's big garage. His exploration leads him to write, "The garage symbolizes driving, moving, loss of neighborhood, community, wealth, poverty. . . ." Now McCovey, alone or with others, could explore this idea further, digging deeper and uncovering new details and complexity. (Or he might choose a different idea from his invention writing to explore further.)

ACTIVITY

1. Use the following questions to explore McCovey's invention writing:

■ Using McCovey's paragraph and your own ideas, explain how the big garage might be symbolic of or stand for driving. For moving. For loss of neighborhood. For wealth and poverty. Develop your responses in the spirit of exploration.

■ Of the six ideas McCovey mentions, which one is the least obvious and why? Which one is the most important and why? Which one is the most interesting and why? (Consider focusing on the least obvious, most important, or most interesting.)

Remember, your purpose in this writing is not just to say what you think or know. Your purpose is to explore and figure out what *might* be thought about the topic.

2. Consider your own invention writing, as you just considered McCovey's. For help, explore ideas further through discussion.

■ What new way of thinking (what insight, what revelation) did you discover?

■ How might you explore the complexities of that idea further? For example:

—How might that thinking be wrong?

—How can you probe more deeply by asking why, how, or so what?

—What contradictions or inconsistencies must be explained?

Public Resonance

Writers do more than focus on a subject, such as a weasel or a porch. They make the subject resonate with the lives of others. The following Invention Questions will help broaden your subject's perspective and make it resonate with others.

❯ Why is this subject important to people? (Why is its uniqueness important?)

❯ Why should your peers know about this subject?

❯ What do people normally experience, understand, or assume about the subject?

❯ Does the presence or action of this subject teach people something—about themselves, about life, about work, about happiness, about materialism, about sincerity, about identity, about relationships, about the past, about the future, about death?

Notice below how McCovey explores the breadth of his subject, using the Invention Question to help him to discover the broad implications of porches and garages:

> **Does the presence or action of this subject teach people something—about themselves, about life, about work, about happiness, about materialism, about sincerity, about identity, about relationships, about the past, about the future, about death?**
> What we see is a loss of community. The big garage shows us we're leaving our own neighborhood a lot. The fact that the garage is connected to the living space shows us that we go from our living area directly, by pushing a button that opens the door, into the street and to another community far enough away that we drive to it. We don't interact with our neighbors (we might not even know their names). We drive past them with our windows rolled up. We maybe don't even smell or feel our neighborhood (I guess that's an exaggeration, but there's something there). Remember, we're not talking about all houses. We're talking about the ones built today. Is loss of neighborhood a loss to the people who live in those neighborhoods? Does big garage/no front porch mean loss of neighborliness? Yes, these relationships—or ones like them—can exist outside one's own neighborhood. But what is the effect of this? What is a neighbor anymore?

Here McCovey explores connections to broader cultural trends. While some subjects have more automatic public resonance, others need to be *made* relevant to the audience, and it is up to a writer to make the connection.

Invention Workshop

An essay does not just relay information; it invites readers to see something new in a familiar world. If you think a topic is boring, you have an opportunity to unpack the boredom, finding something new and worth sharing with others. Instead of allowing a dull topic to stop one's thinking, a good observer uses analysis to make the topic interesting.

1. Share your observation with others and discuss what the subject shows about the way people see the world around them, and how they live. The goal is to develop new insights for your project.

2. After exploring the public resonance of your topic with others and writing down any new insights, return to the Invention Questions on page 112. Respond in writing to these questions again, now that you have focused on the public resonance of the subject. See what else you can find. As you write, think about how to re-approach the questions from a new, more informed perspective. For example, how might you see something else unique about the subject now? Does the subject now seem unique in some less obvious way?

   • What new insights emerged from your second round with the Invention Questions?

   • What new questions emerged?

Thesis

The thesis, whether stated directly or implied, reveals a specific insight on a subject. The more narrow the insight, the more focused and intensive the writing will be. Although it is easy to offer a first-glance statement, try to narrow in on a particular quality. Notice how the following bulleted statements offer broad and predictable ideas. But the maroon statements reveal something unique and specific:

- The people at the local tavern keep to themselves.

  In the dark, smoky quiet of Timothy's Pub, the regulars face straight ahead but share intimate crises in their quick coded exchanges.

- The neighborhood is a quiet place.

  The disappearing porches in the neighborhood signal a shift to a more disconnected, isolating, but technologically advanced time.

- The Fun Factory has a spirit of competition.

  Once the games begin at The Fun Factory, the players shift radically: from unfocused adolescent "dorks" to focused competitive intellectuals.

The more specific theses focus on more particular subjects: people vs. regulars; neighborhood vs. disappearing porches; Fun Factory vs. players. These specific sentences bring the reader up close. (We can even imagine a television camera zooming in to the more particular subjects.) Also, the maroon sentences have stronger verbs: *keep* vs. *face/share; is* vs. *signal; has* vs. *shift.* The stronger verbs do more than create action; they enrich the content, making the nouns work harder. As a result, the sentences push readers through the sentence with more energy.

REVISING YOUR THESIS

Before drafting your essay, develop a thesis to guide you. Then, in groups, discuss your working thesis statements, suggesting more specific nouns and stronger verbs.

Evolution of a Thesis

Imagine a writer is observing students at a community college. She notices many things about the students: their clothes, their ages, and so on. But she decides to focus on a particular point: *The students at Beach Community College spend their time coming and going primarily alone.* Such a statement offers a particular idea about the college students. The essay then would focus on the solitary nature of the students. The point might grow and develop layers throughout the invention process:

Point of Contact:

- The majority of the students coming in and out of the buildings are alone; they do not talk together or in groups. If people are talking, they are talking on cell phones.

Analysis:

- Although I have always associated college with social life, the students at Beach Community College show that college is often a solitary experience.

Public Resonance:

- When most people talk about college, they inevitably bring up campus life: the parties, the Greek system, the study groups, and so on. They think of all the movies and stories about those crazy college years, but the reality may be fundamentally different for many students.

Working Thesis:

- Despite the popular notions of social life on college campuses, the students at Beach Community College show that higher education can be a solitary experience.

Rhetorical Tools

An observing essay shares an insight about a particular subject. While writers discover and develop this insight through careful observation, they communicate it to the readers through a variety of rhetorical tools.

Using Details

The details of the essay should lead the reader to the same conclusion that the writer makes. Refer to your notes from the Point of Contact section and find all the specific details to support your main point. Your essay should be generated only from details that help show that point. For example, because Annie Dillard's observation focuses on the weasel's "purity of living," she provides details that convey that idea. You can imagine many other details (such as where the weasel went after the encounter or general information about weasel life), but this information wouldn't support the main idea. The essay includes details that show the contrast between Dillard's life of motive and the weasel's life of purity.

Using Narrative

Many writers choose to narrate the events of an observation, explaining the events leading up to a particular moment of discovery. Narration can help place the observation in time and help situate the reader. Dillard uses narration at the beginning of her essay, taking the reader through several paragraphs that lead up to her encounter with the weasel. Here, Dillard uses narration to narrow her focus from a broader view of the natural surroundings to a particular animal:

> The sun had just set. I was relaxed on the tree trunk, ensconced in the lap of lichen, watching the lily pads at my feet tremble and part dreamily over the thrusting path of a carp. A yellow bird appeared to my right and flew behind me. It caught my eye; I swiveled around—and the next instant, inexplicably, I was looking down at a weasel, who was looking up at me.

The narration creates a powerful contract between the nonchalant, relaxed feeling of the surroundings and the weasel's intense stare.

Using Allusions

Allusions are references to bits of public knowledge—things, events, or people outside of the main subject being observed. Writers use allusions to help illustrate a point or create a feeling. For instance, McCovey alludes to baseball when discussing the front porch:

> One can see, then, how the exchange occurred. Like an old-fashioned trade in baseball, gone is the home team's beloved front porch, replaced by a big, new garage.

McCovey's allusion calls readers back to an earlier time when people sat outside on front porches and talked to neighbors passing by. The allusion to baseball helps to create the feeling of which McCovey speaks in his conclusion: "I am not prepared here to argue that we are a civilization in deep trouble because of this, though it does seem to me appropriate that we should lament, at least a little, the loss of the front porch." Some (not all) readers will immediately identify with the feeling the allusion conjures, of a time in baseball before free agency when many players began and ended their careers with the same team, when fans became more attached to their hometown players and were more likely to lament their departure, when life was simpler, the pace was slower, and baseball was the national pastime.

McCovey's allusion to the old-fashioned trade in baseball illustrates both the value of and the concern with using allusions. Some readers won't pick up on the baseball allusion. McCovey decides to use it anyway, understanding this. The allusion adds texture and depth of meaning for some readers, but McCovey does not allow the overall meaning of his essay to be lost on a reader who doesn't understand the allusion. (A reader would not say, "I didn't understand his main idea because I don't know what an old-fashioned trade in baseball is.") The following questions will help you develop allusions for your own writing:

> Does my subject relate to any political event or situation?

> Does my subject relate to any social or cultural event or situation?

> Does my subject relate to any person or event in history? In literature? In popular culture (movies, television, music)?

Using Simile and Metaphor

Similes and metaphors are comparisons that point out or create similarities between two or more seemingly different things. (A simile uses "like" or "as.") Writers use them to help create pictures for readers, to make points more engaging and intense. Notice how Dillard compares meeting a weasel to meeting a lover or deadly enemy:

> Our look was as if two lovers, or deadly enemies met unexpectedly on an overgrown path when each had been thinking of something else: a clearing blow to the gut. It was also a bright blow to the brain, or a sudden beating of brains, with all the charge and intimate gate of rubbed balloons. It emptied our lungs. It felled the forest, moved the fields, and drained the pond; the world dismantled and tumbled into that black hole of eyes. If you and I looked at each other that way, our skulls would split and drop to our shoulders. But we don't. We keep our skulls. So.

Figurative language such as similes and metaphors should be used selectively—and sparingly—to direct the reader's perceptions toward main ideas.

ACTIVITY

As writers develop, they learn to insert intellectual space between the writing instructions and their essay. Where the inexperienced writer might read the instructions and then write an essay, the more experienced writer inserts space by first using writing to plan, to ask questions, to invent, and to reflect. Before you draft your essay for this chapter, write down a working thesis and several supporting ideas. For example, how might you use narration, allusions, dialogue, or some other strategy to help readers understand and accept your thesis? Then share your sketch with others to get feedback before you draft an entire essay.

Revision

Writers create essays through invention, drafting, and revision. A draft is a work in progress and must be viewed that way. Writers don't just buff a draft—correcting spelling, punctuation, grammar. Instead, they ask hard questions about their basic approach: Does my thesis and essay *really* express a focused insight about the subject? Drafts often express a variety of general ideas, so revision can involve making painful cuts to focus entirely on the single most valuable insight. Another tough question is whether the thesis and essay are *really* revelatory. Many drafts have not yet revealed something unique and particular enough to make the essay stand out, so revision involves examining the supporting points, returning to the Invention Questions, and exploring *a* less obvious, potentially more interesting point more deeply. Before exchanging drafts with a peer, ask yourself hard questions about your essay's focus and insight.

Peer Review

Exchange drafts with at least one other writer. Before passing your draft to others, underline the thesis, or write it above your essay. This way, reviewers will get traction as they read. As a reviewer, use the following questions to guide your response:

1. Point out any words or phrases in the thesis that could be more specific. (See the Thesis section, page 116, for more guidance.)

2. Where can the writer do more analysis and reveal more about the subject in the observation? (Point to passages that seem most obvious to you. As you read, look for claims that anyone could immediately offer without intensive analysis. Beside these passages, write "more analysis?" If you can suggest an interesting idea, explain it on the back of the writer's draft.)

3. Help the writer illustrate his or her claims with details. As you read, look for broad characterizations—those that anyone could imagine without a close observation. Ask yourself: Could this be more specific? Can we *really* see the particular nuances of the subject? In the margin, write "more details" where the writer could more intensely show the points.

4. Offer some figurative language to help characterize the subject. After you have read the entire draft, offer your own metaphor or simile about the subject. Give your suggestion on the back of the draft. Make sure it is something that fits the writer's voice.

5. If the writer uses narrative, does it help support the main idea of the observation? How? (If you have difficulty explaining how it supports the main point, perhaps the writer should rethink its use in the essay!)

6. Are the paragraphs coherent? Do you ever get the sense that a paragraph is giving details that seem unrelated to one another or unrelated to the point of the essay? If so, write in the margin "check paragraph coherence."

7. The most focused statement possible often makes for a better introduction. Suggest a surprisingly focused opening statement.

8. Consider the writer's voice.
   - If the writer is present (using "I"), is this necessary? Explain how the presence of the writer helps make the point of the observation.
   - If the writer is invisible (no "I"), how is that beneficial?
   - Where could the writer be more informal (breaking some conventions) or more formal?

9. Help the writer avoid common grammatical errors: comma splices, sentence fragments, or pronoun/antecedent agreement.

10. Write down the specific subject of the observation. Then complete the following statement: Ultimately, this essay is not about [the specific subject: a weasel, for example]. It is about _____.

Reflection

As a developing writer and thinker, you should be able to not just write an essay but also articulate ideas about the way it communicates an idea and persuade others to think differently. Now that you have written an observing essay, respond to the following:

1. What does your observation say about life in this place and time?

2. What do people normally experience, understand, or assume about the subject, and how does your essay present a new way of thinking about it?

3. List three rhetorical tools you used in the essay, and explain how each one helps readers understand and accept the thesis.

4. Identify several sentences that are especially lively and well written. What is it about the nouns, verbs, and other sentence parts that make the sentences lively and well written?

Beyond the Essay: Cover Image

Images are often used to represent a movie, novel, album/CD, video game, and so on. How might you use an image to express the main idea of your essay?

1. Create a *collage* as a cover or title image for your observing essay. A collage is a single image made up of various images. For example, a collage expressing the main idea of an observing essay could include photos, newspaper headlines, objects from nature (a leaf, a seed), trash (a candy wrapper or other packaging), and so on. It could be entirely electronic—an *e-collage*. As with an essay, creating a collage involves selecting and combining smaller parts (or ideas) to create a larger, overall message (or idea). The particular pieces to include in the collage will be an early decision, and then you will decide how to arrange the parts into the larger image.

2. Once you have created a collage expressing the main idea of your observing essay, explain the visual rhetoric of your collage. How do the particular visual elements work together to convey one main idea? What is the relationship among the elements, physically (on the page or screen) and conceptually (in the reader's mind)? How do colors, shapes, textures, and the juxtaposition of images work together to create the overall message?

5 Analyzing Concepts

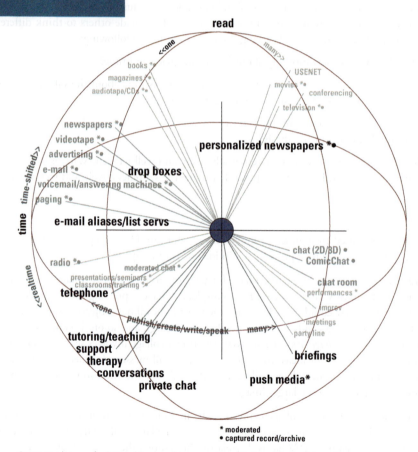

read

<one

many>>

books *•
magazines *•
audiotape/CD *•

USENET
movies *•
conferencing
television *•

newspapers *•
videotape *•
advertising *•
e-mail *•
voicemail/answering machines *•
paging *•

personalized newspapers *•

drop boxes

time-shifted>>

e-mail aliases/list servs

time

radio *•

chat (2D/3D) •
ComicChat •

moderated chat *
presentations/seminars *
classrooms/training *•

chat room
performances *

<<realtime

telephone

<one

improv
meetings
party line

publish/create/write/speak

many>>

tutoring/teaching
support
therapy
conversations
private chat

briefings

push media*

* moderated
• captured record/archive

Conceptual map of relationships in cyberspace. From Nathan Shedroff, http://www
.cybergeography.org/altas/conceptual.html

Chapter Objectives
This chapter will help you to:

- Break down the constituent parts of a concept.
- Use invention questions to explore the tension within and boundaries of a concept.
- Develop a focused and revelatory essay supported with examples, contrary examples, definitions, and outside sources.
- Transpose your thinking into a graphic expression.

"Concepts have no 'real' definitions; instead, they have uses. They are our ways of coming to understand the world and deciding how to behave within it."

—**Susan R. Horton**

INTRODUCTION

Concepts are ideas or abstract formulations. They are generalized notions beyond specifics. For example, we have concepts of *college, marriage, friendship,* or *technology* that go beyond any particular college, spouse, friend, or piece of equipment. And when our colleges, spouses, friends, and machines do not measure up to our concepts, we get frustrated, and we may even alter our concepts.

Within a particular culture, concepts change, sometimes drastically, and people do not always agree on what concepts mean. A dispute over a concept is often the catalyst for major conflict between people, cultures, and countries. For example, think about the intense and extended battles brought on by differing notions of *God* or the political struggles brought on by differing concepts of *woman, man, family, marriage, life, college, torture,* or *freedom.* Analyzing concepts turns out to be important and sticky business.

In academia, students and professors are mired in the process of analyzing, discussing, and arguing about concepts. Consider *sex.* In a biology course, students discuss sex as reproduction. The concept in biology involves the study of hormones and reproductive systems (egg, sperm, gestation periods, embryo, and so on). In psychology, sex might be understood as a complex of drives. Students explore it using Freud's under-standing of sexual development, repression, and parental affiliation. And in sociology, students might approach sex as socially patterned behavior. A sociological understanding of sex may involve the study of social customs (such as dancing, choosing clothing, dat-ing, and marriage). These concepts are obviously different; in fact, many people claim that a discipline's take on a concept partly defines that discipline. For example, part of what defines a sociologist is how he or she understands *sex* or *community* or *family*. Disciplines also focus on and develop their own concepts. *Ego,* for instance, is a concept developed by psychology. And much of your college career will involve exploring and analyzing the main concepts of different disciplines and your chosen field.

The chapter readings will provide insight into various analytical strategies. For example, each essay looks closely at the parts or elements of a concept. This close examination leads to a focused and insightful point about the concept. As you read, try to identify the parts or elements being broken down, and trace what the examination of them reveals. After reading the essays, you can find a concept in one of two ways—go to the Point of Contact section to find a topic from everyday life, or choose one of the Ideas for Writing that follow the essays. After finding a subject, go to the Analysis section to begin developing the analysis.

READINGS

Why "Natural" Doesn't Mean Anything Anymore
Michael Pollan

At first thought, we probably imagine we know what "natural" means. In the following essay, author and activist Michael Pollan acknowledges that on one level, common sense should determine this meaning. But on another level—for example questioning whether certain products should be labeled "natural"—the concept is complicated and difficult to define. Pollan, a professor of journalism at the University of California, Berkeley, has written five New York Times Best Sellers and numerous essays. This essay, published April 28, 2015 in *The New York Times Magazine,* explores the complexity of the word "natural."

It isn't every day that the definition of a common English word that is ubiquitous in common parlance is challenged in federal court, but that is precisely what has happened with the word "natural." During the past few years, some 200 class-action suits have been filed against food manufacturers, charging them with misuse of the adjective in marketing such edible oxymorons as "natural" Cheetos Puffs, "all-natural" Sun Chips, "all-natural" Naked Juice, "100 percent all-natural" Tyson chicken nuggets and so forth. The plaintiffs argue that many of these products contain ingredients—high-fructose corn syrup, artificial flavors and colorings, chemical preservatives and genetically modified organisms—that the typical consumer wouldn't think of as "natural."

Judges hearing these cases—many of them in the Northern District of California—have sought a standard definition of the adjective that they could cite to adjudicate these claims, only to discover that no such thing exists.

Something in the human mind, or heart, seems to need a word of praise for all that humanity hasn't contaminated, and for us that word now is "natural." Such an ideal can be put to all sorts of rhetorical uses. Among the antivaccination crowd, for example, it's not uncommon to read about the superiority of something called "natural immunity," brought about by exposure to the pathogen in question rather than to the deactivated (and therefore harmless) version of it made by humans in laboratories. "When you inject a vaccine into the body," reads a post on an antivaxxer website, Campaign for Truth in Medicine, "you're actually performing an unnatural act." This, of course, is the very same term once used to decry homosexuality and, more recently, same-sex marriage, which the Family Research Council has taken to comparing unfavorably to what it calls "natural marriage."

If nature offers a moral standard by which we measure ourselves, and a set of values to which we should aspire, exactly what sort of values are they?

Michael Pollan, "Why 'Natural' Doesn't Mean Anything Anymore," from *New York Times Magazine,* April 28, 2015.

So what are we really talking about when we talk about natural? It depends; the adjective is impressively slippery, its use steeped in dubious assumptions that are easy to overlook. Perhaps the most incoherent of these is the notion that nature consists of everything in the world except us and all that we have done or made. In our heart of hearts, it seems, we are all creationists.

In the case of "natural immunity," the modifier implies the absence of human intervention, allowing for a process to unfold as it would if we did nothing, as in "letting nature take its course." In fact, most of medicine sets itself *against* nature's course, which is precisely what we like about it—at least when it's saving us from dying, an eventuality that is perhaps more natural than it is desirable.

Yet sometimes medicine's interventions are unwelcome or go overboard, and nature's way of doing things can serve as a useful corrective. This seems to be especially true at the beginning and end of life, where we've seen a backlash against humanity's technological ingenuity that has given us both "natural childbirth" and, more recently, "natural death."

This last phrase, which I expect will soon be on many doctors' lips, indicates the enduring power of the adjective to improve just about anything you attach it to, from cereal bars all the way on up to dying. It seems that getting end-of-life patients and their families to endorse "do not resuscitate" orders has been challenging. To many ears, "D.N.R." sounds a little too much like throwing Grandpa under the bus. But according to a paper in The Journal of Medical Ethics, when the orders are reworded to say "allow natural death," patients and family members and even medical professionals are much more likely to give their consent to what amounts to exactly the same protocols.

The word means something a little different when applied to human behavior rather than biology (let alone snack foods). When marriage or certain sexual practices are described as "natural," the word is being strategically deployed as a synonym for "normal" or "traditional," neither of which carries nearly as much rhetorical weight. "Normal" is by now too obviously soaked in moral bigotry; by comparison, "natural" seems to float high above human squabbling, offering a kind of secular version of what used to be called divine law. Of course, that's exactly the role that "natural law" played for America's founding fathers, who invoked nature rather than God as the granter of rights and the arbiter of right and wrong.

"Traditional" marriage might be a more defensible term, but traditional is a much weaker modifier than natural. Tradition changes over time and from culture to culture, and so commands a fraction of the authority of nature, which we think of as timeless and universal, beyond the reach of messy, contested history.

Implicit here is the idea that nature is a repository of abiding moral and ethical values—and that we can say with confidence exactly what those values are. Philosophers often call this the "naturalistic fallacy": the idea that whatever *is* (in nature) is what *ought to be* (in human behavior). But if nature offers a moral standard by which we can measure ourselves, and a set of values to which we should aspire, exactly what sort of values are they? Are they the brutally competitive values of "nature, red in tooth and claw," in which every individual is out for him- or herself? Or are they the values of cooperation on display in a beehive or ant colony, where the interests of the community trump those of the individual? Opponents of same-sex marriage can find examples of monogamy in the animal kingdom, and yet to do so they need to look past equally compelling examples of animal polygamy as well as increasing evidence of apparent animal homosexuality. And let's not overlook the dismaying rates of what looks very much like rape in the animal kingdom, or infanticide, or the apparent sadism of your average house cat.

The American Puritans called nature "God's Second Book," and they read it for moral guidance, just as we do today. Yet in the same way we can rummage around in the Bible and find textual support for pretty much whatever we want to do or argue, we can ransack nature to justify just about anything. Like the maddening whiteness of Ahab's whale, nature is an obligingly blank screen on which we can project what we want to see.

Any food product that feels compelled to tell you it's natural in all likelihood is not.

So does this mean that, when it comes to saying what's natural, anything goes? I don't think so. In fact, I think there's some philosophical wisdom we can harvest from, of all places, the Food and Drug Administration. When the federal judges couldn't find a definition of "natural" to apply to the class-action suits before them, three of them wrote to the F.D.A., ordering the agency to define the word. But the F.D.A. had considered the question several times before, and refused to attempt a definition. The only advice the F.D.A. was willing to offer the jurists is that a food labeled "natural" should have "nothing artificial or synthetic" in it "that would not normally be expected in the food." The F.D.A. states on its website that "it is difficult to define a food product as 'natural' because the food has probably been processed and is no longer the product of the earth," suggesting that the industry might not want to press the point too hard, lest it discover that *nothing* it sells is natural.

The F.D.A.'s philosopher-bureaucrats are probably right: At least at the margins, it's impossible to fix a definition of "natural." Yet somewhere between those margins there lies a broad expanse of common sense. "Natural" has a fairly sturdy antonym—artificial, or synthetic—and, at least on a scale of relative values, it's not hard to say which of two things is "more natural" than the other: cane sugar or high-fructose corn syrup? Chicken or chicken nuggets? G.M.O.s or heirloom seeds? The most natural foods in the supermarket seldom bother with the word; any food product that feels compelled to tell you it's natural in all likelihood is not.

But it is probably unwise to venture beyond the shores of common sense, for it isn't long before you encounter either Scylla or Charybdis. At one extreme end of the spectrum of possible meanings, there's nothing *but* nature. Our species is a result of the same process—natural selection—that created every other species, meaning that we and whatever we do are natural, too. So go ahead and call your nuggets natural: It's like saying they're made with matter, or molecules, which is to say, it's like saying nothing at all.

And yet at the opposite end of the spectrum of meaning, where humanity in some sense stands outside nature—as most of us still unthinkingly believe—what is left of the natural that we haven't altered in some way? We're mixed up with all of it now, from the chemical composition of the atmosphere to the genome of every plant or animal in the supermarket to the human body itself, which has long since evolved in response to cultural practices we invented, like agriculture and cooking. Nature, if you believe in human exceptionalism, is over. We probably ought to search elsewhere for our values.

WRITING STRATEGIES

1. What is Pollan's main idea about the word "natural"?

2. The essay uses examples to help discuss the meaning of "natural." Choose one example and explain how it helps develop the main idea.

3. How does Pollan explain his claim that "any food product that feels compelled to tell you it's natural in all likelihood is not"?

4. What does Pollan mean when he alludes to Scylla and Charybdis?

5. How do values fit into Pollan's discussion of "natural"?

EXPLORING IDEAS

1. The language used to express an idea, such as "do not resuscitate" versus "allow natural death," can affect people's decisions. Do an Internet search to discover another example of an idea expressed in different language to influence people's decisions.

2. What does Pollan mean by "nature is an obligingly blank screen on which we can project what we want to see"?

3. Explain the FDA's difficulty defining "natural."

4. Explain what Pollan means by "nature is over."

IDEAS FOR WRITING

1. Find a common word and explore its meaning. For example, fill in the blank: So what are we really talking about when we talk about _____?

2. What word, or concept, that applies to food can be explored in an essay? (You might also consider words/concepts that apply to education, family, or work.)

If responding to one of these ideas, go to the Analysis section of this chapter to begin developing ideas for your essay.

Black Like I Thought I Was
Erin Aubry Kaplan

Over the centuries, Americans have struggled with race and ethnicity. We have built laws, institutions, and schools of thought around widely held categories. But collectively, we have not made up our minds about difference, diversity, or sameness. As with many concepts, the more we explore, the more we rediscover our own misconceptions. In short, it seems that the concept of race keeps escaping us. In this essay, originally printed in the *LA Weekly,* Erin Aubry Kaplan shows how some deeply grounded assumptions about race may be shattering.

Wayne Joseph is a 51-year-old high school principal in Chino whose family emigrated from the segregated parishes of Louisiana to central Los Angeles in the 1950s, as did mine. Like me, he is of Creole stock and is therefore on the lighter end of the black color spectrum, a common enough circumstance in the South that predates the multicultural movement by centuries. And like most other black folk, Joseph grew up with an unequivocal sense of his heritage and of himself; he tends toward black advocacy and has published thoughtful opinion pieces on racial issues in magazines like *Newsweek.* When Joseph decided on a whim to take a new ethnic DNA test he saw described on a *60 Minutes* segment last year, it was only to indulge a casual curiosity about the exact percentage of black blood; virtually all black Americans are mixed with something, he knew, but he figured it would be interesting to make himself a guinea pig for this new testing process, which is offered by a Florida-based company called DNA Print Genomics Inc. The experience would at least be fodder for another essay for *Newsweek.* He got his kit in the mail, swabbed his mouth per the instructions and sent off the DNA samples for analysis.

Now, I have always believed that what is now widely considered one of slavery's worst legacies—the Southern "one-drop" rule that indicted anyone with black blood as a nigger and cleaved American society into black and white with a single stroke—was also slavery's only upside. Of course I deplore the motive behind the law, which was rooted not only in white paranoia about miscegenation, but in a more practical need to maintain social order by keeping privilege and property in the hands of whites. But by forcing blacks of all complexions and blood percentages into the same boat, the law ironically laid a foundation of black unity that remains in place today. It's a foundation that allows us to talk abstractly about a "black community" as concretely as we talk about a black community in Harlem or Chicago or South-Central (a liberty that's often abused or lazily applied in modern discussions of race). And it gives the lightest-skinned among us the assurance of identity that everybody needs in order to feel grounded and psychologically whole—even whites, whose public non-ethnicity is really ethnicity writ so large and influential it needs no name. Being black may still not be the most advantageous thing in the world, but being nothing or being neutral—the rallying cry of modern-day multiculturalists—has never made any emotional or real-world sense. Color marks you, but your membership in black society also gives you an indestructible house to live in and a bed to rest on. I can't imagine growing up any other way.

Wayne Joseph can't, either. But when the results of his DNA test came back, he found himself staggered by the idea that though he still qualified as a person of color, it was not the color he was raised to think he was, one with a distinct culture and definitive place in the American struggle for social equality that he'd taken for granted. Here was the unexpected and rather unwelcome truth: Joseph was 57 percent Indo-European, 39 percent Native American, 4 percent East Asian—and zero percent African. After a lifetime of assuming blackness, he was now being told that he lacked even a single drop of black blood to qualify.

"My son was flabbergasted by the results," says Joseph. "He said, 'Dad, you mean for 50 years you've been passing for black?'" Joseph admits that, strictly speaking, he has. But he's not sure if he can or wants to do anything about that at this point. For all the lingering effects of institutional racism, he's been perfectly content being a black man; it has shaped his worldview and the course of his life in ways that cannot, and probably should not, be altered. Yet Joseph struggles to balance the intellectual dishonesty of saying he's black with the unimpeachable honesty of a lifelong experience of *being* black. "What do I do with this information?" he says, sounding more than a little exasperated. "It was like finding out you're adopted. I don't want to be disingenuous with myself. But I can't conceive of living any other way. It's a question of what's logical and what's visceral."

Race, of course, has always been a far more visceral matter than a logical one. We now know that there is no such thing as race, that humans are biologically one species; we know that an African is likely to have more in common genetically with a European thousands of miles away than with a neighboring African. Yet this knowledge has not deterred the racism many Europeans continue to harbor toward Africans, nor the wariness Africans harbor toward Europeans. Such feelings may never be deterred. And despite all the loud assertions to the contrary, race is still America's bane, and its fascination; Philip Roth's widely acclaimed last novel set in the 1990s, *The Human Stain,* features a Faustian protagonist whose great moral failing is that he's a black man who's been passing most of his life for white (the book has been made into a movie due in theaters next month). [The movie was released in 2003.]

Joseph recognizes this, and while he argues for a more rational and less emotional view of race for the sake of equity, he also recognizes that rationality is not the same thing as fact. As much as he might want to, he can't simply refute his black past and declare himself white or Native American. He can acknowledge the truth but can't quite apply it, which makes it pretty much useless to other, older members of his family. An aunt whom he told about the test results only said that she wasn't surprised. "When I told my mother about the test, she said to me, 'I'm too old and too tired to be anything else,'" recalls Joseph. "It makes no difference to her. It's an easy issue."

After recovering from the initial shock, Joseph began questioning his mother about their lineage. He discovered that, unbeknownst to him, his grandparents had made a conscious decision back in Louisiana to *not* be white, claiming they didn't want to side with a people who were known oppressors. Joseph says there was another, more practical consideration: Some men in the family routinely courted black women, and they didn't want the very public hassle such a pairing entailed in the South, which included everything from dirty looks to the ignominy of a couple having to separate on buses and streetcars and in restaurants per the Jim Crow laws. I know that the laws also pointedly separated mothers from sons, uncles from nephews, simply because one happened to be lighter than the other or have straighter hair. Determinations of race were entirely subjective and imposed from without, and the one-drop rule was enforced to such divisive and schizophrenic effects that Joseph's family—and mine— fled Louisiana for the presumably less boundary-obsessed West. But we didn't flee ourselves, and didn't expect to; we simply set up a new home in Los Angeles. The South was wrong about its policies but it was right about our color. It had to be.

Joseph remains tortured by the possibility that maybe nobody is right. The essay he thought the DNA test experience would prompt became a book that he's already 150 pages into. He doesn't seem to know how it'll end. He's in a kind of limbo that he doesn't want and that I frankly wouldn't wish on anyone; when I wonder aloud about taking the $600 DNA test myself, Joseph flatly advises against it. "You don't want to know," he says. "It's like a genie coming out of a bottle. You can't put it back in." He has more empathy for the colorblind crowd than he had before, but isn't inclined to believe that the Ward Connerlys and other professed racial conservatives of the world have the best interests of colored people at heart. "I see their point, but race *does* matter, especially with things like medical research and other social trends," he says of Connerly's Proposition 54, the much-derided state measure that seeks to outlaw the collection of ethnic data that will be voted on in the recall election next Tuesday. "Problems like that can't just go away." For the moment, Joseph is compelled to try to judge individually what he knows has always been judged broadly, to reconcile two famously opposed viewpoints of race not for the sake of political argument—he has made those—but for his own peace of mind. He's wrestling with a riddle that will likely outlive him, though he doesn't worry that it will be passed on to the next generation—his ex-wife is black, enough to give his children the firm ethnic identity he had and that he embraced for most of his life. "The question ultimately is, are you who you say you are, or are you who you are genetically?" he muses. The logical—and visceral—answer is that it's not black and white.

WRITING STRATEGIES

1. What is Kaplan's main point about the concept of race?

2. This article relies heavily on the story of Wayne Joseph. Explain how his story works—how it helps Kaplan to make a complex point.

3. In ¶5, Kaplan explains that "Joseph struggles to balance the intellectual dishonesty of saying he's black with the unimpeachable honesty of a lifelong experience of *being* black." Why does Kaplan italicize *being*? What distinction is she making?

4. In ¶6, Kaplan says that race "has always been a far more visceral matter than a logical one." How does this statement work in the essay? What kind of distinction does it help readers to make?

5. Kaplan's article makes a classic academic move: it reveals the complexity in something that seems simple. In other words, she *complicates* our understanding of a concept. She shakes up common and comfortable ways of thinking. Find a passage in which you see Kaplan complicating an idea. Describe the comfortable way of thinking and how Kaplan shakes it up.

EXPLORING IDEAS

1. What is the difference among race, ethnicity, nationality, and lineage?

2. White Americans sometimes imagine themselves as nonethnic—as having no ethnicity. Carefully reread ¶4 in Kaplan's article. What is her response to this way of thinking?

3. A close examination of identity requires debunking common sentiments or clichés. Consider, for instance, the notion that people should simply *be themselves*. What does this sentiment assume about ethnicity or identity? What does it ignore?

4. Kaplan reports that "Joseph remains tortured by the possibility that maybe nobody is right." In other words, he fears that there is no clear answer about his racial identity—about racial identity in general. Why is such a possibility so frightening?

IDEAS FOR WRITING

1. In what ethnic category have you always seen yourself? How has that category fused to your everyday life? How has it shaped the way you live?

2. Beyond race and ethnicity, what other category has determined your identity? Closely examine that label. Interrogate the assumptions that keep it in place.

If responding to one of these ideas, go to the Analysis section of this chapter to begin developing ideas for your essay.

STUDENT ESSAY

The Real, the Bad, and the Ugly
Cassie Heidecker

Cassie Heidecker is an art student at Northwestern Michigan College. She developed the following essay about reality television. At first, she struggled not to defend these guilty pleasures but to analyze the concept itself. In this essay, she manages to avoid an explicit argument about the programs, instead revealing how they work on viewers. In her analysis, she discovers key differences among reality, realism, and realistic. And she discovers that reality shows contain a hint of viewers' everyday lives. (Portions of Heidecker's invention work are shown in later sections of this chapter.)

Reality television is a unique form of reality. It's not really real. (Everyone knows that, right?) After all, reality shows have theme music, background sounds, engaging hosts, narrators, sizzling graphics, and makeup artists. The shows are edited so that dialogue is framed and situated for maximum effect. Whatever the contestants say seems snappy, targeted, deliberate, or perfectly stupid. The shows have scenes with pitch-perfect tension, climax, and resolution. But real life has none of these. Real life is mostly boring, uselessly noisy, stagnant, uncertain, ill-defined, repetitive, hopelessly dumb, and sometimes it's quietly and privately beautiful. Such things can't be filmed and put on television for mass viewing. In short, it only takes a moment (or paragraph) to underscore some major differences between reality television and the mundane reality of everyday life.

> Describes the obvious tension or apparent contradiction in the concept.
>
> Shows aren't real like life. Life is contradictory—dumb, boring, beautiful.

But reality TV contains something. It draws millions of people away from the Internet and toward their television screens every night. The attraction might simply amount to what it's not: Shows like *Survivor, the Real World, Big Brother, Hell's Kitchen* are not the traditional television fakery where beautiful and two-dimensional humans live two-dimensional lives. These shows are not the plastic, soulless, and formulaic fiction of most primetime sit-coms and dramas. They are something else.

> Alludes to specific shows.
>
> Hints at the complexity in the concept—at this "something else."

My husband and I watch culinary reality shows like *Hell's Kitchen* and *Top Chef.* We're embarrassed about it. We don't tell our

> Personal testimony—and a detailed confession.

Cassie Heidecker, "The Good, the Bad, the Real." Reprinted with permission of the author.

friends. These shows are trash TV and we don't think of ourselves as trash TV people. But when we watch (when we literally run down from our respective work or domestic duties and avoid the phone for that ridiculous hour), we stay glued to the situation. We laugh in all the places we're supposed to laugh. We holler at all the appropriate moments. We laugh at ourselves laughing. We are the unapologetic groundlings at a Shakespearean drama. We yell at the lecherous old men, the conniving women, the smug adolescents, the deceit, the flawed personalities, the near misses, and the moments of predictable victory. We talk about the obvious low-brow appeals of *Hell's Kitchen* and how the quick-fire editing makes the show totally gripping, hilarious, and winky. We discuss the intricate appeals that *Top Chef* makes on our sympathies and the complex character development that works over an entire season.

And we're not alone. Despite the results of a Pew Research Center poll indicating that 63% of the American public thinks that reality TV shows signal our cultural decline, the ratings continue to climb. In fact, "What viewers say they want and what they really watch are not the same" (Carter). So what's the appeal? My husband and I know the shows aren't real. We know we're not watching realism. But we wouldn't be caught dead watching these shows if they featured actors pretending to hope they're going to win the next prize. (Imagine someone like Jennifer Aniston or Zach Braff playing socially awkward but earnest fry cooks.)

What then is the *reality* of reality TV?

Hoping to nail down *reality*, I made the risky move of consulting our unabridged *Webster's* dictionary. As I expected, the definition of reality is tricky—maddening even. The first definition: "The quality or state of being real." The definitions go on in a similar fashion until definition 2c, which states, "What actually exists: what has objective existence: what is not a mere idea: what is not imaginary, fictitious, or pretend." This definition clinches something important. While conventional television dramas are entirely pretend—mere ideas—the people on reality TV shows are real in the sense that they (probably) haven't spent years training to be on stage or behind a camera. In short, they're not actors in the artistic sense. They haven't studied moods and posture and tonality and craft and the thousands of other things that actors study. Instead, they've (probably) spent most of their lives like the rest of us—working day-to-day in some "objective existence" at some job we'd rather not have. They are folks who

Allusions and explanations show a complexity to the shows.

They understand the rhetoric of the shows.

Outside source gives public resonance to the previous testimony.

Specific allusions intensify the public resonance—and support the point about reality shows' unique quality.

A breakthrough point: The contestants are not practiced at being contestants. They are not imagined people.

Refers to the most complex aspect of the definition and explains how it sheds light on the concept.

(probably) want another life—who are taking a momentary swing at something beyond their everyday lives. At least, that's the implied story of so many reality television shows. The contestants are from the world we occupy. And they'll most likely return to it when the season ends, when the show gets canceled, when they get kicked off, sent home, chopped, voted out, fired, or whatever the case may be.

Despite the ridiculous situations, the dopey and over-complicated rules (that flash by us at the end of the show), reality television has something that viewers automatically sympathize with: the reality behind the characters—not the show itself but the world that the contestants belong to, the world that is unscripted, the world that will surround the contestants again. Maybe the reality part of reality shows is the unfilmed everyday life that bookends the episodes themselves. This reality lingers in the air each week and becomes increasingly palpable, increasingly real, as the season draws to a close.

American Idol is the reigning champion of reality television. Every season, millions of callers dial in to make sure that the winners keep on winning, that losers keep on losing. The sheer number of calls gets at something critical about these shows: they're participatory. The shows are imbued with the life outside of them. Pop culture critic James Poniewozik explains, "Reality is more than a TV genre now. . . . It's everywhere. When Scott Brown won an upset Senate victory in Massachusetts, he was joined onstage by his daughter Ayla, an *American Idol* semifinalist from Season 5." He goes on to trace the trajectory of reality TV from mere entertainment to a kind of reality in itself: "In 1992, reality TV was a novelty. In 2000, it was a fad. In 2010, it's a way of life." In 2014, Charles B. Slocum, assistant executive director of the Writers Guild of America, West, explained that reality TV has spanned the whole continuum of popular entertainment—from innocent observation of family life in *Kids Say the Darndest Things* to sexual allure in *Taxicab Confessions*.

In the world of high art, such as literary fiction, the writer works to create a fictive dream—a coherent and impenetrable fantasy. The hope is that readers enter the dream and forget the real world. When we read a novel, for instance, our hopes become tied to Gatsby, Frodo, Ishmael, Antonia, Anna, and so on. We suspend our disbelief. And in turn, we are suspended in an ornate web of un-reality. But in reality television, part of the experience is the interplay between the fabricated scene (the kooky kitchen challenge limited to rutabagas and pig liver) and the invisible everyday lives of the contestants. We

The heaviest analytical passage—which also contains the thesis of the essay.

So viewers always know, quietly, that real life awaits the contestants.

Alludes to the most popular example to support the point.

Reality TV is part of everyday life. It's as real as this building.

Uses the source to underscore the point made at the start of the passage.

Contrary examples (allusions to novels) show the particular nature of these shows and how they work on viewers (see page 147 for more on "contrary examples").

Reality TV isn't high art, but it's not simply trash either.

know that Angelo, if that is his real name, has a life beyond the one in *Top Chef.* And we know that he's probably, at least a little, like the guy we're watching. We know that the same dude making dim sum will be out on the highways, at the grocery store, at the local coffee shop, at the bar, and late to work right along with us. That's a captivating idea. The real and the fabricated are dancing together in our heads.

A more figurative way of expressing the thesis.

For viewers, this is a powerful aesthetic experience. We know that the contestants are from our world. Most likely, just before shooting the show and being told how to stand, whom to complain about, and what to wear, they were living normal lives. And when the show is over, they'll come back to the non-limelight, to this side of the screen. They'll go back to their own couches and watch their fabricated and edited selves. Maybe this is the appeal. Maybe reality TV attracts so many viewers because of its crafty intermingling of fiction and reality, its tug on the distinctly American belief "that everybody should have a shot. That sometimes being real is better than being polite. That no matter where you started out, you can hit it big, get lucky and reinvent yourself" (Poniewozik), or even that you can temporarily play the game and then go home again.

In fact, it's an aesthetic experience—not just a guilty pleasure.

Yet another figurative way of expressing the complexity of the thesis.

Some people proclaim self-righteously that reality television is a big hoax—that the winners are hand-selected, that the contestants have been carefully chosen to maximize viewing pleasure, and so on. But these spoilers are focused on the obvious. They're saying, "Look! It can't possibly be real!" And they're right—of course! *The Amazing Race, Top Chef, American Idol,* and all their cousins are not real*istic.* They're not real*ism.* They are reality television—a unique and weird phenomenon that is as much about the viewers and our world as anything.

Acknowledges and then counters those who might dismiss the complexity of the concept.

We are the reality of reality TV.

Works Cited

Carter, Bill. "Tired of Reality TV, but Still Tuning In." *The New York Times,* 13 Sept. 2010, nyti.ms/1Ibjnub.

Current Decade Rates as Worst in 50 Years: Internet, Cell Phones Are Changes for the Better. Pew Research Center for the People & the Press, 21 Dec. 2009, www.people-press.org/files/legacy-pdf/573.pdf.

Poniewozik, James. "Reality TV at 10: How It's Changed Television—and Us." *Time,* 22 Feb. 2010, content.time.com/time/magazine/article/0,9171,1963739,00.html.

"Reality." *Webster's Third New International Dictionary, Unabridged,* Merriam-Webster, 1993, p. 2021.

Slocum, Charles B. "The Real History of Reality TV Or, How Allen Funt Won the Cold War." *Writers Guild of America, West,* www .wga.org/organizesub.aspx?id=1099. Accessed 5 Jan. 2014.

WRITING STRATEGIES

1. Explain what Heidecker reveals about reality television. What aspect of these shows does she help us understand?

2. How does Heidecker's personal testimony function in this essay?

3. Consider the paragraph about novels. How does Heidecker's point about literary fiction figure into the broader point about reality television?

4. In ¶10, Heidecker integrates a quotation by Poniewozik. Explain how the quotation helps support Heidecker's point about the "reality" of reality television.

EXPLORING IDEAS

1. Heidecker nudges readers beyond an easy judgment of reality television shows. Instead, she prompts us to consider the nature of their appeal. What else can be said about the nature of the appeal? Why else do you think millions of viewers tune in to reality television?

2. Heidecker explains that in reality television, "the real and the fabricated are dancing together in our heads." In your own words, how does this work? How does reality "dance with" the un-real aspects of the shows?

3. Heidecker explains that she and her husband "discuss the intricate appeals that *Top Chef* makes on our sympathies and the complex character development that works over an entire season." Do you have a program that works in a similar fashion on you? What show appeals to your sympathies? How does it work?

4. Given Heidecker's points, what do you think are the differences between realism, realistic, and reality television?

5. Do you have any guilty pleasures? Why do you feel guilty about them?

IDEAS FOR WRITING

1. What concept is at the root of your favorite television show?

2. What do current reality television programs suggest about the concept *competition?*

If responding to one of these ideas, go to the Analysis section of this chapter to begin developing ideas for your essay.

Outside Reading

Analyzing concepts is common work across academic disciplines. Writers in philosophy, education, psychology, history, sociology, economics, engineering, law, and even practical fields such as nursing explore shared concepts. They break down the layers or dimensions of concepts such as *self, community, learning, anxiety, pathology, currency, trade, balance, fairness, equality, individual right, assistance, power,* and so on. The discoveries writers make about such concepts help to define the purpose of their fields.

Focus on your academic major, or one you are considering, and find a journal or magazine article that analyzes a basic disciplinary concept. To conduct an electronic search of journals and magazines, go to your library's periodical database and perform a keyword search. Experiment by typing in various concepts related to your chosen field. Avoid using phrases or articles such as *a, an, the;* instead, use nouns separated by *and.* The results will yield lists of journal and magazine articles. After you find an article, apply the following questions:

1. What is the thesis, or main insight, of the article? Try to narrow in on the most revealing point the writer offers.

2. Describe how the writer goes beyond the obvious, beyond a cursory understanding of the concept. Point to passages in which the writer tries to reveal some complexity that wouldn't otherwise be seen.

3. Identify the major rhetorical strategies (such as narration, description, or figurative language). In other words, describe how the writer defends or supports the thesis.

4. Identify any passages in which the writer attempts to create public resonance. The writer might, for instance, try to connect the concept to some broader understanding or some broader social issue.

5. Finally, consider the audience. Who reads the particular publication? Why? Does the audience know certain things or care about certain issues? How does the writer tap into or connect with that knowledge or set of concerns?

INVENTION

"What does it mean that success is as dangerous as failure? Whether you go up the ladder or down it, your position is shaky."

—Tao Te Ching

For the writing in this chapter, you must seek out meaning beyond your initial thoughts about a concept. The following sections are designed to help you through this process: to find a particular concept (in Point of Contact), to examine the concept closely (in Analysis), to make it relevant to a community of readers (in Public Resonance), to develop a focused point (in Thesis), and to develop support for that point (in Rhetorical Tools). The Invention Questions in each section are not meant to be answered directly in your final essay. They are meant to prompt inventive thinking and intensive writing.

Point of Contact

We carry concepts around with us and, for the most part, do not question them. But writers are willing to get underneath concepts that would otherwise go unquestioned. As you consider a possible topic, imagine the concepts that go unnoticed in your everyday life. To find a concept, investigate the world around you for a concept that goes unchallenged and uninspected. The following suggestions, questions, and images may prompt a possible topic:

- **Work:** Success, employment, boss, customer, profit, hours, wage, honesty, freedom, career, experience.

- **School:** Education, study, discipline, learning, science, humanities, grade, teacher, student, intelligence.

- **Home:** Parent, mother, father, pet, living room, divorce, values, God, marriage, privacy, faith.

- **Public Life:** Friend, recreation, commitment, travel, woman, man, patriotism, romance, trash, environment.

- **Sports:** Team, entertainment, audience, fan, loser, victory, competition.

- **Your Major:** Someone majoring in education could analyze a concept such as learning, success, assessment, or high school. Your major itself might be seen as a concept. For example, engineering is a concept, and how one works in that field depends upon one's concept of it.

■ **Television:** What does the local news focus on, and what does this suggest about "news"? What does *The Kardashians* suggest about America, family, celebrity, or fame? What does twenty-four hour news (CNN, Fox News, MSNBC) suggest about government, politics, the United States, Americans, education, the news, the weather? What do house hunting shows suggest about living? What does a cell phone commercial suggest about freedom? What does an insurance commercial suggest about neighbors?

As you reflect on the program or commercial, ask yourself if the concept is somehow oversimplified or misrepresented. Or does the program or commercial fairly represent the concept? Remember that you are not evaluating the television program but rather using it to prompt an idea, to discover a concept that may need analysis and explanation.

ACTIVITY

Imagine more concepts that define your everyday life. If this can be done in a small group, take turns offering concepts until each participant has chosen a potential topic.

Analysis

Analysis involves investigating particular parts within the whole. If we were to analyze an object, we might take it apart and look inside. We might, for instance, analyze a computer by opening the case and looking at the internal wires, the cards, and the connections. But when examining a concept, we cannot take off its cover and simply look inside—at least, not physically. Instead, we have to depend on intellectual inquiry.

Rather than physical tools (screwdrivers or wrenches), we have to develop questions that get inside the abstraction and point to the particular elements of the concept. And the more

Library of Congress

Caio Cassoli/StockXchng

particular we get, the more we are apt to discover. In other words, we should try to understand the concept in the most narrow terms possible. Consider *college*. To analyze the concept, we must break it down and look at particular issues: What does college suggest for people's lives? Is it a time and place for learning specific skills or for exploring boundless ideas? Is it a place for making choices or for generating options? Such questions are analytical; they help shed light on specific issues inside the broader, more abstract idea. As you analyze a concept, use the following Invention Questions to break it down:

> How does your chosen concept influence or change people's lives?

> What emotions, behaviors, or ideas are associated with it?

> What hidden role does it play in everyday life?

> Are there complexities to the concept that people overlook?

Phestus/MorgueFile

Laura Kennedy/StockXchn

© Cengage

Invention Workshop

As you consider the Invention Questions, avoid skimming the surface of broad ideas. Make sure you get specific and discover some new idea or way of thinking about the concept. This won't happen right away. You must explore beyond the ideas that come to mind quickly. For help, enlist the help of at least two other writers and use one of the Invention Questions to launch a focused discussion. As you address the question, avoid chatting (which is always tempting). Instead, pursue any new ideas that surface. For example, in the following discussion, Cassie Heidecker discovers an important complexity to the concept *reality television*:

Are there complexities to the concept that people overlook?

DIANA: Yeah, those shows aren't real. They're not reality at all. Everything is scripted and the characters are all predictable. There's the quiet, good-looking guy, the mean bitch that no one likes, the bully with big muscles, the ditz. It's like a cast of stereotypes.

CASSIE: And it's great entertainment. People love watching. I think it's because the contestants are often rough around the edges. Some are rough in the middle too. But it's the lack of refinement that I like.

MICHAEL: And because the contestants aren't actors. They're people. They have day jobs and families back home.

CASSIE: You think people watch *American Idol* because the contestants have real lives?

MICHAEL: Exactly. That's part of it. They have real lives. That's why they show the small hometown once they start whittling down the contestants. They show the bedroom, the street, the place waiting for them at the end of the season. The point is, these people have real lives.

DIANA: Real lives. That's pretty funny. The reality is supposed to refer to the show, not the contestants.

CASSIE: Well, maybe it's like Michael says. The reality of their lives—outside of the show itself—might be the key. That's the big attraction.

Thinking Further

To explore further, writers look and listen for statements that bend away from the obvious. For example, in an Invention Workshop, Heidecker begins to realize something beyond the simple distinction, realistic versus unrealistic. She can pursue the idea further by asking more questions:

- How are reality television shows different from scripted dramas?

- If reality television is still scripted and edited heavily, why do the shows feel so different from conventional programs?

Watch what happens when Heidecker takes these questions and runs. She begins to discover something.

> **If reality television is still scripted and edited heavily, why do the shows feel essentially different from conventional programs?**
> On one hand, it feels like anything could happen. One of the characters might freak out or leave the show or cut her finger off. But realistically, viewers know that only a certain kind of anything will happen. Does that make sense? I mean, the shows we watch were likely filmed months beforehand and edited and tweaked. And I guess we know that at some level of thinking. (I'm trying to imagine myself watching *Top Chef* and thinking this way.) I know that a winner will be announced at a particular point, that a car chase isn't going to start up, that Jennifer isn't going to run into the room naked. In other words, the shows really are very predictable. But here's the thing: inside of that overall script are these contestants who could be the person next door. And as I'm watching the show (months after filming), most of those people have returned to their lives. They're real again. That's the catch. The people I'm watching are temporary celebrities and then full-time non-celebrities afterward. That's the weird attraction to it all. That's the "reality" of it.

Heidecker is thinking further; she's doing the work of academic writing. She avoids simple answers and easy responses. Her thinking is increasingly complex—and it yields a sophisticated analysis essay. (See page 133.) As you consider your own topic, explore your invention writing. Look for statements that seem unusual, that bend away from the obvious, and then generate probing questions of your own.

Public Resonance

It is up to the writer to make a concept relevant to readers. At some level, your concept already resonates with others, because a concept is, by definition, beyond particulars. Whether it is *reality, college,* or *student,* a concept necessarily involves others. Still, a concept is not always entirely understood—even by those who would, presumably, understand it. Consider *freedom:* As Americans, we often speak of it, sing about it, and even go to war over it, but do most Americans really understand the concept? And, couldn't they understand it better or differently? Even though freedom is part of our collective language, we might not realize its complexities and meaning. As you consider the social significance of your own topic, use the following questions:

❯ Is the concept generally agreed upon?

❯ Why is it important that people have an appropriate understanding of this concept?

❯ Does the concept need to be rethought? Why?

❯ What is the possible connection between the topic and some public concern?

If you choose not to directly state the public resonance of your concept, answering these questions serves another goal—to help you envision the relationship between your audience and your topic. In thinking about the public resonance of the concept, you may come across your *purpose*—the reason you are writing. If you believe that the concept is often misunderstood, then the purpose of your analysis might be to educate your audience. Or if your concept is overlooked, the purpose may be to elevate the status of the concept in your readers' mind.

Imagine a writer who is analyzing the concept "student." On some level, we all know what a student is, but as with all concepts, we can complicate our thinking and explore into the complexities of the concept. This writer has heard students referred to as customers, and believes there's an important difference between a "student" and a "customer": Students take pieces of information and actively work to create meaning, while customers passively receive meaning that has been created for them. For example, a student at a culinary school takes ingredients and makes a hamburger while a customer at a restaurant receives a hamburger that is made for her.

In the following excerpt, our writer discovers why *student,* as a concept, is necessary and why people should rethink it. Instead of giving up early in his exploration, he imagines specific effects, and in doing so, draws out the difference between customer and student:

Is the concept generally agreed upon?
No! That's the whole problem. Many students don't know what it means to be a student.

Why is it important that people have an appropriate understanding of this concept?
If college students really understand what it means to be a student (and not a consumerist student), their experience at college will be defined by self-discovery and enlightenment rather than petty frustration and grumbling. If colleges across America continue to confuse "student" with "consumer," education will suffer. Much of the time spent in college will be on customer service (keeping students happy) rather than challenging their beliefs, developing their minds, and broadening their horizons. Customers ultimately do not want their ideas about themselves to change; they want products and services to support what they think. If college continues down the present path, it is not hard to imagine colleges being devoid of genuinely new ideas.

The writer's essay grows out of this concern for the potential harm to students and higher education. We can see these ideas in his essay's conclusion:

There is no way higher education can counter the incredible momentum of consumerist culture. It is far more pervasive than the discourses of physics or composition studies. However, if we continue to allow the term "customer" to replace "student," I fear that students will become increasingly blind to the difference between consumerist culture and college culture.

Thesis
You probably have many different things to say about your topic, but your project will gain focus and intensity with a thesis statement, a single claim that expresses your particular view on the concept. Look over your notes from the Analysis and Public Resonance sections. Find a theme or pattern running through those notes and try to articulate that idea in a sentence. Your project might:

- **Explain how particular parts or qualities make up a concept.**

  —Maturity involves both recognition of past failures and attempts to retune behavior with those failures in mind.

  —Punk rock involves an explicit and dramatic disdain for common wisdom, popular aesthetic, and accepted manners.

- **Reveal a side or layer of a concept that normally goes unnoticed.**

  —Health is not simply an internal condition but a sound relationship between body and an immediate environment.

  —Behind the common image of trees, lakes, and loose critters, *nature* is a verb, an unyielding cyclical process.

- **Show a quality that distinguishes one concept from another.**

  —Contrary to the passive, personalizing, self-perpetuating, desire-driven customer, students are encouraged to be active. (Simon Benlow)

  —Childhood is not pre-adulthood but an existence fundamentally distinct and characterized by a peculiar mixture of wonder and fear.

- **Explain the inner workings of a concept.**

  —Education involves building new concepts and the ongoing destruction of well-established ideas.

  —In today's use of the term, *patriotism* demands a persistent turning away from self-evaluation.

Evolution of a Thesis

Remember that a thesis does not materialize out of thin air. It develops over time. It may involve a long process of reflection and discussion. And often, a good thesis emerges only after a writer has thoroughly analyzed the topic. Consider the example from the Analysis section, in which Cassie Heidecker's topic, reality television, is developed through a discussion. Her thesis evolves slowly as she tries to get a handle on the complexity of the idea:

- Reality television is not real in the sense that anything could happen.

- Reality television contains both highly edited fiction and some unscripted reality.

- We watch reality television because we understand that the contestants are, for the most part, real people.

- The reality part of reality shows is the unfilmed everyday life that bookends the episodes themselves.

As you consider your own thesis, remember that narrower statements yield more interesting writing. At first, you might think, "I can't possibly write more than a paragraph about something so narrow." However, the process of developing the ideas will generate content for your writing. And the more focused thesis will help you illustrate particular points rather than listing many marginally related issues.

REVISING YOUR THESIS

After you have developed a single statement, take time to reconsider: What do people normally say or assume about the concept? How have you complicated or enriched the common way of thinking?

Rhetorical Tools

Explaining a concept means using rhetorical tools. Writers decide on the tools below, and other support strategies, by asking: Will this help the reader understand and possibly accept the thesis.

Examples

Each writer in this chapter puts forth a particular way of seeing a concept, and each must support that way of seeing with scenarios (hypothetical accounts), allusions (references to bits of public knowledge), and examples. Because analyzing concepts requires abstract thinking, writers must be extra careful to illustrate points with concrete examples. In his introduction, Michael Pollan helps the reader understand the basic issue by giving specific examples of products involved in lawsuits over the word "natural":

> During the past few years, some 200 class-action suits have been filed against food manufacturers, charging them with misuse of the adjective in marketing such edible oxymorons as "natural" Cheetos Puffs, "all-natural" Sun Chips, "all-natural" Naked Juice, "100 percent all-natural" Tyson chicken nuggets and so forth.

These quick examples (just being specific instead of general, really) don't require elaboration. But other examples do. In his third paragraph, Pollan uses the antivaccination crowd as an example to help the reader see a particular way the word "natural" gets used. Pollan makes his claim in the first two sentences and then supports it with a developed example:

> Something in the human mind, or heart, seems to need a word of praise for all that hasn't contaminated, and for us that word now is "natural." Such an ideal can be put to all sorts of rhetorical uses. Among the antivaccination crowd, for example, it's not uncommon to read about the superiority of something called "natural immunity,"

brought about by exposure to the pathogen in question rather than to the deactivated (and therefore harmless) version of it made by humans in laboratories. "When you inject a vaccine into the body," reads a post on an antivaxxer website, Campaign for Truth in Medicine, "you're actually performing an unnatural act." This, of course, is the very same term once used to decry homosexuality and, more recently, same-sex marriage, which the Family Research Council has taken to comparing unfavorably to what it calls "natural marriage."

In some cases, writers may use details to illustrate how *not* to conceptualize an idea. They use **contrary examples** (situations or accounts that show the opposite of the writer's point). For example, Cassie Heidecker uses contrary examples to help her distinguish between genuine fiction and reality television:

> In the world of high art, such as literary fiction, the writer works to create a fictive dream—a coherent and impenetrable fantasy. The hope is that readers enter the dream and forget the real world. When we read a novel, for instance, our hopes become tied to Gatsby, Frodo, Ishmael, Antonia, Anna, and so on. We suspend our disbelief. And in turn, we are suspended in an ornate web of un-reality. But in reality television, part of the experience is the interplay between the fabricated scene (the kooky kitchen challenge limited to rutabagas and pig liver) and the invisible everyday lives of the contestants.

The contrary examples (which are actually allusions to literature) help her to narrow in on particular elements about her topic. They allow Heidecker to draw clear intellectual lines—to demarcate what something is and what it is not.

Definitions and References

While definitions are necessary to good writing, dictionary definitions can be over-used, or used ineffectively, especially as a way of starting an essay. These definitions can be trite and unhelpful. But sometimes a dictionary definition is key to a writer's take on a concept. For Heidecker, a definition helps to make an important distinction:

> **What then is the *reality* of reality TV?**
> Hoping to nail down reality, I made the risky move of consulting our big Webster's dictionary. As I expected, the definition of *reality* is tricky—maddening even. The first definition: "The quality or state of being real." The definitions go on in a similar fashion until definition 2c, which states: "What actually exists: what has objective existence: what is not a mere idea: what is not imaginary, fictitious, or pretend." This definition clinches something important. While conventional television dramas are entirely pretend—ideas only—the identities on reality TV shows are real in the sense that they (probably) haven't spent years training to be on stage or behind a camera.

In addition to longer definitions, writers define words or concepts quickly within an essay and move on to a larger point. Notice how Pollan defines "naturalistic fallacy" in the second sentence below:

Implicit here is the idea that nature is a repository of abiding moral and ethical values—and that we can say with confidence exactly what those values are. Philosophers often call this the "naturalistic fallacy": the idea that whatever *is* (in nature) is what *ought to be* (in human behavior). But if nature offers a moral standard by which we can measure ourselves, and a set of values to which we should aspire, exactly what sort of values are they?

As you consider your topic, apply the following rhetorical tools to help show increasingly complex dimensions of the concept:

- **Examples:** What specific examples in everyday life illustrate my point about the concept?

- **Contrary Examples:** What programs, ads, or other examples from everyday life illustrate an inappropriate or oversimplified way of understanding the concept?

- **Scenarios:** What hypothetical account could demonstrate the concept?

- **Allusions:** What person or event from history, current events, popular culture, or literature illustrates the point about the concept?

Invention Workshop

In small groups, collectively develop support for one another's projects. Each writer should announce his or her thesis to the group. Each group member then should offer at least one response to each of the following questions:

1. What specific examples in everyday life illustrate the writer's point?

2. Name something from popular culture (such as a television show, a movie, an advertising campaign) that illustrates the writer's point. Explain how the writer could allude to it.

3. Name something from history (a person, an event, a trend) that reveals or supports something about the writer's point.

4. Explain how the writer's point is different from how people normally think about the concept.

As the group members offer ideas, the writer should record the group members' responses so they can be integrated later.

Outside Sources

Writers are often surprised to find how many others have addressed their topics and explored the same intellectual pathways. On one hand, outside sources can help a writer substantiate points, and on the other, they can help to add dimension, creating intellectual twists and turns. Notice how Cassie Heidecker uses sources in both ways. In the first passage, she cites a Pew poll that adds public resonance to her personal reaction to reality television. In the second, she uses a quotation from a cultural critic who supports her own sophisticated claim:

> And we're not alone. Despite the results of a Pew Research Center poll indicating that 63% of the American public thinks that reality TV shows signal our cultural decline, the ratings continue to climb. In fact, "What viewers say they want and what they really watch are not the same" (Carter).
>
> The sheer number of calls gets at something critical about these shows: they're participatory. The shows are imbued with the life outside of them. Pop culture critic James Poniewozik explains, "Reality is more than a TV genre now. . . . It's everywhere. When Scott Brown won an upset Senate victory in Massachusetts, he was joined onstage by his daughter Ayla, an *American Idol* semifinalist from Season 5." He goes on to trace the trajectory of reality TV from mere entertainment to a kind of reality in itself: "In 1992, reality TV was a novelty. In 2000, it was a fad. In 2010, it's a way of life."

Heidecker illustrates a common move when using outside sources. She begins her paragraphs with her own assertion—her own understanding of the topic. Then she brings in the outside source to reinforce a complex idea that she has already begun describing. (For more guidance on integrating ideas from sources, see Chapter 16: Integrating and Documenting Sources.)

Revision

Revision is the most difficult step for many writers. We have to genuinely face what we've said and analyze rigorously. We have to take apart what feels complete, finished, and sealed up. If we analyze well, we may find passages that work better than others—those that better support the thesis and those that veer away or simply repeat a bland point. Also, the closer we look, the less apt we are to make generalizations: *It all works. The whole thing is terrible.* Before you pass your draft to review, give it one last read and decide for yourself which passages are the most supportive, which are the most focused and intense, and which are the least focused, the least vitalized.

Peer Review

Exchange drafts with at least one other writer. Before passing your draft to others, underline the thesis, or write it above your essay. This way, reviewers will get traction as they read. As a reviewer, use the following questions to guide your response:

1. Which words or phrases in the thesis could be more focused?

2. Point out passages or sentences that could use more specific illustration. Suggest an example from everyday life that illustrates the writer's point. For example, in an essay about athletics, you might read:

Athletics are the great motivator of many students. Without sports, many would not feel compelled to attend school at all.

You might suggest that "the great motivator" could be illustrated more specifically.

3. Suggest an allusion (to popular culture, literature, or history) that illustrates the writer's point. Rather than accept claims as they are, help the writer make a connection to some other time, place, or text so that the concept (whatever it is) connects to a broader set of ideas.

4. The writer might rely on a dictionary to get started, but the ideas should extend beyond that definition. (The essay may take you beyond a definition that you could easily look up yourself.) Where do you feel that "liftoff" away from a standard definition? If there is no liftoff, where might the writer concentrate attention? If you can, offer a path beyond the definition.

5. Consider the paragraphs: Do they focus on one specific point? Point to any paragraphs that seem to stray into several ideas.

6. In which passages does the writer's voice seem most engaging? (Where do you feel yourself, as a reader, most inspired by the ideas?) Why?

7. Referring to Chapter 19, Vitalizing Sentences, point to particular sentences and phrases that could gain intensity.

QUESTIONS FOR RESEARCH

If the writer used outside sources:

- Where must he or she include in-text citations? (See pages 478–479 and 496–498.)

- Are quotations blended smoothly into the argument and punctuated correctly? (See pages 467–476.)

- Where could more direct textual cues or transitions help readers? (See pages 474–476.)

- Is the Works Cited or References page formatted properly? (See Chapter 16.)

Reflection

As the chapter introduction says, "Writers are willing to get underneath concepts that would otherwise go unquestioned." In this sense, academic writers are not simply reporting information or expressing personal opinions. They are excavating, digging, sneaking into intellectual alleys, and exploring the cultural trash bins. They are revealing the quiet, or sometimes loud and obnoxious, complexities of everyday life.

Now that you've invented, written, revised, and edited a project, you probably have a much deeper understanding of the concept. To draw out that understanding, analyze your essay's rhetoric by answering these questions:

1. How did you get beneath a concept?

2. What was the most revelatory insight? Was it your thesis?

3. What was your most powerful supporting passage? What does it accomplish?

4. How does your project explore the intellectual back roads and alleys? How does it go behind the conventional, obvious ways of thinking about the concept?

5. Given what you've written, will readers think or behave differently?

6. What might be the benefits to others? How might others be impacted?

Beyond the Essay: Conceptual Map

A conceptual map is a graphic presentation of ideas. Using words, shapes, lines, or photographs, the creator of a conceptual map attempts to depict the relationship and complexity of ideas. This strategy is well suited for illustrating the various layers of a concept. For instance, in the image that opens this chapter, a conceptual map depicts the relationships in cyberspace. With the placement of each term, line, and graphic, the designer Nathan Shedroff suggests particular connections. Notice, for instance, that one of the outer spheres is "time," and it turns in tandem with "read." This suggests that time, in cyberspace, is dependent on the act of reading.

1. For this assignment, develop a conceptual map to accompany your writing project:
   - Try to depict the complexity of your ideas using only key words or phrases from your essay.
   - Graphically show how those words and phrases relate.
   - Use lines, arrows, and other shapes to depict the relationship between ideas.
   - Use colors (if possible) to group ideas or to distinguish between types of ideas.

Consider including your conceptual map as a visual aid within your essay.

2. Present your conceptual map to others. Explain how the map represents the complexity of the ideas in your essay. Explain where it succeeds in reinforcing, and falls short of representing, those ideas.

6

Analyzing Written Texts

John Mauk

Chapter Objectives

This chapter will help you to:

- Break down and examine specific rhetorical elements of a written text.
- Identify and explain context, subtext, and intertextuality.
- Develop a focused analytical essay that explains the rhetorical function of various elements in a written text.

"Curiosity begins as an act of tearing to pieces or analysis."

—Samuel Alexander

INTRODUCTION

A nalysis is the act of breaking something down to see how it works. When doctors analyze a heart, they break it down to ventricles and valves. When critics analyze a film, they break it down to plot, characters, acting, and cinematography. And when musicians analyze a song, they break it down to melody, lyrics, chords, and ensemble. In other words, analysis involves pulling apart the subject (heart, film, song) and seeing how each element functions. But the goal is not merely dismantling. Ultimately, we are hoping to understand something about the subject, to discover its patterns, rhythms, and functions. In short, we are hoping to generate an insight, to develop a better understanding of the thing itself.

If you have worked through other chapters in this book, you have already been doing analysis. You have, for instance, broken down places, concepts, even your own memories. But this chapter focuses exclusively on written texts. The goal, here, is to discover how texts work.

In academic life, analyzing written texts (or what we will call *textual analysis*) is crucial work, fundamental to all disciplines and the careers they generate: lawyers analyze court decisions, policies, and transcripts; historians analyze government documents, letters, diaries, or any text produced by the human hand; business leaders analyze sales projections and budget rationale; and when they are not examining patients, physicians analyze the latest medical research. In these examples, notice that we use the term *analyze* rather than *read*. You can probably sense the point: Textual analysis is a kind of intensive reading, a way to interact with an article, essay, book, or blog. The process requires that we understand the ideas *and* how they develop. It involves comprehending the points while tracing how they get made.

Textual analysis also relies on (what many teachers and scholars call) *reading critically*, which is different than skimming, browsing, or reading for content. Reading critically involves a deep understanding of the text—an awareness of how it works: what it's trying to accomplish, what it asserts, how it supports ideas, what positions it pushes against, what it implies, what it asks of readers, and so on. Reading critically is reading analytically—not for the sake of judgment or criticism but simply for more insight.

The essays in this chapter model a range of approaches to analyzing texts. As you read, you will notice some obvious differences. For example, our sample analysis examines a traditional academic essay, Adrienne Carr takes on a commencement address, and Alison Block examines a newspaper editorial. Each also takes on slightly different elements. Our analysis focuses on argumentative *appeals*, Carr focuses on the speaker's attempt to engage the audience, and Block focuses on *appeals, context,* and *subtext*. Although different in scope, these analyses all seek to discover something. Each goes beyond breaking down the text in question and draws out insights from the analytical process. After reading the sample analyses, you can find a text to analyze in one of two ways—go to the Point of Contact section to find a topic from everyday life or choose one of the Ideas for Writing following the essays. After finding a text, go to the Analysis section to begin developing your thoughts.

WHAT ABOUT LITERATURE?

Although stories, novels, plays, poems, and songs are, indeed, written texts, they have some unique qualities—worthy of their own study and exploration. In fact, an entire field of study known as literary criticism focuses on the analysis of literary texts. This chapter, however, focuses on nonliterary written works such as essays, articles, speech transcripts, and blog posts.

The Weight of Sanity: A Sample Analysis of Ann Marie Paulin

MINDTAP
From Cengage
Complete the auto-graded
quiz for this reading.

We developed the following textual analysis of Ann Marie Paulin's essay (printed in Chapter 8, page 230). Ours is only one possible approach. Someone else could write a compelling analysis of Paulin's essay and draw attention to other rhetorical elements. Our strategy was to call out and explain the function of Paulin's purpose, thesis, and main support strategies. And along the way, we discovered an interesting layer to Paulin's essay.

In recent decades, an army of writers has condemned mass media for its fixation with slimness. Thousands of professors, physicians, psychologists, teachers, journalists, and students have argued vehemently about the emotional and physical injury caused by popular culture's parade of super-thin models. In her essay, "Cruelty, Civility, and Other Weighty Matters," Ann Marie Paulin goes a step beyond blaming mass media. She shows how incessant imagery and messaging have shaped public consciousness. Paulin is not out to blame mass media but to exorcise the value system that has taken root in everyday life.

Paulin begins with a blast of personal testimony: "I swear, if I have to sit through one more ad proclaiming that life is not worth living if you aren't thin, I'll slug somebody." Of course, the most demanding element here is Paulin's voice—her willingness to air such frustration and, of course, to slug somebody. But the opening also establishes two key points: First, the problem involves an immense volume of messages that has accumulated into something inescapable. Second, the message is not simply that being thin is better than being fat. It's that being fat is the worst fate possible. Fat people are portrayed in mass media as "sorrowful empty losers."

In her second paragraph, before she launches into a range of support strategies, Paulin heads off a potential mischaracterization of her stance: "I'm not advocating that everyone in America go out and get fat." This brief qualifier is a defense against bad thinking—the illogical extremes that drive American diets. We are a culture, Paulin explains, that consumes mass quantities of donuts along with toxic diet pills: "We may talk tofu but we gobble glazed." In other words, when it comes to eating, not eating, and all the behaviors in between, American mainstream culture is nowhere near reasonable. And in the next paragraph, she references two articles that show how often and why diets fail. The references, examples, and allusions show a culture with confused reflexes—one that "encourages obesity . . . yet breeds a prejudice against fat people."

The next point in her line of reasoning takes the majority of her essay. In fact, Paulin devotes the next eight paragraphs to the notion that normal everyday people, not the mean old media, are the agents of discrimination. She explains how a majority of respondents (79%) to two personal ads preferred to date a drug addict rather than an overweight person. She describes a university study in which men and women ranked "an obese person as the least desirable sexual partner" over those with mental or physical disabilities. And then Paulin moves methodically through everyday life, calling out people in charge of learning (teachers), medical care (doctors), and even growing up (parents). In each case, the bigotry is highlighted with surveys and data. And over the course of twelve packed paragraphs, the point becomes clear: the average citizen who lives, works, browses the Internet, and watches television accumulates a general bigotry about body shape: "The constant repetition of this message in various forms does the damage to the humans who watch and learn."

Throughout these passages, Paulin also describes cause and effect. She shows the harm of such persistent bigotry: lower wages, persistent loneliness, and condemnation from family members and associates. Each effect gets its own full paragraph of grim statistics. And as her essay develops, the argument comes full circle. As it turns out, Americans accept the characterization of obese people as sorrowful losers. We dutifully treat the non-skinny with as much open disdain as they can handle—and then a little more.

Much of Paulin's argument, then, is a kind of cultural analysis—an examination of how mass media creates a value system and how that value system, in turn, creates daily life. But beneath this analysis, Paulin appeals to a basic sense of fairness. After all, the statistics and anecdotes show a civilization methodically discriminating against a group of people who have less power, less money, and less social mobility than their slimmer counterparts. She calls out the "harm," "insensitivity," the "virulently negative attitudes" that obese people encounter. And whenever a writer works so hard to report unfairness, she is usually—as in this case—nudging readers toward the opposite.

But the most consistent appeal—the one that begins, ends, and weaves through Paulin's argument—involves moderation. She calls on readers to think in more rational terms, to recognize (and therefore turn away from) the ridiculous, the illogical extremism, "wrongheaded notions," "nonsense," "hugely oversimplified" thinking, "less than accurate" portrayals, "fanatics," "foolish notions," and "crazy ideas" that populate mainstream thinking about obesity. In her seventh paragraph, she describes an advertisement for Slim Fast. She contrasts the ad's world (that celebrates thinness above all else) to a different world (that values family and sanity and health). This stark contrast establishes a kind of choice: stay crazy or get smart; accept the unreasonable or start resisting it.

In her final passage, Paulin reinforces her main appeal. After working through all the cruelty and incivility related to body size, she nails down the main distinction of her argument. It is not fat vs. skinny, kindness vs. cruelty, or acceptance vs. shame. While those distinctions matter, and probably lurk in the subtext of every passage, Paulin's main distinction is sane vs. crazy:

While I was watching the evening news, a story came on about a young woman who was run over by a bus. I vividly recall that as the station played the footage of the paramedics wheeling the woman away on a stretcher, I said to myself, "Yeah, but at least she's thin." I've been lucky enough to have gained some wisdom (as well as weight) with age: I may be fat, but I'm no longer crazy. There are some things more important than being thin.

WRITING STRATEGIES

1. Identify the thesis. What sentence best characterizes our main insight about Paulin's essay?

2. Paragraph 7 relies on a series of brief quotations. Explain how those quoted phrases work in our analysis. What specific point are we trying to establish?

3. How does this analysis deal with context? Explain where context comes up, where it gets discussed—even indirectly.

4. We conclude with a lengthy quote from Paulin. Explain what analytical point that quote helps us to make.

5. Do you sense any form of evaluation (praise, blame, celebration, judgment) in our analysis? Can you tell if we find Paulin's claims important or valuable? Explain where any subtle evaluation may take place.

EXPLORING IDEAS

1. In our analysis, we deal briefly with Paulin's voice. What else could we have done with Paulin's voice? Why might her voice be more important than we suggest?

2. In our opening paragraph, we claim that "an army" of writers has taken on the issue of media and body image. Why do you think so many writers have taken on the issue in recent years?

3. Despite that army of writers, mass media still rely almost exclusively on super-thin models and perfectly sculpted bodies to sell everything from phones to yogurt. Why? Does Paulin's essay hold some answer?

4. Consider our title, which is an intertextual play on Paulin's title. What are other possible titles for this analysis? How else could we have played with Paulin's language?

5. We claim that Paulin's essay is "a kind of cultural analysis." In your own words, explain the relationship between textual and cultural analysis. How do they overlap? How does one rely on the other?

IDEAS FOR WRITING

1. Find an online article that argues about mass media's impact on women's body image. Analyze that argument. Be careful not to get pulled into the claims; instead, stay outside of the argument and explain *how it works*.

2. Find an online article about the connection between mass media and men's health. Analyze that argument—and, again, be careful not to get pulled into the argument itself.

The Default Setting: An Analysis of David Foster Wallace

Adrienne Carr

Adrienne Carr is a writer and artist. In this essay, she analyzes the now famous 2005 commencement address by David Foster Wallace. Carr explains rhetorical elements such as context and support, but she focuses most attention on Wallace's overt attempts to connect with his audience. It's in those attempts— when Wallace stops to manage the audience's reflexes—that Carr finds the most compelling insights. (For a better understanding of this analysis, you might first search for and read Wallace's address.)

In 2005, David Foster Wallace delivered the commencement address for Kenyon College. At the time, Wallace was a celebrated literary figure, a relatively young and rising star known for his scathing critiques of popular culture and fantastically dense fiction. But in the address, he is neither scathing nor dense. The David Foster Wallace speaking at Kenyon is not a heavy-hitting writer or powerhouse intellectual. Instead, he is an earnest voice, a member of an older generation trying desperately to impart a difficult and "unsexy" message.

The context of the address is key. Wallace is delivering a commencement for one of the nation's top liberal arts colleges, so his audience is postured to launch into the privilege awaiting those from an esteemed institution. But Wallace does not condemn that privilege. He is not out to hammer his audience about class issues. He is up to something else. He uses the grand occasion to highlight the opposite: the uninteresting, uncelebrated, and most forgettable moments of everyday life. And he argues that these moments, the boring and unsexy ones, provide an opportunity to apply the skills learned from a college like Kenyon. In other words, higher education, he explains, does not provide knowledge, disciplinary skills, or facts. Instead, it provides the ability to shift away from one's "default" response to tedium. This is his main point—one that he asserts, reinforces, and even insists upon throughout the address.

To support his point, Wallace depends on some unfancy rhetorical moves. His speech is not full of witty insider references or arcane allusions. It relies, instead, on some basic scenarios—imagined situations that place the audience in the unglamorous sights and sounds of everyday life:

> [L]et's say it's an average adult day . . . . You haven't had time to shop this week because of your challenging job, and so now after work you have to get in your car and drive to the supermarket . . . . And the store is hideously lit and infused with soul-killing Muzak or corporate pop and it's pretty much the last place you want to be but you can't just get in and quickly out; you have to wander all over the huge, over-lit store's confusing aisles to find the stuff you want and you have to maneuver your junky cart through all these other tired, hurried people with carts (et cetera, et cetera, cutting stuff out because this is a long

ceremony) and eventually you get all your supper supplies, except now it turns out there aren't enough check-out lanes open even though it's the end-of-the-day rush. (Wallace 67–70)

The level of detail forces Wallace's point: there is no escaping everyday life—no way to diffuse the ongoing, nonstop labor of getting through the week. And the detail in this early passage sets Wallace up for more scenarios later in the address, where he dramatizes the shift out of default setting, where he explains, for instance, that people—especially those who are supposedly educated—can shift into a better mindset, one that recognizes others' struggles, others' absolute agony in getting through the day. His early scenarios come from the solipsistic

Peter Strain

lens—the one that thinks only "about MY hungriness and MY fatigue and MY desire to just get home" (Wallace 77), while his latter scenarios project a human open to the world of others.

Wallace's address, then, embodies a kind of evolution—a movement from self-centered default thinking to intellectual freedom. That is the unmistakable structure of the address. But as he moves along, Wallace stops in mid-passage (sometimes in mid-sentence) to draw attention to his own rhetoric. In nearly every paragraph, Wallace talks directly about his own attempts to keep his audience engaged. He dances with his listeners' expectations—their anticipation of standard lines, common sayings, and conventional elements of the commencement address. He calls out and grapples with those expectations. For example, Wallace begins with an old tale of two young fish and a wise older one. The unmistakable point of the story is that the younger fish swim along oblivious to the stuff around and within them. They don't understand, as the wise fish does, that they are in water. Wallace then steps out the story—out of the speech itself—and deals with his listeners' potential reaction:

> This is a standard requirement of US commencement speeches, the deployment of didactic little parable-ish stories. The story "thing" turns out to be one of the better, less bullshitty conventions of the genre, but if you're worried that I plan to present myself here as the wise, older fish explaining what water is to you younger fish, please don't be. I am not the wise old fish. (Wallace 5–7)

Shortly after, Wallace again draws attention to the conventions of the genre—and this time, he acknowledges a cliché:

> Of course the main requirement of speeches like this is that I'm supposed to talk about your liberal arts education's meaning, to try to explain why the degree you are about to receive has actual human value instead of just a material payoff. So let's talk about the single most pervasive cliché in the commencement speech genre, which is that a liberal arts education is not so much about filling you up with knowledge as it is about quote teaching you how to think. (Wallace 11–12)

In effect, Wallace has bridged a gap between himself and his audience. He and his listeners now know—if they didn't already—the conventions and formulas of the rhetorical situation. They are all rolling their collective eyes at what is supposed to be said. The conventional cards are on the table. Then Wallace makes an important move: he defends the "pervasive cliché." For the remainder of his speech, he argues for the power and significance of that cliché. But even as Wallace is arguing his case (helping his listeners to imagine the full value of shifting from their default mindsets), he pauses: "Again, please don't think that I'm giving you moral advice, or that I'm saying you are supposed to think this way, or that anyone expects you to just automatically do it" (Wallace 88). And later, after laying out rationale for moving out of default, he pauses again: "But please don't just dismiss it as just some finger-wagging Dr. Laura sermon" (Wallace 127). In these overt attempts to engage listeners, Wallace shows an open desperation. So many apologies and qualifiers reveal his estimation of the immediate audience—their skepticism, their reflex toward boredom, their over-familiarity with institutional life, their unwillingness to take advice. He seems to know that his audience might tune out at any second, that his most immediate listeners are resistant to advice, to lectures, to older people handing down edicts. And so Wallace says repeatedly that he isn't one of those and isn't doing any of that—all while being one of those and doing all of that. Wallace is, in fact, the older fish. He does give sage advice. He does impart wisdom. And he does, in the end, explain what water is: the tedium of everyday life that calls out our (everyone's) default settings:

> The plain fact is that you graduating seniors do not yet have any clue what "day in day out" really means. There happen to be whole, large parts of adult American life that nobody talks about in commencement speeches. One such part involves boredom, routine, and petty frustration. The parents and older folks here will know all too well what I'm talking about. (Wallace 63–66)

Wallace's speech is about the invisible stuff all around and within us—the stuff that flows through people's proverbial gills and makes us breathe, think, and swim in particular ways. And what's most interesting is his own desperate strategy to manage his audience's default setting—the graduates' suspicions and reflexes in that very moment.

After Wallace's untimely death in 2008, the address attracted a huge readership. "It became a treasured piece of writing reprinted in *The Wall Street Journal* and the *London Times,* commented on endlessly in blogs, and emailed from friend to friend" ("This Is Water"). Something about this particular text generated millions of views and ultimately prompted Little, Brown and Company to publish it as a stand-alone mini-book. Now millions of people experience the work in a different context—not only in print but also after Wallace himself is gone from the podium. It's difficult to say what ignited the immense appeal—maybe the terrible irony that Wallace committed suicide after years of depression, maybe the everyday clarity that the address provides, or maybe Wallace's recognizable struggle to reach through this foggy default life.

Works Cited

"This Is Water." Little, Brown and Company, www.hachettebookgroup.com/titles/david-foster-wallace/this-is-water/9780316068222/. Accessed 15 Jan. 2014.

Wallace, David Foster. *This Is Water: Some Thoughts, Delivered on a Significant Occasion, about Living a Compassionate Life.* Little, Brown, 2009.

WRITING STRATEGIES

1. Identify Carr's thesis. What sentence best characterizes her main insight about the Wallace address?

2. Carr uses a significant amount of quotations from Wallace's address. Explain why those quotations are necessary. What do they help Carr to accomplish?

3. Unsuccessful conclusions simply restate or summarize the author's thesis. But Carr's conclusion offers an idea about Wallace's purpose. Explain how that idea relates to the rest of her essay.

4. Carr gets dangerously close to at least one analytical "pitfall." Where do you think this happens? Do you think she falls entirely? Or does she manage to stay on safe analytical ground? Explain your answer. (For a detailed explanation of "pitfalls," see page 183–185.)

5. Do you sense subtle praise or any form of evaluation in Carr's analysis? Explain how Carr either avoids evaluation or veers close to it.

EXPLORING IDEAS

1. Writer's voice is the presence of the writer in the text. Explain Carr's voice. Where do you see (or hear) Carr's voice in this analysis?

2. If you haven't already, read the Wallace address or find the audio recording online. After you have read or listened to the address, explain why you think the address has become so popular.

3. What other rhetorical elements do you detect in Wallace's address? What are the most significant elements that Carr does not describe here?

4. In your own words, explain *default setting* as it applies to people and everyday life.

5. How does Wallace's death figure into your understanding of the Kenyon address?

IDEAS FOR WRITING>

1. Famous writers, politicians, artists, actors, and entrepreneurs often give commencement addresses. Search for possible addresses to analyze. (Make sure to consider the specific context—both the school and the date.)

2. Consider your favorite professional writer: a novelist, journalist, poet, or reporter. Visit that writer's website or publisher-sponsored site. Search for a speech, manifesto, open letter, or formal correspondence to analyze.

If responding to one of these ideas, go to the Analysis section of this chapter to begin developing ideas for your essay.

STUDENT ESSAY

Politics and Audience: *The New York Times'* Appeal to Undecided Voters in 2016

Alison Block

Writing about politics is tricky business. It's easy to move away from analysis and fall headlong into argumentation. In this essay, Alison Block stays on firm analytical ground. Her strategy involves focusing as much as possible on the rhetorical elements of *The New York Times* editorial. She also makes an important analytical move: she *contextualizes* the editorial. In other words, she places it within a broader history of political endorsements. Block is a professional writing major at Miami University. She wrote this analysis directly after the 2016 presidential election.

The 2016 American presidential election will likely go down as one of the most divisive election seasons in American history. The two final candidates, Hillary Clinton and Donald Trump, encountered both fervent support and fervent opposition. Many companies, organizations, and public figures endorsed one candidate or the other, and *The New York Times* continued its century-and-a-half old tradition of endorsing one presidential candidate. In 2016, the Editorial Board chose Hillary Clinton, publishing a concise argument simply entitled "Hillary Clinton for President" in late September, six weeks before the election. The article—that the authors admit writing for the sole purpose of persuading undecided readers—employs a variety of rhetorical strategies that respond directly to the surrounding context and subtext.

Contextualizes the target text.

Articulates the broad purpose of the text.

The editors begin by admitting that "in any normal election year," they would directly compare presidential candidates issue by issue, but that such an action in this particular election would be, in their opinion, futile. They openly state they are "aiming instead to persuade those . . . who are hesitating to vote for Mrs. Clinton," constructing the remainder of the article with reasons why they believe Clinton should be president. The authors' main purpose is intentionally, blatantly obvious: they are attempting to persuade their audience to vote for Clinton; more specifically, they are endorsing her. That much is clear immediately. What is less obvious is the implicit second purpose: to inform, or warn, the readers against voting for Donald Trump. Though they will later write an article in condemnation

Uses the authors' own words to characterize the specific purpose of the text.

There's a secondary, and implied, purpose.

of Trump to mirror their Clinton endorsement, the warning is originally implied in the phrases, "Donald Trump discloses nothing concrete about himself or his plans while promising the moon and offering the stars on layaway," and, "we believe Mr. Trump to be the worst nominee put forward by a major party in modern American history." The brief warning against Trump keeps the focus on their endorsement of Clinton. This is a powerful rhetorical move because it amplifies the argument for Clinton. That is, lauding her accomplishments without comparing her to anyone else would be ineffective for lack of perspective; comparing her to their portrayal of Trump boosts her credibility, while also intensifying their argument.

> *The secondary purpose reinforces the primary purpose.*

This endorsement came at a critical time in the election season. Published in late September, two months after the candidates were officially chosen and six weeks before Election Day, the editorial responds to the public's intense focus on the election. It is aimed specifically at undecided voters, a group larger than usual such a short time before an election. In an election season more polarizing than most, the *Times* editors entered the political context. Yet the endorsement is not a break from nonpartisan journalistic integrity. *The New York Times* has endorsed one candidate in every American presidential race since 1860 (endorsing President Lincoln twice). With such a long-running tradition, this editorial not only responds to the public's need for reasonable, fact-based arguments for (or against) candidates, but also to the *Times'* readers, who expect an endorsement each election cycle. Additionally, much of the discourse surrounding the election was based on voting "against" candidates, not "for" them—in other words, many claimed to vote for Trump simply to vote against Clinton, and vice versa. Yet the *Times'* endorsement provides reasons why readers should vote *for* Clinton, arguing, "The best case for Hillary Clinton cannot be, and is not, that she isn't Donald Trump." By condemning the action of voting against a candidate, the *Times* attempts to give a solid political stance that many voters at the time lacked.

> *Here, intended audience and context seem to fold together.*

> *So the* Times *editors subtly addressed a rhetorical problem for the intended audience.*

The endorsement methodically enumerates Clinton's accomplishments and credits—examples from her forty years in public service. Still, the *Times* considers its audience undecided. While the endorsement constantly praises Clinton's accomplishments, it also engages opposing claims and concedes her shortcomings:

> *The endorsement indirectly counterargues and directly concedes.*

She helped promote the Trans-Pacific Partnership, an important trade counterweight to China and a key component of the

Obama administration's pivot to Asia. Her election-year reversal on that pact has confused some of her supporters, but her underlying commitment to bolstering trade along with workers' rights is not in doubt. Mrs. Clinton's attempt to reset relations with Russia, though far from successful, was a sensible effort to improve interactions with a rivalrous nuclear power.

This strategy is important. People hesitant to support Clinton would not simply forget what they see as her shortcomings, so the *Times* acknowledges them but explains why they are forgivable. Non-supporters of Clinton critiqued her for "flip-flopping" on issues such as TPP, but the *Times* highlights the positive aspect of her indecision—namely, that it shows her commitment to doing what she sees as right for the benefit of trade and workers.

Here, Block shows how the endorsement counters and concedes.

While the editors acknowledge, as her critics did, that she was largely unsuccessful in improving America's relationship with Russia, they praise her effort to do so. By referring to Russia as "a rivalrous nuclear power," the *Times* subtly reminds readers of Russia's dangerous potential, amplifying the importance of Clinton's efforts, even if they were ultimately not successful. This strategy appears throughout the article. For example, the editors say:

Small phrases, then, can do some significant rhetorical work. Here, the language suggests an entire argument.

> Mrs. Clinton and her team have produced detailed proposals on crime, policing and race relations, debt-free college and small-business incentives, climate change and affordable broadband. Most of these proposals would benefit from further elaboration on how to pay for them, beyond taxing the wealthiest Americans. They would also depend on passage by Congress. That means that, to enact her agenda, Mrs. Clinton would need to find common ground with a destabilized Republican Party, whose unifying goal in Congress would be to discredit her.

They begin by appealing to logic, listing a string of related facts—her legislative proposals—that emphasize her productivity in terms of public service. Then, they make a concession to Clinton's opponents. They admit to flaws within her proposals. But they qualify their own concession, pointing out that Clinton's success does not rest on her shoulders alone; it requires the cooperation of Republican lawmakers. The subtext of this qualifier is twofold: one, readers are reminded that while they might not think Clinton will be effective, she can only be as effective as the Republican party allows her to be, thereby distributing the blame equally between Clinton and a Republican Congress.

Language after the block quote details how the quote itself works.

Second, it serves as an encouragement: for Clinton to pass proposals, they must be approved by Republicans, meaning the legislation enacted would likely be more moderate than the proposals. The *Times* editors employ this strategy throughout most of the article, ensuring that they address the many arguments against Clinton while providing a realistic look at her accomplishments and challenges.

Block has found a pattern— some significant and recurring move in her target text.

The article's final paragraph is only two sentences, yet it contains multiple rhetorical techniques:

> Through war and recession, Americans born since 9/11 have had to grow up fast, and they deserve a grown-up president. A lifetime's commitment to solving problems in the real world qualifies Hillary Clinton for this job, and the country should put her to work.

The phrase "through war and recession" alludes to the past fifteen years of trials America has gone through. It subtly reminds readers that Clinton held public office during much of that time, and implies the need for stability in the present. Americans born since September 11, 2001, were, at the time of the article's publication, all under the age of fifteen. By saying "they deserve a grown-up president," the *Times* editors implore their readers to think of those children, a common appeal to emotion—because in our culture, protecting children and their future is one of our greatest responsibilities. Additionally, it implies that Trump is not a "grown-up," which subtly alludes to many instances in which Trump's behavior was deemed childlike. They also clarify that Clinton's career has solved problems in the "real world," subtly critiquing Trump's history in television. Finally, with the words "the country should put her to work," the *Times* editors call readers to action. So with final allusions to their belief in Clinton's capability, Trump's incompetency, and their purpose in writing the article, the Times editors reinforce their multifaceted and urgent argument.

Again, short phrases can suggest a great deal. Block articulates the thinking implied by the short phrase.

Many layers of implication—or subtext.

The argument has urgency or exigence that comes from the nature of that particular election.

Based on a precedent set in the previous thirty-eight elections, and the widespread modern tradition of newspapers choosing a candidate, the *Times* was expected to take a stance, and in their thirty-ninth endorsement chose Clinton. The purpose of endorsements is to provide readers with reasons to vote *for* a particular candidate. It is important to realize that this article is one of countless such articles written at the time. Of course, Clinton did not win the presidency. This fact may reveal the *Times* endorsement, and by extension its genre, as merely symbolic. But the election itself is a different rhetorical situation. It is still important that the *Times* endorsement

Despite the election results, the endorsement genre still lives.

fulfilled its purpose by providing undecided readers with potentially persuasive reasons to choose—and vote for—one candidate.

Work Cited

Editorial Board. "Hillary Clinton for President." *The New York Times*, 24 Sept. 2016, nyti.ms/2cZtKJM.

WRITING STRATEGIES

1. Identify Block's thesis—her main analytical insight about the *Times* endorsement.

2. What is subtext? And how does Block use the concept to understand the *Times* endorsement?

3. Block explains that the *Times* editors qualify their own concession. What does this mean? In your own words, explain how someone can qualify a concession. (You can read about qualifiers and concessions in this chapter and in Chapter 8.)

4. Genre is a category of writing with established expectations. In her concluding paragraph, Block refers to the endorsement genre. How does her reference to genre relate to her main idea?

5. The *Times* endorsement came at a specific moment in history. How does Block put the endorsement in a bigger (or broader) context?

EXPLORING IDEAS

1. Where do you get news about politics? What outlets or people? How do you know the information is reliable?

2. For centuries, newspapers have endorsed political candidates in both national and local elections. Why do you think that tradition has remained central to American politics?

3. Political endorsements are as much about the endorser as the endorsee. How does this notion relate to the *Times* support for Hillary Clinton?

4. The *New York Times* is one of America's oldest and most widely read newspapers. It is often used by mainstream politicians (liberal and conservative) to support arguments, but it also gets condemned by those same politicians. Why do you think that happens?

5. In most of its thirty-nine presidential election endorsements, the *Times* backed the winning candidate. That wasn't the case in 2016. What do you think happened? What forces or factors were most influential?

IDEAS FOR WRITING

1. Find another written endorsement of a political candidate. (Nearly every major U.S. newspaper endorses candidates and ballot issues.)

2. The Supreme Court, the White House, and Congress (all three branches of government) store and chronicle famous opinions and speeches. Search the websites of these institutions to find a text. (And make sure that you are, indeed, at a government site, which should end in *gov*.)

INVENTION

In some ways, analyzing a written text is relatively easy because the elements are literally printed or posted in black and white. However, written texts have many elements, not just words but layers of implication and suggestion. There are subtleties lurking between, beneath, and around the text itself. No matter what you are analyzing—a blog, magazine article, journal article, or even a book—the process involves a sizable set of questions.

Point of Contact

Your target text can be any written published document. We suggest that you choose something easily accessible—a text that you can review often or even annotate as you read. Consider one of the following options for your analysis. And for more information on each category, see pages 442–445 in Chapter 15:

- Journal Articles: Journals are written for scholars in a specific academic field such as history, linguistics, rhetoric, engineering, nursing, or chemistry. The information is specialized—sometimes so highly specialized that following the logic proves difficult to those outside of the field. Still, not all journal articles require years of study or expertise. In fact, finding a journal related to your chosen field may generate good analytical focus. If you are studying psychology, for instance, you might find an interesting article in *Psychology Quarterly*.

- Magazine Articles: Magazines are aimed at general audiences rather than scholars in a specific discipline. The information is presented so that nonspecialized readers can easily follow the ideas and consider the claims. You might think of magazines in two—very broad—categories: the widest possible readership and special interest. The first category usually provides highly accessible articles. They are brief (less than 500 words), accompanied by photos, and come to quick conclusions. Some titles include *Better Homes and Gardens, Cosmopolitan, Men's Health, Sports Illustrated, Women's Day*. The second category offers more in-depth reporting, longer analyses, and even personal essays written by specialists in a field. Titles include *The Economist, Forbes, National Geographic, Orion, Scientific American*.

- Books: An entire book could serve as a target text—especially if the book makes a single and coherent argument or stays focused on a particular event. The upside of taking on a book is the sheer amount of material. There is plenty to consider. However, the amount of text could also pose a challenge. If you are dealing with hundreds of pages, you might find it difficult to narrow down the main idea—the thesis, the supporting premises, or even the purpose.

- Speech Transcripts: Speeches have a unique rhetorical dimension. They were delivered on a particular date, for a particular occasion, to a particular audience. And even if they are centuries old, they echo the occasion. A written transcript of nearly any formal speech can be found on the Internet. Consider historic speeches such as Abraham Lincoln's Gettysburg Address or a more recent State of the Union address. (See the analysis of David Foster Wallace's commencement speech in this chapter.)

- Websites: Websites are as varied as books. They can be immense—with a huge range of contributors, individual articles, and even kinds of text. For instance, CNN's website contains news articles, government reports, blogs, and editorials. Taking on an entire website could prove challenging. We suggest narrowing your focus to a specific article or blog post. With a narrower focus, you will find it easier to trace textual elements— a coherent writer's voice, a thesis or main claim, consistent rhetorical tools, and so on.

Analysis

Textual analysis requires that we look at the whole and find smaller elements within it. And while written texts have a huge range of potential elements, the following steps are crucial for sound analysis:

Analyzing Purpose Textual analysis requires that we understand what a text is trying to accomplish. In other words, we should try to understand the purpose of the text—what it attempts to do for or to readers. Is it out to change minds, promote a service, argue for institutional change, celebrate a public figure, defend a policy, or something else? If we can determine the specific purpose, other elements come into focus. But if we misinterpret the purpose, we might get all kinds of things wrong. Consider, for instance, what happens when you misinterpret the purpose of an e-mail or text. Imagine that a friend texts you to suggest a meeting place and time. You interpret the text as an agreement rather than a suggestion. You show up but she doesn't because her purpose was to start a conversation about, rather than to confirm, the meeting place.

John Mauk

DavidPinoPhotography/Shutterstock.com

There are several long-standing ways to categorize purpose. One classic approach makes three divisions: to inform, to persuade, to entertain. According to this classic view, any given rhetorical act (such as a speech, text, report) seeks to inform, persuade, or entertain an audience. Although these categories are somewhat helpful, they only get us so far. For instance, we can understand only so much if we say that a report is *informative*. There are more specific purposes that we can sense if we focus on how information is presented. The report might be warning its readers, historicizing an issue, connecting ideas that seem otherwise disconnected, filling in intellectual gaps, and so on. If we understand *a more specific purpose,* we will have a better understanding of the text—and be in a better position to explain other elements.

Broad Purpose: to inform.

Specific Purposes: to amend, to explain, to expose, to historicize, to warn, etc.

The same goes with argumentative or persuasive texts. We might decide that an article is trying to persuade its readers, but persuasion is a broad category. If we can sense something more specific, we will understand the text better. We also stand a better chance of sensing the claims and rhetorical tools used throughout.

Broad Purpose: to persuade.

Specific Purposes: to accuse, to calm, to condemn, to celebrate, to correct, to counter, to defend, to dismiss, to incite, to justify, to overturn, to praise, to provoke, to rally, to silence, to solve, etc.

Although this brief list may seem somewhat repetitive, each term—*each potential purpose*—has some important function and unique quality. Imagine the difference between two widely read articles on an international news site. Article A condemns a school loan policy. Article B counters that policy. The first expresses a harsh judgment; the second explains the logic of a competing policy. These are two very different articles that would likely have different kinds of rhetorical tools.

And to make matters more complicated, written texts often have more than one purpose. They try, for instance, to predict and solve, to amend and historicize, to defend and calm. In fact, any combination you can imagine has likely been at the heart of more than one article, essay, or blog written in the past month alone! A good analysis attempts to recognize and describe that combination.

ACTIVITY

The essays in this book have been categorized, in part, according to rhetorical purpose. Essays in Chapter 2, for instance, primarily *remember* a key experience from the past; those in Chapter 4 *analyze* a concept; those in Chapter 9 *evaluate* a place or thing. But there are two problems with our categories: (1) They are a bit too broad, and (2) they suggest that each essay has a singular purpose. Choose any essay in Chapter 2 through 13. Read the essay closely and then describe the purpose as narrowly and accurately as possible. Consider the possibility that the essay may, in fact, be more specific than the chapter title suggests and that it may have a dual or multifaceted purpose.

Analyzing the Thesis/Main Idea It may come as no surprise that academic essays are not the only written texts with thesis statements. Articles, editorials, and reports of all kinds usually have a single insight that drives the content. And if we are doing textual analysis, we should try to understand that insight. From there, we can determine how all other elements come into play. Remember, however, that thesis statements are not always—or often—at the end of the first paragraph. (That conventional placement of the main idea works in scholastic writing, but in college, professional, and popular contexts, the main idea may come in the middle of a text, in the conclusion, or anywhere at all. It might also be implied—not stated directly but suggested by all the other elements.)

Analyzing Support/Rhetorical Tools You are likely familiar with a major aspect of rhetorical analysis—the elements that writers use to support their claims. If you have written an academic essay (and chances are that you have written a number of them!), you have worked to support and develop your ideas with common *rhetorical tools*. You have likely used allusions, narration, secondary sources, definitions, examples, and so on. For the analytical work in this chapter, you will identify and explain how other writers use them. The following list contains rhetorical tools from other chapters. Depending on the nature of your chosen text, some will be more relevant than others:

- **Allusions:** references to history, science, nature, news events, films, television shows, or literary texts (see pages 52 and 118)

- **Authorities/Outside Sources:** references to published sources (see page 148)

- **Definitions:** denotative (dictionary) or connotative (commonly agreed upon) meaning for words (see page 147)

- **Description:** focused and specific detail (see page 86)

- **Dialogue:** direct discussion between two or more people (see page 53)

- **Examples:** specific cases or illustrations of a phenomenon (see page 146)

- **Facts:** agreed-upon events or truths, or conclusions drawn from investigation (see page 255)

- **Figurative Language:** metaphors, similes, analogies, or any statement that changes the literal and denotative (dictionary) definition of words (see page 87)

- **Narration:** any form of storytelling (see page 51)

- **Personal Testimony/Anecdotes:** individual accounts or experiences usually in narrative form (see page 255)

- **Scenarios:** hypothetical or fictionalized accounts (see page 255)

- **Statistics:** information (often given as numerical value) collected through experimentation, surveys, polls, and research (see page 255)

And this list is only the beginning. There are other rhetorical tools to explore and identify, especially if you are analyzing an argumentative text—one that is evaluating, persuading, or taking a stand on an issue. In that case, be on the lookout for argumentative support strategies:

- **Appeal to Logic:** relates the argument to the audience's sense of reason, *or* creates a line of reasoning for the audience to follow.

- **Appeal to Emotion:** relates the argument to an emotional state, or it attempts to create a particular emotional state in the audience.

- **Appeal to Character:** relates the argument to a quality of the author/speaker.

- **Appeal to Need:** relates the argument to basic human needs (economic, physical, sexual, spiritual, familial, political, etc.).

- **Appeal to Value:** relates the argument to shared values (judgments about right/wrong, success, discipline, selflessness, moderation, honesty, chastity, modesty, self-expression, etc.).

Finally, argumentative texts have an additional layer: They engage opposing claims and positions directly. In fact, some argumentative texts devote significant passages to confronting the opposition. They engage what others have said about the issue at hand. Following are three common elements related to opposing or outside positions:

- **Counterargument:** anticipates and refutes claims or positions that oppose those being forwarded by the writer.

- **Concession:** acknowledges the value of others' claims.
- **Qualifier:** acknowledges the limitations of, or makes clear boundaries for, the writer's own argument.

ACTIVITY

Read April Pedersen's article, "The Dog Delusion," in Chapter 8: Making Arguments. In small groups, try to identify rhetorical tools from the preceding list. Seek out support strategies (such as allusions, personal testimony, and examples), as well as argumentative elements such as appeals, counterarguments, concessions, and qualifiers.

Analyzing Organization The arrangement of all these elements also matters. As you are well aware, writers consider all the ramifications of introductions, conclusions, and everything in between. A text might build from the broadest to the most specific point. It might begin with narration and then return to it in the final sentences. It might clump all counterarguments together or counter only in the conclusion. Each organizational strategy can impact the overall effect of the text. Imagine the difference between an article that starts with personal testimony and one that begins with a string of statistics. The two strategies would impact audiences differently and may also create different voices. A sound textual analysis explains how the order of elements plays into the overall development of the text.

Analyzing Voice and Vitality Voice is the presence of the writer in the text—more specifically, the character or tonality of that writer. We're not talking about the real human who is off somewhere in the world (or in history) but the identity that is lurking within the elements of the text itself. As we explain in Chapter 1 and Chapter 18 all texts—even the most formulaic—have voice. From the thesis to its placement, from figurative language to popular allusions, everything that happens in a text shapes the way a writer sounds. For example, imagine an article that begins with an allusion to punk rock, specifically to the Sex Pistols, and how that article might differ from one that begins with an allusion to Beethoven. Of course, these are extreme differences, but they show how one single element can impact the overall feel of a text—and the way the author sounds in the readers' thinking.

Analyzing Context Translated directly, context means *with text*. In other words, context involves all the cultural, human, and physical stuff around the text itself—all the forces that motivated the writer, influenced the claims, and even shaped the nature of the audience. If we want to understand a text, we must examine the context and its constituent parts:

- **Publication:** the journal, magazine, or website that first brought the text into public view. Focusing on the publication can tell us a great deal about text—primarily the kind of audience the writer expected to reach.

- **Intended Audience:** the type of readers most likely to read the text. An analysis of the intended audience includes some basic demographic factors such as age, gender, sex, race, socioeconomic class, political affiliations, religion, even geographical location. Once we narrow in on these factors, we can develop an understanding of the audience's values and assumptions. For example, if we are analyzing a declaration from Black Lives Matter published in a popular magazine such as *The Nation,* we can quickly draw some conclusions about the intended audience's values—that the readership supports policies that yield greater forms of social justice, especially for African Americans. If we know that, we can understand why the declaration may not spend lengthy passages trying to convince the audience of that value.

- **Exigence:** the specific provocation for the text. Exigence is a Greek term that usually translates as *crisis.* For example, a major winter storm, a government shutdown, and a breakdown in peace negotiations are public exigencies that may provoke a range of articles, reports, and blogs. But exigence can also be thought of as an issue or occasion. A parade, a commemoration, a solar eclipse, or an uptick in employment might spur writers into action. If we can discern the exigence driving a text, we might better understand its claims, appeals, allusions, and examples.

- **Cultural Context:** the prevailing values and beliefs that shape everyday life around the text. Writers and readers belong to communities, cultures, and civilizations. They live within a huge network of events: political upheavals, entertainment trends, national tragedies, weather patterns, and so on. And public texts shimmer with all that collective activity. From direct references to subtle traces, a text includes elements of the culture around it. A good analysis includes those traces.

Analyzing Intertextuality Texts often speak back to or depend on other texts to make meaning. They exist in dialogue with other written works. This dialogue is called *intertextuality.* For example, the signs shown in Figure 6.1 make meaning, and humor, by echoing or referencing some other statement.

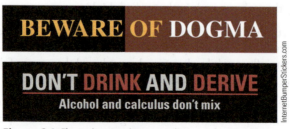

Figure 6.1 These signs use intertextuality to make meaning.

Figure 6.2 "Got faith" ad campaign

Although each sticker makes some sense alone, they all have more meaning if we know the references—if we know, for instance, the old saying about making lemonade when life hands you a lemon. We (as readers) participate in the meaning-making process. We bring our prior knowledge forward and create a compound text—a kind of chemical reaction (at least in our thinking) that's ignited by the two statements: one directly in front of us and one swirling around in our prior experience. In recent years, advisers have picked up on this intertextual strategy. Consider the "Got Faith" ad campaign, Figure 6.2, which echoes the famous "Got Milk" ads that came several years before. In this way, intertextuality adds layers of meaning to any text. When designers and advertisers make a text speak to other familiar texts, they tap into the public domain.

Analyzing Subtext If people have ever told you to "read between the lines," they were hoping you would sense a layer of implied ideas—those suggested but not directly stated or written. This layer of implication is sometimes called *subtext*—meaning that it is under (sub) the more visible and obvious layers. Subtext might also be thought of as a collection of assumptions and hidden values, messages that are not obvious but are present nonetheless. For example, when someone asks what you do for a living, the question involves more than your job. It involves issues of status, identity, economic situation, schedule, even personality. And if you offer a short answer ("I'm in marketing"), that answer has subtext. The same goes with a formal written text. Many of the claims, questions, and supporting statements have subtext. And a good analysis calls out that subtext.

ACTIVITY

Humor relies on subtext. We laugh at jokes because we know what's left unsaid. Laughter, in a sense, is the sound of us acknowledging what we understand but leave unexpressed. Consider, for instance, these fake state mottos. What ideas are implied in each statement?

Arizona: But It's a Dry Heat

California: As Seen on TV

Colorado: If You Don't Ski, Don't Bother

Florida: Ask Us about Our Grandkids

Indiana: 2 Billion Years Tidal Wave Free

Finally, it is important to approach your target text with a sense of discovery. Although this chapter has listed a number of important elements, your target text probably contains other crucial and interesting layers—elements that we have not considered, named, or even imagined. Perhaps your target text relies on a particular term or concept known only among a small group of readers. Or maybe your text repeats a certain phrase that helps to create a logical rhythm over the course of its argument. Or maybe it makes some elaborate move such as shifting voice to accommodate a shift in focus. The possibilities are unlimited. Anything can happen—especially if we're attentive to subtlety. Use the following Invention Questions to begin analyzing your target text:

> What is the specific purpose?
> What is the thesis—the single insight that drives the content?
> What specific rhetorical tools support the thesis?
> How does the text appeal to readers?
> How does the text engage opposing positions or claims?
> How does the organization influence the development of ideas?
> How does the writer's voice show up in the text?
> How do the contextual elements (publication, intended audience, exigence, or cultural context) figure into the text itself?
> How might the text echo or quietly reference another text to make meaning?
> What is the subtext? What implications are made?
> What other unique elements operate in the text? How do they intensify the ideas, support the thesis, or develop some other element?

Thinking Further

Although textual analysis involves identifying and explaining rhetorical elements, the goal is always discovery—to develop a better and richer understanding of the text itself. Successful analyses reveal some pattern, connection, or subtle layer of the target text that might otherwise be missed. And one of the most direct ways to make such a discovery is to combine elements—to ask how different elements work together, influence one another, or intersect in some way. The following Invention Questions can get you started:

> How does the context impact or shape the purpose?
> How might the context shape the subtext?
> How might opposing opinions show up quietly in the subtext?
> How does the intended audience impact the organization or voice?
> How might the audience shape the nature of the support strategies used throughout?
> What patterns or repeating elements do you detect, and how might they impact other elements?

In her invention writing, Adrienne Carr makes some important discoveries about her chosen text (a commencement speech by David Foster Wallace). In the following excerpts, you can see how Carr begins developing an idea about Wallace's voice. In the first passage, she senses a complexity in the voice. In the second passage, she follows up with the idea:

How does the writer's voice show up in the text?

Wallace begins by admitting that he'll perspire through the event. This calls attention to his own anxiety, his own effort. He is, from the start, establishing a presence, a character that is aware of the situation and maybe even humbled by it. He is not aloof or nonchalant. On the other hand, he openly condemns or dismisses the whole commencement genre and its "bullshitty" qualities. So Wallace's voice is complex. It's earnest and dismissive—hopeful and gruff. In a sense, there are at least two tones or notes at work.

How does the intended audience impact the organization or voice?

Most of that argument involves detailed scenarios—driving home from work, going to the grocery store, and so on. In or between these scenarios, Wallace consistently stops and draws attention to his own argument. These moments always involve some correction for his audience: *Don't think I'm doing this; please don't believe that I'm saying that.* It's as though Wallace is trying to get out in front of his audience's biases—as if he's imagining their worst prejudices and trying to fix them so that they can follow his next point. These correctional rest stops make up much of the speech. There are at least eleven passages (depending on how you count) in which Wallace addresses and tries to tweak his audience's assumptions. And it's these passages where Wallace is most earnest or at least most present. It's where we see him building up to his most intense and difficult points. The longer and more involved the rest stop, the more complex and taxing the point that follows. Wallace's voice works almost like a huddle between him and the audience—where he gets to call "time-out," gather his listeners, and make sure that everyone is with him.

Good invention writing often works in this fashion: The writer senses some quality, question, or even a kind of trouble—something that doesn't sit easily or fit into a simple category. If the writer is attentive, she keeps working with that quality. As in Carr's case, she might even discover something crucial.

Thesis

Remember that this project is about your target text and the way it works. As the previous section suggests, there are many elements and, therefore, many ideas that you can develop about the text. You can write about any, all, or some combination of the elements you have discovered, and so it helps to develop a main point, an analytical thesis that can anchor your ideas. Consider the following sample thesis statements—how they might anchor a textual analysis.

Statements that focus on one key element:

- In her article about animal rights, Marlow Henderson uses stark detail to reveal the traumatic life of stray dogs in the Detroit area.

- In his editorial "Making the Grade," Gary Mueller supports his claims primarily with statistical evidence, but the whole argument depends upon his unstated belief that students can make the right choices.

- Rosa Delmonico's article "Having It All" methodically counters a series of mainstream assumptions about successful women.

Statements that highlight the interaction of several elements:

- Chloe Holloway's "Race and Pet Patterns" relies exclusively on personal testimony to suggest—but not state directly—big questions about the gulf between white and black America.

- The subtext of Michael Krug's blog post depends on the audience's familiarity with the income tax laws.

- In his book chapter "Late Night Feeding Frenzies," Khalil Khan uses cultural context to show how food choices are tied to historical variables.

These samples are only the beginning of what's possible. So much depends upon the nature of the target text, the specific elements, and your own understanding—your take on what's most significant. For instance, consider the statement about Holloway's "Race and Pet Patterns." While one writer might see unstated "big questions" as the most significant element in the article, another might focus more on the function of Holloway's voice and how it softly manages a difficult political issue.

COMMON THESIS PROBLEMS

As we explain in the Rhetorical Tools section, textual analysis comes with some unique problems or *pitfalls*. The two most frequent pitfalls are summary and evaluation. In other words, writers often get caught up in summarizing too much or evaluating the target text. But there are also some more subtle traps that can settle into your project early on—even when you're developing a working thesis statement. See "Four Common Pitfalls" (pages 183–185).

Evolution of a Thesis

A focused thesis seldom, if ever, falls from the sky or congeals instantly in our brains. Thesis statements develop over time. They become more intensive, more concentrated, as writers work through ideas. For Adrienne Carr, the thesis started with an interest in David Foster Wallace's voice. Notice how the following statements evolve. The first acknowledges a distinct quality about the voice. The second explains how that quality works within the text—how it functions throughout the speech. The third and fourth refine the idea with narrower terms (*manage* rather than *address*, *default setting* rather than *assumptions*).

- Wallace's voice is complex. It's earnest and dismissive—hopeful and gruff. In a sense, there are at least two tones at work.

- Throughout his speech, Wallace steps out of one voice and into another, which allows him to address his audience directly.

- The most distinct element through the speech is Wallace's strategic management of his audience's assumptions.

- Wallace strategically manages his audience's default setting—the graduates' suspicions and reflexes in that very moment.

Notice, too, that the last two statements get more focused: "manages" is more focused than "address," and "default setting" is more focused than "assumptions." Each statement gets more narrow and, therefore, more revealing about the target text.

Of course, it doesn't always work like this. Thesis statements morph in any number of ways. For Carr, the voice issue, which she discovered early in her invention work, carried over to other issues and other questions. She saw a distinct quality, explained how that quality interacted with another element (the audience), refined the nature of that interaction, and then connected it to the text as a whole. The thesis, then, shows up toward the end of Carr's analysis:

> Wallace's speech is about the invisible stuff all around and within us—the stuff that flows through people's proverbial gills and makes us breathe, think, and swim in particular ways. And what's most interesting is his own desperate strategy to manage his audience's default setting—the graduates' suspicions and reflexes in that very moment.

Rhetorical Tools

This may sound redundant, but textual analysis is mostly about the text. That means most of your writing will stay focused on specific elements of your target text. Only rarely should you venture away from it and describe some other issue or source.

Identifying and Explaining Textual Elements A good textual analysis identifies the text's elements and explains how they work—for instance, how they support the thesis, how they reinforce the purpose, how they correspond to the intended audience and so on. In the following passage, Carr identifies the context of Wallace's speech and explains how it works. She doesn't simply point out the element. She explains how it functions, how it figures into the purpose and main idea:

> The context of the address is key. Wallace is delivering a commencement for one of the nation's top liberal arts colleges, so his audience is postured to launch into the privilege awaiting those from an esteemed institution. But Wallace does not condemn that privilege. He is not out to hammer his audience about class issues. He is up to something else. He uses the grand occasion to highlight the opposite: the uninteresting, uncelebrated, and most forgettable moments of everyday life. And he argues that these moments, the boring and unsexy ones, provide an opportunity to apply the skills learned from a college like Kenyon.

These two moves are critical for rhetorical analysis: *identifying an element and explaining its function*. In fact, the most successful analyses develop insights from the second move. As they come to understand the function of all the elements, they discover something about the inner workings of the text. As Carr's analysis develops, she discovers an important connection among the elements in Wallace's speech: the details of the scenario and the overarching organization. In the following passage, she explains this connection:

> The level of detail forces Wallace's point: there is no escaping everyday life—no way to diffuse the ongoing, nonstop labor of getting through the week. And the detail in this early passage sets Wallace up for more scenarios later in the address, where he dramatizes the shift out of default setting, where he explains, for instance, that people—especially those who are supposedly educated—can shift into a better mindset, one that recognizes others' struggles, others' absolute agony in getting through the day. His early scenarios come from the solipsistic lens—the one that thinks only "about MY hungriness and MY fatigue and MY desire to just get home," while his latter scenarios project a human open to the world of others.

Focusing on Specifics As analysts get closer and closer to their texts, they begin to see the significance of individual sentences, phrases, and even word choices. Some of the most powerful insights, in fact, come from that close attention. In the following passage, Alison Block focuses on specific language in her target text. She discovers not only how that language functions but also how similar language shows up repeatedly:

> By referring to Russia as "a rivalrous nuclear power," the *Times* subtly reminds readers of Russia's dangerous potential, amplifying the importance of Clinton's efforts, even if they were ultimately not successful. This strategy appears throughout the article.

After this passage, Block gives more examples and explains how they relate to the purpose of the text:

> They [editors] begin by appealing to logic, listing a string of related facts—her legislative proposals—that emphasize her productivity in terms of public service. Then, they make a concession to Clinton's opponents. They admit to flaws within her proposals. But they qualify their own concession, pointing out that Clinton's success does not rest on her shoulders alone; it requires the cooperation of Republican lawmakers.

Finding Patterns A pattern is any meaningful repetition. The presence of a recurring element may help to show something about a text. Imagine, for instance, if a text had four paragraphs that began with a similar kind of concession:

> "My opponents believe, rightly, that . . ."

> "My opponents believe in a sound theory of . . ."

"My opponents accept a fine principle . . ."

"My opponents also cling to an important value system . . ."

Such a pattern would be hard to ignore. And it would likely figure heavily into the voice. At the least, it would determine how other argumentative elements function. But not all patterns are as easily identifiable. For example, in his commencement speech, David Foster Wallace consistently and directly grapples with his audience's expectations. And in her analysis, Carr discovers this recurring move and explains its significance:

> In these overt attempts to engage listeners, Wallace shows an open desperation. So many apologies and qualifiers reveal his estimation of his audience—their skepticism, their reflex toward boredom, their over-familiarity with institutional life, their unwillingness to take advice.

This is an important discovery for Carr. In fact, it is, in her own words, "the most interesting" quality to Wallace's speech:

> Wallace's speech is about the invisible stuff all around and within us—the stuff that flows through people's proverbial gills and makes us breathe, think, and swim in particular ways. And what's most interesting is his own desperate strategy to manage his audience's default setting—the graduates' suspicions and reflexes in that very moment.

Summarizing To understand how a text works (analysis), we must understand what it is saying (summary). The *how* depends upon the *what*. Usually, rhetorical analysis relies on an initial, brief summary. For instance, Carr begins her analysis with a brief (one-paragraph) summary of her target text. Such an introductory summary is a conventional and effective strategy. It allows writers and readers to get a good sense of the text. Without that initial basic understanding, analysis is nearly impossible.

And even after we summarize, when we enter analytical territory, we still need summary. Even when we're doing analysis, we need to summarize briefly. For instance, notice how the following passage relies on a brief summary (highlighted). In this case, summary and analysis are working together. The power of the analysis depends upon a close and accurate summary:

> The next point in her line of reasoning takes the majority of her essay. In fact, Paulin devotes the next eight paragraphs to the simple notion that normal everyday people, not the mean old media, are the agents of discrimination. She explains how a majority of respondents (79%) to two personal ads preferred to date a drug addict rather than an overweight person. She describes a university study in which men and women ranked "an obese person as the least desirable sexual partner" over those with mental or physical disabilities. And then Paulin moves methodically through everyday life, calling out people in charge of learning (teachers), medical care (doctors), and even growing up (parents).

Although summary is important to good analysis, it can also become a problem. It can over-shadow the analytical moves. If we are doing analysis (if analysis is the goal), then we must be careful to keep summary from taking over—from eclipsing our explanation of how the argument works. This can be a difficult path. Notice the differences among the following moves: summary, almost analysis, and analysis. In the first, the writer strictly summarizes. In the second, the writer identifies Paulin's appeal to value but then shifts into summary—merely restating Paulin's points rather than analyzing the appeal. And in the third, the writer genuinely analyzes Paulin's move:

Summary
In Paulin's seventh paragraph, she explains a Slim Fast advertisement that sends a sad message—that diet products are more important than one's children or family.

Almost Analysis
In Paulin's seventh paragraph, she appeals to value by describing a Slim Fast advertisement. In the advertisement, a woman announces that Slim Fast "is the best thing that ever happened to me." Paulin explains how sad it is that the woman did not put the product at least second to her child.

Analysis
In her seventh paragraph, she describes an advertisement for Slim Fast. She contrasts the ad's world (that celebrates thinness above all else) to a different world (that values family and sanity and health). This stark contrast establishes a kind of choice in readers: stay crazy or get smart; keep on accepting the unreasonable or start resisting it.

To accomplish genuine analysis, a writer has to both identify the element and then explain how it works. For instance, if we discover an appeal to value, we have to describe what values, what cherished ideals, the writer appeals to and how that drives the argument forward or how it supports the main claim.

Quoting Strategically Most textual analyses depend on quotation. The writer narrows in on specific words, phrases, and sentences to illustrate points and develop ideas. In this sense, quotation is a type of textual evidence; it is support from the target text. For example, consider Carr's analysis of David Foster Wallace. She gives several quotations from the text, which allow her to make the following claim:

> In these overt attempts to engage listeners, Wallace shows an open desperation. So many apologies and qualifiers reveal his estimation of the immediate audience—their skepticism, their reflex toward boredom, their over-familiarity with institutional life, their unwillingness to take advice. He seems to know that his audience might tune out at any second, that his most immediate listeners are resistant to advice, to lectures, to older people handing down edicts.

If Carr hadn't integrated Wallace's own words, her characterization would be groundless. After all, she is a drawing a conclusion about Wallace. To do so, she must rely heavily on his text. Wallace's words give credence to the way Carr understands his effort.

ACTIVITY

Chapter 5: Analyzing Concepts describes conceptual maps or graphic presentations of ideas (see page 151). Conceptual maps are often used to help writers understand abstract relationships—how ideas correspond, overlap, intersect, and so on. This practice can be especially helpful with textual analysis. Before you write a draft, make a graphic presentation of your chosen text. Use circles to categorize the text's rhetorical elements, arrows to show how the ideas develop from point to point, and other shapes to show opposing positions. You might even draw out the context—the values and assumptions swirling in the culture around the text.

Caution: Four Common Pitfalls

Rhetorical analysis comes with a few unique dangers—four pitfalls to avoid. This first pitfall is **evaluating the text**. In evaluation, we make and defend judgments about the worth of an argument. We condemn it, celebrate it, or explain that it's okay but not great. Analysis does none of that. It avoids judging the success, the worth, the soundness, or acceptability of the text. Analysis avoids taking a side for or against. In the first list that follows, the statements judge the worth of the target texts. They are evaluative statements. The second list makes analytical points:

Evaluative
Wallace does a good job of supporting his main idea.

Stanton's ideas are right on target.

Paulin convinces me that a change is definitely in order.

I don't accept these claims.

I am suspicious of Wallace's ideas because they seem ungrounded.

Analytical
Wallace relies on personal testimony to ground his most complex points.

Stanton echoes Jefferson's Declaration as a way to reinforce shared values.

Paulin develops an appeal to value with several paragraphs.

Wallace directly addresses his audience's assumptions about the situation.

Stanton appeals to emotion by connecting the power of the nationalism to the power of gender equality.

Now, let's look at the difference between evaluation and analysis in a full paragraph. In the first passage, the writer openly celebrates Wallace's speech. This passage is clearly evaluative because it judges the soundness of Wallace's points. The second passage (taken from Carr's analysis on page 158) is clearly analytical. It avoids judging Wallace's points and, instead, explains his rhetorical strategies:

Evaluative

Wallace's level of detail makes the speech successful. As he lays out the tedium and daily grind of getting to the grocery store, waiting in line, and battling one's way home, he creates a gripping scenario that a reader simply cannot ignore. The masterful scenario dramatizes the solipsistic life of the average person and makes readers, no matter who they are, ashamed to even imagine that life. And the scenarios that come later in the speech do the opposite: they create a vision of someone open to the world of others.

Analytical

The level of detail forces Wallace's point: there is no escaping everyday life—no way to diffuse the ongoing, non-stop labor of getting through the week. And the detail in this early passage sets Wallace up for more scenarios later in the speech, where he dramatizes the shift out of default setting, where he explains, for instance, that people—especially those who are supposedly educated—can, if they choose—shift into a better mindset, one that recognizes others' struggles, others' absolute agony in getting through the day. His early scenarios come from the solipsistic lens—the one that thinks only "about MY hungriness and MY fatigue and MY desire to just get home," while his latter scenarios project a human open to the world of others.

Second, some writers get lured inside the points of the text they are analyzing, and rather than remain outside of that text, on solid analytical ground, they begin **making a case**. In the first passage that follows, the writer further develops—makes a case for—Ann Marie Paulin's idea. It's as if the writer has suddenly been possessed by Paulin. In the second passage, we stay on solid analytical ground:

Making a Case

Paulin shows how the average citizen, who lives, works, browses the Internet, and watches television, accumulates a general bigotry about body shape. The normal response to fat people is one of disgust and condemnation. Even drug addicts are held in higher regard than someone over the recommended weight. Landlords, dates, teachers, even parents all share the belief that fat people are inherently unworthy.

Analyzing

Paulin shows how the average citizen, who lives, works, browses the Internet, and watches television, accumulates a general bigotry about body shape. She moves methodically through everyday life and calls out people in charge of housing (landlords), learning (teachers), and even growing up (parents). In each case, the bigotry is highlighted with surveys and testimony.

The third pitfall involves **describing the effect of the original argument**. In this situation, the writer describes how the argument (or a part of it) might affect an audience. This is not inherently wrong. After all, rhetorical analysis does involve an examination of the argument's impact on an intended audience. But this quickly gets dangerous whenever the original argument (the text being analyzed) is left behind and the focus shifts to imagined audience responses. After all, we don't know exactly how an audience will respond. We cannot assume that readers or viewers will automatically laugh, think, cry, or get angry. The following passage crosses into dangerous territory because it begins to move away from Paulin and emphasizes particular audience responses:

Readers feel Paulin's anger and desperation. They begin to understand the incredible unfairness surrounding the everyday lives of so many Americans. As they internalize the injustice, they understand exactly what drives Paulin's argument.

Again, we don't know for certain what readers feel or understand. But we do know how the text works; we know how it attempts to appeal to readers. And that is the safer analytical focus. In the following passage, we appropriately describe the relationship between Paulin's text and her readers:

> Paulin's argument appeals to readers' sense of fairness. After all, the statistics and anecdotes all show a civilization methodically discriminating against a group of people who have less power, less money, and less social mobility than their slimmer counterparts. She calls out the "harm," "insensitivity," the "virulently negative attitudes" that obese people encounter. And whenever a writer works so hard to report unfairness, she is usually—as in this case—nudging readers toward the opposite.

While the previous pitfall focuses too much on an imagined audience, the fourth pitfall involves **describing the author's intent**. This strategy is fraught with problems. Because we cannot genuinely know a writer, advertising agency, or movie director's thoughts, we must be careful not to conjure them based on one argument. In the following example, the writer leaves behind an analysis of the argument and begins imagining the interior life of the author (Paulin):

> Ann Marie Paulin was hoping to wake people up, to stop dieting, and to live a better and freer life. She didn't want people to suffer the way she has—or the way she did when she was younger. That's why she wrote the essay the way she did. She put her full force into it because she knew that's what it would take to make people listen.

Reflection

Textual analysis requires that we switch off a basic intellectual motor: skimming. When we zoom through a news website or take in a quick billboard advertisement, we skim and consume meaning as a whole. We usually don't break it down or ask hard questions. Instead, we glide over the surface and accept whatever it offers. Many of the texts we encounter in mainstream consumer culture have been written with this mind. The messages, brief reports, and ads are written to provoke an automatic feeling or thought. This chapter calls on you to stop skimming, to consider the textual particles and elements that might otherwise be missed. And now that you've written a text, try your hand at analyzing it as thoroughly as possible. In other words, try to analyze your own analysis!

1. Thesis: What is your single most compelling discovery about your chosen text? What single analytical statement do you make about it?

2. How do you go about breaking down your chosen text? What elements do you pull apart? What do you call them?

3. How do you deal with context? How does the publication or delivery of your chosen text figure in to your writing?

4. Do you explore intertextuality and/or subtext? How do they shape your understanding of the chosen text, and how far do you get into them?

5. How do you structure your analysis? What organizational strategies do you rely on? For instance, do you walk through your chosen text paragraph by paragraph? Do you handle rhetorical elements separately?

6. Consider your voice. Sometimes analysts adopt the tone—or just subtle echoes—of their chosen texts. (This is not necessarily bad. If anything, it shows a subtle intertextual play.) Did this happen to you? Explain any specific passages.

Revision

Genuine revision requires intellectual distance from the draft. Some writers create this distance by taking time between writing and revising sessions. They complete a draft, sleep on it, and return the next day. If your schedule won't allow a full night or day, you might—at the least—insert some other activity between writing and revising. The break will allow a fresh perspective. If you are able to work closely with other writers, in real-time or online, use the prompts and questions in the following section.

Peer Review

Underline your thesis or write it at the top of your essay so that reviewers will understand your focus as they read your draft. Then, exchange drafts with at least one other writer. Reviewers should use the following questions to guide a helpful response:

1. Based on the writer's summary, do you have a good sense of the text? If you can, explain the text in a brief passage.

2. Where could the writer get more specific about his or her chosen text? Check for general or vague phrases such as "appeals to readers" or "supports the thesis." If such statements are not followed up with specific descriptions, the writer can likely get more specific.

3. Has the writer fallen into any pitfalls? (See pages 183–185 for specific descriptions.) If so, point them out. Consider each separately:

   a. Evaluating (praising or condemning) the text

   b. Making a case for the text's argument or claims

   c. Describing the effect of the text on an intended audience

   d. Describing the author's intent rather than the text itself

4. Consider the writer's paragraphs. Are they coherent? Do they take on one rhetorical element and explain that element thoroughly? Point out any paragraphs that take on too much—that explain (or try to explain) too many rhetorical elements.

5. Underline any sentences or phrases that could be more readable and concise. (Hint: In textual analysis, sentences sometimes become long and cumbersome because the writer is trying to manage her own language *and* that of the text in question. Watch out for especially lengthy sentences. If you have a hard time following the logic, suggest strategies for shortening and vitalizing.)

6. Finally, check for some important conventions of textual analysis:

   a. Make sure the writer is using present tense to discuss the text (unless the writer is discussing the delivery of a speech).

   b. Make sure the writer uses "quotation marks" for direct statements, phrases, and words taken from the chosen text.

   c. Make sure the writer has explained where the chosen text was delivered or published.

Beyond the Essay

As we explain earlier in this chapter (page 175), subtext is a collection of assumptions and unstated messages that operate between the lines of a text. And every text has this layer: To some degree, your chosen text (the one that you analyzed) relies on readers to make some connections, to fill in some intellectual gaps, to understand the value of some concept, and apply it to the situation at hand. In other words, texts don't say everything required of readers. Readers do much of the work. For example, consider the messages in the following passage from Ann Marie Paulin's essay (page 230):

> At the least, given the reports and studies, we can conclude that weight prejudice is not merely aesthetic judgment. It's an alarming trend, just like obesity itself, that hurts real people. When people are denied a place to live or a means of support not because of any bad behavior or lack of character or talent on their part but because of someone else's wrongheaded notions, then we need to get our minds straightened out.

Such a passage implies, but does not state, ideas such as: *Prejudice is bad. Aesthetic judgments are easier to dismiss than other forms of judgment. People should not be denied basic rights. People internalize what others think of them. Weight does not represent someone's character. Many people operate as though weight does represent character.* As readers, we pick up on these points. We formulate them and then use them to understand the nature of Paulin's argument.

Return to your chosen text and focus exclusively on all the things that are not said. This does not mean that you're looking for secret messages. It means you're looking for shared messages, ideas that are so widely accepted—or so finely stitched into the text—that they go unstated. After developing a list of those ideas, present them in some form other than a conventional essay. For example, chart them out in a conceptual map. If possible, clump the implied statements together according to topic. You can take this process a step further by listing other texts (articles, websites, novels, films, television programs) that are, somehow, related to each clump of statements. In other words, you might show the subtle intertextuality at work in the subtext!

7

Analyzing Images and Videos

Chapter Objectives

The sample essays and invention prompts in this chapter will help you to:

- Explain the rhetorical function of elements in an image or video.
- Explain the role of context, subtext, intertextuality, and genre conventions in an image or video.
- Develop an analytical essay that remains focused on the function and interplay of rhetorical elements in an image or video.

"At the speed of light, policies and political parties yield place to the charismatic images."

—**Marshall McLuhan**

INTRODUCTION

Mainstream life in the United States is saturated with images—not random pictures and photographs, but carefully selected images designed to " what we think and how we feel. Drawings, computer graphics, digitized photos, and airbrushed faces surround us. The minute details appeal to our values, desires, needs. They hook into and activate our assumptions and desires. Even after the image itself is gone, it still influences how we see the rest of the world.

There is no doubt about it: The barrage of images in our culture dramatically influences how we think, how we live, what we value, what we believe. But are we victims of everything we see? Is each advertisement, poster, graphic, and illustration another intellectual demand? Can we do more than see and accept? What value is gained from seeing inside the workings of images? Living in an image-soaked culture prompts such questions. Especially since most of the images we encounter were designed to influence our thinking, such questions may be vital.

As images in consumer society become increasingly sophisticated, consumers need to become more sophisticated seers. When we break down an image, we can better understand how it works, how it conveys meaning, how it conceals values and beliefs. And we can also better understand how that image relates to the world around it. In short, the more analytical we become, the more we see.

Figure 7.1 Window display at a GNC store

At first glance, images might seem silent, void of assertions. However, even the most simplistic image can speak. Just like a written text, images have rhetorical tools, strategies for persuading readers of some idea. For example, the advertisements in Figure 7.1 were displayed in the window of a health food store. The poster on the far left relies on the image of a young woman. She is sassy and vibrant. She asserts herself outward. The image connects the product and health with youth, vitality, and even a fashionable hairstyle and makeup. The poster on the right features a sunflower, a symbol of nature and purity. The sunflower, along with the promotion for a "new look," sits on a green background, which suggests newness and freshness. Such details are no accidents. They are closely scrutinized and designed to impact consciousness in particular ways. But even if they were accidents, the elements still impact readers.

As previous chapters explain, analysis is the act of breaking something down to its basic elements and coming to a better understanding of how that thing works. This chapter applies the analytical process to images and videos. The sample essays demonstrate a range of analytical strategies. First, Elizabeth Thoman examines how advertising images have worked in recent American history. Rebecca Hollingsworth focuses on the interplay of text and image. Nick Fendinger explains how an ad's voiceover interacts with specific visual elements. After reading the essays, you can find an image or video in one of two ways: (1) go to the Point of Contact section to explore your everyday life, or (2) choose one of the Ideas for Writing that follow the essays. After finding an image or video, go to the Analysis section to begin developing your ideas.

Rise of the Image Culture: Re-Imagining the American Dream

Elizabeth Thoman

Americans are so used to watching TV that they take the commercials for granted and don't consider the impact these images have on their lives. As Elizabeth Thoman, founder of *Media & Values* magazine, says, "Each commercial plays its part in selling an overall consumer lifestyle." Throughout her essay, Thoman explains how television commercials have become fused with the patterns and habits of everyday life and how that fusion might be staved off with a new critical awareness.

Like most middle-class children of the 50s, I grew up looking for the American Dream. In those days there were no cartoons in my Saturday viewing, but I distinctly remember watching, with some awe, *Industry on Parade*. I felt both pride and eager anticipation as I watched tail-finned cars rolling off assembly lines, massive dams taming mighty rivers and sleek chrome appliances making life more convenient for all.

When I heard the mellifluous voice of Ronald Reagan announce on *GE Theatre* that "Progress is our most important product," little did I realize that the big box in our living room was not just entertaining me. At a deeper level, it was stimulating an "image" in my head of how the world should work: that anything new was better than something old; that science and technology were the greatest of all human achievements and that in the near future—and certainly by the time I grew up—the power of technology would make it possible for everyone to live and work in a world free of war, poverty, drudgery, and ignorance.

I believed it because I could see it—right there on television.

The American Dream, however, was around long before television. Some believe the idea of "progress" goes back to when humankind first conceived of time as linear rather than cyclical. Certainly the Judeo-Christian heritage of a Messiah leading us to a Promised Land inspired millions to strive for a better world for generations to come.

Indeed, it was the search for the "City on the Hill" that brought the Puritans to the American colonies and two centuries later sent covered wagons across the prairies. In 1835, Alexis de Tocqueville observed that Americans "never stop thinking of the good things they have not got," creating a "restlessness in the midst of prosperity" that drives them ever onward.

Even the U.S. Constitution, remember, only promises the pursuit of happiness. It doesn't guarantee that any of us will actually achieve it.

It is this search for "something-more-than-what-we've-got-now" that is at the heart of the consumer culture we struggle with today. But the consumer culture as we know it could never have emerged without the invention of the camera and the eventual mass-production of media images it made possible.

REPRODUCING PICTURES

In 1859 Oliver Wendell Holmes described photography as the most remarkable achievement of his time because it allowed human beings to separate an experience or a texture or an emotion or a likeness from a particular time and place—and still remain real, visible, and permanent. He described it as a "conquest over matter" and predicted it would alter the physics of perception, changing forever the way people would see and understand the world around them. Holmes precisely observed that the emergence of this new technology marked the beginning of a time when the "image would become more important than the object itself and would in fact make the object disposable." Contemporary advertising critic Stuart Ewen describes the photographic process as "skinning" the world of its visible images, then marketing those images inexpensively to the public.

But successive waves of what might be called reality-freezing technology—first the photograph, followed by the phonograph and the motion picture camera—were only some of many 19th-century transformations that paved the way to our present image culture. As the wheels of industrialization began to mass-produce more and more consumer goods, they also increased the leisure time available to use these products and the disposable income required to buy them. Soon the well-being of the economy itself became dependent on an ever-expanding cornucopia of products, goods, and services. The Sears-Roebuck catalogue and the department store emerged to showcase America's new abundance and by the turn of the century, as media critic Todd Gitlin notes, "production, packaging, marketing, advertising, and sales became functionally inseparable." The flood of commercial images also served as a rough-and-ready consumer education course for the waves of immigrants to America's shores and the thousands of rural folk lured to the city by visions of wealth. Advertising was seen as a way of educating the masses "to the cycle of the marketplace and to the imperatives of factory work and mechanized labor"—teaching them "how to behave like human beings in the machine age," according to the Boston department store magnate Edward A. Filene. In a work world where skill meant less and less, obedience and appearance took on greater importance. In a city full of strangers, advertising offered instructions on how to dress, how to behave, how to *appear* to others in order to gain approval and avoid rejection.

Granted, the American "standard of living" brought an end to drudgery for some, but it demanded a price for all: consumerism. Divorced from craft standards, work became merely the means to acquire the money to buy the goods and lifestyle that supposedly signified social acceptance, respect, even prestige. "Ads spoke less and less about the quality of the products being sold," notes Stuart Ewen, "and more about the lives of the people being addressed."

In 1934, when the Federal Communications Commission approved advertising as the economic basis of the country's fledgling radio broadcasting system, the die was cast. Even though early broadcasters pledged to provide free time for educational programs, for coverage of religion, and for news (creating the famous phrase: the "public interest, convenience, and necessity"), it wasn't long before the industry realized that time was money—and every minute counted. Since free enterprise dictates that it's better to make money than to lose it, the American commercial broadcasting system was born. But it was not until the 1950s that the image culture came into full flower. The reason? Television.

Television was invented in the 1930s, but for many years no one thought it had any practical use. Everyone had a radio, even two or three, which brought news and sports and great entertainment right into your living room. And if you tired of the antics of *Fibber McGee and Molly* or the adventures of *Sergeant Preston of the Yukon,* you could always go to the movies, which was what most people did at least once a week.

So who needed television? No one, really. What needed television, in 1950, was the economy. The post-war economy needed television to deliver first to America—and then to the rest of the world—the vision, the image, of life in a consumer society. We didn't object because we thought it was, well, just "progress."

WHAT PRICE PROGRESS?

Kalle Lasn, a co-founder of the Canadian media criticism and environmentalist magazine *Adbusters,* explains how dependence on television first occurred and continues today each time we turn on our sets: "In the privacy of our living rooms we made a devil's bargain with the advertising industry: Give us an endless flow of free programs and we'll let you spend 12 minutes of every hour promoting consumption. For a long time, it seemed to work. The ads grated on our nerves but it was a small price to pay for 'free' television. . . . What we didn't realize when we made our pact with the advertisers was that their agenda would eventually become the heart and soul of television. We have allowed the most powerful communications tool ever invented to become the *command center of a consumer society* defining our lives and culture the way family, community and spiritual values once did."

This does not mean that when we see a new toilet paper commercial we're destined to rush down to the store to buy its new or improved brand. Most single commercials do not have such a direct impact. What happens instead is a cumulative effect. Each commercial plays its part in selling an overall *consumer lifestyle.* As advertising executive Stephen Garey noted in a recent issue of *Media & Values,* when an ad for toilet paper reaches us in combination with other TV commercials, magazine ads, radio spots, and billboards for detergents and designer jeans, new cars and cigarettes, and soft drinks and cereals and computers, the collective effect is that they all *teach us to buy.* And to feel somehow dissatisfied and inadequate unless we have the newest, the latest, the best.

Just like our relatives at the turn of the century, we learned quickly to yearn for "what we have not got" and to take our identities from what we own and purchase rather than from who we are or how we interact with others. Through consuming things, through buying more and more, we continue the quest for meaning which earlier generations sought in other ways—conquering the oceans, settling the land, building the modern society, even searching for transcendence through religious belief and action. With few places on earth left to conquer today, the one endless expanse of exploration open to us is the local shopping mall.

TRANSCENDING MATERIALISM

Thus the modern dilemma: While few of us would turn in our automatic washing machines for a scrub board or exchange our computers for a slide rule, neither can we expect the images of the past to provide the vision for the future. We must recognize the trade-offs we have made and take responsibility for the society we have created.

For many today, the myth of "progress" is stuttering to a stop. The economic slowdown of the early '90s presents only the most recent example of the human suffering created by the boom and bust cycles of the consumer economy. But even if some magic formula could make steady economic growth attainable, we can no longer afford it. Material limits have been set by the Earth itself. Unlimited exploitation in the name of "progress" is no longer sustainable.

True progress, in fact, would be toward a materially renewable lifestyle that would fulfill the physical, spiritual and emotional needs of all—not just some—of the world's people, while allowing them to live in peace and freedom. Under such a system, communication's most important aim would be to bring people together. Selling things would be a part of its function, but not the whole.

Disasters like Chernobyl and the Alaskan oil spill raise hard questions about the long-term social impact of technological innovation. In the U.S., the loss of whole communities to the ravages of drugs, crime, and homelessness threatens the very principles which allow any humane society to flourish.

At the same time, the global events of 1991—the breakup of the Soviet Empire, the struggles for national identity, even the rise of fundamentalist governments in many parts of the Third World—bear witness to a growing desire for meaningful connections as well as material and political progress.

In many ways we are living in a new world, and around that world hungry eyes are turning toward the Western democracies' longstanding promises of freedom and abundance—the promises the media has so tantalizingly presented.

Yet behind the media culture's constantly beckoning shop window lies an ever-widening gap. West or East, North or South, the flickering images of the media remain our window on the world, but they bear less and less relationship to the circumstances of our day-to-day lives. Reality has fallen out of sync with the pictures, but still the image culture continues.

We'll never stop living in a world of images. But we can recognize and deal with the image culture's actual state, which might be characterized as a kind of mid-life crisis—a crisis of identity. As with any such personal event, three responses are typical:

1. *Denial.* Hoping that a problem will go away if we ignore it is a natural response, but business as usual is no solution.

2. *Rejection.* Some critics believe they can use their television dials to make the image culture go away, and urge others to turn it off, too. But it's impossible to turn off an entire culture. Others check out emotionally by using drugs, alcohol, addictions of all kinds to vainly mask the hunger for meaning that comes when reality and images don't converge.

3. *Resistance.* A surprisingly active counterculture exists and is working hard to point out the dangers of over-reliance on the image culture. But such criticism is negative by its very nature, and critics tend to remain voices crying in the wilderness.

A positive alternative is needed. What I have called *media awareness*—the recognition of media's role in shaping our lives and molding our deepest thoughts and feelings—is an important step. The three steps I have outlined above provide simple but effective tools for beginning to work through this process. Although they seem basic, they have their roots in the profound state of being that Buddhism calls *mindfulness:* being aware, carefully examining, asking questions, being conscious.

Even a minimal effort to be conscious can make day-to-day media use more meaningful. Being conscious allows us to appreciate the pleasure of a new CD album and then later turn it off to read a bedtime story to a child. Being conscious means enjoying a TV sitcom while challenging the commercials that bait us to buy. Being conscious allows us to turn even weekend sports events into an intergenerational get-together.

But however achieved, media awareness is only a first step. Ultimately, any truly meaningful attempt to move beyond the image culture will recognize the spiritual and emotional emptiness that the material objects it sells cannot fill.

By convincing us that happiness lies at the other end of the cash register, our society has sold us a bill of goods. To move beyond the illusions of the image culture we must begin to grapple with some deeper questions: Where is the fine line between what I want and what all in society should have? What is the common good for all?

Or to rephrase Gandhi: "How do we create a society in which there is enough for everyone's need but not everyone's greed?"

Thousands of years ago a philosopher wrote of a cave of illusion in which captive humans were enraptured by a flood of images that appeared before them while they ignored the reality outside the cave. This prophetic metaphor contained its own solutions. Once again we are summoned into the light.

WRITING STRATEGIES

1. What is Thoman's thesis?

2. How does Thoman use history to develop the main idea? What other strategies does she use?

3. What connection does Thoman make between images and lifestyle?

4. How is Thoman's essay a call to action?

EXPLORING IDEAS

1. In ¶8, Thoman quotes Oliver Wendell Holmes as saying the "image would become more important than the object itself and would in fact make the object disposable." With others or alone, think of examples to support Holmes's point.

2. Interview others to find out how they think advertising influences them. Based on the interviews, to what degree would you say others have media awareness? (See ¶15.)

3. In her conclusion, Thoman references Plato's Allegory of the Cave. Read Plato's allegory, which can easily be found on the Internet. How does Plato's point about image and reality support Thoman's insight?

4. What is the difference between *advertising* and *education*?

IDEAS FOR WRITING

1. Explore the relationship between advertising images and the economy, education, family, health, or the environment.

2. Thoman says, "Most single commercials do not have such a direct impact. What happens instead is a cumulative effect" (¶15). Use a certain type of image to support or refute this theory.

If responding to one of these ideas, go to the Analysis section of this chapter to begin developing ideas for your essay.

An Imperfect Reality
Rebecca Hollingsworth

In the following essay, Rebecca Hollingsworth goes beyond the first glance and shows readers how an image (an autism-awareness magazine ad) interacts with and even relies on written text. Through analysis, Hollingsworth breaks down the particulars of an image and shows how the ad appeals to shared values and hopes.

Every day we hear more and more about developmental disorders that afflict children in the United States, disorders that have been misunderstood, downplayed, or ignored. With recent advances in child development and behavior studies, and, perhaps to a large extent, with the explosion of pop psychology personalities like Dr. Phil, Americans are paying more attention than ever to children's mental health. Of course, the general public isn't necessarily any more educated about developmental disorders than it was in the past, but experts and non-experts alike are now insisting that it's okay, even fashionable, to acknowledge and address the ways in which our children aren't "perfect."

> Allusions to pop culture help to place the ad in context.

One health epidemic at the forefront of public consciousness is autism, a brain disorder that impairs a person's ability to communicate, socialize, and participate in group behavior. Often surfacing by the time a child is three years old, the symptoms of autism include stifled speech and difficulty in displaying joy or affection. According to a 2012 study by the U.S. Centers for Disease Control and Prevention, about 1 in 150 American children are autistic—a staggering number that makes autism the fastest-growing developmental disorder in the United States. Since the release of these findings, nonprofit organizations across the country have been working to raise public awareness of this national health crisis. The largest of these organizations, Autism Speaks, recently launched a multimedia campaign aimed at parents of autistic, or potentially autistic, children.

> Another passage that explains cultural context—this narrowing to the specific issue in the ad.

The 2006 autism awareness campaign sponsored by Autism Speaks challenges common notions of the "perfect kid" by revealing how the reality of autism crushes unrealistic ideals of young American girls and boys. The campaign features a series of television, radio, online, magazine, and billboard advertisements that emphasize the prevalence of the disorder. The campaign's magazine ads show kids doing "kid things"—that is, playing dress-up for girls and playing

> This calls out the ad's rhetorical function: It challenges common notions.

Odds of a child becoming a top fashion designer: 1 in 7,000

Odds of a child being diagnosed with autism: 1 in 150

Some signs to look for:

No big smiles or other joyful expressions by 6 months. | No babbling by 12 months. | No words by 16 months.

To learn more of the signs of autism, visit autismspeaks.org

AUTISM SPEAKS®
It's time to listen.

Autism Speaks

Figure 7.2 Autism Speaks ad

sports for boys. In one ad (see Figure 7.2), a young girl adorns herself with brightly colored clothes and jewelry as proud mom looks on.

The girl wears a cropped, short-sleeved, light pink jacket unzipped to reveal a billowing fuchsia-and-black striped tie and matching fuchsia beaded necklace. She commands the attention of her mother and of us; she stands in a fashionable pose with one leg slightly bent as she looks down to tie a light pink belt around her waist. She towers above her mother, who sits in the lower-left corner of the ad, watching her daughter from the sidelines. The mother's gaze creates a direct line of vision to the young girl, drawing the viewer's eye to this fashionable focal point. Like mom, we look on as the young girl tries on one piece of clothing after another, suggested by the pink, white, and blue clothes draped over furniture in the background. The girl's jewelry—the chunky necklace and the dangly charm bracelet—and her sophisticated tie clash with her long, stringy pigtail braids and big white teddy bear in the background. The pink-and-white washed walls covered in a busy pastel pattern remind us that this is a child's room and that we are witnessing child's play.

The text of the ad jolts us into a reality that is discordant with the idealistic image. Bannered text across the bottom of the image

This passage explains how details function within the ad itself—how they generate and reinforce ideas.

reads, "Odds of a child becoming a top fashion designer: 1 in 7,000. Odds of a child being diagnosed with autism: 1 in 150." This startling statistic of the likelihood that this young girl—any young girl— is autistic turns our viewing experience upside down. As we watch the young girl over her mother's shoulder, we must confront the prevalence of this developmental disability in American children— and the very real possibility that our own child may be that 1 in 150.

<aside>This examines the relationship between image and text—how the two work together.</aside>

The text of the ad goes on to educate parents about the warning signs of autism: a child's inability to show joy by six months, to babble by twelve months, and to talk by sixteen months. And all this text, along with the sobering 1 in 150 statistic, fences us off from the image. In fact, the text separates us from the scene. It's behind the mother's shoulder, but in front of our eyes. We know something she doesn't. In classic dramatic irony, we see the looming, or probable, reality that neither child nor mother can imagine in the ideal bedroom.

<aside>This further examines the text/image relationship—how the layout itself functions.</aside>

The sponsor's logo (a puzzle piece in the shape of a child) and slogan ("Autism Speaks: It's time to listen") appeal to a parent's responsibility to pay attention to her child's behavior, to monitor each developmental step or lack thereof, to hope for the best, to fear the worst. And like all such ads—those that appeal to the complex tangle of parent responsibility and fear—the message begs many questions: Does autism really speak, or does it whisper? How will I know? Once I hear it, what do I do? How could autism affect my child's chances in the world? Is it curable? Is it deadly?

<aside>Dramatic irony: The audience understands something—a tension between reality and the ideal—that the characters do not.</aside>

<aside>The ad appeals to—or attempts to engage—specific emotions and thoughts in parents.</aside>

In this sense, the ad does what numerous other campaigns do: it scares us. But this one aims at a particularly vulnerable place: the intersection of our idealism and our fear. It contrasts deluded notions of success—defined here as becoming a top fashion designer—with a statistically harsh truth. We can no longer bask in the old *one in a million* cliché. Like the pretty imagery in the fictional bedroom, that number has been upstaged by a more demanding probability.

<aside>The conclusion gets more specific. It doesn't wrap up or get general but narrows in on the particular "intersection" of emotions.</aside>

Work Cited

United States, Department of Health and Human Services, Centers for Disease Control and Prevention. "Prevalence and Characteristics of Autism Spectrum Disorder Among Children Aged Eight Years: Autism and Developmental Disabilities Monitoring Network, Eleven Sites, United States, 2012." *MMWR Surveillance Summary*, vol. 65, no. SS-3, 1 Apr. 2016, www.cdc.gov/mmwr/volumes/65/ss/ss6503a1.htm.

WRITING STRATEGIES

1. According to Hollingsworth, what does the Autism Speaks advertisement encourage us to think?

2. Hollingsworth breaks the ad down into its basic elements. Which specific elements are most important to her analysis? How, according to Hollingsworth, do those elements work on the consciousness of readers?

3. In your own words, explain the relationship between image and text in the Autism Speaks ad.

4. Hollingsworth generally avoids first-person pronouns in her essay. When she uses them (such as in her opening sentence and in ¶5), she uses the plural *we* and *us* instead of the singular *I* and *me*. Why might Hollingsworth have decided to use the plural instead of the singular? What is the effect created when she does use the singular *I* in ¶7?

5. Study Hollingsworth's use of subjects and verbs. Choose two sentences in which the verbs are especially lively, and explain how they communicate an idea that is important to the main point.

EXPLORING IDEAS

1. Which additional detail of the image Hollingsworth could discuss? How would the additional detail strengthen her analysis?

2. Look up "dramatic irony" and explain Hollingsworth's statement, "In classic dramatic irony, we see the looming, or probable, reality that neither child nor mother can imagine in the bedroom." How is this irony important to Hollingsworth's main point?

3. With a group of peers, examine all the details of an ad, and then decide: What is the main idea of the ad? How does it encourage viewers to think or act? How do images help readers understand and accept the ad's main idea? How do text and image work together? Seek out and explain the importance of one hidden, or less obvious, detail.

4. How are you like an ad? What visual details have you created about yourself, and what main idea do you want these details to communicate?

IDEAS FOR WRITING

1. Hollingsworth says, "In this sense, the ad does what numerous other campaigns do: It scares us." Find a particular ad and explain how it scares us. What vulnerability does it take aim at? How does it strike fear? What does the ad achieve beyond scaring viewers?

2. Find an ad that you consider to be educational. How does the ad connect with readers beyond providing educational information? How does it get the readers' attention? How does it appeal to the readers' basic values or beliefs?

If responding to one of these ideas, go to the Analysis section of this chapter to begin developing ideas for your essay.

STUDENT ESSAY

Look on My Works: *Breaking Bad's* Final Season Trailer

Nick Fendinger

Many modern television programs rely on characters and themes from literature. In this essay, Nick Fendinger explains how an extended advertisement, or trailer, for the popular program *Breaking Bad* relies on a 19th-century poem. He explains how the two texts (a modern television ad and an old poem) converge into a unique form. As you read, keep track of the different names and voices: the 19th-century poet Percy Bysshe Shelley; Ozymandias, the poem's emperor; Bryan Cranston, the modern actor; Walter White, Cranston's *Breaking Bad* character; Heisenberg, White's pseudonym.

In 1818, Percy Bysshe Shelley composed "Ozymandias," a poem about a fallen emperor and the fleeting nature of his accomplishments. Now nearly two hundred years old, "Ozymandias" has been adapted to proclaim the demise of yet another emperor: Walter White. Prior to the release of the final episodes of *Breaking Bad*, AMC (the company which co-produced *Breaking Bad*) published a trailer in which actor Bryan Cranston recites the nineteenth century poem over a montage of stop motion shots depicting landmarks of the show and the deserts of Albuquerque, New Mexico. Cranston, speaking in the persona of Walter White, then acts as the prophet of his own demise. The poem takes on new meaning as it suggests the eventual fall of White's drug empire which had been built in the prior four seasons of the series. As Cranston recites the lines, the trailer becomes a prophecy of destruction: the legendary crystal meth "cook" Heisenberg is doomed.

   The opening scenes instill a sense of dread. Barbed wire fences, towering telephone wires, and a lone tree are all shown in a desolate landscape most commonly associated with death: the desert. The bleak visual introduction establishes an ominous mood that is reinforced throughout the trailer. These initial scenes are void of human life. Not a single character is shown. But over the lifeless terrain comes the gravelly voice of Walter White, Albuquerque's public enemy number one. By withholding the genre expectation of depicting the show's main character and instead featuring a lone voice in the desert, the trailer cultivates an aura of mystique, a mystery that temporarily disguises what should be expected. It also merges the past (the nineteenth century poem) with the present (a twenty-first century television antihero).

   As with any trailer, the one for *Breaking Bad* provides a lens for understanding the coming season and perhaps the whole series. The lens is proposed in the first two lines of the poem as the narrator adopts the voice of "a traveler from an antique land." The whole series, then, adopts an ancient persona. The tale of Walter White becomes timeless, even exotic and mythical. By adopting a nineteenth century poem as its voice, the trailer, and thus the series, emphasizes the persistence of its themes through time. It suggests that Walter White is playing the role of Ozymandias, that the series' antihero is more akin to a mythical emperor whose scale and potency are biblical in proportion as he declares himself, in the voice of Shelley's exotic traveler, a "King of Kings."

Following the chilling introduction, the trailer's visual scenes progress randomly. Each image does not logically demand the next. Rather, the scenes are organized to provide an emotional climax. For example, at around the thirty second mark, a shot depicting a barbed wire fence is shown immediately prior to Walter White's residence, which suggests the iron grip that Walter's business has on his family. As the trailer progresses, each scene becomes faster paced, including rapid motion traffic. In contrast, the opening scenes feature languidly floating clouds. The disparity of pace creates a visual climax; like an opera, the tempo continuously rises until a monumental crash completes the crescendo. Rhetorically speaking, the climax fosters an urge to tune in and alleviate the dramatic pressure built through rapidly progressing images.

The pace is reinforced by the recitation of "Ozymandias." The lines of the poem, in harmony with the visual scenes, accelerate the momentum. In other words, the poem acts as a rhetorical engine driving the story. After all, without Walter White's iconic voice and the narrative of Ozymandias, the story within the images would not be an advertisement; the images alone would lack the necessary context provided by the voice of one of TV's most infamous antiheroes. The poem, then, establishes scenes like the one depicting the hat of Walter White (55 second mark) as symbolic landmarks. The hat is no longer just a drug lord's trademark fashion statement, it is now the "colossal Wreck" of Shelley's poem, some "shattered visage" sunk in desert sands. By working in harmony, the poem and the visual scenes construct a storyline in which the hat serves as a resolution. The story, while incomplete, stimulates interest and a desire to fill the holes in the coming season—for example, how the modern empire, like the ancient one, will crumble to ruins.

Apart from connecting the visual scenes into a flowing story, the poem's early nineteenth century language clashes with the salient themes of *Breaking Bad*. After all, an early nineteenth century sonnet may—especially in the instance of a drug lord whose partner's quintessential phrase is "Yeah, bitch!"—seem overly proper for this particular trailer; in fact, it may be seen as the fashion equivalent of wearing a tuxedo to dine in McDonald's. But the contrasting tones increase the emotional gravity of the show. The narrative is no longer about a chemistry teacher who happens to be a novice meth dealer; instead, it is about a meth *emperor* willing to extinguish all human life that obstructs his path. The increased gravity even heightens the intellectual merit of the show and makes it stand out from hundreds of other contemporary dramas.

Another device implemented to increase the intensity is the brief pause just before the final scene. After the trailer reaches its emotional peak, with the images travelling at their quickest pace and Cranston proclaiming the stirring line "Look on my Works, ye Mighty, and despair," there is a cut to black. The cut emphasizes the scene that follows: a "boundless and bare" landscape is now embedded with the accumulated tension of all prior scenes. In other words, the brief pause acts as a rhetorical floodgate, storing the waters of emotion only to let them burst forth in a crescendo signaled by Cranston describing the "colossal Wreck" coupled with the image of his hat. The final seconds are a crucial dramatic blow.

The "Ozymandias" trailer for *Breaking Bad* relies on intertextuality. Two works converge and create a dynamic conversation between the past and the present. One text works with the other; both get changed in the process. The modern ghastly plot of *Breaking Bad* gets some historical (even educational) ambience from the classic poem. Intertextuality acts not merely as a savvy literary device, it enhances the intellectual merit of a modern television drama.

Works Cited

AMC. "Ozymandias – As Read by Bryan Cranston: Breaking Bad." *YouTube*, 29 July 2013, youtu.be/T3dpghfRBHE.

Mikics, David. "A Poem to Outlast Empires." *Poetry Foundation*, www.poetryfoundation.org/learning/guide/238972. Accessed 27 Oct. 2017.

Shelley, Percy Bysshe. "Ozymandias." *The Complete Poetical Works of Percy Bysshe Shelley*, edited by Thomas Hutchinson, vol. 2, Oxford UP, 1914, pp. 546–49. *Gleeditions*, 17 Apr. 2011, gleeditions.com/ozymandias/students/pages.asp?pg=4.

WRITING STRATEGIES

1. What is Fendinger's thesis?

2. Explain how *pacing* is crucial to Fendinger's analysis.

3. In your own words, how is the *Breaking Bad* trailer *intertextual*?

4. Explain how Fendinger uses quotations from the Shelley poem to help develop his analysis.

5. What does Fendinger do in his concluding paragraph? (Hint: He does more than summarize or wrap up his essay!)

EXPLORING IDEAS

1. Try to find the *Breaking Bad* trailer on the Internet. What details, beyond those Fendinger explains, suggest forthcoming doom in the television show?

2. Consider your favorite television program or film. How does it rely on or borrow from some other text—for instance, an old storyline about vampires, ghosts, heroes, criminals, or crime fighters?

3. Commercials (both still images and videos) are often intertextual: They borrow from other commercials to make their assertions or humor. Find a commercial on the internet and explain its *intertextuality*.

4. Fendinger points to the trailer's "emotional peak." Return to the commercial you found (for the previous question). What is its emotional peak? What elements help to develop that peak?

5. In his third paragraph, Fendinger explains how the trailer—and the show itself—takes on an ancient persona. Consider your favorite program or film. What is its persona? How does that persona get developed and maintained from scene to scene or episode to episode?

IDEAS FOR WRITING

1. Find a video trailer for your favorite television program or film. How does the trailer establish expectations for the program or film itself? Like Fendinger, work slowly—frame by frame—through the video. Take no detail or element for granted.

2. Return to the second question in Exploring Ideas. Focus exclusively on the ways your favorite program or film borrows from some other text.

If responding to one of these ideas, go to the Analysis section of this chapter to begin developing ideas for your essay.

INVENTION

Most of the images and videos that constitute everyday life are meant to prompt an idea or emotion—not to be analyzed. (This, say many scholars, is all the more reason to analyze them.) In developing ideas for this project, we should work against what most images ask of us. We should examine how they work by breaking down the parts and then reassembling them. The following sections are designed to help you through this process, specifically, to find a particular an image or video (in Point of Contact), to examine its elements closely (in Analysis), to develop a focused point (in Thesis), and to develop support for that point (in Rhetorical Tools). The Invention Questions in each section are not meant to be answered directly in your final essay, but to prompt inventive thinking and intensive writing.

Point of Contact

Explore the following possibilities to find an image or video for your own analysis. Consider all the elements: the pictures, text, colors, placement, models, clothing, blank space, audience, and even the surrounding materials such as stories and columns.

Print Advertisements

Print ads range from dense collages of pictures and words to a single image with one slogan (see examples in Figure 7.3). Browse any magazine or newspaper. Also consider print advertisements that lurk in more inconspicuous places, such as your credit card bill, a public bathroom, a phone book, a calendar, and so on.

Volkswagen recycling

Advertising Archives

Mmm...Classic.

Advertising Archives

Figure 7.3 Print advertisements

David Pollack/Getty Images

Figure 7.4 A poster

Posters

Most often, posters work like billboards. They are designed to catch a passing eye—to shout loudly enough so that anyone in the vicinity will notice the message (see Figure 7.4).

Internet Images

Images found on the Internet range from shocking photos of war to wondrous shots of outer space. Consider sites such as Newsmap (newsmap.jp) or Buzztracker.org in which stories of the world are represented graphically (see Figure 7.5).

Billboards

Billboards are made to distract people, to yank attention away from the road (see Figure 7.6). Examine one closely to understand how it works toward that goal.

Analysis

Your approach to analysis will depend on your chosen subject—whether a single image, an image with text, a video with voiceover, or some combination of image, text, and video. Apply the following sections and questions that best fit with your chosen subject.

Figure 7.5 Internet image

U.S. Department of agriculture

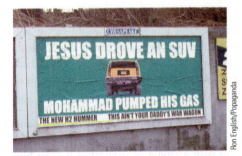

Ron English/Popaganda

Bill Aron/PhotoEdit

Figure 7.6 Billboards

Image

Analyzing an image involves looking at the content (the subject matter) of the image, and then the particular visual elements:

Content: The subject, information, or objects that are pictured. Everything within an image is important—from the largest to the tiniest object or detail. They all figure into the nature of the image; they all impact the consciousness of viewers.

Framing: What has been placed within the boundaries of the image. Whether by choice, by accident, or by necessity, certain objects are included in the image while other objects are left out. Whether a photographer's (or designer's) deliberate move or pure accident, the framing impacts what is seen. It closes in on a particular range of objects and closes out the rest of the world.

Composition: The way the visual elements of the image are arranged within the frame. Some objects stand in the foreground, others in the background or off to the side. Objects may be crowded, touching, overlapping, far apart. The spatial relationships can be both aesthetic— that is, pleasing to the eye—and meaningful.

Focus: The degree to which some areas of the image are sharp (or clear) and other areas are blurry. The focus impacts the movement of the eye. Sharper objects automatically attract attention away from blurry or fuzzy objects, thereby prompting viewers to see and understand the image in a particular way.

Lighting: The degree to which some areas of the image are brightly lit and other areas are in low light or in shadows. An entire image may be dark or light, or some parts of the image may be in shadows or in bright light. Although shadows and light may be a natural consequence of a sunny day or a tall building blocking a photographer's light, the way the elements are lit creates an effect.

Texture: How the image, or certain objects in the image, looks like it would feel if you could touch it. Images can suggest, or appear to have, texture. Just as tree bark and a marble countertop have different textures, visual images can suggest how they might feel if touched. Even if content, framing, composition, and such are all the same in two images, a smooth or rough texture may suggest a different idea about the content.

Angle and Vantage Point: The angle at which the image is presented, or the vantage point or perspective from which a photograph, for example, is taken. Every image suggests a perspective. A photograph of a politician speaking with a crowd of supporters behind him suggests one meaning, while a shot of the same politician from behind and speaking to a mere handful of people suggests something else. A low-angle shot of the politician might suggest power; a high-angle shot looking down on the politician might suggest weakness.

Significance: The collective meaning or impact of all the elements. Our ultimate goal is to figure out how all these elements work together to express ideas, just as the elements of an essay, novel, poem, or movie work together. When analyzing, we focus on one element at a time, but we are always looking at more than one element. For example, when we consider how an image is framed or composed, we are also considering the image's content. When we talk about composition, we are looking at how these various formal elements work together.

Consider the image of the man playing guitar (Figure 7.7): A man, presumably a farmer, plays an acoustic guitar in an open field. The background is nearly empty except for the lower part of a distant building. The distance behind the man matters—perhaps as much as the man himself. Directly beside him sits a small electric amplifier. The man and the amplifier—adjacent, focused, well lit, in the foreground—seem like a mixed pair, like they do not belong together, especially surrounded by an open field of dirt. But all the elements of the image insist that we see them together. Even the angle—seeing both of them from the front—makes us (the viewers) feel like an audience. What do all these elements prompt us to think, to imagine, to assume? What feelings are conjured by the interplay of the elements?

Figure 7.7

Examine the image you have chosen for your project. The following Invention Questions will help you analyze how the image works to affect viewers.

- **Content:** What content—subject or information—is presented in the image? What are the main objects in the image? Of the main elements, which appear to be most prominent? Which are less prominent?

- **Framing:** How is the image framed? What has been placed within the boundaries of the image? What has not been included? How do the boundaries influence your focus?

- **Composition:** How are the elements of the image arranged? Are visual elements symmetrical (distributed evenly) or asymmetrical (not distributed evenly)? Are elements touching, overlapping, close together, or far apart? Are elements above or below each other, or to the left or the right of each other? What is in the background? What might the relationship of elements encourage someone to think?

- **Focus:** How is the image focused? That is, what objects or areas appear most clear or sharp? What objects or areas are not clear? Is anything unusual or striking about the focus? How does the focus draw your attention? How does it affect the relationship of certain elements?

- **Lighting:** How is the image lit? That is, what objects or areas are well lit? What areas are dark, or in shadow? Is the light harsh or soft? Is there a contrast of tones from light to dark? What is darkest, and what is lightest? How does the lighting affect what is pictured? How might different lighting change the image?

- **Texture:** What is the texture of the image? If you could touch what is pictured, how would it feel? How does the photograph's texture relate to its content?

- **Angle and Vantage Point:** From what angle is the photograph taken? Is it straight-on? Is it exaggerated? How does the angle affect the composition of the image? That is, are some elements more in the foreground or background? Are some more prominent?

You may, in your analysis, consider other elements as well. Colors, for example, may be subdued or bright and splashy. Such details may have significance.

Video

Many of the elements related to image analysis can be applied to videos; after all, a video is a series of moving images. Television commercials, online commercials, music videos, films, trailers, and so on, are carefully crafted. Directors make deliberate decisions about camera angle, lighting, composition, framing, and focus. Consider, for instance, a trend in pop music videos: Cameras often look "up" at singers and performers, so the performers stare down at the viewing audience. The camera angle has significance. It influences how the performer is propped up or hailed. Or consider how *framing* works in music videos. Singers are most often centered in each shot. All other musicians, people, and objects stay in the margins or background. This framing technique reinforces the centrality of the singer and the lyrics. Of course, plenty of music videos feature other characters, objects, and performers. The point here is that videos rely on the elements explained in the previous section, and a fine analysis could be developed by attending to those elements. But videos include some additional elements:

Pace: The speed of events, scene changes, or camera angles. When images are moving, their speed matters. Fast scene or camera changes intensify action. In movies such as the *Bourne* series, the camera shifts every few seconds. Those rapid changes reinforce the physicality of the plots and underscore the main character's actions, not his planning, strategizing, or moral uncertainty. He is not meditative or reflective but decisive and already headed into some new situation. Cameras move more slowly—or barely at all—in other types of media. In talk-shows, for instance, the camera generally stays put. It looks straight at the host and moves slightly only when a guest speaks. Or consider the typical horror movie scene in which the main character (not the killer) is moving into a potentially dangerous situation—a dark room or thick forest. The camera remains fixed behind the character's shoulder. In this case, the lack of fast movement creates tension. Pace is created not so much by the scene itself but the length of a scene or the time before the camera angle shifts.

Narrative: The storyline, either implied or explicit, that develops over the course of the video. It's easy to recognize narrative, or storyline, in a movie. For instance, a character finds herself in trouble, meets someone who can help her, and together they set out to solve the problem. But narrative also operates, often more subtly, in music videos and commercials. The narrative may be quick—only a sliver of the entire commercial. Imagine, for instance, the common laundry detergent ad: A kid gets muddy, his parent wonders how to remove the stains from his clothes, and along comes some helpful neighbor or spokesperson with the magic bottle. In short, narrative finds its way into all kinds of videos. Despite their length, most have some conventional elements: an introduction to the character(s), the onset of a problem, an escalation of the problem and/or action, the climax or peak, a resolution to the problem, and a de-escalation.

Genre: Conventions established by the type of video or text. Genre is a category that carries some automatic conventions or standard elements. For instance, consider the horror movie genre. Any specific horror movie includes some conventional—*generic*—elements: a mysterious and evil force at work, innocent people, often teenagers, targeted by that evil force, a direct conflict between the evil force and those innocent people. The same goes with pop music videos, a very broad genre that usually features the song, the singers/performers, or a loosely spun narrative that relates to the song lyrics. A deviation from those generic elements would confuse viewers. For instance, imagine a pop music video that features thirty minutes of news footage or two people playing chess. Such footage would fall outside the genre conventions.

Genre determines much more than content. It also shapes other elements: framing, composition, focus, pace, and so on. You might think of genre as an overarching rhetorical element, one that controls the usual behavior of all others—and even how audiences engage with the specific video. For instance, when you are watching a music video, you are probably not confused when you see your favorite singer walking down a busy street mouthing the words to a song—with no mic, no band, no instruments whatsoever. The pop music video genre has established that this otherwise very strange behavior is normal and expected.

One powerful way to analyze a video (or any type of text) is to ask how it follows and breaks from genre convention. While most popular commercials and music videos closely follow convention and, therefore avoid confusing the audience, some programs openly deviate from genre. They do so to make fun of the conventions themselves or to break new ground. For example, Stephen Colbert's original talk show, *The Colbert Report*, famously employed dramatic camera shifts while he sat still at his desk. The sudden shifts had a comedic effect because nighttime talk shows *aren't supposed to be action-packed*. Recently, the company Dove launched a campaign that deviated from the conventions of beauty care commercials by arguing against standards of beauty. These examples (Colbert and Dove) show that genre establishes common boundaries that can be followed or, occasionally, abandoned.

ACTIVITY

Most genres can be broken down into subgenres—smaller categories that come with distinct expectations. Punk rock, for instance, is a subgenre of rock-n-roll. And from there, emo-punk is an even smaller subgenre with its own conventions—attitudes, sounds, ensemble, and fashion sense. In a small group, articulate another subgenre of popular music and then list the specific elements that are seen in a typical video. (Caution: Be careful not to characterize a specific performer as a subgenre. Any given performer, no matter how popular, belongs to a genre and subgenre.)

Expectations: Genres create specific expectations. Once we know we're watching a music video, for instance, we expect certain things to happen: to see some glimmer of the singer or performers, not long periods of news footage or people playing chess. So genre establishes initial expectations. But the video itself also establishes expectations. The first few seconds or frames of any video create thoughts about what should or might happen. Those thoughts get reinforced or violated as the video goes on. For instance, imagine a music video that begins with a singer staring at the camera. That image, paired with genre conventions, creates an expectation that she will begin mouthing lyrics when the song starts. Imagine, however, if she were to begin laughing wildly or run into the distance when the song starts. The expectation established by the video would be violated. Most videos, of course, avoid such explicit violations. Instead, they establish expectations and then fulfill them. The important point is that every new frame or scene is doing something with (reinforcing, fulfilling, diverging from, violating) expectations established earlier.

If you've chosen a video for your project, apply the following questions:

> How do elements such as composition, focus, lighting, and camera angle influence the overall mood of the video?

> What is the pace? Where or when does the pace change? How do changes in pace influence the narrative?

> What is the genre or subgenre of the video? How does it follow and/or deviate from genre conventions?

> What expectations get established in the first frames or seconds of the video? How do those expectations get reinforced or violated as the video continues?

Text

Images often depend on written text—language inscribed on or positioned with the image itself. Likewise, videos usually come with a voiceover. Images and language, then, function together. In her essay, Rebecca Hollingsworth explains the crucial interaction between image and text:

> The text of the ad jolts us into a reality that is discordant with the idealistic image. Bannered text across the bottom of the image reads, "Odds of a child becoming a top fashion designer: 1 in 7,000. Odds of a child being diagnosed with autism: 1 in 150." This startling statistic of the likelihood that this young girl—any young girl—is autistic turns our viewing experience upside down.

Sometimes, text relies on other texts to make meaning. As we explain in Chapter 6 (page 174), text often speaks back to or depends on other texts to make meaning. That is, text often exists in dialogue with other texts. When that dialogue or interplay is explicit, it is called *intertextuality*. In his essay, Nick Fendinger characterizes the relationship between a television trailer's imagery and the voiceover as *intertextual*:

> The "Ozymandias" trailer for *Breaking Bad* relies on intertextuality. Two works converge and create a dynamic conversation between the past and the present. One text works with the other; both get changed in the process. The modern ghastly plot of *Breaking Bad* gets some historical (even educational) ambience from the classic poem. Intertextuality acts not merely as a savvy literary device, it enhances the intellectual merit of a modern television drama.

Chapter 6 explains *subtext* as a layer of unwritten ideas that lurk beneath the written words (page 175). Just like text, images also have subtext. Even if they have no written text, they can still suggest, or imply, ideas. In advertising, images and text often work together to suggest a layer of subtext. Subtext is invisible, so finding it is hard work. We have to look closely at all the elements and connect them with common values and assumptions. Examine the image you have chosen for your project and answer the following questions:

> What does the image suggest? (Besides the obvious statements or ideas, what subtle assumptions or beliefs lurk in the image?)

> How do content, framing, composition, focus, lighting, texture, angle, or vantage point suggest subtle assumptions or beliefs?

If the image has accompanying text, answer the following questions:

> How does the text correlate with the significance of the image?

> How do content, framing, composition, focus, lighting, texture, angle, and vantage point help to convey the ideas?

> Does the text, image, or video echo other texts? (How does the language depend on our familiarity with other texts?)

Context

Analyzing an image or video involves examining how it relates to its context—the things and people surrounding it. The specific context is the real physical space that surrounds the image—the building, the magazine, the neighborhood, the campus, the wall, and so on. Every image is affected by the specific context in which it appears. In the images shown in Figure 7.8, da Vinci's *Mona Lisa* (one of the world's most reproduced work of art) is surrounded by different contexts. In the first image, the crowded room at the Louvre influences how the *Mona Lisa* is viewed and what it means. In the other images, the *Mona Lisa* has been re-contextualized (recast in different graphic surroundings, even different clothes!).

The contexts change how da Vinci's original image works.

You can also think of context more broadly. Beyond the physical space surrounding an image or video, the broader culture provides meaning. The values and beliefs that shape everyday life also impact the way an image, video, or any text works—why it gets made, how it gets received. Examine the image or video you have chosen for your project and answer the following questions:

> What beliefs, attitudes, values, or morals does it support or appeal to?

> What beliefs, attitudes, values, or morals does it push against?

> What public concern does the image speak to?

> How might people benefit by exploring the possible meanings of the image?

Invention Workshop

In a small group, use the Invention Questions to explore ideas in depth. First, share your image or video with others in your group. Then apply one of the Invention Questions. Once someone

Figure 7.8 Mona Lisa in different contexts

in the group offers a possible answer, record the response. Someone else in the group should then continue that thinking by asking how the first responder arrived at his or her point.

Thesis

The purpose of this project is to analyze how an image or video works to impact viewers. The analysis should reveal something that readers would not otherwise see or imagine. It should show the insides, the mechanics, of the image or video. Consider the following examples:

- In trendy music videos, the camera looks up from the ground at the performers, which reinforces the notion that the performers have power over, and speak down to, their audiences.

- Beyond the main image of the Cadillac, the sophisticated background elements make the pitch to potential consumers.

- Presidential campaign commercials rely on the imagery of middle-class America so that candidates will be seen as "average Joes."

Notice that each statement explains the significance, the meaning or impact, of a particular element. Take, for example, the third statement. It explains how *the imagery of middle-class America* (a particular element) casts the candidates as average Joes (the element's significance, its meaning or impact). A good thesis for this project has two important qualities: a focus on a particular element and an explanation of its significance. Look over your invention writing and focus on a particular element (something in the content, the composition, the framing, etc.). Then explain its significance—how that element works to convey meaning or develop a feeling.

Common Thesis Problems

As in most writing projects, the more specific the claims, the more intensive the ideas will be. If you can point to a particular element in the image or video and explain how that element works, then you are probably on your way to a focused thesis. The following statement lacks significance and focus. It targets "many" ads and offers a sweeping statement about them:

Many *Sports Illustrated* ads use women as the main focus.

The statement does not explain how something in those ads works, how they influence people, or how the individual elements create messages. The following statement also lacks focus:

Rolling Stone magazine makes one thing clear: sex sells.

Rolling Stone is a good-sized magazine—with a table of contents, album lists, pictures, ads, articles about politics, music reviews, movie reviews, and so on. Of course, someone could associate all those elements with sex, but the project would probably lack focus. A writer with such a statement needs to look more closely at something specific in *Rolling Stone*.

Evolution of a Thesis

Thesis statements do not always evolve in a neat fashion, progressing from a broader to a more focused insight. Sometimes (maybe most times), they wander, circle back, and jump around as the writer tries to get traction. In the following, we can see Rebecca Hollingsworth searching out meaning through single sentences. She is trying to connect two things: a particular element of the ad and the meaning of that element for viewers. The following statements are attempts, some better than others, at forging that connection.

- Many ads, like that for the Autism Speaks, appeal to Americans hopes for their children.

- The language and image of the Autism Speaks ad pushes against some grand hope that parents may have for their children.

- The language of the Autism Speaks ad contrasts harshly with the hope and innocence implied by the image.

- The ad for Autism Speaks contrasts deluded notions of success—defined as becoming a top fashion designer—with a statistically harsh truth.

Revising Your Thesis

Develop a working thesis statement that includes attention to a specific element and explains its significance. Then in a small group, discuss each person's statement. Apply the following:

- Does the statement focus on a specific element (something in the content, composition, framing, angle, focus, etc.)? How could the specific element be narrower?

- Beyond the writer's statement, what is the significance (possible meaning or impact) of that specific element? (What else might it suggest about people, lifestyles, nature, America, clothing, social class, race, gender, politics, domestic life, art, music, and so on?) Be creative. Imagine that the significance is not what people initially assume!

- Make a case for the most surprising or hidden significance in the image. Make a connection that seems, at first, outrageous. Try to convince others in the group that your point is valid.

Rhetorical Tools

For this project, the main support strategy involves using details directly from the image or video itself. In fact, the goal is to maintain intense focus on specific elements and explain how they function—how they make meaning, relate to context, other texts, or other elements in the image or video itself. In her analysis, Rebecca Hollingsworth shows readers how details make meaning:

> Like mom, we look on as the young girl tries on one piece of clothing after another, suggested by the pink, white, and blue clothes draped over furniture in the background. The girl's jewelry—the chunky necklace and the dangly charm bracelet—and her sophisticated tie clash with her long, stringy pigtail braids and big white teddy bear in the background. The pink-and-white washed walls covered in a busy pastel pattern remind us that this is a child's room and that we are witnessing child's play.

Hollingsworth's analysis shows the power of subtle details that might get overlooked:

> As we watch the young girl over her mother's shoulder, we must confront the prevalence of this developmental disability in American children—and the very real possibility that our own child may be that 1 in 150.

Because we are looking over the mother's shoulder (at the girl from her mother's vantage point), the image confronts us with a real possibility—about American children and about *our own child.* Hollingsworth's careful analysis adds up to a main point:

> In this sense, the ad does what numerous other campaigns do: It scares us. But this one aims at a particularly vulnerable place: the intersection of our idealism and our fear. It contrasts deluded notions of success—defined here as becoming a top fashion designer—with a statistically harsh truth. We can no longer bask in the old *one in a million* cliché. Like the pretty imagery in the fictional bedroom, that number has been upstaged by a more demanding probability.

Remember that any image or video is part of a genre, which means that it uses some conventional elements and expectations. In his essay, Nick Fendinger explains how a video trailer relies on but withholds expectations to create a specific mood:

> The opening scenes instill a sense of dread. Barbed wire fences, towering telephone wires, and a lone tree are all shown in a desolate landscape most commonly associated with death: the desert. The bleak visual introduction establishes an ominous mood that is reinforced throughout the trailer. These initial scenes are void of human life. Not a single character is shown. But over the lifeless terrain comes the gravelly voice of Walter White, Albuquerque's public enemy number one. By withholding the genre expectation of depicting the show's main character and instead featuring a lone voice in the desert, the trailer cultivates an aura of mystique, a mystery that temporarily disguises what should be expected.

Return to any notes you generated from the Analysis section of this chapter. Ask yourself the following questions about the image or video:

> What details (about the content, focus, composition, framing, lighting, texture, angle, and significance) best illustrate my main point?

> What specific text best illustrates my main point?

> Does the context help to support my main point?

Research

Using a periodical database or an Internet search engine, explore how others have discussed the image or video you are analyzing. Most likely, you won't find sources about the specific image or video (unless you are analyzing a historic piece of art or popular culture). However, you'll likely find sources about a genre—an automobile ad, a billboard, a movie trailer, and so on. (Remember that keyword searches require several restarts with substitutions and small changes. For instance, changing *automobile* to *car* or *ad* to *advertisement* may yield different results. For more assistance with using databases and online catalogs for research, see Chapter 14: Finding Sources.

Revision

Your analysis should reveal something readers would not otherwise see or imagine. This involves inventing your way to a focused and insightful thesis and then using rhetorical tools to help readers understand and accept that thesis. Before exchanging your draft for peer review, return to the questions in the Analysis, Public Resonance, and Rhetorical Tools sections, and explore further from your new perspective (the perspective you developed last time you worked through those questions). See how you can improve your focus, insight, and support before getting feedback from a peer.

Peer Review

Write down what you think your analysis reveals, and then exchange drafts with at least one other writer. After reading your draft, the other writer should write responses to the following questions:

1. What did the analysis reveal? That is, what didn't you see or imagine about the image or video until you read the essay?

2. How might the thesis be more specific and revealing? Offer particular rewording, or a whole new direction, even if you think the thesis is good as is.

3. What additional details from the image might be used to strengthen or refocus the analysis?

4. Are there any blueprinting passages? Can they be eliminated? Suggest a strategy that keeps readers focused on the ideas rather than on the structure of the essay.

5. What sentences can be combined through subordination? Combine two sentences in the opening paragraph, subordinating one idea to the other. Combine at least two sentences elsewhere in the essay.

6. Consider the following vitality strategies explained in Chapter 19: Vitalizing Sentences:

   —Mark any clichés. Explain how the cliché conceals or blurs thinking, and then suggest an alternative to the cliché.

   —Note any stilted language. Suggest an alternative approach to the passage.

   —Help the writer experiment with sentence length and brevity. Reconstruct one paragraph, extending some sentences and abbreviating others. Try to create intensity with shorter sentences.

—Change vague nouns to specific nouns.

—Change *be* verbs (*is, are, was, were*) to active verbs.

—Change clauses to phrases.

—Change phrases to words.

—Combine sentences.

—Repeat structures.

—Intensify verbs.

7. What grammatical or proofreading issues make reading difficult or create small distractions for readers?

Reflection

Before moving on to another writing project, reflect on this one. The following questions ask you to consider your own rhetoric. The writing you do in response to these questions is sometimes called *meta-writing*, which is when you take a step back to think and write about your writing. Getting this distance can help you see and learn new things, even after you've written your essay.

1. What is the essay's thesis?

2. How does your analysis of a particular visual element (or several elements) reveal a new way of understanding the image or video?

3. How does a particular reference to evidence from outside the image or video help readers understand and accept your thesis? If you didn't use any outside evidence, what outside evidence might you have used and why?

4. What is the essay's most intense passage and why?

5. How did the essay evolve through the process of inventing, drafting, and revising?

6. How did writing this essay help you develop as a writer and thinker?

Beyond the Essay: Video Briefing

1. "What was your analyzing images essay about?" We are often asked such questions, not only about essays we have written, but also about other aspects of our lives. A boss may ask, "What happened last night with the customer who called this morning to complain?" A professor may ask, "How is your writing project coming along?" A family member may ask, "How'd Cindy's softball game go?" In some cases we can simply

answer, "Not much" or "Fine." But sometimes we must give a clear and accurate account of events or an appraisal of progress—a briefing—either verbally or in writing.

Some briefings are impromptu, such as those called for by the previous situations: We don't have time to prepare and must answer on the spot. Other briefings are more prepared and formal: for example, each day the president's press secretary briefs the press on important issues.

For practice with briefings, create a two-minute video briefing of your analyzing images essay. Your briefing should include your main idea (thesis), your main supporting ideas, and any important details necessary to fill in any gaps for the audience. You may decide to write out the entire text of your briefing. If you do, try not to simply read the text for your briefing. Or, you may decide to jot down key points. However you do it, record your briefing using a computer or smartphone and review and redo it until you are happy with your delivery.

Consider including your video file as part of your essay.

2. In several paragraphs, explain how effectively your briefing communicates the ideas from your essay. For example, in what way does the video more effectively communicate your ideas? In what way is the essay more effective? How might viewing the video help someone better understand your essay, and why?

John Metz

Chapter Objectives

The sample essays and invention prompts in this chapter will help you to:

- Develop a focused and revelatory argument related to your everyday life.
- Recognize and apply different forms of support: examples, allusions, testimony, scenarios, statistics, authorities, facts, and artistic appeals.
- Recognize and apply counterarguments, concessions, and qualifiers.
- Recognize and avoid a range of logical fallacies.
- Transpose your argument into an open letter.

"Someone who makes an assertion puts forward a claim—a claim on our attention and to our belief."

—Stephen Toulmin

INTRODUCTION

Argument is the art of persuading people how to think. This may sound absurd since most people, we hope, already know how to think, or at least *what* to think about particular issues. But with argument, we can change how people view things, even slightly, and so affect how they approach and process ideas.

Arguments come to us in different forms. We hear them given in speeches, debates, and informal discussions. We hear them every day on talk shows, in break rooms, college hallways, and public meeting places like restaurants and pubs. Arguments get delivered through action. They come explicitly in protests, parades, sit-ins, labor strikes, and elections. They also come in more subtle forms: People donate to charities (thereby expressing their favor of a particular cause); they patronize or boycott a particular store; they choose not to vote (thereby expressing their stance against the entire political process). Arguments get made through art in all media: sculpture, painting, music, and so on. And arguments are major elements of literature. For example, it has been said that Aldous Huxley's book *Brave New World* argues against the extremes of materialism and industrialization and that Kate Chopin's *The Awakening* argues for a new vision of women's identity. Even poems offer arguments: Walt Whitman's masterpiece *Leaves of Grass* argues for the value of common American workers and their common language.

People in all occupations make or deal with arguments. For example, a human resources manager for a packaging company argues in a report that more supervisors should be hired in the coming fiscal year; several department store sales associates collectively write a letter to store and regional managers in which they claim current scheduling practices minimize sales commissions; the public affairs director of a major automobile company argues that a new advertising campaign should not be offensive to a particular demographic group; the lawyers for a major computer software company argue in a district court that the company's business practices comply with federal antitrust laws.

In any situation, those who can deliver the most sophisticated and engaging arguments tend to have the most influence. Of course, a sophisticated and engaging argument involves a great deal of strategy. For instance, in academic argument (arguments made in academia or college), blatant personal attacks, outright aggression, and sugarcoated language are not valued, nor are empty phrases ("don't question what's in my heart") and mean-spiritedness ("your ideas are simply idiotic"). But although academic writers are not out to squash an opponent or cuddle up to audiences, they do more than simply present their opinions. In providing a new way of thinking about a particular topic, academic writers must also analyze others' ideas and explain how their own claims relate to those of others.

The chapter readings will provide insight into various argumentative strategies. For example, every argument has a main claim (thesis) that can be expressed in a single sentence, and particular support strategies such as examples, scenarios, and so on, that unpack that claim. As you read, look for the main claim (it may be explicitly stated or implied) and the support strategies that help readers understand and accept it. After reading the essays, you can find a topic in one of two ways—go to the Point of Contact section to find a topic from everyday life, or choose one of the Ideas for Writing that follow the essays. After you find a topic, go to the Analysis section to begin developing your argument.

READINGS

The Dog Delusion
April Pedersen

Sometimes writers examine the behaviors and reflexes that seem most harmless. When a trend seems uncritically accepted in everyday life, writers step forward. In this essay, April Pedersen, a writer and illustrator living in Reno, Nevada, goes after a seemingly innocent behavior: dog idolization. As the argument develops, Pedersen deals with a range of opposing positions and assumptions.

There was a time when "Dog is my co-pilot" was merely a fun slap at the "God is my co-pilot" bumper sticker, and it was funny precisely *because* nobody would ever think to elevate their dog to such a height. Within the past decade, however, pets—primarily dogs—have soared in importance. ("Dog is my co-pilot" is now the slogan of *Bark,* a magazine of dog culture, and the title of an anthology—published by *Bark*'s editors—billed as essays, short stories, and expert commentaries that explore "every aspect of our life with dogs.") Canines, with their pack instincts and trainability, are by far the most likely pet to be anthropomorphized as a family member, a best friend, or a "fur baby," treated accordingly with gourmet meals, designer apparel, orthopedic beds, expensive therapy, and catered birthday parties. Some people even feel (and in some cases, demonstrate) that their dogs are worth dying for. Others say the animal lovers are going too far.

In a Pew Research Center study, 85 percent of dog owners said they consider their pet to be a member of their family. However the latest trend is to take that a step further in seeing the animal as a child. A company that sells pet health insurance policies has dubbed the last Sunday in April as "Pet Parents Day." Glance through magazines like *Bark, Cesar's Way* (courtesy of "Dog Whisperer" Cesar Millan), and other mainstream publications, and the term "pet parent" crops up regularly. The "my-dogs-are-my-kids" crowd isn't being tongue-in-cheek, either. They act on their beliefs, buying Christmas presents, photos with Santa, cosmetic surgery, and whatever-it-takes medical care for their animal. In fact having a puppy, claimed one "mother," is "exactly the same in all ways as having a baby." And while pushing a dog around in a stroller would have gotten you directions to a mental health facility twenty years ago, today it's de rigueur to see a canine in a stroller (or a papoose), and some passersby are downright disappointed to discover a human infant inside.

Who's to say what a pet's value is (aside from the purchase price)? Shouldn't people be free to spend whatever they want on things for their dog? What real harm is there in believing one's schnauzer is a "child who never grows up?" The implications are more ridiculous

April Pedersen, "The Dog Delusion," from *The Humanist Magazine*, November/December 2009. Reprinted with permission of the author.

MASTER DOG   OWNER BEST FRIEND   GUARDIAN 4-LEGGED FAMILY MEMBER PARENT CHILD WORSHIPER GOD

and far reaching than you might expect. Take the widely held notion that dogs give us unconditional love and nonjudgmental loyalty. Praising dogs for being incapable of acting like bad people is not only junk logic, it turns the animal into an idealized (godlike?) version of ourselves, to be rewarded with all manner of pampering. How can the comparatively complex human being compete with creatures said to exude unwavering faithfulness, forgiveness, trust, love, and innocence? Pets are pegged as more loving, more pure, more giving, more devoted. They are implied to be our moral superiors for not stealing money, starting wars, or judging people by their physical appearance. They accept us for who we are, while we come across as scheming, judgmental malcontents who love on condition only. I have quite a collection of misanthropic utterances from dog lovers, most along the lines of "I'll take dogs over humans any day," and "dogs love without having an agenda!" It's no surprise that many dog lovers would rather be stranded on an island with a dog than with their spouse (or with any other person for that matter). Then there's the CEO who said he doesn't trust clients who don't have pets. How sadly similar to the religious who say they don't trust nonbelievers.

    Further undermining humans, dogs trained for various tasks are routinely referred to as soldiers, officers, actors, therapists, heroes, or athletes. But a police dog simply can't know the moral difference between a stash of cocaine and an old sock. One of the most absurd examples of anthropomorphism I've seen was a funeral for a drug-sniffing dog. The sheriff's department went all out with a motorcade, flag-draped casket, bag pipers playing "Amazing Grace," a eulogy from a pastor, and a rose-adorned easel on which the dog's portrait rested. Officers from all across the Western United States paid their respects, and the service received heavy local media coverage. All this for an animal that couldn't even grasp what a "law" was.

    "Dogs are for people who can't have kids," a gay newspaper columnist told me recently. It's true that homosexual (and straight) couples who can't or don't want children of their own often migrate towards dogs as child substitutes and view the arrangement as a different kind of family, but a family nonetheless. Such dog-based "families" may at first blush seem benign or even beneficial. After all, people with a family mentality are more likely to form stable, safe neighborhoods and have a vested interest in the community. Those without children may benefit from nurturing a living creature and learning to be less self-centered. But doesn't it make more evolutionary sense to want to care for the young of your own species over another species? Couples without kids for whatever reason could still opt to be foster parents, mentors, or Big Brothers/Sisters to make a positive difference in a child's life instead of funneling all their concerns into dogs. And what about devoting one's time to saving endangered species of animals (whose survival also affects that of humans)?

Yet each day dogs gain more and more importance, protection, and access to realms once reserved for humans. Michigan is considering a bill that would allow pet care as a tax write-off. What's next? Dogs counted as residents in the U.S. Census?

This shift in the status of dogs hasn't gone unnoticed by animal rights advocates. Already thirteen U.S. cities have ordinances that ditch "pet owner" for "pet guardian." The change is intended to be merely symbolic, its fans claim. If so, why make the effort? I worry it's a foot in the door to gradually desensitize society to the outlandish idea of pets being the equals of minor children. Allowing ourselves to glance down the slippery slope, we might foresee absurd lawsuits over injuries to pets, murder charges for those suspected of negligence in a pet's death, and laws requiring guardians to strap their fur kids into car seats, or to walk them twice a day, or giving any number of rights to the animals. Recently dog owners have begun to demand off-leash beaches and trails, under the premise that dogs have a "right" to run free. What's next, making spaying or neutering a crime, because pets should have the right to reproduce? Or allowing dogs to bite people or chase livestock in order to fulfill their right to behave as predators? Where would the "pet" line for special status be drawn? At gerbils? Ferrets? Canaries? Hermit crabs? The funny part is, not even the pet industry can decide if pets are children or property. In ads hawking pet supplies, dogs and cats are promoted as family members, loved ones, and babies. Yet the defense strategy, if sued over, say tainted pet food or a defective squeaky toy, is to focus only on the economic aspect of the pet.

Viewing dogs as our children extends to risking life and limb to save them as well. What would evolutionary psychologists make of healthy people of reproductive age leaping to their deaths into scalding hot springs, icy rivers, or smoke-filled infernos in an attempt to rescue a possibly neutered animal? Among surveyed pet owners, 93 percent, which includes the young and childless, would do just that. Of course, most dog owners fully expect their pet to save them, Lassie style, should the need arise. But if not trained for rescue work, most dogs would simply stare, hide, or eat the contents of their owner's picnic basket as their master sinks under the lake's surface. Cases abound where pets happen to save people from perilous situations, but they, the pets, were acting as animals, not as humans.

One can always argue that, from an environmental perspective, the pets-as-kids thing makes sense. With the human population reaching unsustainable numbers, pets can fill our desire to nurture without adding to the surplus of humans. Even so, dogs still eat a lot and produce a lot of waste (which has to be cleaned up unless the status lift requires potty training). And don't forget that dogs have to come from somewhere, and parents will show preferences for certain breeds. Puppy mills would be happy to meet the increased demand for dogs, if it can be considered ethical in the best of circumstances to take puppies away from their mothers and litter mates and give them to another species to raise them. Interestingly, our popular pets such as the domestic dog play no balancing role in any ecosystem; they are human-developed and human-maintained. Even feral dogs prefer to hang around our villages, urban areas, and garbage dumps instead of returning to the woods to dance with wolves. And if too many people opted against having children in favor of pets, the result couldn't be good for economies; children are the future workforce, consumers, voters, tax payers, innovators, you name it.

Let's outsmart dogs a little by cutting back on the over-the-top stuff. The dogs won't notice. Funds spent on a dog's blueberry facial or in-room canine massage at a swanky hotel ($130 an hour) are about as close to setting a pile of cash on fire in front of a destitute person as I can imagine. Ditto on buying a sweater for an animal covered in fur, or a carob-coated eclair for a scat eater, or personalized cookies for the species that can't read (that would be all species except us). Certainly dogs can't visualize themselves as Homo sapiens of any age, and are becoming obese and even ill-mannered at the hands of their besotted owners. It makes no sense whatsoever to pour so much time, money, and emotion into an animal whose main "goal" in life is to leave its scent on a tree. Think about it—how would you like to be a dog? To be unable to talk, write, or question. To look upon a masterpiece of art without an ounce of admiration, to gaze at the starry night without an iota of wonder, to see a book and have not the slightest inclination to open it, or stare without comprehension at a voting booth.

It's fine to enjoy a pet. I've had several myself, including a cat that lived eighteen years. When his kidneys failed, a $12,000 kidney transplant was off the radar (a case can be made that such surgery on an animal is unethical anyway), and I didn't consider him to be my son. This need not diminish pets. We can enjoy them for what they are, without the anthropomorphic delusion.

WRITING STRATEGIES

1. Plenty of pet owners would disagree with Pedersen's claims. Explain how Pedersen takes on opposing views. Describe a particular passage and explain how she pushes back or refutes the opposition.

2. How does Pedersen concede to the opposition or qualify her points? Describe particular passages. (For information on concessions and qualifiers, see pages 259–260.)

3. Explain how Pedersen uses appeals to logic. (See pages 256–257 for an understanding of appeals.)

4. Read about logical fallacies on pages 260–262. How does Pedersen's use of *slippery slope* impact her argument?

5. Pedersen appeals to values throughout her argument. What particular appeals to value do you detect?

EXPLORING IDEAS

1. Pedersen explains that "our popular pets such as the domestic dog play no balancing role in any ecosystem; they are human-developed and human-maintained." Why is this point important to her argument?

2. Explain why it would be wrong to characterize Pedersen as "anti-dog."

3. Pedersen compares some pet owners to "the religious who say they don't trust nonbelievers." Consider this comparison. How might dog ownership resemble religious belief or practice?

4. Even if you disagree vehemently with Pedersen, why might she have a sound position?

IDEAS FOR WRITING

1. Consider some other widely accepted form of ownership. How might it be undermining human development?

2. What particular aspect of dog ownership makes people more humane?

If responding to one of these ideas, go to the Analysis section of this chapter to begin developing ideas for your essay.

Cruelty, Civility, and Other Weighty Matters

Ann Marie Paulin

As with most engaging essays, Paulin's originates in personal circumstance. (See her invention writing on page 248.) Also, as with most engaging essays, the writer extends her thinking into the public sphere. As you read "Cruelty, Civility, and Other Weighty Matters," notice how Paulin puts forth an argument while keeping herself in the background, only briefly referring to herself in the essay's introduction and conclusion. As you will see, Paulin goes beyond the increasingly common argument against the media's portrayal of women; she reveals something about the subtle effects of that portrayal. Paulin, who teaches English and gender studies at Owens Community College in Toledo, Ohio, shows that a writer's voice matters—that savvy use of voice actually creates layers to an argument. That is, her voice rehumanizes the issue and the people involved. If the media have dehumanized "fat people," Paulin does more than argue against the media; she strikes back with an intense, multifaceted presence.

A strong, emphatic (but informal) voice.

"You" makes the voice more informal.

"Our" is a direct strategy to create public resonance.

I swear, if I have to sit through one more ad proclaiming that life is not worth living if you aren't thin, I'll slug somebody. So much for the theory that fat people are jolly. But, contrary to what magazines, talk shows, movies, and advertisements proclaim, we aren't all a bunch of sorrowful, empty losers with no friends and no self-esteem, either. As with most complex issues—religion, politics, human relationships—most of what we see in mass media is hugely oversimplified and, therefore, wrong. So, if many of us recognize the media are notorious for getting things less than accurate, you might wonder why I let these images bother me so much. Well, if you were one of the millions of fat Americans living in a culture where you are constantly depicted as some sort of weepy loser, ill-dressed buffoon, or neutered sidekick, your good nature might wear a bit thin as well. But far more important than my ill temper is a creepy sense that these inaccurate images have shifted our vision of what is

"Cruelty, Civility, and Other Weighty Matters," by Ann Marie Paulin. Reprinted with permission of the author.

important in life way out of whack, so far out that people are being hurt. What I'm proposing here is that we need to get some perspective on this issue.

First of all, let me make it clear that I'm not advocating that everyone in America go out and get fat. According to the news media, we are doing that very handily on our own, in spite of all the messages to the contrary and the shelves of diet food in every supermarket. (One of my colleagues came by today with a newspaper article on the Krispy Kreme Donut chain; evidently, Americans eat three million Krispy Kreme donuts each day. We may talk tofu, but we gobble glazed.) Americans all need to work on eating healthier and getting some exercise. Of course, the thin fanatics claim to advocate a healthy lifestyle as well, but I question how healthy people are when they are living on low-calorie chocolate milk drinks, or taking herbal supplements containing goodness knows what, or loading up on the latest wonder diet pill. Remember Fen-phen?

And most diets don't work. An essay by Rebecca Puhl, Ph.D., and Chelsea Heuer, MPH, in the *American Journal of Public Health,* cites studies which found:

> Most weight losses are not maintained and individuals regain weight after completing treatment. Patients who have lost weight through lifestyle modification typically regain 30% to 35% of their lost weight during the year following treatment, and regain most (if not all) of their lost weight within five years. ("Obesity Stigma" 1021)

The authors go on to quote from a study by Mann, et al. "Dieters who gain back more weight than they lost may very well be the norm, rather than an unlucky minority" (qtd. in Puhl and Heuer 1021). My point here is not to argue that overweight people should not try to lose weight for health reasons. Indeed, even a modest weight loss of ten percent of a person's body weight is beneficial to one's health (Puhl and Heuer, "Obesity Stigma" 1021). But such modest weight loss, while healthy, is rarely enough to earn a person fashionably thin status. And despite what the cultural messages suggest, most of us fat folks are trying to eat more sensibly, but the environment does play a role. In a culture where most of us are rushed from work to classes to other activities, the temptation to grab fast food is huge. Sugary or fatty foods are often available in grab and go packages that are so much easier to take to work or eat in the car than making a healthy

An important qualifier: "I'm not advocating that …."

Counterargument.

Integrates (introduces) information from an authority for support.

Long quotes—more than four lines—are indented. This is called a "block quote."

The writer qualifies her point (My point here is not …), makes a concession (Indeed, even a modest weight loss …), and then counterargues (But such modest weight loss, while healthy, is rarely enough ….)

Integrates information from an authority for support.

Engages the reader by anticipating a reader's response.

Takes the reader from one claim (culture encourages obesity) to another claim (culture breeds a prejudice against fat people).

snack. And, there is evidence to suggest we may even be wired to prefer junk food. Brownell and colleagues, in an essay in *Health Affairs*, cite studies which show: "Animals given access to food high in sugar and fat—even when healthy food is freely available—consume calorie-dense, nutrient-poor food in abundance, gain a great deal of weight, and exhibit deteriorating health" (379). I know, I know. We aren't rats. We are thinking beings, but this article goes on to point out that it is not so different for people: "Research has shown consistently that people moving from less to more obese countries gain weight, and those moving to less obese countries lose weight" (379).

So we are surrounded by a culture, even an infrastructure, that encourages obesity, yet the culture also breeds a prejudice against fat people. Various articles and news magazine programs have reported that Americans of all sizes make far more than simple aesthetic judgments when they look at a fat person. Fat people are assumed to be lazy, stupid, ugly, lacking in self-esteem and pride, devoid of self-control, and stuffed full of a host of other unpleasant qualities that have nothing to do with the size of a person's belly or thighs. But, as

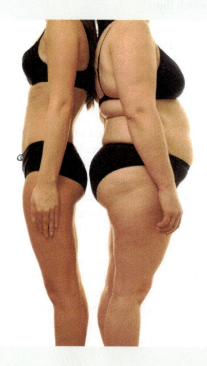

© iStock.com/hartphotography1

anyone who has ever been the victim of such prejudice can tell you, the impact such foolish notions have is real and harmful. For example, Marilyn Wann, in her book *Fat! So?*, cites an experiment in which "[r]esearchers placed two fake personal ads, one for a woman described as '50 pounds overweight' and the other for a woman described as a drug addict. The drug addict received 79 percent of the responses" (59). So, in spite of the agony addiction can cause to the addict and those who love her, people would rather get romantically involved with an addict than a fat person. And not much has changed. In a 2008 article, "The Stigma of Obesity: A Review and Update," Puhl and Heuer report:

> One study asked college students (N=449) to rank order six pictures of hypothetical sexual partners, including an obese partner, a healthy partner, and partners with various disabilities (including a partner in a wheelchair, missing an arm, with a mental illness, or described as having a history of sexually trans- mitted diseases. Both men and women ranked the obese person as the least desirable sexual partner compared to the others. (10)

While it is certainly good news to see that people can look beyond disabilities, such as a wheelchair or a missing arm, and see the value of the whole human being, it is distressing that Americans refuse to do the same for a person's weight. Why would anyone want to date someone who will land them in the STD clinic? How dangerous is that? And yet, such a person is clearly seen as a better romantic choice than a heavy person. Here is a case where weight prejudice is certainly more dangerous to the person with the prejudice than it is to the fat person.

Another area of discrimination based on weight is in employment, both in getting hired in the first place and in receiving equal pay for equal work. In 1998, Wann pointed out that the average fat woman earns about $7000 less per year than her thinner sisters (80). Today, things are still not improving. As of 2004, a study from the National Longitudinal Survey of Youth found that obese men and women suffered a "wage penalty" for their excess weight. For men, wages ranged from 0.7–3.4% less than their slimmer coworkers, while for women the wage losses ranged from 2.3 to 6.1% (qtd. in Puhl and Heuer, "The Stigma of Obesity" 10). Here, as in other areas, we find that obese women are penalized more by society than obese men. Either way, in many jobs, a person's weight has nothing to do with the quality of their performance. In my case, I teach

Introduces an example by integrating information from a source.

Comments on the idea from the source.

Invites the reader to think about disabilities, weight.

The first sentence is a claim. The rest of the paragraph is support.

Information from sources supports the claim.

The essay writer comments on the support information above.

English at a community college. Jobs in academia require an advanced degree, so I happen to have a Ph.D., which has nothing to do with my body size, unless you want to count the weight I gained from thousands of hours sitting reading, sitting at a keyboard, sitting grading papers.

At the least, given the reports and studies, we can conclude that weight prejudice is not merely aesthetic judgment. It's an alarming trend, just like obesity itself, that hurts real people. When people are denied a place to live or a means of support not because of any bad behavior or lack of character or talent on their part but because of someone else's wrongheaded notions, then we need to get our minds straightened out.

The messages are particularly insidious when they suggest that being thin is more important than a man's or, more often, a woman's relationships with her loved ones or even than her health. The media churn the images out, but the public too often internalizes them. For example, in one commercial for Slim Fast, the woman on the ad is prattling on about how she had gained weight when she was pregnant (seems to me, if you make a person, you ought to be entitled to an extra ten pounds) and how awful she felt. Then there is a shot of this woman months later as a thin person with her toddler in her yard. She joyously proclaims that Slim Fast is "the best thing that ever happened to me!" The best thing that ever happened to her?! I thought I heard wrong. What about that little child romping by her heels? Presumably, there is a daddy somewhere for that little cherub. What about his role in her life? The thought that losing that weight is the most important thing that ever occurred in her life is sad and terrifying. It's even worse for the folks who share that life with her. I kept hoping that was not what she meant. I'm sure her family is really most important. But she didn't say, "Next to my baby, Slim Fast is the best thing that ever happened to me." Advertisers don't spend millions of dollars creating ads that don't say what they intend them to; this message was deliberate. Granted, this is only one ad, but the message is clear: The consumer is the center of the universe, and being thin is the only way to ensure that universe remains a fun place to live. The constant repetition of this message in various forms does the damage to the humans who watch and learn.

While we can shrug off advertisements as silly, when we see these attitudes reflected among real people, the hurt is far less easy to brush away. For instance, in her essay, "Bubbie, Mommy, Weight

Allusion to a popular item, Slim Fast, as support for the claim above it.

Thinness ads damage minds lives.

Addresses an opposing point: that ads are harmless.

Watchers and Me," Barbara Noreen Dinnerstein recalls a time in her childhood when her mother took her to Weight Watchers to slim down and the advice the lecturer gave to the women present: "She told us to put a picture of ourselves on the 'fridgerator of us eating and looking really fat and ugly. She said remember what you look like. Remember how ugly you are" (347).

Provides an example, from an essay, as support.

I have a problem with this advice. First, of course, it is too darn common. Fat people are constantly being told they should be ashamed of themselves, of their bodies. And here we see another of those misconceptions I mentioned earlier: the assumption that being fat is the same as being ugly. There are plenty of attractive fat people in the world, as well as a few butt-ugly thin ones, I might add. Honestly, though, the real tragedy is that while few people in this world are truly ugly, many agonize over the belief that they are. Dr. Pipher reported: "I see clients who say they would rather kill themselves than be overweight" (91). Pipher wrote of these attitudes in 1995, but there is not much evidence to suggest we have become any more reasonable or sensible. In fact, in the article "Stigma and Discrimination in Weight Management and Obesity," Brownell and Puhl cite a 2001 study which showed that "28% of teachers in one study said that becoming obese is the worst thing that can happen to a person" (21). Statements like this make me despair for my profession. We are supposed to encourage critical thinking, not mindlessly parrot nonsense and pass it on to the younger generation. And if people think being fat is the worst thing that can happen, they have not watched the world news lately. How would people feel if the attitude was reversed: *The worst thing you can be is thin. All those skinny students must be lazy and stupid. They haven't got enough sense to eat enough or to look the way we want them to. Why bother with them?* And don't think that idea doesn't apply to fat prejudice. Brownell and Puhl cite another study that shows "controlling for income and grades, parents provide less college support for their overweight children than for their thin children" (21). What is up with that? A person's weight certainly has nothing to do with his or her intellect or curiosity about the world. Plus, based on the data I've reported so far, we plus size folks need all the education we can get just to struggle up to a living wage.

Analysis of the opposing logic.

And don't think teachers are the only educated people with crazy ideas about overweight folks. Based on my research, the medical profession is full of people who despise us. "Stigma and

Transition from the field of education to the medical profession.

Discrimination in Weight Management and Obesity" reports that "24% of nurses say they are 'repulsed' by obese persons" (21). That's a virulently negative attitude to get from someone upon whom your life may depend. And according to Puhl and Heuer, things are just as depressing with the doctors: "In a study of over 620 primary care physicians, 50% viewed obese patients as awkward, unattractive, ugly, and noncompliant" ("Stigma of Obesity" 4). But how many people are willing to be compliant with someone who makes them feel awkward, unattractive, and ugly? The article goes on to explain that "one-third of the sample [of doctors] further characterized obese patients as weak-willed, sloppy, and lazy" (4). That's a lot of judgments to make after a ten-minute office visit. Shoot, my doctor is a republican, and if I'm willing to overlook that, the least he can do is overlook a few extra pounds. But, all kidding aside, this prejudice may have real and dangerous effects. Overweight people often do not seek medical care, especially preventive care. Puhl and Heuer go on to report:

Support from various sources is introduced and cited.

> Several studies show that obese persons are less likely to undergo age-appropriate screenings for breast, cervical, and colorectal cancer. Furthermore, research shows that lower rates of preventive care exist independently of factors that are typically associated with reduced health care use, such as less education, lower income, lack of health insurance, and greater illness burden. ("Stigma of Obesity" 7)

Family, too, may ridicule the overweight.

This bullying of the overweight is not only coming from professional and public life. Sadly many people face the cruelest ridicule from family, those we count on most for love and support. Another example of this bullying comes from Pipher's book *Hunger Pains: The Modern Woman's Tragic Quest for Thinness.* Pipher recounts a conversation she overheard one day in a dress shop:

> I overheard a mother talking to her daughter, who was trying on party dresses. She put on each dress and then asked her mother how she looked. Time after time, her mother responded by saying, "You look just awful in that, Kathy. You're so fat nothing fits you right." The mother's voice dripped with disgust and soon Kathy was crying. (89)

Pipher goes on to suggest that Kathy's mother is a victim of the culture, too, because she realizes how hard the world will be on her fat daughter. Unfortunately, what she doesn't realize is how much better her daughter's quality of life would be if she felt loved by her mother. Puhl and Heuer cite the results of a 2006 study of 2,449 overweight and obese women. "Participants were provided with a list of 22 different individuals and asked how often each individual had stigmatized them because of their weight. Family members were the most frequent source of weight stigma, reported by 72% of participants" (qtd. in "Stigma of Obesity" 10).

And the familial insensitivity doesn't stop at adulthood. In Camryn Manheim's book *Wake Up! I'm Fat,* the actress discusses her battle with her weight. She expected many of the difficulties she encountered from people in the entertainment industry, which is notorious for its inhuman standards of thinness for women. But when she gained some weight after giving up smoking, she was stunned when her father told her she should start smoking again until she lost the weight (78). In *The Invisible Woman: Confronting Weight Prejudice in America,* W. Charisse Goodman cites a 1987 study that concluded: "When good health practices and appearance norms coincide, women benefit; but if current fashion dictated poor health practices, women might then engage in those practices for the sake of attractiveness" (30). Like taking up smoking to stay slim.

Certainly everyone is entitled to his or her own opinion of what is attractive, but no one has the right to damage another human being for fun or profit. The media and the diet industry often do just that. While no one can change an entire culture overnight, people, especially parents, need to think about what they really value in the humans they share their lives with and what values they want to pass on to their children. We need to realize that being thin will not fix all our problems, though advertisements for diets and weight loss aids suggest this. Losing weight may, indeed, give a man or woman more confidence, but it will not make a person smarter, more generous, more loving, or more nurturing. It won't automatically attract the dream job or the ideal lover. On the contrary, people who allow the drive to be thin to control them may find that many other areas of their lives suffer: They may avoid some celebrations or get-togethers because of fear they may be tempted to eat too much or the "wrong" foods. They may cut back on intellectual activities like reading or enjoying concerts or art museums because those activities cut into their exercise time too much. The mania for thinness can cause a person to lose all perspective and balance in life. I know. It happened

The writer continues her claim/support approach, beginning the paragraph with a claim then using authorities (Manheim and later Goodman) as support.

The closing paragraph drives home the argument:
- everyone is entitled to his or her own opinion
- but no one has the right to damage another human being for fun or profit
- the media and diet industry do that
- no one can change an entire culture overnight
- but people, parents need to think about what they really value
- we need to realize . . . .

Back to the personal situation and relaxed voice.

to me. My moment of revelation came about twelve years ago. I was a size ten, dieting constantly and faithfully keeping lists of every bite I ate, trying to lose fifteen more pounds. While I was watching the evening news, a story came on about a young woman who was run over by a bus. I vividly recall that as the station played the footage of the paramedics wheeling the woman away on a stretcher, I said to myself, "Yeah, but at least she's thin." I've been lucky enough to have gained some wisdom (as well as weight) with age: I may be fat, but I'm no longer crazy. There are some things more important than being thin.

Sanity is better than insane thinness. The conclusion ties back to the intro.

Works Cited

Brownell, Kelly D., et al. "Personal Responsibility and Obesity: A Constructive Approach to a Controversial Issue." *Health Affairs*, vol. 29, no. 3, Mar.-Apr. 2010, pp. 378–86.

Brownell, Kelly D., and Rebecca Puhl. "Stigma and Discrimination in Weight Management and Obesity." *The Permanente Journal*, vol. 7, no. 3, Summer 2003, pp. 21–23.

Dinnerstein, Barbara Noreen. "Bubbie, Mommy, Weight Watchers and Me." *Worlds in Our Words: Contemporary American Women Writers*, edited by Marilyn Kallet and Patricia Clark, Prentice Hall, 1997, pp. 347–49.

Goodman, W. Charisse. *The Invisible Woman: Confronting Weight Prejudice in America*. Gurze Books, 1995.

Manheim, Camryn. *Wake Up! I'm Fat*. Broadway Books, 1999.

Pipher, Mary. *Hunger Pains: The Modern Woman's Tragic Quest for Thinness*. Ballantine Books, 1995.

Puhl, Rebecca, and Chelsea Heuer. "Obesity Stigma: Important Considerations for Public Health." *American Journal of Public Health*, vol. 100, no. 6, June 2010, pp. 1019–28. *PubMed Central*, doi:10.2105/AJPH.2009.159491.

---. "The Stigma of Obesity: A Review and Update." *Obesity*, vol. 17, no. 5, May 2009, pp. 1–23. *Wiley Online Library*, doi:10.1038/oby.2008.636.

Wann, Marilyn. *Fat! So? Because You Don't Have to Apologize for Your Size*. Ten Speed Press, 1998.

WRITING STRATEGIES

1. Why do you think Paulin refers to "overweight" people as "fat"? What is the effect of this word on readers?

2. Paulin helps readers to understand her main ideas by stating them at the beginning of paragraphs. Find three paragraphs in this essay that begin with the main idea. Do those sentences also connect the paragraph to the previous paragraph? If so, describe how.

3. Paulin uses written sources to support her argument. In some places she directly quotes the sources; in others she paraphrases or summarizes (that is, she puts what the source says in her own words). Find an example of each (quote, paraphrase, summary). How do you know the information is from a source? Does Paulin make that clear? Notice how Paulin introduces the information and punctuates it.

4. Paulin's conclusion does not merely summarize points she has already made. Reread the conclusion and describe how it goes beyond mere summary. What does it try to do?

5. Paulin seems to know that her audience needs to be nudged along to accept her point. In your view, what particular rhetorical strategy is most effective at nudging readers to see the real harm of the media's portrayal of weight?

EXPLORING IDEAS

1. How is weight a public issue?

2. In her opening paragraph, Paulin says that inaccurate images about weight "have shifted our vision of what is important in life way out of whack, so far out that people are being hurt." Then she calls for perspective. What support can you provide for her claim that our vision of what is important is out of whack? What support can you provide that people are being hurt?

3. Why should or shouldn't comedians refrain from making fat jokes about specific individuals?

4. In her conclusion, Paulin says, "[P]eople who allow the drive to be thin to control them may find that many other areas of their lives suffer." Apply her thinking to some other situation besides body weight, and explain how a particular drive has led to suffering.

IDEAS FOR WRITING

1. In what subtle ways are short people marginalized or dismissed in everyday life?

2. What are the quiet hardships of beauty? Focus on one particular struggle that traditionally attractive girls, boys, men, or women encounter.

If responding to one of these ideas, go to the Analysis section of this chapter to begin developing ideas for your essay.

Hive Talkin': The Buzz around Town about Bees

Teresa Scollon

For years, scientists and journalists have been calling on the public to acknowledge the crisis of declining bee populations. The issue has been described and argued about in many books, television programs, and articles. In this essay, Teresa Scollon makes an important move: She localizes the issue and argues about the response from her hometown. Scollon is the author of *To Embroider the Ground with Prayer*, a poetry collection focusing on rural life in Michigan.

Consider the honeybee: *Apis mellifera*. Shipped from Europe to Jamestown in 1622, it spread and thrived and multiplied, often in feral colonies. It is as familiar to us as Pooh Bear, another import, who loved his honey, too. The honeybee is sometimes the symbol of the stinging insects we fear, lumped together with all the bugs that sport similar stripes. Or it appears as the wholesome symbol of nature, winged and cute, hovering on the labels of sweet drinks and waxy balms.

Its intricate social arrangements fascinate us. As Thomas Seeley writes in *Honeybee Democracy*, "It is a bee that is beautifully social. We can see this beauty in their nests of golden combs, those exquisite arrays of hexagonal cells sculpted of thinnest beeswax. We can see it further in their harmonious societies, wherein tens of thousands of worker bees, through enlightened self-interest, cooperate to serve a colony's common good."

In 1944, Karl von Frisch at the University of Munich discovered that honeybees communicate directions to food sources by dancing, specifically in a move called the "waggle." He won the Nobel Prize. Thomas Seeley, quoted above, spent decades studying the honeybees' collective decision-making processes, and goes so far as to wistfully surmise that if only humans would take a few cues from bees, we might be better off.

The honeybee, of course, makes honey from the nectar and pollen it collects from flowers. And by virtue of its appetites and its fuzz, the bee, like other pollinators, is the necessary accomplice to the reproductive lives of plants.

In other words, the bee completes the circuit, jumps the gap, closes the loop that figures importantly into the food chain. Without bees and other pollinators, one-third of the foods we eat would no longer be available to us. An unknown quantity of food necessary to other forms of life would no longer be available. We'd be in big trouble.

But wait—we **are** in big trouble. Because the bees are.

North America is home to some 4,000 species of native bees, 420 of them in Michigan, but we aren't so good at tracking their number or even recognizing their presence, as most of them live as solitaries (bumblebees the social exception). Honeybees, whose pollination services have become much more economically significant than their honey products, are animals we raise, rent out and keep track of. We can say for sure that honeybee colonies have drastically declined, and because native bees are subject to the same perils, we deduce that native bees are likely suffering as well.

WHAT'S GOING ON?

While bees have always been vulnerable to long winters, disease, pests, drought and storms, they've been able to bounce back. Normal annual loss of bee colonies ran at about 10 percent. But the winter/spring of 2006/2007 saw a dramatic change in the resilience of domestic bee populations. Bee colony losses in that year reached 30 percent, and have hovered around that figure ever since. Some beekeepers lost more than 80 percent in 2006. USDA statistics count wintertime die-offs, but now beekeepers were seeing die-offs all year round. The phrase "Colony Collapse Disorder" was coined in 2006 to describe a mysterious phenomenon in which adult bees simply and suddenly disappeared. Beekeepers would open a hive to find only the queen and brood (developing) bees.

A resulting period of intense research points to a complex set of pressures on both domestic and wild bees that includes "disease, a parasite known as the varroa mite, pesticides, extreme weather and poor nutrition tied to a loss of forage plants," according to an article in the May 14 *New York Times*. USDA documents add "sublethal effects of pesticides," gut microbes and lack of genetic variation to the list.

Harvard School of Public Health studies in 2012 and 2014 determined a link between post-winter colony collapse and the increased use of a family of systemic pesticides called neonicotinoids, or neonics for short. These chemicals are used as sprays for plants or marinades for seeds. The plants take the chemicals up into their vascular systems, and any creature that feeds on the leaves, pollen or nectar ingests the poison. While a neonic dose may not kill an individual bee, the aggregate effect on a hive can be deadly. The neonics impair the bees' neurological functions, perhaps including the ability to navigate back to a hive.

Nutritional deficiencies are due to increasing conversion of bee-friendly fields to monocropping of soybeans or corn, which provide little bee sustenance. The hyper-manicuring of lawns in commercial developments and sprawling suburbs destroys wild habitat and forage. Gone are the strips of wildflowers and so-called "weeds" that supported native insects. Finally the drift and increasing use of herbicides kills off wild vegetation, starving bees and forcing them to feed on pesticide-treated crops.

DOWN-HOME RESPONSE

Several concerned organizations, including Michigan State University, are collaborating in the Integrated Crop Pollination Project, trying to better understand the role of bees in cropping systems. Nikki Rothwell, PhD, coordinator of the Northwest Michigan Horticultural Research Center, notes that growers and beekeepers are working together with honeybee health in mind.

Some municipalities have allowed urban beekeepers to set up shop, and several states have established grant and other supportive programs for beginning beekeepers. With more small backyard hives, says Rothwell, we are adding more bees to an area, which may contribute to increased genetic diversity of honeybees.

In December 2012, Traverse City joined in, amending zoning rules to allow beekeeping within certain constraints. The amendment was proposed and championed by a group of interested citizens, Slabtown resident Kima Kraimer chief among them. According to Kraimer, supporting the local cultivation of honeybees supports this area's priorities and way of life.

For a region increasingly eating—and banking on—locally grown food, food products and the tourists they bring, a local supply of pollinators is crucial. The typical city lot has plenty of room for hives and bee-friendly plantings. And, says Kraimer, for a city and region so dependent on agriculture, it was simply incongruent to have an ordinance against bees. She felt it was important to get Traverse City up to speed with the rest of the world in regards to urban beekeeping.

The ordinance in question is *Chapter 610: Animals*. And while the description of prohibited animals that cause "annoyance or disturbance in a neighborhood, by making sounds common to its species" might bring to mind a human neighbor or two, the ordinance's intended focus is pesky bees, crowing roosters and the like. The original ban on bees and other livestock dates to 1966 in an effort to attract city tourists to the area and shed Traverse City's self-image as a rural backwater. But as TC residents are discovering, there are some good things about rural backwaters, including better access to food production and healthy ecosystems. And now the pendulum is swinging back.

A 2009 amendment allows for keeping chickens, and the 2012 amendment allowing bees was written in a similar format, according to Missy Luick, planning and engineering assistant for the city. Compared to other municipalities, she says, the Traverse City ordinance is relatively simple but strict, allowing only two colonies per parcel. The amendment did not pass unanimously at either the planning or the commission level and discussion unearthed fears of litigation and bees on the move. The inclusion of city notification of a beekeeper's neighbors appeared to pacify nervous commissioners.

By way of contrast, an Ypsilanti ordinance begins with language that acknowledges a larger purpose: "Whereas, honey bees are beneficial to mankind and to Michigan in particular … " and quiets possible fears with "Whereas, gentle strains of honey bees can be maintained within populated areas in reasonable densities to fill an ecological niche … without causing a nuisance if the honey bees are properly located, carefully managed and maintained."

Whatever its language, with the Traverse City ordinance in place, six parties applied for the beekeeping permit in 2013, and four in 2014. Education about bees has picked up. Cherryland Garden Club and ISLAND offer workshops, and Oryana Natural Foods spent the month of June educating the public about bees and pollinators with information and novel displays. They pulled black cloth over produce that requires pollination to show that without bees and other friends, we simply wouldn't have many of our favorite and most nutritious foods.

Says Sandi McArthur, Oryana's education and outreach coordinator, "All these factors are coming down on this tiny bee, which is responsible for the amazing bounty that we enjoy every day. As humans we need to see the fragile relationships, the connections between ourselves and the natural world, so we can live more synchronistically and in balance. We need to look at what we are doing and change those practices that we know are harmful and support practices that are supportive of all life. We know what we need to do; now we just need to follow through and do it."

That connection, ultimately, is not only a smart move, but a deeply fulfilling one, as Kraimer, who kept bees until their collapse this winter, attests. "Taking on beekeeping isn't just a task or project," she says. "It's a deep, fulfilling connection to ecology. When you're actually working with hives, that's magic. You're tapping into a deep, mysterious ecological process, and being reminded, as a human, of our role in that."

Kraimer hopes that even residents who don't keep bees will keep asking themselves about their role and responsibility relative to ecological systems. What we are doing in our own yards will have an impact, for better or worse, on the ecosystem. The more we are aware of that, the better we can redirect our impact to reduce pollution and the demise of species. "Bees are dying," she says. "And thinking that we are somehow apart from that is not correct." In fact, she says, most of us already have bees making honey in our yards—we just don't know it's happening.

If our yards are part of an ecosystem, the online boast of a *Ticker* respondent who keeps a "bug-free" yard just doesn't make sense. Why have a yard at all? Why not sling up a hammock in a concrete box? And what does that guy/gal plan to eat for the rest of his/her over-scrubbed days? And what, exactly, should we do about our human propensities for alienation, hyper-vigilance, taking an impulse too far? The best strategy seems to lie in paying attention to connections and how human beings are part of a larger ecological system in which every creature, beautiful or not, plays a crucial part. Our crucial part is, at the very least, to pay attention and to change those activities and practices that we already know do harm.

Funny how talk of bees soon lights on traits we wish, perhaps, to cultivate in ourselves: harmony, cooperation, industry, beauty, service. And the perils bees face—the intersecting effects of chemicals, land use, climate change—are perils we face as well. Maybe we are getting the hang of investigating multi-faceted issues. Maybe the primal pull to see ourselves as part of something bigger will be irresistible and productive. Maybe bees, in one more service to humans, will teach us to step into our role of understanding and supporting the web of life.

The poet Rainer Maria Rilke would agree. For him, the physical world was the entry into the invisible, or spiritual, world. "It is crucial," he wrote in 1925, "not only that we not corrupt and degrade what constitutes the here and now, but … [that it] be comprehended by us in a most fervent understanding and transformed.

"Transformed? Yes, for our task is to imprint this provisional, perishable earth into ourselves so deeply, so painfully and passionately, that its essence can rise again 'invisibly' inside us. We are the bees of the invisible. We wildly collect the honey of the visible, to store it in the great golden hive of the invisible."

WRITING STRATEGIES

1. What is the essay's main claim (or thesis)?

2. How would you describe Scollon's writer's voice? Do you think her voice changes, even slightly, throughout the essay? Use particular passages to support your response.

3. What passages most clearly convey the public resonance of Scollon's essay?

4. Where does the essay effectively use one of the following support strategies: example, allusion, personal testimony, scenario, statistic, authority, facts, appeal to logic, emotion, character, need or value?

5. While Scollon's argument focuses on bees, it suggests something more. Explain what the essay suggests (or argues indirectly) about people. Identify key passages in Scollon's essay to support your point.

EXPLORING IDEAS

1. What makes Scollon's essay an argument and not just a report on bees?

2. What does Scollon mean by "there are some good things about rural backwaters"? How might Traverse City residents have changed their thinking about this?

3. In what way does Scollon think our human propensities can affect bees?

4. What are the reasons why bees could be struggling to survive?

IDEAS FOR WRITING

1. In what other way is your yard part of an ecosystem, and how is that important?

2. In what less obvious way are humans connected to some other wild animal?

If responding to one of these ideas, go to the Analysis section of this chapter to begin developing ideas for your essay.

INVENTION

Academic audiences demand more than "three reasons why I believe X" arguments. They want to experience more in an argument than a writer's personal beliefs; they want to learn a new way of thinking. So academic writers often look for a way to make people rethink an issue. They try to create a new position on a familiar topic or assert a position on an entirely fresh topic. And good writers do not merely *choose* topics; instead, they *build* topics from the novel and surprising moments of everyday life.

The following sections are designed to help you develop ideas for your argument: specifically, to discover a topic (in Point of Contact), develop particular points about the topic (in Analysis), make it relevant to a community of readers (in Public Resonance), focus your position (in Thesis), and create support for that position (in Rhetorical Tools). The questions in each section will help you generate intense ideas and start writing. Your responses to the Invention Questions may take you in various directions, and some of your responses may get left behind. That is to be expected in academic work—or in any work that seeks to discover something valuable.

Point of Contact

Some situations in everyday life are obviously significant—what they mean for our lives, or for the lives of others, is apparent. When our country goes to war or when a new president is elected, for example, most Americans understand the significance. Many situations, however, are far more subtle; their potential meaning is hidden by life's hustle and bustle. To understand their meaning, we must stop in our tracks and focus on them. Use the following suggestions, questions, and images to explore possible topics. If a question seems engaging to you, or if you associate some emotion or idea with the question, start writing. Ask yourself: "Can I change someone's mind about this situation or issue?"

School

What lurking attitude is ruining the learning process? If we're a country of progress, why should history be taught anyway? How is mainstream fashion brainwashing even the smart kids? Will football be the end of serious public education? How was *Napoleon Dynamite*'s portrayal of high school right on target? How are high schools destroying students' ability to cope with the first year of college? How is high school its own form of religion?

Work

What doesn't the public understand or appreciate about my work? Are the work expectations fair? Are the hours fair to workers? What hidden forces or assumptions work against productivity? Why don't people in my line of work get paid more? Are they paid way too much?

George Zimzores/MorgueFile

Napster

Frankie Manning/Getty Images

NASA

Home

What does my neighborhood layout suggest about being a human? How does the layout of my house or apartment or dorm help me to be a better person? What is the central appliance in my living space and how does that affect my thought process? Should more people have gardens? What do cathedral ceilings (or some other architectural feature of our homes) make people think about themselves?

Community

Does my town know what to do with teenagers? Does the water taste funny? Does my town offer ample mass transit? How does the police force function—as keepers of the peace or as something else? How important are trees?

Pop Culture

Can a democracy seriously thrive without a good punk scene? What is a culture without a vibrant funk subculture? Should we be leery or supportive of a whole channel dedicated to food? What does the Discovery Channel do for science? Should there be a fun show about language and writing? Calculus?

Your Major

Look through a current journal in your field to find controversial issues: Are entry-level personnel in my field treated fairly? Is some research in my field or major controversial? Is my field undervalued by the public? Has my field changed any of its practices, for better or worse, in recent years? Should my field be more diverse (in gender and/or ethnicity)?

> ### ACTIVITY
> Make a list of other questions that draw attention to troubling situations in the world around you. What attitude or basic assumption lies beneath some troubling behavior or policy?

Analysis

Analysis cracks open the layers of a topic—and helps writers see more than their initial thoughts. Without analysis, writers may find themselves with little new to say. Avoid answering the Invention Questions too quickly. Instead, use them to search for deeper understanding, which will translate into more intensive writing. Allow time and space for your own thinking to develop:

> What is the particular point of crisis or tension?

> How has the situation (or condition, behavior, policy) come about, and why does it continue?

> What are the effects of the situation (or condition, behavior, policy)?

> Why do I have an opinion on this topic?

> Why is my belief valuable?

In her Invention writing, Ann Marie Paulin looks beneath the initial tension or problem and discovers a hidden layer. She goes beyond being "angry" and discovers that media trends indirectly support, even "encourage," mistreatment and incivility:

Why do I have an opinion on this topic?

I have been fat since I was a kid. For about two days in my twenties I starved my way down to a size ten, thereby earning this head-turning compliment from the guy I was then dating: "You'd be a real fox if you'd just lose a few more pounds." I've had complete strangers say the most astonishing things to me on the street. For example, on my way through a parking lot to get to my car, I passed a young man who looked over at me and shouted: "I don't !, #$ fat chicks!" Who was asking? While these behaviors have sometimes hurt me, they mostly make me angry. And when I look around at the society in which I live, I don't see any signs that this kind of behavior is discouraged. Indeed, the media seems to suggest that fat people, by their very existence, seem to deserve contempt and abuse.

How has this situation come about?

Where it gets tricky is that by the media's definition, damn near everyone is fat. How has this situation come about? I'm not sure, but I've watched it develop. When my mother was young, a size ten or twelve was a respectable dress size. When I was in my twenties, a size eight was a respectable size. Now, you must be a size four, two, or even better, a zero to be considered thin. Now, a six-foot-tall model who wears a size twelve dress is considered plus size. She only gets her photo in Lane Bryant ads and such. It's as if society has completely forgotten the concept of "normal size," and so a person is either thin (if you can count all her bones when she appears in a bathing suit) or she's fat. And that leaves the majority of women believing they are fat and hating themselves for it).

Paulin's thinking shows how writers work: In the process of analyzing ideas, they create various possible writing directions. However, as they begin to develop their projects, they become more focused and revelatory; they grab onto one point and take it somewhere, going beyond the common complaints and revealing a particular quality, effect, or layer of the issue.

Invention Workshop

Enlist the help of another writer in answering one of the Invention Questions. Use the question to initiate a discussion that explores further by questioning one another's responses to the questions. For example, below, Jack is focusing on his high school education. Notice how the discussion with Marcus goes beyond Jack's initial response:

What is the particular point of crisis or tension?

JACK: My high school education was inadequate. I graduated with a B average, and I came to college having to take developmental courses before I could even begin taking credit courses.

MARCUS: But is that the high school's fault?

JACK: Well, if I couldn't cut the mustard in entry-level college courses, why did I get mostly Bs in high school? It seems like something's out of whack.

MARCUS: OK. So the standards are too low in high school?

JACK:	Yeah, I think so.
MARCUS:	Were you ever warned about the standards in college?
JACK:	Sure. All the time, teachers would scare us with things like, "Wait 'til you get in college; you've got to work constantly to keep your grades up."
MARCUS:	But did anyone ever share specifics with you? Did you know what kinds of writing, for instance, you would be doing in college?
JACK:	Not really. It's all been a big surprise.
MARCUS:	Maybe that's the issue: high school students (and maybe teachers and administrators) don't really know what kinds of things go on in entry-level college courses.
JACK:	Yes—and so there's this huge gap in between, and some students fall right into it.

It would be easy to reinforce Jack's initial idea—the inadequacy of high school—by sharing examples of bad teachers or rotten classes, but Marcus and Jack do better. They develop the initial idea into something more specific and revealing: the gap between high school and college standards.

Thinking Further

Analysis is not about answering a question and finding an answer. The real insights lie beneath the answers. Return to your responses to the Invention Questions and try to find the most valuable ideas:

- What statements reveal something specific?
- Which statements or phrases seem new to you?
- Which statements or phrases make a new connection, one that you had not considered before?

Now use the statements you found to develop increasingly intense ideas for your argument. If nothing stands out at this point, consider re-approaching the Invention Questions and invite another person to join your exploration. This time, use the following questions to explore further:

> What behavior, policy, or quality is at the heart of the topic? (What is beneath the tension you initially discovered?)

> What attitude, value system, or assumption rests beneath the actions of people who are involved?

Public Resonance

Writers transform issues or personal concerns into arguable topics, issues that matter in some way to other people. Making a personal concern resonate with a public issue is simply a process of extension. To this end, the following Invention Questions can be used as springboards from personal concerns to public issues. For example, examine the following question: *Is my living situation conducive to my goals as a student?* You may have answered: "Yes. I live at home with my parents and commute to school." Your situation is not unique. Many college students struggle with their living situations—with the decision of living on campus, in a nearby apartment complex, or at home with their parents, away from the campus altogether. This decision involves more than a simple personal choice. It has something to do with college funding, with the success of college students, with the entire college experience. In this sense, your situation resonates with a more public issue. The initial (more personal) question might evolve into a more public question: *Is it beneficial for college students to live at home while going to school?* As you consider your own topic, use the following questions to move from a personal concern to a public issue:

- Who might care about this issue? Why?

- Who *should* care about this issue? Why?

- How are my readers involved in this issue? How *could* they be involved?

- What group of people might understand or sympathize with my situation?

- Is this issue an example of some trend?

- Why is it important that others hear my opinion about this issue?

- What else has been said about this issue, and how are my ideas different?

Public resonance is key in Ann Marie Paulin's project. Her essay shows that the more a topic affects people, the more attention it may deserve. In her responses to the Invention Questions, she explores the hidden messages in ads and the unstated assumptions lurking in the public domain. Paulin's responses show her making connections between her own situation and many others. By extending her thinking outward, she is developing the public dimensions of her idea:

Who might care about this issue? Why?

This is certainly a very public issue because it is almost impossible to escape the media: magazines, newspaper ads, billboards, radio, TV, movies, ads plastered in public restrooms and on the walls of buses, ads in your e-mail every day. And every one of those images that deals with weight or beauty makes it clear that to be fat is completely unacceptable and completely fixable if only a person tries hard enough and buys the right products.

Now, if this were just an issue of vanity, it might be something that could be shrugged off. But it goes much deeper than that. If you really pay attention to those ads, their real message is often that if you are fat, no one will love you. Your husband will leave you (if you ever manage to get one to begin with). Your children will be ashamed of you. Your friends will give up on you. You will be alone and unloved because you are fat. That is the message that really hits us where we live. Who wants to be some lonely outcast? We must conform to whatever it takes.

And so, most of us try the diets, the pills, the exercise classes, the wonder machines, and sometimes even more extreme measures like stomach stapling surgery. But in spite of all the time, money, and effort we expend, most of us are still fat. If you look at the studies done, the results are all about the same: Anywhere from 90% to 98% of the people who lose weight gain it all back within five years.

Sometimes writers need to go beyond the *actual* effects or consequences of an issue and *imagine* the possible ways others are involved. Consider the following: A writer is arguing about college students living at home. The issue seemingly affects only college students, and maybe their parents. But the writer makes the issue resonate with many other potential readers by transforming a personal issue into a more public one:

How college students live is not simply a matter of personal choice and comfort. It is a public issue, a public education issue. At the federal, state, and local levels, Americans are increasingly focused on the out-of-school living conditions of elementary and secondary students. Whenever people talk about the quality of education, invariably they end up discussing the living situation of students—the stability of their homes, the qualities of the neighborhoods. Why? Because people are beginning to realize that education does not occur in a vacuum, that how and where students live impact how they learn. But for some reason, we don't seem to be concerned once students are in college. Consequently, millions of college students swarm off to school every fall, often without deeply considering the implications of where they will live. And when millions of dollars of loans and grants go down the drain when students fail out their first year, we don't seem to ask the same questions we ask about elementary and secondary students.

RESEARCH

Consider using outside sources to help you invent—not just so you can report what others have said, but to help you imagine the hidden values, assumptions, and attitudes people have about the topic. Discover what has been said about your topic, what people have argued, why they have taken certain positions, or why they have ignored it altogether. (See Chapter 14 for help with finding sources.)

Thesis

An argumentative thesis invites debate or suggests that opposing claims exist. For example:

But far more important than my ill temper is a creepy sense that these inaccurate images [about body type] have shifted our vision of what is important in life way out of whack, so far out that people are being hurt.

The process of narrowing down an argument to an intensive single sentence helps writers to understand the heart of their idea. At an early stage in your project, you need not settle into an exact wording, but trying to generate a focused statement can help your ideas gain intensity.

An argumentative thesis should have four qualities:

Arguability

It should be arguable. That is, an arguable thesis should take a stand on an issue that has two or more possible positions. If you can conceive of other possible positions on the topic, you are probably in arguable territory.

Scope

It should be appropriately narrow. Scope—or focus—can be addressed by asking narrow enough questions. Be careful of broad questions: *Is my town boring?* To answer such a question, one would have to consider all of the town's complexities, all of its goings-on, all of its people, all of its places, and so on. However, the question *Does my town offer sufficient activities for teens?* is more easily answerable—and ultimately arguable.

Public Resonance

It should address an issue that resonates with the readers. A good argument addresses a concern that others have *or that a writer thinks they should have.* In other words, a thesis should express something that matters (that has some significance) to readers. It should involve others.

Revelation

Academic writers attempt to do more than argue for their own opinions. They try to *reveal* an unfamiliar topic or reveal a new layer to a familiar topic. *Revelatory*—or insightful—thesis statements change readers' (and the writer's) thinking because they show something new. They clear away the mundane thinking and reveal the roots of an issue. Often, revelatory thesis statements:

- Include a reference to the opposition.

- Overturn or contradict popular opinion.

- Show a particular effect or relationship.

- Uncover a hidden layer.

ACTIVITY

1. Transform the following into revelatory thesis statements:

   - The Internet has changed the world.

   - Video games are bad for kids.

   - Sixteen-year-olds who commit crimes should be punished as adults.

2. In a small group, choose one of the following topics and develop at least one revelatory argumentative statement:

   - Leash laws in your town

   - The process for choosing presidential nominees

   - Product placement in movies

   - The cost of college textbooks

   - High school English courses

Evolution of a Thesis

Writers can always increase the focus and revelation of a thesis. The following idea evolves into an increasingly sophisticated point:

- College students benefit from living at home.

- Traditional college students still need the support structure of their home lives to deal with the new challenges of college.

- Because college culture demands intense intellectual and social change from high school culture, traditional college students need the support structure of home.

The first statement announces a simple opinion. The second narrows in on a specific tension, "the new challenges of college," but is still a bit vague and can intensify with more focus on that tension. The third statement brings us close to the primary tension and shows us something that might otherwise escape our awareness: the "intense intellectual and social change" between high school and college culture. Readers of the last two theses, especially the third, are offered a novel insight about schooling. In this way, revelatory thesis statements are more than personal opinion; they are particular and persuasive insights.

Common Thesis Problems

The Question Problem: A question is not a thesis, because it offers no stance. People sometimes use questions to imply a stance: *Isn't that the point of college? Why can't you be like your sister?* But this is generally an informal strategy—something people do in everyday talk. A formal argumentative stance should suggest a particular position amid a realm of many others.

The Obvious Fact Problem: An argument that simply announces a commonly known condition is no argument at all. Imagine someone arguing: *Many people go to college for their futures; Americans love cars;* or *Space exploration is expensive.* Such statements do not invite opposition because they are widely held beliefs. They are safe statements about the condition of our civilization. But the statement *Space exploration is too expensive to continue at its present pace* invites opposition.

The Personal Response Problem: Argument depends upon the presence of several other perspectives peering at the same topic. However, when people proclaim a personal response (about their tastes, likes, dislikes, or desires), they merely make public their own state of mind. *I really liked the movie* is not an argumentative stance. It is a statement about a person's tastes. But the statement *Johnny Depp's portrayal of a wayward pirate illustrates his superior range as an actor* invites opposition. Other positions can engage the point critically.

REVISING YOUR THESIS

Before moving on, try to express the main point of your argument in a single sentence. Then evaluate the statement using the following questions:

- How is the statement arguable? (What other positions might be taken?)

- Can the statement be narrower? (What words are too vague or broad?)

- With what public issue or concern does the statement resonate?

- How does the statement reveal a unique insight or hidden layer of the issue?

You might also exchange your working thesis statement with peers and use these questions to generate helpful responses.

Rhetorical Tools

Crafting an essay, or any written text, is a recursive process: Writers move back and forth, drafting, rethinking, redrafting. The strategies in this section will help you move through the process, building an engaging text from your ideas. Academic argument involves four basic ingredients or elements:

- Main claim/thesis
- Support

- Counterargument

- Concession

Support

Support gives substance and legitimacy to an argumentative claim and comes in a variety of forms. Consider the following as a collection of usable support strategies, a toolbox for persuading readers of your position, despite the particular topic.

© Cengage

Examples: Specific cases or illustrations of a phenomenon. (See Pedersen ¶4 and 6, Paulin ¶7.)

Allusions: References to history, science, nature, news events, films, television shows, or literary texts. (See Paulin ¶2, Scollon ¶1.)

Personal Testimonies/Anecdotes: Individual accounts or experiences. While testimony comes from an eyewitness ("I saw the train coming around the mountain …"), an anecdote is told by the arguer as though he or she is an objective reporter of events ("The incident on the train tracks started with the train coming around the mountain …"). (See Pedersen ¶11, Paulin ¶1 and 2.)

Scenarios: Hypothetical or fictionalized accounts. (See Pedersen ¶7.)

Statistics: Information (often given as numerical value) collected through experimentation, surveys, polls, and research. (See Pedersen ¶2, Paulin ¶4.)

Authorities: References to published (most often written) sources. When using authorities, writers must formally document the use of any information, ideas, and expressions taken from sources. For an extended explanation of formal documentation and integration of sources, see Chapter 16: Integrating and Documenting Sources. (See Paulin ¶2, Scollon ¶2–3, 12.)

Facts: Agreed-upon events or truths, or conclusions drawn from investigation. (See Scollon ¶10–11.)

Too often, writers limit themselves by assuming that facts and statistics are the primary support tools for a good argument, when the truth is that facts and statistics are merely a fragment of what's possible—and what's most valuable. Writers have the whole world of culture and history within reach. They can make connections (allusions) to historical or current events, literary texts, science, nature, and their personal lives. For example, perhaps you see a connection between your topic and a recent news event. You could briefly explain details of the event and then describe what it means for your topic—how it reveals something significant and ultimately validates your opinion. The same thing goes for a movie, an ad, or a historical event. For instance, imagine a writer developing the argument about college residence policies. He might bring popular culture to his aid:

> In movies and popular television shows, college is nearly always portrayed as a raucous social engagement. The typical movie college student (like those in *American Pie* or *Animal House*) is a dormitory, apartment, or frat or sorority house dweller who thrives or suffers in the family-free environment. The whole point of college in mainstream movies is to create a living situation in which the students just tread the line between responsible participation in society and utter immersion in bohemian life. It's no wonder that going to college seems synonymous with "going away" to college. When students long to avoid living in the chaotic social climate of campus life, they are working against more than some college policies. They are working against popular culture.

If you see a connection, especially one that others might not see, you can create a new way of thinking about the topic. Use the following questions to develop allusions, testimony, and scenarios for your argument:

> ❯ Does a historical situation or trend (say, the rise of a particular fashion, organization, or individual) illustrate something about my topic?

> ❯ How has popular culture treated my topic? Does it show up in television shows, movies, or commercials? If so, how is it characterized, mishandled, or celebrated?

> ❯ Have fictional characters illustrated something important about the topic or some behavior related to it?

> ❯ How does nature (animals, life cycles, plants, biological processes, and so on) demonstrate something about my topic?

> ❯ What has science taught people about my topic?

> ❯ Do any news events illustrate my point or stance?

> ❯ What have I witnessed or experienced that illustrates my point?

> ❯ What hypothetical situation could illustrate my point?

> ❯ What do other writers or authorities on the matter say about the topic?

Additionally, arguments depend on appeals, which make a connection between the topic and the audience's thoughts, values, and feelings. In fact, appeals have such rhetorical force that they give meaning to and can even dominate over other forms of evidence. The first three appeals that follow (to logic, emotion, and character) are often discussed using three classical Greek terms: *logos* (for logic), *pathos* (for emotion), and *ethos* (for character). These are sometimes referred to as the Classical appeals.

Appeal to Logic: Relates the argument to the audience's sense of reason. When writers create a line of reasoning, they create an intellectual path for readers—several steps (sometimes called premises) that lead to an argumentative claim or even the writer's thesis. (See Pedersen ¶7, Paulin's conclusion.)

Appeal to Emotion: Relates the argument to an emotional state of the audience, or attempts to create a particular emotional state in the audience. (See Paulin ¶1 and conclusion.)

Appeal of Character: Relates the argument to a quality of the author/speaker. (See Pedersen ¶11.)

Appeal to Need: Relates the argument to people's needs (spiritual, economic, physical, sexual, familial, political, etc.). (See Scollon ¶25.)

Appeal to Value: Relates the argument to people's values (judgments about right/wrong, success, discipline, selflessness, moderation, honesty, chastity, modesty, self-expression, etc.). (See Paulin ¶4–5, Scollon ¶26.)

While these appeals are listed separately, it is important to remember that they often function together. They overlap and even depend on one another in subtle ways. For example, imagine a line of reasoning that walks through the consequences of defunding an animal shelter. The line of reasoning itself appeals to logic: *If this happens, then this will happen.* But the consequences, hundreds of dogs and cats suffering, have an emotional appeal. Even if the writer does not amplify that suffering with detailed description, the suffering would still matter. It would still function as part of the argument. In this way, emotions, values, and needs often intensify logical appeals.

Additionally, the appeals often rely on other forms of support. Consider the topic from the previous section: college students living at home. If we want to convince readers to believe that college should not require students to live on campus, we might create the following appeal to logic or line of reasoning:

Premise: The shift from high school to college culture is significant.
Premise: Many students experience a kind of culture shock in the transition.
Claim: This culture shock negatively impacts their academic performance.

Each of these statements would involve further explanation, examples, facts, allusions, and testimony. In other words, this line of reasoning might require several lengthy passages of text and a range of different support strategies. If the readers could accept each premise, they would be led directly to the thesis—that college policies should not require on-campus residence for all first-year students. In this way, writers can generate several logically connected paragraphs that build toward their thesis statements. As you consider your own topic, use the following questions to develop appeals:

> What line of reasoning can I create for readers to follow? What premises do readers have to accept before they accept my thesis?

> How can I connect the topic to people's values (sense of right and wrong, success, discipline, selflessness, moderation, honesty, chastity, modesty, self-expression, etc.)?

> How can I connect the topic to people's basic needs (spiritual, economic, physical, sexual, familial, political, etc.)?

> How can I connect the topic to people's emotions (fear, hope, sadness, happiness, etc.)?

> Does my life (my role in a relationship, on a job, in school, on a team, etc.) lend credibility to my position on this topic?

ACTIVITY

Generate a variety of appeals for each of the following claims:

- Although war illustrates human cruelty and malice, it also illustrates human compassion and sympathy.

- Most proponents of capital punishment fail to consider the impact on the executed person's loved ones.

- Democracy cannot thrive in a two-party system.

- Excessive marketing leads to a lack of civility and respect among citizens.

Counterargument

Counterarguments anticipate and refute claims or positions that oppose those being forwarded by the writer. Writers must account for positions outside of, or opposed to, their own claims(s) and include reasoning to offset that opposition. For example, a savvy teenager who wants to attend a party will imagine his parents' concerns and work those concerns into his argument about why he should be allowed to go. A politician will anticipate her opponent's position on an issue and formulate her speech accordingly.

The most successful arguers are good counterarguers. They address and even dismantle the specifics of opposing claims. In her essay, Ann Marie Paulin counterargues by summing up advice given to Barbara Dinnerstein: "She told us to put a picture of ourselves on the 'fridgerator of us eating and looking really fat and ugly. She said remember what you look like. Remember how ugly you are." In the paragraph that follows this advice, Paulin explains why she disagrees:

> I have a problem with this advice. First, of course, it is too darn common. Fat people are constantly being told they should be ashamed of themselves, of their bodies. And here we see another of those misconceptions I mentioned earlier: the assumption that being fat is the same as being ugly. There are plenty of attractive fat people in the world, as well as a few butt-ugly thin ones, I might add. Honestly, though, the real tragedy is that while few people in this world are truly ugly, many agonize over the belief that they are. Dr. Pipher reported: "I see clients who say they would rather kill themselves than be overweight" (91). I never have figured out how trashing a fellow being's self-esteem is going to help that person be healthier.

In academic argument, opposing claims are vital. Instead of ignoring or fearing them, good writers *use* them to develop points. Addressing opposing claim will make an argument more complex, more developed, and more persuasive.

Some writers integrate a counterargument directly into their thesis statements. For example, let's examine the working thesis: *College students benefit from living at home while attending school.* Now let's imagine the opposition: Someone might argue that the college experience depends on moving away from home, that intellectual growth requires leaving one's family and familiar turf. This opposing position might be supported with personal testimony and stories in literature that tell of heroes leaving their homeland to seek knowledge or wisdom in the world. We would do well to consider these points, and perhaps work against some, or one, of them directly. We might even work part of the logic into our own thesis: *Despite the attraction of living away from home and experiencing life in unfamiliar territory, college students benefit from living at home while attending school.* The thesis now contains a counterargument. It is both an assertion and a response to an opposing point.

Invention Workshop

This activity is designed to generate counterarguments:

- Assemble writers into small groups.

- The first writer should read his or her thesis statement to the group.

- Taking turns, each group member should refute the position given in the statement. The idea is to play devil's advocate, to complicate the writer's ideas.

- The writer should write down each opposing.

- After everyone in the group has given an opposing claim, repeat the process with another writer.

Concession and Qualifier

While counterarguments refute others' claims, concessions acknowledge the value of others' claims. Put another way, if the writer says that an objection or alternative is wrong, the response is a counterargument; but if the writer says that the objection or alternative is right, that response is a concession. Paulin makes concessions in her argument:

> While it is certainly good news to see that people can look beyond disabilities, such as a wheelchair or a missing arm, and see the value of the whole human being, it is distressing that Americans refuse to do the same for a person's weight.
>
> Certainly everyone is entitled to his or her own opinion of what is attractive, but no one has the right to damage another human being for fun or profit.

Paulin's concessions (it's good to look beyond disabilities; people are allowed their own opinion of what is attractive) propel her argument forward. Her concessions are an important part of her line of reasoning.

Conceding in academic argument does not make an argument wishy-washy. In fact, a good concession shows that a writer understands the broader context—other opinions, values, hopes, and perspectives. A good writer might discuss the logic of another position and show, *to some degree,* how that position has validity. This does not mean that the writer's own point is weak; on the contrary, it means that his or her point is strong enough to acknowledge the soundness of other positions.

Qualifiers are related to concessions. They acknowledge the limitations of, or make clear boundaries for, the writer's own argument. For example, when we say *some, most, many* or *often, frequently, occasionally* we are using qualifiers. When giving a speech on the evils of corporate tax evasion, a senator qualifies her statements: "Granted, *most* companies in America pay taxes responsibly, but we must focus on those *few* rogue and politically powerful companies." When arguing for a salary increase, a union leader acknowledges a point made by the opposition: "We understand that economic times ahead *could be* perilous and that a salary increase *could* make the company more financially vulnerable to outside forces, but the future of the company certainly depends upon the well-being of its loyal employees." In her argument, Paulin employs an explicit qualifier, which may keep readers from mischaracterizing her position:

> First of all, let me make it clear that I'm not advocating that everyone in America go out and get fat. According to the news media, we are doing that very handily on our own, in spite of all the messages to the contrary and the shelves of diet food in every supermarket.

ACTIVITY

Before drafting an essay, plan out your main elements. Write out your working thesis and then, below it, create five headings:

- Personal testimony
- Examples, allusions, or scenarios
- Evidence from sources or reference to authorities
- Opposing positions
- Counterarguments, concessions, or qualifiers

Under each heading, list the ideas or information you've generated so far.

Caution: Logical Fallacies

Logical fallacies are flaws in the structure of an argument that make the claims invalid. A fallacy is a falsehood, so a logical fallacy is a logical falsehood that makes no sense within a given situation. For example, consider this familiar line:

> If you break a mirror, you'll have seven years of bad luck.

We may recognize this as superstition. In academic terms, it is called *faulty cause/effect*. That is, the broken mirror does not actually cause misfortune in one's life. The statement seems categorically faulty. However, the success (or logic) of any argument depends on the particular situation. All argumentative statements exist in situations that give those statements credibility.

(If someone's entire fortune were tied to a mirror, then the previous statement would be more logical!) Statements are logical or illogical based on the situation.

In academia, recognizing logical fallacies is part of being a critical thinker in all disciplines. Academic readers become suspicious when an argument contains any of the following fallacies:

Ad hominem (Latin for to the person): Attacks a person directly rather than examining the logic of the argument:

- We cannot possibly consider Ms. Smith's proposal because she is a Catholic.
- Mr. Mann's argument is suspicious because he is a socialist.

Strawperson: Exaggerates a characteristic of a person or group of people and then uses the exaggeration to dismiss an argument:

- Islamic fundamentalists are crazy. They only want to destroy Americans. We cannot accept their claims about imperialism.
- Environmentalists are radical. They want to end everyone's fun by taking cars and boats away.

Faulty Cause/Effect: Confuses a sequential relationship with a causal one. Assumes that event A caused event B because A occurred first:

- Since the construction of the new baseball stadium, homelessness in the downtown area has decreased.
- The tax cut made energy rates drop.

Either/or Reasoning: Offers only two choices when more exist:

- Either we destroy Russia or it will destroy us.
- The American people will choose to control their own lives or give away their wills to socialist candidates.

Hasty Generalization: Draws a conclusion about a group of people, events, or things based on insufficient examples (often, the logical flaw behind racist, sexist, or bigoted statements):

- Men are too possessive. My ex-boyfriend would never let me go out alone.
- French people are rude. When I went to France, the civilians grunted French statements when I asked for help.

Non sequitur (Latin for it does not follow): Skips several logical steps in drawing a conclusion:

- If we do not trash the entire tax code, the downtown area will slowly deteriorate.
- A new baseball stadium downtown will help with the homelessness problem.

Oversimplification: Does not acknowledge the true complexity of a situation or offers easy solutions to complicated problems:

- If we could give kids something to do, they wouldn't get depressed.

- This credit card will end all of my financial problems.

Slippery Slope: Assumes that a certain way of thinking or acting will necessarily continue or extend in that direction (like a domino effect). Such an argument suggests that once we begin down a path, we will inevitably slip all the way down, and so the effects of a particular action or idea are exaggerated:

- If the college makes students take more mathematics, the next thing we know, advanced calculus and quantum physics will be requirements for all graduates.

- If North Vietnam succeeds in making South Vietnam communist, it will eventually threaten the shores of the United States of America.

False Analogy: Makes a comparison between two things that are ultimately more unlike than alike. The differences between the things make the comparison ineffective or unfair, or the comparison misrepresents one or both of the things involved:

- Writing is like breathing: you just do what comes naturally.

- Like Galileo, Bill Clinton was breaking new ground, but no one understood him.

Begging the Question: Attempts to prove a claim by using an alternative wording of the claim itself:

- Girls should not be allowed into the Boys' Military Academy because it is for boys only.

- I believe that all cigarette smoking should be banned from public places because I truly believe in smoking bans.

ACTIVITY

1. What logical fallacies might you overhear in everyday situations? Consider the following scenarios: a customer trying to return an item; a store clerk trying to sell an extended warranty; a teacher explaining why a student cannot receive credit for a late assignment; a student arguing that he or she should receive a better grade; two politicians debating a tax cut; a husband explaining why he should go fishing with his cousin all weekend.

2. In groups, write an example for each of the fallacies listed in this chapter.

3. In groups, write short argumentative essays loaded with logical blunders. Someone in each group should read the completed essay aloud, and the class should attempt to point out and name the fallacies.

Revision

Some argumentative essays take on too much. Their focus is too broad, which results in vague, unconvincing support. Take one last look at your thesis—the main argumentative assertion of your essay. Does it focus on a particular tension, a particular aspect of an issue, a specific element or dimension of a broader topic? What words or phrases (*things, people, society*) can be more specific? How might you focus on one aspect of an issue rather than the whole issue?

Peer Review

Underline your thesis or write it at the top of your essay so that reviewers will get traction as they read. Then, exchange drafts with at least one other writer. Reviewers should use the following questions to guide a helpful response:

1. How well can you follow the writer's line of reasoning? (See Appeal to Logic, pages 256–257.) Imagine the line of reasoning as though it is a stone path. If the path is well laid out, you should feel a stone at every step. If it is not, you might miss a step; you might feel like some intellectual step is missing.

2. Can you think of another cultural, literary, historical, or political allusion that relates to the writer's position?

3. Suggest specific points that the writer should concede or qualify. For instance, the writer's position might seem too extreme; the claims might include too many people or a large, diverse group without making any distinctions. Point out such claims, and help the writer to see the need to acknowledge subtlety, complexity, and exceptions.

4. Can you imagine another opposing point that the writer could address in a counterargument? Although the writer may have dealt with several opposing positions, you might think of an additional issue that should be addressed.

5. Consider the writer's voice. Circle passages or sentences that shift mood and speak *at,* rather than *with,* readers. Suggest an alternative strategy or phrasing.

6. Do paragraphs focus on one main point? Point to sentences in paragraphs that stray from the initial idea put forth in the paragraph.

7. What is the most engaging passage in the draft so far? Why?

8. Check for sentence vitality.
   - Where can the writer change linking verbs to active verbs?
   - Where can the writer avoid drawing attention to *I* and *you?*
   - Consider vitality strategies from other chapters:
     —Help the writer change unnecessary clauses to phrases.
     —Help the writer change unnecessary phrases to words.

—Point to expletives (such as *there are* and *it is*).

—Help the writer change passive verbs to active verbs for more vitality.

—Help the writer avoid common grammatical errors: comma splices, sentence fragments, or pronoun/antecedent agreement.

QUESTIONS FOR RESEARCH
If the writer used outside sources:

- Where must he or she include in-text citations? (See pages 478–479 and 496–498.)

- Are quotations blended smoothly into the argument and punctuated correctly? (See pages 467–476.)

- Where could more direct textual cues or transitions help readers? (See pages 474–476.)

- Is the Works Cited or References page formatted properly? (See Chapter 16: Integrating and Documenting Sources.)

Reflection
Academic essays are not merely vehicles for communicating thought. They are intellectual playing fields—places for writers and readers to discover something. Those discoveries do not exist in the vacuum of an essay; they resonate outward through the lives of the writers and readers. An argument essay in particular sets out to assert something about the world, and that assertion is bound to impact reality—because people live according to the arguments they accept. Now that you have written an argumentative essay, consider its rhetorical layers:

1. How does your thesis reveal something about everyday life?

2. How does your essay challenge something about the way most people live and think?

3. How important are appeals to your argument?

4. How do you engage opposing positions? How do they make your argument more complex?

5. How do you concede or qualify?

Beyond the Essay: The Open Letter
Argumentative essays have changed the world. They've started revolutions, supported religious movements, initiated new scientific organizations, spotlighted atrocities, and prompted a broad range of political events. But sophisticated arguments can impact the world through other genres too.

The open letter is closely related to the essay. It is aimed at a particular audience, a particular reader or set of readers, but it also resonates with a broader audience. An open letter draws both writer and readers, and an otherwise private discussion, into a public setting. For example, Martin Luther King, Jr.'s "Letter from Birmingham Jail" was originally aimed at nine fellow clergy members, but the letter also speaks to millions of others. In effect, King's response to a particular audience is also for a broader audience. The conversation occurs among a few particular people, but the issues and claims involve many. Or consider the apostle Paul's letters to the Romans that now constitute part of the New Testament. They have become known to millions of readers, but they were originally aimed at a particular group of people. Or more currently, newspapers and magazines often print open letters to the president, to an editor, or to corporate heads. Hundreds, thousands, or millions of others read and are influenced by these letters. And one might argue that these others are really the main audience.

Because letters are written with a particular audience in mind, they may draw attention to specifics about the readers' lives, such as specific behaviors, policies, attitudes, or events. The writer may then draw out the significance, explaining the impact on or meaning for others (the public resonance).

Return to your essay and imagine a particular person or group of people who should read and accept your claims. Then develop an open letter addressed to that particular audience. But don't just make a few simple changes in your essay and call that a letter. Instead, *take a big step back*: Imagine a different rhetorical situation, this one having a different audience, a different method of delivery, and a different purpose. Although you may end up using some especially nice strategies from the essay, approach the letter as if writing from scratch.

The following questions may help shape your ideas:

- Who is the primary audience? Who is being explicitly addressed in the letter?

- What other audience is there? Who else might read the letter and what might their response be? Can they take action based on the letter? How might they think or act differently because of reading it?

- How can you appeal to the primary audience? How can you make a specific connection between them and the issue? How might the letter also appeal to others reading it?

- What pieces (phrases, sentences, ideas, strategies) can you take from the essay and include in the letter? Why these pieces? What pieces should you leave behind? What new pieces should you create for the letter?

9

Responding to Arguments

John Metz

Chapter Objectives
This chapter will help you to:

- Identify the main claim (thesis), support strategies, counterarguments, and concessions operating in a specific argument.
- Identify warranting assumptions operating in a specific argument.
- Develop an analytical/argumentative essay that responds to a specific argument.
- Develop your ideas with a range of analytical and argumentative support strategies.

"We hold these truths to be self-evident, that all men are created equal, that they are endowed by their Creator with certain inalienable Rights, that among these are Life, Liberty, and the pursuit of Happiness."

—The Declaration of Independence

INTRODUCTION

Arguments are all around us. They lurk in nearly every situation—public or private—and we often respond to arguments that hover but are not stated directly. Some situations generate a huge range of arguments. Like magnets, they attract a storm of claims, facts, testimony, appeals, counterarguments, concessions, and qualifiers. Consider, for instance, the border between the United States and Mexico. In recent years, it has created a litany of arguments about federal and state budgets, immigration, race, national identity, drug use, poverty, labor, minimum wage, taxes, health care, education, and human rights. As with many political issues, the border has developed its own argumentative cosmos, filled with radical new claims, traditional platforms, and competing interpretations of founding national documents. The positions get bantered around on radio talk shows, blogs, and of course political campaign ads. Entering that cosmos can be tricky. With so many issues and positions swirling around, it can be difficult to find a particular point of contact.

In academia, writers understand the power and peril of big argumentative issues. Rather than take on a huge swirl of claims, they often focus and respond to specific texts: A psychologist responds to Freud's theory of ego development, explaining that such a theory is not valuable in treating female patients. A political science student supports a revised historical account of U.S. foreign policy that holds Henry Kissinger partly responsible for atrocities in Chile during the 1970s. Law students respond to a Supreme Court ruling that upholds the rights of law enforcement officers to detain citizens for traffic violations. They argue that the ruling erodes protections against "unreasonable search and seizure." An English professor reviews a controversial new book and defends its claims against rampant consumerism.

As these examples suggest, responding to an argument does not necessarily mean disagreement. The initial argument (whether a court ruling, a book, an essay, or a historical account) provides the position on a topic. A writer has many options beyond agreement or disagreement. For instance, he or she might agree with the initial argument and extend the ideas with additional points, disagree with a particular point, redefine the issue, or point out some logical flaws. As you can imagine, this is a somewhat more sophisticated task than what we examined in Chapter 8: Making Arguments. However, responding to arguments is an engaging activity, one that is not only vital to and valued in academia, but also necessary for maintaining a democracy. Although a writer can respond to many different kinds of argument, this chapter focuses primarily on arguments that are formally delivered.

The chapter readings will illustrate a variety of strategies for responding. Early in each essay, the author refers to a particular aspect of the original argument, and this reference provides purpose and traction for the response. As you read, notice how this reference to the original argument is made. After reading the essays, you can find an argument in one of several ways: Go to the Point of Contact section to find an argument from everyday life; choose one of the Ideas for Writing that follow the essays; or respond to any argumentative essay from another chapter in this book. After you find a topic, go to the Analysis section to begin developing your response.

READINGS

Entitlement Education
Daniel Bruno

We often respond to the people (and arguments) that we agree with the most. In the following essay, Daniel Bruno agrees with most of Peter Sacks's original argument. His introduction explains: "But he fails, it seems, to emphasize enough a most harmful effect of this sense of entitlement." Bruno's response does not disagree but rather *emphasizes* a crucial point in an attempt to make *readers* more aware of it. (Portions of Bruno's invention work are shown in later sections of this chapter.)

In his book *Generation X Goes to College,* Peter Sacks describes, among other things, the sense of entitlement that some students in today's consumerist culture have toward a college education. One entire chapter explores this issue alone, providing examples of this "sense" and looking into its "humble beginnings." Sacks shows how consumerism has invaded education, leading some students to expect good grades for little effort. But he fails, it seems, to emphasize enough a most harmful effect of this sense of entitlement. The biggest problem, as I see it, is that although students are able to graduate from high school (and even some colleges) with minimal effort, those students may find themselves cheated in the long run.

> Overall summary of original argument.
>
> Entitlement: expecting to get good grades for little effort.
>
> Main response to the original argument.
>
> (Attention to "I") Bruno's thesis, and distinction between his argument and the original.

How might they be cheated? One might argue that students get cheated because entitlement doesn't go on forever. At some point it stops. For example, a college graduate with a marketing degree, but especially weak thinking or writing skills, may find himself disadvantaged on the job. It is not that his boss puts her foot down; instead, the job does. Our student finds himself not well prepared for it. He gets cheated because he is disadvantaged at his job—a job that he paid money to learn how to do. Of course the point isn't about marketing majors. The same is true of students in any field. (Marketing is just what came to mind.)

One might also claim that students will be cheated because their lives will somehow *be less.* This argument claims that a person's

Analysis of several possible arguments about the results of student entitlement.

intelligence contributes to his quality of life. Here we must remember that "intelligence" is not just "knowledge." Instead, it is being able to use knowledge, to make connections and figure things out, to see causes and solve problems. A person may have much knowledge—that is, he may have accumulated a lot of facts—but not have much intelligence . . . or so the argument goes. As one goes from first grade to twelfth, from twelfth grade to college, and from freshman to senior, education shifts focus from mere accumulation of information (knowledge) to application of information (intelligence). And while we may accumulate more knowledge as a senior in college than we did as a senior in high school, the focus in college has (or should have) shifted from mere knowledge to intelligence—that is, to the ability to make good use of one's knowledge.

Intelligence = being able to use knowledge.

Other standard arguments claim other ways students might be cheated. For example, we might feel sorry for someone who doesn't get a joke—or a reference. Allusions to literature, history, philosophy, and so on allow us to say much in few words. But does the listener understand? If a person is unaware of common references—the Battle of the Bulge, Normandy, Existentialism, T. S. Eliot, World War I, Rasputin, John the Baptist, Gandhi, apartheid, Jonas Salk, Johnny Appleseed, Lewis and Clark, the Trail of Tears, slavery, the Donner Party, and so on—he misses out on conversations, on meaning, on *connecting with his fellow inmates.* Of course, here one might counter that you don't need to know all of these things. And, I agree, you don't. People tend to hang out with people who have similar interests and tastes.

Transition.

Cheated out of standard cultural knowledge.

Uses historical and other allusions to prove his point about allusions.

Concession.

One more argument claims that because we live in a democracy, we must be well-educated. Since all the citizens are responsible for the government, our forefathers promoted public education so that all citizens—not just the wealthy and elite—would know how to read and write. Thomas Jefferson wrote,

This gives the topic extra public resonance (since the democratic process is at stake).

Cheating the whole democracy.

> I know no safe depository of the ultimate powers of society but the people themselves; and if we think them not enlightened enough to exercise their control with a wholesome discretion, the remedy is not to take it from them, but to inform their discretion by education. This is the true corrective of abuses of constitutional power. (278)

In what ways can educated citizens correct abuses in a democracy? A person's way of life, his purchases and activities—not just a person's vote or protest march—is part of the responsibility. Thus, consumers and neighbors and co-workers and so on should behave responsibly and think intelligently. It is our responsibility as citizens of a democracy.

True enough, these are all ways that students who are allowed to just slide by end up getting cheated. But another way (and one less talked about) strikes me as being far more offensive. This reason hinges on the fact that many students are not just sliding by.

Transition paragraph that leads us to Bruno's particular stance.

In *Generation X Goes to College,* Peter Sacks illustrates that all of today's college students cannot just be thrown in the same big barrel. In describing the modern/post modern clash in education, he spends the majority of his time talking about those students who are underprepared, who lack the basic study skills required in academic work, and who demonstrate little real commitment to their own education. Yet, he does not discuss this problem in isolation. He also mentions another type of student. For example, he introduces the reader to Marissa and Carol: "As very good students, [their views] were virtually excluded by The College in order to accommodate the whiners and complainers" (61). And he says they "suffered not only educationally" (63). In addition to discussing specific good students, an entire chapter presents survey results about students' attitudes toward education. While he makes claims such as "nearly a quarter of the students . . . harbored a disproportionate sense of entitlement," this very statement tells the reader that a full three-quarters (that is, three out of four) students *do not* "harbor a disproportionate sense of entitlement" (54-59). He wraps up the book by focusing on another student, Andie, who he describes as "a good student, constantly picking [his] brain for information and feedback on her work" (186-87). His final paragraph, before the Epilogue, says, "Let's create a system that encourages people like Andie at least as much as the ones who don't give a damn" (187). Thus, Sacks shows that today's students are a more diverse group—in skill level, background, and attitude toward education—than has ever before been gathered together in the college classroom.

Return to the original argument.

Quotations illustrate particular points of the original. A properly used colon—to introduce a quote with words that could be punctuated as a sentence—provides coherence. Readers know immediately the relationship of the words on the left and right of the colon. Quotation marks provide coherence by making clear that the words inside them are from a source.

More summary of the original argument.

Now when we connect two things—the present grade-inflated, entitlement-driven education system that has got a foothold in most of America's high schools and colleges AND the diversity in skill and attitude toward education of today's college students—two problems appear.

Transition paragraph.

One problem is that the motivated students are not being as challenged as they could be. Although their situation is not ideal, it is far from hopeless. They have at least three options: (1) take

Motivated students are cheated.

advantage of the easy system and learn a little along the way; (2) motivate themselves, working harder (and learning more) than the system requires them to; and (3) attend a more academically rigorous school (of course such schools still exist, though they are likely to cost more to attend).

While motivated students suffer in our too-lax system, so do the un- (or under-) motivated ones. And these students, who need our help the most, are the ones most cheated. As Sacks says, "I now believe the students are the real victims of this systematic failure of the entitlement mindset" (189). The students who are allowed to slide by, who are content to slide by, who perhaps don't even realize that they are sliding by because sliding by is all they know—those students find themselves arriving at college less prepared and less motivated than the "better students." And what happens next? Sadly, the gap between these two groups grows even wider.

The motivated student with good study skills (the one who has had at least an adequate high school education) attends class, takes notes, understands reading assignments, follows instructions, develops even better habits of mind, gains even more knowledge, and learns ways of making that knowledge work for her and her fellow humans. But in a system where B's are average and C's might indicate that although a student "tried" she did not demonstrate understanding or skill, the poorer students continue to advance through the system while remaining trapped at the bottom. Their level of thinking does not change much, while that of their better-prepared peers does.

The injustice, then, has been done to the students (as Sacks says, the students are the victims). While the student has happily skipped (or unhappily slogged) along through sixteen years of formal education, she is allowed, if she wants, to come away with very little in terms of education. She is allowed, unfortunately, to escape practically unscathed by learning. The problem, of course, is that the two students have entered college on different academic levels and the one on the higher level has graduated on an *even higher* level while the one on the lower level has remained pretty much the same.

Students would do well to look around them, at the room full of fellow classmates. They should imagine that many of those students will be graduating one day. And they should imagine the students

---

Undermotivated students are cheated.

Sacks's quotation supports Bruno's argument.

Gap between students grows bigger.

Scenarios are the main support tool.

Sacks and Bruno argue the same point.

They do not even realize they are being cheated.

in the classroom next door and across the hall and in all the other buildings on campus. They will be graduating, too. They should also imagine all those students at the more than 4,000 other colleges throughout the country: Ohio State, Michigan, Michigan State, Findlay College, Iowa State, Oklahoma A&M, The University of Utah, California This or That. (*The Chronicle of Higher Education*'s 2000–2001 "Almanac" lists 4,096 colleges in the United States.) Many of those students are well-prepared, working hard, and developing even better habits and thinking skills.

In our competitive world, the sad truth is that even some of the very good students, though their college dreams were to be doctors and lawyers and pharmacists and engineers, will be waiting tables. Don't get me wrong: There is no shame in that. The point is, that's not why they went to college. The truth is that for some students, college will be a tough uphill climb (a climb that could have been avoided with a more adequate high school education). A sadder truth, I am afraid, is that because of skills and attitudes developed in high school, for some students the reality of genuine learning (as opposed to just getting by) might already be too late.

Competition for jobs and status.

Qualifier.

The "I" draws attention to Bruno's personal concern.

It's too late for many!

Works Cited

"The Nation." *The Chronicle of Higher Education: Almanac Issue 2000–01,* 1 Sept. 2000, p. 6.
Sacks, Peter. *Generation X Goes to College.* Open Court Publishing, 1996.

WRITING STRATEGIES

1. Are you able to understand Bruno's response to Peter Sacks, even if you have not read *Generation X Goes to College?* What helpful background information does Bruno provide? What other information might have been helpful?

2. What is Bruno's thesis?

3. Bruno defines "intelligence" in his essay. How is this definition important? How does it work to support his point about education?

4. Explain how Bruno's essay has public resonance. That is, how is his argument important to others besides himself?

5. What evidence does Bruno provide to support his thesis? What other kind of evidence might he have provided?

EXPLORING IDEAS

1. With a group of peers, explore how the education system you have experienced is or is not "too lax." Provide specific examples.

2. What is the purpose of education in elementary school? High school? College? After you write out responses, explore further with a group of peers: What else might be the purpose, or *a* purpose, of education?

3. How might high school better prepare students for college? How might it better prepare them for life?

4. Bruno says, "[academically] poorer students continue to advance through the system while remaining trapped at the bottom" (¶12). Explore Bruno's claim further: Is it true? Can you provide examples for support? Why do some students get trapped at the bottom? Is it okay for them to be trapped there? What, if anything, should be done about this?

IDEAS FOR WRITING

1. What does Bruno get wrong?

2. If you agree with Bruno, what new and important point might you add?

3. If responding to one of these ideas, go to the Analysis section of this chapter to begin developing ideas for your essay.

If responding to one of these ideas, go to the Analysis section of this chapter to begin developing ideas for your essay.

"Have It Your Way": Consumerism Invades Education
Simon Benlow

Arguments come at us in many forms, sometimes in basic everyday language—an online ad, a billboard, or an office memo. In the following essay, Simon Benlow responds to a widely accepted statement in consumer life. He responds not only to the statement itself but also to underlying assumptions that come along with it.

Two weeks ago, the faculty and staff received a memo regarding "National Customer Service Week." We were urged to take special efforts in serving our customers—presumably, our students. Certainly, I have no objections to extending extra efforts in helping students feel comfortable and situated in the college environment. However, I am troubled (as are many instructors and professors) by use of the term "customer" to refer to students. I am concerned about the slow and subtle infiltration of consumerism into education (by companies buying access to students' brains), and I am downright hostile to the way "customer" has suddenly replaced the word (and maybe idea of) "student" in higher education. And because my concerns may seem ungrounded, I'd like to offer a brief analysis—a quick examination of the basic and not-so-basic differences between "customer" and "student."

"The customer is always right." We hear this hollow phrase resound through the corridors of mainstream consumerist culture. The motive behind the phrase is painfully clear: to keep customers happy, to keep them from complaining, and most importantly, to keep them coming back. (The meaninglessness of the phrase is well known, too—for those of us who have had the displeasure of holding for customer service.) The phrase is meant to maintain a climate in which the substance of anyone's concerns or complaints is obfuscated by friendly and diplomatic clichés—"your business means so much to us"; "we'll do everything we can to address the problem." Ultimately, the goal of customer service, in this sense, is to lull customers into a sense of complacency—even though their phones may not be working or their washers are throwing sparks.

"Have it your way!" We all know the song and the friendly fried food establishment associated with this slogan. It's a harmless phrase, in and of itself, and one that works particularly well for the franchise. It suggests to customers that their particular appetites can be catered to, that their specific tastes, no matter how eccentric (within the continuum of dip n' serve fried food) can be easily satisfied. It promotes the idea that the institution will shift its entire set of processes to meet the desires of the individual.

The meal deal bargain. In our hyper-drive-thru culture, we've been given a quicker and easier way to get fast food (and a host of other things as well): the combo or meal deal. In the old days, we had to pull up to the drive-thru board, search under "Sandwiches" and

THEN go through the labor of exploring "Sides" and "Beverages." It was all too much. Now, we can simply pull up, and say a number. We don't even have to trouble ourselves with uttering all the stuff we want to eat. We just say, "#1 with a diet." The meal deal craze is, of course, not limited to fast food; it is, simply, most explicitly manifested in the fast food industry. In the fast food world, we can see the motives of an increasingly consumerized culture: (1) to limit the interaction between the provider and the customer, (2) to limit the time the customer has to reflect on his/her wants, and (3) to limit the energy the customer has to exert.

Passivity. Customers are encouraged to be passive. We are prompted in a variety of ways not to be agents of our own making. Our needs and desires are met by the work of others. As customers, we pay for someone else's work, for someone else's acts of invention, creation, and production. And we not only hire out our activities (painting our homes, cooking our dinners); we also hire out our imaginations. We don't even have to imagine what is possible. Others have already done the imagining, created a product or service and have told us how we can use it. (They've even taken the extra step of telling us what NOT to do: "Women who are pregnant or who may become pregnant should not take, or even handle, these pills.") In short, *the world of the customer is based on intellectual inactivity;* we merely have to dial the phone, click the icon, say a number. We don't have to reflect, invent, produce, or research. Nor do we have to shop: they will deliver. Being a customer means being driven by simple and personal desires—and ultimately demanding that those desires be met.

But here's the issue. Contrary to the passive, personalizing, desire-driven customer, students are encouraged to be active. In college, students cannot simply consume knowledge. Even in its most packaged form, the textbook, knowledge must be regenerated, revised, reinterpreted, and remembered so that it is more than an answer on a multiple-choice test. Students who read textbooks, literature, and articles passively will get nothing from them. Certainly, they will be able to read something aloud, or even to themselves, and maybe summarize a main point; however, they will not know how to imagine the implications or significance of a textbook chapter. (And this is what academics mean when they say, "Our students don't know how to *make meaning*.")

Students who come to college with a consumerist attitude are lost. Because they are anticipating their most basic desires will be stimulated (because that's how people are massaged into buying stuff they don't need), consumerist students come to college waiting to be tickled, waiting to see the big boom, the car chase or the sex scene, the french fry, the Cherry Coke. What they encounter, however, are rooms filled with ingredients. They see only black and white words where they anticipate smashy colors and extravagant tools for getting their attention. In the face of pure ingredients (the stuff for making meaning), they will be confused and terribly bored.

Consumerist students (or those who have been tricked into thinking like consumers) will also have a difficult time understanding principles. Principles, established doctrines which are to be followed or evaluated in the processes of making knowledge, don't really exist in consumer culture unless you count slogans as doctrines. Because everything is based on the eccentricities of the individual ("hold the pickle, hold the lettuce"), the individual need not ever think outside of his/her own desires and the reality that is created from projecting those desires onto everything and everyone in view. In higher education, principles establish how a discipline works. Physics works on principles of matter and energy. The goal of a physicist is to discover the principles and understand how they can be used. Composition works on principles—conventions of grammar and persuasion. This is not to say that all knowledge is prescribed. On the contrary, students in such classes are encouraged to invent, to break rules, to go beyond. But in order to do so, they need certain ground rules; they need to understand that certain principles exist in the world outside of their own desires. (One cannot do chemistry and simply dismiss algebra because it is distasteful.)

When I think back to the best teachers and professors in my education, I recall those who demanded everything contrary to the consumerist mentality. They insisted on active students; they made us read staggering amounts of material and then actively put that material to use; they prompted us into confusion and disorientation; they made us uncomfortable, and then, sometimes, offered paths to clarity. In short, they made us into critical, reflective agents of our own becoming, rather than passive bags of desire. Everything valuable about my education came from instructors and professors who were free from the ridiculous tyranny of consumerism.

There is no way higher education can counter the incredible momentum of consumerist culture. It is far more pervasive than the discourses of physics or composition studies. However, if we continue to allow the term "customer" to replace "student," I fear that students will become increasingly blind to the difference between consumerist culture and college culture. I fear they will become increasingly more confused by the expectations of college, and that in the nightmarish long run, colleges will become simply another extension of the consumerist machine in which everyone is encouraged to pre-package knowledge, to super-size grades, and to "hold" anything even slightly distasteful.

WRITING STRATEGIES

1. According to Benlow, what is the essential difference between *student* and *customer*? How does Benlow make this difference clear?

2. Explain how Benlow uses personal testimony. How does it help to support his argument about students and customers?

3. Benlow is concerned about the "subtle infiltration of consumerism into education." What passages characterize the subtle infiltration? In other words, how does Benlow point out the subtlety of consumerism?

4. How does Benlow apply counterargument, concession, or qualifiers? Point to specific passages in your response.

5. Explain how the fast food slogan "Have It Your Way" functions in Benlow's argument. What does the slogan help him to do?

EXPLORING IDEAS

1. Analysis involves investigating specific elements, or ideas, within the whole. What are the particular elements, or ideas, within *consumerism?*

2. Benlow claims that consumerism "is far more pervasive than the discourses of physics or composition studies." Offer some support for this claim. How are the discourses of consumerism more dominant in your life than those of academic disciplines?

3. Benlow explains that consumerist students have difficulty with principles. Explain how a consumerist mindset might be a hindrance to learning a principle that you've learned.

4. In what ways have you been addressed or labeled as a customer? How has your college tried to make you into a customer rather than a student? Do you think it has worked against you?

IDEAS FOR WRITING

1. Consider some other widely accepted slogan. What does it suggest about everyday life and how might that suggestion be harmful or inaccurate?

2. Take on a common saying—one widely used but rarely examined. How might that saying mischaracterize a process such as learning, voting, or growing old?

If responding to one of these ideas, go to the Analysis section of this chapter to begin developing ideas for your essay.

STUDENT ESSAY

The Power of Failure: J. K. Rowlings' 2008 Harvard Commencement Speech
Liz Winhover

The following essay is a rhetorical analysis, an essay in which the writer, Liz Winhover, steps back and—instead of getting involved in *what* is being argued—examines the argument's rhetoric. In other words, Winhover's essay focuses on *how* J. K. Rowling communicates her ideas. Notice that Winhover mentions Rowling's ideas, in places summarizing what Rowling says, but that her essay focuses on *how* Rowling develops and supports her points.

In the summer of 2008, J. K. Rowling took to the podium to deliver the commencement speech for the graduates of Harvard University. At the time, Rowling had published the final installment of her successful children series, *Harry Potter*, and had movies in the works for those same books ("J. K. Rowling"). She was not an odd choice for Harvard's commencement. Her widespread success as an author represents the grand accomplishment one might associate with Harvard University, one of the top institutions in the world.

The addressees were the graduates of Harvard's 2008 class. The intended audience, however, stretched further to include the entire audience present on the day of the commencement. Because the timing has now passed for the delivery of the speech, the audience now is anyone who reads a transcript or watches a recording of the speech. Today's audience's detachment from the genuine occasion means they will have a different reaction to the speech than the graduates had on the day it was delivered.

The urgency of the situation is interesting. Rowling is giving a commencement speech, a type of delivery that requires specific timing because there is only one day on which to give a commencement speech—the day of the graduation. Additionally, there is the occasion—the graduation itself. While the occasion includes talking about the future lives of the graduates, the exigence (the situation that requires attention) could relate to the declining American economic status ("2008"), prompting Rowling to speak about "the benefits of failure" (Rowling) because graduates are entering an increasingly selective workforce. However, the speech is still fueled by the need to address the graduates on their accomplishments and comment on the possibilities of their future.

Rowling focuses on two main subjects— the benefits of failure and the importance of imagination. She talks first about her own failures: "I had failed on an epic scale. An exceptionally short-lived marriage had imploded, and I was jobless, and a lone parent, and as poor as possible." But she also explains the benefits those failures brought her because,

"The Power of Failure: J. K. Rowlings' 2008 Harvard Commencement Speech," by Liz Winhover. Reprinted with permission of the author.

she says, "failure meant a stripping away of the inessential." Next she focuses on her work with Amnesty International and how this helped to expand her imagination and empathy for others. She also underscores how empathy for other human beings is needed to combat evil in the world.

The first line of reasoning involves the "benefits of failure." This can be seen by breaking the reasoning down and looking at the grounds, the support for the claim: Rowling failed early in her career, which she talks about extensively. The first warrant (an idea that connects claim and support) following this statement is that everyone fails in life (failure being relative to each person's expectations and hopes). Rowling backs this up when she says, "Talent and intelligence never yet inoculated anyone against the caprice of the Fates." When she points out the unavoidable "caprices of the Fates," she suggests that failure is widely experienced. In other words, it's something Rowling and her audience shares. This leads to the claim that failure can have benefits, as Rowling shows with her own story of "rags to riches."

While Rowling's speech resonates with such basic presuppositions as *higher education is good* and *success is good*, she explores another presupposition more in depth and pushes against it: *failure should be avoided*. She explains that failing meant stripping away all distractions around her, which allowed her to "direct all [her] energy into finishing the only work that mattered to [her]." However, she doesn't completely reject the presupposition that failure should be avoided, but argues that failure can have positive benefits. It showed her that she "had a strong will, and more discipline than [she] had suspected." She is suggesting that failure taught her more about herself.

Another appeal seen throughout the speech is ethos. Rowling doesn't have to laud her own credentials and accomplishments, partially because Harvard has a history of choosing only well-established and accomplished persons and because of the widespread success of her book series and movie series. However, she does have to establish her credentials as a failure, a side of her the audience would know less. She spends several paragraphs discussing the range and depth of her failures, establishing that she is qualified to talk about such a subject. She also speaks about her experiences with Amnesty International, creating a pathos–ridden passage about the empathetic and imaginative lessons this job taught her.

Rowling's second line of reasoning focuses on the importance of imagination. Specifically, she claims that imagination can make us more empathetic. The grounds, or support, for this claim can be seen as Rowling herself. It can be argued that she *is*, or carries, the ethos to back this claim. Because of her far-reaching success as an author of fiction/fantasy stories, she can be relied on to have a solid imagination and, therefore, state its importance. This logic relies on a two-part warrant—an idea that connects a claim and its support. The first warrant states, *imagination can allow us to see beyond ourselves*. If we are able to see beyond ourselves, then the second warrant follows that *we can imagine other people's experiences and accept the validity of those experiences*. Rowling backs this warrant with considerable information about her work with Amnesty International, which she cites as "One of the greatest formative experiences of my life…[that] informed much of what I subsequently wrote in those [Harry Potter] books," suggesting that being aware of the stories of those around us can lead to greater imagination. This leads to the unstated claim that with the information imagination brings us, we can be more empathetic.

Rowling's 2008 address came at a time when the United States housing market was experiencing a decline and later that year would crash. The message of Rowling's speech would speak to the graduates' future struggles because as she says, "Talent and intelligence has never yet inoculated anyone against the caprice of the Fates."

I believe that Rowling's focus on her life story, highlighting her failures and her road to accomplishment, was suitable for a Harvard graduation speech. She allowed the new graduates to see that her success wasn't built over night but required passion and determination. A work ethic accompanies success, and graduates must be willing to struggle toward their goals despite being rejected time after time. The kind of honesty she provides about her path to success is important if not necessary. Success, after all, is a powerful magnet. It draws attention to itself, and so people too easily forget how failure works or how often it shows up in everyday life. At places like Harvard, failure is probably a foreign, if not exotic, concept. One could argue that many Harvard students have never confronted the realities of failure, and yet Rowling pushed the relevance of failure because no one is immune to it.

As a college student, I am not as far removed from failure as a Harvard graduate. For myself, the small yet formative experience of quitting my high school sports team really felt like failure. But from that disappointment came self-respect for my actions and the opportunity to focus on other interests. What I saw as failure strengthened the trust I placed in my decision-making and my love for writing. And now that I'm in college, I fear failing in the classroom and ruining my chances for the future. But if the past and J. K. Rowling have taught me anything, it's that failure can contain the lessons that influence the future.

Works Cited

"2008." *Wikipedia, The Free Encyclopedia*, 5 Mar. 2017, en.wikipedia.org/w/index.php?title= 2008&oldid=768738519. Accessed 7 Mar. 2017.

"J. K. Rowling." *Wikipedia, The Free Encyclopedia*, 27 Feb. 2017, en.wikipedia.org/w/index .php?title=J._K._Rowling&oldid=767706893. Accessed 3 Mar. 2017.

Rowling, J. K. "Text of J. K. Rowling's Speech." *Harvard Gazette*, 5 June 2008, news.harvard .edu/gazette/story/2008/06/text-of-j-k-rowling-speech.

WRITING STRATEGIES

1. Even though you have not read or heard Rowling's speech, why can you understand Winhover's response to it? What strategies does Winhover use to help the reader understand.

2. Based on Winhover's essay, summarize Rowling's argument.

3. Winhover reveals warrants—or warranting assumptions—that are key to understanding Rowling's line of reasoning. Closely examine the fifth paragraph. In your own words, explain how a specific warrant operates within Rowling's "first line of reasoning."

4. Describe the public resonance of Winhover's essay.

5. In her final two paragraphs, Winhover gives her opinion about failure and its importance. In your own words, characterize Winhover's opinion.

EXPLORING IDEAS

1. What does Winhover assume about students at Harvard? And why do you, or don't you, share her assumption?

2. What significance does Winhover draw from Rowling's speech?

3. Provide your own example of how failure can be beneficial by stripping away the inessential.

4. Winhover suggests Rowling's message was influenced by "declining American economic status." What might her message have been in a robust and growing economy?

5. Describe a failure of your own. What did that failure do for you? What idea or reflex might it have sparked?

IDEAS FOR WRITING

1. Find a commencement speech online and analyze its rhetoric, ultimately explaining the message's significance to you.

2. Find an important warranting assumption (or warrant) in a speech and argue for its value, making sure to help the reader understand the warrant's role in the speech.

INVENTION

Responding to an argument involves sophisticated thinking and planning. In a sense, this project is an argument[2]—an argument to the second power. You are not only taking on another argument (with its own layers and nuances), but you are also developing a layered argument of your own. The following sections are designed to help you through the invention process, specifically, to find an argument (in Point of Contact), to discover the mechanics of that argument (in Analysis), to understand how the points relate to a community of readers (in Public Resonance), to invent a focused stance of your own (in Thesis), and to develop your own support (in Rhetorical Tools).

Point of Contact

In this chapter, the point of contact is an actual argument. You will be responding to an explicit argument that someone else has formulated or to an argument expressed by many people. Remember that an argument need not be an essay; arguments are also made by advertisements, posters, and billboards. To find an argument that may relate directly to the goings-on of your life and community, examine the following options:

- **Local/City/Campus Newspapers:** Search the editorial pages and letters to the editor for arguments.

- **National Newspapers:** Publications such as the *New York Times, USA Today,* and *The Wall Street Journal* have editorial pages and columnists who offer arguments on various political and social issues.

- **Magazines:** Popular weeklies (such as *Newsweek, The Nation, Time,* and *US News and World Report*) and monthly or quarterly magazines (such as *Utne Reader* or *The New Republic*) are filled with argumentative articles and personal columns on social and political issues.

- **A Publication from Your Major** (such as *Education Journal, Nursing, Applied Science and Engineering*): Examine not only main articles but also reviews and personal columns.

- **Disciplinary Databases** (databases that focus on specific disciplines): Go to your library and check the electronic databases for your major or a closely related one.

- **Websites:** Go to your favorite search engine and enter topical keywords (*dogs, skateboards, economy,* etc.). You might find argumentative sites or pages more quickly if you combine potential topics with words such as *law, policy, argument, crisis,* or *debate.*

You can also focus your search on arguments made by bloggers by using blog searchers such as Google Blog Search (blogsearch.google.com), or a blog directory such as the one found at technorati.com.

Once you have found a potentially interesting argument, answer the following question:

- Why does the argument interest me?
  —Because something or someone has been omitted?
  —Because something or someone has been misrepresented?
  —Because I disagree or agree with it?
  —Because it raises an important issue that should be further discussed?

—Because it changed my mind on a topic?

—Because it is potentially important (helpful or dangerous)?

Analysis

To analyze the argument, think of it as having two layers: (1) the four elements of argument (claim, support, counterargument, and concession) and (2) the underlying warranting assumptions.

The First Layer: The Four Elements of Argument

Thesis Before we can respond to an argument, we must know *exactly* what is being argued. That is, we must figure out the thesis, the particular stance the writer takes on the topic. Finding the thesis for a written argument can be trickier than it seems. Although some essays have explicit theses (stated directly), others are implied (not stated, but suggested by the supporting points). Once we locate the thesis (or understand it based on the details of the argument), we can then see how it is supported.

Support Initially, the thesis might seem outlandish, but good support strategies will invite readers to accept even the most extreme thesis statements. Remember that support comes in a variety of forms:

Statistics	Scenarios
Authorities	Appeal to Logic
Facts	Appeal to Emotion
Examples	Appeal of Character
Allusions	Appeal to Need
Personal Testimonies/Anecdotes	Appeal to Value

Depending on the medium of the argument (essay, poster, etc.), the support may be varied. Or the writer may depend on one key support strategy. We might ask: *How well does the support strategy connect to the thesis?* or *Given this argument, how appropriate is the support strategy?* For a detailed explanation of support strategies, see pages 254–262 in Chapter 8: Making Arguments.

Counterargument Sophisticated arguments anticipate and refute opposing claims. In fact, the success of an argument may depend on its counterarguments—on the ability of the writer to fend off opposing claims. A key counterargument strategy is the turnabout paragraph, in which a writer explains an opposing perspective and then responds.

Concession Concessions acknowledge the value of opposing claims. Writers who concede acknowledge that others' positions may offer worthwhile insight outside of the writers' own claims. When writers concede points, their arguments do not lose force; instead, they appear more fair-minded. A writer who concedes shows that he or she has considered a range of other ideas.

To fully understand the first layer of the argument, answer the following questions for the argument to which you are responding:

> What is the main claim/thesis?

> What are the means of support for the main claim?

> Do the support strategies sufficiently prove the thesis?

> How does the argument address opposing claims? Are those claims sufficiently refuted?

> Does the argument concede to outside positions? What is the effect of those concessions?

> Does the writer define the issue correctly?

Daniel Bruno uses one of these Invention Questions as a springboard to discover a specific shortcoming in Peter Sacks's book:

Does the writer define the issue correctly?
Sacks defines the issue correctly as far as he defines it. Entitlement education has the negative effect that he says it does, but he fails, it seems, to discuss or focus on an important aspect of the issue, which is that some students, who don't have an entitlement mentality, learn a great deal in school while others, who do, don't learn a great deal, or very much at all. The students who have the entitlement mentality slide by while their classmates are learning more and more. The gap between the two groups widens. So, what does this mean to those students who feel entitled to good grades because they showed up (high school) or paid the tuition (college)? They get grades, but did they learn anything? Did they get an education?

The Second Layer: Warranting Assumptions

Beneath the first, most visible, layer of an argument lurk warranting assumptions: the ideas that connect the points in an argument. Warranting assumptions (or *warrants*) are the root system of an argument. Although they usually go unstated (or remain underground, like the root system of a tree), they are as important to an argument as the explicitly stated points. When we dig up warranting assumptions and investigate them closely, we can decide if they are reasonable and if the overall argument holds together.

Philosopher Stephen Toulmin developed a powerful analytical system for digging up assumptions. In his perspective, every argument has a structure with interrelated parts. Using this, we can see how those parts relate and how well they function. Here are the three basic elements:

Claim: The main argumentative position (or thesis) being put forward
Grounds: The support for the position (evidence, examples, illustrations, etc.)

Warranting Assumption: The idea, often unstated, that connects the claim and the grounds—or that justifies the use of the grounds for the claim

The warranting assumption lies (often hidden) between the claim and the grounds. See how the elements work in the following example:

Claim:	Sport utility vehicles are dangerous.
Grounds:	Many models roll over easily.
Warranting Assumption:	Vehicles that roll over easily are dangerous.

The assumption lies between the claim and the grounds, connecting them logically. In this example, the rollover frequency of SUVs supports the claim that they are dangerous. The warranting assumption (vehicles that roll over easily are dangerous) lies between the claim and the grounds. The assumption is entirely acceptable; few people would challenge it. But consider a different argument:

Claim:	Sport utility vehicles are valuable to the average American driver.
Grounds:	The extra-large carrying capacity and four-wheel drive capability meet traveling needs.
Warranting Assumption:	Extra-large carrying capacity and four-wheel drive are valuable for the average American driver's traveling needs.

The assumption here is less acceptable. Someone might argue against this warranting assumption on the grounds that the average American driver does not need extra-large carrying capacity and four-wheel drive, and that these aspects are unnecessary for most drivers. Stating the assumption thus reveals a particular weakness in the argument and provides an opportunity to respond.

Dissecting arguments in this fashion allows for various critical opportunities. Writers can focus attention on (take exception or agree with) two different layers of an argument: grounds and/or assumptions. Consider, for example, the first claim: *Sport utility vehicles are dangerous.* Although the assumption *vehicles that roll over easily are dangerous* is acceptable, the grounds for the claim *many models roll over easily* can be challenged. Someone might agree with the assumption but cite statistics showing that only a few models are prone to rollover accidents.

Claim:	Sport utility vehicles are dangerous.	
Grounds:	Many models roll over easily.	(Questionable)
Warranting Assumption:	Vehicles that roll over easily are dangerous.	(Acceptable)

Responding with such statistics could help a writer challenge the original argument. In this case, the responding writer would be challenging the grounds. For other arguments, both the grounds and assumption might be arguable:

Claim:	The environment is not in danger from human influence.
Grounds:	The environment is supporting (Questionable) the Earth's population today.
Warranting Assumption:	The present human population (Questionable) directly illustrates the health of the environment.

Here, both the grounds and the warranting assumption are questionable. Although the grounds could be refuted on their own terms (by illustrating the vast numbers of people starving throughout the world), the more interesting response might point to the warranting assumption. The mere presence of people does not indicate the health of the environment. For instance, someone might point to dramatic increases in skin and other cancers to illustrate the effects of greenhouse gases and environmental contamination. In this case, discovering the warranting assumption would allow a responding writer to point out a flaw in the logic.

The following questions can help you develop a response to the argument you have chosen to examine.

> What is the warranting assumption?
> Is the assumption acceptable or arguable?
> Can I prove that the assumption is incorrect?
> What else does the author of the argument assume (about life, identity, society, people's behavior, time, politics, human nature, etc.)?

Public Resonance

Public resonance refers to the way in which an argument relates to a community. In most cases, any published argument that you find will already have public resonance, especially if it comes from a newspaper, magazine, or journal. Your job, however, is not complete. As a responding writer, you can draw attention to the effects of the original argument on its readers and on the community at large.

To develop public resonance, examine the argument to which you will respond, and answer the following questions:

> Has the argument had an impact on readers? Any specific person or people?
> How *could* the argument affect people (negatively or positively)?

> ❯ What other issues or situations does the argument relate to or address?
>
> ❯ How can I relate the argument to the needs/wants of my audience (or anyone who is involved in the topic)?

Invention Workshop

In a small group of writers, use one of the Invention Questions to start a discussion about your topic. First, explain the original argument (the argument to which you are responding). Then, pose the question. (So the question does not get lost in the discussion, write it down where everyone can see it.)

In the following excerpt, Daniel Bruno explores *what* and *how* people might think about student entitlement. Here, Bruno has narrowed in on a particular issue from the original argument. It's not merely that students shouldn't feel entitled to high grades. Bruno goes further and discovers the double jeopardy of entitlement: Those who feel entitled are "missing out" on their own educations:

> **How can I relate the argument to the needs/wants of my audience (or anyone who is involved in the topic)?**
> Some students feel entitled, which means expecting a good grade automatically, without working or learning anything. Some don't. The wants of the entitlement students are different than their needs. They want a grade or degree but need to learn and work. Interestingly, the students who feel entitled are the ones missing out, while the ones who don't feel entitled benefit. Maybe the students who believe they are entitled would benefit from thinking about the students who think differently, the ones who they will be competing against in the future, the ones who perhaps will be better prepared and have a better work ethic. The entitlement-minded students may find out too late that others are working hard and developing good skills and attitudes.

RESEARCH

What have others said about your topic? If you are responding to a specific text, go beyond that author's views and seek out other perspectives. Examine your invention writing and search keywords in a periodical database search. (Remember that periodical databases, such as InfoTrac® College Edition, rely on keywords rather than phrases.) Enter main nouns linked together with *and*. If you have no luck, keep changing the nouns, replacing them with synonyms. For instance, Bruno might enter: *students and college and entitlement*. Then, he might try: *students and college and attitude*. He might replace *attitude* with *achievement, success, study skills, apathy,* or a combination of these.

Thesis

Responding to arguments is complicated because another set of claims must be engaged. But do not let those other claims confuse you. Resist chasing ideas throughout the original argument, and instead focus on a particular issue and then springboard into your own reasoning. Your argument might do one or more of the following:

- Redefine the issue according to your understanding.

  Sacks shows how consumerism has invaded education, leading some students to expect good grades for little effort. But he fails, it seems, to emphasize enough a most harmful effect of this sense of entitlement.

- Argue for the value of a particular point or assumption in the original text.

  In "Technology, Movement, and Sound," Ed Bell argues against our culture's increasing love affair with technology. The real value of his argument is its focus on the relationship between personal technology and public effects.

- Argue against a particular point or assumption in the original text.

  Simon Benlow insists that students are increasingly more consumerist in their approach to education, but consumption is not inherently passive or anti-educational.

- Extend the original argument to include a broader set of ideas.

  April Pedersen concludes, "When his kidneys failed, a $12,000 kidney transplant was off the radar (a case can be made that surgery on an animal is unethical anyway), and I didn't consider him to be my son." Although it might be hard to argue that $12,000 is too much to spend on saving a human life, Pedersen's point can be applied to humans as well as dogs: Far too many receive medical care that is unnecessary and arguably unethical, even if it is life-saving.

- Narrow the argument and suggest an important emphasis.

  As Jayme Stayer argues in "Whales R Us," theme parks such as SeaWorld are a "reflection of American culture . . . not a promoter of political change." His argument shows us that mainstream American culture may entirely lack a language for political change.

As you can see in these statements, it is not enough to say "I disagree" or "I agree." Instead, a project such as this benefits from a more focused point—one that shows something (important, harmful, inaccurate, valuable, etc.) in the original argument. The following questions can help generate the thesis of your argumentative response:

> With what *particular* point do I agree or disagree?

> How are my assumptions different from or similar to those of the writer?

> How is the original argument too narrow or too exclusive?

> What particular point in the original argument might readers fail to see? Why is it so important?

> How can I extend or broaden the original argument?

Evolution of a Thesis

Notice how the following idea evolves from summary, to gut reaction, to analytical insight:

- In "Crimes Against Humanity," Ward Churchill argues that the use of Native American symbols for sports teams is racist.   **Summary**

- Churchill's argument made me mad, and I think it may do the same to a lot of people. It basically suggests that everyone who supports certain professional sports teams is somehow tied to genocide.   **Gut reaction**

- Mainstream America might need to be pushed before it will accept new ideas.   **Analytical insight**

- Churchill's "Crimes Against Humanity" reminds us that mainstream opinions often do not change unless people encounter shocking, even offensive, claims.   **Focused statement**

Throughout this intellectual journey, the writer, by discovering something specific about Churchill's argument and its potential effect on readers, moves from dismissing the argument to revealing a quality in it.

Thinking Further

Although gut reactions can get a writer started, they are often too vague. The following statements show what someone might feel directly after reading an argument. While these initial feelings are valuable, they are only the beginning:

- Ann Marie Paulin's argument is right on target.

- April Pedersen's argument is important for dog lovers to hear.

- In "Crimes Against Humanity," Ward Churchill is just making a mountain out of a molehill.

These initial reactions must be explored. The writers might ask:

- What particular idea or assumption of Paulin's argument is insightful or valuable? Why is it insightful or valuable?

- Why is Pedersen's argument important? What particular aspect is valuable to animal lovers?

- Why might the issue really be a mountain?

In asking such questions, the writers can take their gut reaction to the next level—to more focused ideas:

- Ann Marie Paulin reveals the quiet everyday prejudices against overweight people.

- April Pedersen's argument correctly challenges the common misconception that caring for pets as one would care for humans is harmless.

- Churchill describes a view of American history and sports that most people do not consider.

REVISING YOUR THESIS

With a group of peers, explore your thesis statements. Try to narrow statements by going after broad adjectives (*valuable, wrong, irresponsible, good, intense,* etc.), replacing them with more specific descriptors or explanations. Also, check out the Common Thesis Problems in Chapter 8: Making Arguments on page 254. The same problems may lurk in this project as well.

Rhetorical Tools

Even though you are responding to someone else's argument, you are still creating your own argument. Consider all the argumentative strategies introduced in Chapter 8.

Using Support

Remember you have the whole world beyond the original argument to support your points. You can use various forms of evidence (such as personal testimony, examples, and facts, as well as allusions to history, popular culture, and news events) and appeals.

- What particular examples from everyday life show my point?

- Does a historical situation or trend (say, the rise of a particular fashion, organization, or individual) illustrate something about my topic?

- How has popular culture treated my topic? Does it show up in television shows, movies, or commercials? If so, how is it characterized, mishandled, or celebrated?

- How has literature (novels, poetry, drama, short stories) dealt with my topic? Have fictional characters illustrated something important about the topic or some behavior related to it?

- How does nature (animals, life cycles, plants, biological processes, and so on) demonstrate something about my topic?

- How can this topic relate to people's sense of logic? What line of reasoning can I create for readers to follow?

(See pages 254–257 in Chapter 8: Making Arguments, for more help in developing evidence and appeals for your argument.)

Counterarguing

Good writers address opposing claims. As you develop your own argument, ask yourself the following questions:

- Apart from the author of the original argument, who might disagree with my position? Why?

- What reasons do people have for disagreeing with me?

- What evidence would support an opposing argument?

Conceding and Qualifying Points

When responding to an argument, a writer should be especially mindful of giving credit to others' points. Exploring the following questions will help you to see possible concessions for your own argument.

- Does the original argument make any valid points?

- Does my argument make any large, but necessary, leaps? (Should I acknowledge them?)

- Do I ask my audience to imagine a fictional situation? (Should I acknowledge the potential shortcomings of a fictional or hypothetical situation?)

- Do I ask my audience to accept generalizations? (Should I acknowledge those generalizations?)

ACTIVITY

After responding to the preceding questions, discuss with peers the extent to which you should concede and qualify each point you discovered. For example, if you discovered that your argument made a large but necessary leap, should you acknowledge the leap in a phrase, a sentence, or an entire paragraph?

Remembering Logical Fallacies

Examine the original argument for logical fallacies. Finding fallacies in an argument can help you generate a response. For example, in the following passage, the writer points to a logical shortcoming in the original argument:

> Smith argues that incoming college students cannot handle the intellectual rigors of academia. He characterizes an entire generation as "undisciplined and whimsical." But like all arguments about entire generations, Smith's depends upon a hasty generalization. The truth about today's college students is far more complex than Smith's assertions, and any statement that seeks to characterize them as a whole should be looked upon with suspicion.

See a list and examples of logical fallacies in Chapter 8, pages 260–262.

ACTIVITY

Write a one-paragraph summary of the essay you plan to write, stating your thesis and main supporting ideas. Share your summary with peers and look for logical fallacies. (See pages 260–262.) Although such fallacies are common in one's early thinking, they can be hard to spot. To find them, you may have to discuss the summaries and examine ideas carefully.

Revision

The Invention Questions in this chapter are not meant to be answered just once. The value of these questions is in responding to them as a way of discovering and developing new ideas, then returning to them and exploring further from your new perspective. Before you exchange drafts with a peer, revisit the questions in the Analysis, Public Resonance, Thesis, and Rhetorical Tools sections of this chapter and try to ratchet up your thinking even further.

Peer Review

Exchange drafts with at least one other writer. Before exchanging, underline your thesis (or write it at the top of the first page) so that others will more quickly get a sense of your main idea. Use the following questions to respond to specific issues in the drafts:

1. Can any phrases or terms in the thesis be narrowed? If so, circle them and make some suggestions for more focus.

2. Is the main idea of the original argument sufficiently summarized? (Could the summary be shorter? How?)

3. Where could the writer support broad statements with specific evidence (allusions, examples, facts, personal testimony, scenario)? Writers often fall into the habit of making broad claims that should be illustrated. For instance, someone might argue, "All students learn differently." But such a statement needs to be supported with specifics. Otherwise, readers have no reason to accept it, no reason to see it as true.

4. Where might the writer oversimplify the original argument/issue or mischaracterize the original author's position? (Look especially for ad hominem or strawperson logical fallacies. See pages 260–262.)

5. What paragraphs shift focus? Where do you sense gaps in the lines of reasoning? How could the writer fill those gaps?

6. Circle any clichés or overly broad statements that could be transformed into specific and revelatory insights.

7. Consider sentence vitality:

- What sentences are over-embedded? (Point to any clauses that overlap with other clauses, causing a disconnect between ideas.)

- Examine attributive phrases. Point out unnecessary phrases or sentences that could be boiled down.

- Consider other vitality strategies explained in Chapter 19.

  —Where can the writer change linking verbs to active verbs?

  —Where can the writer avoid drawing attention to *I* and *you*?

  —Help the writer change unnecessary clauses to phrases.

  —Help the writer change unnecessary phrases to words.

  —Point to expletives (such as *there are* and *it is*).

  —Help the writer change passive verbs to active verbs for more vitality.

  —Help the writer avoid common grammatical errors: comma splices, sentence fragments, or pronoun/antecedent agreement.

QUESTIONS FOR RESEARCH
If the writer used outside sources:

- Where must he or she include in-text citations? (See pages 478–479 and 496–498.)

- Are quotations blended smoothly into the argument and punctuated correctly? (See pages 467–476.)

- Where could more direct textual cues or transitions help readers? (See pages 474–476.)
- Is the Works Cited or References page formatted properly? (See Chapter 16.)

Reflection

Just as we discuss ideas with others as part of the invention process, we also play out discussions in our own minds. We have both external and internal dialogues. For example, to invent for this essay, you may have written responses to Invention Questions, discussed publicly (with others), and created internal dialogues (imaginary discussions inside your head). We create internal dialogues while driving, walking the dog, working out, and so on. These dialogues—like invention writing and public discussions with others—use rhetorical tools to explore and develop new ways of thinking.

1. Which did you rely on most for invention: written responses to Invention Questions, public dialogue, or internal dialogue? Which might you have utilized more and why?

2. List two key points in your essay.

   a. For each point, did you invent the point through written responses to Invention Questions in the text, public dialogue, internal dialogue, a combination of the three, or some other way? Explain.

   b. How did each key point function in the essay? Was it the thesis? A support strategy? An opening (introduction) strategy? Part of the conclusion?

3. If you can recall any internal dialogue from your invention process, describe how it worked:

   a. Who was your imaginary discussion partner?

   b. What was the nature of the discussion? Was it cooperative, combative, or something else?

4. How was your essay a response to an ongoing public discussion? What specific ideas from that public discussion was your invention (writing as well as public and private dialogues) a response to?

Beyond the Essay: Tattoo Design

If designing a tattoo for a college writing class sounds crazy, consider the rhetoric of the tattoo and the prevalence of tattoos in the United States, in the world, on your college campus, in your classroom, on TV, and so on. Tattoos (body art)—like essays, letters, videos, or speeches—do rhetoric; they communicate ideas through particular strategies (colors, images, words, placement, and so on). Given their prevalence, tattoos must be communicating something important.

1. Design a tattoo that expresses the main idea of the essay you've written for this chapter. Whether you design your tattoo on paper or on the computer, consider both the idea you want to communicate and the visual elements that will present that idea. What image or images might you use? What words? What font size or style? Where on one's body should the tattoo go, and how does the location affect the message?

2. In several paragraphs, explain the rhetoric of the tattoo you designed.

10 Evaluating

John Metz

Chapter Objectives

This chapter will help you to:

- Identify and articulate the purpose of a given subject.
- Identify and articulate criteria for evaluating the success or worth of that subject.
- Develop a focused evaluative essay that argues about the success or worth of that subject.
- Explore how criteria and evaluation function beyond academic writing.

"I criticize by creation . . . not by finding fault."

—**Marcus Tullius Cicero**

INTRODUCTION

Evaluating is the act of judging the value or worth of a given subject. We make informal judgments constantly throughout our daily lives: We decide that we like a particular car more than another, or that one song on the radio is better than another. Such evaluations are informal because they involve little analysis; that is, we do not usually take the time to thoroughly analyze each song we hear on the radio as we are sweeping through stations. We also take part in formal evaluation, a process that goes beyond an expression of likes and dislikes: Teachers must evaluate student performance; jury members must evaluate events, people, and testimony; voters must evaluate political candidates; members of unions must evaluate contracts; managers must evaluate employees; executives must evaluate business proposals; citizens must evaluate laws and lawmakers. In such situations, mere personal tastes cannot dictate evaluative decisions. Instead, a formal process—sometimes entirely intellectual, sometimes organized in visible steps—is necessary for sound evaluation.

Much literary work is also evaluative. Barbara Kingsolver's *Poisonwood Bible,* for example, condemns twentieth-century missionary work in Africa. Yann Martel's *Life of Pi* critiques scientific rationality. Ralph Ellison's *Invisible Man* reveals a range of racist assumptions and practices. And Jonathan Swift's *Gulliver's Travels,* perhaps one of the most famous examples of evaluative literature, critiques (or satirizes) political and economic institutions of eighteenth-century England. Whether one is an author, jury member, civil engineer, or voting citizen, the person who can evaluate well and make judgments outside of his or her personal tastes is able to make valuable decisions, to help distinguish the best course of action, to clarify options when many seem available. And in a culture that is increasingly filled with choices (among political candidates, retirement plans, religious paths, and lifestyles, to name just a few), it is increasingly important for literate citizens to evaluate well.

The essays in this chapter all make judgments and, in doing so, present their subjects to readers in a particular light. In other words, each writer gives an opinion about a subject (be it a video game, a television show, or film) and then supports that opinion by showing selected details of the subject. Although the writers give some form of overview (a general summary about the subject), they also focus the readers' attention on the details that support their judgments. This is fair play. In drawing attention to certain details (and ignoring others), they are simply creating argumentative positions—the positions they want readers to accept. Notice, also, that the writers tend to draw on support outside their subjects; that is, they refer to other similar subjects to show particular points, which gives credibility to their arguments. As you read this chapter's essays, notice how the claim, support, and organization are shaped by one or more criteria. After reading the essays, you can find a subject in one of two ways: (1) go to the Point of Contact section to find a topic from your everyday life, or (2) choose one of the Ideas for Writing that follow the essays. After finding a subject, go to the Analysis section to begin developing the evaluation.

READINGS

Talibanned
Benjamin Busch

Benjamin Busch is an actor, poet, essayist, photographer, film producer, and retired Marine lieutenant colonel. As an actor, he played memorable characters on programs such as *Homicide, The Wire,* and *Generation Kill.* As a Marine, he served two tours in Iraq and was awarded the Bronze Star. He has, then, an acute understanding of the tension between reality and fiction. In this article, Busch uses one criterion to evaluate a video game: realism. This essay was recorded in an edited form as "A Video Game Does Not a Soldier Make" on National Public Radio's *All Things Considered.*

My Grandfather fought the Nazis and was wounded. For years afterward, my father re-created that war in games in his Brooklyn neighborhood, where some of the children playing had lost their fathers overseas. But war games require two sides, and someone in Brooklyn always had to play the Germans.

When I was a boy, I was given plastic army men. They were posed already fighting. I arranged them in the sandbox behind our house, and I killed them. I voiced their commands and made the sounds of their suffering. I was every one of them, and I was their enemy. I imagined their war—and I controlled it. I was a child. But I lost those magical powers as a Marine in Iraq.

We know children are immersed in digital interactivity now, and the soldier of today has grown up on video games. It is becoming a new literacy of sorts. Playing and risking your life are different things, of course. In the video war, there may be some manipulation of anxiety, some adrenaline to the heart, but absolutely nothing is at stake.

The military has recognized the attraction of trigger based combat games and has incorporated them into recruitment and training. There is an official U.S. Army Game called *America's Army.* Gamers are encouraged to download a free video game where they can "play *America's Army 3* on Steam and earn Steam Achievements, ranking up among your friends as you earn distinguished status, badges, medals, and ribbons." Without leaving home, players can comfortably attain rank and recognition online as imaginary soldiers on a game platform designed to transform their entertainment into military service. On the same site the U.S. Army places ads picturing members in uniform. One says:

> Meet PVT Alaniz. He joined the Army to pay for a college education and is proud to follow in his grandfather's footsteps. Free room, board and laundry allow him to put money toward some of the important things in life: like treating his girlfriend and buying a plasma TV to play Xbox 360. Check out the opportunities the Army created for PVT Alaniz.

There is something disingenuous about this interactive advertising. Player characters cannot be killed in *America's Army 3*. As their "avatars" become distinguished soldiers, players can more easily see themselves in uniform. Video game training continues after enlistment. The Army now uses games like *Full Spectrum Warrior* and *Full Spectrum Command* to develop leadership skills in virtual combat environments.

Electronic Arts (EA) developed a modern combat game with members of the U.S. Special Forces. It is called *Medal of Honor* after the highest American military decoration for heroism, and it is based in the current Afghanistan war. *Medal of Honor* allows gamers to play as the Taliban as well as U.S. Forces in multi-player contests. This brought immediate outrage from members of allied leadership in England, where Defense Secretary Dr. Liam Fox called for a ban on the sale of the game because players choosing to play as Taliban could "kill" allied soldiers. Pressured by this objection, the U.S. military followed suit, banning the sale on its bases. Despite the controversy, AE did nothing more than change the name of "the enemy" from "Taliban" to "Opposing Forces." Changing the name of the enemy doesn't change who it is.

I honestly don't like that *Medal of Honor* depicts the war that is happening in Afghanistan right now because—even as fiction—it equates war with the leisure of games. Hundreds of

Courtesy of Benjamin Busch

combat games use historical conflicts, especially World War II, as their subject but there is a great deal of psychological separation from these events. There has been time to recover from loss, and to mourn. A game that claims "authenticity" played during the same conflict it depicts is not emotionally distant from it but is, instead, emotionally parallel. Furthermore, the age of the game's target audience is the same as that of the soldiers fighting so the line between casual entertainment and traumatic reality blurs.

But what nation or military has the right to govern fiction? Banning the representation of an enemy is imposing nationalism on entertainment. The game cannot train its players to be actual skilled special operations soldiers, nor is it likely to lure anyone into Islamic fundamentalism. It can grant neither heroism nor martyrdom. What it does do is make modern war into participatory cinema. That is its business.

Despite my objections to certain aspects of the video war game, I don't know that game makers have any particular responsibilities to any of us. They are a market based entertainment business. Their sales are subject to mature audience restrictions like film and pornography, but game ratings are not enforced by any government agency in the United States. We can only hope that business values social decency, and respects essential humanism but a gaming company is only truly concerned with market reception in the form of product sales. The responsibility is placed on the consumer and parents. At the age of 18, an American citizen can vote, and can enlist in the armed services without parental consent. We should assume that they can also choose their entertainment for better or for worse. Issues of responsibility arise when our military develops war games with private companies and then allows them to be sold publicly. The game then partially becomes a governmental, even military, product and its messages are unable to speak free of politics or real war.

The more our imagination is disengaged from our environment, the more we detach from visceral experience, and that is a problem if soldiers are being trained on video games for artificial wars. Part of their comprehension of the real war may be based on this manufactured fantasy of it.

But imagine how frustrating this game would be if, just as you began to play it, an invisible sniper shot you dead every time. The game would not be popular because being killed that way isn't fair—just like war. Reality has a way of correcting misconceptions.

The power of controlling your situation, to be able to stop the war and rest, is something that our soldiers are quietly desperate for. For those who patrol the valleys of Helmand, it is a way to impose limits on the uncertainty of war, and the constancy of vulnerability. A video game can produce no wounds, and take no friends away. The soldier understands the difference.

The games of my youth seem more innocent than the fully articulated violence delivered for the modern day boy, but so did the films, news, and books. There is a truth common to all, and that is that playing war in any medium is not combat, and for a gamer, it's not even political. It's just sedentary adventurism in need of a subject. In the real "war gaming" of the invasion and occupation of Afghanistan, perhaps the Pentagon should have allowed someone to play as the Taliban.

The truth is that there are two ways out of Afghanistan: wounds or luck. Proficiency is only part of surviving the randomness of death, and playing games will not protect or endanger soldiers or governments. If gamers are inspired to join the Taliban, they should talk to John Walker Lindh first. And for those who truly want to play for a Medal of Honor, recruiters are standing by. Only eight have been awarded since we invaded Afghanistan. All but one have been posthumous.

WRITING STRATEGIES

1. Busch begins his essay with some family history and personal testimony. Explain how these two introductory paragraphs help to launch his evaluation.

2. What is the essay's most powerful statement against *Medal of Honor*?

3. In ¶9, Busch says, "We can only hope that business values social decency, and respects essential humanism but a gaming company is only truly concerned with market reception in the form of product sales." How does this subtle appeal to decency help with his evaluation of the video game?

4. How does Busch counterargue or concede to opposing positions? Describe particular passages.

5. Explain how Busch's conclusion reinforces his position on *Medal of Honor*.

EXPLORING IDEAS

1. Consider Busch's point: that *Medal of Honor* "equates war with the leisure of games." Why might that equation be something to evaluate, even if (or especially if) you are an avid gamer?

2. Busch explains that the U.S. military works closely with private corporations to develop software. Why might that interaction be a concern for both soldiers and citizens?

3. Busch describes gaming as "sedentary adventurism in need of a subject." How is this phrase an indictment of gaming? How is *sedentary adventurism* negative?

4. In his conclusion, Busch alludes to John Walker Lindh—a U.S. citizen who traveled to Afghanistan in 2001, trained with Taliban forces, and fought against the U.S. military. He was captured that year, detained as an enemy combatant, and is currently serving a twenty-year prison sentence. How does Lindh's story figure into the argument about games such as *Medal of Honor*?

IDEAS FOR WRITING

1. Video games are often condemned for their levels of violence. Choose a particular game and develop an evaluation. Avoid simply attacking or defending the portrayal of violence. Consider other criteria.

2. Focus on an advertisement for military recruiting. Evaluate its moves, its strategies, its realism, or even its parallels to popular video games.

If responding to one of these ideas, go to the Analysis section of this chapter to begin developing ideas for your essay.

Important and Flawed
Kareem Abdul-Jabbar

Artistic works do not live in a vacuum. They are always understood, received, and evaluated according to prevailing values and beliefs. Sometimes, artists themselves are evaluated along with their works. In this review, Kareem Addul-Jabbar—former NBA basketball star and cultural critic—evaluates a controversial film, *Birth of a Nation*. He argues about the worth of the film itself and about its co-writer and director, Nate Parker. This review was published in *The Hollywood Reporter*, September 2016.

Telling the story of Nat Turner's 1831 slave rebellion seems to have a cursed history. In 1967, William Styron wrote the best-selling novel *The Confessions of Nat Turner*, which won the Pulitzer Prize. However, despite popularizing an important event in American history, the novel was met with angry criticism from some African-Americans in part because Styron, who told the story from Nat Turner's point of view, was white. Even though the novel was supported by black literary giants Ralph Ellison and James Baldwin, a book of criticism by 10 black writers was published dissecting what they deemed blatant cultural appropriation. Today, African-American Nate Parker, the co-writer, director, co-producer and star of the Nat Turner biopic *The Birth of a Nation*, faces an equal level of harsh public scrutiny that threatens to overshadow his impressive, important and flawed film.

Before I discuss the film, I want to address the controversy about whether or not people should go see a movie made by a man who 17 years ago was tried for rape. It is the same issue of equating the art with the artist that comes up every time a film is released by Roman Polanski or Woody Allen, two significant filmmakers whose works no longer can be judged outside public debates about what they may or may not have done. This raises the question of whether or not we should support any artist who has done wrong: Norman Mailer stabbed his wife; Anne Perry murdered her mother; H.P. Lovecraft, Flannery O'Connor and Patricia Highsmith were racists; Ezra Pound, T.S. Eliot, Degas and Wagner were anti-Semites. Before writing *Lord of the Flies*, a high school favorite, William Golding attempted to rape a 15-year-old girl. Despite creating powerful female characters in his plays, Shakespeare cruelly hobbled his own daughters by keeping them illiterate. And William S. Burroughs, the darling of the Beat generation, killed his wife while drunkenly trying to shoot a glass off her head. The difference for most of us is that, in many cases, we can pry the art from the artist because they are dead and cannot profit from our support. In the case of living artists whose morality we are judging, supporting their work can make us feel like accomplices.

I am always reluctant to judge a person's guilt or innocence based on an accusation because it smacks of the kind of rough vigilantism that justified lynching. Yet I appreciate that we live in a society that even asks the question of whether or not seeing a movie is a moral act, and I respect those that grapple with the decision, as I have. But we have to be especially careful about making public judgments solely based on our sympathies about the nature of the alleged crime.

I wasn't at Nate Parker's trial, so I can't know all the specifics. I tried to do due diligence. I read many articles and interviews, including Goldie Taylor's articulate and thoughtful article in *The Daily Beast* in which she, as a victim of sexual assault and someone who read the trial transcript, says she believes Parker is guilty, yet still encourages people to see the film because of its significance in teaching African-American history. I also read the statement in support of Parker and *The Birth of a Nation* co-writer Jean Celestin (who was at first convicted but later exonerated on appeal) by Penn State alumni who were present during the investigation and trial. In their document, they state that "some of us [supporters] are women who have survived sexual violence," and they detail allegations of racism and bullying by the investigators. Because I can't know what really happened, and because there is so much conflicting information, I have to rely on the determination of the judicial system.

Innocent until proven guilty.

I'm glad I made that decision because there's a lot to love in this movie. The story unfolds like an epic poem, with each scene a finely crafted stanza beautifully photographed and often enhanced by a rousing gospel song or a plaintive "Strange Fruit." The massive seas of cotton, the grand trees hung with Spanish moss and the gorgeous landscapes create a taunting Eden, the heavenly place in which the slaves reside but may never live. Equally impressive is the layered development of Nat Turner as he transitions from hopeless slave to baptizing himself as a free man, however brief that taste of paradise. The most emotionally engaging moments won't soon be forgotten: slave owners knocking out the teeth of a slave in order to force-feed him; the young black boy holding up a sign that reads, "Slaves for Sale"; Turner wielding a hatchet while leading a charge. Particularly unforgettable is the image of a young white girl skipping across the veranda, a black girl following behind her with a rope around her neck like a leash or noose. What makes this latter image so provocative and memorable is the blank obliviousness of the black girl as she skips along behind. We can see in Nat's face the realization bloom that if something isn't done, another generation will grow up thinking this is how things have to be—or worse, should be.

Equally compelling is the scene in which Nat and his owner's son, Sam, play hide and seek. Sam smiles at Nat as if they will always be lifelong pals, but that hope is crushed as the older Sam (Armie Hammer) increasingly treats his childhood friend with detached indifference and inhumanity. Their final violent confrontation is as much about personal betrayal as it is about slavery.

Though the film is a marvel in so many ways, there are also a few missteps. People of color, myself included, long have complained about the whitewashing of history that does not accurately reflect our experiences in or contributions to America. Last year, a black high school student in Texas noticed his geography textbook referred to slaves as "workers," which prompted national scrutiny of textbooks filled with historical inaccuracies and omissions, especially when it comes to minorities. I have written several books trying to reclaim and popularize African-American history: *What Color Is My World: The Lost History of African-American Inventors, On the Shoulders of Giants: My Journey Through the Harlem Renaissance,*

Black Profiles in Courage: A Legacy of African-American Achievement, and *Brothers in Arms: The Epic Story of the 761st Tank Battalion, WWII's Forgotten Heroes*. However, as much as I dislike whitewashing history, I'm also opposed to blackwashing it by canonizing a person by sanitizing their story. What makes Spike Lee's *Do the Right Thing* one of the best films ever made is its affection for the characters, not despite their flaws but because of them. When his characters overcome cultural inertia to do something heroic, it taps into that part of us that says we, too, could be heroic.

What makes Nat Turner's story an inspiration for oppressed people is that he was an ordinary man with strengths and weaknesses who made an extraordinary choice to lead a revolution against tyranny, not unlike the progenitors of the American Revolution. His transformation is uplifting because he is so human. But Parker chooses to mythologize Turner by turning him into a Moses/Christ-like figure. In the movie's opening scene, a tribal ceremony echoing the characters' African roots, an elder pronounces Nat a "prophet" and "leader" because of his birthmark moles. This is based on Turner's own testimony about himself in *The Confessions of Nat Turner*, which was transcribed by Thomas Ruffin Gray, a lawyer for several of the other slaves in the rebellion—though not Turner—after Turner's capture. The difference between Turner seeing himself as a prophet of God and being pronounced one by others during this overwrought scene is the attempt to transform Turner from a man with a crisis of faith into the familiar archetype of the epic hero—"The One," like Neo in *The Matrix* or Katniss in *The Hunger Games*. That trivializes the real man. Turner did not turn himself in because he wanted to sacrifice himself to save others; he hid out for two months before being discovered. And, according to records, Turner's rebels killed at least 10 men, 14 women and 31 infants and children. That's a harsh reality that should be acknowledged rather than buried because it says a lot about the effects of dehumanizing people until they are left with no other option but behaving inhumanely. Slavery, whether with chains and shackles or institutional racism that destroys hope for a better future, breeds violence. Sometimes that violence takes the form of a revolution targeting the oppressors, but sometimes it's chaotic, even self-destructive. The black-on-black crime ravaging our inner-city communities is a legacy of this oppression. As is the pattern of unnecessary police violence against unarmed people of color.

A filmmaker is under no obligation to balance the portrayal of whites and blacks, but it can hurt the veracity of the film to have almost all whites portrayed in such stereotypically villainous fashion when all the black characters are portrayed as humble, loving, heart-of-gold men, women and children. If this film is meant to preserve African-American history, this lopsided racial presentation makes it less accessible. The single exception is the wife of Nat's owner, who, in a limited way, encourages his education. The dinner scene in which she has tears in her eyes as she watches her drunken son act in the same loutish way as her deceased husband is truly touching. More of that kind of nuanced characterization would have helped.

It's impossible to present a fictionalized account of a historic event that is completely accurate. That would make for a dull film. All the artist can hope to do is represent the spirit of the events and people, seeking to tell a larger truth rather than merely recount facts. In the case of *The Birth of a Nation,* Parker partially succeeds. He captures the truth of the spirit of defiance necessary for all people to remain free. But in an attempt to romanticize Nat Turner, he overlooks what truly made him heroic and his rebellion a warning bell for the future. But these flaws don't make the film's strengths any less effective or admirable. Many of the scenes will continue to haunt me for years to come.

And Parker's intense performance is a marvel. As a whole, the poetic film reminds me of the final two stanzas of another poem, "This Skin that Carry My Worth," by Earl Mills, an African-American poet in his 60s who was illiterate until he was 48:

> So when you look at me.
>
> This skin that may be darker than you like.
>
> Has been to hell and back.
>
> Yet we stand tall with our heads up and shoulders back.
>
> This dark skin that carry my worth,
>
> Was not my choice it was my birth.
>
> This Skin That Carry My Worth.

WRITING STRATEGIES

1. Abdul-Jabbar's thesis is implied by the title, "Important but Flawed." What specific sentence in the review fleshes out this point?

2. In your own words, explain Abdul-Jabbar's estimation of the film—both its social worth and its shortcomings.

3. Examine Abdul-Jabbar's allusions to past literary and artistic figures in ¶2. What argumentative point do these allusions help to make?

4. What criteria (standards of judgment) does Abdul-Jabbar use to guide his evaluation of the film? What criteria guides his evaluation (or verdict) of Nate Parker?

5. Describe any counterarguments, concessions, or qualifiers operating in Abdul-Jabbar's argument.

EXPLORING IDEAS

1. In your own words, explain cultural appropriation.

2. Give one reason why artists should be careful about cultural appropriation. Give one reason why they shouldn't.

3. Consider another artistic work (a film, song, album, novel) that has helped to shed light on race and American history. Explain what particular idea or understanding that work brought forward.

4. Should artists' lives be judged along with their artistic works? Why or why not? (Are there any boundaries or situations that should be considered?)

5. What rules, guidelines, or principles—beyond trying to sell tickets—should filmmakers follow? Anything specific? None at all? Give reasoning for your answer.

IDEAS FOR WRITING

1. Focus on another controversial film. Consider the criteria people use (or have used) to evaluate the film. How might the criteria be flawed or misapplied?

2. Consider a classic novel, play, or film. As you begin evaluating, try to characterize the prevailing values and beliefs of its day—what audiences expected and understood about the genre and the content. (You may need to research the era.)

If responding to one of these ideas, go to the Analysis section of this chapter to begin developing ideas for your essay.

STUDENT ESSAY

Star Trek: Where No Man Has Gone Before

Jaren Provo

Most people have a favorite television program, but few of us consider how that program resonates with broader cultural trends—how it speaks to, addresses, or challenges common biases and prejudices. In this essay, Jaren Provo takes a close look at *Star Trek*. She goes beyond merely celebrating its attributes; she evaluates *Star Trek* according to its role in shaping attitudes about and within popular culture. Provo wrote this essay for her first-semester college writing course.

> "The greatest danger facing us is ourselves, and irrational fear of the unknown. But there's no such thing as 'the unknown,' only things temporarily hidden, temporarily not understood."
>
> —Captain James T. Kirk

The epigraph establishes a way of thinking before the essay begins.

Since its stunning and innovative debut in 1966, *Star Trek* has given modern culture a new promise for the future, one of peace, cooperation, and tolerance not seen in such tenacity or splendor before or since. Yet, despite the significant cultural contribution *Star Trek* has made, many see this legendary universe as unreachable, non-applicable, influencing only the stereotypical Klingon-quoting, uniform-donning, convention-going fan. However, this view is false. *Star Trek* empowers mainstream America to imagine a future of hope-filled opportunity rather than horrific obliteration.

Takes on a misperception and explains the rhetorical function of the show.

Each of us is familiar with *Star Trek* in some manner, whether it be the phrase "Beam me up, Scotty" (which, actually, was never said verbatim in the series), the *USS Enterprise,* the . . . very . . . long pauses . . . of William Shatner's portrayal of Captain Kirk, or its groovy theme music. *Star Trek* is best described, by Roddenberry himself, as the 1960's television show set "close enough to our own time for continuing characters to be fully identifiable as people like us, but far enough into the future for galaxy travel to be fully established" ("*Star Trek* Is"). It is not until much later in the franchise that we realize *Star Trek* is set in the 2260s AD, focusing on the crew and

Gives widely recognizable allusions from the show.

voyages of the starship *Enterprise* as it carries out its five-year mission of peaceful exploration. As the *Enterprise* travels through space, it encounters various worlds with attributes reminiscent of Earth, and discusses numerous issues of political, social, and human nature. *Star Trek* shows us, through a cast of recurring dynamic characters and a space-oriented view, a reflection of humanity and its possibilities.

Briefly overviews the show's plot. (Several paragraphs of overview are unnecessary.)

The specific focus here is Roddenberry's first series, the original series (or what Trekkies refer to as TOS). There have been five television spin-off series and ten movies deriving their roots from TOS, but each successive reiteration of *Star Trek* brings an even more commercialized version of Roddenberry's standard-defying innovation. In these new series, special effects have replaced meaningful plots; de rigueur characters have replaced dynamic ones. Roddenberry's vision rose above the need for believable explosions, unrecognizable aliens, and shoot-em-up alien-invader plots, such that *Star Trek* struggled to remain on the air during its short (but syndicate-able) three-year stint; it was a vision that broadcasting officials placed little promise in, as it was most certainly not a mainstream science fiction show.

Distinguishes the original show from spin-offs that turned more toward mainstream tastes.

But this vision was so powerful and so magnificent that it opened an avenue to engage humans in their own universe. While popular culture at the time focused on the individual and his or her worldly place in society, *Star Trek* expanded the horizons of the human mind toward the furthermost reaches of space. In the *Star Trek* future, there are no physical boundaries or burdens, for the greatest, most inaccessible reaches of the universe are merely a warp speed away, the unknown cultures of a million worlds much like Earth are open for communication and exploration. Indeed, one of the core principles of *Star Trek* is the "parallel worlds concept"—that there are billions of planets with conditions comparable to Earth that could harbor similar social, ecological, and humanlike development ("*Star Trek* Is"). It is this principle that shapes the core mission of the *USS Enterprise* herself: "to boldly go where no man has gone before."

A key feature that distinguishes Star Trek *from most other shows of the day.*

The passage narrows in on that distinguishing feature.

And in so doing, the humans of the twenty-third century do not have to face a decimated, physically and culturally broken world similar to those in many recognizable pop culture realms, such as *Terminator* or *The Matrix*. Instead, they are a functioning global culture. These individuals are able to realize their own humanity by exploring and relating to alien cultures in the depths of the universe, offering aid and relief to struggling civilizations, but willing to observe and maintain the customs of the native peoples. This core

Here's a key element of the show: "the prime directive."

idea constitutes the Prime Directive, a predominant theme throughout *Star Trek*. The Prime Directive advocates involvement with, but not indoctrination of, other cultures (unless there is a lack of a progressing, stable culture). To each world the *Enterprise* travels, it promotes a mission of peace and negotiation, rather than conquest.

Through this process, humans become increasingly tolerant of groups within their own species. Bigotry or intolerance in any form is seen as a horrendous trait and a mark of low character. On the bridge of the *Enterprise,* such individuals as an African woman, Asian American man, Scottish engineer, pointed-eared alien without emotions, nationalistic Russian youngster, and even an Iowan hunk with a rhythmically related speech deficiency are regular residents, each respected for his or her own talents and merit as a member of the crew. Even representatives of such backgrounds as German, French, Irish, Indian, British, Native American, and more are seen frequently on the *Enterprise.* Jeff Greenwald, author of *Future Perfect: How "Star Trek" Conquered Planet Earth,* echoes this idea: "[*Star Trek*] has given us a model of a truly multicultural world, where all races and creeds are afforded equal respect and rights" (qtd. in Schrof 8). Together, this diverse and accepting group explores the human condition, such items as the role of good and evil (in such episodes as "The Savage Curtain" and "The Enemy Within"), maturity and age (in the episodes "Miri," "Charlie X," and "The Deadly Years"), and an ambition-free life ("This Side of Paradise").

However, some feel that *Star Trek*'s diverse cast is not as accepting and multicultural as it appears. In his piece, "Carved From the Rock Experiences of Our Daily Lives: Reality and *Star Trek*'s Multiple Histories," Lincoln Geraghty concedes that TOS casts "token" minority members as crew and is deficient because of its lack of an openly homosexual crewmember (161). In this way, he argues, *Star Trek* repeats the "mistakes other popular television series made" (161). However, it is important to observe the cultural climate of the 1960s, especially in popular media. If indeed minority groups were portrayed, they were often playing roles of servants (Asian Americans), slaves (African Americans), or senseless and vicious warriors on the Western plains (Native Americans). The latter was not often represented by those from this culture; often, individuals of Italian descent were given the roles of Native Americans. Though perhaps not main characters with substantial parts (with the exception of Spock, who is an alien and would in a sense be considered a member

Star Trek presents an ethnically diverse crew with a shared mission. These are held up as values.

A counterargument paragraph: The opposition calls minority characters tokens; Provo explains them as groundbreaking.

A small quaifier within the broader counterargument.

of a "minority" group), these individuals are not degraded, but are respected on the merit of their performance and contributions to the ship itself. These individuals also took on a more active role as *Star Trek* progressed; in the third season, *Star Trek* was even so bold as to portray the first interracial kiss on television ("Plato's Stepchildren"). Given the exclusive nature of the times, *Star Trek*'s role was an advanced platform (unlike other pop culture outlets) upon which racial, ethnic, and gender acceptance could be built.

The latter half of the paragraph responds to (counters) the opposing view.

Together, these humans learn from past mistakes, attempting to avoid their occurrence in other cultures developing in similar manners (as in the episodes "Patterns of Force" and "A Taste of Armageddon"). Indeed, as William Blake Tyrrell states in his 1977 article (around the peak of *Star Trek*'s syndication-led revival), "*Star Trek* creates a future world where the glories of the past are pristine and the failures and doubts of the present have been overcome. It gives us our past as our future, while making our present the past, which . . . is safely over and forgotten" (qtd. in Geraghty 167). But in *Star Trek,* the past is not so much forgotten as it is no longer dwelled upon; it is often revisited for comparative and developmental purposes. Humanity in the future does not degrade; it matures and refines itself toward a more ideal form.

Quotation from Tyrrell reinforces Provo's claim about the show's value.

Notably absent from *Star Trek*'s list of qualities is the predominant science fiction theme regarding space aliens: "When they come, they'll destroy us all." This permeated view is reflected in numerous locales, such as *Independence Day, Invasion of the Body Snatchers,* and H.G. Wells' *War of the Worlds.* Yet in *Star Trek,* the first contact with aliens is a diplomatic one, in which logical, peaceful Vulcan representatives come to Earth to note their presence and encourage future technological development. After this contact, more connections are forged with other alien worlds, such that the United Federation of Planets develops (with a flag suspiciously reminiscent of that of the United Nations) to promote peaceable cooperation among these cultures. Alien cultures are not (generally) out to conquer Earth and all of humanity in a blazing inferno of death and destruction, but are civilized, developing worlds willing to forge ties with others in the universe to assure mutual survival.

Contrasts *Star Trek* to other popular sci-fi dramas.

Also uncharacteristic of *Star Trek* but common in the sci-fi realm is the element portraying humans as slaves of technology, hopelessly existent only in body. This concept is perhaps most prevalent in the *Matrix* trilogy. Yet *Star Trek* foretells humans as harnessing the

Another way *Star Trek* differs from other works in the genre.

resources of technology to propel themselves outward into space, to explore, to contact, to impact in a positive way. The transporter and warp drive allow for expedient, efficient movement among planets and realms; the communicator (predecessor to the flip-phone?) and universal translator aid in interpersonal and intercultural contact; the scientific tricorder (a handheld programmable scanning device) and ship's scanners enhance exploration purposes; and medical tricorders and unknown, but apparently technical, whirring devices devised from salt 'n' pepper shakers exist for medical purposes. True, some matters of technology are dangerous and destroy human independence, such as the M-5 Multitronic Computer in the episode "The Ultimate Computer." Essentially, this device is meant to save lives by replacing the human presence on a starship, yet it manages to entirely control the ship and destroy hundreds of innocent lives in the process. However, this technology is not typical, and ends up being destroyed. M-5 reminds us to maintain a fine balance between technology serving and subverting humankind.

Some, however, disagree with the assertion that *Star Trek* promotes a palate of peace, tolerance, and diplomacy, pointing to the predominant enemy throughout the series: the Klingon Empire. They observe the constant conflict between the Klingons and the Federation, between their opposing interests of complete colonization and diplomatic cooperation. Certainly the Federation is not peaceful toward or tolerant of this group of aliens. Yet, the Klingon Empire is an imperialistic, dictatorial force of conquest interested in destroying the diplomatic network of the Federation and its promotion of freedom and democracy. Actions taken against the Klingons are in matters of defense, not of aggression, and peace negotiations between the Klingons and Federation persist throughout and beyond the series. Eventually, internal political movements bring the dictatorial regime to its knees, and even the Klingons themselves are incorporated into the Federation.

Many also claim that *Star Trek* is merely a scripted TV show, unrealistic and inaccessible to all but the most obsessive fans. However, *Star Trek* has reached and influenced some of the leaders of technology and society, including individuals such as Bill Gates, several NASA scientists and engineers, and even the late Dr. Martin Luther King, Jr. The message of *Star Trek* resonates through these and other individuals familiar with *Star Trek*'s ideals, such that all in society are influenced by this series. Many outlets

[margin notes]

Details substantiate the claim about harnessing technology.

Qualifies but maintains the claim about technology.

Another counterargument paragraph: The opposition points out ongoing conflicts; Provo explains nuances of the conflicts.

Another counterargument: The opposition says *Star Trek* is inaccessible; Provo says it's highly influential.

in society and the media also carry *Star Trek*'s concepts into their settings on an entertainment level. Considering entertainment's pivotal role in our society (take, for instance, the large number of individuals who gain current events knowledge from comedy shows such as *The Daily Show, The Tonight Show with Jay Leno,* and *Saturday Night Live*), the sheer entertainment quality of *Star Trek* brings it into our everyday lives. Furthermore, the core concepts of *Star Trek* are not fictional and far-reaching, but are based on events and themes within the Vietnam War era and relating to the human condition.

> A broader defense: popular television shows, generally, influence politics and culture.

Imagine a world in which *Star Trek* is absent. We would miss more than the phrases "He's dead, Jim" and "Beam me up, Scotty," more than warp drive and the same men in red shirts dying before the introductory theme each week. Our culture would be void of a revolutionary promise, a promise of tolerance, peace, exploration, and humanity in our future. Without *Star Trek,* modern pop culture would be filled only with bleak visions for tomorrow, of aliens ruthlessly invading and destroying Earth, of a humanity decimated and barely clinging to the edge of existence, of survival depending upon backstabbing and cruelty. *Star Trek* is one of the few (perhaps the only) candles flickering in the darkness of popular apocalypticism, a guarantee of a secure future where tomorrow may not be such a horrible thing after all.

> A world with *Star Trek* ≠ a world without its distinct vision of a promising future.

We must be sure not to violate the magnitude of *Star Trek* and its whispers of truth for the days ahead. We must not be intolerant of that which heralds a tolerant tomorrow, doubtful of a harbinger of hope, or disparaging toward a beacon of peace or humanity. The zeitgeist bestowed upon our culture by *Star Trek* must be appreciated for its complexities and considered in its hopeful message to the people of today.

> Provo's voice lifts, becomes grand, in its final defense.

> The value of *Star Trek* is its vision of the future and its effect on pop culture.

Works Cited

Geraghty, Lincoln. "Carved from the Rock Experiences of Our Daily Lives: Reality and *Star Trek's* Multiple Histories." *European Journal of American Culture,* vol. 21, no. 3, Nov. 2002, pp. 160–76. *Academic Search Elite,* doi:10.1386/ejac.21.3.160.

Schrof, Joannie M. "A World of Trekkies." *U.S. News and World Report,* 29 June 1998, p. 8.

"Star Trek Is." *Memory Alpha,* memory-alpha.wikia.com/wiki/Star_Trek_is. . . . Accessed 8 Apr. 2014.

WRITING STRATEGIES

1. How does Provo address the common dismissal about "Trekkies"?

2. Although she does not state them directly in the essay, what can you infer about Provo's criteria (standards of judgment)? In other words, in her view, what makes a good television program? Why does *Star Trek* meet those standards?

3. How does Provo counterargue? Explain how particular counterarguments add dimension and value to her essay.

4. Although Provo praises *Star Trek*, she also qualifies and concedes some points. Explain how a specific qualifier or concession functions in her argument.

5. How does Provo's sentence structure influence her voice? Focus on a particular paragraph and explain how the sentences impact the "sound" of the argument.

EXPLORING IDEAS

1. Provo argues that television programs are more than entertainment—that they deal with important culture issues within a given era. What current television dramas attempt to deal with the political and cultural tensions of our era? How do they succeed or fail?

2. Provo celebrates *Star Trek* because it challenged racial prejudices of the 1960s. Do you think television can genuinely challenge or overturn common assumptions about race or gender? Why or why not?

3. Provo argues that most science fiction in popular culture, other than *Star Trek*, predicts a future of "horrific obliteration." What recent movies or television programs reinforce Provo's point? Do any challenge her notion?

4. From ancient times to the present, civilizations imagine other nations, tribes, people, or species as inherently wicked or debased. Oral stories, religious traditions, novels, and popular movies often characterize some faraway, unknown group as hostile, weird, or even corrupt. How does *Star Trek* fit into that long tradition?

IDEAS FOR WRITING

1. What particular program works to break down common prejudices or stereotypes? How does it succeed or fall short?

2. Consider a current commercial or ad campaign. How does it subtly reinforce negative stereotypes about people? Why don't viewers tend to acknowledge such stereotypes?

If responding to one of these ideas, go to the Analysis section of this chapter to begin developing ideas for your essay.

INVENTION

"The trouble with normal is it always gets worse."

—**Bruce Cockburn**

Invention is the primary strategy for generating new ideas. As you work through the following sections, imagine possibilities beyond your initial thoughts. The Point of Contact section will help you to find a subject for the evaluation; Analysis will help you to develop particular points about the subject; and Public Resonance will help you to make it relevant to a community of readers. The Thesis and Rhetorical Tools sections will help you develop a specific claim and support it appropriately. As in the other chapters, the Invention Questions in each section are not meant to be answered directly in your final written assignment. They are meant to prompt reflection and discovery; however, your answers may translate directly into your drafts.

Point of Contact

Evaluators need to have insight into their subject, so choose something that you can examine carefully. Your instructor may provide subjects, or you can use the following suggestions and questions to seek out and focus on a subject. As you proceed through the Invention Questions, take ample notes. Record as much information about the subject as possible.

Attend an Event Choose a carnival, circus, beauty pageant, dance, tractor pull, art show, concert, poetry reading, company meeting, college class, etc. What happens before the event? What is the mood? How are the participants treated during the event? What kinds of interaction occur during the event? Where does the event take place? What impact does the location have on the event?

Investigate a Person Evaluating a person (a government official, doctor, religious leader, talk show host, roommate, professional athlete, work supervisor or manager, work associate, etc.) can be tricky because it is easy to fall into an explanation of one's likes and dislikes. Instead, focus on the qualities or actions of the person in terms of his or her particular position or title. Is he or she willing to listen to people? For how long? What does he or she do while listening to someone? How do people respond or react to this person? Are people comfortable around this person? Is this person entertaining, enlightening, engaging, comforting, informative, energizing (or the opposite of any of these)?

Visit a Place Pick a restaurant, movie theater, night club, amusement park, college classroom or campus, shopping mall, grocery store, etc. Gather information about the place. How do people behave? What behavior is tolerated, supported, ignored? What is on the walls? How does this influence the mood of the place? How much open space is available? Is the place empty, crowded, stuffy, clean, lonely, isolated, intense?

Watch a Movie or Show Pick a motion picture, sitcom, documentary, television drama, or music video. Gather information and details, going beyond simple likes and dislikes. Does the dialogue reveal something about the characters that their actions do not? What kinds of graphic or sexually explicit images appear? Is the movie/show humorous or frightening in some way? How? What message(s) does the movie/show offer? Does the movie/show have stereotypes (of rich people, poor people, women, men, racial groups, children, the elderly)?

Read a Text Consider a book, article, poster, letter, website, etc., related to your major. In this case, go to one of the journals for your major, or to a database in your library. In some ways, evaluating a text is easy because it can be examined closely without having to rewind

John Mauk

or travel somewhere. However, a written text can be a complicated mass of elements. What is the main idea or main argument of the text? What kind of evidence or support is used? How formal is the language? What is the tone of the text? If the text is an argument, does it address counterarguments? Does it use concession? What strategies are used to draw readers into the ideas of the text?

Analysis

Imagine taking your car to a mechanic because you hear a strange knocking sound when you accelerate. As you pull into the garage, the mechanic smiles and exclaims, "Hey, nice car! I love Ford Mustangs! There's nothing wrong with *that* car." Obviously, you'd be a bit disoriented, and maybe a little grumpy. You'd also probably complain: "Hey, I want you to tell me what's wrong with the car—tell me why it's making that sound!" The problem with this scenario is that the mechanic does no analysis and uses no *criteria* (the standards on which judgments are based). The evaluation of the car is based on the mechanic's own likes and dislikes.

Or imagine reading a review of a fine Italian restaurant. While ignoring the wine list, entrees, and presentation of the food, the reviewer gives the restaurant a very low rating because of a limited number of ice cream flavors. In this scenario, the reviewer uses the *wrong* criteria. The reviewer evaluates a fine dining establishment with criteria for judging an ice cream shop. This would be similar to judging a historical drama negatively because it is not funny: Historical dramas are not, usually, supposed to be funny, nor are fine Italian restaurants supposed to have wide varieties of ice cream.

Discovering the Purpose of the Subject

The first analytical step is to discover the subject's purpose or goal—to understand, in other words, what the subject is attempting to achieve. We can only develop criteria and then evaluate a subject if we know the subject's purpose and audience. For example, we can evaluate a movie only if we understand what the movie is attempting to do: to succeed as a comedy for teens, to maintain high action for adults, or to retell a classic fairy tale for children. Evaluating something means understanding what that subject is attempting to do.

> What does your subject try to achieve? (Be specific. For example, an Italian restaurant may be attempting to provide an elegant dining experience with a particular ethnic cuisine. This is different from the goal of a general chain restaurant such as Denny's, which attempts to provide economically priced food from a general menu.)

> What do other like subjects try to achieve? (Think about subjects similar to yours— other teachers, other comedic movies, other restaurants, and so on.)

> Who is your subject's audience? (Whom does your subject attempt to engage or attract?) If you have not already considered the audience, imagine who might use, benefit from, and interact with the subject.

> What goals *should* your subject, or all subjects like it, have? (It might be argued, for instance, that a restaurant should attempt to elevate the dining experience, to transform the mundane act of eating into a cultural and social event. Once this criterion is established, someone might then use it to judge a particular restaurant.)

In the following, a writer, Linda, applies some key invention questions to her subject:

What does this subject try to achieve?

Chunky's is trying to create a local dining experience—like the place belongs exclusively to our town. There are aerial photos of the region on most of the walls, some pennants of the Bengals, Reds, and a few of the area high schools. But the most blatant cue is the sign when you walk through the front door: *your local hangout.* It's a bold statement. Less subtle cues show up on the menu. Instead of "specials," it's "local favorites." Instead of "cocktails," it's "what you're drinking." The food itself is like any straight-up American grill: sandwiches, chili, pasta salad, maybe a ribeye special or stew in the winter. In other words, it's not trying to elevate the dining experience but simply make easygoing food available for most middle range tastes. It's all presented on easygoing plates by easygoing servers, always dressed in basic brown slacks and a white button-down.

What do other like subjects try to achieve?

It wouldn't make sense to compare Chunky's to a fast food chain—whose goals are to make easily consumable food extremely fast and economic. Maybe it's fair to call Victoria's—just down the street from Chunky's—a "like subject." Victoria's is a local dining establishment—has been around for decades. It attempts to elevate the entire dining experience so customers go through something beyond just sitting down and consuming food that tastes good. The climate of Victoria's—from the threshold to the restrooms, from the chairs to the lighting—is geared to make people slow down, look around, and savor. It's especially clear when the servers first come to your table. They don't give the quick address: "Hi, my name's _____. What can I get you?" They ask if you've been in before, what you're interested in—something elegant, something hearty, etc. And when they explain specials, they don't just say what's in the dish. They explain how it's prepared, what the chef was thinking, sometimes where the ingredients come from. It's obvious from the start: this place is up to something beyond consumption. It's fostering a kind of meditation on eating and drinking. (This is all different from Chunky's, which isn't about a slow, meditative, or intimate experience but a social, cheery outing.)

Applying Criteria to the Subject

Now that you have a sense of the subject's purpose, you can begin making specific evaluative points. Refer to your notes from the Point of Contact section and answer the following:

> In what particular ways does the subject achieve its goal? What specific parts, tools, or strategies help the subject to achieve its goal?

> In what particular ways does the subject fall short of achieving its goal?

> What goals does the subject ignore?

> How does the subject compare to and contrast with other similar subjects?

> What is unique about your subject's approach or strategy to achieving its goal?

Public Resonance

A meaningful evaluation considers how the subject affects or influences people—how it resonates with people's lives and concerns. For example, a movie critic might argue that children's
movies carry the responsibility of developing notions of right and wrong. Or someone might
suggest that a restaurant affects the health and well-being of a community and influences the
image of a neighborhood. Ultimately, it is up to the writer to reveal the influence of a subject.

Each of the writers featured in this chapter (Busch, Abdul-Jabbar, and Provo) develops
public resonance by connecting the specific subject to broader social issues. In her essay, Jaren
Provo makes an explicit case about *Star Trek*. She, in fact, argues about the show's influence
on American pop culture:

> Imagine a world in which *Star Trek* is absent. We would miss more than the phrases
> "He's dead, Jim" and "Beam me up, Scotty," more than warp drive and the same men
> in red shirts dying before the introductory theme each week. Our culture would be void
> of a revolutionary promise, a promise of tolerance, peace, exploration, and humanity
> in our future. Without *Star Trek*, modern pop culture would be filled only with bleak
> visions for tomorrow, of aliens ruthlessly invading and destroying Earth, of a human-
> ity decimated and barely clinging to the edge of existence, of survival depending upon
> backstabbing and cruelty. *Star Trek* is one of the few (perhaps the only) candles flicker-
> ing in the darkness of popular apocalypticism, a guarantee of a secure future where
> tomorrow may not be such a horrible thing after all.

In his article, Benjamin Busch also deals explicitly with public resonance. In the following
passage, he transitions from his own objections to broader, and murkier, problems associated
with video games and the portrayal of war. The paragraph begins with a kind of concession
about legal responsibilities but then ends with some larger (social or humanistic) layers of
responsibility:

> Despite my objections to certain aspects of the video war game, I don't know that
> game makers have any particular responsibilities to any of us. They are a market based
> entertainment business. Their sales are subject to mature audience restrictions like film
> and pornography, but game ratings are not enforced by any government agency in the
> United States. We can only hope that business values social decency, and respects essen-
> tial humanism but a gaming company is only truly concerned with market reception in
> the form of product sales. The responsibility is placed on the consumer and parents. At
> the age of 18, an American citizen can vote, and can enlist in the armed services with-
> out parental consent. We should assume that they can also choose their entertainment
> for better or for worse. Issues of responsibility arise when our military develops war
> games with private companies and then allows them to be sold publicly. The game then
> partially becomes a governmental, even military, product and its messages are unable to
> speak free of politics or real war.

As Busch and Provo illustrate, public resonance can become an integral part—maybe the most critical part—of your argument. Use the following questions to help develop public resonance for your own evaluation:

> How does the subject influence people's lives (their health, attitudes, living conditions, etc.)?

> Why is this subject important in people's lives?

> What do people expect from the subject?

Invention Workshop

With at least one other writer, use one of the Invention Questions to launch an intensive and focused discussion about your subject. Try to go beyond your first thoughts on the subject. For example, Linda, who is evaluating a new restaurant in her town, transcends her initial thoughts. Her discussion leads to a more complicated understanding of the subject and its relationship to people's lives:

Why is this Subject Important in People's Lives?

LINDA: That's easy . . . a restaurant serves people food. And people need food.

MARCUS: But do restaurants just provide food?

JACK: No, they also provide service—someone bringing you the food. And they also make eating a social event.

LINDA: But that isn't the important part.

MARCUS: Well, it isn't the main part, but I'd say people need that social aspect in their lives, and eating is naturally a social activity. That's what's so enjoyable about eating out—you get to feel social.

LINDA: But eating is also a personal thing, right? It's about the home and family, too.

JACK: I would say that restaurants are important because they provide a place where people can feel slightly special—like they're somewhere besides their living room with a bowl of cereal. They make eating feel elevated.

LINDA: If that's the case, what's the deal with all these restaurants saying they're "just like home"?

MARCUS: Well, that's the goal of those chain restaurants, which really aren't like home at all. They're trying to make people feel close to home.

LINDA: So these restaurants provide something psychologically to people. I guess that's why restaurants spend so much on atmosphere and advertising.

MARCUS: So what about the particular restaurant Chunky's? Does it make people feel "at home"?

LINDA: Not really. It feels like a chain restaurant that's attempting to not feel like a chain restaurant.

Linda has discovered something subtle, less obvious, about the subject's purpose: Restaurants aren't simply about food; they are also about familiarity. This discovery kicks up a range of interesting questions about the psychology of food service. These could impact how she evaluates the particular restaurant.

RESEARCH

Consider using outside sources to help you figure out what others have said about the subject. Do not expect to find writers who share your perspective. Instead, explore for various perspectives. Have people generally found the subject valuable, worthy, deficient, dangerous, helpful? If your subject is very specific (such as a local diner) you might search for evaluations in that general category (local diners). See Chapter 14: Finding Sources for help.

Thesis

An evaluation makes a judgment about a subject. An evaluative thesis statement gives focus to that judgment: The thesis sheds light on a particular element of the subject. For instance, a movie has many elements, such as characters, plot, cinematography, themes, special effects, and dialogue. A thesis can help create focus, telling readers that the evaluation will deal primarily with plot, not character development and costumes:

The movie's plot is unnecessarily confusing.

An evaluative thesis need not be completely positive or completely negative. It need not, for example, claim that a particular movie is absolutely great or downright rotten. Many evaluative thesis statements are a mixture of judgments. A statement might concede some value but focus primarily on a shortcoming as in the following:

While the movie's cinematography is engaging, the plot is unnecessarily confusing.

Although the student government has been more public than in previous years, it has still failed to address the student body's most significant concerns.

Even with the new ensemble tricks, which provide an interesting layer of ear candy, Ebenezer Typhoon's new collection of songs still lacks any substantive message.

The menu at Robinson's Grill may lack diversity, but it does what so many other restaurants cannot: deliver a genuinely local dining experience.

Evolution of a Thesis

A good thesis gives focus to an entire project. Linda's evaluation of a restaurant (in the Public Resonance section) gains focus as she works to craft a thesis. First, she discovers the subject's purpose. Then, while exploring public resonance, she discovers another, less obvious, layer. From there, she refines the idea into an evaluative claim:

- Chunky's attempts to give people a variety of good food and friendly service.

- People like to feel attached to their surroundings, to the places they shop and eat. Therefore, restaurants such as Chunky's try to create the illusion that diners are patronizing a friendly neighborhood grill.

- Although Chunky's attempts to make people feel comfortable in a small neighborhood grill, it doesn't work very well.

- Although Chunky's tries to make people feel comfortable in a small neighborhood grill, the attempt itself overwhelms the dining experience.

Linda's thesis evolved as she worked through the complexities of the subject. She discovered a subtle gap between the restaurant's purpose and the actual dining experience. This insight reveals something that might otherwise go unnoticed.

Common Thesis Problems

The Blurry Focus Problem A sufficiently narrow focus can mean all the difference between intensive and bland writing. First, a writer needs to home in on a particular subject, such as a particular band, a particular college campus or program. But that is often not enough. As in the following examples, the specific subjects still do not provide intensive points:

- Green Day is a great punk band.

- Big River Community College is a good school.

These statements need more focus. The writers could examine more particular elements (such as the themes of Green Day's songs or the accessible class times at Big River). Or the writers could develop more vital statements by avoiding the broad predicates "is a great . . ." and "is a good. . . ."

The Obvious Fact Problem The goal of evaluative writing is to help readers see the subject in a new light—to help them see some particular value or shortcoming. But writers sometimes fall into the trap of stating the obvious:

- Howard Stern offends people.

- Although some purists did not like it, the *Lord of the Rings* trilogy made a lot of money at the box office.

Both of these statements announce common knowledge, facts about the radio shock jock and the Peter Jackson movies. But neither statement offers an evaluation. The stated facts say nothing about the value or shortcoming of the subjects. Offending people, for instance, may be a good thing. And making lots of money may not mean much about the movies' artistic success.

The Noncommittal Problem An evaluation is an argument; therefore, the writer should put forth a position. But it may be tempting to back away from the evaluation and to let readers make up their own mind about the subject. The following examples back away; they lack a committed stance:

- The new building will please some and offend others.

- It's up to individual readers to decide whether or not they appreciate Kingsolver's *Poisonwood Bible*.

The noncommittal problem is related to a broader issue: Some writers are afraid of pushing too hard. They want to avoid forcing readers into a perspective. Although this seems like a legitimate concern, we should remember that readers need not be *forced* into an opinion or new perspective. Instead, they can be invited, lulled, guided, nudged, or attracted. Writers should seek to make their opinions so attractive, reasonable, enlightened, and compelling that readers feel as though they must adopt them. In short, don't fear commitment! Readers are waiting around for their minds to be changed.

REVISING YOUR THESIS

Develop a thesis by asking a basic question: On what particular value or shortcoming do I want to focus? Try various wordings for your thesis. Let the idea evolve, tighten, over several attempts. Then, share the thesis statement with two other writers. As you look over their statements, look for all three common problems: blurry focus, obvious fact, and noncommittal stance. Suggest strategies for narrowing and intensifying the statements.

Rhetorical Tools

An evaluation is a type of argument, so it may include a range of argumentative support strategies. All the support strategies listed in Chapter 8: Making Arguments can be applied to this chapter. Additionally, counterarguments, concessions, and qualifiers are especially valuable in evaluative writing.

Using Support

Most of the claims made in evaluations are supported with specific information about the subject itself. The writer points out particular details that illustrate the main idea and show the value or shortcoming of the subject. For example, Abdul-Jabbar calls up specific scenes from his subject, *The Birth of a Nation*:

> The most emotionally engaging moments won't soon be forgotten: slave owners knocking out the teeth of a slave in order to force-feed him; the young black boy holding up a sign that reads, "Slaves for Sale"; Turner wielding a hatchet while leading a charge. Particularly unforgettable is the image of a young white girl skipping across the veranda, a black girl following behind her with a rope around her neck like a leash or noose. What makes this latter image so provocative and memorable is the blank obliviousness of the black girl as she skips along behind. We can see in Nat's face the realization bloom that if something isn't done, another generation will grow up thinking this is how things have to be — or worse, should be.

You might also go beyond the subject itself—beyond your particular text, show, person, place. As explained in Chapter 8, writers have the world of history and culture at their disposal. This applies to evaluation as well. To prove a point about the subject, you can borrow from other moments in history, from science, nature, popular culture, or merely point out other like subjects. For example, Jaren Provo goes beyond her topic, *Star Trek,* to reinforce her thesis:

> Many also claim that *Star Trek* is merely a scripted TV show, unrealistic and inaccessible to all but the most obsessive fans. However, *Star Trek* has reached and influenced some of the leaders of technology and society, including individuals such as Bill Gates, several NASA scientists and engineers, and even the late Dr. Martin Luther King, Jr. The message of *Star Trek* resonates through these and other individuals familiar with *Star Trek*'s ideals, such that all in society are influenced by this series. Many outlets in society and the media also carry *Star Trek*'s concepts into their settings on an entertainment level. Considering entertainment's pivotal role in our society (take, for instance, the large number of individuals who gain current events knowledge from comedy shows such as *The Daily Show, The Tonight Show with Jay Leno,* and *Saturday Night Live*), the sheer entertainment quality of Star Trek brings it into our everyday lives. Furthermore, the core concepts of *Star Trek* are not fictional and far-reaching, but are based on events and themes within the Vietnam War era and relating to the human condition.

To develop claims using outside support, consider the following Invention questions:

> ❯ Does a historical situation or trend (such as the rise of a particular fashion, organization, or individual) illustrate something about my topic?

> Does my topic or situation appear in any movies or television shows? If so, how is it handled?

> Does my topic appear in any works of literature? If so, how is it handled?

> Has science taught us anything about my topic?

> Have I witnessed or experienced someone or something that illustrates my point?

> Can I construct a scenario to illustrate my point?

BEWARE OF TOO MUCH SUMMARY

A writer should present some basic facts about, or summarize, the subject as part of the evaluation. The presentation or summary of the subject should *not* constitute the majority of an evaluation, but it should offer only the relevant details about the subject. For example, an evaluation using the thesis *While the movie's cinematography is engaging, the plot is unnecessarily confusing* would not devote long passages to the dress or appearance of the characters. Such information would be unnecessary and irrelevant to the evaluation.

Counterarguments and Concessions

Evaluations can also involve counterarguments and concessions (see Chapter 8, pages 258–260). Because evaluations are argumentative, they must acknowledge that other opinions (other judgments about the subject) are possible. In another passage from Provo's essay, she explains an opposing position, and then in a classic turnabout paragraph, she counters:

> However, some feel that *Star Trek's* diverse cast is not as accepting and multicultural as it appears. In his piece, "Carved From the Rock Experiences of Our Daily Lives: Reality and *Star Trek's* Multiple Histories," Lincoln Geraghty concedes that TOS casts "token" minority members as crew and is deficient because of its lack of an openly homosexual crewmember (161). In this way, he argues, *Star Trek* repeats the "mistakes other popular television series made" (161). However, it is important to observe the cultural climate of the 1960s, especially in popular media. If indeed minority groups were portrayed, they were often playing roles of servants (Asian Americans), slaves (African Americans), or senseless and vicious warriors on the Western plains (Native Americans). The latter was not often represented by those from this culture; often, individuals of Italian descent were given the roles of Native Americans. Though perhaps not main characters with substantial parts (with the exception of Spock, who is an alien and would in a sense be considered a member of a "minority" group), these individuals are not degraded, but are respected on the merit of their performance and contributions to the ship itself.

Invention Workshop

This activity is designed to generate counterarguments. The process involves an intensive group exchange. Follow these steps: Assemble writers into small groups (three or four per group work best). Each writer should have his or her thesis statement (main evaluative claim about the subject) written down. The first writer should read his or her thesis statement aloud to the group. Taking turns, each group member then should attempt to refute the position given in the statement. The idea is to play devil's advocate, to complicate the writer's ideas. The writer should record each opposing claim that is offered. After everyone in the group has given an opposing claim to the first writer, the second writer should recite his or her thesis, and the process begins again.

Revision

Revision requires sound evaluation. As with all forms of evaluation, writers should judge their work according to particular criteria—standards beyond the writers' own likes and dislikes. In a college writing course, these standard are often made explicit on syllabi, assignment prompts, or rubrics. The criteria often come in some of the following broad categories: *focus, support, depth, development, organization, documentation, grammar,* and *mechanics.* Like the sections of this chapter, common criteria often begin with the more difficult or abstract issues, such as *focus* or *depth,* and work toward more concrete or rule-based issues such as *grammar.* Look carefully through your course materials for these standards so that your revision is guided by shared criteria.

Peer Review

Exchange drafts with at least one other writer. Use the following questions to respond to specific issues in the drafts:

1. Can any phrases or terms in the thesis be narrowed? If so, circle them and make some suggestions for more focus. Does the thesis avoid the common problems? (See pages 324–325.)

2. Does the evaluation summarize or describe the subject thoroughly? (Where might the summary or description be unnecessary or unrelated to the main idea?)

3. Where could the writer support broad evaluative claims with specific details about the subject? For instance, someone might argue "the plot is unnecessarily complicated" but avoid pointing to specific points in the plot. (This is a critical omission for an evaluative argument, so examine the claims closely.)

4. Where might the writer go beyond the specific subject (the place, text, person, etc.) and allude to some other like subject? How could other like subjects help readers to see the main idea?

5. What other evaluative claims could be made about the subject? How could the writer address other, perhaps opposing, opinions?

6. Do any paragraphs shift focus from one point about the subject to another? Write "shifts focus" in the margins.

7. Identify any passages of harsh description. (See page 543.)

8. As a reviewer, point to particular sentences and phrases that could gain vitality and intensity. Use the following:

   a. Look for unnecessary interrupting clauses and phrases. Underline them and/or draw an arrow to show where the phrase or clause can be moved.

   b. Rewrite a sentence to create more intensity with a repeating pattern.

   c. Cross out wordy phrases, and write in more concise options.

   d. Consider other vitality strategies explained in Chapter 19: Vitalizing Sentences.

   - What sentences are over-embedded? (Point to any clauses that overlap with other clauses, causing a disconnect between ideas.)
   - Examine attributive phrases. Point out unnecessary phrases or sentences that could be boiled down.
   - Where can the writer change linking verbs to active verbs?
   - Where can the writer avoid drawing attention to *I* and *you*?
   - Help the writer change unnecessary clauses to phrases.
   - Help the writer change unnecessary phrases to words.
   - Point to expletives (such as *there are* and *it is*).
   - Help the writer change passive verbs to active verbs for more vitality.
   - Help the writer avoid common grammatical errors: comma splices, sentence fragments, or pronoun/antecedent agreement.

Reflection

Writers of all stripes struggle to evaluate their own work. We often fall on one side of a perilous fence: either celebrating our ideas too enthusiastically or cutting ourselves down too quickly. Quite often, those extremes (*I did a great job* verses *I'm a terrible writer*) keep us from understanding what we've accomplished. But good writers try to look honestly at their own rhetoric. They apply some criteria beyond their own likes, fears, and hang-ups. Now that you've written an evaluation, evaluate *it*. (That's right. Evaluate your performance as an evaluator.) Avoid the extremes: exuberant enthusiasm and self-deprecation. Instead, consider the following questions that focus on the essay's rhetoric, and let these questions guide you to an honest look at your work:

1. How did you do more than express a personal opinion? How did you help readers to genuinely re-see the subject?

2. Could you have better engaged opposing positions? Did you do more than dismiss or refute the opposition? How could you have more genuinely dealt with other perspectives, values, or assumptions?

3. How inventive were your allusions? How well did you use support outside of the subject itself?

4. How did your voice engage readers? Was it boring? Did it do something other than speak in academic monotone?

Beyond the Essay: Evaluation Form

Student course evaluations, those forms that you fill out at the end of every semester, are a topic of debate in higher education. Although evaluations are meant to measure the success of a course, some administrators and professors argue that course evaluations are too prone to bias—that students who do well give good evaluations and students who do poorly give poor evaluations, or that many students through no fault of their own cannot really understand the goals and the value of the course. Others argue that student evaluations are popularity contests that encourage professors to inflate grades. All these arguments *evaluate* evaluations.

An important part of the conversation about course evaluations involves *criteria*— the standards that should be used to make the evaluation. These criteria might include rigor of the material, convenience for students, entertainment (enjoyment), entertainment (motivation), the students' interests, the instructor's appearance, instructor personality, grading policies, academic standards, quality of the syllabus, schedule of assignments, clarity, adherence to course or departmental objectives, individual student needs, and acknowledgment of a student's personal life and complications that occur throughout the semester. (More issues than these exist, and as a student you may have a quite different list than your professor. Why?)

1. As a class, discuss what criteria you think should be used to create a course evaluation. Then, with a group of peers, create a course evaluation form for a college class. Ask yourselves: What criteria should be used in a college classroom evaluation? Then create the form and discuss its pros and cons with the class.

2. In several paragraphs, argue for the criteria you generated.

11 Searching for Causes

Chapter Objectives

The sample essays and invention prompts in this chapter will help you to:

- Examine a range of possible conditions (behavioral, economic, social, psychological) related to a social phenomenon.
- Develop an analytical/argumentative essay that ties a specific cause to a social phenomenon.
- Develop the essay with a range of support strategies, counterarguments, and concessions.
- Express or enrich your argument with a collage of images.

"One great cause of failure is lack of concentration."

—Bruce Lee

INTRODUCTION

When something happens in a community, everyone wants to know why. Why did the apartment building catch on fire? Why did the incumbent mayor's campaign lose momentum? Why are so many kids absent from school? What causes the traffic jam on I-95 every day? Why did the stock market suddenly drop? Why did the terrorists attack? Of course, everybody has guesses, but it takes a close analysis to discover the possible causes of such phenomena. Fire officials inspect the ashes of a burned apartment building; political scientists examine candidates' speeches and poll results; civil engineers look closely at travel patterns and highway capacity; economists deliberate over consumption trends and overseas markets. In all these cases, the people searching for causes are detectives attempting to find answers amid a dizzying array of possibilities.

The search for causes constitutes much of the workload in many occupations. Doctors diagnose patients looking for the cause of particular symptoms. Psychologists try to understand the causes of personality disorders or behavioral problems. Business executives hold weekly meetings and discuss the causes of production failures. Education specialists work with children to find the cause of scholastic problems.

The search for such causes is not easy. Any number of factors can contribute to an effect. Take, for example, low proficiency test scores in public schools: School administrators might argue that poor teaching is the cause; teachers may point to poor parenting and discipline problems in the classroom; parents may point to bullying on school grounds or drug abuse; others might point to the tests themselves as the cause. The search for this cause, as it turns out, is a heated debate.

Academia prepares people to understand causes in different fields—that is, that the study of a particular discipline gives students the critical perspectives necessary for asking the right questions within their fields. But despite the particular field or discipline, the process of discovery (of focusing and analyzing) is much the same, and the act of communicating one's discoveries is key in every situation.

The chapter readings will provide insight into necessary writing strategies. For example, each essay in this chapter puts forth a particular claim about what caused or causes something—about *why* something happens. The author might not state it this way, but readers could write down the main claim as *X causes Y,* filling in X with the *cause* and Y with the *behavior, event, or trend.* The entire essay then helps readers understand and possibly accept that claim. As you read, identify the X and Y parts of the main claim and the particular support strategies (examples, explanations, facts, statistics, and so on) that help readers accept it. After reading the essays, you can begin looking for a particular relationship in one of two ways—go to the Point of Contact section to find a problem from your everyday life, or read the following essays and choose one of the Ideas for Writing that follow. After finding a subject, go to the Analysis section to begin developing the evaluation.

READINGS

MINDTAP
From Cengage
Complete the auto-graded
quiz for this reading.

Is Google Making Us Stupid?
What the Internet Is Doing to Our Brains
Nicholas Carr

The following essay appeared in the July/August 2008 issue of *The Atlantic*. While the title asks if Google is making us stupid, the essay examines how not just Google but technology in general (typewriters, clocks, the Internet) changes the way we think. Nicholas Carr is author of *The Shallows: What the Internet Is Doing to Our Brains*.

"Dave, stop. Stop, will you? Stop, Dave. Will you stop, Dave?" So the supercomputer HAL pleads with the implacable astronaut Dave Bowman in a famous and weirdly poignant scene toward the end of Stanley Kubrick's *2001: A Space Odyssey*. Bowman, having nearly been sent to a deep-space death by the malfunctioning machine, is calmly, coldly disconnecting the memory circuits that control its artificial brain. "Dave, my mind is going," HAL says, forlornly. "I can feel it. I can feel it."

I can feel it, too. Over the past few years I've had an uncomfortable sense that someone, or something, has been tinkering with my brain, remapping the neural circuitry, reprogramming the memory. My mind isn't going—so far as I can tell—but it's changing. I'm not thinking the way I used to think. I can feel it most strongly when I'm reading. Immersing myself in a book or a lengthy article used to be easy. My mind would get caught up in the narrative or the turns of the argument, and I'd spend hours strolling through long stretches of prose. That's rarely the case anymore. Now my concentration often starts to drift after two or three pages. I get fidgety, lose the thread, begin looking for something else to do. I feel as if I'm always dragging my wayward brain back to the text. The deep reading that used to come naturally has become a struggle.

I think I know what's going on. For more than a decade now, I've been spending a lot of time online, searching and surfing and sometimes adding to the great databases of the Internet. The Web has been a godsend to me as a writer. Research that once required days in the stacks or periodical rooms of libraries can now be done in minutes. A few Google searches, some quick clicks on hyperlinks, and I've got the telltale fact or pithy quote I was after. Even when I'm not working, I'm as likely as not to be foraging in the Web's info-thickets, reading and writing e-mails, scanning headlines and blog posts, watching videos and listening to podcasts, or just tripping from link to link to link. (Unlike footnotes, to which they're sometimes likened, hyperlinks don't merely point to related works; they propel you toward them.)

For me, as for others, the Net is becoming a universal medium, the conduit for most of the information that flows through my eyes and ears and into my mind. The advantages of having immediate access to such an incredibly rich store of information are many, and they've been widely described and duly applauded. "The perfect recall of silicon memory," *Wired*'s Clive Thompson has written, "can be an enormous boon to thinking." But that boon comes at a price. As the media theorist Marshall McLuhan pointed out in the 1960s, media are not just passive channels of information. They supply the stuff of thought, but they also shape the process of thought. And what the Net seems to be doing is chipping away my capacity for concentration and contemplation. My mind now expects to take in information the way the Net distributes it: in a swiftly moving stream of particles. Once I was a scuba diver in the sea of words. Now I zip along the surface like a guy on a Jet Ski.

I'm not the only one. When I mention my troubles with reading to friends and acquaintances—literary types, most of them—many say they're having similar experiences. The more they use the Web, the more they have to fight to stay focused on long pieces of writing. Some of the bloggers I follow have also begun mentioning the phenomenon. Scott Karp, who writes a blog about online media, recently confessed that he has stopped reading books altogether. "I was a lit major in college, and used to be [a] voracious book reader," he wrote. "What happened?" He speculates on the answer: "What if I do all my reading on the web not so much because the way I read has changed, i.e., I'm just seeking convenience, but because the way I THINK has changed?"

Bruce Friedman, who blogs regularly about the use of computers in medicine, also has described how the Internet has altered his mental habits. "I now have almost totally lost the ability to read and absorb a longish article on the web or in print," he wrote earlier this year. A pathologist who has long been on the faculty of the University of Michigan Medical School, Friedman elaborated on his comment in a telephone conversation with me. His thinking, he said, has taken on a "staccato" quality, reflecting the way he quickly scans short passages of text from many sources online. "I can't read *War and Peace* anymore," he admitted. "I've lost the ability to do that. Even a blog post of more than three or four paragraphs is too much to absorb. I skim it."

Anecdotes alone don't prove much. And we still await the long-term neurological and psychological experiments that will provide a definitive picture of how Internet use affects cognition. But a recently published study of online research habits, conducted by scholars from University College London, suggests that we may well be in the midst of a sea change in the way we read and think. As part of the five-year research program, the scholars examined computer logs documenting the behavior of visitors to two popular research sites, one operated by the British Library and one by a U.K. educational consortium, that provide access to journal articles, e-books, and other sources of written information. They found that people using the sites exhibited "a form of skimming activity," hopping from one source to another and rarely returning to any source they'd already visited. They typically read no more than one or two pages of an article or book before they would "bounce" out to another site. Sometimes they'd save a long article, but there's no evidence that they ever went back and actually read it. The authors of the study report:

> It is clear that users are not reading online in the traditional sense; indeed there are signs that new forms of "reading" are emerging as users "power browse" horizontally through titles, contents pages and abstracts going for quick wins. It almost seems that they go online to avoid reading in the traditional sense.

Thanks to the ubiquity of text on the Internet, not to mention the popularity of text-messaging on cell phones, we may well be reading more today than we did in the 1970s or 1980s, when television was our medium of choice. But it's a different kind of reading, and behind it lies a different kind of thinking—perhaps even a new sense of the self. "We are not only *what* we read," says Maryanne Wolf, a developmental psychologist at Tufts University and the author of *Proust and the Squid: The Story and Science of the Reading Brain,* "We are *how* we read." Wolf worries that the style of reading promoted by the Net, a style that puts "efficiency" and "immediacy" above all else, may be weakening our capacity for the kind of deep reading that emerged when an earlier technology, the printing press, made long and complex works of prose commonplace. When we read online, she says, we tend to become "mere decoders of information." Our ability to interpret text, to make the rich mental connections that form when we read deeply and without distraction, remains largely disengaged.

Reading, explains Wolf, is not an instinctive skill for human beings. It's not etched into our genes the way speech is. We have to teach our minds how to translate the symbolic characters we see into the language we understand. And the media or other technologies we use in learning and practicing the craft of reading play an important part in shaping the neural circuits inside our brains. Experiments demonstrate that readers of ideograms, such as the Chinese, develop a mental circuitry for reading that is very different from the circuitry found in those of us whose written language employs an alphabet. The variations extend across many regions of the brain, including those that govern such essential cognitive functions as memory and the interpretation of visual and auditory stimuli. We can expect as well that the circuits woven by our use of the Net will be different from those woven by our reading of books and other printed works.

Sometime in 1882, Friedrich Nietzsche bought a typewriter—a Malling-Hansen Writing Ball, to be precise. His vision was failing, and keeping his eyes focused on a page had become exhausting and painful, often bringing on crushing headaches. He had been forced to curtail his writing, and he feared that he would soon have to give it up. The typewriter rescued him, at least for a time. Once he had mastered touch-typing, he was able to write with his eyes closed, using only the tips of his fingers. Words could once again flow from his mind to the page.

But the machine had a subtler effect on his work. One of Nietzsche's friends, a composer, noticed a change in the style of his writing. His already terse prose had become even tighter, more telegraphic. "Perhaps you will through this instrument even take to a new idiom," the friend wrote in a letter, noting that, in his own work, his "'thoughts' in music and language often depend on the quality of pen and paper."

"You are right," Nietzsche replied, "our writing equipment takes part in the forming of our thoughts." Under the sway of the machine, writes the German media scholar Friedrich A. Kittler, Nietzsche's prose "changed from arguments to aphorisms, from thoughts to puns, from rhetoric to telegram style."

The human brain is almost infinitely malleable. People used to think that our mental meshwork, the dense connections formed among the 100 billion or so neurons inside our skulls, was largely fixed by the time we reached adulthood. But brain researchers have discovered that

that's not the case. James Olds, a professor of neuroscience who directs the Krasnow Institute for Advanced Study at George Mason University, says that even the adult mind "is very plastic." Nerve cells routinely break old connections and form new ones. "The brain," according to Olds, "has the ability to reprogram itself on the fly, altering the way it functions."

As we use what the sociologist Daniel Bell has called our "intellectual technologies"—the tools that extend our mental rather than our physical capacities—we inevitably begin to take on the qualities of those technologies. The mechanical clock, which came into common use in the 14th century, provides a compelling example. In *Technics and Civilization,* the historian and cultural critic Lewis Mumford described how the clock "disassociated time from human events and helped create the belief in an independent world of mathematically measurable sequences." The "abstract framework of divided time" became "the point of reference for both action and thought."

The clock's methodical ticking helped bring into being the scientific mind and the scientific man. But it also took something away. As the late MIT computer scientist Joseph Weizenbaum observed in his 1976 book, *Computer Power and Human Reason: From Judgment to Calculation,* the conception of the world that emerged from the widespread use of timekeeping instruments "remains an impoverished version of the older one, for it rests on a rejection of those direct experiences that formed the basis for, and indeed constituted, the old reality." In deciding when to eat, to work, to sleep, to rise, we stopped listening to our senses and started obeying the clock.

The process of adapting to new intellectual technologies is reflected in the changing metaphors we use to explain ourselves to ourselves. When the mechanical clock arrived, people began thinking of their brains as operating "like clockwork." Today, in the age of software, we have come to think of them as operating "like computers." But the changes, neuroscience tells us, go much deeper than metaphor. Thanks to our brain's plasticity, the adaptation occurs also at a biological level.

The Internet promises to have particularly far-reaching effects on cognition. In a paper published in 1936, the British mathematician Alan Turing proved that a digital computer, which at the time existed only as a theoretical machine, could be programmed to perform the function of any other information-processing device. And that's what we're seeing today. The Internet, an immeasurably powerful computing system, is subsuming most of our other intellectual technologies. It's becoming our map and our clock, our printing press and our typewriter, our calculator and our telephone, and our radio and TV.

When the Net absorbs a medium, that medium is re-created in the Net's image. It injects the medium's content with hyperlinks, blinking ads, and other digital gewgaws, and it surrounds the content with the content of all the other media it has absorbed. A new e-mail message, for instance, may announce its arrival as we're glancing over the latest headlines at a newspaper's site. The result is to scatter our attention and diffuse our concentration.

The Net's influence doesn't end at the edges of a computer screen, either. As people's minds become attuned to the crazy quilt of Internet media, traditional media have to adapt to the audience's new expectations. Television programs add text crawls and pop-up ads, and magazines and newspapers shorten their articles, introduce capsule summaries, and crowd their pages with easy-to-browse info-snippets. When, in March of this year, *The New York Times* decided to devote the second and third pages of every edition to article abstracts, its design director, Tom Bodkin, explained that the "shortcuts" would give harried readers a quick "taste" of the day's news, sparing them the "less efficient" method of actually turning the pages and reading the articles. Old media have little choice but to play by the new-media rules.

Never has a communications system played so many roles in our lives—or exerted such broad influence over our thoughts—as the Internet does today. Yet, for all that's been written about the Net, there's been little consideration of how, exactly, it's reprogramming us. The Net's intellectual ethic remains obscure.

About the same time that Nietzsche started using his typewriter, an earnest young man named Frederick Winslow Taylor carried a stopwatch into the Midvale Steel plant in Philadelphia and began a historic series of experiments aimed at improving the efficiency of the plant's machinists. With the approval of Midvale's owners, he recruited a group of factory hands, set them to work on various metalworking machines, and recorded and timed their every movement as well as the operations of the machines. By breaking down every job into a sequence of small, discrete steps and then testing different ways of performing each one, Taylor created a set of precise instructions—an "algorithm," we might say today—for how each worker should work. Midvale's employees grumbled about the strict new regime, claiming that it turned them into little more than automatons, but the factory's productivity soared.

More than a hundred years after the invention of the steam engine, the Industrial Revolution had at last found its philosophy and its philosopher. Taylor's tight industrial choreography—his "system," as he liked to call it—was embraced by manufacturers throughout the country and, in time, around the world. Seeking maximum speed, maximum efficiency, and maximum output, factory owners used time-and-motion studies to organize their work and configure the jobs of their workers. The goal, as Taylor defined it in his celebrated 1911 treatise, *The Principles of Scientific Management,* was to identify and adopt, for every job, the "one best method" of work and thereby to effect "the gradual substitution of science for rule of thumb throughout the mechanic arts." Once his system was applied to all acts of manual labor, Taylor assured his followers, it would bring about a restructuring not only of industry but of society, creating a utopia of perfect efficiency. "In the past the man has been first," he declared; "in the future the system must be first."

Taylor's system is still very much with us; it remains the ethic of industrial manufacturing. And now, thanks to the growing power that computer engineers and software coders wield over our intellectual lives, Taylor's ethic is beginning to govern the realm of the mind as well. The Internet is a machine designed for the efficient and automated collection, transmission, and manipulation of information, and its legions of programmers are intent on finding the "one best method"—the perfect algorithm—to carry out every mental movement of what we've come to describe as "knowledge work."

Google's headquarters, in Mountain View, California—the Googleplex—is the Internet's high church, and the religion practiced inside its walls is Taylorism. Google, says its chief executive, Eric Schmidt, is "a company that's founded around the science of measurement," and it is striving to "systematize everything" it does. Drawing on the terabytes of behavioral data it collects through its search engine and other sites, it carries out thousands of experiments a day, according to the *Harvard Business Review,* and it uses the results to refine the algorithms that increasingly control how people find information and extract meaning from it. What Taylor did for the work of the hand, Google is doing for the work of the mind.

The company has declared that its mission is "to organize the world's information and make it universally accessible and useful." It seeks to develop "the perfect search engine," which it defines as something that "understands exactly what you mean and gives you back exactly what you want." In Google's view, information is a kind of commodity, a utilitarian resource that can be mined and processed with industrial efficiency. The more pieces of information we can "access" and the faster we can extract their gist, the more productive we become as thinkers.

Where does it end? Sergey Brin and Larry Page, the gifted young men who founded Google while pursuing doctoral degrees in computer science at Stanford, speak frequently of their desire to turn their search engine into an artificial intelligence, a HAL-like machine that might be connected directly to our brains. "The ultimate search engine is something as smart as people—or smarter," Page said in a speech a few years back. "For us, working on search is a way to work on artificial intelligence." In a 2004 interview with *Newsweek,* Brin said, "Certainly if you had all the world's information directly attached to your brain, or an artificial brain that was smarter than your brain, you'd be better off." Last year, Page told a convention of scientists that Google is "really trying to build artificial intelligence and to do it on a large scale."

Such an ambition is a natural one, even an admirable one, for a pair of math whizzes with vast quantities of cash at their disposal and a small army of computer scientists in their employ. A fundamentally scientific enterprise, Google is motivated by a desire to use technology, in Eric Schmidt's words, "to solve problems that have never been solved before," and artificial intelligence is the hardest problem out there. Why wouldn't Brin and Page want to be the ones to crack it?

Still, their easy assumption that we'd all "be better off" if our brains were supplemented, or even replaced, by an artificial intelligence is unsettling. It suggests a belief that intelligence is the output of a mechanical process, a series of discrete steps that can be isolated, measured, and optimized. In Google's world, the world we enter when we go online, there's little place for the fuzziness of contemplation. Ambiguity is not an opening for insight but a bug to be fixed. The human brain is just an outdated computer that needs a faster processor and a bigger hard drive.

The idea that our minds should operate as high-speed data-processing machines is not only built into the workings of the Internet, it is the network's reigning business model as well. The faster we surf across the Web—the more links we click and pages we view—the more opportunities Google and other companies gain to collect information about us and to feed us advertisements. Most of the proprietors of the commercial Internet have a financial stake in collecting the crumbs of data we leave behind as we flit from link to link—the more crumbs, the better. The last thing these companies want is to encourage leisurely reading or slow, concentrated thought. It's in their economic interest to drive us to distraction.

Maybe I'm just a worrywart. Just as there's a tendency to glorify technological progress, there's a countertendency to expect the worst of every new tool or machine. In Plato's

Phaedrus, Socrates bemoaned the development of writing. He feared that, as people came to rely on the written word as a substitute for the knowledge they used to carry inside their heads, they would, in the words of one of the dialogue's characters, "cease to exercise their memory and become forgetful." And because they would be able to "receive a quantity of information without proper instruction," they would "be thought very knowledgeable when they are for the most part quite ignorant." They would be "filled with the conceit of wisdom instead of real wisdom." Socrates wasn't wrong—the new technology did often have the effects he feared—but he was shortsighted. He couldn't foresee the many ways that writing and reading would serve to spread information, spur fresh ideas, and expand human knowledge (if not wisdom).

The arrival of Gutenberg's printing press, in the 15th century, set off another round of teeth gnashing. The Italian humanist Hieronimo Squarciafico worried that the easy availability of books would lead to intellectual laziness, making men "less studious" and weakening their minds. Others argued that cheaply printed books and broadsheets would undermine religious authority, demean the work of scholars and scribes, and spread sedition and debauchery. As New York University professor Clay Shirky notes, "Most of the arguments made against the printing press were correct, even prescient." But, again, the doomsayers were unable to imagine the myriad blessings that the printed word would deliver.

So, yes, you should be skeptical of my skepticism. Perhaps those who dismiss critics of the Internet as Luddites or nostalgists will be proved correct, and from our hyperactive, data-stoked minds will spring a golden age of intellectual discovery and universal wisdom. Then again, the Net isn't the alphabet, and although it may replace the printing press, it produces something altogether different. The kind of deep reading that a sequence of printed pages promotes is valuable not just for the knowledge we acquire from the author's words but for the intellectual vibrations those words set off within our own minds. In the quiet spaces opened up by the sustained, undistracted reading of a book, or by any other act of contemplation, for that matter, we make our own associations, draw our own inferences and analogies, foster our own ideas. Deep reading, as Maryanne Wolf argues, is indistinguishable from deep thinking.

If we lose those quiet spaces, or fill them up with "content," we will sacrifice something important not only in our selves but in our culture. In a recent essay, the playwright Richard Foreman eloquently described what's at stake:

> I come from a tradition of Western culture, in which the ideal (my ideal) was the complex, dense and "cathedral-like" structure of the highly educated and articulate personality— a man or woman who carried inside themselves a personally constructed and unique version of the entire heritage of the West. [But now] I see within us all (myself included) the replacement of complex inner density with a new kind of self—evolving under the pressure of information overload and the technology of the "instantly available."

As we are drained of our "inner repertory of dense cultural inheritance," Foreman concluded, we risk turning into "'pancake people'—spread wide and thin as we connect with that vast network of information accessed by the mere touch of a button."

I'm haunted by that scene in *2001*. What makes it so poignant, and so weird, is the computer's emotional response to the disassembly of its mind: its despair as one circuit after another goes dark, its childlike pleading with the astronaut—"I can feel it. I can feel it. I'm afraid"—and its final reversion to what can only be called a state of innocence. HAL's outpouring of feeling contrasts with the emotionlessness that characterizes the human figures in the film, who go about their business with an almost robotic efficiency. Their thoughts and actions feel scripted, as if they're following the steps of an algorithm. In the world of *2001,* people have become so machinelike that the most human character turns out to be a machine. That's the essence of Kubrick's dark prophecy: as we come to rely on computers to mediate our understanding of the world, it is our own intelligence that flattens into artificial intelligence.

WRITING STRATEGIES

1. What is the essay's thesis?

2. Explain how Carr uses a combination of support strategies to help readers understand and accept the thesis.

3. Describe the essay's opening strategy.

4. Carr draws attention to an assumption of Sergey Brin and Larry Page—that we'd all "be better off" if our brains were supplemented, or even replaced, by an artificial intelligence. Why does Carr think this assumption is unsettling? How is questioning the assumption important to Carr's point?

5. Identify a concession Carr makes and explain how it is important to his argument.

EXPLORING IDEAS

1. Explain how you have taken on certain qualities of an intellectual technology (a tool that extends one's mental capacities).

2. What is Taylor's ethic, and how is it beginning to govern the mind?

3. Why do you think companies get an economic advantage from consumers' distraction? In other words, why is distraction profitable?

4. What does Carr think we will sacrifice if we lose the "quiet spaces opened up by the sustained, undistracted reading of a book, or by any other act of contemplation"? Do you agree or disagree? What evidence can you provide to support your position?

IDEAS FOR WRITING

1. What besides technology has caused people's minds to function differently?

2. What particular aspect of the media has changed the way people's minds work?

If responding to one of these ideas, go to the Analysis section of this chapter to begin developing ideas for your essay.

Why We Binge-Watch Television
Kevin Fallon

In "Why We Binge-Watch Television," Kevin Fallon, a senior entertainment reporter at *The Daily Beast*, suggests the cause of why so many of us, apparently 61 percent, regularly binge-watch TV. As you read, consider Fallon's reasoning—how he supports his understanding of the main cause.

We correspond with each other in 140-character bursts. We consume news in sound bites and blog posts. We're, by all accounts, an increasingly distracted society, with the attention span of a house fly sipping on Red Bull in a room lit by a strobe light while dubstep plays. Knowing that, it makes absolutely no sense that we are also a society that enjoys binge-watching TV.

But we do. Oh, for the love of Walter White, we do.

According to a new study by Harris Interactive on behalf of Netflix, 61 percent of us binge-watch TV regularly, which is to say that we watch at least 2-3 episodes of a single series in one sitting. Or, some of us (many of us), devour 14 in a row with breaks just for bathroom and answering the door for the delivery man. Almost three-quarters of us view binge watching as a positive experience, and nearly 80 percent say that feasting on a show actually makes it better.

Given how many times we've heard people use the word "binge-watch" this past year and how many times we've alarmed our friends by disappearing from society for a week to marathon a show, it shouldn't be surprising that the practice is quickly becoming the new normal when it comes to consuming television. But it is remarkable that such a highly fragmented world is actively seeking out—and even preferring—longer form, more complex storytelling at the same time we want everything else in life easy and breezy.

It shouldn't compute. So why does it?

All of the elements of a perfect storm brewed at the same time, explains Grant McCracken, a cultural anthropologist who worked on the study. More accurately, it's a storm cycle: TV has gotten better, making viewers smarter, making TV even more complex, making binge-watching more fun. And because we're living in a world where too many things are constantly competing for our attention, developing a habit of binge-watching is like seeking shelter in the calm eye of that storm.

"I was illuminated to hear people say, 'Look, it's precisely because there's so much distraction that this is a special pleasure,'" McCracken says of the 1,500 streamers he interviewed as part of the study. While TV marathons have always been events, the rise of binge-watching is a byproduct of necessary and sufficient conditions that have only surfaced in recent years, with the easy availability of streaming, season DVDs, and TiVos compounded with the rise in quality of the shows available.

Plus, there's the undeniably fun appropriation of the word "binge."

"You hear that people are slightly embarrassed to spend four or five hours watching TV, that there's something reckless or indulgent or ill-advised about it," McCracken says. "That was the origin of the research project: to find out if 'binge' is the right metaphor, and if not then what is."

As it turns out, the entire connotation of "binge"—a word tinged with the shame of eating an entire roll of cookie dough—has changed into something prideful and brag-worthy. "Finally some people get that there's something ironic about the term," McCracken says. "People aren't watching *Dukes of Hazard*. They're watching great TV, not bad TV."

Indeed, the successive-episode viewing couldn't be as popular as it is—especially, again, in the age where people discuss everything and anything on social media and attempting to avoid a major plot spoiler online is a fool's errand—if the series being binged weren't as creatively evolved and dramatically complex as *Breaking Bad*, *The Wire*, *Game of Thrones*, *Orange Is the New Black*, and other popular binging series are.

"Remember on *Dallas* when somebody shot J.R.?" says McCracken. "If you found out who did it after the fact, what would be the point of going back and watching that season? But with something like *The Wire*, even if a friend accidentally let a key character's death slip it doesn't' really destroy the point of watching the show." There's so much more to pick apart, dissect, and become emotionally and intellectually engaged with that watching it, despite the unintended spoiler, is still enjoyable.

The late-in-its-run success of *Breaking Bad* is the perfect example of that. The show's final season premiered to double the series' previous ratings high and almost four times the ratings for the show's debut in 2008. The five years in between saw hordes of people finally caving to the "you *have* to watch *Breaking Bad*!" pressure of their colleagues, thanks to the availability of the entire series for streaming on Netflix.

"I think Netflix kept us on the air," Vince Gillian, *Breaking Bad*'s creator, said after his show won the Emmy for Best Drama Series in September. "Not only are we standing up here [with the Emmy], I don't think our show would have lasted beyond Season Two. It's a new era in television and we've been very fortunate to reap the benefits."

Netflix is notorious for keeping its data locked away in that same bunker where the UFOs and the still-alive Elvis Presley are kept, but the company does confirm that binging is more popular than ever with its subscribers. "Our viewing data shows that the majority of streamers would actually prefer to have a whole season of a show available to watch at their own pace," said Ted Sarandos, Chief Content Officer of Netflix.

The habits even shape its original programming choices, including *House of Cards* and *Orange Is the New Black*. "Netflix has pioneered audience choice in programming and has helped free consumers from the limitations of linear television. Our own original series are created for multi-episodic viewing, lining up the content with new norms of viewer control for the first time."

The result, not just because of strides in original programming from Netflix but because of the "binging" now becoming a legitimate alternative to most first-run broadcast airings, is that we are rejecting in at least one crucial aspect of our lives—entertainment—the idea of instant gratification. It's what McCracken calls the "in case of emergency, break glass" phenomenon. And we all can identify with it.

There's a new series that you're excited about. You can't wait to try it out. "Then there's a small tension," McCracken says. "Do you watch it right away or do you set it aside for some eventuality like a terrible flu or a terrible snow storm?" Anyone who just snuggled under a blanket with Olivia Pope during Snowstorm Hercules to watch an entire season of *Scandal* and gasped because OMG HE'S HER FATHER!? knows exactly what he means. "You have a great show on hand. You're protected in event of emergency. And then there's something delicious about having a great show on standby, in reserve."

Binging, as we used to do it, was a hindsight act of embarrassment, an action realized only after its completion when staring at an empty Doritos bag. Now we're planning to do it. In a world moving faster than ever and our focus more split than ever, who would have thought that it would be the medium of television, once called "a vast wasteland" by former FCC Chairman Newton Minow, that would finally slow us down.

WRITING STRATEGIES

1. What is Fallon's thesis, or main claim?

2. What support strategies unpack, or develop, the thesis?

3. Describe Fallon's voice. Provide specific passages or phrases from the article to support your description.

4. Point to any counterarguments, concessions, or qualifiers in Fallon's article. Explain the rhetorical function of each—how each serves the overall argument.

EXPLORING IDEAS

1. Come up with a better term than "binge-watch." Explain what your term highlights or suggests that "binge-watch" misses.

2. Explain why, according to this essay, the final season of *Breaking Bad* premiered to double the series' previous ratings.

3. What program would you like to binge-watch and why? Describe the binge-watching experience? Will it involve food? friends? What time of year? Describe the experience you anticipate.

4. Beyond television, where else do you witness binge-like behavior? What do you think is the cause?

IDEAS FOR WRITING

1. What is the cause of binge-watching TV? If you have ever done it, begin with your own experience, and then explore further with outside research.

2. Develop another explanation—or cause—for why we might prefer longer, more complex storytelling at the same time we want everything else to be easy and breezy.

If responding to one of these ideas, go to the Analysis section of this chapter to begin developing ideas for your essay.

Why Millennials Are Weak
Quinn Greenwell

Essays and ideas can emerge from formal writing assignments or from passing comments. "Why Millennials Are Weak" was prompted when Quinn Greenwell's brother mentioned an online reader comment, which Greenwell considered further through discussion and research. As you read, notice that Greenwell moves directly from the phenomenon itself (the apparent weakness of Millennials) to the cause of that phenomenon.

My brother turned me on to this Reaction (what is sometimes called a Reader Comment), which followed a Yahoo SNL (*Saturday Night Live*) recap November 13, 2016—the Saturday after Donald Trump was elected president:

The essay emerges from (is a response to) a Reader comment.

> Millennials are the weakest group of people ever. Once all the boomers die the Chinese will walk across America with ease.

So, we talked about this and wondered, "Are Millennials the weakest group of people ever? And, if they are, will their contemporaries in China be weak too?" Of course this led me to a Google search, and I found a study saying that Millennials are literally weaker than their parents—at least in the sense that, according to the study, they have weaker handshakes. NPR reported, "In a study of Americans ages 20–34, occupational therapists found that men younger than 30 have significantly weaker hand grips than their counterparts in 1985 did. The same was true of women ages 20–24, according to the study published online by the *Journal of Hand Therapy....*" (Jacewicz). In the study, 237 participants squeezed a hand dynamometer, which measures grip force: "Men's hand strength decreased by 20 pounds and women's hand strength decreased by 10 pounds" (Best).

These paragraphs discuss physical strength, which the writer learned about while researching for something else.

This isn't what I was thinking I'd find. But it was interesting. The title of one of the articles got right to the point: "Why Millennials Have WEAK Handshakes: Lack of 'Hard Work' Means Young People Today Have Less Grip Strength." That made sense. While some Millennials have strong grips, others don't because they don't work the same types of jobs as people worked in 1985. While jobs have changed, so has everyday life: raking a yard full leaves would probably strengthen one's grip more than using a leaf blower; washing dishes by hand might strengthen one's grip more than putting them in and taking them out of the dishwasher; dialing a rotary phone might strengthen one's grip more than saying, "Hey, Siri. Call Mom." As with a lot of studies, the participants might not have been representative. Perhaps the hard workers didn't participate because they were out working hard. Still, the nature of work has changed, which is the point.

Enough about grip strength though. A *Wall Street Journal* article got at another point. Social psychologist Jonathan Haidt suggests that Millennials may be weak because of antifragility, a concept developed by Nassim Nicholas Taleb in his book *Antifragile: Things That Gain from Disorder*. Taleb proposes that "people/systems/organizations/things/ideas can be described in one of three ways: fragile, resilient, or antifragile" (McKay and McKay).

Introduces a concept: antifragility.

Things that are fragile "break or suffer from chaos and randomness," from "adversity or volatility." Things that are resilient "remain steady in times of both adversity and tranquility." In "Beyond 'Sissy' Resilience: On Becoming Antifragile," Brett and Kate McKay explain, "Buddhism and Stoicism promote psychological resilience, as both philosophies teach indifference to change. When you're mentally resilient, you don't care if you're rich or if you lose your wealth in a single day." According to Taleb, resilience is settling for the status quo. The McKays say, "To be truly effective in a world swirling with complexity, randomness, and risk, you can't stop at sissy resilience. Whenever you can, you should always find opportunities to actually *grow* from disorder, volatility, and adversity. The goal should be to move beyond resilience to becoming antifragile." They say, "Things that are antifragile grow and strengthen from volatility and stress. ..."

Information from sources (Taleb and the McKays) explain the concept.

Haidt says children need unsupervised time "to get in over their heads and get themselves out," that they're not getting enough of that, and "that it greatly decreased in the 1980's," which by the way coincides with the hand grip thing. According to Haidt, "millennials come to college with much thinner skins." (He's being figurative, I'm sure, but I wonder if their skin, like their handshakes, might be studied and found to be literally thinner than their parents' skin.) What caused this, according to Haidt, is child-rearing: "With the rise in crime, amplified by the rise of cable TV, we saw much more protective, fearful parenting. Children since the 1980s have been raised very differently—protected as fragile."

The writer puts forth a claim of cause: What caused this is child-rearing.

We're all familiar with helicopter parents. Melanie Thernstrom, in "The Anti-Helicopter Parent's Plea: Let Kids Play!" says:

Research suggests that students with controlling "helicopter" parents are less flexible and more vulnerable, anxious and self-conscious, as well as more likely to be medicated for anxiety or depression. Similarly, children whose time is highly structured—crammed with lessons and adult-supervised activities—may have more difficulty developing their own "executive function" capabilities, the ability to devise their own plans and carry them out. Conversely, the more time children spend in free play, the better they develop these capabilities.

And Mike Lanza, a father who says that "kids have to find their own balance of power," believes the following:

> Basic developmental psychology posits that if children develop a fundamental sense that they (not their parents) are masters of their own destiny, they will be successful adults, and that without that belief they will flounder: It's easy to want to rid yourself of a life that doesn't feel truly your own. (Thernstrom)

The final sentence above refers to "the rash of suicides among Palo Alto high school students in recent years," which Lanza believes are "extreme examples of the larger problem." Lanza thinks "organized sports fail to teach the critical life skills that he and his friends learned in pickup games they had to referee themselves [when they were] forced to resolve their own disputes, because if they didn't, the game would end." Lanza embraces the idea of antifragility, and sees helicopter parenting as the cause, or as *a* cause, of fragility and, therefore, weakness.

Central to Mike's philosophy is the importance of physical danger: of encouraging boys to take risks and play rough and tumble and get—or inflict—a scrape or two. Central to what he calls mom philosophy (which could just be described as contemporary parenting philosophy) is just the opposite: to play safe, play nice and not hurt other kids or yourself. (Thernstrom)

If Millennials are weak—or *the weakest group of people ever*—one cause might be their parents' parenting style, and that had to be caused by something—the Millennials grandparents? the role of technology? Of course Millennials have virtues too. And handgrip aside, we might think more about what it means to be "weak."

Works Cited

Best, Chivali. "Why Millennials Have WEAK Handshakes: Lack of 'Hard Work' Means Young People Today Have Less Grip Strength." *Daily Mail*, 22 June 2016, www.dailymail.co.uk/sciencetech/article-3654089/Why-millennials-WEAK-handshakes-Lack-hard-work-means-young-people-today-grip-strength.html#ixzz4Pw4mocrA.

Chan, Robert. "'SNL' Recap: Dave Chappelle Hosts a Dignified Evening of Comedy." *Yahoo TV*, Yahoo / ABC News Network, 13 Nov. 2016, www.yahoo.com/tv/snl-recap-dave-chappelle-hosts-a-dignified-evening-of-comedy-124858880.html.

Haidt, Jonathan. "Our Weak, Fragile Millennials." *The Wall Street Journal*, 22 Feb. 2016, www.wsj.com/articles/our-weak-fragile-millennials-1456185268.

Jacewicz, Natalie. "Millennials May Be Losing Their Grip." *NPR*, 13 June 2016, www.npr.org/sections/health-shots/2016/06/13/481590997/millennials-may-be-losing-their-grip.

McKay, Brett, and Kate McKay. "Beyond 'Sissy' Resilience: On Becoming Antifragile." *The Art of Manliness,* 3 Dec. 2013, www.artofmanliness.com/2013/12/03/beyond-sissy-resilience-on-becoming-antifragile.

Thernstrom, Melanie. "The Anti-Helicopter Parent's Plea: Let Kids Play!" *The New York Times*, 19 Oct. 2016, nyti.ms/2jBf8pd.

WRITING STRATEGIES

1. What is the essay's main claim, or thesis?

2. Explain the connection between the introduction and Greenwell's thesis.

3. How relevant is handgrip to Greenwell's larger point? Why might Greenwell have mentioned it to support a larger point in the essay?

4. Choose one source that Greenwell uses as support and explain what particular point it reinforces.

EXPLORING IDEAS

1. Explain "antifragility." (How is it different than fragile or resilient?)

2. According to the McKays, why can't you stop at resilience?

3. Do you think today's parents are more protective and fearful than earlier parents? If so, why? What caused this? Should they be more protective and fearful? What are the consequences of this protection and fear?

4. Are Millennials weak? And, if so, what does it mean to be "weak"?

IDEAS FOR WRITING

1. What caused helicopter parents?

2. Why are Millennials weak? Or why are they strong? (Or why are they something else?)

If responding to one of these ideas, go to the Analysis section of this chapter to begin developing ideas for your essay.

INVENTION

"All human beings should try to learn before they die what they are running from, and to, and why."

—**James Thurber**

Invention, an act of discovery, involves asking questions where we had assumed we knew the answers. For this chapter, it means asking why something occurs (or has occurred) and going beyond the first (and second) guess.

The following sections are designed to help you through the invention process: in Point of Contact to find a topic; in Analysis to imagine unseen causes; in Public Resonance to consider the ways your topic extends outward and affects the public; in Thesis to focus your ideas to a particular insight; and in Rhetorical Tools to explore a range of possible support strategies. The Invention Questions in each section are not meant to be answered directly in your final written assignment; they are meant to help you explore and develop revelatory ideas.

Point of Contact

The search for a cause begins with a question: Why did something happen? Why does something continue? What causes some phenomenon? The following questions can help you to explore possible topics. After you have decided on a particular topic, go to the Analysis section to continue your search for causes.

Work

- Why are some sections/groups/teams more successful than others?
- Why is workplace efficiency up or down?
- Why are profits for the company or organization up or down?
- Why are some workers more content or fulfilled than others?

Local Events

- Why is urban sprawl taking place in your community?
- Why is a local sports team winning or losing?
- What makes one school perform better than others?
- Why are some areas of town more policed than others?
- Why do so many yards look the same?

Social Trends

- What causes road rage? Teenage rebellion? Conformity to fashion trends?
- Why are the elderly isolated?
- Why is depression on the rise in the United States?
- Why do Americans love sport utility vehicles?
- Why does the condition of streets change throughout a city?
- Why doesn't anyone care about the future?

Campus Issues

- Why do college students binge drink?
- Why do some students cheat? Procrastinate?
- What causes boredom?
- Why are some classes more difficult for large numbers of students?

Politics

- Why do younger generations tend not to vote?
- Why does a certain community consistently vote Democratic or Republican?
- What has made political discourse so uncivil?

Your Major

- What has caused the field to thrive (or deteriorate) in recent years?
- What has fueled a recent debate in the field? Why has the debate continued?
- Find the cause of a phenomenon in your field, for example:
  —*History:* a revolution, a military victory or loss
  —*Art:* a style (such as impressionism), an artistic revolution
  —*Biology:* an organism's short life span
  —*Criminal Justice:* a jury decision, a Supreme Court decision to hear a case
  —*Business Marketing:* the success or failure of a marketing campaign

Analysis

Now that you have a topic (any phenomenon from the Point of Contact section), the next step is to begin searching for possible causes. (We use the term *phenomenon* here to refer to anything you are exploring—any behavior, event, situation, attitude, issue, idea, and so on.) You

John Metz

may already have some guesses about the cause. But keep an open mind. Any phenomenon can be a consequence of many factors, both physical and abstract. Respond to the following Invention Questions, and refer back to your notes as you continue the process.

> What events or behaviors led to the phenomenon?
> What social conditions or prevailing attitudes led (or could lead) to the phenomenon?
> What economic conditions led to the phenomenon?
> What state of mind or psychological need may have led to the phenomenon?
> What are all the possible reasons someone would carry out this behavior?

Invention Workshop

Use one of the Invention Questions to initiate a discussion about your topic. Stay focused on the responses and keep asking questions so that your initial thoughts evolve. For example, in the following workshop, the participants take on Jack's topic: why people join cults. The conversation progresses because Jack keeps asking questions and others offer focused responses along the way. In the brief exchange, Jack moves from an obvious position to something more complex.

What State of Mind or Psychological Need May have Led to the Phenomenon?

JACK: These people are obviously sick—mentally ill.

DIANA: What kind of mental illness?

JACK: I don't know . . . probably some kind of schizophrenia or something.

DIANA: But a lot of the people who join cults are otherwise productive members of society—with jobs, families, homes, social responsibilities. I've even heard that some cults attract people who are smarter than average. It doesn't seem like these people are downright mentally ill—at least in the way most people talk about mental illness.

JACK: So if they aren't sick in some way, why would they possibly leave behind their families and friends, give all their money to a group of strangers, and lose their identities?

MARCUS: Well, I've heard that a lot of those people don't have friends—they're lonely.

JACK: How can people be lonely if they have families and jobs?

MARCUS: Working a job and supporting a family doesn't necessarily make someone truly connected to others. Think about midlife crises—where people run out and have wild flings or buy ridiculously expensive sports cars. They're obviously unfulfilled.

JACK: But wouldn't you say that joining a cult is a little more extreme than buying a car or having an affair?

DIANA: Sure, but remember that a lot of people long for something more than sex and fast cars. They wonder what's out there, what their purpose is, what's beyond this life.

JACK: And religious cults have all those answers—well, at least that's the argument.

DIANA: Yeah, so the whole issue may be related to loneliness and longing rather than sickness.

Thinking Further

Invention is not simply answering a few questions. Instead, it is a process of exploring, discovering, and developing ideas. Ideas that emerge from initial responses should be explored even further. For example, in his dialogue with Diana and Marcus, Jack's thinking evolves:

Beginning of the dialogue:	Sick people join cults.
End of the dialogue:	Loneliness and longing, which run rampant in mainstream culture, drive people to wonder what they're missing. This is where cults come in.

With this new understanding, Jack might come to more insightful conclusions about the perspective of people who join cults:

> I guess in the eyes of a potential cult member, a cult doesn't look like a cult. I mean, a group doesn't hang a "Cult" sign on the door. They don't say, "Hey!! Join our cult!! We'll all kill ourselves next year! It'll be great!!" No. A cult is merely a group of people who offer a web of relationships and a clear purpose in life. Isn't that why people go to college even though they hate it?! Isn't that why people join the Army?? A clear sense of purpose?!! Is college a kind of cult? Is the Army?!! Here's the message of both institutions: "Leave behind everything—your family, etc. Come here. Stay with us. And . . . you have to follow our strict schedule of events. But in the end, you'll be way better off." Holy crap! We're a culture of . . . cults.

Jack's continued exploration of why people join cults has taken him into new intellectual territory. He is exploring the relationship between something he thinks is dangerous (cults) and something he thinks is normal (college, the army).

Use the following questions to further explore your topic:

> ❯ How has your understanding of the cause developed? What new idea has entered your thinking?

> ❯ Why didn't you think about this before?

RESEARCH

Find an outside source (a website, article, or book) about your concept. (Consult Chapter 14: Finding Sources to help you explore.) The author(s) of the source may have a different understanding of the causes. Summarize the main points of the source, then answer the following questions:

- Does the source suggest a cause for the phenomenon?

- If not, does the source imply or assume a cause?

- Does the source account for the most direct cause?

- Does the source account for indirect or multiple causes? Hidden causes?

Public Resonance

Some topics automatically resonate with public concerns, while others seem more difficult to connect with. Local or intensely personal topics, for instance, may seem less linked to broader concerns. Imagine how your topic involves others who are not directly associated with it. Use the following questions to help generate a sense of public resonance for your topic:

> What are the effects of this phenomenon?

> Whom does it affect? How does it affect them?

> How does it affect people indirectly?

> How does my position or understanding relate to popular perspectives on the topic?

Jack's topic of cult membership might seem to affect only specific people—cult members, their families, maybe the communities surrounding a cult. But Jack goes further than that and imagines the broader and subtler factors:

How does it affect people indirectly?
If people are drawn to cults through deep loneliness, then cults potentially relate to everyone—that is, anyone who cares about family, friends, the quiet neighbor, etc. Our days are filled with constant inattention to others. Most people choose their narrow paths (their jobs and their small circle of friends) and leave everyone else. Many of us will go weeks without truly acknowledging anyone outside of our little circles. Rarely do we invite the quiet guy from work out with us; rarely do we call our cousin to see how she's doing. We leave lonely people behind us every day.

Jack discovers that cults might relate to everyone. He can now explore this idea even further, examining the messages that popular culture sends to people: that we must have intense social engagement to achieve happiness and fulfillment, that solitude should be avoided, that excitement and purpose should define every minute of our lives. Jack would then be exploring the culture surrounding cults. He would be thinking like a sociologist and assuming that any one behavior is linked to a broad system of attitudes, messages, and group behaviors.

While searching for public resonance, writers might find not only public resonance but new angles on the topic. For example, if Jack's exploration of public resonance raises ideas about pop culture and social engagement, these discoveries could lead Jack to think about social networking and then about Facebook and its relationship (or similarity) to cults.

ACTIVITY

1. Present your ideas to a small group of peers, explaining the phenomenon's cause and its public resonance. Ask group members how the phenomenon affects their lives.

2. Explain how the group discussion helped you discover and develop ideas regarding public resonance and the topic in general. What new ideas emerged, and how might they help shape your essay?

Thesis

The kind of writing done in this chapter is both analytical and argumentative. Each author offers an analysis of the topic and an argument for his or her understanding of the cause. Each has a thesis that focuses on the causes or set of causes most responsible for the phenomenon. As you consider your main point, examine all possible avenues. (You may even begin writing and drafting before your ideas take shape.) Your thesis might do any of the following:

- Argue for a particular cause.

  Professional sports have gotten more violent because of the intensity of sports coverage in the media.

- Argue that several factors equally cause the phenomenon.

  Writing proficiency among American high school students continues to diminish because of a broader cultural disinterest in reading and a fundamental misunderstanding of language.

- Argue against an apparent cause or widely held belief and for a less obvious or more complicated cause.

  People drive gas-guzzlers not because they are selfish and insensitive but because they are uneducated about their real choices.

  The music industry is losing profits not because college kids are insatiable thieves but because the industry has not evolved with the listening habits of the new generation.

As you consider your topic, decide on your emphasis: Will it be important to thoroughly describe several causes or to focus on one?

Evolution of a Thesis

Your main idea may not come into focus immediately. Notice how Jack's thesis evolves from his initial thoughts into a sophisticated point.

Jack focuses on a particular phenomenon:

- What makes people leave everything and everyone behind and join cults?

He uses the Invention Questions on page 353 to probe for causes:

- *What state of mind or psychological need may have led to the phenomenon?* Some form of mental disease makes people join cults.

He works through his initial thoughts and discovers a less obvious cause:

- Deep loneliness and lack of purpose in life cause people to leave their families and join cults.

Jack struggles to integrate public resonance into his understanding of the cause:

- The deep loneliness and loss fostered by our hurried society create desperate searches for belonging and purpose, and cults sometimes fulfill those needs.

ACTIVITY
Reflect on how your main idea, like Jack's, came into focus:
- What phenomenon did you focus on?
- What Invention Question(s) did you use to probe for causes?
- What less obvious cause did you discover?
- How did you integrate public resonance into your understanding of the cause?

Common Thesis Problems
Perhaps the two most common thesis problems are psychological, striking before the writer ever touches a key or marks a paper:

1. **Fear of Ongoing Invention:** Some writers assume that thesis statements are fixed, unchangeable structures that must be strictly adhered to throughout a writing project. As they draft ideas and generate support for their initial point, they avoid asking hard questions and making new connections; that is, they fear continued invention once they've started drafting. But thesis statements are not traps. They are statements that help writers focus and intensify their thinking *as they are writing*. The human brain functions in new ways once serious writing and shaping begin; therefore, writers should allow their own writing to help them with new ideas.

2. **Fear of Commitment:** In contrast to the first fear, some writers avoid committing to a focused statement. They wander around without attempting to establish a particular idea, without digging in to a specific intellectual place. Such wandering, if it goes on too long, can lead to shallow ideas—saying lots of different things about lots of different things.

Although invention is key throughout the process, invention is not general wandering. Better ideas come when writers dig in their intellectual heels.

For more related common thesis problems, see Chapter 8: Making Arguments, page 254.

Revising Your Thesis

Write out responses to these questions: *Am I afraid of ongoing invention? Why? Am I afraid of commitment? Why?* Then discuss your responses with a group of classmates:

1. How many people in your group have a fear of, or resistance to, ongoing invention or commitment?
   - What reasons do group members give for their fear of, or resistance to, ongoing invention? (What caused their fear or resistance?)
   - What reasons do group members give for their fear of, or resistance to, commitment? (What caused it?)

2. Discuss how each group member arrived at his or her thesis for this chapter's essay. Which group members might have committed to a rigid thesis too early? Choose an Invention Question from earlier in the chapter that they should explore further for ongoing invention.

3. Help group members who have trouble committing to one idea focus their statement. Choose an Invention Question they should explore to help narrow and deepen their thoughts.

Rhetorical Tools

Remember that you are not simply explaining a cause. You are arguing that a particular cause (or set of causes) could be responsible for a phenomenon, and you also are arguing that your understanding of the cause/effect relationship is worth considering. Therefore, consider the support strategies of argument (from Chapter 8: Making Arguments), and use the following questions to develop support for your thesis:

> How can I illustrate the relationship between the cause and the effect? (What line of reasoning can I use?)
> Does a historical event or figure help to show the cause?
> Can I allude to a similar phenomenon (with a similar cause) to support my point?
> Does a literary work (novel, poem, drama) or popular culture text (movie, television program, song) support my point?
> How do other writers discuss this cause?
> Does something in nature (in animal or plant life) support my point?

> Has anyone done scientific study on this phenomenon? Does it support my point?

> Have I witnessed or experienced someone or something that illustrates my point?

> Can I construct a hypothetical situation that illustrates my point?

Integrating Authorities (Outside Sources)

Outside sources must be integral to your own points and carefully integrated into your argument, not just inserted. For example, notice how Carr integrates an outside source to support his personal testimony about having trouble reading:

> I'm not the only one. When I mention my troubles with reading to friends and acquaintances—literary types, most of them—many say they're having similar experiences. The more they use the Web, the more they have to fight to stay focused on long pieces of writing. Some of the bloggers I follow have also begun mentioning the phenomenon. Scott Karp, who writes a blog about online media, recently confessed that he has stopped reading books altogether. "I was a lit major in college, and used to be [a] voracious book reader," he wrote. "What happened?" He speculates on the answer: What if I do all my reading on the web not so much because the way I read has changed, i.e., I'm just seeking convenience, but because the way I THINK has changed?"

Carr introduces his main point in his own words, and then he introduces an outside source, Scott Karp, as support. Notice that Carr provides Karp's credentials: "Scott Karp, who writes a blog about online media, . . ." When using authorities as support, it is important to provide readers with information about the source:

> Bruce Friedman, **who blogs regularly about the use of computers in medicine**, also has described how the Internet has altered his mental habits.

> But a recently published study of online research habits, **conducted by scholars from University College London**, suggests that we may well be in the midst of a sea change in the way we read and think.

> But it's a different kind of reading, and behind it lies a different kind of thinking—perhaps even a new sense of the self. "We are not only *what* we read," says Maryanne Wolf, **a developmental psychologist at Tufts University and the author of** *Proust and the Squid: The Story and Science of the Reading Brain.* "We are *how* we read."

For more help with this support strategy, see Chapter 16: Integrating and Documenting Sources.

Counterarguing and Conceding

Counterarguments defend against—or counter-argue—opposing claims. Writers must anticipate and account for positions outside of or opposed to their own claims(s) and include reasoning to offset that potential opposition. In many cases, writers must contend directly with arguments that forward another cause. The following questions can help you develop counterarguments:

> What other causes could be attributed to this phenomenon? (Why are these other causes less acceptable or less valid?)

> What other reasons do people have for disagreeing with me?

> What support will most effectively respond to opposing positions?

Concessions acknowledge the value of positions or claims other than those being forwarded by the writer. Remember that good writers (with a broad understanding of the topic) are able to concede the value of some points or qualify their own points well. As you consider your own argument, your own position about a cause, use the following questions to develop concessions and qualifiers:

> Are there legitimate reasons for taking another position on this topic?

> Does the argument make any large, but necessary, leaps?

> Do I ask my audience to accept generalizations?

Invention Workshop

For this workshop, generate opposing positions for each project. The goal here is to play devil's advocate—to imagine causes that the writer has not yet imagined. Each writer should announce his or her thesis. Group members should then take turns offering responses. Use the following questions:

> What other causes (different from the one forwarded by the writer) could be attributed to this phenomenon?

> Are there legitimate reasons for taking another position (different from the writer) on this topic?

Revision

Now get help from other writers. Before exchanging drafts with at least one other writer, underline your main idea (your thesis) or write it at the top of your draft.

Peer Review

Use the following questions to respond to specific issues in the draft:

1. Can any phrases or terms in the thesis be narrowed? If so, circle them and make some suggestions for more focus. Does the thesis avoid the common problems? (See page 254.)

2. Can you follow the writer's line of reasoning? Do you accept the cause the writer asserts? Why or why not?

3. What other support strategies could the writer employ? (Consider examples, allusions, scenarios, and so on. See pages 254–257.)

4. Mark any paragraphs that shift focus from one point about the subject to another.

5. If the writer uses outside sources, are they integrated smoothly into the argument? (See pages 467–477 in Chapter 16: Integrating and Documenting Sources for specific strategies.)

6. Consider the writer's voice.

    a. Identify any passages that seem preachy.

    b. Does the writer seem credible? What passages support your decision?

    c. Identify a passage that seems flat, without intensity. Suggest a strategy for the writer to create a sense of wonder.

7. What sentences and phrases could gain vitality and intensity? Consider the strategies explained in Chapter 19: Vitalizing Sentences. For example:

- Look for unnecessary interrupting clauses and phrases. Underline them and/or draw an arrow to show where the phrase or clause can be moved.

- Cross out wordy phrases and write in more concise options.

- What sentences are over-embedded? (Point to any clauses that overlap with other clauses, causing a disconnect between ideas.)

- Examine attributive phrases. Point out unnecessary phrases or sentences that could be boiled down.

- Where can the writer change linking verbs to action verbs?

- Where can the writer avoid drawing attention to *I* and *you*?

- Help the writer change unnecessary clauses to phrases and phrases to words.

- Point to expletives (such as *there are* and *it is*).

- Help the writer change passive verbs to active verbs for more vitality.

Reflection

Writing about a cause can have consequences for readers, the writer, and a community as a whole. To consider the possible consequences of your essay, reflect on its rhetoric:

1. The chapter introduction states that "people searching for causes are detectives attempting to find answers amid a dizzying array of possibilities." As a detective, what answer did you find?

2. What rhetorical tools most help readers understand and accept the answer you found?

3. Based on their new understanding, how might readers think and behave differently? How might this behavior affect others?

4. What particular paragraph or sentence might have the strongest impact on readers and why?

5. How does your essay contribute to an ongoing discussion, and how might it prompt readers to make a further contribution?

Beyond the Essay: Photo Essay

A photo essay is built not of paragraphs but of photographs. Consider Figure 11.1. In some parts of the country, salt is put on the roads to melt snow and ice. This salt rusts cars. The photo essay makes a point about the economics of road salt and its cost to average drivers:

Figure 11.1 "Road Salt," a photo essay

Drivers pay by washing the salt off their cars, getting their cars repaired, and ultimately by purchasing new vehicles.

1. Now that you have invented ideas for your essay, look for images that communicate the same way of thinking about the topic, and arrange them into a photo essay. Consider using the photo essay within your written essay to help readers understand and accept your thesis.

2. Explain in several paragraphs how the images work together to make your point.

12 Proposing Solutions

Chapter Objectives

This chapter will help you to:

- Examine a problem related to your everyday life and seek out underlying causes.
- Explore a range of solutions directly tied to the underlying causes of the problem.
- Develop an analytical/argumentative essay that proposes and defends a solution.
- Develop the essay with a range of support strategies, counterarguments, and concessions.
- Express your argument in a medium beyond the academic essay.

"I believe that if you show people the problems and you show them the solutions, they will be moved to act."

—Bill Gates

INTRODUCTION

In everyday life, crisis is a constant. Problems emerge in every facet of our existence. In professional life, problems arise in working conditions, policy implementation, coworker relations, labor/management relations, and government standards. Our communities face problems such as homelessness, pollution, school violence, terrorism, and urban sprawl. At home, the list of possible problems can seem endless. Although many of us have the privilege of ignoring such problems, someone in some capacity has to address them. Whether elected official, shift supervisor, environmental scientist, department chair, or student, someone ultimately has to address daily crises and propose solutions.

When writers propose solutions to problems, they are involved in many layers of analysis. They must analyze the problem to discover its causes—some of which may lie hidden in abstraction. They must also consider all the possible ways for addressing the problem and then come to some conclusion about the most appropriate solution.

Proposing solutions involves argument. Writers have to convince readers that the problem must be addressed, that action is necessary. They must also argue for the value of their particular solution. This is what politicians do for a living; members of

Congress, after all, spend much of their time arguing, first, that particular problems deserve allocated funds and, second, that those funds should be used in particular ways.

You might think of proposing a solution as a double-layered argument: First, you must argue that a problem exists and, second, that a particular solution will best solve it. Proposing a solution involves all the elements of an argument (thesis, support, counterargument, and concession). Writers who acknowledge the true complexities of their problems and solutions will better engage their readers and meet with less opposition. Some solutions are not necessarily complicated physical solutions, but rather simple reconsiderations—that is, new ways of thinking about familiar problems.

The readings in this chapter illustrate strategies for proposing solutions. They help readers understand the problem and then propose a solution through a main claim (thesis) and support. After reading the essays, you can uncover a problem to write about in one of two ways—go to the Point of Contact section to find a problem from your everyday life, or choose one of the Ideas for Writing that follow each essay. After finding a subject, go to the Analysis section to begin developing ideas for your essay.

READINGS

Hi, I'm a Digital Junkie, and I Suffer from Infomania
Manoush Zomorodi

Manoush Zomorodi, host and managing editor of "Note to Self," a tech podcast produced by WNYC, searches for answers to life's digital quandaries. In the following essay, published January 19, 2016, she explores the problem of infomania, and proposes a solution. As you read, you consider your own relationship with infomania.

I was recently described, to my face, as a "modern digital junkie."

This diagnosis was given to me, half in jest, by Dr. Dimitrios Tsivrikos, consumer psychologist at University College London, when I described my symptoms to him. After spending my workday tapping, swiping and emailing, I come home and—despite my exhaustion and twitching eyes—I want to consume more online. But I'm not even absorbing the articles, tweets and posts that I peruse. I'm just skipping from page to page, jumping from link to link.

There's another word for my problem. It's infomania, defined by the Oxford dictionary as "the compulsive desire to check or accumulate news and information, typically via mobile phone or computer." And I'm far from alone.

Kelsey Lakowske, a listener in California, emailed me in desperation. "I want to read all these articles about everything from the latest scientifically engineered sugar substitute to an in-depth analysis of Donald Trump's hair," she said. "It's like a different flavor of FOMO.... It's fear of missing out, but missing out on content—and on knowledge. With limited time and mental resources, there's no way to get through it all."

Tsivrikos told me he sees this issue most frequently in city folks like us, who think that stuffing their brains will make them better educated, more informed and more connected. But we can't possibly absorb or retain all the digital media we try to consume. Not only is this undertaking futile, it's stressing us out. Our gadgets' ability to keep us "in the know" has changed social expectations—and is exceeding our brains' processing power. We say that we're "maxxed out" or we "don't have the bandwidth," jargon that reflects this sense of inadequacy. It's time for us to make working within our brains' capacities, rather than the Internet's, socially acceptable.

Psychologists have done studies on the negative effects of multitasking and decision fatigue, but the long-term consequences of this kind of information overload is unknown. In a survey done a few months ago by the digital mapping and analytics company Esri UK, 61% of respondents called "the need to read and keep track of information from too many sources" a serious concern in their daily lives and 45% said that "the stress of data overload has affected either their sleep or relationships with family or colleagues." Fully a third of respondents

Zomorodi, Manoush. "Hi, I'm a Digital Junkie, and I Suffer from Infomania." *Los Angeles Times.* 19 Jan. 2016.

reported that they had difficulty absorbing the content from all the emails, social media posts, news and documents they encountered.

We already know that we read differently and retain less when getting information online. And there's been lots of research about how digital media are changing our attention spans. But human-computer interaction researchers are just beginning to study why a full day of digital tasks and interruptions makes us crave even more digital tasks and interruptions. Why would we spend hours at work on a computer, then go home and mindlessly tap away on Facebook or Pinterest?

For one thing, when we're tired, we fall prey to this tendency more easily. Professor Gloria Mark at UC Irvine's Department of Informatics recently completed study that suggests that the less sleep we get, the shorter our attention span is on any computer screen the next day—and the more likely we are to gravitate toward social media. "If you're really tired," she said, "you're not really mentally prepared to do heavy-duty work. You tend to do lightweight activities like Facebook. It's easy. It doesn't involve a lot of mental effort. And, of course, you have a shorter attention duration, which translates into more switching between different computer screens and different activities because you just don't have the mental resources to be able to focus and concentrate."

For many of us, this becomes a self-perpetuating cycle. We know our attention span is limited, but even if our phone doesn't buzz with a text, we self-interrupt. We check email one more time. We look at our Twitter or Instagram feed. We don't resist clicking on that link. It could be funny! Or contain life-changing information! Or at least provide conversation material for that holiday party tonight! We are inadvertently training our minds to seek digital interaction with little deeper intellectual payoff.

I don't know if there's a cure for infomania, but I believe we can put our symptoms in check. We need to put a higher value on taking the time to synthesize, interpret and reflect on the information we take in every day. The next step in digital literacy is not just understanding how to find reputable online sources but refining our content consumption according to our personal priorities and values.

Part of the problem is simply sorting through the mountains of information we're dealing with. Daniel Levitin, professor of psychology and neuroscience and author of the book "The Organized Mind: Thinking Straight in the Age of Information Overload," explains the difficulty we have distinguishing and prioritizing among various bits of content on our screens. "During the day, when information comes in, you're not quite sure how important it is or how important it's going to be. You have no system for it... You put it in your brain and you kind of toss it and turn it around . . . because it doesn't attach to anything." He advocates for moments of mindfulness. "Just take a beat, take a breath and pay attention." If there's something actually important to you, take a moment to mentally "mark" it.

We also need to ask ourselves: What's the point of this insatiable hunger for information? When it comes down to it, what do we really want to get out of it? We can set limits by setting personal goals, figuring out what we want to learn or do more of. Maybe you just want to be more up-to-date on the news and current events. Or you want to come up with more original ideas. Perhaps you've decided it's time for you to really master a skill or subject. Maybe you want to put greater emphasis on your personal life and be in better touch with friends and family—or even yourself. Maybe you want to simply be calmer and more relaxed.

The information you consume should reflect this personal choice. Tsivrikos suggests creating goals for going online, writing them down and putting them in the place where you do most of your data consumption. That way, he says, you'll know what you're looking for, channel your efforts and be less likely to wander off. Having goals and sticking to them spares our brains the effort of processing unneeded information. It also releases us from the feeling of never being satisfied.

Earlier and earlier, children need to be given this responsibility, taught the value in thinking through goals and understanding the consequences of a life spent skimming. If they don't choose, our gadgets and the delightful pre-loaded activities on them will decide for them.

Above all, we need to reset our own and society's expectations. It has to be OK to say, "I didn't see it/read it/watch it." Otherwise, you'll have spent life catching up on Netflix, reading a backlog of top-ten lists, or looking at GIFs from co-workers. If those activities fit in with your goals, go for it. But if they get you no closer to achieving what you really want to achieve tomorrow, next year, or in the next five years, downgrade their relevance in your life.

WRITING STRATEGIES

1. What problem does Zomorodi write about? What solution does she propose?

2. Explain how Zomorodi uses argumentative appeals. For instance, how does she appeal to logic or value?

3. How does the essay use an authority to explain why we go home and tap away on Facebook after having worked on a computer all day? How persuasive is this support?

4. Describe Zomorodi's sentence-level writing style, using a few key sentences to support your overall description.

EXPLORING IDEAS

1. What role does self-interrupting play in your life?

2. What do you really want to get out of the information on your phone?

3. What does the information you consume on your phone and computer say about *you*?

4. What do you want to achieve, and how does the information you have been consuming help you achieve it, or how does it make achieving it more difficult?

5. Why might this essay be outdated in three years?

IDEAS FOR WRITING

1. Research and describe decision fatigue and then propose a solution.

2. Research and describe multi-tasking and then propose a solution.

3. Research and describe some other issue Zomorodi identifies and then propose a solution.

If responding to one of these ideas, go to the Analysis section of this chapter to begin developing ideas for your essay."

Your Kids Bored at School? Tell Them to Get Over It
Laura Hanby Hudgens

Is school boring? Is it exciting!? Is it always exciting, or ever exciting, or is it interesting enough? Two students sitting next to each other in the same classroom can have different responses—one finding a class engaging and worthwhile and the other feeling bored and ripped off. In the following essay from *The Miami Herald* online (July 2016), Laura Hanby Hudgens, a part-time high school teacher, a freelance writer, and a mom of four, proposes a solution. Hudgens lives with her husband and children on a buffalo farm in the Ozark Hills.

Any discussion about the problems in American education – and what is to blame for these problems—will likely include one or all of the usual suspects: inadequate and unequal funding, a lack of resources, underpaid and overworked teachers, over-testing, poverty and heavy-handed legislation.

As a teacher and the mother of four public-school-educated children, I can tell you that all of these things have negatively impacted our schools. All of these things are problems.

But there is another problem, one that is plaguing many of America's classrooms and jeopardizing the future of our children, yet it is rarely addressed—at least not as it should be. That problem is apathy. In classrooms all over the country, the teacher cares more about her students' grades, learning and futures than they do.

Teachers are expected to combat apathy by continually finding new and innovative ways to reach students—through multimedia lessons, group work, games, alternative assessments or whatever it takes. To ensure student engagement and skill acquisition, we must teach to the individual learning styles, interests and abilities of each of our students. If a student can't learn the way we teach, we must teach the way he learns—times infinity.

Sadly, all the attempts to dazzle and awe eventually wear some teachers down. They burn out. They leave a profession they are good at and once felt called to.

However, the loss of good teachrs isn't even the worst effect of the be-all-things-to-all-people mentality. The real danger is that this way of thinking has shifted the responsibility of learning, and of caring about learning, from the student to the teacher. Because it isn't just administrators and parents who believe that it is a teacher's job to make learning fun. Kids believe it, too. As a result we have a generation of students who think that if a lesson or an assignment or a class is not interesting, if it isn't engaging and fun and inspiring, then it simply isn't worth caring about. They are not obligated to care about it. It's a teacher's job to make all learning exciting. If the teacher hasn't lived up to her responsibility, why should the child?

In a workshop I recently attended, teachers were told that kids are so attracted to video games because of the constant feedback—the progress, praise and prizes. We were

Hudgens, Laura Hanby. "Your Kids Bored at School? Tell Them to Get Over It." Special to *The Washington Post Miami Herald.* 18 Jul. 2016.

encouraged to design our instruction more like a video game. How else can we expect to hold their attention?

That is a frightening mentality because it has created a generation of consumer learners. Many students don't see education as a privilege. They see it as a product. And if they don't like the salesperson, if they aren't impressed with how it's packaged, they aren't buying.

But our kids have to learn to be self-motivated because at some point in every person's life, either at school or in a job or in a marriage, he or she will have to buck up and say, "This is hard. This is boring. I don't want to do this. But I'm doing it anyway. And I'll do my best."

Many students don't see education as a privilege. They see it as a product. And if they don't like the salesperson, if they aren't impressed with how it's packaged, they aren't buying.

So how do parents and educators teach kids to be self-motivated? There are no easy answers. But there are two things that need to happen.

First, we have to change the national conversation about education. This doesn't mean that educators should stop trying to improve instruction, but it does mean that there have to be more conversations about the role students play in ensuring their own learning. Teachers, parents, administrators and, of course, the students have to start making self-motivation an educational focus and priority. Self-motivation should be the new educational buzzword—every bit as prevalent and powerful as any we've seen shape our classrooms in the last few decades.

In the meantime, teachers and parents need practical strategies for encouraging students to take responsibility for their own learning. That is the second thing that has to happen. On a basic level we need to help our kids develop habits and discipline that will lead to academic success.

Unfortunately in a consumer-oriented educational system, words such as habit and discipline have all but gone by the wayside. We emphasize concepts like differentiation, higher-order thinking, cooperative learning and data-driven instruction over student responsibilities like organization, perseverance and hard work.

The good news (at least for kids) is that the best hope for developing any habit is to start small - especially when good habits need to replace bad ones.

I've used the start-small strategy with my kids. Maybe it's because he's the baby of the family, but I have somehow let 12 years go by without helping my youngest son develop good habits when it comes to keeping his room clean and taking care of his things. Now his room is a disaster.

The solution isn't to insist he do one massive overhaul. If I do that, I am likely to walk into a seemingly spotless room only to discover 400 baseball cards, half his spring wardrobe and last year's Halloween candy stashed under his bed. Instead, I'm encouraging him to take one thing at a time and do it little by little. Twenty minutes a day. First the closet. Then the drawers. Then under the bed. This keeps him from becoming overwhelmed and frustrated and allows him to experience several small successes.

When the job is done, not only will he have a clean room, but he will have learned that perseverance pays off.

This is the same approach I take with my students who struggle with apathy. I encourage them to start small, to start with one class and to give 100 percent in that class. I talk to them about specific strategies: Sit in the front. Take notes. Ask questions. Be organized. Do all the work.

Find a study partner. It might be difficult for a struggling student to take on that kind of responsibility seven periods a day, but often students are willing to commit to 100 percent in one class.

And when students experience hard-won success in one class, they will be empowered by that success and likely apply that newly learned work ethic to other classes and pursuits.

Success breeds success, and success is an excellent motivator.

Not only does success motivate, but it can also inspire, and here is where we move from sheer determination to passion - the true goal of education. No matter how innovative the instruction, it's unlikely that a student will grow to love a class if he is just getting by. But the kid who started out just trudging through history might find that he has a passion for it once he applies himself. A student who once wrote half-hearted essays might find her talent and her voice when she begins to take writing seriously.

The fact is that it's rare (except in the movies) that even the most brilliant teacher can motivate an apathetic student to embrace a lifetime of learning. On a really good day, we can spark a child's interest in the lesson. But in the long term, the desire to learn and improve has to come from within.

The world isn't a video game. It doesn't always offer fun and exciting paths through the mazes of life. So unless we change the way we approach education to include an emphasis on student responsibility, and unless we give our students the basic tools they need to accept that responsibility, we really haven't taught them much at all.

WRITING STRATEGIES

1. According to Hudgens, what is the problem, and what solution does she propose?
2. How does Hudgens support her claim about self-motivation? How persuasive is her support? What other support might she have provided?
3. Who is the audience for Hudgens' essay? What passages best indicate what audience she is writing to?
4. What is Hudgens' line of reasoning?
5. How does Hudgens acknowledge various problems but then focus on one?

EXPLORING IDEAS

1. What does Hudgens mean by "the be-all-things-to-all-people mentality"?
2. Do you agree or disagree with Hudgens that "kids have to learn to be self-motivated"? Why?
3. Has over-testing been a problem in your education? A benefit? Explain.

IDEAS FOR WRITING

1. What habits and disciplines will lead to academic success?
2. *If* the desire to learn and improve has to come from within, how can we motivate students to learn and improve?

If responding to one of these ideas, go to the Analysis section of this chapter to begin developing ideas for your essay."

Different Jobs
Dana Stewart

MINDTAP
From Cengage
Complete the auto-graded
quiz for this reading.

We interact daily with other people's jobs, sometimes with judgement and frustration. In the following essay, Dana Stewart, a writer and teacher, explores the degree to which we understand the complexity of other people's jobs, and then proposes a solution.

Have you ever heard somebody say, "The world would be a boring place if everybody was the same?" This expression, or a variation of it, is a cliché. And it's also probably true. If everyone thought the same thoughts, liked the same things, had the same strengths and weakness, the same personalities, and so on, we might all get along better, or maybe not. But the point is, we aren't all the same. We like different things; we have different strengths and weaknesses; and that's the reality of our existence.

Introduction speaks directly to the reader: Have YOU ever heard . . . .

A few weeks ago I heard some fans discussing why their local football team lost a big game, and one of them said, "The *second* easiest thing to do is beat up on a high school football coach." When someone asked what the easiest thing to do is, she said, "Beat up on a barista." She said this because that's what she does. But you can fill in the blank: "The easiest thing to do is beat up on [say your job here]." One morning I was listening to a sports talk show in the car. Three basketball coaches were talking, and one of them quoted another coach who said, *coaching basketball is the only job where people who don't know anything about it think they know more than you do*. The coaches all agreed and had a good laugh about this, assuring each other that their profession was the only one like this. They were wrong, of course.

Two short anecdotes help develop the main idea, which the writer states later in the essay.

Most, if not all, jobs are like this. People can be judgmental about other people's jobs. Here we are talking about the motorist who doesn't understand the complexity of driving a semi-truck and so becomes frustrated or angry by something the truck driver does; or the passenger who doesn't understand the complexity of flying a jet or being a flight attendant. Think of any job—a fast food worker, doctor, bank teller, highway worker, electrician, cleaning lady, president, barber, receptionist, college professor—and that job involves complexity that someone *not* doing it isn't aware of.

Two quick examples illustrate the claim that people can be judgmental about other people's jobs.

Readers are invited to add to the previous examples by thinking of their own examples.

"Different Jobs," by Dana Stewart. Reprinted by permission of the author.

Since we don't understand the complexity of other people's jobs, we can become frustrated. And some people get mired in this frustration. To avoid or reduce this problem, we should be mindful of the abstract relationship we have with other people's jobs. "Abstract" means "existing in thought or as an idea but not having a physical or concrete existence" ("Abstract," def. A1). So when someone else's job exists for you only "in thought or as an idea" and has no "physical or concrete existence [to you]," it is natural to *oversimplify* that person's job and by extension to oversimplify that person's *existence*.

To solve this problem we could walk a mile in that person's shoes. For example, we could do her job for a while to see what it's like, to experience its complexities. But walking a mile isn't the same as walking thousands of miles, day after day, year after year. So while we might see the light and truly understand the complexity we didn't see before, we might also mislead ourselves into thinking we know what it's like to wait tables for a living because we did it for a few days. The television show *Undercover Boss* is a good example of this. The boss does someone else's job to get a sense of it, but this is like spending a weekend in prison to see what prison is like. You'd learn some things about it, but not be an actual convict doing real time. Another thing we can do is just be nice and more understanding, but what can help us get more into this state of mind?

In his book *Public Opinion*, Walter Lippmann explains the concept *pseudo-environment*. He describes a triangular relationship between the actual environment (for example, an actual class), what he calls a *pseudo-environment* (your idea of that class), and your actions (the actual things you say and do, which are based on the pseudo-environment but play out in the actual environment). Lippmann illustrates this with a story: Some Englishmen, Frenchmen, and Germans live on an island. A British ship comes to the island every 60 days, bringing supplies and the news of the day—or the last 60 days. When the ship finally arrived in September of 1914, the islanders learned that England and France were at war with Germany. Since they didn't know this, their pseudo-environment was that they were friends when, in fact, their countries were at war and for the last six weeks they were enemies (3).

Lippmann's story illustrates "how indirectly we know the environment in which we nevertheless live" (4). Until the ship came with current news, each man on the island "was still adjusted to an environment that no longer existed" (4). In the same way, a student might struggle in an English class because her idea of the class (her pseudo-environment) does not accurately match the actual class. For example, she loved and did well in Mrs. Beetle's high school English class, so when she takes Professor Gowan's college English class, she imagines it (in her mind of course) as Mrs. Beetle's class was, not as Professor Gowan's class is. She works hard but doesn't do well because her actions are based on her pseudo-environment but play out in the actual environment.

Another example helps clarify the previous example.

If we apply Lippmann's *pseudo-environment* to other people's jobs, we can see how indirectly we know someone else's job. We see the parts of it that we see, but not the parts of it we don't see. So we run the risk of thinking the entire complexity of the job is what we see when, in fact, the complexity is hidden from us. I worked out at the University Rec Center, lifting weights in the free weight room, running on the track, swimming laps, sitting in the sauna, playing racquetball, squash, badminton, and volleyball, and stretching underneath the stairs where there were mats for stretching. An acquaintance, Rob, played basketball at the Rec Center, but didn't do anything else there. To play basketball, he walked down the stairs, where he sometimes saw me stretching, and onto the court. When he was done, he walked up the stairs, where he sometimes saw me stretching, and left. One day he said to me, "Is that all you do here—stretch?" Since Rob only saw me stretching, he had an oversimplified idea of my workout routine. And this is how we tend to see other people's jobs.

Personal testimony as support— to help the reader understand and possibly accept the main claim.

Being aware that we all, by necessity, have pseudo-environments (because we cannot know the complexity of others' jobs or their lives), we can alleviate our own frustration *and* appreciate others more. By realizing that our understanding of their work is just our own pseudo-environment, not their actual work or life, we don't simply come to understand how complex (how physically hard, how mentally exhausting, how overwhelming, or downright undoable) their job is. We also realize we can't really understand their job's complexity and their life's travails.

The previous paragraphs lead up to (they support) this proposed solution.

Works Cited

"Abstract, *Adj. 1.*" *Oxford Living Dictionaries*, Oxford UP, 2016, en.oxforddictionaries.com/definition/us/abstract. Accessed 30 Nov. 2016.

Lippmann, Walter. *Public Opinion*. Harcourt, Brace, 1922. *Internet Archive*, archive.org/stream/publicopinion00lippgoog#page/n6/mode/2up.

WRITING STRATEGIES

1. According to Stewart, what is the problem and what is the solution?

2. What is one supporting claim (a claim that supports the main claim or thesis) and what support strategy does Stewart use to support, or unpack, that claim?

3. Stewart uses "I" and "you" in the essay: "A few weeks ago **I** heard some fans ..."; "**You**'d learn some things about it, but not be ..."; "**I** worked out at the University Rec Center ..."; "So when someone else's job exists for **you** only 'in thought or as an idea.'" Are these pronouns okay, or should they be avoided? If Stewart avoided "I" in the next to last paragraph, how else might that information be presented and would this strengthen, weaken, or not affect the essay?

4. How do the first two paragraphs of the essay establish a tone or expectation for the rest of the essay?

EXPLORING IDEAS

1. How effective is Stewart's explanation of *pseudo-environment*? Demonstrate your understanding of the concept by giving your own example.

2. Explain how your understanding of someone else's work is just your pseudo-environment and not their actual environment.

3. According to Stewart, what is the problem with walking a mile in someone else's shoes? Why is or isn't Stewart's support here convincing?

IDEAS FOR WRITING

1. Propose a solution to a frustrating situation.

2. Propose a solution to a misunderstanding involving work.

If responding to one of these ideas, go to the Analysis section of this chapter to begin developing ideas for your essay.

INVENTION

"No problem can withstand the assault of sustained thinking."

—Voltaire

For this chapter, your topic will be a particular problem—some situation that needs to be changed or an idea that needs to be rethought. Be wary of global problems like hunger, poverty, or racism. They are not unapproachable or unsolvable, but such big problems usually have local or particular expressions, and it is the local or particular that is often the most appropriate place to start. Focusing on a particular problem also sets the ground for a manageable solution. For example, solving financial difficulty for single-parent students is more manageable than solving poverty in general.

The following sections are designed to help you through the invention process: specifically, to discover a problem (in Point of Contact), to develop an understanding of its causes and develop a possible solution (in Analysis), to make it relevant to a community of readers (in Public Resonance), to develop a focused statement about the problem and solution (in Thesis), and to develop support for your argument (in Rhetorical Tools). The Invention Questions in each section are not meant to be answered directly in your final written assignment. They will, however, help you to think further into your topic, to develop intense claims and insightful points.

Point of Contact

Social problems are not necessarily physical or material; they can be intellectual, spiritual, or psychological. Consider problems related to bad policies (all first-year students must live on campus), narrow thinking (a government administration that assumes energy must come from fossil fuels), or troubled systems (a bureaucracy in which all decisions must be made at the executive level before action can be taken).

Writers often do best with topics with which they are familiar, or those with which they can become familiar. To discover particular problems, consider the different circles of your life. Use the following suggestions and questions to help dig up a problem that you, as a writer, witness or experience, and attempt to see problems that others might disregard. See the problems that lurk behind the obvious. If one of the suggestions prompts you to see a problem, begin by recording details—that is, try to explain the particulars of the problem.

School

- Are students missing too many classes?

- Do my instructors communicate poorly with students?

- Are my peers lazy?
- Are enough courses offered to students?
- Do instructors give enough or too many exams?
- Did my high school education adequately prepare me for college?
- Is the curricular gap between high school and college too wide?

Government

- Does the city government do enough for children? For senior citizens?
- Does state government overlook the particular needs of my community?
- Are citizens sufficiently involved in local government?
- Do average citizens know how tax dollars are spent?
- Are there enough minorities in public office?

Television

- Is prime-time television too adolescent?
- Are sports televised too often?
- Is there something wrong with the way sports are televised?
- Are talk shows tasteless, moronic, or disrespectful?
- Has art been abandoned by popular culture?

Your Major

- What are the problems related to employment in my field?
- What about job security? Safety for the workers? Safety for the public?
- Do people enter their major or career field for the wrong reasons?

Community

- Are the elderly people in my family or community isolated?
- Do people in my neighborhood ignore one another?

Ronnie Bergeron/MorgueFile; Rich Stern/StockXchng

- Are there too few animals in people's lives? (Too many?)

- Does traffic in my community interfere with daily life?

- Are billboards tasteless or boring?

- Are there too many chain stores or strip malls in my community?

ACTIVITY

Now go beyond these suggestions. In groups or alone, develop more strategies for encountering and exploring social problems. Imagine what might be wrong, or what can be better than it is.

Analysis

Proposing a solution involves first analyzing the problem and then considering the pros and cons of the possible solutions.

Problems: Any solution must address the causes of a problem. Therefore, analyzing a problem to discover all possible causes is essential to developing a good solution. Often the causes of a problem are not clear, however. A problem may originate from an abstract source, such as a long tradition, a widely held attitude, or a flawed assumption. And writers must search through such abstractions to find the possible causes. To understand the full complexities of your problem, respond to the following questions:

> What are the causes of the problem?

> What are the most troubling or alarming images associated with the problem?

> What are its short-term effects? Long-term effects?

> What other situation (event, attitude) does this problem resemble?

Consider Dana Stewart's Invention writing below:

What are the causes of the problem?

The problem is that people don't understand my job, so when they talk to me about it, they oversimplify it. I hate it when people who don't do my job, who have never done my job, think they know more about it than I do. It bugs me when my boss, or other higher ups, who don't deal with the complexities of my job have simple suggestions about what I should do about complex issues. So, there are various causes—higher ups who are too willing to make suggestions. I think the cause here might be that they have to solve problems and make people happy, but they don't really understand the complexities of the situation. Still, they speak up. Some customers are like this too. They see things from their perspective only, even when they say or think they are understanding. They don't understand. So the cause of the problem is, they don't understand the complexities of someone else's job, but they get into that person's business anyway.

Stewart's writing is not definite at this point; instead, it is explorative. Stewart is seeking a cause and through the writing above—which is a starting place, not an endpoint—is coming to terms with a *potential* cause and a *possible* focus for an essay. Stewart hits on several causes: too willing to make suggestions; have to solve problems and make people happy; don't understand complexities; see things from their perspective only. Stewart will ultimately focus on not understanding the complexities of someone else's job because we see it from our own perspective, and then will use research and the concept *pseudo-environment* to develop a solution.

RESEARCH

You may respond to the Invention Questions on different levels, first providing your own initial responses and then gathering information from outside sources. Such sources may include friends, coworkers, family members, websites, articles, and books. (Consult Chapter 14:

Finding Sources and Chapter 15: Analyzing, Synthesizing, and Evaluating Sources to help you explore.) As you research, look not just for ideas that support your initial responses but, more importantly, for ideas that might change the way you think.

Solutions: Before settling on a solution, consider how the solution will work, how it will address the causes of the problem, and how it might fail. Answers to the following questions will be vital to developing your solution and to making it persuasive to readers. While you will benefit from understanding all of the following issues, your readers may need some points emphasized over others. Ask yourself what points seem least obvious, or most debatable, to your audience. Respond to the following questions to develop your solution:

> What action (solution) will best address the causes of the problem?

> What might stand in the way of this solution?

> How will the solution change the situation?

> Does this solution have potential shortcomings or limitations?

Below, Stewart explores solutions, not just settling for the first idea that comes to mind but continuing to write—to explore—beyond the shortcomings of the first idea. While this still might not be the greatest solution, the writer has forged beyond the initial idea and into new, potentially interesting, territory.

What action (solution) will best address the causes of the problem?

Will BEST address it? This reminds me of the basketball coaches on the radio who spent ten minutes (maybe five) talking about how coaching basketball is the only profession where people think they know more than you. No it's not. Probably everyone's job is like that. People driving cars don't like people riding bicycles. And people riding bicycles don't like people driving cars. The guy riding a bike doesn't like cars then when he's driving a car he doesn't like bikes. So, the action is that everyone could just do someone else's job—or walk a mile in their shoes. But, that's too easy, like that TV show where the boss wears a disguise and works at his own company. You still don't really know what it's like. Instead, you have to understand and always try to keep in mind that you don't really know what that other person's job is like or what kind of stuff that person's dealing with.

Public Resonance

Some topics may seem difficult to connect to a broad public concern, but good writers bring *seemingly* marginal topics into the center of public consciousness. The problem you have chosen may obviously affect (or potentially affect) a community or society at large. However, no matter how much your problem involves or affects people, you still must connect it to a public concern. As you consider your own topic, respond to the following questions:

> Who should care about this issue? Why?

> What particular community, place, or group does this issue affect?

❯ How might my reader(s) be involved in this issue?

❯ Why is it important that others hear my opinion about this issue?

Notice how Stewart uses ideas from the Analysis writing to explore further and formalize some ideas about public resonance:

How might my reader(s) be involved in this issue?
So the cause of the problem is, *people* don't understand the complexities of someone else's job. This isn't unique to my job. It's true of all or nearly all jobs, and of life in general. People think this way about my job and about other people's jobs too. And I think this way about other people's jobs, of course. I think someone's doing a lousy job, which some of the time they just plain are, but other times I just don't understand the complexity of their job. So, this is definitely relevant to any reader—because it's how we all think.

Invention Workshop

The public resonance may not be clear at first, but working through all the possibilities can help your topic to expand in interesting ways. Enlist the help of other writers, and in a small group, answer one of the questions for your topic. As a group, work at collectively building a sophisticated answer to the question.

In the following, Marcus has discovered a problem in his community: Elderly people in nursing homes and senior living centers are isolated from others. In a discussion with peers, Marcus develops his initial thinking:

"What Particular Community, Place, or Group Does this Issue Affect?"

MARCUS: Primarily the elderly. Senior citizens are primarily concerned about this issue, and as medical advances allow people to live longer, it seems like we all should be worried—because we'll all be old someday.

LINDA: But shouldn't the younger generations be concerned about the isolation of the elderly, too—I mean beyond just caring about themselves as they age?

DIANA: Yeah . . . even if they don't care, it seems like stuffing the elderly away from mainstream society can't be a good thing, for anybody.

MARCUS: It's like we are ignoring a huge group of people—the group that probably has the most insight and experience about big social problems.

LINDA: And I would even say personal and family problems. I know in my family, it was always my grandmother who understood everyone's problems and could talk through them without getting angry or mean. She was the one who gave everyone a sense of direction.

MARCUS: So when society shuts away its elderly, maybe the biggest victims are the younger generations. Of course, it's bad for the elderly, but in a more indirect and long-term way, maybe their absence from mainstream society is an even bigger wrong.

Maybe the younger generations feel the effects in the long term without their patience, insights, and experience.

Thesis

A thesis for this project should offer a specific strategy for addressing a specific problem. The following examples show a range of possible strategies:

- If the sales associates at Dalworth's had more discretion over break time, the management/employee tension would decrease significantly.

- The budget crisis at Midland State College can only be addressed with a tuition increase.

- Small-group work can help writers get beyond their frustration with invention.

- The degradation of rural areas cannot be stopped with peaceful public rhetoric. Significantly higher gasoline taxes would, however, keep people from building homes farther away from their jobs.

- If the country could begin to take back the airwaves from corporate interests, democracy might then begin to flourish.

- When America's hunters and fishermen see their shared interests with strong environmental groups, their combined political force will help counter the unchecked movement into wildlife areas.

Thesis statements tend to go off track for a few reasons. Before committing to a statement (to something that may impact everything hereafter!), see the Common Thesis Problems on page 254 in Chapter 8: Making Arguments.

Evolution of a Thesis

Notice how a thesis might evolve out of the invention process. Marcus's topic (isolation of the elderly) can be developed into a focused and sophisticated point. He begins by articulating the problem. Then he tries to make the problem more specific. Finally, he works to integrate the solution:

- In the long run, younger generations may feel the effects of the elderly's isolation.

- Older generations are isolated—their experiences, insights, and wisdom cut off from the people who need it most: everyone else.

- We have to make our grandparents the center of our families, not the marginal human satellites they are presently.

- Because older generations are isolated, their experiences, insights, and wisdom cut off from those who need them most, families should rethink how grandparents figure into everyday life.

- The lost experiences, insight, and wisdom of the older generations can be reintegrated into culture only through families; therefore, each family should work to place its grandparents at the center of everyday life.

Try to express your own problem and your solution in a sentence or two before moving on.

REVISING YOUR THESIS

Writers sometimes seek out problems that are simply too big: hunger, racism, sexism, political deceit, and so on. But such giant problems have too many causes and too many forms. Writers are more apt to create a focused argument and offer an important insight if they take on a specific problem—one that can be located in a particular place and time. Before moving on, make certain that your problem is as narrow as possible.

Rhetorical Tools

Remember that proposing a solution is a form of arguing. In fact, the process may involve two layers of argument: (1) persuading readers about the nature or degree of the problem and (2) showing the value of a particular solution. The goal is not necessarily to convince readers that only one solution is possible but that a particular solution to an important problem has merit.

Although the act of proposing solutions can vary greatly, good proposing solutions essays have certain key elements (which you have already begun to develop):

- **Problem:** Includes illustrations or examples, an explanation of causes, and a picture of short- and long-term effects.

- **Solution:** Includes an explanation of how that solution will address, confront, or stop the causes of the problem.

- **Counterargument:** Addresses concerns about or opposing claims to the solution or the articulation of the problem.

- **Alternative Solutions:** Include any other potential strategies for addressing the problem. Articulating alternative solutions requires an explanation of why these are less desirable than the main solution being offered.

- **Concession/Qualifier:** Acknowledges any possible shortcomings of the solution or concedes value to some opposing claim or alternative solution.

The development of these elements depends upon your particular problem and solution. Some problems, for instance, require significant explanation; that is, you might need to work hard just to make readers aware of the complexities of the problem. Or perhaps you have a problem that is rather apparent (such as abandoned buildings plaguing an entire section of town). Consider how your audience may view the problem, and make certain to convince your readers to see the problem as you do.

Also, remember the strategies from Chapter 8: Making Arguments. Writers have the whole world of culture, history, and science within reach. By alluding to key historical moments, relevant literary texts, news events, or popular culture figures, you can make claims more persuasive to readers or show that your position is shared by others. Use the following questions to help construct supporting points for your argument (and see the examples in the chapter readings):

> Does a historical situation or trend (the rise of a particular fashion, organization, or individual) illustrate something about my topic?
> Has science taught us anything about my topic?
> Have I witnessed or experienced someone or something that illustrates my point?
> Can I construct a hypothetical situation that illustrates my point or dramatizes my solution?

Discovering Counterarguments and Alternative Solutions

In proposing a solution, you are arguing that a problem exists *and* that a particular solution will address it. But someone might argue with you about several points: that the problem is no problem at all, that your solution will not work, that your solution is inappropriate—too costly, inhumane, unmanageable, and so on. A good arguer addresses those possible objections and may even dig into opponents' assumptions.

Every problem has many possible solutions, and a good writer acknowledges other possibilities. But acknowledging solutions other than your own involves explaining their shortcomings. That is, as you mention other solutions, you must also make it clear that they are not as valuable as yours for some reason. Other solutions, for instance, might be less efficient, more dangerous, less ethical, less manageable, or simply inadequate.

Considering other solutions can also help you understand the strengths and shortcomings of the solution you are promoting. For instance, a solution to Marcus's problem from the Public Resonance section, isolation of the elderly, might involve refiguring the concept of the nuclear family to include grandparents, uncles, aunts, and cousins. He might argue that only in reconceptualizing the basic family unit will elderly members of society find more genuine social engagement. But he might also address other solutions, such as programs that bring together schoolchildren and nursing home residents. According to his argument, such solutions might fall short of creating deep and lasting relationships for the elderly.

As you consider your own topic, apply the following questions:

> Who might not see this as a problem? Why?

> Why might my solution not work?

> What other solutions could be (or have been) attempted?

> Why is the solution I am proposing better or more effective?

Avoiding Logical Fallacies

Logical fallacies are flaws in the structure of an argument that can make readers call the claims into question. (See further explanation of logical fallacies in Chapter 8: Making Arguments, pages 260–262.) In proposing solutions, be especially cautious of logical fallacies. When considering the possible long-term effects of a solution, writers may make any of several logical errors:

- Imagining an effect unrelated to present causes (**faulty cause/effect**)

- Skipping several logical steps between a cause and a possible effect (**non sequitur**)

- Extending present circumstances to their most dramatic or disastrous conclusion without sufficient logical cause (**slippery slope**)

Consider Marcus's topic: *Mainstream society isolates the elderly.* It might be valuable for Marcus to project the long-term effects of this problem. However, he should be cautious and not overstate the effects.

Logically Sound:

- Without the insight of older generations, mainstream society may continuously forget the social crises of the past and have to relive many burdens.

- As older generations are further isolated, the difficulties they have lived through are isolated with them. And without constant real-life reminders in our midst, younger generations are likely to ignore a past that is not written by official voices of history.

Logically Unsound:

- The United States will have to go through another two world wars because it has completely forgotten the past.

- Everyone will eventually think like children without the elderly in everyday life.

- Society will eventually keep everyone over fifty years old locked away.

Revision

Academic audiences value directness and intensity. They do not want to struggle through overly wordy phrases and jumbled sentences. And they don't like boredom any more than anyone else. In short, academic audiences are people too. They want to stay awake and be engaged. Examine your draft, focusing on the following issues:

- **Delete the Obvious:** Consider statements or passages that argue for or detail what you and your peers already assume. Although you might use some common assumptions or common knowledge to build an idea, avoid telling readers what they already accept.

- **Intensify the Least Obvious:** Think about your essay as a declaration of new ideas. What is the most uncommon or fresh idea? Even if it's a description of the problem or a slightly different take on solving it, develop it further. Draw more attention to it.

Peer Review

Exchange drafts with at least one other writer. Before passing your draft to others, underline the thesis or write it at the top of your essay. This way, reviewers will get traction as they read.

As a reviewer, use the following questions to guide your response:

1. Is the problem the writer describes worthy of attention? Is it a problem worth solving? If not, what might the writer do to make the problem more significant?

2. Is the writer's solution appropriate for the problem? Will it address specific causes? Is it manageable? Realistic? Humane?

3. Try to imagine a reason why the writer's solution will not work. What unforeseen forces or variables should the writer consider?

4. What other solutions might be as or more productive in solving the problem?

5. Consider the organization of the essay. Do any paragraphs shift focus without sufficient cues? Do any paragraphs move away from their initial points without taking you along? Point to specific places in the essay that move too abruptly from one idea to another.

6. How would you describe the writer's tone? (See page 547.) Do you feel invited into the topic, or do you have to work at keeping your attention focused? (Is the writer's voice too flat, too uninteresting, too typical?) Rewrite a short passage of the draft using a different voice. Help the writer imagine how a different voice might sound.

7. Consider sentence vitality:

   a. Help the writer avoid obvious content. Circle any sentences or passages that seem obvious to you.

   b. Help the writer avoid padding. Underline phrases that inflate simple ideas and draw out sentences unnecessarily.

c. Help the writer "call a fool a fool." Rewrite any phrases or sentences that seem to hedge, that circle around a more direct and intense wording.

d. Consider other strategies from Chapter 19: Vitalizing Sentences.

Reflection

One powerful way to better understand your own work is to analyze its basic elements or perform what is often called *rhetorical analysis*. In rhetorical analysis, writers describe how arguments work. Looking at the essay you've written, develop a final analytical statement:

1. How does the essay confront a problem and offer a solution?

2. How does the essay go beyond the common intellectual reflexes related to the problem? For instance, does it show things in a different light? Does it assert something that others don't see? Does it call for a solution that has not been attempted?

3. How does the essay take on opposition? How does it counterargue or concede? Or why doesn't it?

Beyond the Essay: Exploring Other Media

Students sometimes see education—or certain college courses such as this one—as separate from their actual lives. However, the course is not only related to your major; it is directly related to your major, and it is, more importantly, directly related to your *life*. Writing courses such as this one look at what really goes on in everyday life, and they present what goes on (invention strategies, rhetorical strategies, and so on) in an organized way. Admittedly, a college writing course can be a confusing and seemingly irrelevant place. But if you can remember that the invention strategies in this book are a description (not a prescription) of how everyday people think and communicate effectively, you can more successfully fuse schoolwork and real life. Now that you have written a proposing solutions essay, communicate your solution in some other form such as a letter, speech, poster, bumper sticker, website, photo essay, T-shirt, poem, song, performance, or comic strip.

13 Thinking Radically: Reseeing the World

Bankoo/Shutterstock.com

Chapter Objectives
The chapter will help you to:

- Recognize status quo thinking related to a specific issue or topic.
- Develop a revelatory, analytical, argumentative essay that transcends the status quo, questions common sense, or digs into a root issue.
- Develop the essay with a range of support strategies, counterarguments, and concessions.
- Transpose your new/radical thinking into a visual essay.

"We must therefore look in the obscurest corners and summon up courage to shock the prejudices of our age if we want to broaden the basis of our understanding of nature."

—**Carl Jung**

INTRODUCTION

L iving in a society demands a certain degree of conformity. As individuals in a society, we conform to laws, clothing styles, hairstyles, and even culinary tastes (most Americans like french fries but not raw oysters). We also conform to ways of thinking; we learn to follow intellectual conventions. This is not to say that we all think alike, but we do buy into conventional patterns of thought that, on the one hand, allow us to participate in shared knowledge but, on the other hand, limit intellectual possibilities.

Mainstream thought invites us to accept a particular view of reality, and with it, certain assumptions. Consider the following:

- Progress involves technological advancement.
- The past is behind us.
- People who make lots of money are successful.
- Poor people are worse off than rich people.

- We make individual choices.
- Time is constant.

Such ideas are what we might call *common sense,* in that they represent widely held and largely unexamined beliefs. But some people have examined and even challenged such common ideas. For example, thinkers such as Wendell Berry challenge the idea that human progress necessarily involves increased dependence on technology; several important religious figures (Jesus, Buddha, Muhammad) overturned the inherent value of monetary riches; and Albert Einstein showed the world that time is not constant but relative. We might say that such figures transcend and challenge commonsense thinking. They call into question those beliefs that rest beneath layers of intellectual practice and everyday life. They show us questions where we may have assumed solid answers.

People who transcend conventional thinking are not *radical* in the sense that they want to destroy mainstream life. (We are not talking here about anarchists, religious zealots, or specific political positions.) Rather, they are radical *thinkers*—they escape conventional thought patterns. Although convention calls on us to think within the lines, radical thinkers work to see beyond those lines and then communicate what ideas are possible. Their writing seeks to reform conventional thinking.

Radical thinking is not a matter of topic choice. Topics are not, in themselves, radical. Radical thinking involves an adventurous *approach* to a topic and offers a new way to think. For example, in 1784 Benjamin Franklin first put forth the idea of daylight savings time. After waking at an unusually early hour in the morning and finding that the sun had risen, he imagined that people could change their clocks to coincide with sunrise throughout the seasons.

In 1543, Nicolaus Copernicus challenged the conventional theory that the Earth is the center of the universe. He defied Church law and common sense of the day and claimed that the Earth rotates around the sun. History is filled with such intellectual adventurers, those who transcended norms to see relationships beyond the obvious, to find meaning outside of cultural norms, and to imagine perspectives beyond the present:

- W. E. B. DuBois argued against mainstream thinking about African Americans' place in society. Although most politicians, educators, and civic leaders walked a moderate line, assuming that black people in the United States could thrive in subservient positions, DuBois imagined that African Americans should act as leaders for national and global change.

- Psychologist Carl Jung broke away from his colleague Sigmund Freud (and the conventional wisdom of the psychological community) to argue that human unconscious is, in part, a collective rather than an individual phenomenon.

- Georgia O'Keeffe transcended artistic conventions by focusing on the organic. While art and popular culture were increasingly transfixed on the abstract, O'Keeffe sought out the most pure and basic forms of identity in images such as flowers and landscapes.

Radical thinkers have changed how laws, government, and institutional policy work. People such as Thomas Jefferson, Mahatma Gandhi, Eleanor Roosevelt, Martin Luther King Jr., and Martin Luther articulated ideas and policies that were beyond conventional thinking of their times.

In academic study and everyday life, methods often evolve because real people transcend the common sense of their fields; that is, they imagine the possibilities beyond what is assumed. The people who are able to think beyond *what is* and to conjure images of *what could be* are those who most often provide direction for improvement in the quality of daily work and daily life. As you explore this chapter, remember that all those people who have helped bring about change are those who first had to imagine a reality beyond the status quo.

The chapter readings will provide insight into various strategies. For example, in "Unemployed and Working Hard," Simon Wykoff transcends conventional thinking about the homeless. As you read, look for how Wykoff and the other writers provide carefully selected details to help readers see through common thinking and imagine the topic differently. After reading the essays, you can find a topic in one of two ways—go to the Point of Contact section to find a topic from everyday life, or choose one of the Ideas for Writing following the essays. After finding a subject, go to the Analysis section to begin developing your thoughts.

Celibate Passion
Kathleen Norris

In the following essay, Kathleen Norris, a writer and oblate in the Benedictine Order, offers an alternative vision of celibacy. Norris is author of various books and poems including *Dakota: A Spiritual Geography.* "Celibate Passion" was published in *The Christian Century* (1996).

Celibacy is a field day for ideologues. Conservative Catholics tend to speak of celibacy as if it were an idealized, angelic state, while feminist theologians such as Uta Ranke-Heinemann say, angrily, that celibate hatred of sex is hatred of women. That celibacy constitutes the hatred of sex seems to be a given in popular mythology, and we need only look at newspaper accounts of sex abuse by priests to see evidence of celibacy that isn't working. One could well assume that this is celibacy, impure and simple. And this is unfortunate, because celibacy practiced rightly is not at all a hatred of sex; in fact it has the potential to address the troubling sexual idolatry of our culture.

One benefit of the nearly ten years that I've been affiliated with the Benedictines as an oblate, or associate, has been the development of deep friendships with celibate men and women. This has led me to ponder celibacy that works, practiced by people who are fully aware of themselves as sexual beings but who express their sexuality in a celibate way. That is, they manage to sublimate their sexual energies toward another purpose than sexual intercourse and procreation. Are they perverse, their lives necessarily stunted? Cultural prejudice would say yes, but I have my doubts. I've seen too many wise old monks and nuns whose celibate practice has allowed them to incarnate hospitality in the deepest sense. In them, the constraints of celibacy have somehow been transformed into an openness. They exude a sense of freedom.

The younger celibates are more edgy. Still contending mightily with what one friend calls "the raging orchestra of my hormones," they are more obviously struggling to contain their desire for intimacy and physical touch within the bounds of celibacy. Often they find their loneliness intensified by the incomprehension of others. In a culture that denies the value of their striving, they are made to feel like fools, or worse.

Americans are remarkably tone-deaf when it comes to the expression of sexuality. The sexual formation that many of us receive is like the refrain of an old Fugs song: "Why do ya like boobs a lot—ya gotta like boobs a lot." The jiggle of tits and ass, penis and pectorals assaults us everywhere—billboards, magazines, television, movies. Orgasm becomes just another goal; we undress for success. It's no wonder that in all this powerful noise, the quiet tones of celibacy are lost.

But celibate people have taught me that celibacy, practiced rightly, does indeed have something valuable to say to the rest of us. Specifically, they have helped me better appreciate both the nature of friendship and what it means to be married. They have also helped me recognize that celibacy, like monogamy, is not a matter of the will disdaining and conquering the desires of the flesh, but a discipline requiring what many people think of as undesirable, if not impossible—a conscious form of sublimation. Like many people who came into adulthood during the sexually permissive 1960s, I've tended to equate sublimation with repression. But my celibate friends have made me see the light; accepting sublimation as a normal part of adulthood makes me more realistic about human sexual capacities and expression. It helps me better respect the bonds and boundaries of marriage.

Any marriage has times of separation, ill health, or just plain crankiness in which sexual intercourse is ill advised. And it is precisely the skills of celibate friendship—fostering intimacy through letters, conversation, performing mundane tasks together (thus rendering them pleasurable), savoring the holy simplicity of a shared meal or a walk together at dusk—that help a marriage survive the rough spots. When you can't make love physically, you figure out other ways to do it.

The celibate impulse in monasticism runs deep and has an interfaith dimension. It is the Dalai Lama who has said, "If you're a monk, you're celibate. If you're not celibate, you're not a monk." Monastic people are celibate for a very practical reason: The kind of community life to which they aspire can't be sustained if people are pairing off. Even in churches in which the clergy are often married—Episcopal and Russian Orthodox, for example—their monks and nuns are celibate. And while monastic novices may be carried along for a time on the swells of communal spirit, when that blissful period inevitably comes to an end the loneliness is profound. One gregarious monk in his early 30s told me that just as he thought he'd settled into the monastery, he woke up in a panic one morning, wondering if he'd wake up lonely for the rest of his life.

Another monk I know regards celibacy as the expression of an essential human loneliness, a perspective that helps him as a hospital chaplain when he is called upon to minister to the dying. I knew him when he was still resisting his celibate call. The resistance usually came out as anger directed toward his abbot and community, more rarely as misogyny. I was fascinated to observe the process by which he came to accept the sacrifices that a celibate, monastic life requires. He's easier to be with now; he's a better friend.

This is not irony so much as grace: In learning to be faithful to his vow of celibacy, the monk developed his talent for relationship. It's a common story. I've seen the demands of Benedictine hospitality—the requirement that all visitors be received as Christ—convert shy young men who fear women into monks who can enjoy their company.

Celibates tend to value friendship very highly. And my friendships with celibate men, both gay and straight, give me some hope that men and women don't live in alternate universes. In 1990s America, this sometimes feels like a countercultural perspective. Male celibacy, in particular, can become radically countercultural insofar as it rejects the consumerist model of sexuality that reduces a woman to the sum of her parts. I have never had a monk friend make an insinuating remark along the lines of "You have beautiful eyes" (or legs, breasts, knees, elbows, nostrils), the kind of remark women grow accustomed to deflecting. A monk is supposed to give up the idea of possessing anything, including women.

Ideally, in giving up the sexual pursuit of women (whether as demons or as idealized vessels of purity) the male celibate learns to relate to them as human beings. That many fail to do so, that the power structures of the Catholic Church all but dictate failure in this regard, comes as no surprise. What is a surprise is what happens when it works. For when men have truly given up the idea of possessing women, a healing thing occurs. I once met a woman in a monastery guest house who had come there because she was pulling herself together after being raped, and she needed to feel safe around men again. I've seen young monks astonish an obese and homely college student by listening to her with as much interest and respect as to her conventionally pretty roommate. On my 40th birthday, as I happily blew out four candles on a cupcake ("one for each decade," a monk in his 20s cheerfully proclaimed), I realized that I could enjoy growing old with these guys.

As celibacy takes hold in a person, as monastic values supersede the values of the culture outside the monastery, celibates become people who can radically affect those of us out "in the world," if only because they've learned how to listen without possessiveness, without imposing themselves. In talking to someone who is practicing celibacy well, we may sense that we're being listened to in a refreshingly deep way. And this is the purpose of celibacy, not to attain some impossibly cerebral goal mistakenly conceived as "holiness," but to make oneself available to others, body and soul. Celibacy, simply put, is a form of ministry—not an achievement one can put on a résumé but a subtle form of service. In theological terms, one dedicates one's sexuality to God through Jesus Christ, a concept and a terminology I find extremely hard to grasp. All I can do is catch a glimpse of people who are doing it, incarnating celibacy in a mysterious, pleasing, and gracious way.

The attractiveness of the celibate is that he or she can make us feel appreciated, enlarged, no matter who we are. I have two nun friends who invariably have this effect on me, no matter what the circumstances of our lives on those occasions when we meet. The thoughtful way in which they converse, listening and responding with complete attention, is a marvel. And when I first met a man I'll call Tom, I wrote in my notebook, "Such tenderness in a man . . . and a surprising, gentle, kindly grasp of who I am."

I realized that I had found a remarkable friend. I was also aware that Tom and I were fast approaching the rocky shoals of infatuation—a man and a woman, both decidedly heterosexual, responding to each other in unmistakably sexual ways. We laughed a lot; we had playful conversations as well as serious ones; we took delight in each other. At times we were alarmingly responsive to one another, and it was all too easy to fantasize about expressing that responsiveness in physical ways.

The danger was real but not insurmountable; I sensed that if our infatuation were to develop into love, that is, to ground itself in grace rather than utility, our respect for each other's commitments—his to celibacy, mine to monogamy—would make the boundaries of behavior very clear. We had few regrets, and yet for both of us there was an underlying sadness, the pain of something incomplete. Suddenly, the difference between celibate friendship and celibate passion had become a reality; at times the pain was excruciating.

Tom and I each faced a crisis the year we met—his mother died, I suffered a disastrous betrayal—and it was the intensity of those unexpected, unwelcome experiences that helped me to understand that in the realm of the sacred, what seems incomplete or unattainable may be abundance after all. Human relationships are by their nature incomplete—after 21 years my husband remains a mystery to me, and I to him, and that is as it should be. Only hope allows us to know and enjoy the depth of our intimacy.

Appreciating Tom's presence in my life as a miraculous, unmerited gift helped me to place our relationship in its proper, religious context, and also to understand why it was that when I'd seek him out to pray with me, I'd always leave feeling so much better than when I came. This was celibacy at its best—a man's sexual energies so devoted to the care of others that a few words could lift me out of despair, give me the strength to reclaim my life. Celibate love was at the heart of it, although I can't fully comprehend the mystery of why this should be so. Celibate passion—elusive, tensile, holy.

WRITING STRATEGIES

1. Write down a thesis statement for "Celibate Passion."

2. Explain Norris's strategy for helping readers understand and accept the thesis. What support strategies (from pages 254–260 in Chapter 8: Making Arguments) are especially helpful, and why?

3. Focus on Norris's use of personal testimony. Identify one especially important passage of personal testimony, and explain how it helps readers understand Norris's radical point.

4. What does Norris mean by "celibate passion"? How does she make this concept clear to readers?

5. Describe Norris's voice as a writer, and provide several excerpts from her essay to support your description.

EXPLORING IDEAS

1. What does Norris mean by "celibates become people who can radically affect those of us out 'in the world'"?

2. What might readers have the most trouble understanding about Norris's argument, and why? What assumptions, values, or beliefs might make Norris's argument difficult for some people to understand?

3. Based on Norris's essay, what is the purpose of celibacy? How does being celibate achieve this purpose?

IDEAS FOR WRITING

1. What, like celibacy, can you argue is a subtle form of service?

2. How has a close connection to something (a group, a cause, a goal) helped you to understand an idea in a different way than most people?

If responding to one of these ideas, go to the Analysis section of this chapter to begin developing ideas for your essay.

Build the Wall
Ed Bell

In "Build the Wall," Ed Bell takes an idea—that if we're going to build a wall, we should *build a wall*—and runs with it. While some Americans are for building a wall on the U.S./Mexico border (and enjoy chanting "Build the Wall, Build the Wall") others, for various reasons, are against it. Bell looks at the issue differently, proposing that a more radical way of thinking about a border wall would not just keep undocumented immigrants (referred to by some as "unauthorized immigrants," "illegal immigrants," "illegal aliens," or "illegals") out of the country. It would be the Nation's and one of the world's greatest tourist attractions and money makers.

The Great Wall of China attracts over 10 million tourists a year ("World's Most Visited Tourist Attractions"), along with all the money those tourists spend getting there, being there, and going back home. After the September 11, 2001 attacks on the World Trade Center and Pentagon, President George W. Bush told the traveling public in a speech at O'Hare International Airport, "Get on board. Do your business around the country. Fly and enjoy America's great destination spots. Get down to Disney World in Florida. Take your families and enjoy life, the way we want it to be enjoyed."

Obviously, consumerism is important to the American economy. Even though we talk about bringing back the old-time mining and manufacturing jobs, they might because of technology and American wages be gone for good. CEOs, shareholders, and the consumers themselves demand that products be manufactured outside the country. Anyway, according to the documentary *The Century of the Self*, way back in 1928 President Hoover, an engineer, announced to an influential group of advertisers and public relations men, "You have taken over the job of creating desire and have transformed people into constantly moving happiness machines. Machines which have become the key to economic progress" (Curtis). The United States still produces some things. But it is mostly a service and information economy. And its citizens are largely customers/consumers.

When Donald Trump won the 2016 presidential election, one of his most popular appeals was to build a wall along the entire American-Mexican border. This drew chants of BUILD THE WALL, BUILD THE WALL. In his speech announcing his candidacy, Trump said, "I will build a great, great wall on our southern border, and I will make Mexico pay for that wall. Mark my words" ("Donald Trump Transcript"). Later he said it would be "a real wall. Not a toy wall like we have now" ("Donald Trump Emphasizes").

A February 2016 *Washington Post* article focused on Trump's inconsistent remarks about the actual height of the wall. And in response to critics' comments about his wall, Trump himself enjoyed saying, "The wall just got higher" (Bump). I think common sense says it's not likely a 2,000-mile-long wall would be one height the entire distance or that anyone could accurately

---

state the entire length's height at the start of the project. The terrain would be uneven, and the building material, style, and height could change along the way, I would think.

Without pinpointing how, Trump said he would make Mexico pay for it. After the crowd finished chanting BUILD THE WALL, Trump's next line was, "And who's going to pay for it?" And in unison, thousands of Americans would shout, "MEXICO!" (Bump). The pundits reveled in this debate. Google *Who will pay for the wall?* and you can read for days about how much the wall might cost and how it *might*—but probably *won't*—be paid for. All this debate is small-minded though. If done correctly, the wall will pay for itself.

As soon as Trump was elected, we heard that he might not intend to build the wall. During the campaign he said he would, if elected, try to put Hillary Clinton in prison; then two weeks after his election, in a meeting with *The New York Times* he said:

> [H]e was no longer interested in pursuing Mrs. Clinton, in part because he wanted to heal the wounds of a divisive campaign. "I don't want to hurt the Clintons, I really don't," Mr. Trump said during the interview. "She went through a lot and suffered greatly in many different ways, and I am not looking to hurt them at all. The campaign was vicious." (Davis and Shear)

So, did he think the same way about the wall? Some news outlets said he had downgraded the plan to a fence. And some said his supporters might not be too upset about this because while they took Trump's promises *seriously*, they did not take them *literally*. But what if Trump's promise about building the wall wasn't just serious? What if it was literal too? And what if his thinking was radical?

What is a wall?

Some walls are thin. You can punch a hole through them. Other walls are thicker. Then there's the Great Wall of China that people walk along eight or ten people wide. Does Trump mean to build a thirty-foot wall that's a couple feet wide? Or would the wall be two walls with a walkway, or a roadway, in between? And why would the height be the same all the way across? In places the wall could be a pit, the dug-out earth used to create other parts of the wall that rise up twenty, fifty, or a hundred feet high in nearby stretches.

According to *The Times of India*,

> The [Great Wall of China] spanned mountainous terrain, conforming to the territory's numerous peaks and valleys. Some stretches have watch-towers placed at regular intervals along the top of the wall with space for soldiers to march. At its most impressive, it measured at least 7.6 metres [about 25 feet] in height and up to 9 metres [about 30 feet] in width. These dimensions varied greatly at other points. ("What Is")

Of course the Great Wall of China is wider at the bottom than at the top. And, it's really more like two walls, the area inside filled with rocks and dirt. So, why not make the Trump wall even wider and fill it with stores, restaurants, and casinos? Anything else would be thinking small and, some might say, a waste of a good wall building.

The Great Wall of China had watch-towers and enough space for the guards to march along it. Trump's wall could have that too, but with more width for driving, riding, and walking and more towers for watching, dining, gambling, and anything else a good entrepreneur can imagine. What about an eight-lane highway, at least in parts, with biking and hiking lanes with picnic and pet areas, and on each side of the wall a fenced-off No-Man's land. Like ranch land in the Western U.S., travelers can drive through this area but must stay on the road. If it sounds like things are getting complicated, they're not really. A simple wall won't work, but a Really Great Wall with a fence around it will.

People will get married at the wall. They will run, Forrest Gump–like, from one end to the other—some to raise money for their favorite cause. They will bike it, the nice weather along the border making this possible year-round.

Like the annual bike ride across Iowa, the Appalachian Trail, or our nation's longest highways, travelers will want to bike or hike or drive the length of the wall. And one industry to emerge will be helping travelers do that. There will be bus tours, motorcycle rentals, and perhaps a high-speed train—and perhaps an old-fashioned low-speed one too. You can see the Great Wall of China from space, some say, so as space tourism develops, people will go there in part to view the Great Wall of Trump—if he builds it big enough.

But won't all of this just facilitate more illegal, or undocumented, immigration? Won't undocumented immigrants still tunnel under, climb up, or rappel down the wall? No. The wall will stimulate so much business that people will flock to it—not over it and beyond. The steepest part of the wall will become a great tourist attraction. People will want to see the highest part of the wall. They will pay to climb it and to rappel back down or jump off—bungee, hang-glider, or wingsuit style. Because of the hot dry landscape and rising columns of hot air called *thermals*, hang-gliding records have been set from Zapata, Texas, with gliders taking off from the border and gliding more than 400 miles north (Choi).

And other parts of the wall will have their own appeal. Communities along the border will no longer regret their location as a dangerous crossing point for undocumented immigrants and drug traffickers. Just as the canals, railroads, and interstate highways built thriving communities out of desolation, the Great American-Mexican Wall will immediately and for a long time after draw people and money to small border towns and cities. The existing towns will thrive, and new ones will emerge. The land along the border will become financially valuable beyond anything its owners currently imagine.

Is this what they want to happen to their land? And will it happen to everyone's borderland? They didn't vote for Trump because there were any guarantees or because these problems are easy to solve. Some old-timers may long for the way things were. And not everyone will prosper at first. But that's just the *fittest-survive* style capitalism Trump supporters value. In time, any creative, ambitious entrepreneur can get rich.

The Great Wall will offer variety. People will have to spend money to get there, to eat there, to sleep there, to drink there. This will create jobs at the wall and many miles away—in the U.S., Mexico, Canada, China. People will want to spend the night, in a plush hotel or a rustic campground. The tours will have themes, and Americans and Mexicans and Germans and Japanese will look forward to taking different tours, one tour making them want to experience another. A new band starting out, a new idea for sunglasses, a new way to ride a bicycle, a new mixed breed of dog—the Wall will be the place to market these new creations. The Wall will compete hard and fast with the Grand Canyon, New York City, and Las Vegas. Tourists will buy tee-shirts that say *What Happens at the Wall Stays at the Wall*. Of course BUILD THE WALL has a metaphorical meaning too, which troubles many.

Metaphorically it means to not let some people into the country and to remove others who are already here. And that is an important issue—more important probably than building a literal wall. But on some level, perhaps building a wall like the one discussed here can do more than talking about (and trying to build) metaphorical bridges. President Trump will probably not deport 11 million undocumented immigrants. He might deport 10,000 (or 100,000) and then advertise this so visually and repeatedly that it seems like he's deported millions. And based on that, along with making undocumented immigrants uncomfortable (by not providing them with healthcare, education, or jobs for example), many may, as Mitt Romney and Donald Trump have both suggested, self-deport. What difference that will make, if it happens, we will see.

The Great Wall of China exists, and tourists from around the world flock to it. The U.S. is talking about building a wall along its border with Mexico. If serious, this wall could draw crowds and create revenue. Certainly, if construction of a really great wall begins, some people will want to see it. So they will drive or fly, and they'll want to enjoy themselves (spend money) when they get there. If the problem is keeping undocumented immigrants out of the country, they can work at the wall. And the Mexican side just might do better than the American side, all things being equal.

This raises another point: If consumerism is important to the economy (of the U.S. *and* of Mexico); if our national leaders want to build a wall; if the U.S. expects Mexico to pay for it; and if this wall could be one of the largest tourist attractions, job creators, and money-makers in the history of the world, then why doesn't Mexico build the wall itself, a few miles south of the border, in its own sunny climate with its own money and investors, keeping all the profit for itself?

Works Cited

Bump, Philip. "Donald Trump's Mexico Border Wall Will be as High as 55 Feet, According to Donald Trump." *The Washington Post*, 26 Feb. 2016, www.washingtonpost.com/news/the-fix/wp/2016/02/26/so-how-high-will-donald-trumps-wall-be-an-investigation.

Bush, George W. "At O'Hare, President Says 'Get on Board.'" United States, White House, Office of the Press Secretary, 27 Sept. 2001, georgewbush-whitehouse.archives.gov/news/releases/2001/09/20010927-1.html.

Choi, Charles Q. "Hang Glider Aims to Break Long-Distance Flight Record." *Live Science*, 19 June 2016, www.livescience.com/55117-hang-glider-attempts-record-breaking-flight.html.

Curtis, Adam. "The Century of the Self (Full Documentary)." *YouTube*, uploaded by David Lessig, 9 July 2015, youtu.be/eJ3RzGoQC4s.

Davis, Julie Hirschfeld, and Michael D. Shear. "Donald Trump Drops Threat of New Hillary Clinton Investigation." *The New York Times*, 22 Nov. 2016, nyti.ms/2mCBWnY.

"Donald Trump Emphasizes Plans to Build 'Real' Wall at Mexico Border." *CBC News*, 19 Aug. 2015, www.cbc.ca/news/world/donald-trump-emphasizes-plans-to-build-real-wall-at-mexico-border-1.3196807.

"Donald Trump Transcript: 'Our Country Needs a Truly Great Leader.'" *Washington Wire*, Wall Street Journal, 16 June 2015, blogs.wsj.com/washwire/2015/06/16/donald-trump-transcript-our-country-needs-a-truly-great-leader.

"What Is the Length and Width of the Great Wall of China." *The Times of India*, 28 Nov. 2004, timesofindia.indiatimes.com/home/sunday-times/What-is-the-length-and-width-of-the-Great-Wall-of-China/articleshow/938685.cms.

"World's Most Visited Tourist Attractions: No. 26 Great Wall of China." *Travel and Leisure*, www.travelandleisure.com/slideshows/worlds-most-visited-tourist-attractions/27. Accessed 28 Nov. 2016.

WRITING STRATEGIES

1. How does Bell transcend, or go beyond, the common way of thinking about the U.S./Mexico border?

2. How does Bell build a bridge to readers who might resist his thinking?

3. How would you describe Bell's writer's voice? Provide a couple specific passages to illustrate your description. Why is or isn't Bell's voice appropriate for this essay's content?

4. How does the essay anticipate and respond to the idea that the wall would just encourage more illegal immigration? What evidence from the essay most persuasively counterargues this point?

5. Explain Bell's line of reasoning. In other words, how does he develop a series of connected premises that lead to a specific claim?

EXPLORING IDEAS

1. How convincing is Bell that the wall will pay for itself? Explain.

2. How realistic is Bell's proposal? Why is or isn't it a real possibility?

3. How effectively do you think a wall like the one Bell proposes would compete for tourist dollars with the Grand Canyon, New York City, or Las Vegas? Explain.

4. What does Bell mean when he says building a wall might do more than building a metaphorical bridge?

IDEAS FOR WRITING

1. Focus on a current political issue, but avoid taking the usual positions. Instead, try thinking beyond the common statements and beliefs.

2. How else might we think about the U.S./Mexico border? Other than a wall, what is possible?

STUDENT ESSAY

Unemployed and Working Hard
Simon Wykoff

Radical thinkers help others reimagine conventional ways of thinking. In the following essay, written for his first-year writing class, Simon Wykoff provides carefully selected details from an average day to help others reimagine the common stereotype of the "lazy bum." Using personal testimony and a few outside sources, Wykoff flips the stereotype upside down.

A common stereotype in today's society is that of the lazy bum. People see a homeless man on the side of the road, waiting for handouts, and assume that's all he ever does. In reality, this couldn't be further from the truth. As the painter Willem de Kooning once said, "The trouble with being poor is that it takes up all of your time" (qtd. in "Willem de Kooning Quotes"). This is absolutely true, and I think you'll find that homeless people are incredibly busy doing the most important job to all of us: surviving.

The essay begins with a common stereotype.

The essay pivots quickly to an alternate way of thinking

According to a fact sheet available from the National Coalition for the Homeless, the best approximation of the total number of homeless people comes from a study done by the National Law Center on Homelessness and Poverty, which states that roughly 3.5 million people in the United States will experience homelessness every year ("How Many"). For most of my childhood, my father was one of these many homeless people. While growing up, I spent a large amount of my time living on the streets with him. I can tell you from my experiences that the process he went through every day in order to find food and shelter was one of the roughest "jobs" I have ever seen.

Personal testimony as support.

Before I begin, something you need to understand is that my father did not make use of services like shelters during his many years of homelessness. His opinion, which I have seen held by many other homeless people, was that these services were usually crowded, of poor quality, and often more dangerous than simply living on the streets. While this did make life more difficult in some ways, he (and I) felt it kept him safer in the end.

From Wykoff, Simon, "Unemployed, and Working Hard." Reprinted with permission.

Begins explaining his father's daily activities—as an example that supports the main claim.

The first thing my father did upon waking up was check his belongings. Depending on the place he was sleeping, there was a good chance that something could have been stolen from him in the middle of the night. It was not uncommon for him to find the clothes in his backpack gone, or to discover that he was missing money he had stashed away.

After checking through his items, he would look over the money he had remaining from his efforts on the previous day. If he had enough, he would buy himself breakfast, usually at one of the cheaper coffee shops around town. If he had no money, he went to the dumpsters behind several bakeries in the town to fish out the four-day-old bread they had thrown away. If the bread wasn't moldy, it was his morning meal.

Details—such as "dumpsters behind several bakeries," "four-day-old bread," and "moldy"—help bring the description to life.

Once he had some food in his belly, he usually tried to locate a current paper. This often meant waiting around in coffee shops until someone left one on the table after their breakfast. Sometimes this step could take him hours, but he was determined not to waste the precious money on a newspaper when he could get it for free with patience.

His father is looking for work.

As soon as he had the paper, he thumbed through it, looking for jobs he could feasibly apply to. Due to his particular circumstances, he was without official identification. This, of course, made the search much more difficult. If he found something, he would tear off the piece of the paper and store it to refer to later.

I should interject here and explain how he got around the city. While my father was homeless, he was lucky enough to have a bicycle, which he treasured beyond everything else. It's not uncommon in a larger city to have the place you get food, the place you sleep, and the place you go to try and earn money be miles and miles apart. Because of this, even on a bike my father spent a considerable amount of time traveling. He would often ride from one end of the city to the other several times a day. This takes an incredible amount of endurance, especially when you are doing it on an empty stomach, as he often was. Many times, just a trip from the place he was sleeping to the closest bakery in the morning was a marathon!

Another good detail: a paragraph about a bicycle.

The next thing he did after looking for job opportunities was to get money in order to buy food for the rest of the day. While you may see many homeless panhandling, I think people don't realize that a large number of homeless actually do small-time work for their daily bread. As mentioned in an online editorial, the homeless these days are increasingly working menial tasks for extra cash, or just to survive (Hilton). For all the people you see standing outside

Clarifying a possible misconception: not all homeless panhandle.

John Metz

of stores with signs, others are playing instruments on street corners, gathering cans for recycling, or washing windows.

My father fell into the category of musicians. To make money, he sat in a high-traffic area and played his pennywhistle for the people passing by. He didn't heckle pedestrians, or openly beg. He didn't even display a sign. He was simply a man on the street with an upturned hat in front of him, playing Irish jigs.

After a few hours of tiring playing, my father went off to buy his lunch and dinner for the day. He had no place to store food, like a refrigerator, so he was forced to buy items that wouldn't perish. His diet was made up largely of things like chips, bread, and vegetables that could be eaten raw. This was hardly an ideal diet, but he managed nonetheless.

"Tiring playing": His father is working hard.

After he finished his lunch, my father went looking for things he could sell or use himself. The best way for him to do this was dumpster diving. He would go to the areas of town where the richer college students lived, and wade through the communal dumpsters for things like VCRs or microwaves that could be carried to nearby stores and

Another example of working hard.

Another *task*.

sold. This was often difficult work, as he had to strap any large items to the back of his bicycle and ride with them for some time.

Once he finished searching through the dumpsters, he went on to his next task, applying for any jobs he had found in the paper. This was difficult, as most of the places he could apply to were on the edges of town, away from the college districts. He would ride all the way across town to submit his barren résumé, only to have it rejected.

Finally, as his arduous day neared an end, my father looked for a place to sleep at night. This was not always easy, and he had to switch locations fairly often. If he didn't, he would begin to raise the suspicions of the property owner, or become a target for the more dangerous people on the streets.

The writer draws a conclusion for the reader, based on the evidence provided in the previous paragraphs.

As you can see, my father's day was far from that simplistic stereotype of the bum who sits on street corners all day and waits for people to help him out. What people don't seem to realize is that to survive on the streets, you have to take things into your own hands. You need to have perseverance, stamina, and a little bit of luck. Though it may seem outlandish, I think you'll find that many homeless people work just as much, or more, than you.

Works Cited

Hilton, Dan G. "Designer Java for a Regular Joe." *Homeless Man Speaks*, 2 Nov. 2006, homelessmanspeaks.com/facts-arguments-nov-2-2006/.

"How Many People Experience Homelessness?" *National Coalition for the Homeless*, July 2009, www.nationalhomeless.org/factsheets/How_Many.html.

"Willem de Kooning Quotes." *The Quotations Page*, www.quotationspage.com/quotes/Willem_de_Kooning/. Accessed 14 Nov. 2016.

WRITING STRATEGIES

1. How is the essay a response to conventional thinking?

2. What is the essay's thesis?

3. Choose one paragraph from the essay and explain why it is especially effective in helping readers reimagine the homeless.

4. Identify several details and explain how they help bring Wykoff's narrative to life.

5. Describe how the essay is organized. What other organizational strategy might Wykoff have used?

EXPLORING IDEAS

1. What important qualities does Wykoff's father have? What other qualities might be important to surviving as a homeless person?

2. What skills are most important for the survival of someone who isn't homeless?

3. With a group of peers, explore Wykoff's closing sentence: "Though it may seem outlandish, I think you'll find that many homeless people work just as much, or more, than you." Does that seem outlandish? Do group members agree with Wykoff's statement?

IDEAS FOR WRITING

1. What common stereotype couldn't be further from the truth?

2. What don't people realize?

If responding to one of these ideas, go to the Analysis section of this chapter to begin developing ideas for your essay.

Outside Reading

Read a *New York Times* article online, along with its Readers' Comments. (Not all articles have Readers' Comments.) Find one comment that you think illustrates radical thinking and respond to the following:

1. What is the main claim (or thesis) of the comment? Is the main claim stated or implied?

2. In what way(s) does the comment transcend or challenge conventional thinking?

   Which of the support strategies discussed in Chapter 8: Making Arguments—example, allusion, personal testimony, scenario, statistic, authority, facts, appeal to logic, emotion, character, need, or value—help readers understand and accept the main claim and how?

   (See the Rhetorical Tools section of Chapter 8 for help understanding support strategies.)

3. How does the comment engage opposition: Does it respond directly to any points in the article or to any other reader comments? Does it make any counterarguments or concede any points?

4. Describe the writer's voice and why it might be inviting or alienating to readers.

5. Write your own Readers' Comment in response to the article or more specifically in response to the comment you found radical.

INVENTION

"Uncertainty can be a guiding light."

—U2

On the one hand, the focus of this chapter may seem rather abstract; we are, after all, attempting to imagine new intellectual ground. On the other hand, these ideas can have their beginnings in familiar, everyday terrain. Although the goal may be to extend thinking beyond familiar ideas, we can still start with everyday life.

For this chapter, nothing is more important than the act of invention. As in previous chapters, the writer should attempt to discover something interesting or valuable—or even bizarre. Unlike in previous chapters, the goal is to escape conventional thinking and imagine something outside of common intellectual activity. The following sections are designed to help you through this process—specifically, to discover a topic (in Point of Contact), to develop particular points about the topic (in Analysis), to make it relevant to a community of readers (in Public Resonance), to invent a focused position (in Thesis), and to develop support (in Rhetorical Tools). Use the Invention questions in each section to explore further.

Point of Contact

The prompts in this section are designed to generate possible writing topics. Fill in the blanks with as many possibilities as you can until you find an engaging topic, imagining possibilities within and beyond your experiences.

Imagining New Connections Radical thinkers see connections not normally seen: an important connection between the economy and nature, oceans and people, music and politics, and so on. Imagine various possibilities, and fill in the blanks in the following statements:

Most people do not see the connection between _____ and _____.

Even though it is not apparent, _____ and _____ are deeply connected.

Imagining Different Possibilities The policies and procedures of society often blind us to alternatives. Imagining those alternatives might reveal a new way to live. For example, someone might imagine something even better than democracy, or a new way to fund college, or an alternative to war. Fill in the blanks with possible ideas:

Presently, most people _____, but they could _____.

Presently, the law requires that people must _____, but the law could state that _____.

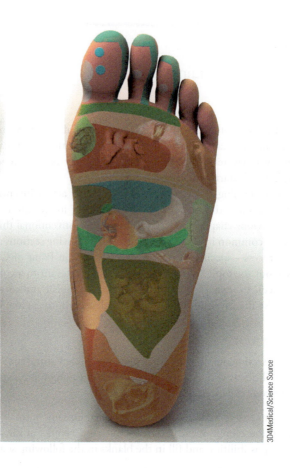

3D4Medical/Science Source

Questioning Common Sense Living in a society means participating in common practices and beliefs. But a common belief is not always the best belief. Imagine possibilities for the following and fill in the blanks:

Most people in my community want _____ without examining the underlying meaning.

I have always been taught to think _____ but now see a different way.

Exploring the Past and Future A radical vision sees beyond the confines of the present. A radical thinker might imagine what the world would be like if the American Revolution had not occurred, or how work in the United States will be defined in fifty years. As you imagine time beyond the present, fill in the blanks for the following:

In the past, people's perspective of _____ was fundamentally different from our present understanding.

In the future, people will probably understand _____ differently than we do.

Going to the Root The term *radical* comes from the Latin *radix,* which means *root* or *source.* Radical thinking might be seen as a process of finding the root or essence. For example, someone might explore the essence of womanhood or manhood, the true meaning of growing old, or the essence of education. Fill in the blanks in the following questions:

What is the essence of _____?

What is the most fundamental quality of _____?

ACTIVITY

In a small group, use the categories in this section to ask more questions. After generating more questions, try to create more categories, and then create several questions for each new category. Do not stop generating questions until everyone participating has encountered a potential topic.

Analysis

The intellectual activity in this chapter involves *theory*—reasoning that is divorced from practical or physical particulars. When people theorize, they explore the realm of ideas and assumptions and make generalized claims. For example, when Sigmund Freud theorized about the nature of the unconscious, he was not making guesses about his own mind, but that of the *human* mind. He theorized that psychological ailments emerge from childhood crises. His theory, like all theories, could be applied to particular situations; he used the general notion to help cure problems within specific patients.

Everyone has theories (general accounts or concepts that inform how we receive ideas and act on the world), but theories are usually not discussed openly. They most often lie undetected in our minds. For instance, people may have a theory about knowledge acquisition; that is, they may have a general account of how people come to know things. This theory may be fairly complicated and may involve memory, experience, and language use—but rarely do people examine such theories closely and ask hard questions: *How does language acquisition relate to knowledge acquisition?* Doing theory, then, is the act of examining and developing our concepts. As you can imagine, theorists take little for granted. They are not willing to accept the answers they have been given, but rather look around them and imagine what other answers may be possible.

ACTIVITY

Doing theory requires a degree of intellectual play, as well as some deliberate and constructive probing. With several peers, choose one of the following topics:

- The difference between men and women
- When a child becomes an adult
- The relationship between individual and community
- The relationship between humans and nature

Each participant should explain his or her theory about the topic in one minute—or one paragraph if using e-mail or instant messaging. After each participant has a turn, start again. Everyone should take another turn and build upon or speak back to particular points made in the previous round. After the second round, start again. After several rounds, each participant should write a brief paragraph explaining how the theory session changed, developed, confirmed, expanded, or highlighted his or her ideas.

Now, *theorize* about your topic: Explore freely, beyond prior assumptions or quick answers. Ponder your topic for as long as possible before coming to any conclusions. Keep a notepad with you for a day or for several days while you rethink your ideas. Record even the most offbeat or seemingly irrelevant notions. The following questions will help you make connections and discover meaning:

> What is the basic or essential quality of the topic?
> How does the topic affect or influence thinking?
> How does conventional thought or practice keep people from a radical perspective on this topic?
> What is the origin of the topic?
> What do people normally not consider about the topic?

Use these questions to begin a process of exploration that you will continue through writing. For example, Linda, a business major, has chosen to explore the *essence of business*. In a discussion with peers, she begins to explore the topic:

What is the Basic or Essential Quality of the Topic?

LINDA: Well, I wonder if this topic can even be thought about radically, but let's try it: I think the basic quality of business is competition.

MARCUS: Competition with other people?

LINDA: Yes . . . I think so. Other people or companies—or even countries.

MARCUS: For that matter, what about towns and communities?

LINDA: Yeah, I guess so. Towns and communities do compete for customers, for market, for tourism dollars.

DIANA: So are all these people and communities competing for money?

LINDA: Ultimately, yes. But at first, they are competing for more customers or clients.

MARCUS: So . . . is it always about more customers? More money?

LINDA: Well, I'd think so. Certainly, for retail stores, the daily goal is getting more people through the doors and to the cash register than the store across the street.

DIANA: What if we looked at it like the companies are living organisms? I just saw something about bears on the Discovery Channel: Every summer and fall, before hibernation, the bears try to consume as much food as possible. But they also need to conserve their strength. They don't want to exert a lot of energy while trying to eat all this food. The ultimate goal isn't the amount of food. It's survival. The bears are competing for food, like salmon, but the essence of their competing is survival.

LINDA: So . . . back to business . . . companies are not necessarily competing for just money; they're competing for survival, for life.

MARCUS: That makes a lot of sense. Surviving in business involves making a lot of money (more than others), but it also involves conserving. Think about it: Companies that are out just to make a lot of money go down quickly because they didn't conserve.

The important moment here is Diana's brave reference to the Discovery Channel. Although bears and business have little in common, Diana is thinking about the essence of things—how entities stay alive. Her inventive connection makes the group rethink the essence of business. And now Linda's thoughts on the essence of business are beginning to take flight. She is going beyond the quick, easy response and exploring some hidden dynamics of business. If she continues developing these ideas, she could transcend conventional wisdom and make valuable discoveries.

Thinking Further

Everyday language is filled with sayings that suggest indisputable truths. Widely used yet unexamined, these sayings, sometimes called *clichés,* conceal more truth than they communicate. They might even misguide our thinking. Consider the following: *What doesn't hurt you only makes you stronger. Bigger is better. Back to the basics. Boys will be boys.* Such clichés might get in the way of exploring your own topic, but they can also mark the exact spot where radical thinking is most needed. The following questions may help you explore beyond conventional thinking:

> Can you think of any clichés related to your topic?

> How do they limit thinking?

> Might the opposite of the cliché be true?

ACTIVITY

In a small group, share topic ideas. Then list the common sayings, assertions, and opinions related to each topic. Capture all the conventional wisdom associated with each topic. What do people normally think, feel, and say about each? What are the common opinions, complaints, and hopes? The goal is to give each writer a clear sense of the conventional so that he or she can think beyond it.

In his invention writing about the future, Ed Bell explores building a border wall:

What do people normally not consider about the topic?

They don't consider what else a wall can be or do. They think a wall is a wall. There's a wall already in places along the border. I've never seen it. But it sounds like a privacy wall between two houses—something like that but bigger. Just a wall to keep people on their own side. But the Great Wall of China is a different kind of wall. Photos show crowds of tourists walking along it as far as you can see. It's crowded. People flock to it. It's a tourist *attraction*. So, that's ironic, or something. We all know that wall functions that way, but we don't consider that for this situation. The economically successful places are scenic; they tend to be in warm, sunny places; they rely on tourists. Think Las Vegas, Los Angeles, Miami .... Anyway, people consider a wall is just a wall, a simple wall, that keeps people out. What they don't consider is that a wall can be like a mall or have malls (stores) inside it—an economic attraction. Why couldn't it? Why wouldn't it? We all know if you build it they will come. (Cliche?) If you build a really great wall, will it simply keep people out. (Most people seem to think it won't.) Or, will it be a place—like the Great Wall of China—that people want to see and walk along and spend money at? And so, can you think about it that way?

Bell's Invention writing is explorative. His ideas are not final or definite at this point. Instead, he is exploring possibilities. After exploring and discovering the ideas above, he forces himself to think—and write—about other Invention questions, and through this writing, which builds on his previous discoveries, he uncovers additional less-obvious thinking:

How does conventional thought or practice keep people from a radical perspective on this topic?

Well, the argument is the U.S. needs a wall to keep people out, and that this wall would just be a wall and nothing else. So, the conventional thought is 1) it's just a wall and nothing else and 2) you have to get someone else to pay for it. I haven't heard anyone say, "Hey! Let's hurry up and build that wall before someone else does—because, we could build a really big, cool wall that would draw people to it, for fun and entertainment and who knows what else." Instead, the conventional thought is, we don't want a wall, and we're certainly not going to pay for it. The U.S. might regret it if Mexico started building it a few miles south of the border, because it'd be their wall and their tourist attraction, job creator, and money maker. You might end up having a race to build the wall. Or, some cooperation or collaboration in building it.

Public Resonance

In one sense, your topic may already have public resonance. Because you are theorizing (exploring general ideas rather than particular situations), your topic may easily connect to others. However, radical thinking runs the risk of alienating others. When writers transcend conventional wisdom, they must invite others into the new vision, which is no small task (consider Galileo's fate!). Use the following questions to help connect your ideas to readers' concerns:

> What is conventional thought on the topic?

> What nonconventional claims have been made about the topic?

> What keeps people from understanding the thing/idea in nonconventional ways?

> How would a new understanding of the topic help people? (Who, particularly, would a new understanding help?)

In his Public Resonance invention writing, Ed Bell uses ideas he has already invented in response to the Analysis questions. Instead of imagining he has already invented these ideas and can't think of anything else, he uses some earlier (Analysis) discoveries as launchpads for even more radical thinking:

What is conventional thought on the topic?
Conventional thought is that a wall is just a wall. So this involves redefining what a wall can be. We have an example. The Great Wall of China. It is a tourist attraction. So, at least on the idea level, it could be interesting to think about building a wall that is the new American/Mexican tourist attraction. It could be state of the art, sweet! Conventional thought is it's just a wall and somebody has to pay for it—not *somebody gets to profit from it.* Which is ironic considering Donald Trump appeals to many because he's a businessman.

Bell's intellectual persistence, curiosity, and playfulness allow him to run with his ideas. The more he writes, the more he comes up with and the more insightful, less-obvious ideas he discovers.

Thesis

A thesis provides focus. Because the ideas for a Thinking Radically essay are potentially abstract and far-reaching, a focused thesis will help keep the text from wandering. Notice how the following thesis statements focus on a particular topic, acknowledge a conventional view, and offer an alternative way of seeing. For example,

> Behind our desire to drive bigger vehicles and own bigger homes lurks more than an attraction to symbols of personal success; it is, rather, a deep hostility toward other people and the environment.

This thesis focuses on a particular topic: the desire to drive bigger vehicles and own bigger homes. It acknowledges a conventional view: This desire is related to one's personal success. And it offers an alternative way of seeing: The desire actually has more to do with one's hostility toward other people and the environment. Consider the focused topic, conventional view, and alternative way of seeing in the following thesis statements:

- Although a glass ceiling may prevent women from climbing the ladder of success, women and men both would have a better quality of life if they participated on the lower rungs only.

- Though *Jeopardy* is often perceived as a test of intelligence, it is really a test of knowledge. A better test of intelligence is *Survivor* or *The Amazing Race,* which requires more analytical thinking skills.

- More gunfights and car crashes actually make a movie duller, not more exciting.

- Because people have come to believe it is the ultimate power, modern medicine has ironically done more harm than good in most people's lives.

- It is commonly thought that the North defeated the South in the Civil War. In fact, the South now controls the American government.

- Even just a cursory look at one's own life will turn up evidence that every American's primary function these days is to consume.

- Although the American school system prepares citizens for employment, it allows (and perhaps encourages) them to be helpless against propaganda.

- Farmers or dogcatchers as politicians would serve the people better than professional politicians do.

- A president who doesn't understand why terrorists might fly planes into buildings is ultimately far more dangerous than the terrorists.

- The poor are better off than the wealthy.

- Had the electric guitar not been invented, the accordion would have continued its reign as the most popular instrument among American youth.

- Although students should feel comfortable in a college classroom, the uneasiness some students feel is necessary to learning.

- All animals, not just humans, should be given the right to life, liberty, and the pursuit of happiness.

- Because of credit and debt, most Americans today are unknowing slaves to the wealthy.

- College professors aren't any smarter than the average Joe.

- Eggs are more valuable than gold.

- Mundane tasks, like weeding a garden or doing the dishes, are a form of meditation that most Americans should indulge in more often and more earnestly.

- The way that Americans communicate with each other is a bigger threat than terrorism.

ACTIVITY

Choose one of the sample thesis statements in this section. Describe how it is or is not radical. Does it transcend or speak back to some particular conventional way of thinking? Does it reveal something usually overlooked or dismissed? How does the wording and construction of the sentence help readers see something new?

Evolution of a Thesis

Do not be in a hurry to solidify your thesis. As you write and think, ideas will evolve, and this *evolution* of ideas is the goal of academic writers. In the previous example, when Linda explored the topic of business, her ideas transformed over time. She started by trying to discover the essence or root of business. In her early discussion with peers (see the Analysis section, pages 411–413), she discovered an alternative way of thinking, as illustrated in the move from the first and second statements. More focused and inventive thinking led her to the final statement.

Linda begins with a widely held understanding of her topic:

- The essence of business is making money.

She develops a position different from conventional thinking:

- Like any organism, the essence of business is survival.

She shapes the idea as she writes:

- Beneath the everyday affairs of making money, the essence of business is survival, which involves consuming and conserving.

Because this chapter invites you beyond your initial opinion, you might be wondering: *Am I supposed to give my opinion, or what?* This is a fair question. A radical statement is an opinion insofar as a single writer is offering a new way to see a topic. But it is more than a personal opinion. It is a writer's attempt at rethinking something, and an invitation to others to rethink.

Although you may begin your exploration with an opinion, your thinking will evolve. When a writer provides support for an opinion, the opinion becomes a claim. By supporting a claim, the writer is now making an argument, not just expressing an opinion or saying what he or she thinks.

REVISING YOUR THESIS

How do you know that your opinion is speaking back to conventional views? How do you know that you've gone far enough in your thinking? To answer these questions, you might enlist the help of others in reevaluating your thesis. In a small group, present your topic. Have the group members describe all the conventional opinions they can imagine. Then present your thesis and explain why you think it responds to or transcends conventional thinking. The group should then ask:

- Does the thesis uncover something new?

- Does it offer a new way of seeing the topic?

- If not, what is holding it back?

Rhetorical Tools

It will take various rhetorical tools to help readers understand and possibly accept an entirely new vision. In addition to the ones mentioned here, consider the strategies discussed in other chapters, particularly Chapter 8: Making Arguments.

Using Narration

Narration draws readers into a set of events. A narrative or story can help writers illustrate a broader point; when making adventurous claims, a narrative can help bridge the gap between conventional and radical ideas. Throughout his essay, Simon Wykoff uses narration to help readers understand his broader point about how hard some homeless people work:

> Once he had some food in his belly, he usually tried to locate a current paper. This often meant waiting around in coffee shops until someone left one on the table after their breakfast. Sometimes this step could take him hours, but he was determined not to waste the precious money on a newspaper when he could get it for free with patience.

> As soon as he had the paper, he thumbed through it, looking for jobs he could feasibly apply to. Due to his particular circumstances, he was without official identification. This, of course, made the search much more difficult. If he found something, he would tear off the piece of the paper and store it to refer to later.

Using Description

Writers making adventurous or radical claims must consider the intellectual positions of their audience. Because readers may have no mental pictures of the ideas being put forth, it is up to the writer to sufficiently describe or characterize ideas. Notice Bell's description, which helps readers to see evidence of his claims:

> The Great Wall will offer variety. You'll have to spend money to get there, to eat there, to sleep there, to drink there. This will create jobs at the Wall and many miles away— in the U.S., Mexico, Canada, China. You'll want to spend the night, in a plush hotel or a rustic campground. The tours will have themes, and Americans and Mexicans and Germans and Japanese will look forward to taking different tours, one tour making them want to experience another. A new band starting out, a new idea for sunglasses, a new way to ride a bicycle, a new mixed breed of dog—the Wall will be the place to market these new creations.

Building Intellectual Bridges

Writers who make radical (or new) claims cannot simply dismiss the beliefs of others; they must build an intellectual bridge between conventional thought and new thought. In a sense, this is the primary objective of the writing in this chapter. When making adventurous claims, it is especially important to make these connections, so your ideas have genuine significance and are more than vague abstractions. Simon Wykoff begins and ends his essay with a connection to readers' beliefs:

> A common stereotype in today's society is that of the lazy bum. People see a homeless man on the side of the road, waiting for handouts, and assume that's all he ever does. In reality, this couldn't be farther from the truth. As the painter Willem de Kooning once said, "The trouble with being poor is that it takes up all of your time." This is absolutely true, and I think you'll find that homeless people are incredibly busy doing the most important job to all of us: surviving.

Wykoff immediately speaks to what many people believe: "A common stereotype in today's society. . . ." He helps readers see that stereotype: "People see a homeless man on the side of the road, waiting for handouts, and assume that's all he ever does." Then he offers an alternate way of thinking: "I think you'll find that homeless people are incredibly busy doing the most important job to all of us: surviving." The details throughout the essay help readers understand and accept an alternate viewpoint to the common stereotype. Then in his conclusion, Wykoff makes an explicit connection between this alternative and others' beliefs:

> As you can see, my father's day was far from that simplistic stereotype of the bum who sits on street corners all day and waits for people to help him out. What people don't seem to realize is that to survive on the streets, you have to take things into your own hands. You need to have perseverance, stamina, and a little bit of luck. Though it may seem outlandish, I think you'll find that many homeless people work just as much, or more, than you.

Counterarguments and Concessions

Especially when their claims are unconventional, writers must anticipate and account for positions opposed to their own. Counterarguments anticipate and refute opposing positions while concessions acknowledge their value. In one sense, a Thinking Radically essay, or any essay that makes an argument, is like one big counterargument to a more conventional way of thinking. Notice how Wykoff frames his entire essay as a counterargument, or response, to another position:

> A common stereotype in today's society is that of the lazy bum. People see a homeless man on the side of the road, waiting for handouts, and assume that's all he ever does. In reality, this couldn't be further from the truth. . . .

Bell's overall essay, too, is a counterargument to another position. And, within his overall counterargument, he directly takes on a particular counterargument:

> But won't all of this just facilitate more illegal immigration? Won't illegals still tunnel under, climb up, or rappel down the Wall? No. The Wall will stimulate so much business that people will flock to it—not over it and beyond. The steepest part of the wall will become a great tourist attraction. People will want to see the highest part of the wall. They will pay to climb it and to rappel back down or jump off—bungee, hang-glider, or wingsuit style. Because of the hot dry landscape and rising columns of hot air called *thermals*, hang-gliding records have been set from Zapata, Texas, with gliders taking off from the border and gliding more than 400 miles north (Choi).

Outside Sources

Radical or adventurous claims do not exist in a vacuum; they exist alongside other similar claims and discoveries. While Wykoff develops his argument primarily through a personal narrative about his father, notice how he reinforces this position with an outside source:

> The next thing he did after looking for job opportunities was to get money in order to buy food for the rest of the day. While you may see many homeless panhandling, I think people don't realize that a large number of homeless actually do small-time work for their daily bread. As mentioned in an online editorial, the homeless these days are increasingly working menial tasks for extra cash, or just to survive (Hilton). For all the people you see standing outside of stores with signs, others are playing instruments on street corners, gathering cans for recycling, or washing windows.

RESEARCH VERSUS MESEARCH

Finding outside sources that confirm our positions and support our worldviews is usually easy. But such work, what we might call *mesearch,* misses the spirit and goal of *research,* which is to explore beyond our own initial suppositions, to read and rethink topics. Researching can be an inventive process—one that catapults us beyond initial ideas.

AVOID:

- Collecting statistics without questioning them, reflecting on them, and evaluating their significance.

- Limiting your exploration to sources that share your opinion or perspective.

- Merely "proving" your position with others' words.

TRY:

- Gathering perspectives from a variety of sources.

- Closely examining writers who oppose your perspective or who see the world differently.

- Directly addressing the unstated assumptions and values in the sources. Try to discover what the writers value, hope for, or dismiss. What is their basic view of the world, and how does that influence their approach to the topic?

Revision

Because you are asking readers to resee an idea so completely, you must first participate in that reseeing by revising carefully. Before exchanging drafts with another writer, revisit the Invention Questions in the Analysis and Public Resonance sections to see how they might help you write an even more focused, more revealing thesis. Then revisit the Rhetorical Tools section to see how else you might help readers understand and accept your thesis.

Peer Review

Exchange drafts with at least one other writer. First underline the thesis or write it at the top of your essay. This way, reviewers will get traction as they read.

As a reviewer, use the following questions to guide your response:

1. Does the thesis offer a new way of thinking about the topic? Why or why not?

2. In what sense does this essay transcend or speak back to conventional thinking?

3. Where is the writing most descriptive and specific? Where could the writer be more specific? Remember that it is easy, but less valuable, to remain entirely abstract and general. If the writer makes a general statement (about business, students, women, and

so on), it must be exemplified. As a reader, you should come away from the essay with some specific image or impression imprinted on your thoughts. Have you?

4. Where does the writer use appeals to logic? Can you follow the line of reasoning? If not, at what point does it break down? (See the discussion of logos in Chapter 8: Making Arguments, page 256.)

5. Play devil's advocate for a moment: What points seem entirely ungrounded or unreasonable? Why? What could the writer do to make the point more reasonable?

6. Suggest specific points that the writer should concede or qualify. For instance, the writer's position might seem too extreme; the claims might include too many people or include a large, diverse group without making any distinctions. Point out such claims, and help the writer to see the need to acknowledge subtlety, complexity, and exceptions.

7. Does the writer do anything unconventional or especially engaging with the organization? Is the introduction especially intense? The conclusion? Where does the writer seem to rely on old standard strategies?

8. Consider the writer's voice:

   a. Describe how it engages you with the ideas. Do any passages seem unengaging? Why?

   b. Describe the level of formality. Is it appropriate for the topic, the writer's approach, the assignment?

9. What is the most engaging passage in the draft so far? Why?

10. Check for sentence vitality:

    a. Offer a strategy for a stylistic fragment.

    b. Consider other strategies from Chapter 19: Vitalizing Sentences.

       • If you encounter any noun clusters, suggest a revision of the sentence.

       • When possible, change nouns (such as in *make a decision*) to verbs *(decide)*.

       • Circle any unnecessary modifiers (*very, really, certainly*, and so on).

       • Where can the writer avoid drawing attention to *I* and *you?*

       • Where can the writer change linking verbs to active verbs?

       • Point to expletives (such as *there are* and *it is*).

       • Help the writer change passive verbs to active verbs for more vitality.

QUESTIONS FOR RESEARCH

If the writer used outside sources:

- Where must he or she include in-text citations? (See pages 478–479 and 496–498.)

- Are quotations blended smoothly into the argument and punctuated correctly? (See pages 467–476.)

- Where could more direct textual cues or transitions help readers? (See pages 476–478.)

- Is the Works Cited or References page formatted properly? (See Chapter 16: Integrating and Documenting Sources.)

Reflection

Now that you have challenged conventional thinking and explored new possibilities, step back and analyze your essay's rhetoric. As you respond to the following questions, write well, crafting complete sentences and supporting your claims:

1. How does your essay transcend the intellectual norm and reveal a new pattern of thinking?

2. How did you use rhetoric to discover and develop a new way of thinking through your response to a particular invention question in this chapter?

3. What particular support strategy (or rhetorical tool) was most important in helping readers understand the essay's main idea?

4. Why is your writer's voice effective for this particular essay? Describe your voice, and refer to several sentences from your essay as examples.

5. How did you use grammatical and sentence-level strategies to intensify your points?

Beyond the Essay: Visual Essay/Collage/Poster

Conventional thinking gets challenged in different ways. We have all seen posters, photographs, videos, movies, letters, speeches, and even bumper stickers that question conventional thinking and offer alternatives. Now that you've written an essay that challenges a conventional way of thinking, combine several images (as the collage in Figure 13.1 does) to create a visual essay that challenges common thinking.

1. On paper or on a computer, select and arrange images and words that make the point of your Thinking Radically essay. Consider including your collage as part of your essay.

2. In several paragraphs, explain how the different images of your collage combine to put forth a unified main claim about the topic.

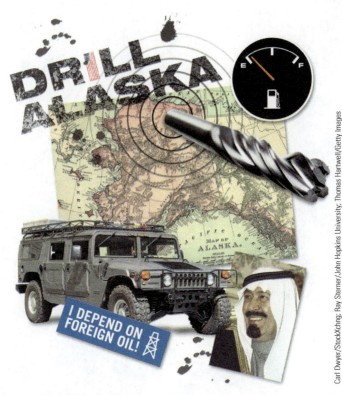

Figure 13.1 A visual collage

14 Finding Sources

Chapter Objectives
This chapter will help you to:

- Use online catalogs and databases to find a range of secondary sources.
- Conduct focused and formal interviews related to your writing topics.
- Conduct focused surveys related to your writing topics.

USING CATALOGS AND DATABASES

When writing instructors refer to sources, they most often mean nonfiction published works such as books and periodicals (journals, magazines, and newspapers), government documents, and reference texts, as well as audio recordings, video recordings, and digital texts like blogs and e-mails. In short, a source is anything that has been written, reported, recorded, or performed—everything from a blog to a formal academic study. In many ways, the process of finding, reading, and analyzing sources is a process of invention. It involves not simply gathering information but also engaging the theories, assumptions, perspectives, and outright arguments of others. For this reason, researchers should not see themselves as *finding and consuming information* but rather *building ideas* with the help of (many) others.

Online Catalogs

Almost universally, libraries use online catalogs for their book and government document collections. A few simple moves can streamline the search process: Adding words narrows a search, while using fewer words broadens the scope. For instance, "economics" by itself tells the catalog to find any and all works with "economics" in the title or description. (At Northwestern Michigan College, this search yielded 1,387 works.) "Economics and consumers" narrows the search (and yielded nine works—a much more reasonable number to browse).

Most catalogs give search options: *an author search, a title search, a subject search,* or *a keyword search.* Author and title searches are appropriate only if you are seeking out a particular source or author by name. Subject searches, which are organized by common headings such as *agriculture, government,* or *gender,* may be valuable for early stages of research—before writers have begun narrowing their insights. Keyword searches are most helpful after you have generated a list of possible words and phrases related to your topic.

Periodical Databases

Newspapers and magazines most often have their own websites. But researchers can rely on electronic databases such as Academic Search Elite, JSTOR, or Academic One File to navigate through the millions of available articles. Like online catalogs, periodical databases give a range of search options: author, title, subject, keyword. Adding words to a search tends to narrow the focus (and limit the number of returns). For example, the keyword search for "weight" on one database produced 804 entries. Narrowing the search by typing "weight and body" produced only 146 entries. Thus, if you are seeking sources about weight and the body, "weight and body" would narrow the results to more relevant sources.

Database searches can be made more efficient by using the following words (called *Boolean operators*):

- Using *and* between words narrows a search by finding documents containing multiple words—*weight and body.*

- Using *or* between words broadens a search by finding documents with either word in a multiword search—*weight or body.*

- Using *and not* between words finds documents excluding the word or phrase following "and not"—*weight and not body* (that is, *weight* only, without any references to *body*).

- Using *near* between words finds documents containing both words or phrases that are near, but not necessarily next to, each other—*weight near body.*

Also, remember that a simple keyword search can turn up thousands of returns. Narrowing one's focus by typing "weight and body and media," for example, will eliminate irrelevant returns found by typing just "weight."

Sources themselves can also lead the way to more sources. If an article, for instance, seems particularly helpful or in tune with your claims, examine its works cited or references list. Chances are, the author has already made some connections or used sources that are directly relevant to your topic and position.

In the old days of walking through library stacks and looking for a particular book, researchers would invariably scan adjacent titles—and often find a number of similar sources. That still happens today! People *still* find important sources in print form. Also, many databases and online catalogs have added tools that connect researchers to related material. For example, after a researcher has clicked on a source, the database may give a list of related search words or subjects. In other words, the database may "know" what you want. (Databases are smart—and getting smarter.) In Figure 14.1, the database offers a link, in the left margin, that connects users to similar sources. Once you have found a key article, this "SmartText" feature connects you to sources that are often directly related.

Figure 14.1 Periodical database of the kind you might find at your school's library

WHERE ARE WE? THE WEB OR A DATABASE?

Periodical databases are not necessarily on the web. They are their own special island. Although they are accessible via an Internet service, they are not websites. Databases such as Academic Search Elite function like resource centers. They collect and categorize articles—most of which have been published in print prior to being uploaded in the electronic format. In other words, database administrators and editors have already done significant work for you. They have compiled sources, created abstracts, and uploaded them into searchable categories and sub-categories. And some have even created the formal citations (MLA, APA, Chicago, and so on) for each source. Such databases are usually not open to everyone on the Internet. They are for subscribers only—or for students who attend a school that has paid the subscription fee.

ACTIVITIES

1. In a periodical database, try several keyword approaches for each of the following questions: In what ways might organized sports harm the young children who participate in them? What is the impact on the environment of people relocating to western states? What novel written in the last half of the 20th century has been most influential?

2. List the different types of sponsors for websites that you found. For example, did you find government-sponsored websites? Websites created and maintained by businesses? Individuals? Nonprofit organizations?

CONDUCTING INTERVIEWS

At a basic level, interviewing involves gathering information from a single person. But it can mean a great deal more. Good interviewers seek to engage interviewees in intensive conversations. They probe for knowledge and ideas, but they also allow interviewees to explore and develop ideas. A good interview, like a good essay, goes beyond basic knowledge; it provides insight.

Asking the Right Questions

Good interview questions create focus, yet allow interviewees to explore. Although they may seek out specific information (data, facts, dates), interview questions should go beyond collecting basic knowledge. (In fact, asking interviewees basic information that can be retrieved through print sources undermines the interview process.) A more valuable strategy is to prompt interviewees to reflect on the meaning of issues or to make connections between ideas. Notice the difference between the following:

What's it like being a doctor?

How has working in the medical field influenced your personal life?

The first question does not focus attention; the interviewee could talk about anything related to the profession. The second question, however, invites the interviewee to consider a particular relationship. It is more specific than the first question but still calls for a certain degree of exploration.

Effective questions can come from thorough planning, but good interviewers also depart from their scripted questions when they see an opportunity to further engage the interviewee. Following up on an interviewee's answers, in fact, is the interviewer's most powerful research tool. Although a survey can only ask a list of preformulated questions, an interview can follow a line of thought that comes from an interviewee's response. Imagine the following scenario, in which a researcher is interviewing a civil engineer:

INTERVIEWER: Is being a civil engineer interesting?
ENGINEER: Sure. I get to deal with all kinds of people and very real situations.
INTERVIEWER: Is being a civil engineer hard?
ENGINEER: Well, some of the work can be difficult. Trying to figure in all the variables in a given project can be a mathematical nightmare.
INTERVIEWER: What would you tell someone who wants to become a civil engineer?

Here, the interviewer comes up short in several ways. First, the questions are mundane. As worded here, such questions would probably not yield focused and insightful answers; they prompt the engineer to respond in general terms. They are surface questions (the kind one might ask at a party), which yield short and uncomplicated answers. Also, the interviewer ignores opportunities to follow up. After the engineer's first responses, the interviewer could have asked about the "very real situations" or the "mathematical nightmare" but leaves both ideas and, instead, moves to the next question. This interview does not probe for insight or engage the thoughts of the interviewee, but merely poses a list of unrelated questions.

The following example shows a different approach. Here, the interviewer starts with a more insightful question. Rather than rely on a vague quality (whether civil engineering might be "interesting"), the interviewer asks about a potential relationship (between civil engineers and society) and consequently receives an insightful response. Also, the interviewer in the following scenario springboards from the engineer's answers, thereby extending the initial thoughts:

INTERVIEWER: How is a civil engineer important to society?

ENGINEER: Well, civil engineers conceptualize living space for the public. They envision what it might be like to live in particular place, say, a downtown area, and then lay out plans to make a park, an intersection, even an entire downtown livable—and they do it all while considering how an area will grow and how people's needs may change.

INTERVIEWER: So civil engineers have to be visionaries?

ENGINEER: Yes! They are not simply figuring formulas about buildings and zones and land; they are imagining what it might be like to live and work within a given area in the present and future.

INTERVIEWER: And they do all this while accommodating the demands of city officials?

Integrating Interviews into Your Writing

Ideas from an interview can be incorporated into various writing situations and purposes. An interview can be used to support claims made in argument, to help explain an idea, or even to help explain the history or significance of some topic. In the following example, notice how the information helps support an idea:

> Most often the water sewers can withstand the runoff from storms, but the past season has illustrated the inadequacy of the current sewer system. According to Harold Johnston, director of utilities, the sewer system was overwhelmed twice in the past three and a half months, and the result was that untreated sewage flowed out into Silver Lake. When an overflow occurs and untreated water spills into the natural water system, the high amounts of bacteria affect the wildlife and jeopardize the health of swimmers and water enthusiasts. In essence, anyone or anything in the lake for days after an overflow is swimming in sewage.

Here, the writer is trying to persuade readers that the water treatment system in her town is inadequate. The claim made by the director of utilities supports the idea. Although the writer probably collected extensive information about the treatment system, she used only one particular point in this paragraph because it directly supports the main idea. (Other information might be used in different passages.)

Planning an Interview

When setting up an interview, be sure to respect the interviewee's position and accommodate his or her schedule. Researchers should never impose themselves on potential interviewees. Use the following hints and strategies:

- Always request an interview well in advance of your own deadlines.

- When making a request, introduce yourself and the reason for the interview: Explain the nature of your research and how the interview will be integrated.

- Beforehand, negotiate a reasonable amount of time for the interview (such as thirty minutes)—and stick to it so as not to impinge on the interviewee's time.

- Plan out the method of recording responses—writing, audiotaping, or videotaping. Ask the interviewee if his or her answers can be recorded, and if his or her name can be used in the research.

- At the end of the interview, thank the interviewee for his or her time, and leave promptly.

FIELD RESEARCH

Interviews are one type of field research, which is often referred to as *primary* research because the researcher interacts directly with the subject(s) and is engaged in the activities and behavior of the thing being studied. Other kinds of field research include experiments, observations, and surveys.

CREATING SURVEYS

Although an interview is based on an individual's knowledge, a survey attempts to find public opinion on a topic. An interview is driven, in part, by the interviewee; his or her insights may influence the direction or emphasis of the interview. But with surveys, the researcher prearranges the direction and emphasis with carefully formulated questions.

Generating Questions

In generating survey questions, a researcher should consider three points:

1. Questions should not lead the respondent to an answer. Good survey questions avoid influencing the respondents' thinking about the issue. For instance, a question that asks *Is our current president completely out of touch with public opinion?* leads the respondent toward a negative evaluation of the president. Such questions prompt respondents to take up a certain position even before answering. A better approach is to state the question without leading the respondent, such as: *Is the current president in touch with labor issues in the United States?*

2. Questions should narrow the focus of the respondents on a specific topic. Although good survey questions should not influence the respondents' thinking on an issue, questions should create a particular focus. For instance, a question that asks *Has the president taken an appropriate stance on international trade?* is more focused than *Do you like our current president?*

3. Questions should use common or unspecialized language. Because survey respondents may come from different walks of life, survey questions should avoid technical jargon or specialized terminology.

Choosing Respondents

Surveyors must consider the demographics (or characteristics) of their potential respondents:

What is the age range in the respondent group?

What is the racial makeup of the respondent group?

What is the gender makeup of the respondent group?

What is the occupational makeup of the respondent group?

What is the geographical origin of the respondent group?

People's occupations, gender, ethnicity, age, and geography impact their understanding of the world—and how they are likely to respond to an issue. For instance, imagine a survey about college life: If all the respondents are college instructors, the answers will probably reflect certain biases and assumptions—which may be entirely different from those of students or people not associated with college life.

Recording and Using Responses

Responses can be recorded in various ways. Perhaps the easiest means is to elicit written responses by asking the respondents to write or check off their answers. But if that is not possible, the researcher must do the recording by writing or taping. (If you plan to record answers, either with video or audio equipment, you must always ask the respondents' permission.)

Survey responses are most often used to show public opinion about a topic or to illustrate common trends in everyday life. For example, a writer researching work issues among students at her college might discover important trends. She could use information from the survey to enhance the significance, or the public resonance, of her topic. In the following passage, she sets up the idea in her first sentence and then plugs in the information from the survey:

> Although many students take a full course load, they also work late on weeknights and throughout the weekends. In an informal survey, 24 of 35 respondents reported that they work at least 25 hours each week—and 21 of those 35 work over 30 hours each week. One student explained her situation bluntly: "No one told me that a full load of classes would compete with my work schedule. I thought I could do both, but it's nearly impossible."

The sample survey that follows offers room for the respondents to write in answers and to develop their thoughts. You could imagine someone responding to this survey fairly quickly because the questions are limited in number and fairly simple. Although it could offer some valuable insights about working hours, it is also limited in its scope, like all surveys. Because this survey does not ask for personal information from the respondents (age, sex, education, etc.), the researcher should be careful not to make broad statements about salary and job satisfaction in the United States, but to stay focused on the amount of time people dedicate to their jobs.

SAMPLE SURVEY: WORKING HOURS

Please respond to the following questions. Use the back of the page if you need more space.

1. Do you currently hold a full-time or part-time job? If so, what is the nature of the work?

2. If you work part time, how many hours per week?

3. How many hours per week are you contracted to work? (Or how many hours per week are you supposed to work, according to the job description?)

4. How many hours per week do you normally work (at or away from the job site)? Do you work on weekends?

5. How much time do you spend preparing for and/or traveling to and from work? (Feel free to give specifics.)

6. Is overtime mandatory or voluntary at your job? (What kinds of incentive are offered for overtime?)

7. Do you feel sufficiently compensated for the work you do? Why or why not?

15 Analyzing, Synthesizing, and Evaluating Sources

Chapter Objectives

This chapter will help you to:

- Analyze sources for content and context.
- Understand differences among common source types.
- Synthesize a range of sources in your writing.
- Evaluate sources for relevance, reliability, credibility, timeliness, and diversity.

DEVELOPING CRITICAL LITERACY

In the age of digital information, researchers must make constant decisions about the nature and use of sources. They must decide how a Wikipedia entry, for instance, may differ from a journal article or a historic document. They must *analyze* the intended audience of sources, *evaluate* sources according to standard criteria, and *synthesize* sometimes contradictory voices. The process can be dizzying. Researchers must develop the ability to sift through the mountains of opinions, reports, images, theories, and data—and to make sound judgments about the nature of all that information. Scholars and teachers across the disciplines often refer to this ability as *critical literacy*.

"Just the Facts, Please"—Or Maybe Not

In a world saturated with information (news reports, breaking news reports, blogs, tweets, documentaries, and talk shows for every political persuasion), people sometimes long for simple facts. They want to read or hear something without an overt opinion attached to it. But this can be a naïve and even dangerous hope. Facts are tricky. They can *appear* unbiased, but they often emerge from a particular worldview, from a specific way of interpreting a situation. For instance, consider the following two reports about the same event:

A. Today in Milford, rush hour traffic was slowed when over two thousand protesters gathered around the town square to challenge a new city ordinance that will allow Pemblebrook Industries to open another facility in the city limits. The new facility will bring thirty to forty new jobs into Milford. Construction is to begin by early fall.

B. Today in Milford, over two thousand people gathered downtown in a peaceful protest against a new city ordinance that will change zoning of the Stark's wetland area. The ordinance, passed in an unpublicized overnight council meeting, was celebrated by Pemblebrook Industries, which hopes to drain and pave the wetland to make way for a new bottling facility.

Both passages report facts, and the facts themselves may seem unbiased. However, the selection of facts in each portrays a particular slant on the situation. In passage A, the situation itself is framed by traffic. In passage B, the situation is framed by the cause of the protest. In A, we learn about new jobs but do not learn about the destruction of wetlands. In B, we learn about an overnight meeting but not the jobs. Each report invites us to see the Milford protest in a particular light. If these passages were published in a newspaper, the headlines might read:

Headlines for A:	**Headlines for B:**
New Bottling Facility Coming to Town	Backroom Deal Dooms Stark's Wetlands
Forty New Jobs for Milfordians	Quiet Zoning Change Concerns Milford Citizens
City Council Paves the Way for New Facility	Public Outrage at Overnight Rezoning
Outraged Environmentalists Hit the Streets	The End of Milford's Wetlands

These headlines seem factual—like they are beyond opinion. But they all select and emphasize a single dimension of the situation. And that selection supports a way of valuing, devaluing, supporting, or ignoring a set of concerns. Both selections, both sets of headlines, are biased *and* factual.

Collectively held opinions can also parade around as facts. When an entire community (or civilization) believes something without question—as every community does—the idea functions as a fact. Here are some commonplace beliefs that were, at one time, considered facts:

- Women cannot make rational decisions but can only mimic the decision-making process of men.

- If she doesn't drown, she's a witch.

- People of African descent are naturally prone to criminality.

- People of Mediterranean descent are naturally more passionate than northern Europeans and Asians.

- We can determine personality traits by feeling the shape of an individual's skull.

- The Earth is flat.

- Mental disorders are caused by an unacknowledged sin.

- Bleeding supports good health.

- Jews are the root cause of economic hardship in Europe.

- The Iraqi government was involved in the 9/11 attacks.

Of course, most people in the United States now look on these beliefs as terribly sexist, racist, tragic, or just wrongheaded. But at given points in the past, these were collectively asserted as uncontested truths. In some cases, they were taken for granted.

"Numbers Don't Lie"—Or Do They?

Sometimes we can be convinced that numbers are beyond opinion—that they simply represent a truth about the world. Again, this is a dangerous assumption. Numbers, like any text or symbol system, can be used for a range of purposes. We should see statistics as argumentative statements based on various assumptions and variables. As readers, we rarely have access to the assumptions and variables. Most often, about 78 percent of the time, we see only the conclusion—only the number. We are not invited to understand the research situation or the reasoning behind the numbers. For this reason, statistics can be more difficult to evaluate than a well-developed argument.

Of course, plenty of statistics are generated in a careful and sound manner, but many are produced under questionable circumstances or through flawed procedures. If the procedure is flawed, then the numerical conclusions are flawed—and they can distort the reality and urge people to accept ideas that simply are not true. The following flaws or misuses occur frequently, and they may even support some popular claims about medicine, health, and politics:

- Biased sampling

- Data dredging

- Data manipulation

- Discarding of unfavorable data

- Misapplication

- Overgeneralization

When we see statistics in an argument (or used as evidence to support an argumentative statement), we should think through the reasoning. Without a sound line of reasoning, an argument does not benefit from all the statistics in the world. In the following passage, the numbers might distract us from the logical fallacies (such as *begging the question* and *non sequitur*):

> According to the Learning Styles Institute, three out of five students are visual learners. That means 60 percent of all students learn best from pictures and charts. Therefore, teachers should use more visuals. If teachers use more visuals, students will get better grades and perform better on standardized tests.

The percentage has a kind of automatic persuasive power to it. But the overall line of reasoning is fraught with logical problems. The Learning Styles Institute provides nothing in this passage that explains how it defines *visual learner*. Does the study show how a person responds consistently—over weeks, months, years, or decades—to the same stimuli? If not, how can the Learning Styles Institute justify the label? Furthermore, we don't know what *learning* means in this situation. Does it mean consuming and remembering the content of a picture? Does it mean developing increasingly sophisticated insights? We simply do not know. And the answer would certainly change how we accept the argument. Furthermore, we don't know the demographics of the sample. Who was involved in the 60 percent? Were there 10, 100, 1,000 students? Were they tested under a variety of situations, seasons, times of day? The problem with statistics in this case is clear: They can eclipse critical questions and prompt uncritical readers to be persuaded by flawed reasoning. Like a fancy paint job on a bad car, they can keep us from looking under the hood—or even starting the engine.

SUMMARIZING AND ANALYZING SOURCES

Research requires an understanding of the content and context of sources. We should try to understand not only what is being said (content) but also who is being addressed and where the conversation takes place (context). Every source—from book to article to blog—exists in a context of other voices and assertions. And if we don't understand that broader conversation, deciphering a source can be like walking into a dark cave and hearing nothing but weird echoes. For more on analyzing written texts, see Chapter 6: Analyzing Written Texts.

Content

To understand the content of a source, we must understand the source on its own terms. In the same way that a good traveler enters another country and tunes into its sensibilities, good researchers tune into their sources' sensibilities. For instance, we cannot hope that a sophisticated essay will loudly announce its main idea or give a bullet list of solutions. Academic essays simply do not behave like breaking news updates.

Each type of source has unique purposes and functions. A newspaper article, for instance, updates readers on a current event; an academic essay walks carefully through a focused and sophisticated idea; a blog expresses the opinions or experiences of an individual; a scholarly book takes on the assumptions or collective knowledge of a discipline. Obviously, such generalizations do not hold true for every source, but we gain more insight when we can shift our own readerly expectations according to the specific text in front of us. An academic essay, for instance, might build slowly to the main idea. A newspaper article may announce the main idea in the first passage or the headline. In a book, the main idea may come at the end of the introduction—after the author has explained a range of other opinions. If we know such patterns (and don't expect an essay to function like a report), we'll likely understand far more.

A key strategy for understanding content is summarizing the source—reading and then explaining the main idea as accurately as possible. This can be a challenge. We should avoid skimming the surface and blurring away a source's specific insight. For instance, notice how the first statement in the following examples vaguely characterizes John Steinbeck's essay (from Chapter 3) while the second statement gives a more focused characterization of his *insight*.

> **Blurred Summary:** In "Americans and the Land," John Steinbeck describes early Americans' treatment of the land.

> **Focused Summary:** In "Americans and the Land," John Steinbeck describes the American settlers' disdain for the frontier and their "childlike" aggression, which destroyed the early forests, extinguished species, and diminished the continent's fertility.

This section introduces summary as a strategy for better understanding a source. Chapter 16: Integrating and Documenting Sources (pages 467–470) goes further and explains how to use summary inside of a research essay. In other words, this chapter introduces summary as a tool for understanding content, and Chapter 16 explains summary as a tool for integrating others' ideas into your own work.

Context

To understand context, we should consider two aspects of a source: audience and publication cycle. *Audience* refers to the intended readership—to the particular people inclined to read, study, or purchase the source. Are they from an academic discipline? Do they know a set of terms and issues that the general population does not? Are they hobbyists? What about their cultural sensibilities? Are they mad at the government or minorities? Do they believe in a god? Are they suspicious of organized religion? Are they older or younger? What is their overall level of literacy? Can they follow a complex line of reasoning for thirty pages? Do they like NASCAR or fine art? Such questions are figured into publication decisions about the source. For instance, *Forbes* magazine, which is pro-corporate and politically conservative, will likely not publish a lengthy treatise against the banking industry, nor will a scholarly journal in chemistry publish an article on how to make a can of soda explode.

As you can probably detect, writers and publishers make an important distinction between academic and popular audiences. Academic readers have different expectations than popular audiences. For instance, a scholar reading *Philosophy of Science* expects a certain level of analytical rigor that will likely be absent in a magazine such as *Newsweek*. And although general distinctions are difficult to maintain for all sources, it may be helpful to understand the following:

Readers of Academic Sources Expect

- Appeals to logic
- Rigorous analyses
- Evidence or theoretical backing for claims
- Formal documentation (such as MLA)

Readers of Popular Sources Often Expect

- Familiar characterizations and descriptions

- Appeals to value and emotion

- References to popular issues, places, and people

Researchers also should consider the publication cycle of their sources. Does the source get updated weekly? Monthly? Every three years? Has it been reprinted from an original publication? If it's an online source, has anyone taken responsibility for updating the information? Have updates attempted to address changes in the issue? Such questions point to the way information is handled—and what is published. Book publishers, for instance, are less apt to print ideas that are bound to fluctuate on a daily, weekly, or monthly basis. Instead, they publish work that will remain relevant through time. If the source does deal with issues that fluctuate (the stock market, important political figures, fashion trends, health care legislation), then researchers should expect sources to monitor those changes and deal with them accordingly. (These issues also correspond to timeliness, one of the criteria for evaluating sources. See page 457.)

ACTIVITY

In a small group, develop a list of imaginary publication failures—instances when the source does not match the audience's expectations. For example:

- An article about lowering one's cholesterol in a punk rock magazine

- A report on best deals among L.A. marijuana distributors published in *Time* magazine

- A lengthy article about shifting epistemological assumptions in literary criticism published in *Sports Illustrated*

UNDERSTANDING COMMON SOURCE TYPES

As more sources move to the Internet, distinctions among them become difficult to detect. But distinctions are crucial to understanding how sources work and what they offer. The following section explains some key features of source types.

Books and e-books

Books and e-books come in a huge variety: fiction (novels, short story collections) and nonfiction (everything else), textbooks (like *The Composition of Everyday Life*) and trade books (everything sold outside of college curricula), and single-authored books and edited collections. One need only browse a bookstore to understand the immense number of subject categories. For academic research, it's important to remember that books generally take years to write, revise, and publish, so they are not the timeliest source of information. People don't value books for their timeliness but for their depth and richness, for their potential to reveal complexity, history, and the subtle nuances within a topic.

Like all sources, books exist in a conversation, but it may take place over years, decades, even centuries. In other words, with a book, the context may be more difficult to detect than with a tweet, blog, or article. The author(s) may be responding to a claim made long ago. Authors and publishers know this, and they have created some tools to help readers get a sense of the context. For instance, on the back cover and inside sleeve of print books, publishers often tell readers about the nature of the broader conversation. They explain how the work responds to a trend, how it engages a problem or debate, and how it contributes something new. In print and e-books, authors (or editors) use the preface and introduction to explain how their work fits into or responds to a tradition.

Periodicals

Periodicals include magazines (for a general audience), journals (for a specialized audience), and newspapers (both local and national). Popular magazines, such as *People* or *Newsweek,* offer information about mainstream news but rarely provide in-depth analysis of issues, and even more rarely deal with issues outside of major social and political topics. However, some magazines support in-depth reporting. *Harper's* magazine and *The New Yorker,* for instance, are well known for publishing incisive articles that go beyond common perspectives. Even entertainment magazines such as *Rolling Stone* often publish lengthy analytical articles on current issues or significant political figures.

Scholarly journals, which are usually specific to one discipline (such as English, engineering, nursing, business, or marketing), offer very detailed analyses and well-developed opinions on an endless range of topics. The writing in academic journals is most often well researched and well documented, so it tends to be more reliable than that of popular magazines. It may also use discipline-specific jargon that could confuse nonexperts.

At first glance, journals and magazines may look alike, but closer inspection will reveal significant differences. Generally, journals are written for academic or highly specialized readers. The articles explain new theories or practices in a field of study (sociology, psychology, nursing, English, chemistry, history, etc.). The goal of academic articles is not necessarily to communicate an opinion but to explain a new idea and thereby help the discipline, as a whole, to evolve. Magazines are written for general readers, who may have an interest (politics, mountain climbing, hunting). If you are not certain what kind of periodical you have, use the following criteria:

Journals

- Seek to advance knowledge in a *field of study*
- Deal with principles, theories, or core practices in an academic discipline

- Are associated with a discipline or field of academic study

- Have few advertisements, which usually appear only at the beginning and end (not between or among articles)

- Have few colors and flashy pictures (unless they are related to a study or article)

Magazines

- Report information/news or offer how-to advice

- Offer the latest technique in a hobby or sport

- May appeal to readers with a particular *interest*

- Have advertisements throughout the pages, even interrupting articles

- Tend to have more colors and pictures

Newspapers

Newspapers are most valuable for highly publicized topics—those that are or have been visible to the public eye: political events, public figures, national or local disasters, and significant cultural events. For this reason, the context of a newspaper article is fairly easy to detect. The headlines alone help readers to understand the issue, the rhetorical or political tension, and the people involved. For instance, we don't have to think much to understand the context of this *New York Times* headline:

> "How Trump Chose His Supreme Court Nominee"

For the most part, newspapers give the latest updates on current issues but refrain from giving lengthy background information. There are exceptions. For instance, *The New York Times* still funds, supports, and features lengthy analyses of political and cultural issues. But generally, newspapers are records of daily or weekly events more than tools of deep exploration.

Although the move to electronic publication has shrunk the number of printed newspapers, researchers still have access to a staggering number of local and national titles, which are increasingly available online, such as the following: *Afro American, American Banker, Amsterdam News, Atlanta Journal-Constitution, Boston Globe, Chicago Tribune, Christian Science Monitor, Denver Post, Detroit News, Houston Chronicle, Los Angeles Sentinel, Los Angeles Times, Muslim Journal, The New York Times, San Francisco Chronicle, St. Louis Post-Dispatch, Times-Picayune [New Orleans], USA Today, Wall Street Journal, Washington Post.*

Government Documents

Government documents include reports, transcripts, pamphlets, articles, speeches, books, maps, and films. State, local, and federal government bodies have accumulated huge amounts of information about everyday life. Government websites may be the best sources for researching general behavioral trends: what we purchase, how we live, how we get sick, how we heal, what we drink, what we eat, how we vote. Although the U.S. government is the nation's largest publisher, state and city governments publish as well. Such documents, which can be of great value in one's research, can be found online with keyword searches or by going directly to the U.S. Government Publishing Office (GPO) website at www .gpo.gov.

Reference Works

Reference works such as encyclopedias and almanacs are sources about sources. In other words, reference works give a general overview about the scholarship on a given topic. They explain what has been thought and said about key issues in a field. Particularly helpful reference works are topic-specific encyclopedias. Consider, for instance, the following titles, which represent a huge number of specialized reference books:

Encyclopedia of Popular Culture

Catholic Encyclopedia

Encyclopedia of Occultism and Parapsychology

Encyclopedia of Literary and Cultural Theory

Encyclopedia of Counseling

Encyclopedia of Chemical Technology

The Encyclopedia of Phobias

The Encyclopedia of Fantasy

Encyclopedia of Popular Music

The Encyclopedia of Quantum Physics

Researchers often consult reference works early in the process—as a way of gathering keywords or concepts that they use for further searches.

Audiovisual Materials

Audiovisual materials include videos, CDs, DVDs, films, photographs, and any type of recording. As organizations and governmental bodies increasingly move to digital storage, researchers can access a growing body of online recordings. For example, the Academy of American Poets offers videos of poets reciting their work; organizations such as Amnesty International offer video reports; and many governmental sites now include recorded speeches and video updates.

SYNTHESIZING SOURCES

As we explained in the previous section, information does not come free of biases and world-views. Information usually comes in the form of theories, arguments, and hypotheses. In other words, research often involves swimming in others' opinions. Good researchers swim well. They understand how to read, question, and accept the ideas around them. Bad researchers grasp at chunks of statistical and factual debris.

It is also important to remember that writers rarely find sources that neatly overlap, or completely agree with, their own positions. In fact, research should not be a process of seeking agreement but rather one of bringing together various kinds of information, viewpoints, and arguments. Sometimes, writers do not find any sources that share their position on a specific topic. Instead, they discover sources that partially overlap in some way. All of these sources, then, help give dimension to the writer's ideas. In Figure 15.1, notice that supporting evidence (some fact or statistic that backs up the writer's stance) is only one possibility:

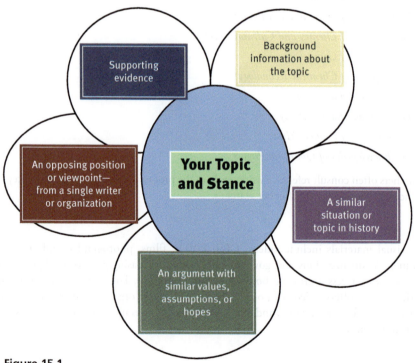

Figure 15.1

For example, consider the topic *light pollution*. Imagine a writer beginning her research with a vague position—that too much light hinders most people from seeing the night sky. A quick search of the web and periodical databases would likely yield some sources that share her position: statistics on the number of Americans who cannot see constellations, background information about the topic, such as when it became a concern for astronomers or how much it impacts plant life. But she can go further. In some invention work, she may discover that the night sky is important because it bestows a sense of wonder and humility in people. She could seek out sources that celebrate the power of wonder—a sociologist who argues that civilizations without a deep sense of wonder quickly fade from history or a religious scholar who argues for the value of humility. Perhaps she finds rationale for parking lots that stay lit all night. She then develops a counterargument to address that rationale. She might also discover a similar but related issue: noise pollution and its effects on agriculture. Although this information about noise pollution may not directly support her main claim, it may show a trend in history—that people have always battled the slow invasion of technology into the natural world. All such sources could help develop an insightful and rich argument. Figure 15.2 represents these sources in relation to the main topic, light pollution.

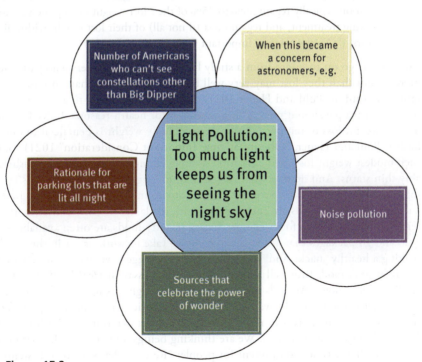

Figure 15.2

Synthesis literally means *bringing together*. So synthesizing sources involves bringing a range of voices and texts together. Academic researchers know they may find closely related sources—for instance, three articles on the local effects of light pollution. But they also know they may find no closely related sources or merely a smattering of texts that are distantly related. In this common scenario, the researcher has to bridge gaps between and among sources. And bridging those gaps often creates exciting insights. When researchers begin writing—formulating the relationships among sources—they often create nuances in their own thinking and discover dimensions of the topic itself.

In the following passage from her essay "Cruelty, Civility, and Other Weighty Matters" (pages 230–239), Ann Marie Paulin assembles a range of sources. Notice how the shaded passages help establish connections among her sources. Paulin does the work of bringing the sources into her own line of reasoning:

And most diets don't work. An essay by Rebecca Puhl, Ph.D., and Chelsea Heuer, MPH, in the *American Journal of Public Health,* cites studies which found:

> Most weight losses are not maintained and individuals regain weight after completing treatment. Patients who have lost weight through lifestyle modification typically regain 30% to 35% of their lost weight during the year following treatment, and regain most (if not all) of their lost weight within five years. ("Obesity Stigma: Important Considerations" 1021)

The authors go on to quote from a study by Mann, et al: "Dieters who gain back more weight than they lost may very well be the norm, rather than an unlucky minority" (qtd. in Puhl and Heuer 1021). My point here is not to argue that overweight people should not try to lose weight for health reasons. Indeed, even a modest weight loss of ten percent of a person's body weight is beneficial to one's health (Puhl and Heuer, "Obesity Stigma: Important Consideration" 1021). But such modest weight loss, while healthy, is rarely enough to earn a person fashionably thin status. And despite what the cultural messages suggest, most of us fat folks are trying to eat more sensibly, but the environment does play a role. In a culture where most of us are rushed from work to classes to other activities, the temptation to grab fast food is huge. Sugary or fatty foods are often available in grab and go packages that are so much easier to take to work or eat in the car than making a healthy snack. And, there is evidence to suggest we may even be wired to prefer junk food. Brownell and colleagues, in an essay in *Health Affairs,* cite studies which show: "Animals given access to food high in sugar and fat—even when healthy food is freely available—consume calorie-dense, nutrient-poor food in abundance, gain a great deal of weight, and exhibit deteriorating health" (379). I know, I know. We aren't rats. We are thinking beings, but this article goes on to point out that it is not so different for people: "Research has shown consistently that people moving from less to more obese countries gain weight, and those moving to less obese countries lose weight" (379).

So we are surrounded by a culture, even an infrastructure, that encourages obesity, yet the culture also breeds a prejudice against fat people. Various articles and news magazine programs have reported that Americans of all sizes make far more than simple aesthetic judgments when they look at a fat person. Fat people are assumed to be lazy, stupid, ugly, lacking in self-esteem and pride, devoid of self-control, and stuffed full of a host of other unpleasant qualities that have nothing to do with the size of a person's belly or thighs. But, as anyone who has ever been the victim of such prejudice can tell you, the impact such foolish notions have is real and harmful. For example, Marilyn Wann, in her book *Fat! So?*, cites an experiment in which "[r]esearchers placed two fake personal ads, one for a woman described as '50 pounds overweight' and the other for a woman described as a drug addict. The drug addict received 79 percent of the responses" (59). So, in spite of the agony addiction can cause to the addict and those who love her, people would rather get romantically involved with an addict than a fat person. And not much has changed. In a 2008 article, "The Stigma of Obesity: A Review and Update," Puhl and Heuer report:

> One study asked college students (N = 449) to rank order six pictures of hypothetical sexual partners, including an obese partner, a healthy partner, and partners with various disabilities (including a partner in a wheelchair, missing an arm, with a mental illness, or described as having a history of sexually transmitted diseases. Both men and women ranked the obese person as the least desirable sexual partner compared to the others (10).

While it is certainly good news to see that people can look beyond disabilities, such as a wheelchair or a missing arm, and see the value of the whole human being, it is distressing that Americans refuse to do the same for a person's weight. Why would anyone want to date someone who will land them in the STD clinic? How dangerous is that? And yet, such a person is clearly seen as a better romantic choice than a heavy person. Here is a case where weight prejudice is certainly more dangerous to the person with the prejudice than it is to the fat person.

Assignment: Summarizing, Analyzing, and Synthesizing Sources

Much academic research is driven by a need to understand what others think—to know how scholars are debating and probing a topic. In other words, academic researchers are not always (or often) driven by the desire to find proof for their own convictions. They are, instead, out to discover the tensions and curiosities about a topic. This assignment focuses on that discovery process. It is designed to help writers explore the boundaries of a topic, to find multiple sources, bring them together, and develop new insights. The goal is not to prove a point or reinforce one's own opinion but to explore how other writers have addressed a topic—what others believe, assume, or imagine. The following steps will help guide you through that process:

1. **Search for Sources:** First, consider a topic—perhaps one that you have already written about. Draw a circle in the middle of a page with your topic and stance (if you have one). Then, in separate circles, write out possibilities for the following: background information; supporting evidence for your position; similar situations or topics in history; the values, assumptions, and hopes underlying your position; and opposing positions and the people or groups that might hold them. Use those circles, then, to generate keywords for searching databases or the Internet.

2. **Summarize the Content:** After finding two or more sources, summarize each. Briefly describe the main idea, or thesis, of the sources. (Be careful not to blur away the particular insight of the source.)

3. **Analyze the Context:** Next, analyze the content and context of the sources. Avoid evaluating the worth or value. In other words, avoid arguing that the sources are good, bad, credible, agreeable, and so forth. Instead, explain how the sources fit into a broader conversation about the topic. Consider the following questions:

   - Who is the intended audience? Scholars? The general public? Any particular group?
   - How do the sources speak to the audience? How do the sources address the values of their audience?
   - What do the writers seem to value? What ideas or principles or hopes do you detect?
   - How do the sources deal with the audience's potential questions, concerns, or doubts? Do they ever address potential concerns or doubts directly?

4. **Synthesize Ideas:** Synthesis involves explaining all the ways sources relate to one another—how they support, inform, or oppose one another. Synthesis can also involve the relationship between sources and the writer's own thinking about the topic. In other words, you might explain how the sources respond to, rub against, undermine, extend, challenge, or reinforce your own ideas. Consider the following questions:

   - How do the sources overlap or contradict? How do they approach the topic differently? Beyond the obvious claims and opinions, what assumptions or unstated values seem to overlap or conflict?

- How do the sources contribute to your understanding of the topic or your ability to engage in this conversation?
- What further questions do the sources provoke?
- How do the sources reveal some layer of the topic that you did not imagine or discuss prior to researching?
- What perspective do the sources offer to you? For instance, do they address some psychological or philosophical layer that you did not imagine?

Sample Synthesis
Exploring Caffeine Views
Jim Crockett

In his essay, "Mugged" (Chapter 3, pages 67–68), Jim Crockett explores the relationship between himself and his coffee mug. As he explores the meaning of that relationship, he suggests in one passage that he may be addicted to caffeine. Although that is not the main assertion in his essay, it gave him a springboard into research. In the following essay, Crockett illustrates three critical moves in academic research: (1) He briefly summarizes two sources related to his topic. (2) He analyzes the content and context of each source. (3) He synthesizes the sources and his own prior thoughts on the topic. In other words, he marries sources and his own understanding of the topic. This marriage of ideas generates new insights. Notice that Crockett does not use the sources to uphold his own initial thoughts. In fact, in the final section of this essay, he corrects part of his prior thinking.

In his magazine article "Caffeine Addiction Is a Mental Disorder, Doctors Say," George Studeville explains that caffeine withdrawal may be officially classified as a psychological disorder. Studeville describes how Roland Griffith, a professor at Johns Hopkins, makes the case for the "syndrome" of caffeine withdrawal. In her article, "Is Caffeine Addictive?—A Review of Literature," Sally Satel concludes that caffeine does not meet the criteria for an addictive drug. While people commonly use the term *addiction* for heavy caffeine use, Satel argues that mild and temporary withdrawal symptoms do not warrant equating the drug with others, like heroin, that are harmful, even ruinous, to individuals and society.

These articles, then, seem to oppose one another: Griffith assumes that caffeine should be considered an addictive drug, while Satel argues that consistent use and mild temporary withdrawal symptoms do not meet the DSM (Diagnostic and Statistical Manual of Mental Disorders) standards for genuine chemical addiction.

Studeville writes for a popular magazine. His readers, then, are not familiar with the jargon of the discipline or its ongoing professional debates. And Studeville himself is a reporter rather than a doctor or professor. His purpose is to inform readers about ongoing research—and a particular argument from Griffith, a professor of behavioral biology and neuroscience. His voice is informal and even a bit dramatic. The title offers the most absurd or extreme characterization of Griffith's argument. "Mental disorder," for common readers, suggests a kind of pathology, a chronic condition. The article offers Griffith's position on caffeine addiction and withdrawal, but it offers no opposing claims. The argument goes unchallenged, uncontested. And according to the title, "doctors" (all or most?) seem to say that Griffith's argument is correct.

Satel is an MD and researcher. She takes on the opposition directly—explaining why some people classify caffeine as an addictive drug. Her section on "methodological problems" reveals some of the flaws and hiccups in this type of research.

The researchers in both articles (Griffith and Satel) seem to value accuracy and a scientific method. Griffith says that he launched his study because "doctors and other health professionals have had no scientifically based framework for diagnosing the syndrome." Satel calls for her colleagues to make fine distinctions in previous studies—and to discount conclusions drawn from studies that lack reliability and credibility. But they differ in an important way— Griffith's argument calls for the collapse of categories: If one cup of coffee creates "physical dependence" (or anything like it), then coffee contains a dependent drug. Satel wants to make distinctions: Some drugs are ruinous to the individual's life, while other drugs (like caffeine) merely create a mild form habituation. Griffith wants to erase degree and difference. Satel suggests that degree of dependence is all the difference in the world.

When We Talk About Drugs and Addictions and Habits, What is the Battle?

As Satel explains, dependence on a drug comes from a need to acquire "physiological homeostasis"—or physical stability. This is, perhaps, different from my acknowledgement about coffee: that drinking it is a daily grounding ritual, a practice that works against the social forces. I suggest that our culture, our *econoculture*, pulls us away from ourselves—that it has left behind its roots in the wilderness. Instead of intimacy and simplicity, we have to blast through everyday life. (The other drivers looked at me angrily—*get the hell out of my way!*—while I meekly tried to rescue my helpless little mug at the busy intersection.) The two sources, and particularly Satel, raise this question: When we talk about drugs and addictions and habits, what is the battle? In my "Mugged" essay, I suggest that the battle might be psychological or philosophical rather than chemical. I focus on the act of drinking, the ritual of carrying my old familiar mug in a society that invites me to buy something new every time I turn around. That's a big battle! Sure, it's not physiologically addictive . . . and maybe I'm not really addicted to caffeine. Maybe that's just a common way of putting it. If Satel's right, after all, I'd just get a headache if I quit. But if I left my mug behind, if I bought (into) the plastic/paper cup world around me, maybe I'd be joining another realm of addiction—a bigger and more ruinous one.

And I don't mean this metaphorically. I mean it for real. I'm thinking, on this morning, of the recent government bailouts: $750 billion to keep the world of super-consumption chugging along. Rather than put serious resources into education, into health care, into the crumbling infrastructure, into alternative energy, we have to inject huge amounts into a habit. And the Treasury Secretary says that the injection will likely create more bad behavior and that we shouldn't monitor it too closely. (The main thing: Get the junkies their fix! And hurry!) There's nothing we can do. We're stuck in a violent cycle. And this resonates with my point about *econoculture*. We're all now working to support the addicts on Wall Street and their political mules in Congress. If the addicts don't get their fix, they'll crumble and the whole economy will shake.

Maybe this is going too far. But Satel's essay makes me think about addiction in social terms. She says that it's not enough for us to simply think about the withdrawal. Instead, we have to think about *harm*. Do the drug and withdrawal hurt the individual and the society? This is where Satel and I overlap, and where I end up wondering: What kinds of addiction am I participating in? What kinds of withdrawal? What addictive behavior does my life encourage? How do I get out of those behaviors? Can I? What personal choices can I make if I am not in control of the drug and its effects?

Works Cited

Satel, Sally. "Is Caffeine Addictive?—A Review of Literature." *The American Journal of Drug and Alcohol Abuse*, vol. 32, no. 4, 2006, pp. 493–502. *Academic Search Premier*, doi: 10.1080/00952990600918965.

Studeville, George. "Caffeine Addiction Is a Mental Disorder, Doctors Say." *National Geographic*, 19 Jan. 2005, news.nationalgeographic.com/news/2005/01/0119_050119_ngm_caffeine.html.

EVALUATING SOURCES

Sources should be relevant, reliable, credible, timely, and diverse. Sources that do not adhere to these criteria can diminish an academic project and even damage an author's credibility.

Relevance

A relevant source is appropriately related to the writer's topic. A writer's first inclination may be to find those sources that directly support his or her thesis statement—that is, sources that speak directly about the writer's particular subject and that espouse his or her particular stance on it. However, such an approach limits the intellectual possibilities—especially because the research process might develop or change how a writer thinks about a subject. Sources do much more than back up someone's opinion. They might help to explain the complexities of the subject, the history of the subject, the writer's position, or even opposition to the writer's position.

Because sources can be used in various ways, one that seems only remotely related to your project might, in fact, be extremely valuable in the long run. Consider the following example: A writer is researching voting practices in his community and wants to make a claim about low voter turnouts in recent elections. He finds a newspaper article about a local school scheduled for demolition that had previously been used as a voting location. This article at first might seem unhelpful. After all, how does this particular school relate to voting trends in the community? It may, in fact, suggest a great deal about voting. That is, one of the factors in voter turnout is proximity to voting locations. This article might, therefore, show a trend in a declining number of voting locations. The same writer might find a government web page about the history of voting in his state. At first this source may not seem valuable because the writer is primarily concerned with recent voter activity. However, the history may provide some clues about the system itself, about the reasons for establishing Tuesdays as election days, about the number of constituents in a given area—all potentially valuable factors in understanding the complexities of recent voter turnout.

Reliability

Reliability refers to the quality of information in the source. A reliable source uses verifiable information and helps readers trace the sources of information. The most reliable sources document the information they offer. (That's why academic audiences value some type of formal documentation, such as in-text citations and a bibliographical list.) In effect, formal documentation says to readers, "Here is the path to relevant research."

For published books and academic journal articles, reliability may not be an issue because such sources endure a process of critical peer review. However, many publications do not have peer reviews. Most magazines and newspapers also do not have room to include formal documentation. Their editorial policies exclude in-text documentation and Works Cited lists.

But there are other ways for writers to signal reliability, such as an appositive phrase. In the following examples, the underlined appositive phrases lend some reliability to the information. Even though the passages lack formal documentation (a formal link to a specific text), they give readers cues about the nature of the source. Notice that the information after the name indicates the source's credentials. When a formal Works Cited list is not possible, writers in many publications use such phrases to document the reliability of their information:

> Kalle Lasn, <u>a cofounder of the Canadian media criticism and environmentalist maga-</u><u>zine *Adbusters*,</u> explains how dependence on television first occurred and continues today each time we turn on our sets.

> Martha Cane, <u>director of Research and Development for Animatrix,</u> argues that power has been consolidated in a few large tech companies.

Remember that most popular magazines are guided by a primary force: money. Editorial policies are driven by the need to make information attractive to consumers. Therefore, claims may be inflated, mitigating details may be played down, and generalizations are common. Also, remember that magazines are funded in large part by corporate advertising and so are not apt to publish articles that might compromise relationships with those advertisers. For these reasons, researchers should always be cautious about quoting popular magazines (or even news magazines) as unbiased truth.

Credibility

Credibility refers to the internal logic of the information presented in the source. A credible source does not attempt to hide its biases or its argument. It makes logical claims and helps readers follow its logic. If the source offers an argument, it makes its position clear and reveals its biases. (And, of course, it is free of logical fallacies.) If the source attempts to inform rather than persuade, it does not spin information or conceal its biases.

The question of credibility may also involve the source's author. Some authors have more credentials than others. However, a book or article by a well-known author should not necessarily outweigh one by a less familiar writer. Many academic and professional writers are not necessarily big names in popular media but are well respected within small communities because they have spent years researching a particularly focused issue. For instance, Patricia Limerick, a highly respected historian, has written a great deal about the American West. Although her name is not recognizable to the general public, it is often noted in history scholarship.

But how would a researcher know this? For instance, if you were not a historian, how would you know about Patricia Limerick's scholarly status? Fortunately, online search engines and databases have made many authors and their bodies of work instantaneously accessible.

First, most periodicals and online news outlets hyperlink author names. If you click on the name, you'll see other works by the same author in that publication. Second, scholarly databases such as Academic Search Complete hyperlink author names as well. If you click on the name, you'll see other works by the same author from *any publication* in the database. Third, you can always Google an author—and here is where plenty of scholars do, in fact, rely on Wikipedia and other open-access sites. Cross-referencing an author name can turn up a list of her works, the sources of publication (magazines, journals, or presses that published her work), and even debates surrounding her works. In short, an online search can show how an author has been received, celebrated, or even condemned by a particular readership. (For more guidelines on such searches, see Evaluating Online Sources, page 458.)

Timeliness

A significant concern in academic research is the date of the sources. It is important that claims are supported with sources that are not obsolete or behind the times. But this criterion depends upon the issue and the claim being made. Some claims require very current sources. For example, a writer making a claim about marriage laws and gay rights would be wise to consider sources published only within two to three years of her research. (Because laws are changing and continue to create significant public debate, sources that are ten years old may be antiquated.) However, that same writer might also want to discuss the concept or development of equality in the United States and discover a valuable text by a 19th-century philosopher. In this case, the writer would use current texts to support claims about time-sensitive topics and would refer to an older source to express an issue that stretches beyond a specific era.

Diversity

Diversity refers to the variety of sources a writer uses. Good writers seek to develop their projects and their perspectives with different voices and media. Writers develop their views on a subject from a range of sources—much in the same way that we develop our views on religion or marriage or education from taking in and making sense of information from various sources. For example, our religious beliefs may have been influenced primarily by our parents, but other sources, such as childhood friends, books, movies, and music, also influence us. Even views that oppose our own are important because they help us to define the borders of our beliefs.

Writers should hope to read and synthesize various sources about their topics; otherwise, their perspectives, and ultimately their positions, can be limited. This means that writers should explore *different perspectives.* They should not seek out conformity of opinion but diversity of thought. For this reason, writers often attempt to seek out different types of sources. They hope to view their topics from as many angles as possible—from different scholarly communities and from popular or mainstream perspectives.

Evaluating Online Sources

Back in the 1990s, when the Internet was first getting traction, teachers and scholars made a clean distinction between print and online sources. That was an important distinction: Although most conventional content (books, journals, academic studies, and so on) was still physically printed and distributed, the Internet was home to any kind of content whatsoever. Because it was mostly ungoverned, the Internet had no conventional ways to filter information. Anyone with a mouse and a little know-how could publish. (A bored seventh-grader could create a homepage that resembled—at least on the surface—a NASA site.) But twenty years have made a big difference. Now, almost everything that counts as a published source in academic writing is—or will soon be—digital and online. So it is increasingly irrelevant to make a distinction between print and online sources—at least when it comes to evaluation. In other words, an article published by *Time, Nursing Science Quarterly*, or *The New Yorker* is no different in terms of credibility or reliability whether you retrieve it in print or online. However, the shift to online sources has created issues that academic researchers must understand:

1. **Authorless-ness:** Some information on the Internet is *unattributed*. In other words, it has no author. Passages, charts, even entire articles are passed around, forwarded, and re-forwarded, with no reference to their origin. Anyone could have generated the information for whatever purpose. This creates a credibility problem. And if the information cannot be cross-referenced, it also creates a reliability problem.

   What to do: Most librarians, researchers, and instructors suggest using only texts (whether they are articles, blogs, reports, or tweets) that can be traced to an author or publisher. In other words, you should be able to identify the author: the individual, company, group, or organization responsible for generating the information.

2. **Misinformation Blitz:** Misinformation, or fake news, is nothing new. Textbooks, history books, television news channels, and politicians have fumbled facts, mischaracterized situations, and skewed numbers. But with the invention of social media, the speed of misinformation has dramatically increased. Now, erroneous information can spread across the globe in a matter of minutes. And once false information has been widely distributed, it becomes its own kind of reality that is difficult or impossible to counter. In fact, a number of studies have shown that corrections to misinformation—if they do get published and distributed via social media—reach *less than half* of the original audience. For instance, imagine that someone tweets erroneous information about a murder trial. That tweet may reach 100,000 people within a few hours. And if the original tweeter discovered that his information was wrong and decided to fix the problem, the correction may only reach 40,000 people—and at a slower pace. In short, misinformation often travels more quickly and more widely than corrections.

   What to do: Avoid using information that comes via social media—such as Twitter or Facebook. If something seems compelling, scan the Internet for competing, corrected, or simply different information about the topic in hand.

3. **Marketplace Bias:** Bias also must be considered. Because the purpose of many sites is to sell something, they may provide information that is slanted. Of course, bias in itself is not bad. Bias is only negative when it is concealed. If a source is trying to sell something, its claims should not be accepted as unbiased truth. And if the source asks for personal information, it may have an alternative agenda. Although some online sources (such as newspapers) require you to register to enter the site, many other sources may ask for personal information so they can market products or services to you.

   What to do: First, always determine the author and publisher of information. If the publisher is a for-profit business (for instance, a website ending in .com), ask yourself if money may have influenced the nature of the information. Second, try to cross-reference claims, facts, or data. If possible, seek out information in not-for-profit publications, such as academic journals. Finally, do not give a website your personal information if you simply want an article. Instead, visit your institution's library and request the article through a database.

4. **Source Confusion:** Now more than ever, it is important for researchers to understand the differences among source types. A blog post, for instance, is different from a traditional article. The two sources come to publication through different processes: even though an article may go through several drafts, with input from various staff writers, and get clearance from at least one or two editors, a blog post may go straight from the writer's screen to the Internet. Even a blog published by an esteemed news organization might go through very little editing or fact-checking. In short, the two sources might be entirely different but look entirely the same.

   This is not to say that a blog—by definition—is less reliable or credible. It may simply offer the kind of argument, interpretation, or angle that a report or journalistic article does not. Imagine the following statement appearing on a news site: "The situation in Fallujah is a catastrophe." Such a claim could come from an unnamed blogger, a journalist in Iraq, the Joint Chief of Staff, or a retired general. Good readers/researchers will always know the origin of such a statement, but good researchers should keep their radar on high. If they know the type of source, they can better trace where the information comes from, who's saying what, and for what reasons.

   What to do: Know your sources. In fact, use labels in your own notes—and try to avoid broad terms such as *website*. Instead, try to determine if you are reading a blog, a feature article from a news site, a report on a government site, and so on.

5. **Abandoned Sites:** In a typical scenario, a student group develops an advocacy website. Over the course of a semester, the site gets loaded with data, statistics, and stories about a key issue. The site stays active for a semester while individuals from the group continue to update the information. Over the summer, the group disintegrates and the site is

forgotten, but it stays on the university server. Three years go by and the site still stands. Although it looks interesting and vibrant, the information is outdated.

As we explain on page 457, timeliness depends upon the nature of the information. Some ideas, assertions, concepts, and theories stay relevant for years or even centuries. But other information can quickly change. If a website deals with time-sensitive topics and does not stay current, it may as well be a dead link.

What to do: If you use information from a website, simply make sure that you can find a date when the site or page itself was last updated. If you cannot find a date, consider cross-referencing the information or even try to contact the site's administrator.

To evaluate the content of websites, ask the following questions:

- Who sponsors this site, and what credibility do they have?

- Is the site attempting to sell something? If so, how might that impact the nature of the information?

- Does the site ask for personal information? (Does it state the purpose of this request?)

- Are statistics/data supported with appropriately documented sources? If not, how can you trace the information and cross-reference it with another source?

- Is the information presented up to date? (When was the site last updated?)

Assignment: Evaluating a Source

Evaluating literally means calling out the value of something. When we evaluate sources, we draw attention to their value—not according to how much we agree with them but according to specific criteria. In other words, evaluating is not about praising sources that support our positions but explaining how sources stack up according to categorical standards: relevance, reliability, credibility, timeliness, and diversity (pages 455–457). For this assignment, find and save a particular source—one that you can read closely. Develop a brief formal evaluation. For each criterion, consider the following key questions:

Relevance

- Does the source speak directly to my specific topic?

- How does the source help to clarify some broader or related point?

- How does the source help to explain the history or complexities of the topic?

Reliability

- Does the source offer formal documentation? Do other sources check out? Are they available?

- If there is no formal documentation, does the source acknowledge authorities with related credentials or qualifications?

- What about the source itself? Is it published by a reputable organization?

Credibility

- Does the source make an argument? If so, are the claims well supported and well reasoned? Do you sense any logical fallacies?

- Does the source attempt to conceal its biases?

- Do you have reason to question the author's credibility? (If so, do a quick web or database search to see if the author has written for or is referenced in other publications.) Is your reason for questioning the author's credibility reasonable? (Are you unnecessarily suspicious?)

Timeliness

- Is this a time-sensitive topic?

- If this is a time-sensitive topic, why might the information in the source be either timely or out of date?

Diversity

- Do my sources represent a variety of viewpoints?

- How do the sources represent different value or belief systems?

SAMPLE SOURCE EVALUATION

Assessing Bond Pittman's "Drink Earlier, Drink Less"

The following essay evaluates a source—in this case, a magazine article by Bond Pittman, "Drink Earlier, Drink Less," published in *The American Spectator* in June 2013.* The first paragraph explains the topic and argumentative approach: We're searching for the cause of binge drinking. The second paragraph summarizes Pittman's article and explains its relevance to our project. The next five paragraphs deal primarily with credibility because that is the most complex criterion for an argumentative article that relies primarily on appeals and examples. More importantly, credibility generates the most concerns or questions when it comes to Pittman's article. The final paragraph deals with timeliness and even reinforces Pittman's relevance. Of course, not every essay that evaluates a source should be organized in this fashion. So much depends upon the topic and the source in question. But this essay illustrates one common and sound way to generate an initial draft.

Binge drinking among college students won't seem to go away. Despite a range of initiatives and campus policies, college students keep on consuming alcohol in dangerous spasms of excess. Plenty of policies, parent groups, and laws aim to manage the behavior by managing alcohol—i.e., trying to keep it as far away from campuses and underage students as possible. But alcohol itself is not the cause of excess. There's something else—something before the alcohol even becomes available—that causes such widespread and persistent binging.

In June of 2013, *The American Spectator* published an essay on binge drinking by Bond Pittman, a senior at Hillsdale College in Michigan. His was the winning entry in the magazine's writing contest: "Each semester, *The American Spectator* holds its college essay contest, an opportunity for undergraduates to show their writing skills and sound off on a pressing issue. Our most recent topic, 'The pros and cons of binge drinking,' elicited this essay by an up-and-coming student from Hillsdale College."

Pittman certainly comes down against binge drinking. He offers some not-so-surprising information about physical effects: weight gain, anxiety, alcohol poisoning, and death. And he argues, in his final passages, for moderation—for restraint even when the surrounding social forces urge indulgence and abandon. But what's most relevant (for this project) is Pittman's analysis of cause. He spends much of his essay exploring the social and institutional forces that cultivate excess. Even though he doesn't enumerate them, he names three: First, he explains the general mainstream attraction to excess:

> We live in a civilization of bingers. Teenagers commonly indulge in irregular and excessive sleeping hiatuses. Credit card companies make fortunes on people's inability to curtail shopping splurges. And it's rare to find victors of the one-potato-chip challenge.

http://spectator.org/articles/55591/drink-earlier-drink-less

I down at least two bowl-sized mugs of Dunkin' every morning, and I waited to watch nine hours of *Downton Abbey* in one sitting because I couldn't bear the week-long wait between episodes.

In other words, the culture at large supports super-consumption—and Pittman, himself, is in the crowd. Second, he argues that the federally stipulated drinking age (twenty-one) "removed [alcohol] from the civic domain and unintentionally given it a clandestine appeal." Third, he blames a lack of role models. His generation, he says, admires no one for his or her noble restraint.

Pittman's credibility depends on his own experience—more specifically, on *the way he explains* his own experience. After all, Pittman is a senior at a Midwestern college. He is literally in the middle of this phenomenon, and so his testimony is crucial. Fortunately, the most detailed and coherent passage of the essay focuses on his experience:

I discovered just how accessible the partying scene was to underage students only hours after my parents dropped me off for freshman orientation. My first night as a college student, I found myself at an off-campus house party packed with upperclassmen and a handful of other freshmen. We were told that free alcohol was available for us. I stood in the middle of the room, squashed between a girl's sequined back and a football player's sweaty arm. I knew I could throw myself into this sea of reckless abandon, or I could stay on solid ground. It was tempting to jump, but after I found my way out of the middle of the crowd, I turned and looked at the spectacle around me. The faces were all those of strangers (no one cared so much as to ask me my name). Everyone was either already drunk or intending to be, and soon.

This passage, even standing on its own, sheds light on binge drinking. It is a kind of exposé about student life. And much of its power comes from what isn't said: the smooth transition from orientation to party. The passage is persuasive not only because of the "reckless abandon" it describes but also for the simple facts of the narrative: Within hours of arriving at college, Pittman is surrounded by free alcohol and serious drinking.

Throughout the essay, Pittman makes some broad claims against his generation and mainstream culture at large, but those claims seem, at the least, in line with his experiences. If he's opinionated, he's not trying to hide it, nor is he trying to scorn his peers. But his credibility does take a hit—not because he's a mere college student or novice writer. (In fact, his writing is clever, engaging, and often careful in its reach.) His credibility diminishes because of his political allegiance.

The American Spectator is openly conservative. Not that there's anything wrong with conservatism, but this conservatism often borders on prejudice and bigotry. In the June issue, along with Pittman's article, writers and longtime contributors rail against gay marriage (that will be, according to George Neumayr, "imposed" on all Americans), openly make fun of President Obama, and offer goofy caricatures of anyone they can deem a liberal. In short, the June 2013 issue upholds a tradition of excessive bias that fills mainstream news magazines across the political continuum. So it is difficult to attribute credibility to *any* text published on its site or in its pages. As with so many similar magazines, its audience expects pot shots and gross portrayals of those who might disagree.

Bond does come out, in his first line, as an adherent to political conservatism. He begins with reigning queen of the American right:

> "You gotta be thinking Sam Adams, not drinking Sam Adams." Sarah Palin gave this advice to the college students attending this year's Conservative Political Action Confer- ence. Just another round fired from her stockpile of one-liners, but her remark was well aimed: College students drink. A lot.

Palin is, then, left behind for the remainder of the essay, and so her presence serves only to announce political allegiance. From there, Pittman's political conservatism shows up in his not-so-veiled hostility toward the federal government:

> If all parents and children followed the letter of the law, most Americans coming of age after 1984 (when the federal government blackmailed the states by withholding federal highway funds if they refused to raise the drinking age to 21) would have their first experience drinking alcohol not in the controlled, safe environment of a home, but in a bar with other freshly turned 21-year-olds.

This is conservative boilerplate: Laws from the federal government are heavy-handed and always against the sanctity of home life. In a more moderate magazine—perhaps one not so comfortable with the shared notion that federal government is always bad—such an historical reference may have been qualified or characterized in less biased terms. And there's one other instance when Pittman seems careless or at least deaf to a broader audience. It happens in his description of the party: "Some girls," he says, "had mascara streaked across their faces, whether due to the hot, sticky atmosphere or from crying, I don't know." Certainly, responsible readers can imagine how sorrow and injury go swirling about a drunken college party, but it's difficult to imagine, from an informed and care- ful understanding, a roomful of college-age women both crying and dancing. (In short, there,s a terrifically naïve argument about women lurking in the off-hand guess at their smeared makeup.)

But the good news for Pittman is that he is not a consistent contributor to *The American Spectator*. He does not make a living fanning the flames of political hostility. Unlike the usual contributors (such as Ben Stein, William Tucker, George Neumayr), Bond does not swing at his political enemies. In fact, he may not even have them yet. More importantly, Pittman does offer insight on the topic. He knows something about "those angsty years" of college. Despite some sloppy characterizations of women and governments, his insights are often lucid—as in the following passage where he reaches beyond the clichés of his peers:

> I have asked people who regularly drink in order to get drunk why they do so, and the answer is generally the same: "It relaxes me to have more fun and helps me to express myself more freely in social situations." But the modern partying scene is the antithesis of community. It involves "dancing" in which human persons are not the essential participants; certain attached body parts are. It presses drinking to the point where the cognitive person behind the red Solo cup is blotted out, and the best nights are often considered to be those that cannot be remembered.

Such passages reveal layers beyond unhealthy behavior. They show something about an unhealthy worldview—more so than a mountain of statistics and legal references. In short, Pittman's firsthand and wide-eyed observation of his peers offers serious insights that more distant (older) writers may not willingly conjure.

Finally, it's easy to say that Pittman's essay is timely. But what's interesting and unfortunate is that it will stay timely for years to come. While binge drinking may find new tools and fashionable avenues on social media (such as the recent NekNominate game), it seems to be firmly rooted in college culture.

16 Integrating and Documenting Sources

Chapter Objectives

This chapter will help you to:

- Summarize sources for different rhetorical purposes.
- Paraphrase and quote sources for different rhetorical purposes.
- Cite and document sources according to conventional formats.

INTEGRATING SOURCES

Sources can add dimension, insight, and depth to your own ideas. They can also add a layer of difficulty. As sources are integrated, sound organizational principles must still apply: Ideas should remain focused, paragraphs must be coherent, and your own line of reasoning should be apparent to readers. Also, information from sources should be blended smoothly into the text so that readers (1) understand its relationship to the writer's own ideas, and (2) know where the information came from. The challenge is to maintain coherence while integrating other voices and opinions. The best way to achieve coherence is to develop an overall plan for your essay before drafting. That is, develop a general strategy for your organization and decide how the sources will function in that plan.

Writers often quote sources directly. But paraphrase and summary are equally important moves. Imagine a writer is doing research on political action. She discovers the following passage from Martin Luther King Jr.:

> Human progress never rolls in on wheels of inevitability; it comes through the tireless efforts of men willing to be co-workers with God, and without this hard work, time itself becomes an ally of the forces of stagnation. We must use time creatively, in the knowledge that the time is always ripe to do right. Now is the time to make real the promise of democracy and transform our pending national elegy into a creative psalm of brotherhood. Now is the time to lift our national policy from the quicksand of racial injustice to the solid rock of human dignity.

The writer decides that this information is valuable because it adds complexity to her ideas. It may be *paraphrased, summarized,* or directly *quoted.*

Paraphrase

Paraphrase is a rewording of the original source using your own words and expressions. It conveys the detail and complexity of the original text. A paraphrase of the King passage might read as follows:

> Humanity doesn't progress without constant struggle of pious and committed individuals. Absence of such struggle means the lack of social and spiritual development. We have to use time to do what is right, to realize the idea of democracy, to change national sorrow into community and collaboration. We have to try to raise the nation up from racist practices into a place of shared honor and respect (King 130).

The paraphrase restates King's ideas, but does so without his particularly figurative language. The writer might find paraphrase valuable because she wants to share the nuances of the idea but does not want the tone of the original text (such as King's poetic voice) to interfere with or take over her own text.

Paraphrasing does not involve merely changing a word or two, or shifting around sentence parts. Inappropriate or lazy paraphrasing leads to *plagiarism:* taking others' ideas or words without attributing proper credit. In the following example, the writer does not rephrase the ideas, but merely shifts some words around and replaces others. If the following appeared in a text, it would be plagiarism:

> Human progress never rolls in on tires of inevitability; it comes by way of the tireless efforts of men willing to be co-workers with God, and without this hard work, time itself becomes an ally of the forces of stagnation. In the knowledge that the time is always ripe to do right, we must use time creatively (King 130).

Notice that in the first sentence, the writer has only substituted one word for another here and there. In the second sentence, the writer has just shifted sentence parts around. This is plagiarism rather than paraphrasing because the passage retains the original flavor and expression of the author. (See more about plagiarism on page 476.)

Summary

Like paraphrase, summary involves expressing a source's ideas in your own words instead of using the words of the source. But unlike paraphrase, summary often removes much of the detail while still dealing with the complexity of the source's idea. A writer may summarize because he or she wants to illustrate a point (made by the original text) and then move on to another idea. In other words, a summary is often used to support a broader claim. For example, consider this brief summary of the original King passage. Notice that King's idea has been entirely reworded, abbreviated, and used as a supporting point:

> Even liberal-minded people believe that minority rights, somehow, evolve quietly through the decades. But Martin Luther King Jr. made the opposite point: that humanity progresses only by the struggle of spiritually motivated people, and those people must use time for social change (130).

Because summary leaves out detail while capturing the main idea, accuracy is essential. Writers should be careful not to misinterpret the source, as in the following summary:

> According to King, only people who go to church regularly can make the world a better place. Racism will thrive without their timely efforts (130).

Summaries can be any length, depending on the writer's purpose. For instance, imagine that a writer is building a line of reasoning about justice. She wants to borrow an idea explained in King's "Letter from Birmingham Jail." She quickly summarizes King's distinction between just and unjust laws without dwelling on specifics:

> But something is not right simply because it is legal. As Martin Luther King Jr. reminds us in "Letter from Birmingham Jail," we must appeal to some principle beyond the law. Because so many laws through history have been unjust and downright oppressive to minority groups, we cannot simply accept legality as the ultimate criterion for righteousness (132-133). In the current debate about gay marriage, we must go beyond legality and explore what is just.

Here, the writer has summarized several lengthy passages from King's text. Rather than get bogged down in the details of King's argument, she abbreviates his ideas in one sentence and then continues developing her own point. A lengthier summary might be appropriate if the writer wanted to carefully detail the difference between a just and an unjust law. She might summarize but offer slightly more detail from King's argument. In effect, she would be summarizing and paraphrasing:

> It is difficult for a population to weigh the justice of its own laws. After all, the laws seem just by virtue of their place in social structures and institutions. But as Martin Luther King Jr. argues, there is a clean and clear distinction between just and unjust laws. First, an unjust law contradicts or opposes moral law—that set of principles above and beyond any particular society. Second, an unjust law diminishes and objectifies people. Segregation, the set of laws that maintained formal racial separation, treated minorities as fundamentally inferior beings—as a group to be removed from the center of society. It was, therefore, unjust. Finally, an unjust law burdens one group of people while passing over another group. In other words, it is not uniformly enacted. And unjust conditions will always come when one group develops a law that targets another group. For instance, the laws in Alabama to keep African Americans from voting were developed by white politicians and their constituents. Such laws maintained oppression, separation, and inequality (132-33). Although the people of the time did not recognize their actions as unjust, they were out of sync with moral law, with God's law.

This lengthier summary of King's argument helps the writer make a point. And if the writer were developing an extensive argument about the distinction between just and unjust laws, she might go even further with her summary. She might take several paragraphs to detail King's logic. But she would have to walk carefully—not allowing King's ideas to take over or push her own ideas aside.

ACTIVITY

In groups, summarize the following passage from Ann Marie Paulin's essay (from Chapter 8). Try to develop two different summaries—one that abbreviates Paulin's point into a single sentence and another that makes the point in a single short paragraph:

> So we are surrounded by a culture, even an infrastructure, that encourages obesity, yet the culture also breeds a prejudice against fat people. Various articles and news magazine programs have reported that Americans of all sizes make far more than simple aesthetic judgments when they look at a fat person. Fat people are assumed to be lazy, stupid, ugly, lacking in self-esteem and pride, devoid of self-control, and stuffed full of a host of other unpleasant qualities that have nothing to do with the size of a person's belly or thighs. But, as anyone who has ever been the victim of such prejudice can tell you, the impact such foolish notions have is real and harmful. For example, Marilyn Wann, in her book *Fat! So?*, cites an experiment in which "[r]esearchers placed two fake personal ads, one for a woman described as '50 pounds overweight' and the other for a woman described as a drug addict. The drug addict received 79 percent of the responses" (59).

Quotation

Quoting involves using the exact words of a source. It puts a spotlight on another writer's language and allows writers to integrate especially important phrasing or passages. The key, however, is to carefully select what ideas and manners of expression are *worth* quoting. When writing down quotes, keep in mind two points:

1. **Quote sparingly.** Quote only when a passage is particularly striking—AND quote only the striking part. For example, do not quote an entire paragraph if you can quote just a sentence; do not quote an entire sentence if you can quote only three words from that sentence.

2. **Put others' words within quotation marks.** Consider the following well-chosen quotation from the original King passage:

> According to Martin Luther King Jr., "Human progress never rolls in on wheels of inevitability; it comes through the tireless efforts of men willing to be co-workers with God, and without this hard work, time itself becomes an ally of the forces of stagnation" (130).

Writers can use various strategies for punctuating quotations:

Quotation marks only: When the quoted matter blends directly into your sentence without a speaking verb (such as *say, says, said, exclaims, proclaims,* or *states*) indicating a change in voice, no punctuation is required before the quotation. The sentence may be punctuated just as it would be if there were no quotation marks:

> According to Anderson's records, before the end of the decade, there were "eighteen million people involved in the crisis" (177).

> Emphasizing her point, Miller demands that "it is now time for something drastic to change here on campus" (43).

Speaking verb followed by a comma: Speaking verbs (such as *say, says, suggests, exclaims,* or *states*) indicate a shift in voice from your voice to the voice of your source. A comma separates the speaking verb and the quotation:

> His final paragraph, before the epilogue, says, "Let's create a system that encourages people like Andie at least as much as the ones who don't give a damn" (Sacks 187).

> Emphasizing her point, Miller suggests, "It is now time for something drastic to change here on campus" (43).

Helpful Verbs for Attributing Quotes

says	describes
considers	insists
argues	tells
shows	offers
explains	informs
demands	claims
suggests	instructs
teaches	points out
emphasizes	

As Martin Luther King Jr. explains, in his "Letter from Birmingham Jail," "One day the South will know that when these disinherited children of God sat down at lunch counters, they were in reality standing up for what is best in the American dream" (130).

A speaking verb combined with a noun creates an attributive phrase that can be placed at the beginning, in the middle, or at the end of a sentence. Quoting involves crafting sentences carefully to create clear and natural-sounding connections between the writer's own ideas and the words of the source. Here are some standard strategies:

Quotation at the Beginning of a Sentence

"All voting is a sort of gaming, like checkers or backgammon, with a slight moral tinge to it," explains Henry David Thoreau (56).

Quotation in the Middle of a Sentence

As Thoreau points out, "All voting is a sort of gaming, like checkers or backgammon, with a slight moral tinge to it" (56), and it is this moral issue that is often overemphasized on ballots.

Quotation at the End of a Sentence

Henry David Thoreau claims that "voting is a sort of gaming, like checkers or backgammon, with a slight moral tinge to it" (56).

Quotation Divided by Your Own Words

"All voting," explains Thoreau, "is a sort of gaming" (56).

Sentence followed by a colon: Sometimes writers use a whole sentence to set up, or explain, the quotation. In this case, they use a colon between their own sentence and the quotation. The colon, in effect, says, "and now, here comes the other person's words":

> For example, he introduced the reader to Marissa and Carol: "As very good students, [their views] were virtually excluded by The College in order to accommodate the whiners and complainers" (Sacks 61).

> As George Williams notes, protection of white privilege is critical to patterns of discrimination: "Whenever a number of persons within a society have enjoyed for a considerable period of time certain opportunities for getting wealth, for exercising power and authority, and for successfully claiming prestige and social deference, there is strong tendency for these people to feel that these benefits are theirs by 'right'" (727).

If an entire sentence is a quotation—that is, if it begins and ends with a quotation mark and contains no reference to the source in between—consider the following approaches: (1) connect the quote, if appropriate, to the preceding sentence with a colon, or (2) add a cue, or transition, as an introduction to the quote.

Special Conditions in Quoting

To integrate quotes smoothly into a text, writers sometimes find it helpful to omit or add certain words for clarity or cohesion. Standard guidelines exist for letting readers know how the writer has altered a quotation. Of course, the writer must be certain that he or she has not changed the source's intended meaning. Note also the standard approach to using long quotations.

Omitting Words: Occasionally, writers want to leave out words or phrases of a passage they are quoting. This is done with ellipses (. . .). They tell readers that words have been taken out of the original passage. Notice how one might quote the following passage from an essay by David Crabtree:

> **Original:** The world is changing at a bewildering pace. Anyone who owns a computer and tries to keep up with the developments in hardware, software, and the accompanying

incompatibilities is all too aware of the speed of change. This rapid change, especially technological change, has extremely important implications for the job market. In the past, it was possible to look at the nation's workforce, determine which of the existing occupations was most desirable in terms of pay and working conditions, and pick one to prepare for. But the rapid rate of change is clouding the crystal ball. How do we know that a high-paying job today will be high-paying tomorrow?

Quotation: According to David Crabtree, "The world is changing at a bewildering pace. . . . This rapid change, especially technological change, has extremely important implications for the job market."

The ellipses indicate the missing sentence from the quotation. The same strategy can be applied to cut any amount of text from a passage. For instance, in the following sentence, a few words have been cut from Crabtree's passage:

Quotation: According to David Crabtree, "This rapid change . . . has extremely important implications for the job market."

Adding Words: Sometimes it is valuable to add a note or comment within a quote. In this case, writers use square brackets to set off their own words. For example, a writer may insert a word in a quoted passage to clarify a vague pronoun or to give a brief explanation:

Original: After months of exhausting research, they had finally come to understand the problem with their design.

Quotation: "After months of exhausting research, [the nuclear scientists] had finally come to understand the problem with their design" (Smith 82).

Here, the writer substitutes the actual noun for the pronoun *they*. Without the noun, readers may not understand the meaning of the quotation. As in this example, inserting bracketed comments within quotes can clear up any potentially confusing information within a quote while maintaining the flow of the sentence.

Noting an Error: If a quotation is grammatically or syntactically flawed, a writer cannot simply change it. In such cases, the quotation must remain intact, and the writer must use square brackets and the three-letter word *sic* directly after the error. Otherwise, readers might assume that the error is on the part of the writer:

In his letter to the editor, Jeremy Miller argues that "Obama should not of [sic] bailed out the auto industry or the banks." He goes on to argue against bailouts in any form.

Using Lengthy Quotes: When writers quote more than four lines, they must use a block quote. As in this passage from Ann Marie Paulin's essay, writers often use a colon before block quotes:

Another example of this bullying someone thin comes from Pipher's book *Hunger Pains: The Modern Woman's Tragic Quest for Thinness*. Pipher recounts a conversation she overheard one day in a dress shop:

> I overheard a mother talking to her daughter, who was trying on party dresses. She put on each dress and then asked her mother how she looked. Time after time, her mother responded by saying, "You look just awful in that, Kathy. You're so fat nothing fits you right." The mother's voice dripped with disgust and soon Kathy was crying. (89)

Pipher goes on to suggest that Kathy's mother is a victim of the culture, too, because she realizes how hard the world will be on her fat daughter. Unfortunately, what she doesn't realize is how much better her daughter's quality of life would be if she felt loved by her mother. Any person surrounded by loving family members at home is much better equipped to deal with whatever the cruel world outside throws at her or him.

Double Quotes: Occasionally, writers quote a passage that contains a quotation or is itself a quotation. In this case, single quotation marks are used inside the double quotation marks:

> As Maria Gallagher has argued, "It is time that we turn the corner on the road of national energy policies and begin to take 'alternative energy' seriously" (23).

Coherence Strategies

Outside sources can make a text more sophisticated, but they can also create confusion if the writer does not make explicit connections between points. Because outside sources often increase the complexity of a text, writers have to employ *textual cues:* sentences, words, and phrases that explain the relationship between ideas and sources. Textual cues are like the road signs of an essay. They help readers keep track of who's saying what within paragraphs and throughout the essay. For example, the following textual cue helps readers keep track of previously mentioned names:

> Most music critics, *such as Smith, Castella, and Sanchez,* see the latest alternative genre as a collective response to the grunge scene of the early '90s.

Here, the critics listed have been discussed prior to this sentence, and the writer simply reminds readers about these voices and how they relate to the present point being made. Simple phrases (such as *for example*) cue readers to make connections between passages in the text:

> Jones's ideas are often seen as radical. Alberta Slavik, *for example,* casts Jones aside as a "hyper-liberal" journalist: "William Jones has gone too far, simply parading his politics at the cost of facts" (76).

In the following paragraph, notice how Daniel Bruno uses a range of textual cues. He blends together, or integrates, what he thinks and what his source says by (1) stating his main idea *(Sacks illustrates that all of today's college students cannot just be thrown in the same big barrel);* (2) directing readers to the source *(he spends, he says, he mentions);* (3) providing the information from the source that supports or explains his idea; and (4) concluding by commenting on the information:

> In *Generation X Goes to College,* Peter Sacks illustrates that all of today's college students cannot just be thrown in the same big barrel. In describing the modern/post-modern clash in education, he spends the majority of his time talking about those students who are underprepared, who lack the basic study skills required in academic work, and who demonstrate little real commitment to their own education. Yet, he does not discuss this problem in isolation. He also mentions another type of student. For example, he introduces the reader to Marissa and Carol: "As very good students, [their views] were virtually excluded by The College in order to accommodate the whiners and complainers" (61). And he says they "suffered not only educationally" (63). In addition to discussing specific good students, an entire chapter presents survey results about students' attitudes toward education. While he makes claims such as "nearly a quarter of the students . . . harbored a disproportionate sense of entitlement," this very statement tells the reader that a full three quarters (that is, three out of four) students *do not* "harbor a disproportionate sense of entitlement" (54-59). He wraps up the book by focusing on another student, Andie, who he describes as "a good student, constantly picking [his] brain for information and feedback on her work" (186-87). His final paragraph, before the Epilogue, says, "Let's create a system that encourages people like Andie at least as much as the ones who don't give a damn" (187). Thus, Sacks shows that today's students are a more diverse group—in skill level, background, and attitude toward education—than has ever before been gathered together in the college classroom.

Writers often rely on Bruno's four steps:

1. Explaining the main idea

2. Referencing the source

3. Giving information from the source

4. Commenting on that information

Essays that rely on outside sources also require good *paragraph transitions* (sentences and phrases that join the content of paragraphs and show the logical connections). Because sources create more dimensions in an essay project, readers require explicit intellectual help as they walk through a line of reasoning. Transition statements usually begin paragraphs and help readers to bridge from one paragraph to the next. The following sentences, which all begin paragraphs, act as bridges from previous points:

- Not all farmers, however, agree with Johnson's strategy.

- Despite this overwhelming amount of evidence, some teachers refuse to acknowledge the way gender and race figure into the classroom.

- But all of the discussion on war distracts voters from significant domestic issues that will impact everyday life in the present and future.

- Because of Smith's recent book, many researchers have begun focusing their attention on the ways technology will change our ability to communicate.

Plagiarism

Plagiarism—failing to acknowledge, or give credit to, a source of information—is intellectual theft. It involves using either (1) an idea or (2) the manner of expression of another person as if it is the writer's own. Plagiarism can take many forms and may be either intentional or unintentional. For example, knowingly turning in another person's paper and claiming it as one's own work is a serious form of academic dishonesty likely to have a severe consequence, such as damage to one's reputation and expulsion from school. Other times, however, writers plagiarize accidentally because they are unaware of the rules. They do not know, for example, that the ideas taken from a source, even if not quoted directly, must be documented.

Just as it is every driver's responsibility to know and obey the rules of the road (for his or her own benefit as well as for the benefit of others), it is every writer's responsibility to know the rules of documentation. To avoid plagiarism, you must acknowledge your source (also referred to as "citing" or "crediting" the source) whenever you express someone else's idea, opinion, or theory, or whenever you provide information such as a fact or statistic that is not common knowledge.

If you use the exact words of the source, you must indicate that by putting them within quotation marks—and also by crediting the source (using quotation marks alone does not count as crediting the source). If you use information from a source but express it in your own words (through paraphrase or summary), you should not put the information inside quotation marks, but you still must credit the source.

Most often, plagiarism occurs because writers are simply not going far enough in their paraphrasing. That is, they are not sufficiently rewording the ideas from the original source. A good paraphrase avoids using the same subjects and verbs as in the original text. To avoid this, read the original passage closely, but rather than writing down the ideas immediately, talk through them first. Remember that any one idea can be phrased in infinite ways.

Writers sometimes plagiarize intentionally because they are desperate to complete an assignment or pass a class. They set out to steal (or buy) others' ideas. In this age of technology, students can easily download text from an online source, and they can even buy college essays from websites and online databases. However, such essays are prepackaged, the topics are generalized, and the writing mundane—essentially, they are the opposite of what most college instructors want, and are contrary to the invention strategies suggested throughout this book. Also, as websites featuring prewritten essays increase, so does the ability of instructors to detect plagiarism.

The consequences of plagiarism are more far-reaching and destructive than what some students may assume. Besides failing an assignment, failing an entire class, or being expelled, students who plagiarize fail to learn essential writing and thinking skills—or even when and how to ask for help. They also establish a low standard for themselves, which is perhaps the worst result of plagiarizing.

DOCUMENTING SOURCES

Why document sources? There are at least three good reasons:

1. **To be honest.** When presenting others' opinions, research, or manner of expression, writers give credit to, or acknowledge, their sources.

2. **To gain credibility.** If a source is credible (see Evaluating Sources in Chapter 15, page 454), then the writer's claims gain credibility. Many times writers are not experts on their subject matter; however, they can write confidently about their subjects as a result of sources. Also, writers are taken more seriously if they appear well informed, having "done their research."

3. **To provide readers with more information.** Listing sources provides readers with access to more information. This allows readers to explore the subject matter further.

Different disciplines rely on different styles of documentation. The two most common styles are MLA (Modern Language Association) and APA (American Psychological Association).

MLA STYLE

English and humanities use MLA style. Like other documentation styles, MLA depends on two basic components: (1) an in-text citation of a work and (2) a list of works cited at the end of the text. These two components function in the following ways:

- In-text citations let readers know that particular ideas come from a particular source.

- In-text documentation corresponds to the complete bibliographic information provided at the end of the text.

- In-text citations lead readers directly to the corresponding Works Cited page.

- Done correctly, the in-text reference lists the first word(s)—whether it be the author's last name or the article title—plus the page reference of the citation on the alphabetized Works Cited page. This allows readers to easily locate the source in the list of works.

- The Works Cited page provides complete information for finding all formal sources. This complete information is provided only once and comes at the end of the entire text so that it doesn't interfere with ease of reading.

In-Text Citation

In-text documentation involves referencing the original text in parentheses within the actual sentences of your text; because it uses parentheses, it is sometimes called *parenthetical citation*.

An in-text citation must occur when a writer does any of the following:

- Quotes directly from a source
- Paraphrases ideas from a source
- Summarizes ideas from a source
- References statistics or data from a source

In general, for MLA style, in-text citations should include the author's last name (unless it is given within the sentence) and page number of the source from which the cited material is taken (unless the source is electronic and lacks page numbers).

"After months of exhausting research, they had finally come to understand the problem with their design" (Smith 82).

A space separates the name and the page number.
The end punctuation comes after the citation.

If the author is referred to in the sentence, his or her name can be omitted from the citation.

Emphasizing her point, Miller demands that "it is now time for something drastic to change here on campus" (43).

If the source has no author, use the first word or phrase of the source's title and punctuate accordingly (quotation marks for an article and italics for a book).

The oil had spread over much of the shoreline and had "already begun its death grip on a vast array of wildlife" ("Black Death" 54).

If the source has two authors, use the last name of both authors.

(Lunsford and Ede 158)

If you have more than one work by the same author, insert the title of the work after the author name, followed by the page number.

(Faigley, *Fragments of Rationality* 43)

If there is more than one author with same last name, include the first initial for both authors or even the authors' full names.

"After months of exhausting research, they had finally come to understand the problem with their design" (A. Smith 82).

If you are citing material that is already quoted in the source, cite the source in which you found the quotation and add "qtd. in" before the author's name or title.

(qtd. in Smith 82)

If you want to acknowledge more than one source for the same information, use a semi-colon between citations within one set of parentheses.

(Lunsford and Ede 78; Smith 82)

If you have an electronic source with no page numbers, simply exclude the page number from the citation. Do not add page numbers, and do not use those that a computer printer assigns.

According to Martha Smith, "untold numbers of children are negatively affected by the proficiency test craze."

Works Cited .

Works Cited pages list the sources that are directly cited in the text. In general, the first piece of information in the Works Cited entry should correspond directly with the first piece of information in the in-text citation. For example, notice the relationship between the in-text citation for Patricia Hampl, below, and the entire bibliographic information in the Works Cited page:

The difference between those who write memoirs and those who write fiction is that "memoirists wish to tell their mind, not their story" (**Hampl** 330).

Works Cited

Hampl, Patricia. "Red Sky in the Morning." *Reading Culture: Contexts for Critical Reading and Writing*, edited by Diana George and John Trimbur, 7th ed., Longman, 2010, pp. 329–31.

The most essential elements of any Works Cited entry are Author, Title, Publication Information, and for many sources, Location (an exact page number, URL, or physical place where a source can be found).

- **Authors**
  - The author is the person or people who wrote or otherwise created the source.
  - The author name(s) comes first in the citation and is inverted (last name first), with a comma between last and first names.

- **Titles**
  - All words in titles are capitalized except prepositions (such as *on, in, between*), articles (*a, an, the*), coordinating conjunctions (*and, but, for, nor, or, so, yet*), and *to* in infinitives (such as *to run, to go*).
  - The titles of shorter works or works that are part of a larger whole (like an article in a magazine) are set in quotation marks, while the titles of longer or stand-alone works (books, magazines, newspapers, films, websites) are set in italics.
  - If no author is listed for a source, then your citation will start with the title of your source.

- **Publication Information**
  - Publication information will usually include the name of the publisher or sponsoring organization and the copyright or publication date.
  - Publishers should be listed for books, films, television shows, and similar sources. Use complete names for publishers, but omit business words and abbreviations such as *Company (Co.)*, *Incorporated (Inc.)*, and *Corp.* from publisher names in your Works Cited entries. Use the abbreviation *UP* for the words University Press in the names of college publishers (Yale UP, for example).
  - Publisher names should *not* be included in citations for periodicals or articles, for works published directly by authors or editors, for websites for which the publisher's name is the same as the title of the site, or for websites that do not produce the works they house (examples: *YouTube, Hulu,* or databases such as *Academic Search Premier*).
  - If a month is part of the publication date, then abbreviate the names of all months in your Works Cited entries, except for the months of May, June, and July.

- **Location Information**
  - For print sources that are part of a larger whole, such as an article in magazine or an essay in an anthology, provide the specific page number(s) on which the selection appears.
  - For online sources, you will need to include a URL or web address instead of page numbers. If available, it is preferable to provide a permalink or stable URL, rather than copying a URL from your browser. Also, if your source has a DOI (or digital

object identifier), then you should use that identifier number in your citation (preceded by *doi:*) rather than a URL.

- **Access Dates for Online Sources**

An access date should be added to the end of a citation when you are citing an online source that does not have a publication date or date when the site was last modified, or when you are citing an online source that is frequently revised or updated or otherwise changed. If you include a date of access in your citation, that element comes last and is set per this example: Accessed 30 Mar. 2017.

Books

Bibliographic information for books is contained on the title page and the copyright page (the back side of the title page). The title page contains the full title of the book, the author(s), and the publishing company. The copyright page contains date(s) and any edition numbers.

Single Author Print Book

Author Name:
As for all sources in MLA format, the first author name is inverted (last name first).

Title of the Source
Titles of longer or stand-alone works (books, magazines, newspapers, films, websites) are set in italics.

Palmeri, Jason. *Remixing Composition: A History of Multimodal Writing Pedagogy*. Southern Illinois UP, 2012.

Publisher
Publisher names are always found on the title page of a book. Give complete publisher names, but omit business words and abbreviations like Company (Co.) and Inc. from publisher names. Use the abbreviation UP for university presses. Cities or places of publication do not usually need to be included.

Publication Date
The date usually appears on the copyright page of a book, which is the back side of the title page. Always use the most recent date listed. Use a comma between the publisher and the date of publication.

Book with Two Authors

McKee, Heidi A., and James E. Porter. *The Ethics of Internet Research: A Rhetorical, Case-based Approach*. Peter Lang International Academic Publishers, 2009.

Book with Three or More Authors

Kargon, Robert, et al. *World's Fairs on the Eve of War: Science, Technology, and Modernity, 1937–1942*. U of Pittsburgh P, 2015.

Corporate Author or Government Publication

MLA Handbook. 8th ed., Modern Language Association of America, 2016.

United States, Office of Consumer Affairs. *2003 Consumer's Resource Handbook*. Government Publishing Office, 2003.

If an organization or company is both the author and the publisher of the source you are using (as in the *MLA Handbook* example above), then start your citation with the title of the source and list the organization only as the publisher. For government publications, if no specific person is listed as the author, then your citation should list the government entity as the author; start with the name of the government (United States), followed by the agency (Office of Consumer Affairs, in the example above). Many federal publications are published by the Government Publishing Office (GPO).

Subsequent Editions

Wicks-Nelson, Rita, and Allen C. Israel. *Behavior Disorders of Childhood.* 6th ed., Prentice
    Hall, 2005.

When a source has an edition number, find the edition information on the title page of the book. Place the edition number in the Works Cited entry directly after the title or the editor, if there is one. Use the abbreviations *2nd ed., 3rd ed.,* and so on, or *Revised ed.,* depending on what the title page says.

Republished Book

Tolkien, J. R. R. *The Hobbit.* 1937. Ballantine Books, 2003.

Older books may be published by a company other than the original publishers, or a hardcover book may be republished in paperback. In such cases, insert the original publication date after the title, and then give the recent publisher and date.

Edited Book

Busch, Frederick. *The Stories of Frederick Busch.* Edited by Elizabeth Strout, W. W. Norton,
    2014.

When a source has an editor, add *edited by* after the title of the book, followed by the editor's name, not inverted. Use *edited by* even if there is more than one editor.

Translated Book

Bakhtin, Mikhail. *Problems of Dostoevsky's Poetics.* Translated by Caryl Emerson, U of
    Minnesota P, 1984.

When a source has a translator, add *translated by* after the title of the book followed by the translator's name, not inverted.

Online Book

Shaw, Bernard. *Pygmalion.* Brentano, 1916. *Bartleby.com,* www.bartleby.com/138/.

Start by providing complete source information for the print version of the book. Then list the title of the website (italicized) where you found the online book and the URL. If the book is part of an online scholarly project, which is often the case, include information on the sponsoring institution in your citation.

E-book

Doerr, Anthony. *All The Light We Cannot See.* Kindle ed., Scribner, 2014.

Again, provide complete source details as you would for a print version of the book. Include the type of e-reader device you used to view the book and treat that information as you would a version or edition number. In the example above, *Kindle ed.* here stands for *Kindle edition.*

Articles

Articles appear in newspapers and periodicals (journals or magazines). Although newspapers are usually published daily, magazines are usually published weekly or monthly, and journals are published quarterly or even biannually.

ACTIVITY

Decide which type of periodical (magazine or journal) may have published the following articles, and in groups or as a class, discuss the reasoning behind your decisions:

"Heading for the Mountains: An Exciting Getaway for the Whole Family"

"Climatic Shifts in the Mountain Region"

"Coach Fired, Team Responds"

"Enzymes, Nutrition, and Aging: A Twenty-Year Study"

"The Latest in Deep Water Bait"

"Re-inventing the Microscope"

"The Epistemology of Literature: Reading and Knowing"

Article in a Magazine, Accessed Online

Author Name
Regardless of the type of source, the first author name is inverted.

Title of Article
The titles of shorter works or works that are part of a larger whole (like an article in a magazine, or an individual song) are set in quotation marks

Cashion, Matt. "This Commodious Desert." *The Writer's Chronicle*, Feb. 2017, pp. 86-95.

Title of Source
The title of the magazine, journal, or newspaper is italicized.

Publication date
Include month and year directly after the title of the container. For weekly or biweekly magazines, include the full date (day, month, and year). Remember to abbreviate the names of all months except May, June, and July.

Location
For an article accessed online, include a URL (but leave *http://* and *https://* out of the link address) or a permalink or a DOI (digital object identifier) depending upon what is available for your source. If accessing an article in print, include page numbers instead of a URL.

Article in a Print Journal

Leonard, Rebecca Lorimer. "Multilingual Writing as Rhetorical Attunement." *College English*, vol. 76, no. 3, Jan. 2014, pp. 227–47.

Academic or scholarly journals often have a volume number and an issue number, and if available, these need to be included in your citation. The volume number is preceded by *vol.* and the issue number is preceded by *no.* The volume and/or issue number are followed by the publication date (month or season [if available] and year), then inclusive page numbers.

Article in Online Journal

Kingma, Mireille. "Nurses on the Move: Historical Perspective and Current Issues." *OJIN: Online Journal of Issues in Nursing,* vol. 13, no. 2, May 2008, doi:10.3912/OJIN .Vol13No02Man01.

Follow the format for print articles; however, instead of page numbers, you will include a URL or DOI (digital object identifier). Many academic journal articles have a permanent DOI assigned to them by the publisher or have an otherwise stable URL that you can include in your citation.

Journal Article Retrieved from a Database

Glenberg, Arthur M., and Thomas Grimes. "Memory and Faces: Pictures Help You Remember Who Said What." *Personality and Social Psychology Bulletin*, vol. 21, no. 3, Mar. 1995, pp. 196–206. *Academic Search Complete*, doi:10.1177/0146167295213001.

First provide full citation information for the original source, including the volume, issue, year, and page numbers. Then include the name of the database (italicized) and either a DOI or a URL to indicate where the article is located in the database. Remember that academic journal articles in a database often have a specific DOI assigned to them and it is preferable to use a DOI rather than a URL if one is available.

Article in a Print Newspaper

Overbye, Dennis. "With Faint Chirp, Scientists Prove Einstein Correct." *The New York Times*, 12 Feb. 2016, pp. A1+.

For a local newspaper, when the name of the city of publication is not already part of the title of the newspaper, add the city name in square brackets after the title of the newspaper (*The Star Ledger* [Newark]). National newspapers (such as *The Washington Post* or *The New York Times*) do not need any city name included. Add section letters before the page numbers if appropriate. If the page numbers are not consecutive, then list the first page number, immediately followed by a plus sign.

Newspaper or Magazine Article Retrieved from a Database

Turkle, Sherry. "The Flight from Conversation." *The New York Times*, 22 Apr. 2012, p. L1. *Academic OneFile*, go.galegroup.com/ps/i.do?id=GALE%7CA287213303&v=2.1&u =nysl_ me_wls&it=r&p=AONE&sw=w&asid=e70139ddee4d97ee8aa08c5bc06d7342.

First provide full citation information for the original source, including the publication date and page numbers (if available). Then list the name of the database (italicized), and the URL address (or the permalink if available) for the article in the database.

Essay, Story, or Poem in an Anthology (such as a college textbook)

Paulin, Ann Marie. "Cruelty, Civility, and Other Weighty Matters." *The Composition of Everyday Life*, edited by John Mauk and John Metz, 6th ed., Cengage Learning, 2019, pp. 230–38.

Begin with the author, followed by the title of the work (essay, story, or poem). Then give the title of the book, the editors, and the publication information. End with the page numbers on which the article or essay appears.

Encyclopedia Article

Esposito, Vincent J. "World War II: The Diplomatic History of the War and Post-War Period." *The Encyclopedia Americana*, intl. ed., vol. 29, Grolier, 2000, pp. 227–32.

Begin with an author name if one is given. (Check for author names at the beginning or end of the article.) Put the title of the article in quotation marks and italicize the encyclopedia title. Include the edition information (if applicable), volume number (for multi-volume works), publisher name, publication year, and page numbers of the article.

Online-Only Sources

Official Website

Pinsker, Sarah, editor. *Robin Flies Again: Letters Written by Women of Goucher College, Class of 1903*. Goucher College, 1999, meyerhoff.goucher.edu/library/robin/.

Game of Thrones. Home Box Office, www.hbo.com/game-of-thrones. Accessed 6 Feb. 2017.

Begin with the name of the site's editor or author (if available) and the title of the site (italicized). Next, give the name of the publisher of the site or organization that sponsors the site (if available), and the date of online publication or the date of the latest update to the site (if available), followed by the URL.

For websites that do not offer a last modified or other publication date, or that change and are updated often (such as the *Game of Thrones* site), it may be helpful to include an access date at the end of your citation.

Personal or Professional Home Page

McNair, Patricia. *Patricia Ann McNair: Things Writerly and Readerly*. 1 Feb. 2017, patriciaannmcnair.com/.

Begin with the creator's name, followed by the title (or *Home page* if no title is given), publisher or sponsor (if available), the most recent date that the site was updated or revised (if available), and the URL.

Document or Page from Website

Winter, Jana. "FBI Reports Show Terror Suspects Coming from Canada While Trump Stares at Mexico." *The Daily Beast*, 7 Feb. 2017, www.thedailybeast.com/articles/2014/05/04/high-manxiety-thirtysomething-men-are-the-new-neurotic-singles.html.

"SCA Equestrian Handbook." *The Society for Creative Anachronism*, 2012, www.sca.org
/officers/equestrian/pdf/equestrian_handbook.pdf.

Begin with the author's name (if available), followed by the title of the document or page (in quotation marks), the title of the website (italicized), the sponsor or publisher, the date of publication or last update (if given), and the URL. If the web page has no title, then offer a description, such as *Home page* (not italicized) in its place. If the publisher and the title of the website are essentially the same (as in the two examples above), then the publisher name can be omitted from the citation.

Government Website

"Asteroids." *Solar System Exploration*, United States, National Aeronautics and Space
Administration, solarsystem.nasa.gov/planets/asteroids. Accessed 26 Jan. 2017.

If a government agency (like NASA) or other type of organization is both the author and the publisher for a work, then start your citation with the title of the source and list the government agency only as the publisher.

Online Presentation

Groshelle, Zane. "Visualizing Your Pitch." *Prezi*, 19 Feb. 2015, prezi.com/oerqtrj5ie3y
/visualizing-your-pitch/.

Give the author name, the title of presentation (in quotation marks), the title of the website (italicized), the publisher/sponsor of the site (if it is different from the title of the website), and the date of publication or date that the presentation was last modified. End your citation with a URL.

E-mail

Wells, Carson. "Questionable Behavior." Received by Anton Chigurh, 23 Nov. 2013.

Begin with the name of the author/sender of the e-mail, and then treat the subject of the e-mail as the title of the source, setting it in quotation marks. Include the recipient's name; if you were the e-mail's recipient, insert *Received by author* (but not in italics). End with the e-mail's date.

Online Posting

Brown, Fleda. "My Wobbly Bicycle, 129." *Fleda Brown*, 1 Feb. 2017, fledabrown
.com/2017/02/my-wobbly-bicycle-129.

List the author of the posting and the title of the posting (in quotation marks). Then give the name of the website, the date of the posting, and the URL for the posting.

Untitled Online Posting

@metmuseum (Metropolitan Museum of Art). "#SmallWonders features nearly
50 small-scale, intricate carvings created by artists working in the Netherlands in
the 16th cent." *Twitter*, 21 Feb. 2017, 12:22 p.m., twitter.com/metmuseum/status
/834090859570331648.

For a short untitled post like a tweet, provide the author's online user name, followed by the author's real name in parentheses, if known. Include the entire message in your citation and treat the message as the title of the source (enclosed in quotations). Then give the name of the website, the date and time of the posting, and the specific URL for the posting.

Entry in an Online Encyclopedia or Dictionary

"India." *Encyclopædia Britannica Online,* 22 June 2016, www.britannica.com/place/India. Accessed 2 Feb. 2017.

Begin with the title of the entry in the dictionary or encyclopedia, if no author is available. Then list the title of the encyclopedia, the publication or last modified date, and the URL. If you are citing an online dictionary or encyclopedia where the entries are changed and updated regularly (such as *Wikipedia*), then you may also want to include an access date at the end of your citation.

Other Sources

Abstract

Barton, Ellen. "Resources for Discourse Analysis in Composition Studies." Abstract. *Style,* vol. 36, no. 4, Winter 2002, pp. 575–95. *JSTOR,* www.jstor.org/stable/10.5325 /style.36.4.575.

Use the format appropriate for the type of source (book, article, etc.) and add the descriptor *Abstract* after the title. In the case of an abstract found online like this example, include the database title and URL for the article. Note that *JSTOR* provides stable URLs for sources.

Television Episode

"Lisa the Veterinarian." *The Simpsons,* season 27, episode 15, Twentieth Century Fox Television, 2016.

If you are discussing the episode in a general way, provide the title of the episode, the title of the series, the season and episode numbers. Include either the main production company with the year the episode was produced (as in the example above), or include the main distribution company with the original broadcast date (as in the example below).

Smith, Yeardley, performer. "Lisa the Veterinarian." *The Simpsons,* created by Matt Groening, season 27, episode 15, Fox Network, 6 Mar. 2016.

If your paper is focused on a particular character or other person connected with the episode, then start your citation with that person's name (inverted) followed by a description of his or her role. In the example above, the actor who performs the character of Lisa Simpson, Yeardley Smith, is being emphasized.

Film

True Grit. Paramount Pictures, 2010.

If your paper is discussing a film in a general way, then your citation needs only the title of the film, the main or primary distributing company, and the year of release (or re-release, if relevant).

Coen, Joel, and Ethan Coen, directors. *True Grit.* Performance by Jeff Bridges, Paramount Pictures, 2010.

If your essay is focused on the work of a particular person connected with the film, include that person's name with a description in your citation. The example above highlights the film's directors.

Film or Television Episode, Accessed Online

"Unraveling." *The Killing*, season 4, episode 2, AMC, 1 Aug. 2014. *Netflix*, www.netflix
.com/watch/70306003. Accessed 12 May 2016.

Start by providing complete original broadcast information (for a tv episode) or original release information (for a film).
Next give the name of the online site or service (set in italics) where you accessed the tv episode or film, and then the
URL. Because streaming services like *Netflix* and *Hulu* change their content often, you may also want to include an access
date in the citation.

Audio Recording

Tragically Hip. "Morning Moon." *We Are the Same*, Zoe Records, 2009.

Begin with the artist's name. Then list the title of a particular song or section (in quotation marks), the title of the collection or album (italicized), the recording company, and the year of release. If you accessed the recording online, then as
with a film or tv episode accessed online, you would provide the name of the site or service where you accessed the recording (like *Spotify*), set in italics, and then the URL for the recording.

Personal Interview

Mossbacher, Delaney. Personal interview. 4 Dec. 2016.

Begin with the name of the interviewee, inverted. End with the interview date.

Published Letter

Tolkien, J. R. R. "To Christopher Tolkien." 18 Jan. 1944. *The Letters of J. R. R. Tolkien*,
edited by Humphrey Carpenter and Christopher Tolkien, Houghton Mifflin, 2000,
pp. 67–68.

After the date of the letter, give the number of the letter, if available. List the information of the source in which the letter
was published, according to the correct format for the source. (In other words, if the letter is published in a book, as
above, follow the book format.)

Print Brochure

Report Card. Miami U, 2016. Brochure.

Give information in the same format as a book. Include as much publication information as you can locate. Here
University is abbreviated as *U*. Also, for unexpected or unusual sources, you can include a description at the end of the
citation to give readers additional information about the source (*Brochure* in this case).

Print Advertisement

Converse College. "Converse College MFA." *The Writer's Chronicle*, Oct.-Nov. 2015, p. 26.
Advertisement.

Begin with the name of the company that owns or produces the product being advertised, followed by the name of the
product featured in the ad. Then list the complete publication information for the source where you found the ad.
Again, for an unusual sources like this, it can be helpful to include a description at the end of the citation (*Advertisement*
in this example).

Work of Art (painting, sculpture, photograph)

O'Keeffe, Georgia. *Evening Star No. VI.* 1917, Georgia O'Keeffe Museum, Santa Fe.

Include the artist's name (inverted), the title of the work (italicized), the date of composition (if available), the collector or institution that houses it, and the city where it is held.

Lecture or Speech

Obama, Barack. "Remarks by the President on Osama Bin Laden." White House, 1 May 2011, East Room, Washington.

Begin with the speaker's name, and then list the title of the speech or presentation (in quotation marks). Include the name of the meeting and sponsoring organization (if applicable), the date of the event, the venue of the lecture or speech (*East Room*, in this example), and the city.

Performance

Twelfth Night. By William Shakespeare, directed by William Church, Interlochen Center for the Arts, 28 June 2008, Harvey Theater, Interlochen.

For a collaborative performance, like a play, start with the title of the work being performed. Include the author or creator of the work (Shakespeare, in this example), the director, the performers (if available), the sponsoring organization or company (if applicable), the date, the venue or theater, and the city where the performance was held.

SAMPLE RESEARCH ESSAY

Francesca Peck wrote this argument for her first-semester college writing course. Throughout the argument, she brings together, or *synthesizes,* print and online sources to support her case. As you read, take note of documentation strategies, textual cues, coherence devices, and even Peck's voice. She manages to make a formal argument while maintaining an engaging presence in the essay.

Peck 1

Francesca Peck

Professor Mauk

English 111

8 November 2016

A World Made of Pixels

Some art historians argue that America's manifest destiny started with the flash of a camera. In mid-nineteenth century, the government began distributing photographs to endorse tourism, westward expansion, and ultimately, nation building (Stetler). Photography's initial purpose in the United States was intended to *build* American culture, and over time it has *become* our culture, overexposing society to visual representations and compromising the human experience. The crunch of a shuttering aperture marks an incomplete experience, and though the photo *optically* embodies a specific moment in time, the genuine memory subtly fades into the faint distance of our past.

Daughter to an airline pilot, I have flown around the world. By the time I grew mature enough to appreciate

She uses the source (Stetler) to help set up an important distinction that operates throughout the essay.

Personal testimony helps to ground and focus the broader points about American culture and history.

Peck 2

my travel opportunities, I had already become intoxicated with an ardent passion for photography. At this young age, excessive photographing had skewed my priorities: documentation first, experience second. For years I traveled the world without fully participating in the journey because I lurked behind the viewfinder of a camera.

At the age of fifteen, I was introduced to the lush grasses of the Ecuadorian countryside. Arriving at the village of Otavalo, I learned my flashy digital camera was not accepted by the indigenous people. Here, in this town, I recognized the irrelevance of documenting my every blink when real life occurred just beyond my tripod; I realized society's obsession with photography has substituted the human eye for a camera lens, minimizing colossal memories to the 8 × 10 perimeter of experience-thieving photographs.

The overexposure to photography compromises our experience in other ways as well. Its excessive presence in American culture limits the connection we have with our own lives. Ever since the *real* world was introduced to the world of visual representation, specifically photography, the two have been easily mistaken. French philosopher Jean Baudrillard argued that the human mind can mistakenly replace reality with its representation—or simulacrum. Simulacrum has flourished since the trends of social networks and new technology have urged

The personal testimony gets specific and, therefore, more supportive and helpful.

The new paragraph signals a shift back to general points.

The paragraph builds to Baudrillard's complex theory.

Peck 3

their users to share photos on the web. As many now "approach each other and the world through the lens of these media images" (Felluga), our perception of life has begun its descent into two dimensions. We live in what many philosophers call the postmodern age, when "the representation proceeds and determines the real," when "there is only the simulacrum" (Felluga).

Photography itself is not to blame. In fact, photos liberate us from naturally imperfect memory. Studies show a positive relationship between pictures and short-term recollection as they allow us to return to a previous experience. A visual stimulus promotes basic memory, supporting face-to-name recall as well as other details the photo provides (Glenberg). And the value of photography extends far beyond personal use. Advertising, journalism, social media, the arts, and many other industries integrate photos in their work. Photography itself can be considered an industry by the technological advancements it has inspired; for example, funding has already begun to enable mass production of the latest memory assistant, Memoto. This device snaps a picture every thirty seconds, records time, and even tracks its location. The collected data are then organized into a timeline, accessible on computers and smartphones. Casually clipped on a jacket or shirt pocket, Memoto can capture our entire lives on camera for future viewing (Bass).

Peck uses the Felluga quotations to explain the theory of simulacrum. The quotations come at a critical point when the audience must understand a complex idea.

She makes a thorough concession to the use and power of photography. The source (Glenberg) supports the concession.

Peck 4

The paraphrased source (Bass) supports the broader point about the power of photography.

Here, Peck returns to her concern about overexposure. The previous paragraph, then, was a setup for this pointed evaluative claim.

Memoto and its social media predecessors are to blame for the public's overexposure to visual representations. After five minutes on Facebook, we suddenly become world travelers, seeing places we have never physically been. We attended countless parties we were never a part of and gaze at people we have never personally met. This unnatural association between reality and photos has become *normal* in our society; and sadder than it is strange, the places we *actually* go, events we *actually* attend, and people we *actually* meet often fail to live up to our pre-decided expectations.

I cannot doubt the data from scientific studies that imply the human brain has considerably reliable photo-recall ability. Images of real people, landscapes, and even diagrams seem far easier to remember than text; but if we continue with this obsession, there will no longer be a reason to remember an experience without the use of memory aids. The human body is easily manipulated: Overuse of drugs leads to dependency, excessive sugar consumption induces persistent cravings, and contact lenses can worsen natural vision. Clearly overexposure to any form of aid is dangerous to our overall well-being, and photography is no exception.

An appeal to logic: Peck develops a small line of reasoning about the impact of images on brain development.

Peck 5

For the sake of our already imperfect memory and healthy grasp on reality, I am haunted by the dehumanization of future photographic technologies. They encourage the overuse of memory aids, increasing our dependency on technology. Memoto's slogan, "Remember Every Moment" (Bass), eclipses the difference between *memory* and *memory aids*. Memoto supports the simulacrum and disconnects us from the real world. If we rely on visual documentations, would we have any memories at all in their absence?

As a practicing photographer and aspiring photojournalist, I can admit that I too fell to the temptation of over-photographing in the hopes of revisiting my past; but with time, I grew unsatisfied with watching life through the 16.2 megapixels of my beloved Nikon. I learned that what is being experienced outside of the camera is far more important than a documentation of it. As such, we must pick our moments. We must know the more pictures taken, the less valuable each becomes. Fighting against our overexposure to photography allows us to take full advantage of the human experience, always remembering the resolution in which we view our world appears far clearer when we set our cameras down.

Peck 6

Works Cited

Bass, Noel. "Photography, A Crutch for Poor Memory Capacity?" *Noel Bass Photo/Video,* Apr. 2016, www.noelbass.com/photography-vs-memory/.

Felluga, Dino. "Modules on Baudrillard: On Simulation." *Introductory Guide to Critical Theory,* Purdue U, 31 Jan. 2011, www.purdue.edu/guidetotheory/ postmodernism/modules/baudrillardsimulation.html.

Glenberg, Arthur M., and Thomas Grimes. "Memory and Faces: Pictures Help You Remember Who Said What." *Personality and Social Psychology Bulletin,* vol. 21, no. 3, Mar. 1995, pp. 196–206. *Academic Search Complete,* doi:10.1177/0146167295213001.

Stetler, Pepper. "History of Photography." ART 389, 10 Oct. 2016, Miami U, Oxford. Lecture.

Sources are listed in alphabetical order according to the first element—in this case, author last names. The first source is a posting from a personal blog. The next two online sources are from credible, stable sources (a university website and an academic journal in a database). The last source is a lecture that the student writer attended in person.

APA STYLE

The American Psychological Association documentation style is used in psychology, nursing, education, and related fields. But although the format is somewhat different from MLA, the strategies for finding, evaluating, and integrating sources remain the same. And even the basic principles of documentation remain the same across styles: the information in the in-text citation should correspond directly with the References page (the APA equivalent of a Works Cited page).

- In-text (or parenthetical) citations provide unobtrusive documentation of specific information.

- In-text citation lets readers know that particular ideas come from a particular source.

- In-text citation corresponds to the complete bibliographic information provided at the end of the text.

- In-text citations lead readers directly to the corresponding References page.

- Done correctly, the in-text citation lists the first word(s)—whether the author's last name or the article title—plus year of publication and the page number of the citation on the alphabetized References page. This allows readers to easily find the appropriate source on the References page.

- The References page provides complete information for finding the source easily.

- This complete information is provided only once and comes at the end of the entire text so that it doesn't interfere with ease of reading.

In-Text Citation

Like MLA style, in-text documentation for APA involves referencing the original text in parentheses within the actual sentences of your text. An in-text citation must occur whenever a writer:

- Quotes directly from a source

- Paraphrases ideas from a source

- Summarizes ideas from a source

- References statistics or data from a source

For direct quotes, APA in-text citations should include the author name, date (year only) of the source, and page number from which the cited material is taken. If the author name is given within the sentence, however, it does not need to be included in the in-text citation.

> "After months of exhausting research, they had finally come to understand the problem with their design" (Smith, 2008, p. 82).

p. or *pp.* comes before the actual page number(s).

End punctuation comes after the parenthetical citation.

Commas separate elements within the parentheses.

Writers using APA style often include the date directly after the author's name in the sentence.

Emphasizing her point, Miller (2000) demands that "it is now time for something drastic to change here on campus" (p. 43).

If the source has no author, use the first word or phrase of the source title and punctuate the title accordingly (either with quotation marks or italics).

> "Even though most of the nation's coastal shorelines can no longer sustain a full range of sea life, the vast majority of Americans seem unconcerned" ("Dead Seas," 2001, p. 27).

If the source has more than one author, use the last name of both authors. (Notice that APA style uses &, an ampersand, for in-text citations and the References page.)

If the source has two authors, use the last name of both authors. (Notice that APA style uses &, an ampersand, for in-text citations and the References page.)

> (Lunsford & Ede, 2004, p. 158)

If the source has three to five authors, list all last names. For subsequent references, give only the first author followed by *et al.*

> (Smith, Gibson, Fairley, Smith, & Harlow, 1993)

> (Smith et al., 1993)

If the source has more than five authors, give only the first author followed by *et al.*

> (Jones et al., 2000)

If the cited material is quoted in another source, cite the source in which you found the quotation and add *as cited in* before the author name or title.

> (as cited in Smith, 2008)

If you want to acknowledge more than one source for the same information, use a semicolon between citations within one set of parentheses. The sources should be listed in alphabetical order.

> (Lunsford & Ede, 1984; Smith, 2008)

Electronic Sources: Many electronic sources (web pages, for instance) do not have page numbers, but page numbers may appear on the hard copy. Unless the original source has page numbers, omit them from the in-text citation. Instead, either use the paragraph number (after the abbreviation *para.*), if provided, or, if the source has headings, use the heading plus the paragraph number of the source. Electronic texts (especially web pages) may lack authors; in that case, follow the same formula as with print sources, and use the title of the source in the citation.

> (Vince, 2010, Blood to Brain section, para. 2)

References

The References list gives sources that are directly cited in the text. Bibliographies, on the other hand, list all the sources that a writer may have read and digested in the process of researching the project. Entries in a References list must follow strict formatting guidelines. As in MLA documentation, the guidelines may change depending on the type of source, but there are some consistent rules. For instance, the first bit of information in the reference entry should always correspond directly with the in-text citation. In the following example, from Angel's essay (page 504), the entry begins with Price—as does the in-text citation within her essay:

> Drowsiness while driving on the job is the largest contributor to occupational fatalities (Price, 2011).

> Price, M. (2011, January). The risks of night work. *Monitor on Psychology, 42*(1). Retrieved from https://www.apa.org/monitor

The following rules also apply to all sources:

- Author names come first. Last name first, followed by first initial of first name (and first initial of middle name, if given).

- The date comes in parentheses directly after the author names.

- Title of the work comes directly after the date. Article titles are always in regular type, while the sources in which they appear—newspapers, magazines, and journals—are italicized. (Only the first letter of the article title or subtitle is capitalized unless there are proper nouns.)

- If no author appears, the title comes first.

- Publication information follows the title of the source.

- If the source is an article, page numbers come last. If the source is electronic, the retrieval information comes last.

Printed Books

All of the necessary information for books can usually be found on the title page, which is one of the first pages.

General Format for Books

Publication Date:
Comes directly after the author name, in parentheses.

Title:
The first word of the title or subtitle is capitalized, as are any proper nouns. The title is italicized.

Palmeri, J. (2012). *Remixing composition: A history of multimodal writing pedagogy*. Carbondale, IL: Southern Illinois University Press.

Author Name:
Give author last name and initials of first and (if available) middle names.

Location of Publisher:
Provide city and an abbreviation for the state. If the publisher is outside of the United States, give the city and country.

Publishing Company:
Place a colon between the state and publishing company. End with the publisher's name.

Two or More Authors

McKee, H. A., & Porter, J. E. (2009). *The ethics of Internet research: A rhetorical, case-based approach*. New York, NY: Peter Lang Press.

Vasta, R., Haith, M. M., & Miller, S. A. (2005). *Child psychology: The modern science*. New York, NY: Wiley.

Add all additional author names, also inverted, before the title. Use an ampersand (&), not *and*, between the names.

Corporate Author

American Automobile Association. (2007). *Tour book: New Jersey and Pennsylvania*. Heathrow, FL: Author.

Use the name of the corporation for the author name. If the corporate author also published the text, write *Author* for the publisher.

Subsequent Editions

Lauwers, J., & Shinskie, D. (2004). *Counseling the nursing mother* (4th ed.). Sudbury, MA: Jones & Bartlett.

Find the edition information on the title page of the book and place the information in parentheses directly after the title. Use abbreviations: *2nd ed., 3rd ed.*, etc., or use *Rev. ed.* for "Revised edition."

Edited Book

Alarcon, D. (Ed.). (2010). *The secret miracle*. New York, NY: Holt.

If referencing an entire edited book, begin with the editor's name and *Ed.* (for "editor"). Use *Eds.* (for "editors") if the book has more than one editor. Then give the date, the title, the publisher location, and the publisher name.

Translated Book

Bakhtin, M. (2004). *Problems of Dostoevsky's poetics* (C. Emerson, Trans.). Minneapolis, MN: University of Minnesota Press.

Add the translator's name (first and middle initials and last name) and *Trans.* (all in parentheses) after the title of the book.

Printed Articles

Articles appear in newspapers and periodicals (journals or magazines). Although newspapers are usually published daily, magazines are usually published weekly or monthly, and journals are published quarterly or even biannually.

Article in a Magazine

Nussbaum, E. (2017, January 23). Tragedy plus time: How jokes won the election. *New Yorker, 92*(46), 66–68, 70–71.

Osnos, E. (2017, January 30). Survival of the richest: Why some of America's wealthiest people are prepping for disaster. *New Yorker, 92*(47), 36–45.

Include the date (year, month, day) directly after the author name. Do not abbreviate months. If available, give the volume number in italics after the magazine title, followed by issue number in parentheses. If the article appears on non-consecutive pages, list all page numbers separated by a comma.

Article in a Newspaper

Swartz, J. (2014, May 5). Market won't friend social media. *USA Today,* p. B1.

If one is listed, give the author first, followed by the date and the title of the article. After the title of the newspaper, add *p.* or *pp.* and section letters before the page numbers.

Article in a Journal

Leonard, R. L. (2014). Multilingual writing as rhetorical attunement. *College English, 76,* 227–247.

Most academic journals number the pages of each issue continuously through a volume. The second issue does not begin with page 1, but with the number after the last page of the previous issue. For these journal articles, place the volume number in italics directly after the journal title, and before the page numbers. If each issue starts over with page 1, provide the issue number in parenthesis after the volume number, not in italics. Finally, if the article has been assigned a *digital object identifier* (DOI), place that after the period that follows the page number, even if you accessed the article in print. (See information on DOIs, page 501.)

Article or Chapter in an Edited Book

Rodriguez, R. (2014). Achievement of desire. In J. Scenters-Zapico (Ed.), *Identity: A reader for writers* (181–195). New York: Oxford UP.

After the author and date, give the title of the article or chapter. Then write *In* and the first initial and last name of the editor(s). The abbreviation *Ed.* or *Eds.* (in parentheses) should follow the editor(s). End with the title of the book, the page numbers in which the article appears, and the publication information.

Encyclopedia Article

Esposito, V. J. (2000). World War II: The diplomatic history of the war and post-war period. In *Encyclopedia Americana* (9th ed., Vol. 29, pp. 364–367). Danbury, CT: Grolier.

Begin with the author (if given) and date. Then give the title of the article. The name of the encyclopedia (after *In*) should be in italics. The edition number, volume number, and page number(s) should be in parentheses. If an editor is also named, list the first initial and last name before the title (after *In*).

Electronic Sources

As with print sources, citations for electronic sources require author(s), date, title, and publication information. Authors and titles are formatted in the same manner as print sources. The difference occurs with publication information: Publishers of electronic work sometimes assign a *digital object identifier* (DOI), which is a kind of persistent virtual address. The DOI is sometimes, not always, located at the top of the article. If a source has a DOI, you need not include a retrieval date or URL. If no DOI was assigned, however, provide a URL. (When adding the URL to your citation, break it only before slashes [/] or other punctuation and do not add hyphens.) The *Publication Manual of the American Psychological Association* (APA) says, "No retrieval date is necessary for content that is not likely to be changed or updated, such as a journal article or book." In other words, if the content is likely to stay unchanged, no retrieval date is needed. Especially with electronic sources, remember the basic principle behind citing sources: to provide a guide for finding the sources you used. Therefore, the most direct route to the source should always be used in the entry.

Website

Pinsker, S. (Ed.). (1999). *Robin flies again: Letters written by women of Goucher College, class of 1903.* Retrieved from http://meyerhoff.goucher.edu/library/robin

Sierra Club. (2017). Retrieved February 5, 2017, from http://www.sierraclub.org

As with all sources in APA format, begin with the author's or editor's name(s) (inverted), if available, and the date of electronic publication. Give the title of the site (italicized). Write *Retrieved* and then the date of access (if the information is likely to get edited or revised), followed by *from* and the URL (no final period).

Document from Website (Author and Date Stated)

Winter, J. (2017, February 7). FBI reports show terror suspects coming from Canada while Trump stares at Mexico. Retrieved from http://www.thedailybeast.com/articles /2014/05/04/high-manxiety-thirtysomething-men-are-the-new-neurotic-singles .html.

Begin with the author name (normal APA format), followed by the date (in parentheses), the title of the specific document, the word *Retrieved* and the access date if necessary, and finally *from* and the URL.

Document from Website (No Author or Date Stated)

Equestrian handbook. (n.d.). Retrieved February 2, 2017, from http://www.sca.org/

Begin with the title. In place of the date, write n.d. in parentheses for "no date." Then, give the title of the specific document (if applicable), *Retrieved* and the access date if necessary, and finally *from* and the URL.

Personal or Professional Home Page

Brown, F. (2017, February 1). *Fleda Brown: My wobbly bicycle, 129.* Retrieved February 6, 2017, from http://fledabrown.com/2017/02/my-wobbly-bicycle-129/.

Begin with the creator's name, followed by the date of the most recent update, the title, *Retrieved*, the date of access if needed, and *from* and the URL.

Journal or Magazine Article Retrieved from a Database

Ryu, D. (2013). Play to learn, learn to play: Language learning through gaming culture. *Recall, 25*(1), 286–301. doi:10.1017/S0958344013000050

Follow guidelines for a print journal. After the page number, add *Retrieved* and the home page URL of the journal if there is no DOI for the article. If there is a DOI, list it after *doi:* following the page numbers. Whether you provide a URL or DOI, do not include the name of the database.

Journal Article Online

Crow, A. (2000). What's age got to do with it? Teaching older students in computer-aided classrooms. *Teaching English in the Two-Year College, 27*(4), 400–415. Retrieved from http://www.ncte.org

Birmingham, P. (2008). Elated citizenry: Deception and the democratic task of bearing witness. *Research in Phenomenology 83*(2), 198–215. doi: 10.1163/156916408x286969

If the online journal is exactly the same as the print version (which is most common for academic journals), then follow the format for print articles, but conclude the entry with *Retrieved from* and the URL of the journal's homepage if no DOI is assigned. If a DOI is given, list it after *doi:*

Online Presentation

Groshelle, Z. (2014, April 23). *Visualizing your pitch* [Prezi slides]. Retrieved from https://prezi.com/oerqtrj5ie3y/visualizing-your-pitch/

Give the author name, date of publication, and the title of presentation in italics. Then give the digital file format in brackets, *Retrieved from*, and the URL.

Online Book

Shaw, B. (1916). *Pygmalion.* Retrieved from http://bartleby.com/138/index.html

Follow the format for print books, but exclude the original print publication information. End with the URL.

Abstract

Bailey, K.D. Towards unifying science: Applying concepts across disciplinary boundaries. *Systems Research and Behavioral Science, 18*(1), 41–62. Abstract retrieved from http:// onlinelibrary.wiley.com/

Include either the database name or the database URL, but not both.

Other Sources

Brochure

Masonic Information Center. (n.d.). *A response to critics of freemasonry* [Brochure]. Silver Spring, MD: Masonic Services Association.

Use *n.d.* to indicate no date, which is often necessary for brochures. After the title, add the descriptor *Brochure* in brackets before the publication information.

Personal Interview or Letter

(A. Shimerda, personal communication, March 4, 2016)

APA style recommends citing personal communications only with an in-text citation—not in the References list. In the in-text citation, give the name of the interviewee, the title *personal communication*, and the date.

Television Program

Martin, J. (Writer), & Moore, R. (Director). (1992). A streetcar named Marge [Television series episode]. In A. Jean & M. Reiss (Producers), *The Simpsons.* Los Angeles, CA: Twentieth Century Fox.

Begin with the name and title of the scriptwriter, then the name and title of the director and the date. Give the title of the episode or segment followed by the producer and the title of the program (italicized). End with the location of the broadcasting company and the company name.

Government Publication

U.S. Census Bureau. (2007). *Statistical abstract of the United States.* Washington, DC: U.S. Government Printing Office.

If no author is given, use the government agency as the author, followed by the date, the title (in italics), and the publication information that appears on the title page.

SAMPLE RESEARCH ESSAY

Sharon Angel's essay, written for her second-semester English course, is part ethnography and part argument: It reveals the language and social practices of a particular group (third-shift workers) and makes a case for supporting them. Angel also illustrates some important moves for research essays: She brings together, or *synthesizes*, a range of sources and explains how they relate to her own experience. Angel also provides textual cues (see page 474) so that readers understand the relationships among sources. Finally, despite the different sources operating throughout the essay, Angel manages to keep an incisive focus.

Running head: GRAVEYARD SHIFTS   1

Angel provides a separate title page, which is required for APA format.

Graveyard Shifts

Sharon Angel

Northwestern Michigan College

From Sharon Angel, "Graveyard Shifts." Reprinted by permission of the author.

GRAVEYARD SHIFTS 2

Graveyard Shifts

En route to the dumpster with trash bag in tow, I'm working the graveyard shift. Tonight, rogue electrons are brewing a midnight storm. My hair stands on end as if under the spell of a snake charmer. With my empty left hand, I pry open the dumpster enough to sling in the trash with my right. The bag slips into the darkness, and I wonder "just how much pressurized-plankton polyethylene *is* required to make a trash bag?" My wonder is quashed by the sound of dumpster-lid thunder. I know this sound well but it still gives me a start. I return to the building, and the fluorescent light blinds my peripheral vision. I should feel solid, but I funnel, like liquid, into the double glass doors.

Third-shift custodians know all too well how sleep deprivation affects the senses. We know the constant longing for a good day's sleep. And we know that part of our job will always involve managing a kind of persistent "jet lag."

The Bureau of Labor Statistics (2005) reports that approximately 85% of America's labor force works during the day, 15% perform shift work, and only 3% do overnight shift work. The 3% who work overnight, or graveyard, shift form a subculture of little renown. When we think of a subculture (or co-culture), we often imagine a distinct group of people exercising/asserting their freedoms of choice and expression—like hipsters or hackers. As defined by the *Oxford English Dictionary* (1998), a subculture is "A group

> Her personal testimony shows that even heavily researched projects can begin with the writer's own experience.

> The second paragraph connects the writer's experience to others'. It creates public resonance.

> Angel begins with statistics and then uses them to build an interesting point about group identity.

> Two entirely different sources, BLS and OED, help to build a line of reasoning.

GRAVEYARD SHIFTS   3

or class of lesser importance or size sharing specific beliefs, interests, or values which may be at variance with those of the general culture of which it forms part" (p. 19). Third-shift workers are definitely a "group of lesser size," and they do share interests that are "at variance with those of the general culture." But the third-shift subculture is so integrated with the daylight perspective of our 24/7 society that they may not even acknowledge their own night-shift community. Their dual existence seems invisible or at least arguable. So what does distinguish graveyard shift workers from the day-shift majority, and what bonds overnight workers in a unique way?

Typically, a subculture makes its presence known through dress, speech, musical preference, political statements, or social movements—invoking a credo or some external symbolism. But the distinction between daylight workers and overnight workers is more internal than external. What solidifies the midnight subculture is the inherent inclusion of those who have experienced the adjustment of their day/night biological clock (more precisely, the "circadian rhythm"). Yet even graveyard workers may fail to realize the consequences of adjusting one's circadian rhythm.

The circadian rhythm is the internal clock that determines a person's natural sleep cycle within a twenty-four

She goes even further into the nature of the subculture. She's exploring what's not obvious, what's otherwise hidden from plain thinking.

Angel first explains circadian rhythm and then integrates the quotation to further detail its function.

GRAVEYARD SHIFTS   4

hour period. It is heavily influenced by nature's day/night
cycle (with daylight and darkness as external stimuli).
But this internal clock affects far more than just a person's sleep. Michael Price (2011) of the APA *Monitor*
summarizes Charmane Eastman, PhD, (a physiological
psychologist a Rush University in Chicago) as follows:
"The circadian clock is essentially a timer that lets various
glands know when to release hormones and also controls
mood, alertness, body temperature and other aspects of
the body's daily cycle" (para. 5). The American College of
Emergency Physicians (2003) adds that:

> Many bodily functions exhibit circadian rhythms,
> from the best known sleep/wake cycle to all of the vital
> signs. As we become capable of more precise measure-
> ments, more and more circadian cycles are being rec-
> ognized. Even bone length has been found to exhibit
> a circadian periodicity. Most circadian rhythms have
> both an endogenous component (regulated by an
> internal clock located in the suprachiasmatic nucleus
> of the hypothalamus) and an exogenous component.
> The exogenous component is composed of various
> time clues called zeitgebers. One of the most powerful
> zeitgebers is the light/dark cycle. (para. 3)

Recognized or not, these physiological factors dramatically affect the well-being of night-shift workers who

The lengthy quotation is well contextualized by the previous source and Angel's language.

GRAVEYARD SHIFTS   5

Angel follows the lengthy quotation with a thorough connection to her topic. (*The source, then, is made increasingly relevant as the essay continues.*)

must reestablish a circadian rhythm that is not cued by nature's daylight/darkness cycle.

If a steady sleep routine is established, overnight employees can successfully shift their circadian clock to a nocturnal schedule. But the schedule may only be adjusted a certain amount to suit weekend activities, or it will fall out of the established rhythm. This produces, at best, a feeling of jet lag—familiar to most third-shift workers. Enough time for sleep must be set aside, and spent with eyes closed to bright light, in order to establish the "dark" part of the light/dark cycle.

Again, Angel integrates sources only after she introduces the broader point—in this case, the link between sleep patterns and illness.

Extended time spent out of sync with one's circadian rhythm can not only create sleep disorders, but it can increase the risk of stress, diabetes, obesity, heart disease—and even breast cancer. Researchers have also found a direct link between the disruption of circadian rhythm and depression (Gouin, 2010). This is not to mention the fact that night-shift employees working against their circadian rhythm also put others at risk. Hypersomnia and cognitive lapses can be especially hazardous. Drowsiness while driving on the job is the largest contributor to occupational fatalities (Price, 2011). The Exxon Valdez and Chernobyl disasters were attributed in part to the fatigue of overnight workers. And the air traffic controller scandal is a perfect

GRAVEYARD SHIFTS   6

example of what can happen when the scheduling of
night-shift employees is handled without regard for the
increased risks of overnight employment. The management responsible for scheduling employees may never have
worked the overnight shift. That is why support offered by
a fellow third-shifter is especially meaningful—because it
comes from a place of mutual empathy.

    We fellow third-shifters remind each other to drive
safely, offer rides and accompany each other as needed
when walking outside in risky areas. When we arrive
at work, we often discuss who's gotten enough sleep to
function well, as if we're talking about weather conditions. At the end of our shift, there are discussions
about who's craving what for their 6 a.m. dinner—or
the fact that picking up a pizza on the way home is not
an option. And we always know there's a listening ear
when it comes to the disappointments and frustrations
of missing—or being too "out of it" to enjoy social
activities with our diurnal friends and family.

    Mainstream culture's social life revolves around a
diurnal existence. It is often assumed that one who works
nights has their entire day available—and can simply
work their sleep schedule around social activities. But
one's circadian clock can only be finessed to a certain
point. For example, I sleep from 8:00 a.m. to 4:00 p.m.

> The paragraph returns to personal experience.

> Here begins the more explicit argument about mainstream culture's inattention to the third-shift subculture.

GRAVEYARD SHIFTS   7

when I'm in sync with my weekday sleep cycle. So
attending a meeting scheduled for noon is equivalent to
a diurnal worker attending a meeting at 3:00 a.m.

The expectation of overnight workers to function
well in the middle of their sleep cycle is an unrecognized
denial of the overnight subculture. Albeit unintentional,
this denial is a symptom of our failure to recognize
overnight workers as a subculture, to begin with. As
a third-shift worker of eight years, I can testify to the
following: It would be of great advantage to third-shift
employees if we were able to pop out of bed at any
hour, function well, and return to quality sleep—at will.
We would be able to accommodate any schedule as long
as we could piece together seven hours of intermittent,
deep sleep—remaining ever chipper. But that would, in
turn, require humans in general to redefine themselves
by taking control of their "CLOCK gene" which
is "critical to the generation of circadian rhythms"
(*CLOCK*, 2014, para. 1). Of course, if we altered the
CLOCK gene we would be surrendering an aspect of
our physiology in favor of a superhuman mechanism.
That is one more reason why the bond among third-
shift workers is so important. We must remind each
other of our connection with the natural world because
we spend so much time living under an artificial sun.

The CLOCK source is used
within a mini line of reasoning
about mainstream culture's
"failure to recognize."

GRAVEYARD SHIFTS   8

I remember one stressful evening at work when I was racing against the clock, my pupils retracted against the florescent lighting and lungs tightly bound with caffeine. A couple of co-workers rescued me at break time, leading me outside into the fresh air and pointing upward. We spent our break time taking in a sliver of a lunar eclipse. Though we did not fully escape the orange haze of street lamps, we were able to share a bit of nocturnal calm. And though it was left unspoken, it strengthened our camaraderie, and adjusted my priorities. Darkness can not only be soothing, but uplifting. Holly Wren Spaulding (2013) addresses this notion with insight: "When we are estranged from the dark, we lose access to vital human emotions and sensual experiences including wonder, awe and humility" (p. 83). It may be a quirky confession that I look forward to a trip to the dumpster on a blustery night, but it's a chance to briefly navigate away from the realm of artificial light. It's refreshing to spend my break lunching with co-workers at the employee picnic table (as weather permits) rather than squeeze in a trip to the neighborhood 7-Eleven. Third-shift workers stare the neon-lit, 24-7 global economy in the eye.

No longer does a lighted, 7-Eleven sign shine like an oasis in the dark of night. It has been crowded out by competing overnight gas stations, well-lit Wall-Marts and

After more supportive testimony, Angel integrates another source (Spaulding) that speaks to a broader premise about mainstream culture's failure to recognize—or see in the dark.

Angel is careful not to leave her broader points hanging. She supports them with specific background information. Here, the source supports a premise about the mainstream culture.

GRAVEYARD SHIFTS   9

the omnipresent McDonald's drive-thru. In fact there is
irony in the name "7-Eleven." It was adopted in 1947
"to reflect the store's new, *extended* hours (of) 7 a.m.
to 11 p.m., seven days a week" (*History*, 2012, "Toting
Away Your Purchases," para. 2). But apparently, those
hours weren't enough. Consumerism keeps us manufacturing, shipping, and selling goods all night long. After
all, being deprived of a multi-cow, preformed, rewarmed
hamburger at three in the morning would simply be
un-American. But the fact that we can measure time by
an atomic clock and Skype around the globe at all hours
does not mean that being "always open" is the best idea.
Still, we light up the outdoors like a circus and spend
hours of both day and night basking in the blue glow of
television, cell phone, and computer screens.

The lightbulb allusion helps her to build up to Tillett's point at the end of the paragraph.

        Initially, the invention of the lightbulb allowed
Americans to extend their day for work and pleasure. But
who'd have guessed that artificial light might one day
disrupt how well we function? Even for those who work
during the day, lengthening their waking hours into the
night with artificial light may result in an unhealthy
overexposure. "Ocular exposure (the eye, exposed)
to bright, artificial light inhibits the production of
melatonin . . . which helps regulate the body's circadian

GRAVEYARD SHIFTS   10

rhythm and immune function, and also suppresses
(breast cancer) tumor growth" (Tillett, 2006, p. A99).
With all of the associated risks, one might wonder, "Why
would someone *choose* to join a nocturnal co-culture?"

It may seem surprising that "not being able to find
other employment" was ranked in fifth place as a reason
to work overnight. According to two articles published
by the Bureau of Labor Statistics (based on their
monthly Current Population Surveys CPS), one from
1997 and one from 2004, the top four reasons people
chose to work the graveyard shift include "The nature
of the job, personal preference, better arrangements
for family or child care, and better pay" (Beers, 2000).
For some, it is a career choice. In other words, the type
of work they want to do happens to require working
at night. For example, firefighters, police officers, and
emergency medical staff. Individuals who have little or
no problem adjusting their sleep rhythm may simply
prefer to work in solitude, with less interruptions or
perhaps just enjoy less traffic during their commute. The
high cost of hospice and day care may also explain why
one spouse may choose a night shift—so that his or her
partner is always available to care for family members.

We come to work at night in order to serve the
priorities we hold for ourselves or share with our diurnal

The BLS source returns now—at the end of the essay—to help support her argument.

GRAVEYARD SHIFTS   11

loved ones. Although the meaning of "work family" takes on special significance for graveyard shift workers, it is mutually understood that our social life with the diurnal is no less important. In fact, it is especially important for the graveyard shift to remind itself that its existence extends beyond a largely, artificial environment. There is no substitute for the penetrating experience of circadian misalignment in combination with an upside-down social life. Empathizing with others who have shared this experience forms a unique camaraderie. This camaraderie validates our uncommon appreciation for the soothing side of darkness and our longing to connect with the inherent rhythm of our biological world. Graveyard shift workers rely on each other to affirm the existence of these gifts while we toil under artificial light. As we do so, we unwittingly solidify our co-cultural bond.

References

American College of Emergency Physicians. (2010, September). *Circadian rhythms and shift work: Policy resource and education paper.* Retrieved from https://www.acep.org/

Beers, T. M. (2000, June). Flexible schedules and shift work: Replacing the "9-to-5" workday? *Monthly Labor Review.* Retrieved from http://www.bls.gov/opub/mlr/ 2000/06 /art3full.pdf

We now better understand the power of the camaraderie dramatized earlier in the essay.

References are listed in alphabetical order according to the first element in the entry. Publication dates, in APA format, come directly after the title or author names.

Bureau of Labor Statistics. (2005, July 1). [Table of shift data May 2004.] *Shift usually worked: Full-time wage and salary workers by occupation*. Retrieved from http://www.bls.gov /news.release/flex.t05.htm

CLOCK. (2014, April 1). Retrieved January 25, 2017, from http://en.wikipedia.org/wiki/CLOCK

Gouin, J. P., Connors, J., Kiecolt-Glaser, J. K., Glaser, R., Malarkey, W. B., Atkinson, C., . . . Quan, N. (2010). Altered expression of circadian rhythm genes among individuals with a history of depression. *Journal of Affective Disorders*, 126(1), 161–166. doi:10.1016/j.jad.2010.04.002

History. (2012). Retrieved January 25, 2017, from http://corp .7-eleven.com/aboutus/history/tabid/75/default.aspx

Price, M. (2011, January). The risks of night work. *Monitor on Psychology*, 42(1). Retrieved from https://www.apa.org /monitor

Spaulding, H. W. (2013). In defense of darkness. In J. Mauk & J. Metz (Eds.), *Inventing arguments* (brief 3rd ed., pp. 83–87). Boston, MA: Cengage Learning.

Subculture. (1998). In J. A. Simpson (Ed.), *Oxford English Dictionary* (2nd ed., Vol. 17, p. 19). Oxford, England: Oxford University Press.

Tillett, T. (2006, February). Headliners: Breast cancer. *Environmental Health Perspectives*, 114(2), A99. Retrieved from http://www.ncbi.nlm.nih.gov/ pmc/ articles /PMC1367861/

Frequently Asked Questions

Documenting sources involves many moving parts. Even highly trained researchers find themselves wondering about the conventions. The following questions are likely to come up at some point in the process.

What If I Don't Know What Type of Source I Have?

This question often comes up when researching electronic sources. Most online research methods lead to either periodicals (journals, magazines, and newspapers) or websites. (Online books are generally not in the same search paths as periodicals.) If you have an electronic source and are not sure if it is a website or a periodical, check the top of the first page for publication information. If the text has a volume or issue number, or date information, it is most likely a periodical. Also, an electronic article most often lists the title of the magazine or journal at the top of the first page.

How Do I Tell the Difference between a Journal and a Magazine?

In general, a magazine is published more often than a journal. Magazines are published every week *(Time, Newsweek),* every other week, or every month. Magazines are written for nonspecialized, or *general,* readership, whereas journals are written for readers with a specialized field of knowledge (such as nursing, engineering, or pharmacology). Although magazines attempt to inform or entertain the public about various (sometimes even eccentric) topics, journals attempt to investigate ideas, theories, or situations within a discipline or field of study. Check the publication information to see how often the periodical is published, and look at the table of contents to see if the articles are written for general or specialized readers. (See pages 483–485 and 500–501.)

How Do I Find the Publication Information?

Publication information for books can be found on the title page. The front of the title page has the full title, the publisher, and the city of publication, and the reverse (or copyright) page includes the copyright dates and any edition information. For periodicals, the volume and issue number usually appear at the bottom of each page and are often printed on the first page inside the cover along with the table of contents. (However, some periodicals fill the first few pages with advertisements.) Websites can be trickier. If the author, last update, or sponsoring institution does not appear on the opening (or home) page, scroll down to the bottom of the page (or look on the menu for *Information* or *About Us*).

How Do I Know the Page Numbers of an Electronic Source?

Generally, electronic sources do not have page numbers—and documentation styles do not require page numbers for websites or online journal articles. Sometimes, however, a print source will republish its contents electronically and retain page numbers. (In other words, the source appears online exactly as it does in print.) In that case, simply use the page numbers as they appear. Writers can also reference paragraph numbers for electronic sources. Sharon Angel uses this strategy in her essay, formatted in APA style.

Should I Use APA, MLA, or Something Else?

MLA (or Modern Language Association) style is used by writers in the humanities and literature (such as English and communications). APA style is used by writers in the medical field, education, and, of course, psychology. CMS (or Chicago Manual of Style) is used by writers in humanities fields such as religion, history, and philosophy. The sciences (such as physics and chemistry) have particular styles as well. When writing for an academic audience, you should always ask what style to use. Some instructors want their students to use a particular style, regardless of their major or field of study.

Why Are There Different Documentation Styles?

The different styles have emerged over the course of years. They have developed because different research techniques sometimes call for a particular type of documentation. As academic fields grow, they develop and reward research strategies—and one documentation style cannot always account for those strategies.

Why Don't Some Articles Have Works Cited or Reference Pages?

Writers in magazines and newspapers use an informal strategy for referencing their sources. They use *attributive phrases* to link statements or information to particular sources (for example: *According to the English department chair at Pennsylvania State,* grades in first-year college courses have remained relatively stable). However, in scholarly work, writers document sources formally—according to MLA or APA guidelines. These shared guidelines provide a way for readers from other schools, states, countries, or centuries to follow the writer's research trail. In other words, the conventions serve an important purpose: to make certain that others beyond our social spheres can participate in our work.

Standard Abbreviations

MLA	APA	
ed.	Ed.	= Editor or Edited by
eds.	Eds.	= Editors
ed.	ed.	= Edition, usually associated with a number (4th ed.)
Rev. ed.	Rev. ed.	= Revised edition
n.d.	n.d.	= No date
n.p.	n.p.	= No publisher or no place
n. pag.	n. pag.	= No page numbers
trans.	Trans.	= Translator
p.	p.	= Page number
pp.	pp.	= Page numbers
no.	No.	= Number
pars.	para.	= Paragraphs
vol.	Vol.	= Volume

17

Organizing Ideas

John Metz

Chapter Objectives

This chapter will help you to:

- Understand ways of organizing ideas.
- Explore possibilities for organizing ideas in your essays.

INTRODUCTION

A completed text should read like a coherent journey: Readers begin with a sense of direction (a good introduction), pass through various locations (paragraphs), encounter different terrain (foreign concepts or ideas from outside sources), all while following road signs and cues (transitional words, phrases, and sentences). Having traveled an intellectual route, readers arrive somewhere unique and valuable (a good conclusion). This chapter presents strategies for shaping that journey.

BEGINNING

Introductions create focus and establish tone. They are the invitation to *start* thinking. But if an introduction is flat or vague, it can *stop* thinking. Notice this vague introduction:

> There are many critical issues facing today's public schools. They have to consider violence, financial constraints, teacher training, drugs, and student apathy, just to name a few. But in this difficult era, educators have become enamored with a saving grace: technology. Computers are everywhere in our public schools. But the problem is that the technology isn't the saving grace that it seems. Schools should rethink their allegiance to computers.

This introduction illustrates a few mistakes:

- The writer begins with an obvious statement, not an invitation to think or explore an issue.

- Because the introduction begins so broadly, it makes big intellectual leaps to get to the thesis at the end of the paragraph.

- The placement of the thesis at the end of the paragraph makes the earlier information seem contrived and formulaic.

The following introduction, from the essay "Floppy Disk Fallacies" by student Elizabeth Bohnhorst, avoids these mistakes. She takes us directly to the critical issue. She does not need to rush through several vague statements to suggest her position on the issue. She makes it indirectly from the outset:

> "Another boring PowerPoint," responds Jennifer when I ask about her day at school. I might not find these words so discouraging coming from a company executive after a long meeting or even a college student leaving an informative lecture. But these words of an eleven-year-old elementary school student leave me feeling slightly uneasy. PowerPoint presentations are intended to compel students to become more interested in the subject with the use of neon colors and moving graphic images. But these flashy additions to current educational strategies haven't fooled everyone. The text and material covered is still the same boring grammar and spelling lessons but the educator has altered: It is a screen.

The possibilities for introductions are boundless. And the strategy always depends on the voice, the topic, and the assignment itself. Here are some conventional and sound strategies:

- Begin with a specific assertion about the topic. In his essay "Americans and the Land," John Steinbeck begins with a general statement about American settlers and the land:

> I have often wondered at the savagery and thoughtlessness with which our early settlers approached this rich continent. They came at it as though it were an enemy, which of course it was. They burned the forests and changed the rainfall; they swept the buffalo from the plains, blasted the streams, set fire to the grass, and ran a reckless scythe through the virgin and noble timber.

- Begin with a typical belief or stereotype about the topic, and then turn to your particular insight:

> Most people assume they have no relationship with their local police departments. Other than in an emergency situation, most are even reluctant to acknowledge police officers. They often treat them as uniformed specters lurking on the roads of their towns. But the police of any community are deeply connected to the everyday patterns of life. They are serving their communities and participating in daily routines at all levels.

- Begin with a fictional account, or scenario:

> Imagine a community in which the police only appeared for emergencies, in which people had to make a 911 call simply to get a police car to visit the area. Imagine the streets of a crowded city without the occasional police cruiser. Imagine the downtown stores without the presence of a city officer.

- Begin in the past, taking readers back in time from the first sentence. In her essay "How I Lost the Junior Miss Pageant," Cindy Bosley begins narrating and waits until later in her essay to characterize or give meaning to the events:

Every evening of the annual broadcast of the Miss America Pageant, I, from the age of seven or so, carefully laid out an elaborate chart so that I might also participate as an independent judge of the most important beauty contest in the world.

- Re-create the point of contact. Explain how you first encountered the idea. This is often more informal, because it requires some personal narration, as in Manoush Zomorodi's essay "Hi, I'm a Digital Junkie, and I Suffer from Infomania":

  I was recently described, to my face, as a "modern digital junkie."
      This diagnosis was given to me, half in jest, by Dr. Dimitrios Tsivrikos, consumer psychologist at University College London, when I described my symptoms to him. After spending my workday tapping, swiping and emailing, I come home and—despite my exhaustion and twitching eyes—I want to consume more online. But I'm not even absorbing the articles, tweets and posts that I peruse. I'm just skipping from page to page, jumping from link to link.

- Begin with a popular reference. Writers often invite readers into their ideas by alluding to something in popular culture, such as a television program, an advertisement, a song, or a current event. This strategy allows readers to enter the world of the essay through a familiar door. In his article "Is Google Making Us Stupid? What the Internet Is Doing to Our Brains," Nicholas Carr begins with an allusion to the Stanley Kubrick film *2001: A Space Odyssey*:

  "Dave, stop. Stop, will you? Stop, Dave. Will you stop, Dave?" So the computer HAL pleads with the implacable astronaut Dave Bowman in a famous and weirdly poignant scene toward the end of Stanley Kubrick's *2001: A Space Odyssey*. Bowman, having nearly been sent to a deep-space death by the malfunctioning machine, is calmly, coldly disconnecting the memory circuits that control its artificial brain. "Dave, my mind is going," HAL says, forlornly. "I can feel it. I can feel it."
      I can feel it, too. Over the past few years I've had an uncomfortable sense that someone, or something, has been tinkering with my brain, remapping the neural circuitry, reprogramming the memory. . . .

- Begin with the personal and then move to the public. For example, notice how Elizabeth Thoman, in her essay "Rise of the Image Culture: Re-Imagining the American Dream," starts with personal reflection but moves steadily toward the public relevance of her topic:

  Like most middle-class children of the '50s, I grew up looking for the American Dream. In those days there were no cartoons in my Saturday viewing, but I distinctly remember watching, with some awe, *Industry on Parade*. I felt both pride and eager anticipation as I watched tail-finned cars rolling off assembly lines, massive dams taming mighty rivers and sleek chrome appliances making life more convenient for all.

When I heard the mellifluous voice of Ronald Reagan announce on *GE Theatre* that "Progress is our most important product," little did I realize that the big box in our living room was not just entertaining me. At a deeper level, it was stimulating an "image" in my head of how the world should work: that anything new was better than something old; that science and technology were the greatest of all human achievements and that in the near future—and certainly by the time I grew up—the power of technology would make it possible for everyone to live and work in a world free of war, poverty, drudgery and ignorance.

■ Create a shared experience between reader and writer. In short, this strategy is all about public resonance: It makes an explicit intellectual bond among the writer, the issue, and the readers. It often involves the first-person pronouns *we* or *us*. For example, in her essay "An Imperfect Reality," Rebecca Hollingsworth starts by focusing readers on the public nature of the topic:

Every day we hear more and more about developmental disorders that afflict children in the United States, disorders that have been misunderstood, downplayed, or ignored.

CHANGING PARAGRAPHS

Paragraphs guide readers' progress. They tell readers when to refocus attention on the next point. In more conceptual or abstract essays, writers use paragraphs to clearly separate different aspects of a concept. In argumentative essays, paragraphs separate different reasons or counterpoints. Paragraphs can also be used to separate support strategies—for instance, to separate several examples or to move from testimony to an allusion. Paragraph breaks generally help writers to:

■ Change from analyzing one element or quality to another.

■ Shift from a common view to a new or uncommon view of the topic.

■ Move from one support strategy (such as allusion) to another (such as scenario).

■ Transfer from the past to the present.

■ Shift from one memory, situation, or anecdote to another.

Of course, the shift or break cannot be too abrupt. There should be some intellectual bridge or transition. Sometimes making the transition is as easy as choosing the most appropriate information to begin the next paragraph. In these cases, the content of the paragraphs works to bridge the gap. Often, however, the writer needs to create a phrase, sentence, or sentences at the beginning of the new paragraph to clarify the relationship between the old and the new. In his relationship essay "Mugged," Jim Crockett provides a very small, but important, bridge between two paragraphs. The small phrase "in fact" carries readers from an idea to a closer examination of that idea:

> My coffee cup is in my hand a lot.
>   In fact, when it is not in my hand, when I misplace it momentarily, or when, like the other day, I leave it on the bumper of my truck and see a flash in the rearview mirror as my mug goes airborne into the filthy slush of the winter street, I feel a twinge of separation anxiety.

Also, remember that transitions can wait. While developing rough drafts, writers often wait to add the glue between paragraphs. Then they come back through to fill in the cracks—adding transitional phrases, sentences, or entire paragraphs where necessary. With a full draft completed, they can stand back and ask questions: *How do the paragraphs relate? Are they contrary? Is one an extension of the other? Is the second paragraph more particular than the first? Or is the second more broad?*

INTEGRATING OUTSIDE SOURCES

Writers can integrate outside sources by paraphrasing (expressing the ideas of the source in one's own words), summarizing (compacting the ideas of the source and expressing them in one's own words), or quoting (using the exact wording of the source within quotation marks). Passages from research communicate more clearly when the idea has first been set up. In other words, the writer makes the point and brings in an outside source for reinforcement. Then, after a paraphrase, summary, or quotation, the writer may further explain the significance or meaning. In her article "Rise of the Image Culture: Re-Imagining the American Dream," Elizabeth Thoman first explains how commercials influenced consumerism. Then she reinforces the point with a quotation, and finally further explains the idea in the quotation:

> The flood of commercial images also served as a rough-and-ready consumer education course for the waves of immigrants to America's shores and the thousands of rural folk lured to the city by visions of wealth. Advertising was seen as a way of educating the masses "to the cycle of the marketplace and to the imperatives of factory work and mechanized labor"—teaching them "how to behave like human beings in the machine age," according to the Boston department store magnate Edward A. Filene. In a work world where skill meant less and less, obedience and appearance took on greater importance. In a city full of strangers, advertising offered instructions on how to dress, how to behave, how to *appear* to others in order to gain approval and avoid rejection.

These three steps are not required with every use of an outside source. Sometimes, the third step is unnecessary and the writer only sets up the point. In the following passage, Thoman sets up the point about commercials' power, then brings in an outside source (Stephen Garey) to reinforce the point:

> This does not mean that when we see a new toilet paper commercial we're destined to rush down to the store to buy its new or improved brand. Most single commercials do not have such a direct impact. What happens instead is a cumulative effect. Each commercial plays its part in selling an overall *consumer lifestyle*. As advertising executive Stephen Garey noted in a recent issue of Media & Values, when an ad for toilet paper reaches us in combination with other TV commercials, magazine ads, radio spots, and billboards for detergents and designer jeans, new cars and cigarettes, and soft drinks and cereals and computers, the collective effect is that they all *teach us to buy*. And to feel somehow dissatisfied and inadequate unless we have the newest, the latest, the best.

Notice how Hollingsworth begins with a main idea, then introduces the source, paraphrases the supporting information, provides in-text documentation, and then comments on the paraphrased information:

> One health epidemic at the forefront of public consciousness is autism, a brain disorder that impairs a person's ability to communicate, socialize, and participate in group behavior. Often surfacing by the time a child is three years old, the symptoms of autism include stifled speech and difficulty in displaying joy or affection. According to a 2007 study by the U.S. Centers for Disease Control and Prevention, about 1 in 150 American children are autistic—a staggering number that makes autism the fastest-growing developmental disorder in the United States (Rice). Since the release of these findings, nonprofit organizations across the country have been working to raise public awareness of this national health crisis. The largest of these organizations, Autism Speaks, recently launched a multimedia campaign aimed at parents of autistic, or potentially autistic, children.

(For more on integrating sources and documentation, see Chapter 16.)

COUNTERARGUING

Engaging other people's ideas in an essay involves making counterarguments. Counterarguments (responses formed when writers anticipate possible opposition to their claims) are often arranged in separate paragraphs. For example, you might summarize an opposing point in a paragraph, and then in a new paragraph, explain why your understanding is most appropriate, correct, or valuable. The process can be repeated as often as necessary. For example, if you have anticipated three opposing points, you might develop six paragraphs:

Opposing Point A

Your counterargument

Opposing Point B

Your counterargument

Opposing Point C

Your counterargument

Some writers use the *turnabout paragraph* for counterarguments. A turnabout paragraph begins with an opposing position and then includes the writer's counterargument. In other words, the opposing point and the writer's counter are in the same paragraph—usually separated by some explicit change in direction (such as *however, but,* or *on the other hand*). In the following example, the opposing claim (that global warming is not a real problem) is addressed within the paragraph. The paragraph also includes the change of direction:

> Some people argue that global warming is not a problem at all. They suggest that all the discussion about the ozone layer is merely fear-mongering by left-wing political activists. This argument, however, ignores the volumes of evidence compiled by scientists (many of whom are Nobel Prize winners) from around the world—scientists from different cultures, from different religious contexts, from different political systems, and with different political agendas. The amount of data they have collected and the sheer din of their collective voices ought to be enough to convince people that global warming is much more than the delusions of a few environmental groups.

In her essay "Reverence for Food," Rachel Schofield makes a similar move. She directly explains the opposing position ("some would disagree") and then shifts to her way of thinking:

> Food still enables us to survive, but we no longer revere it. Some would disagree, citing the weight problems engorging our country. We see food 24/7 on TV, hear about it on the radio, see it advertised on billboards, and even in Internet pop-ups. Advertising works. We buy what we see, yet the low nutrition levels in our highly processed foods leave our bodies starving for more, and we only give them more junk. We can see the preeminence of food in the dedication of temples to food all along our highways; fast food chains are more popular than ever. However, there is a difference between obsession with food and reverence for it. Our fast food restaurants and freezer aisles are brothels where impure, chemically altered food is bought and sold. Almost gone are the days when honest, unadulterated food can be purchased by the American family.

You might decide that the opposing position requires significant explanation, and that it would be best to group opposing points together before giving your counter. Therefore, you might devote several paragraphs before countering:

Opposing Point A

Opposing Point B

Opposing Point C

Your counterargument to A

Your counterargument to B

Your counterargument to C

Regardless of your general organization strategy, make certain to cue readers when giving a counterargument. Readers need to understand when the focus shifts from the counterargument to the main argument. You might begin a paragraph with an opposing viewpoint: "Some opponents might argue that. . . ." If so, you will need to shift readers back to your logic: "But they do not understand that. . . ." Here is a list of some helpful transitions when doing counterargument:

On the other hand,

Contrary to this idea,

Although many people take this stance,

However, (; however,)

Despite the evidence for this position,

But

SEPARATING PROBLEMS AND SOLUTIONS

When writers propose solutions, they have to manage a range of rhetorical elements: the problem, illustrations or support for the problem, the solution, support for the solution, previously attempted or alternative solutions, shortcomings of those solutions, counterarguments, and concessions. These can be arranged in any order. Here are two standard strategies:

- Problem

    Examples/Illustrations

- My Solution to the Problem

    Examples/Illustrations

- Attempted or Alternative Solution

    Explanation

    Shortcoming

- Attempted or Alternative Solution

  Explanation

  Shortcoming

OR

- Problem

- Attempted/Alternative Solution A and the Shortcoming

- How My Solution Avoids This Shortcoming

- Attempted/Alternative Solution B and the Shortcoming

- How My Solution Avoids This Shortcoming

- Attempted/Alternative Solution C and the Shortcoming

- How My Solution Avoids This Shortcoming

The arrangement of elements depends on the topic. Some problems demand more attention; others less. Some solutions need significant explanation and support; others less. If the problem is fairly obvious—if readers already see it as a problem—then it will not require lengthy supporting passages, counterarguments, concessions, and so on. But if the problem is subtle—if readers don't see it as a problem—then a longer explanation is required. Writers must ask themselves two questions: First, *will readers easily accept this as a problem? If not, I'll have to persuade them.* Second, *will readers easily accept the solution? If not, I'll have to persuade them.* For example, if the problem is a violent elementary school playground, the writer may not have to work diligently to make a case. Readers are not apt to dismiss such a problem. But if the problem is a quiet form of institutional racism, then the writer might need to take more time (more paragraphs) to reveal the problem.

CONCLUDING

As with introductions, the possibilities for conclusions are limitless, but some principles and strategies apply. First, academic writers rarely waste time summarizing or "wrapping up" points they have just made. Instead, they use their conclusions to extend points into the readers' world or to suggest the significance of their ideas. Consider the following strategies:

- End with public resonance, as Dana Stewart does in "Different Jobs":

  Being aware that we all, by necessity, have pseudo-environments (because we cannot know the complexity of others' jobs or their lives), we can alleviate our own frustration *and* appreciate others more. By realizing that our understanding of their work is just our own pseudo-environment, not their actual work or life, we don't simply come to understand how complex (how physically hard, how mentally exhausting, how overwhelming, or downright undoable) their job is. We also realize we can't really understand their job's complexity and their life's travails.

- Simon Benlow makes a similar, but slightly more subtle, move in his essay

"Have It Your Way: Consumerism Invades Education":
   However, if we continue to allow the term "customer" to replace "student," I fear that students will become increasingly blind to the difference between consumerist culture and college culture. I fear they will become increasingly more confused by the expectations of college, and that in the nightmarish long run, colleges will become simply another extension of the consumerist machine in which everyone is encouraged to pre-package knowledge, to super-size grades, and to "hold" anything even slightly distasteful.

Caution: The explicit call to action can move a text into overt argumentation. Of course, that is fine if the assignment is focused on argumentation. But if the assignment calls for more analytical writing, then calls to action should be limited.

- Return to an introductory image or scene. This strategy is often called "framing." Having gone through the complexities of the essay, the readers know something special and different about the opening idea or image. Returning to it does not merely restate the point; instead, it helps the readers understand just how far they've come. They understand a new poignancy, a new sticking point, about the topic. In his article "Is Google Making Us Stupid? What the Internet Is Doing to Our Brains," Nicholas Carr returns to his initial allusion:

   I'm haunted by that scene in *2001*. What makes it so poignant, and so weird, is the computer's emotional response to the disassembly of its mind. . . . HAL's outpouring of feeling contrasts with the emotionlessness that characterizes the human figures in the film, who go about their business with an almost robotic efficiency. . . .

- Allude to something well known to the readers. An allusion can be a powerful conclusion strategy because it projects the point of the essay onto some other subject or idea. It extends the essay's reach outward. In his essay "Americans and the Land," John Steinbeck makes a powerful historical allusion:

   But we are an exuberant people, careless and destructive as active children. We make strong and potent tools and then have to use them to prove that they exist. Under the pressure of war we finally made the atom bomb, and for reasons which seemed justifiable at the time we dropped it on two Japanese cities—and I think we finally frightened ourselves. In such things, one must consult himself because there is no other point of reference. I did not know about the bomb, and certainly I had nothing to do with its use, but I am horrified and ashamed; and nearly everyone I know feels the same thing. And those who loudly and angrily justify Hiroshima and Nagasaki—why, they must be the most ashamed of all.

QUESTIONS FOR ORGANIZING YOUR PROJECTS

There is no secret formula for good academic writing. But there are some helpful concepts and questions. As you consider your own projects, apply the following questions, which correspond to the strategies explained throughout this chapter:

- What introductory strategy will yield the most momentum and intensity?

- What individual points should be developed separately in paragraphs?

- How should I take on opposing positions? In turnabout paragraphs or some back-and-forth strategy?

- Do I have a range of distinct support strategies? Does each warrant its own paragraph?

- Where will outside sources (if applicable) be most helpful? What specific points or passages could use the help of other voices?

- How can a conclusion go beyond summarizing? How can the final paragraph(s) leave readers with a sense that they have traveled through an important idea?

18

Developing Voice

John Metz

Chapter Objectives

This chapter will help you to:

- Understand ways to create and control writer's voice.
- Explore possibilities for your own writer's voice.

INTRODUCTION

When we talk, we project a character or mood by choosing certain words and changing the sound, pitch, and pace of our voices. (Some people talk with dramatic ups and downs; others blab at us in a single-note dirge.) We use physical gestures, too: waving our hands, bowing our heads, opening our eyes wide or closing them. As writers, we don't use our hands or eyes to gesture to readers, but we have other strategies. Because we write in different contexts, for different audiences, and on different occasions, we need to be flexible, adapting our writer's voice to suit the conventions and expectations of each situation. This is one of the most valuable skills for a writer, and it's one you can hone through experiment.

ESTABLISHING PRESENCE

When we write, we enter words, phrases, clauses, and punctuation into a document. That document, in turn, creates a voice. Whether the writer is present (still at the keyboard), far away, or long since gone, the language still has a quality that readers hear in their heads. In other words, voice is *the presence created by the writing itself.* This section explains some common strategies for controlling the nature and power of that presence.

Choosing Details

When writers stay abstract and general, when they do not commit to details, their voices remain less visible. Abstraction often hides a writer's voice. But when writers characterize their subjects by using particular and focused words, their voices become recognizable. For instance, throughout her essay, Jaren Provo makes some grand claims about *Star Trek,* but she grounds those claims in details. In the following, Provo's voice becomes more and more pronounced as the details increase:

> Also uncharacteristic of *Star Trek* but common in the sci-fi realm is the element portraying humans as slaves of technology, hopelessly existent only in body. This concept is perhaps most prevalent in the *Matrix* trilogy. Yet *Star Trek* foretells humans as harnessing the resources of technology to propel themselves outward into space, to explore, to contact, to impact in a positive way. The transporter and warp drive allow for expedient, efficient movement among planets and realms; the communicator (predecessor to the flip-phone?) and universal translator aid in interpersonal and intercultural contact; the scientific tricorder (a handheld programmable scanning device) and ship's scanners enhance exploration purposes; and medical tricorders and unknown, but apparently technical, whirring devices devised from salt 'n' pepper shakers exist for medical purposes.

The nature of details helps to shape voice. In other words, the specifics writers offer influence how they are heard. In her essay, the details Cindy Bosley shares about her hometown help shape her voice, or how she *sounds* to readers. Of the many details Bosley could offer, she chooses ones that help establish a confessional tone:

> Clearly, I lacked the save-the-whales-and-rainforest civic-mindedness required not only of Miss America, but of Junior Miss America, too. Even, although one wouldn't think it, in Ottumwa, Iowa, where my mother would go on to work in a bathtub factory, and then a glue factory, and then an electrical connectors factory (the factory worker's version of upward mobility), and finally, a watch factory where they shipped and received not just watches but cocaine in our town that at that time had more FBI agents in it than railroad engineers. And even in this town where my sister would go to work the kill floor of the pork plant where, for fun, the workers shot inspection dye at each other and threatened each other's throats with hack-knives. And even in this town where my cousin, age 13, would bring a bomb to seventh grade for show-and-tell, and get caught and evacuated, and be given community service to do because the public-school- as-terrorist-ground phenomena hadn't yet been born.

The same goes with observational writing. Details do more than ground the claims. They also characterize the writer's voice. In her essay, Annie Dillard's voice gets fleshed out in details and imagined scenes:

> I would like to have seen that eagle from the air a few weeks or months before he was shot: was the whole weasel still attached to his feathered throat, a fur pendant? Or did the eagle eat what he could reach, gutting the living weasel with his talons before his breast, bending his beak, cleaning the beautiful airborne bones?

Controlling Speed and Time

Having more details slows down time for readers. Like in a film, time slows down when a writer (or producer) focuses in on many particular details. Steinbeck uses details throughout his essay to focus on particular moments in history:

> Quite a few years ago when I was living in my little town on the coast of California a stranger came in and bought a small valley where the Sempervirens redwoods grew, some of them three hundred feet high. We used to walk among these trees, and the light colored as though the great glass of the Cathedral at Chartres had strained and sanctified the sunlight. The emotion we felt in this grove was one of awe and humility and joy; and then one day it was gone, slaughtered, and the sad wreckage of boughs and broken saplings left like nonsensical spoilage of the battle-ruined countryside.

Having fewer details speeds up time for readers. The fewer details readers get, the more quickly they move through the text. Writers decide which ideas they want readers to slow down for—and which ideas they want readers to move through quickly. For instance, in his essay, Benjamin Busch gives two brief anecdotes—something about his grandfather's life and his own. He goes back in time but moves quickly along, choosing to focus only on the most significant details in each case. The passages, then, help the reader to zoom through time and gather up only the most important pieces of information:

> My Grandfather fought the Nazis and was wounded. For years afterward, my father re-created that war in games in his Brooklyn neighborhood, where some of the children playing had lost their fathers overseas. But war games require two sides, and someone in Brooklyn always had to play the Germans.
>
> When I was a boy, I was given plastic army men. They were posed already fighting. I arranged them in the sandbox behind our house, and I killed them. I voiced their commands and made the sounds of their suffering. I was every one of them, and I was their enemy. I imagined their war—and I controlled it. I was a child. But I lost those magical powers as a Marine in Iraq.

Managing the "I"

Some writers make themselves visible in the text. They refer to themselves and their interactions with the subject. In other words, the writerly "I" shows up in the text. But the "I" must be managed, showing up for good cause—for instance, to help create a sense of location or personal experience. In his essay, Chester McCovey includes himself in his observations and refers to his own presence in the scenes or situations. But he does not inject the "I" without good cause. His presence helps to show the lack of front porches in a particular area, and his recollections of his grandparents help make a point about changes that have occurred in American society. His use of "I" gives support to his more general claims:

> My grandparents' garages were small, just enough for one car and a few tools—not much of a garage for today's homeowner. In those days the garage kept a car and a small lawnmower, some rakes, and so on. The garage today must keep much more. One can see, then, how the exchange occurred. Like an old-fashioned trade in baseball, gone is the home team's beloved front porch, replaced by a big, new garage. Of course the trade is much more interesting than that. And a look at how it occurred enlightens us a little about the world in which we live. More importantly, it tells us not so much about how life is now but about how it came to be. And, I would argue, it shows us the way in which things will continue to change.

Cassie Heidecker's present "I" is important to her analysis. Her essay focuses on reality television. While most of her essay focuses directly on that subject, the following passage turns to her own experience. She uses the present "I" (and its plural "we") to make a strategic point. In the latter paragraph below, she moves to a broader point, signaled by a specific transition away from her own experience:

> My husband and I watch culinary reality shows like *Hell's Kitchen* and *Top Chef.* We're embarrassed about it. We don't tell our friends. These shows are trash TV and we don't think of ourselves as trash TV people. But when we watch (when we literally run down from our respective work or domestic duties and avoid the phone for that ridiculous hour), we stay glued to the situation. We laugh in all the places we're supposed to laugh. We holler at all the appropriate moments. We laugh at ourselves laughing. We are the unapologetic groundlings at a Shakespearean drama. We yell at the lecherous old men, the conniving women, the smug adolescents, the deceit, the flawed personalities, the near misses, and the moments of predictable victory. We talk about the obvious low-brow appeals of *Hell's Kitchen* and how the quick-fire editing makes the show totally gripping, hilarious, and winky. We discuss the intricate appeals that *Top Chef* makes on our sympathies and the complex character development that works over an entire season.
>
> And we're not alone. Despite the results of a Pew Research Center poll indicating that 63% of the American public thinks that reality TV shows signal our cultural decline, the ratings continue to climb.

Contrarily, some writers stay invisible. The writerly "I" never appears. Instead, their texts focus entirely on the subject. In his essay, Justin Scott remains invisible in his observation, yet his essay still projects a particular voice:

> One thing is immediately obvious in this cemetery: Those laden with the gifts of life often choose to utilize them in death, and those less fortunate make do with what

they must. Class warfare spills into the afterworld: Business owner is segregated from bricklayer, clergy is separated from atheist. There are large domineering crypts bearing the surnames of the wealthy dead inside, branch-scraping obelisks with ornate script, tombs carefully sculpted to resemble tree stumps, small temples dedicated to their dead in ancient Greek style, and inevitably, the sunken, flat, and nondescript markers of the poor or humble. . . .

Scott's passage illustrates how a voice can be projected not through "I" but through careful word choice and sentence structure. Many writers opt for Scott's strategy. They create powerful, engaging, and intimate voices without drawing direct attention to their own experiences.

Using Allusions

Allusions are references to some public bit of knowledge (such as a historical event, a political situation, or a popular culture figure). An allusion can give a personal essay a broader and more public feeling while also helping to create a particular voice. For example, the following allusion helps to characterize Simon Benlow's voice—especially early in the essay when he sounds intolerant of consumer life. The nature of the allusion (to a seemingly unimportant matter like fast food) helps Benlow to trivialize consumer culture and appear slightly above it:

"Have it your way!" Of course, we all know the song and the friendly fried food establishment associated with this slogan. It's a harmless phrase, in and of itself, and one that works particularly well for the franchise. It suggests to customers that their particular appetites can be catered to, that their specific tastes, no matter how eccentric (within the continuum of dip n' serve fried food) can be easily satisfied.

In her essay, Cassie Heidecker uses a range of allusions. The references to popular and lowbrow television programs impact how readers hear her. Toward the end of her essay, Heidecker adds dimension to her voice when she alludes to a series of novels—such as *The Great Gatsby, Lord of the Rings, Moby Dick, My Antonia,* and *Anna Karenina:*

In the world of high art, such as literary fiction, the writer works to create a fictive dream—a coherent and impenetrable fantasy. The hope is that readers enter the dream and forget the real world. When we read a novel, for instance, our hopes become tied to Gatsby, Frodo, Ishmael, Antonia, Anna, and so on. We suspend our disbelief. And in turn, we are suspended in an ornate web of un-reality. But in reality television, part of the experience is the interplay between the fabricated scene (the kooky kitchen challenge limited to rutabagas and pig liver) and the invisible everyday lives of the contestants.

Promoting Curiosity

One of the primary jobs of a writer is to pique curiosity in readers. Very rarely does a writer (in any situation) seek only to tell readers what they are already thinking. Instead, writers seek to light a small fire in readers' minds, to make them want to *consider* an issue. Perhaps the most important strategy for promoting curiosity is to embody it, that is, to be curious as a writer. Curious writers make curious readers. In the following passage, Kathleen Norris begins making a case for celibacy, and rather than come right out of the gate celebrating the celibate life, she adopts a posture of wonder:

> But celibate people have taught me that celibacy, practiced rightly, does indeed have something valuable to say to the rest of us. Specifically, they have helped me better appreciate both the nature of friendship and what it means to be married. They have also helped me recognize that celibacy, like monogamy, is not a matter of the will disdaining and conquering the desires of the flesh, but a discipline requiring what many people think of as undesirable, if not impossible—a conscious form of sublimation. Like many people who came into adulthood during the sexually permissive 1960s, I've tended to equate sublimation with repression. But my celibate friends have made me see the light; accepting sublimation as a normal part of adulthood makes me more realistic about human sexual capacities and expression. It helps me better respect the bonds and boundaries of marriage.

The person we detect through the language seems full of wonder. And it is not only the content of the passage; also notice the sentence structure. She uses long sentences to keep the reader in her perspective.

Asking questions can also make a reader curious about the subject. In other words, when writers give voice to their own curiosity, they invite readers along for the intellectual ride. For instance, in an essay about his dog, David Hawes asks a series of pointed questions. The answers are far less important than the curiosity developed by the passage:

> Sometimes, though, I have to wonder about him liking his pampered life. Sometimes when he's in a really deep sleep, his legs jerk violently, like he's running. Is he dreaming about retrieving ducks and quail? When fall comes, do those longing looks he gives me mean he's wondering when I'm going to get the shotgun out so he can do what he was bred to do? When he lies down with his head between his paws and heaves one of the heavy dog sighs, is he wishing he could be running through a field somewhere, sniffing out the game? Does he feel like something is missing from his life, but he's not sure what it is? And worst of all, does he blame me for what's missing?

In his essay, "Build the Wall," Ed Bell launches an entire line of inquiry with a series of questions:

> So, did he think the same way about the wall? Some news outlets said he had downgraded the plan to a fence. And some said his supporters might not be too upset

about this because while they took Trump's promises *seriously*, they did not take them *literally*. But what if Trump's promise about building the wall wasn't just serious? What if it was literal too? And what if his thinking was radical?

What is a wall?

Some walls are thin. You can punch a hole through them. Other walls are thicker. Then there's the Great Wall of China that people walk along eight or ten people wide. Does Trump mean to build a thirty-foot wall that's a couple feet wide? If so, what holds it up? Or would the wall be two walls with a walkway, or a roadway, in between? And why would the height be the same all the way across?

As Bell and Hawes show, a series of questions can function for nearly any subject, but writers must be careful not to frustrate readers with too many questions or a tedious question/answer approach that makes the essay drag. Questions also become ineffective if they substitute for a simple but interesting claim.

Using Figurative Language

Figurative language is any phrasing that deliberately bends or changes the literal meaning or dictionary definitions of words. The following figures commonly appear in college and professional writing:

Metaphor: a comparison in which one thing is made to share the characteristics of another

> Her home was a sanctuary where we felt healed spiritually and psychologically.

Simile: a comparison of two seemingly unrelated things using *like* or *as*

> Life is like a box of chocolates.

Understatement: a claim that is deliberately less forceful or dramatic than reality

> Hurricanes tend to create a little wind.

Hyperbole: a deliberate exaggeration

> I'm so hungry, I could eat a horse.

Figurative language does more than support an idea. It also adds tonality to a writer's voice. And because figurative language transforms or bends the usual meaning of words and phrases, it should bend toward the nature of the writer's voice: sobering, comic, condemning, hopeful, absurd. For example, Forrest Gump's simile in the previous example fits with his uncomplicated and easygoing character. A box of chocolates is a simple, pleasant surprise, and so it equates with his character. (It certainly would not be fitting for Gump to say, "Life is like a raging volcanic explosion bursting forth from the fires of the earth.") In other words, the nature of a simile or metaphor directly impacts how the writer's voice sounds to readers. For instance, the first simile that follows would likely create a casual or even slightly humorous tone and the second, a more sophisticated or lofty tone:

> Hardcore punk singers are like public belchers—guys, primarily, with digestion problems and microphones.

> Hardcore punk singers are like angry court jesters, calling attention to their own raucous behavior while slipping in serious social commentary.

Whispering (Drawing Readers in Close)

Writers often use parentheses or dashes to make an aside comment or ask a rhetorical question. The material separated by parentheses or dashes is often a more intimate or personal note (something one might share only with the person sitting closest at the table). These often help create a particular voice because they reveal insights that are less public, or even less directly related to the main idea, than other information. In the following passage, Jaren Provo makes two asides:

> After this contact, more connections are forged with other alien worlds, such that the United Federation of Planets develops (with a flag suspiciously reminiscent of that of the United Nations) to promote peaceable cooperation among these cultures. Alien cultures are not (generally) out to conquer Earth and all of humanity in a blazing inferno of death and destruction, but are civilized, developing worlds willing to forge ties with others in the universe to assure mutual survival.

Provo's first, longer aside effectively winks at the readers. It nudges us in the shoulder as if to say, "On the down-low, we know what that's all about, eh?" The second offers a slight qualifier. Because *generally* is set apart from the main part of the sentence (in parentheses), it slows readers down a bit and makes Provo's voice feel slightly more cautious, more present, more aware of us—her readers. In fact, we might say that all asides function in this way: to make the writer feel more in touch, more in cahoots, with readers. Longer sentences with long phrases can also create a sense of delicacy and can bring readers into the subtleties of a thought. In Jim Crockett's concluding paragraph, the intricacy of his long sentences brings readers into the quiet complexities of the relationship:

> Because, even though my mug is always nearby, whether on the lectern or table in front of the classroom, in the cup holder on the dashboard of my truck, on the desk where I am writing this essay, or just dangling from my hand, all it really signifies is an addiction to caffeine and the need, because I am human, for some small and securing daily grounding ritual.

Yelling (Emphasizing Points)

One way to amp up the volume of a statement is to use an exclamation mark at the end. But other strategies, such as interrupting the natural flow of a sentence with a phrase or clause, can draw attention to an idea. This does not mean that the writer is angry or shouting at readers; rather, it allows the writer to guide the readers' attention to particular ideas. This is often done, as in Jim Crockett's essay, with interrupting words, phrases, or even clauses set off by commas:

> The relationship, or mugging, that has developed with my coffee mug is one-sided and is, because a mug's needs are simple, an easy relationship to maintain.

Repeating words, phrases, or clauses can also highlight an idea. John Steinbeck repeats *us* to highlight the collective nature of the issue:

> No longer do we Americans want to destroy wantonly, but our new-found sources of power—to take the burden of work from our shoulders, to warm us, and cool us, and give us light, to transport us quickly, and to make the things we use and wear and eat—these power sources spew pollution on our country, so that the rivers and streams are becoming poisonous and lifeless.

Short sentences can work as whispers or as yells, depending on content and context. They sometimes create emphasis because of their placement after longer sentences, such as in Cassie Heidecker's essay about reality television. She uses a compact sentence (highlighted below) to announce a key point:

> Reality television is a unique form of reality. It's not really real. (Everyone knows that, right?) After all, reality shows have theme music, background sounds, engaging hosts, narrators, sizzling graphics, and makeup artists. The shows are edited so that dialogue is framed and situated for maximum effect. Whatever the contestants say seems snappy, targeted, deliberate, or perfectly stupid. The shows have scenes with pitch-perfect tension, climax, and resolution. But real life has none of these. Real life is mostly boring, uselessly noisy, stagnant, uncertain, ill-defined, repetitive, hopelessly dumb, and sometimes it's quietly and privately beautiful. Such things can't be filmed and put on television for mass viewing. In short, it only takes a moment (or paragraph) to underscore some major differences between reality television and the mundane reality of everyday life.

Using Sentence Length

Sentence length has a powerful impact on voice. Long, winding sentences that travel in and out of various ideas before returning readers to the original path can create a self-reflective and sophisticated voice, one that considers complexities. Short sentences can create a determined voice. Notice the difference between the following:

Childhood was a gas.

Childhood was a raucous journey of twists and turns in which each moment was its own forever and every day a monument.

Although the metaphors here impact the sound of the sentences, the length matters. The sheer time that readers spend inside of a sentence shapes how they hear it. In her essay, Cindy Bosley uses sentence length to tug and pull at readers. The first sentence of the following passage is short, and because of the content, it is almost a whisper. The rest of the paragraph, consisting of longer sentences, takes readers further into the idea. The movement between long and short sentences creates the sensation of a living person telling a story, and the content of those sentences helps communicate the feelings and emotional complexities of that human:

My mother had secret hopes. Finally divorced for the second time from the same man, my father, she sat with me and gave her own running commentary about who was cute, who smiled too much, who would find a handsome husband. My mother, having always been a little to a lot overweight, excelled at swimming, and she told me much later that she chose swimming because she didn't feel fat in the water. Her sister was the cheerleader, but she was a swimmer, too heavy for a short skirt of her own, she said.

Even analytical writing can take full advantage of sentence variety. For instance, in her essay about David Foster Wallace, Adrienne Carr keeps her passages lively with a range of sentence lengths—some compact and to the point, others more protracted and complex:

The context of the address is key. Wallace is delivering a commencement for one of the nation's top liberal arts colleges, so his audience is postured to launch into the privilege awaiting those from an esteemed institution. But Wallace does not condemn that privilege. He is not out to hammer his audience about class issues. He is up to something else. He uses the grand occasion to highlight the opposite: the uninteresting, uncelebrated, and most forgettable moments of everyday life. And he argues that these moments, the boring and unsexy ones, provide an opportunity to apply the skills learned from a college like Kenyon. In other words, higher education, he explains, does not provide knowledge, disciplinary skills, or facts. Instead, it provides the ability to shift away from one's "default" response to tedium. This is his main point—one that he asserts, reinforces, and even insists upon throughout the address.

(For more on sentence length, see Chapter 19: Vitalizing Sentences.)

BUILDING CREDIBILITY

Good writers are inviting and curious; they avoid preachiness and hostility. They also create a sense of credibility, the quality that makes points believable. In argumentative writing, credibility is especially important for readers to understand and accept claims. This section explains some common ways that writers build or threaten their own credibility.

Drawing on Experience

A credible voice is not necessarily commanding or domineering. It might just be logical, insightful, and believable. Sometimes, credibility gets established with personal experience. Writers such as Anne Marie Paulin use personal experience strategically:

> Certainly everyone is entitled to his or her own opinion of what is attractive, but no one has the right to damage another human being for fun or profit. The media and the diet industry often do just that. While no one can change an entire culture overnight, people, especially parents, need to think about what they really value in the humans they share their lives with and what values they want to pass on to their children. We need to realize that being thin will not fix all our problems, though advertisements for diets and weight loss aids suggest this. Losing weight may, indeed, give a man or woman more confidence, but it will not make a person smarter, more generous, more loving, or more nurturing. It won't automatically attract the dream job or the ideal lover. On the contrary, people who allow the drive to be thin to control them may find that many other areas of their lives suffer: They may avoid some celebrations or get-togethers because of fear they may be tempted to eat too much or the "wrong" foods. They may cut back on intellectual activities like reading or enjoying concerts or art museums because those activities cut into their exercise time too much. The mania for thinness can cause a person to lose all perspective and balance in life. I know. It happened to me. My moment of revelation came about twelve years ago. I was a size ten, dieting constantly and faithfully keeping lists of every bite I ate, trying to lose fifteen more pounds. While I was watching the evening news, a story came on about a young woman who was run over by a bus. I vividly recall that as the station played the footage of the paramedics wheeling the woman away on a stretcher, I said to myself, "Yeah, but at least she's thin." I've been lucky enough to have gained some wisdom (as well as weight) with age: I may be fat, but I'm no longer crazy. There are some things more important than being thin.

Arguing, Conceding, and Qualifying

Argument need not be cast as an act of aggression or belligerence. Although arguments are sometimes heated and intense, they need not belittle others. In fact, the fastest way to alienate, or turn off, a reader is to sound narrow-minded, mean, arrogant, or intimidating. A good argument attracts readers and engages those who might oppose the claims being made. A bad or unsuccessful argument loses readers.

Conceding or qualifying a point can make an argument seem more controlled and more inviting; therefore, even when writers have a strong conviction, they can acknowledge the value of some other point or the limits of their own. Imagine the following argument:

> First-year college students are not mature enough to live on their own, without the guidance of parents and the familiarity of home turf. Dorm life is a celebration of self-destruction and disorientation. The social distractions draw students away from the real purpose of college and defeat even the most focused and determined students. Colleges should rethink the requirements for first-year students to live on campus.

Although these claims unfairly generalize college students (see *logical fallacies*) and therefore threaten the logical soundness of the argument, they also project a hasty or pushy voice. But with a concession, the same argument can be cast with a different voice. The following paragraph acknowledges some value in dorm life and, as a result, seems fairer and less alienating:

> Dorm life does hold some value for young students. It can create a climate of inquiry and academic engagement. However, many young college students are overcome by the utter freedom, lack of genuine guidance, and constant social distractions. And too many students who would otherwise succeed in their first years at college are suffering or failing because they are forced to live on campus. Colleges should, at least, begin to reevaluate requirements for on-campus living.

Conceding can create a more engaging voice, but conceding unnecessarily or too often can have negative results. Imagine the same argument, but with a distracting degree of concession:

> Living in dorms can be the best thing possible for a college student; however, dorm life can also defeat many students. Sometimes, even the brightest and most determined students can be overcome by the social distractions. Although it all depends on the individual student's personality and upbringing, college dorm life can actually work against the whole purpose of going to college. Certainly, each college should consider the characteristics of its own student body, but policies that require students to live on campus should be reevaluated.

All the concessions and qualifiers undermine the importance of the argument. The voice behind the text seems concerned about offending potential readers. But, ironically, such writing makes readers feel distant or detached from the ideas. Because the writer seems uncommitted, readers have no reason to engage the ideas. (Be cautious not to concede away your level of commitment—and your argument.)

Avoiding Harsh Description

It is tempting to use emotionally loaded terms or to proclaim an opposing view as "dumb" or "evil," but such language suggests that the writer has not fully investigated the subject. In the following, Ann Marie Paulin does not attack the media and the diet industry with aggressive adjectives, but argues that they damage people's lives. This is a far more sophisticated and useful strategy than merely dismissing them with a negative word or phrase:

> Certainly everyone is entitled to his or her own opinions of what is attractive, but no one has the right to damage another human being for fun or profit. The media and the diet industry often do just that. While no one can change an entire culture overnight, people, especially parents, need to think about what they really value in the humans they share their lives with and what values they want to pass on to their children.

Be cautious of dismissing a subject by using harsh words. Imagine the following passage, in which a writer evaluates a government official:

> Mayor G. is out of his mind. He has no understanding of the political spectrum and no concept of city governance. He is just some crazy, power-hungry man looking for a soapbox to stand on. If the city really understood the depth of his insanity, it would kick him out of office immediately.

This passage echoes some of the combative language in mainstream politics, which keeps voters from looking closely at a subject. Such language is rife with logical fallacies. Instead of investigating the subject closely, it portrays a writer's unfocused aggression. In the following passage, Benjamin Busch comes down hard against *Medal of Honor*, but his voice is sober, intense, and without nasty condemnation:

> The power of controlling your situation, to be able to stop the war and rest, is something that our soldiers are quietly desperate for. For those who patrol the valleys of Helmand, it is a way to impose limits on the uncertainty of war, and the constancy of vulnerability. A video game can produce no wounds, and take no friends away. The soldier understands the difference.

Talking with, Not Arguing at, Readers

An academic argument is not an argument with readers. It is a *conversation with readers about an argumentative position.* And if that conversation is compelling, readers may find that position valuable. In other words, argumentative writing speaks with readers about a particular position or set of positions and attempts to make one position more logical and/ or valuable than others.

To help visualize the roles of a writer and readers, imagine the following: The writer sits beside a reader, pointing at and directing attention to a set of claims. The writer does not sit in front of and point his or her finger at the reader. This may seem like a subtle difference, but notice how it may change a passage. In the following example, Laura Hanby Hudgens urges readers to consider the problem of disengaged students:

> First, we have to change the national conversation about education. This doesn't mean that educators should stop trying to improve instruction, but it does mean that there have to be more conversations about the role students play in ensuring their own learning. Teachers, parents, administrators and, of course, the students have to start making self-motivation an educational focus and priority. Self-motivation should be the new educational buzzword—every bit as prevalent and powerful as any we've seen shape our classrooms in the last few decades.

But imagine if Hudgens had talked at readers directly. In the following, the writer tries to convince readers ("you") to change their behavior. This passage is more shrill and probably would be less engaging to readers:

> You need to have a serious conversation about your children's learning. First, stop coddling them. Stop telling them they're smart no matter what because they're only smart if they work at it. Also, you need to stop blaming teachers and the education system at large. Instead, tell your children directly: they have to change their attitude about learning. They must get more involved, more engaged.

Applying Rogerian Argument

Because argument can create hostility and turn people away from each other, Carl Rogers developed an argumentative perspective that emphasizes building connections between different positions. People who use *Rogerian* argument look for similarities rather than differences between argumentative positions. Such a strategy creates an engaging voice— one that invites exploration of ideas rather than harsh dismissals. In his essay, Daniel Bruno takes the Rogerian approach. He begins by explaining the value of a text to which he later responds:

In his book *Generation X Goes to College*, Peter Sacks describes, among other things, the sense of entitlement that some students in today's consumerist culture have toward a college education. One entire chapter explores this issue alone, providing examples of this "sense" and looking into its "humble beginnings."

Sacks shows how consumerism has invaded education, leading some students to expect good grades for little effort. But he fails, it seems, to emphasize enough a most harmful effect of this entitlement. The biggest problem, as I see it, is that although students are able to graduate from high school (and even some colleges) with minimal effort, those students may find themselves cheated in the long run.

Creating Reasonable Tone

Tone, the color or mood of a writer's voice, is vital to maintaining the readers' interest. Tone that is too emotional can overwhelm; one that is condescending can alienate. For example, when evaluating a subject, writers must be careful not to force their conclusions *at* readers. Instead, the writer's job is to present a conclusion—one that is reasonable and engaging enough to make readers consider it. For example, in his essay about the video game *Medal of Honor*, Benjamin Busch condemns the game but maintains a reasonable tone:

> I honestly don't like that *Medal of Honor* depicts the war that is happening in Afghanistan right now because—even as fiction—it equates war with the leisure of games. Hundreds of combat games use historical conflicts, especially World War II, as their subject but there is a great deal of psychological separation from these events. There has been time to recover from loss, and to mourn. A game that claims "authenticity" played during the same conflict it depicts is not emotionally distant from it but is, instead, emotionally parallel. Furthermore, the age of the game's target audience is the same as that of the soldiers fighting so the line between casual entertainment and traumatic reality blurs.

It would be easy, and tempting, for Busch to shout at readers about the game. Imagine the following:

> Medal of Honor is a complete disgrace. It claims "authenticity" but cannot deliver anything close. You can die in a real war. In this game, you can only watch digital images collapse. That's authentic? I'm afraid not. But what's more ridiculous and offensive is the game's portrayal of a war currently happening—a war in which real people are dying.

This passage is over the top. It forces the writer's evaluation at readers and demands that they feel a particular emotion. Busch's passage is less confrontational, while still intense. He does not make emotional demands on readers; instead, he leaves readers to reflect on the position he's offered.

FOLLOWING CONVENTIONS

In most academic situations, writers must follow a range of grammatical, syntactical, and formatting rules. But attending to one's voice is not so much about rules as conventions: a set of expectations shared among many readers and writers. This section explains how writers might work within and sometimes beyond the conventions.

Considering Verb Mood

The three verb moods in English are indicative, subjunctive, and imperative:

- Indicative mood makes statements or asserts facts.

  The diners are sitting at the table.

- Subjunctive mood expresses what could or should happen.

  If it were lunchtime, the diners would be sitting at the table.

- Imperative mood issues commands or suggestions.

  For lunch, sit at the table.

Most sentences in this text (and in an essay, article, e-mail, and so on) are in the indicative mood. They make statements about writing. Others are in the subjunctive; they inform readers about possible ways to act, think, or write. And others are in the imperative mood; they order, or command, readers to act, think, or write a certain way.

Imperative mood is rare in academic essays and formal proposals because it tells readers what to do or think. And when done inappropriately, imperative mood seems to boss readers around. Of course, exceptions exist. Imperative can be appropriate in the final passages of an essay. For instance, April Pedersen's article, "The Dog Delusion," is primarily in the indicative mood, as are most of the essays in this book, but she shifts briefly to imperative mood. The following (highlighted) instances come toward the end of her article after her reasoning has been carefully detailed:

Let's outsmart dogs a little by cutting back on the over-the-top stuff. The dogs won't notice. Funds spent on a dog's blueberry facial or in-room canine massage at a swanky hotel ($130 an hour) are about as close to setting a pile of cash on fire in front of a destitute person as I can imagine. Ditto on buying a sweater for an animal covered in fur, or a carob-coated eclair for a scat eater, or personalized cookies for the species that can't read (that would be all species except us). Certainly dogs can't visualize themselves as Homo sapiens of any age, and are becoming obese and even ill-mannered at the hands of their besotted owners. It makes no sense whatsoever to pour so much time, money, and emotion into an animal whose main "goal" in life is to leave its scent on a tree. Think about it—how would you like to be a dog? To be unable to talk, write, or question. To look upon a masterpiece of art without an ounce of admiration, to gaze at the starry night without an iota of wonder, to see a book and have not the slightest inclination to open it, or stare without comprehension at a voting booth.

While Pedersen uses the mood shift well, and sparingly, writers should be careful with imperative mood. If not handled well, it can diminish the intensity of a good argument. Because imperative mood draws attention to readers, it can draw less attention to the topic. The goal of most academic writing is to keep intensive focus on the topic, to build a compelling idea for would-be readers, not to go after the particular person holding the essay. In the following, notice how the first sentence focuses on readers rather than the topic. In other words, the energy of the sentence goes toward a nameless and invisible "you," while the second and third sentences draw more attention to the topic:

- **Imperative Mood:** Do not treat your dog like a human.

- **Indicative Mood:** Treating dogs like humans generates confusion in an already complex relationship.

- **Subjunctive Mood:** Dog owners could discover the genuine benefits of living with a different species.

The differences may seem subtle, but the three sentences radically change the role of a reader. In an imperative sentence, readers are called upon—insisted upon. In indicative and subjunctive sentences, readers join the writer in a mutual examination of the topic. And because academic writing celebrates that mutual examination, indicative and subjunctive are used most often.

Adjusting Formality

Formality is adherence to an established convention. A formal text follows certain expectations and avoids slipping out of conventional language and organizational patterns. Because essays are used in a number of situations and academic disciplines, the conventions vary, and so does the expected level of formality. Generally, writing that draws no attention to the writer's presence is considered more formal. (Of course, this is a general rule, and it does not apply to all writing situations.)

A writer's voice can make the reading experience formal or relaxed, rigorous or casual. Remember that a casual voice does not necessarily mean casual thinking. A very sophisticated analysis can be presented in a casual manner. For instance, Simon Benlow approaches the fast food/customer service issue on its own terms. He borrows the phrases and the lowbrow tone of drive-through culture:

> In the old days, we had to pull up to the drive-thru board, search under "Sandwiches" and THEN go through the labor of exploring "Sides" and "Beverages." It was all too much. Now, we can simply pull up, and say a number. We don't even have to trouble ourselves with uttering all the stuff we want to eat. We just say, "#1 with a diet." The meal deal craze is, of course, not limited to fast food; it is, simply, most explicitly manifested in the fast food industry.

You may detect a slight shift in the last sentence—where Benlow pulls away from the drive-through language and makes a broader point about society. In this sense, Benlow's voice ebbs and flows. It adopts the casual language of consumption and then snaps at those same casual-sounding phrases. (This raises an important aspect of voice, or voicing: It is far more complex than discovering a single, personal, or genuine sound. In our everyday lives, as in speech, we often shift in subtle ways, borrowing tones and phrases from popular culture, academic culture, business, entertainment, and politics. We fuse those elements into our own tongues— and it all ends up sounding like us, like the single person speaking. But don't be fooled! Voice is often, or always, filled with the subtle tones of others.)

Although some writers tend toward a formal, sober tone, others use comedy or informality to connect with readers. For example, Simon Wykoff speaks directly to readers: He is not overly casual, nor is he overly formal or elaborate. Wykoff's language can be described as conversational:

> I should interject here and explain how he got around the city. While my father was homeless, he was lucky enough to have a bicycle, which he treasured beyond everything else. It's not uncommon in a larger city to have the place you get food, the place you

sleep, and the place you go to try and earn money be miles and miles apart. Because of this, even on a bike my father spent a considerable amount of time traveling. He would often ride from one end of the city to the other several times a day. This takes an incredible amount of endurance, especially when you are doing it on an empty stomach, as he often was. Many times, just a trip from the place he was sleeping to the closest bakery in the morning was a marathon.

Exploring the Boundaries

Some writers perform. Their language suggests, "Look at what I'm saying and how I'm saying it!" Some writers lay low. Their language says, "I'm here, but only to give you some information." Some writers hide. Their language says, "I hope no one sees me in this essay." Every writer has a comfort zone, the place where he or she feels most at ease. The problem is that *our most comfortable voices are not always the most appropriate* for the situation, and they do not allow us to explore language. In some situations, the intensely performative writer may need to be invisible and understated. And the writer hiding behind sentences may occasionally need to step forward and be noticed.

The best writers in all disciplines, occupations, and walks of life are not locked into a voice. They can work with various voices, depending on the writing situation. For that reason alone, it's good to recognize—and remember—the range of possibilities available. Take, for instance, two different passages from two different writers—April Pedersen and Ann Marie Paulin, who both appear in the same chapter:

> In a Pew Research Center study, 85 percent of dog owners said they consider their pet to be a member of their family. However the latest trend is to take that a step further in seeing the animal as a child. A company that sells pet health insurance policies has dubbed the last Sunday in April as "Pet Parents Day." Glance through magazines like *Bark, Cesar's Way* (courtesy of "Dog Whisperer" Cesar Millan), and other mainstream publications, and the term "pet parent" crops up regularly. The "my-dogs-are-my-kids" crowd isn't being tongue-in-cheek, either. They act on their beliefs, buying Christmas presents, photos with Santa, cosmetic surgery, and whatever-it-takes medical care for their animal. In fact having a puppy, claimed one "mother," is "exactly the same in all ways as having a baby." And while pushing a dog around in a stroller would have gotten you directions to a mental health facility twenty years ago, today it's de rigueur to see a canine in a stroller (or a papoose), and some passersby are downright disappointed to discover a human infant inside. —April Pedersen

Certainly everyone is entitled to his or her own opinion of what is attractive, but no one has the right to damage another human being for fun or profit. The media and the diet industry often do just that. While no one can change an entire culture overnight, people, especially parents, need to think about what they really value in the humans they share their lives with and what values they want to pass on to their children. We need to realize that being thin will not fix all our problems, though advertisements for diets and weight loss aids suggest this. Losing weight may, indeed, give a man or woman more confidence, but it will not make a person smarter, more generous, more loving, or more nurturing. It won't automatically attract the dream job or the ideal lover. On the contrary, people who allow the drive to be thin to control them may find that many other areas of their lives suffer: They may avoid some celebrations or get-togethers because of fear they may be tempted to eat too much or the "wrong" foods. They may cut back on intellectual activities like reading or enjoying concerts or art museums because those activities cut into their exercise time too much. The mania for thinness can cause a person to lose all perspective and balance in life. I know. It happened to me. —Ann Marie Paulin

QUESTIONS FOR DEVELOPING VOICE

All pieces of writing have a voice. Sometimes those voices are sober and formal. Other voices are comedic, even hilarious. This does not mean that the topic itself is funny; it means that the writer's presentation of ideas is humorous. Some of the best writers can make a potentially dull topic feel quirky, or a light topic have depth and profound significance. Of course, most writings fall somewhere in the middle between serious and comic, between utterly stiff and totally untamed. As you consider your own voice, imagine how it will sound in the minds of readers: clean, vibrant, bored, bashful, disinterested, present, intense, comedic, witty, self-aware, reflective, bare-knuckled, compassionate, knowledgeable, and so on. Each sentence you write will add to that sound. The following questions can help you imagine possibilities:

- Should I adhere to the most formal tone or can I explore the boundaries?

- What details would intensify my voice?

- Can I use figurative language or allusions to intensify and shape my voice?

- Should I put myself in the text? If "I" am in the text, what purpose does it serve? Will my presence help communicate the main idea or distract readers from experiencing the subject?

- Can I get less monotone? Can I whisper in some passages and yell in others?

- Even if my voice is casual, informal, or comedic, is it credible?

- How can I concede or qualify to better moderate my voice?

- Do I veer toward harsh description? If so, can I tone it down?

- Should I break some academic conventions? What might be the consequences?

19

Vitalizing Sentences

John Metz

Chapter Objectives

This chapter will help you to:

- Understand ways to vitalize sentences.
- Explore possibilities for vitalizing sentences in your writing.

INTRODUCTION

Vitalized writing is lively. It involves a broad range of strategies and patterns—from winding clauses that bring readers through intellectual nuances to brief phrases that pop in the reader's mind. The important principle is that sentences account for the whole reading experience: If your sentences are full of empty phrases, stiffened by dull patterns, or slowed by jumbled clauses, they won't call on readers' attention. Your writing will lie flat on the page or computer screen. But if your sentences are lively, they will pull readers along and through whatever dense concept or difficult argument you've developed.

This chapter includes strategies for ratcheting up your writing. Some call for pruning phrases, some call for substituting words, and others call for more radical changes. Throughout the chapter, we assume you have a completed draft—that your work is somewhat developed and ready for close editing. Although the examples belong to specific essays and articles, the strategies themselves can be applied widely—not only to different assignments but also to different genres of writing.

CONTROLLING THE PACE

Even the most patient and attentive readers want to move through a text. They want to experience the flow of one idea to another. So good writers manage the pace of their language. Like film directors, they move their audiences along from scene (idea) to scene (idea). This process usually involves tightening sentences as much as possible—so that longer sentences, when they do come along, mean more to the reading experience. The following strategies focus on controlling the speed of your readers' thoughts.

Turn Clauses to Phrases

A clause (which includes both a subject and verb) can often be shortened to a phrase, which makes the sentence more concise and lively. Notice how the clause in the first sentence below can be reduced to a phrase (that is, to a group of two or more words that do not include both a subject and verb). The second sentence, from John Steinbeck's essay "Americans and the Land," avoids the unnecessary "that were":

> On the East coast, and particularly in New England, the colonists farmed lands *that were* meager and close to their communities and to safety.

> On the East coast, particularly in New England, colonists farmed meager lands close to their communities and to safety.

The same goes for the following sentence. Notice how the second version, from John Steinbeck's essay, trims the clauses into phrases:

> When a super-highway was proposed in California which would trample the redwood trees in its path, an outcry arose all over the land *that was* so strident and fierce that the plan was put aside. And we no longer believe that a man, *because he owns* a piece of America, is free to outrage it.

> When a super-highway was proposed in California which would trample the redwood trees in its path, an outcry arose all over the land, so strident and fierce that the plan was put aside. And we no longer believe that a man, by owning a piece of America, is free to outrage it.

Although these differences are slight, the phrases (rather than the clauses) increase the sentences' vitality. And if the strategy is spread out over several pages of text, the benefits are easy to see. The paragraphs read more smoothly. (Often, when writers are concerned about "the flow" of their essays, this is the strategy to apply.)

Turn Phrases to Words

The same principle can be applied to phrases: They can often be boiled down to single words. Consider the following two sentences. The second, also from Steinbeck's essay, boils down a common phrase to a more succinct word:

> Almost every day, the pressure of outrage among Americans grows.

> Almost daily, the pressure of outrage among Americans grows.

The differences are slight, but small transformations build up throughout an essay, creating the difference between droopy and intensive writing. This strategy also makes writers search for more intense or powerful words, as in the following:

> The decision was not very smart.

> The decision was illogical.

Back in the day, people did not assume that all communication should be instantaneous.

Historically, people have not assumed that all communication should be instantaneous.

Combine Sentences

Sentences cue the readers. A period says, "Stop." A new sentence says, "Go." This stopping and starting creates vitality. But too many starts and stops keep readers from settling into ideas, so writers combine sentences to keep readers gliding along. Sentences can be combined with *coordination* (adding together clauses of equal importance). The underlined conjunctions in the following sentences show where the writers joined ideas together. The ideas before and after the conjunctions are grammatically equal. The grammar cues readers to give them equal intellectual weight:

> My father did not believe in such things for girls as shoes, clothes, haircuts, college, or photographs for Junior Miss, <u>and</u> so there was no way he was going to give a penny for a pageant-worthy dress or a professional photographer's 10-minutes-plus-proofs. (Cindy Bosley)

> Mrs. Rath had an ability to recognize the kids that actually wanted to read and learn and, often times, would send a few of us down to the library where it was quiet <u>and</u> we could have some sanctuary from the usual classroom shenanigans. (Steve Mockensturm)

Sentences also can be combined with *subordination* (making an idea less important than the main part of a sentence). Subordination involves tucking some ideas into others, creating the critical overlapping quality of good writing. The following examples show a variety of possibilities. Each sentence has a main clause (underlined), and other subordinated parts:

> For years <u>it sat empty,</u> the massive entrance looking out on Upton Avenue with no expression.

> As hoped for and expected, <u>a figure appeared out of nowhere.</u>

> Almost half a day later, around midnight, <u>the train crunched into Chicago</u>, where I hopped off, exhausted and exhilarated.

Notice how the third sentence, from Leonard Kress's "A Beat Education," would read differently if the ideas were separated into full sentences:

> Almost half a day later, around midnight, the train crunched into Chicago. I hopped off, and I felt exhausted and exhilarated.

Although the difference is small, this version creates more stops and starts for readers. Those shorter, separated ideas can be valuable, but good writers subordinate less important information. Hopping off the train is necessary information for Kress's narrative, but it's not the main idea, so Kress subordinates it.

Subordinate Less Important Ideas

Vitalized writing establishes a primary intellectual current—an undeniable forward momentum that allows readers to distinguish between dominant and supporting ideas. The following sentence from Rebecca Hollingsworth's essay "An Imperfect Reality" conveys two ideas: a main idea (that autism is a health epidemic at the forefront of public consciousness) and a subordinate idea (the definition of autism):

> One health epidemic at the forefront of public consciousness is autism, a brain disorder that impairs a person's ability to communicate, socialize, and participate in group behavior.

Consider another example from Hollingsworth. She conveys two important ideas (when autism surfaces and what its symptoms are). The first idea is subordinate to the second one because the second idea is expressed in the main, or independent, clause. Subordinating one idea to the other helps to keep the essay moving:

> Often surfacing by the time a child is three years old, the symptoms of autism include stifled speech and difficulty in displaying joy or affection.

But notice how the pace would slow if neither of the sentences included subordination:

> One health epidemic at the forefront of public consciousness is autism. Autism is a brain disorder that impairs a person's ability to communicate, socialize, and participate in group behavior. It often surfaces by the time a child is three years old. The symptoms of autism include stifled speech and difficulty in displaying joy or affection.

Experiment with Length

If writers aren't careful, their language can turn robotic: every sentence having about the same number of words, the same number of clauses, and the same types of phrases. Just as good speakers vary the sound of their voices, good writers vary the length of their sentences. Notice how Rebecca Hollingsworth, in her essay "An Imperfect Reality," varies sentence length in the following passage:

> In this sense, the ad does what numerous other campaigns do: it scares us. But this one aims at a particularly vulnerable place: the intersection of our idealism and our fear. It contrasts deluded notions of success—defined here as becoming a top fashion designer—with the statistically harsh truth. We can no longer bask in the old *one in a million* cliché. Like the pretty imagery in the fictional bedroom, that number has been upstaged by a more demanding probability.

In her first two sentences, Hollingsworth uses a colon to connect an explanation to the preceding sentence part, an independent clause; the next sentence includes an interrupting element set off with dashes; the next sentence is shorter, including just a main clause; and the final sentence includes an introductory phrase followed by an independent (or main) clause. These different ways of combining ideas (with colons, dashes, an introductory clause) keep the writing from sounding robotic.

Short sentences keep readers alert and moving—but only when they are interspersed with longer ones. Short sentences can also help dramatize thought, as in this passage from Chester McCovey's essay "The Front Porch":

> I am not saying there are no front porches. Obviously there are. And I am not saying everyone has a two-car garage instead. In my neighborhood, small garages not connected to the house still reign.

Avoid Unnecessary Interruption

Sometimes writers will inject a phrase or clause between the main parts of a sentence (between a subject and its verb or between verbs and direct objects). A modifying clause or phrase, like this one, comes between main parts of a sentence. Interrupting elements can be appropriate when the subject needs explaining. For example, in the following, the interrupting element, *Bart's distempered father*, helps explain the subject. It does not slow down the reading significantly:

> Homer Simpson, <u>Bart's distempered father,</u> consistently leads his family through a campaign of treacherous buffoonery.   **Appropriate interruption**

But writers sometimes unnecessarily interrupt the flow of a sentence:

> Nothing, <u>in the animated town of Springfield,</u> is worthy of the praise it wants.   **Unnecessary interruption**

> So I asked myself, <u>on my way out of SeaWorld,</u> what I had learned.

In many cases, the interrupting element can be moved to the front of the sentence, which keeps the main parts of the sentence together:

> <u>In the animated town of Springfield,</u> nothing is worthy of the praise it wants.

> <u>So on my way out of SeaWorld,</u> I asked myself what I had learned.

Avoid Over-Embedding

Although a well-placed clause between the subject and verb can help create a clear and lively sentence, too many loose clauses can slow or even derail readers. In the following sentence, two overlapping dependent clauses (both beginning with *that*) interfere with the pace. They embed themselves between the two most important elements of the sentence: the subject (*problem*) and verb (*is*).

> The problem that Thoreau has with the government that depends upon the majority is that the majority often fails to think of what is right and what is wrong.

For better pace, the sentence might be rewritten:

> According to Thoreau, a government of the majority has a key problem: Majorities often fail to distinguish between right and wrong.

As you can see, it's easy to fix over-embedded sentences. The tricky part is seeing them in the first place. As you consider your own writing, remember that over-embedding often happens in the drafting phase when writers are shaping ideas.

Avoid Pileups

Prepositional phrases sometimes pile up and create a dense wall of unreadable words. (A prepositional phrase begins with a preposition, such as <u>in, of, between, on, beside, behind,</u> or <u>for.</u>) Too many prepositional phrases (even two in a row) can slow down or stop readers. You might think of it as momentum: Verbs propel readers through sentences. So when too many phrases pile up, the sentence slows down. Without verbs, the reading gets thick, sentences get muddy, and readers bog down. Good writers avoid too many phrases. The following sentence begins with three prepositional phrases:

> <u>The celebration of the holiday at the end of the month</u> will attract many tourists to the town.

If the sentence has fewer prepositional phrases, the verb (*will attract*) moves closer to the subject (*celebration*), and the sentence becomes less muddy:

> At the end of the month, the holiday celebration will attract many tourists to the town.

Avoid Vague Pronouns

Pronouns such as *these, this, those,* and *it* are often used to refer back to previous ideas so readers feel a sense of familiarity as they move forward. In short, such pronouns help to keep momentum going between sentences and paragraphs. Notice how Elizabeth Thoman in "Rise of the Image Culture: Re-Imagining the American Dream" uses *this* to bring readers from one paragraph to another:

> Even the U.S. Constitution, remember, only promises the pursuit of happiness. It doesn't guarantee that any of us will actually achieve it.

It is <u>this</u> search for "something-more-than-what-we've-got-now" that is at the heart of the consumer culture we struggle with today.

But she also gives us more information, so the transition between paragraphs is smooth: "this search for 'something-more-than-what-we've-got-now.'" The additional information keeps readers in tow. In such a passage, the pronoun offers extra glue between ideas. But imagine if the pronoun had to act alone:

Even the U.S. Constitution, remember, only promises the pursuit of happiness. It doesn't guarantee that any of us will actually achieve it.

<u>This</u> is at the heart of the consumer culture we struggle with today.

Now the pronoun carries all the burden of the transition between paragraphs. If readers are not entirely certain what *this* is, the transition is unsuccessful. For better vitality and pace, writers make pronouns refer directly to specific nouns.

CLEANING THE LANGUAGE

It is easy to fill up pages with useless phrases and clauses. (Perhaps you even know some tried-and-true tactics for adding five words where you might need only one, two, or three. Perhaps you recognize those moves here!) Good writers prune their language. They get comfortable with the delete key. The following strategies will help you to cut the useless stuff from your drafts and to make the remaining words mean more.

Avoid Clichés

Clichés are tired, worn-out phrases. We hear them constantly in everyday life—on greeting cards, in popular songs or political speeches, and in casual conversations. Think of all the times you have heard these phrases:

You don't know what you have until it's gone.

We should expand our horizons.

Follow your dreams.

Anything is possible.

Children are the future.

I believe in my heart that . . .

Hang in there.

Discover who you are as a person.

People are entitled to their own opinions.

Whatever will be will be.

Reach for the stars.

Think outside the box.

Everyone is different.

Different strokes for different folks.

It's all just water under the bridge.

Fight the good fight.

Or even consider smaller phrases that are plugged into sentences but are rarely inspected:

the real world

hard work

the good life

family values

the American people

today's society

common sense

The list goes on. Such common phrases are not tools for thinking—they are substitutes for thinking. Because they have been used repeatedly and in so many different contexts, their meaning has been emptied. We use clichés when there is nothing left to say—or to make it seem like there is nothing else to say. Clichés blur complex thinking. They hide the possibility of further thought. For instance, notice the thinking that might go on behind this cliché: We should expand our horizons.

> What are horizons? How do they form? Are horizons imposed on us, or do we adopt them ourselves? If they are imposed by others, can we simply choose to expand them or do we have to break some rule? How do we know when a horizon expands? What experiences or voices or situations make them expand? Are we just as likely to shrink our horizons? Isn't that human nature? What kind of action broadens our understanding? Is it just a new experience or something else?

All of these questions suggest the complexity behind the idea. But rather than promote hard thinking, clichés invite both writers and readers into quiet, unreflective agreement. In a sense, clichés are strategies for quieting the mind, which is the opposite goal of academic writing.

Avoid Stilted Language

If clichés are the common, overused phrases of the day, stilted language is the opposite—an overly elaborate jungle of pretentious clauses and phrases. Stilted language is unnecessarily elevated. Instead of communicating complex and interesting ideas clearly, it buries ideas in a jungle of language, making readers work hard to sift through a basic, yet overly written, idea. For example, in Writer A's passage, the ideas are vague because they are stretched out over unnecessary, but pretty, phrases:

> *Writer A:*
>
> People, in every walk of this big life, should query themselves about the direction of their occupational goals. And they should do this persistently, both before entering into a projected career path and while enduring the veritable ins and outs of said career path. Is it not fitting to examine the very essence of such matters, which would otherwise remain beyond our consciousness in the mundane existence of work? Certainly, we should endeavor to explore the cracks and folds of our lives and thereby free ourselves of any unknown shackles.

Writer A injects strings of needless constructions ("in every walk of this big life," "the very essence of such matters") and elaborate language ("their occupational goals," "mundane existence of work") that inflate the importance of the ideas. Writer A also mingles two competing metaphors at the end of the passage. As readers, we are left exploring the "cracks and folds" while also freeing ourselves from "unknown shackles." Notice a less stilted approach:

> *Writer B:*
>
> Before entering a job, people should ask themselves if it fits their broader career plans. Even after working at a job for months or years, people should return to this question. Otherwise, the workaday lifestyle can prompt us to believe that a present career path is the best—the one that we should continue to walk.

Writer B uses a metaphor at the end, but it works here because it does not compete with other figurative language in the sentence. Now that the ideas are less ornate, they seem less overwhelming. In fact, stated more plainly, the ideas appear ordinary (which should prompt a writer to explore the ideas further). These passages reveal two major problems with stilted language: (1) it jumbles ideas so that readers are left guessing or wondering, and (2) it inflates ideas so that they seem beyond exploration. Writers and readers should not be impressed with ornate language but rather with intense ideas expressed clearly.

Avoid Unnecessary Attention to I

Most writers are naturally drawn to use the first-person pronouns *I, me,* and *my.* But personal pronouns can distract readers from the ideas and bog down the sentences:

I think that social security ought to be tied to the marketplace.

It is my personal belief that social security should not be a gamble.

In each of these sentences, the main idea is subordinated in a *that* clause. *I* statements such as these are unnecessary in most academic writing because the claims are already attributed to the writer. By attaching his or her name to an essay, the writer has already implied "I believe," "I think," "I feel," "it seems." Saying it again is redundant. However, personal pronouns are sometimes helpful or necessary. When dealing with several claims or outside sources, writers may insert the first-person pronoun to make a clear distinction between their own thoughts and others', as Ann Marie Paulin does here:

> For instance, in her essay, "Bubbie, Mommy, Weight Watchers and Me," Barbara Noreen Dinnerstein recalls a time in her childhood when her mother took her to Weight Watchers to slim down and the advice the lecturer gave to the women present: "She told us to put a picture of ourselves on the 'fridgerator of us eating and looking really fat and ugly. She said remember what you look like. Remember how ugly you are."
>
> I have a problem with this advice. First, of course, it is too darn common.

Paulin could have avoided the first-person pronoun: "But this advice is dangerous to young women." But she chose the first-person pronoun, perhaps because it is less formal and coincides with the voice she has established in her essay. Although writers should generally avoid first-person pronouns, writers like Paulin can make effective, occasional use of them.

Writers also use *I* for personal narratives—telling a story or anecdote involving their own experiences. Such uses are legitimate and important. Narratives draw attention to the relevant experience of the writer, which requires use of the first-person pronoun.

Unnecessary I Statement

I think that history should be taught with more attention to the lives of everyday people.

Appropriate Personal Narrative

When I was in high school, my history courses focused almost exclusively on big battles and big governmental moments.

Avoid Unnecessary Attention to You

The second-person pronoun *you* refers directly to readers—the people reading the text. Because academic essays are invitations to a broad audience (to instructors, peers, and even the broader community of thinkers that they represent), *you* is generally avoided. Like the first-person singular pronouns (*I, me, my*), *you* distracts readers from the issue at hand. But *you* is especially hazardous in academic writing because it makes writers shift into the imperative mood—the mood of commands. Here, the writer shifts focus and mood:

> Political parties do their best to keep people from closely examining issues. Instead, they wash over complexities and invite voters to stand on one side or another. You should consider your allegiance to any political party.

The first two sentences focus on political parties, people, and voters. But the final sentence shifts and suddenly speaks at the readers, telling them what to do. To most academic audiences, this shift is unacceptable.

Clean Up Attributive Phrases

When writers refer to another text, they need to introduce the author's words with attributive phrases. These phrases connect an author to his or her ideas: *according to Biff Harrison; in Jergerson's argument; as Jacobs points out;* and so on. But clumsy phrasing can get in the way:

1. In "Letter from Birmingham Jail," by Martin Luther King Jr., King writes about how society can be unjust.

2. Ann Marie Paulin wrote an essay about incivility and obesity. It is called "Cruelty, Civility, and Other Weighty Matters."

Each of these sentences makes a similar error: Each draws unnecessary attention to the act of writing or to the author's thoughts. Each could be boiled down:

1. In "Letter from Birmingham Jail," Martin Luther King Jr. writes about injustice.

2. Ann Marie Paulin's essay "Cruelty, Civility, and Other Weighty Matters" shows the deeply personal impact of media images.

Avoid Blueprinting

Sometimes writers draw attention to their own plans. That is, they tell readers what they are doing or what they are about to do. This strategy can be called *blueprinting* because it informs readers of the writer's plan (like the blueprints for a house). Blueprinting is not inherently wrong, but it draws attention away from the ideas and toward the writer's processes, and this can distract readers. Rather than announcing plans, writers can simply state the points. Consider this blueprinting passage:

> In the following pages, I will explain how the advertising images on MTV influence the present generation.

Removing the blueprinting leaves a relatively vague sentence:

> Advertising images on MTV influence the present generation.

So the writer might develop a more focused point:

Advertising images on MTV promote the belief that clothes create identity.

When the blueprinting is removed, sentences have more potential because important content can be added. In fact, it must be added. As the previous example shows, blueprinting can fool a writer into thinking that sentences are saying more than they are. And, blueprinting can be subtle:

Next is the composition.

Now, after examining the content, we should explore composition.

These more subtle forms are common because writers use them as paragraph transitions. Although they are generally more accepted, ideas can be connected more effectively:

Closely related to content, composition influences how viewers come to an image.

Condense Wordy Phrases

In everyday life, we use lots of phrases that contain unnecessary words. But in writing, we can clean out the filler:

black in color	*condense to*	black
square in shape	*condense to*	square
try and explain	*condense to*	explain
due to the fact that	*condense to*	because
in this day and age	*condense to*	today (or now)
back in the day	*condense to*	then
at the present time	*condense to*	now
for the most part	*condense to*	mostly (or most)
in the final analysis	*condense to*	finally
in the event that	*condense to*	if
frank and honest	*condense to*	honest
revert back to	*condense to*	revert

Notice the wordy and condensed phrases in action:

Wordy: In the event that your sentences are more vital, your grades will likely improve due to the fact that instructors, for the most part, want intense ideas rather than bloated sentences.

Condensed: If your sentences are more vital, your grades will likely improve because most instructors want intense ideas rather than bloated sentences.

Avoid Expletives

To help keep things lively, writers delete unnecessary words, such as expletive constructions. Expletives begin with <u>there</u> or <u>it</u> and are followed by a form of <u>to be,</u> such as <u>is, are, was,</u> or <u>were.</u> (Note: Not every expletive construction must be replaced, and not every there or it followed by a form of <u>to be</u> functions as an expletive.) Notice how the following sentences can be revised to remove the expletive and make the writing more clean and intense:

There were many students who voiced the need for more evening courses.

Many students voiced the need for more evening courses.

It is this long list of problems that made the community suspicious of the mayor's speech.

This long list of problems made the community suspicious of the mayor's speech.

Throw Away the Obvious

Imagine a protester holding a sign that says, "No More Bank Bailouts!" Given the situation (a protest) and the general state of the economy (a slow recovery), most people can infer—or quietly fill in—the unstated layers of the argument. We know that the protester is against government money supporting bad behavior among bankers. Now imagine another sign that says, "No More Bank Bailouts! I Think They Are Wrong and I Don't Support Them!" The second sign says too much. Everything after the first sentence is obvious. Of course, an academic essay and a protest sign are different. But they are the same in this respect: Too many obvious statements diminish their effectiveness.

As we have argued in previous chapters, college writing is about generating new ideas—not expressing the same old opinions. This point applies even to individual paragraphs and sentences. Good writers learn to throw away obvious statements, those that readers will infer on their own. For example, in the following passage, the second and third sentences are obvious:

When the company executives cheated thousands of employees out of their pensions, they ruined retirement for many families. It is wrong when people cheat others. And the executives should have known better than to do such a thing.

In this case, the first sentence has already done the important work. The words *cheated* and *ruined* make a powerful point. The second and third sentences, however, simply pound out what is already implied. In short, more than half of the words in the above passage can, and probably should, be thrown away.

GETTING SPECIFIC

Many of the strategies in this chapter involve cutting and pruning. But when writers cut, they notice their drafts shrinking, and a shrinking draft creates its own problem: meeting the required word count of an assignment. So what can be done? How can writers develop sufficient drafts while deleting unnecessary or vague phrases? One answer is to get specific—to narrow in on particular actions, situations, people, and ideas. The more particular writers get, the more incisive their ideas become. Potentially bland statements turn into sharper insights and often into more detailed passages.

Vitalize with Verbs

Verbs are the engine of a sentence. And they are the agent of motion for a reader's mind: They move a reader's thoughts. Weak verbs make for little movement. In the following, the first sentence depends on a weak verb:

> Handheld video games are bad for kids to have in the car.
>
> Handheld video games have destroyed the family road trip.

The verb of the first sentence, *are,* is often called a *linking verb.* When linking verbs act as the main engine of a sentence, they limit what's possible. Often, they corner the writer into using a vague adjective, in this case *bad.* The second sentence uses an active and more intensive verb: *destroyed.* The second sentence creates a more engaging image. In the following sentences, linking verbs create unnecessary layers and clauses. Notice how each can be tightened and vitalized with an *active verb:*

> The problem with this *is* that the house is too expensive for our budget.
>
> Here's the problem: The cost of the house exceeds our budget.
>
> The committee *is* not prone to allowing everyone *to be* as free with their money as they want.
>
> The committee will probably not allow everyone to spend resources freely.

Using active verbs rather than linking verbs vitalizes writing. This is not to say that using linking verbs is always a mistake. (Sometimes, they are necessary.) However, changing to more active verbs can dramatically impact your writing, creating more focused statements, more intensive ideas, and more revelatory thinking.

Avoid *Be* Verbs When Possible

Be verbs—*is, am, are, was, were, being, been,* etc.—are a type of linking verb. They link the subject of a sentence to a noun or a quality.

The kittens are cute.

The government is out of control.

Sentences are cues for readers.

Although such verbs are often necessary and valuable, they are often overused—hanging around in a sentence that would benefit from a more active verb. With a small, but important, change to the final example sentence above, we can make the verb active—and shorten the sentence:

Sentences cue readers.

Changing *be* verbs to active verbs throughout an essay can have dramatic effects. For instance, in John Steinbeck's essay "Americans and the Land," verbs pull readers through the ideas:

The great redwood forests of the western mountains early attracted attention. These ancient trees, which once grew everywhere, now exist only where the last Ice Age did not wipe them out. And they were found to have value. The Sempervirens and the Gigantea, the two remaining species, make soft, straight-grained timber. They are easy to split into planks, shakes, fenceposts, and railroad ties, and they have a unique virtue: they resist decay, both wet and dry rot, and an inherent acid in them repels termites. The loggers went through the great groves like a barrage, toppling the trees—some of which were two thousand years old—and leaving no maidens, no seedlings or saplings on the denuded hills.

EXPERIMENTING WITH PATTERNS

Written language is not simply linguistic. Once it enters a reader's thinking, it becomes sonic and rhythmic. Whether it is being read aloud or quietly, language moves along in pulses. It includes pauses, dips, repetition, and stops. Good writers tune in to the way their language works—and to the sound it might create in readers' minds. The following strategies will help you to tune your phrases and sentences and to maximize rhythm and movement.

Repeat Clause or Phrase Patterns

When writers don't invent, they find themselves unnecessarily repeating the same claims throughout their essay. However, repetition is not always bad. In fact, skillful repetition can add vitality and intensity to sentences. When writers re-create a sentence pattern, they create familiar linguistic territory for readers, and drive points home. For example, Jaren Provo's essay "Star Trek: Where No Man Has Gone Before" repeats modifiers—and even replicates the syllable patterns:

> Yet, despite the significant cultural contribution *Star Trek* has made, many see this legendary universe as unreachable, non-applicable, influencing only the stereotypical Klingon-quoting, uniform-donning, convention-going fan. However, this view is false. *Star Trek* empowers mainstream America to imagine a future of hope-filled opportunity rather than horrific obliteration.

Later, Provo repeats both clause patterns and verb structure to create a powerful conclusion:

> We must be sure not to violate the magnitude of *Star Trek* and its whispers of truth for the days ahead. We must not be intolerant of that which heralds a tolerant tomorrow, doubtful of a harbinger of hope, or disparaging toward a beacon of peace or humanity. The zeitgeist bestowed upon our culture by *Star Trek* must be appreciated for its complexities and considered in its hopeful message to the people of today.

Repetition can make sentences feel more deliberate and intense, more dramatic and lively. Readers can actually feel the word patterns insisting on attention.

Intensify with a Series

A series of words creates a pattern for readers. When a chain of words is lined up, readers make an automatic intellectual connection. We most often see single words in a series:

> The land flattens itself out and creates a sense of <u>openness, emptiness,</u> and <u>space</u>.

But phrases can also be put in a series:

> The land flattens itself out and creates <u>a feeling of openness, a sense of emptiness,</u> and <u>an eyeful of space.</u>

Skillful writers can put entire clauses in a series. Here, the repeating clauses create an intellectual pattern, set up a way of thinking, and pull readers briskly through the images:

> They live in a place <u>where the fields lie uninterrupted, where the houses take the full brunt of the wind, where the horizon simply evaporates.</u>

Try Absolutes!

Absolute phrases—which consist of a noun, modifiers, and often a participle—modify an entire clause or sentence, not just a word or phrase. Absolutes can help intensify ideas—weaving them together to create a more sophisticated, yet concise, sentence. Consider the following sentences:

> The beauty pageant had finally concluded and the whole ordeal had finally come to an end. Cindy Bosley could now escape the desperate feelings around her.

Although these sentences are correct and functional, they can be combined with an absolute phrase. The verbs of the first sentence will be omitted and the ideas slightly compressed into an absolute phrase attached to the clause:

> The beauty pageant concluded and the whole ordeal finally over, Cindy Bosley could escape the desperate feelings around her.

If used sparingly, absolute phrases can add subtle variety, helping readers escape the march of subject/verb, subject/verb, subject/verb sentence patterns.

Try the Stylistic Fragment

Sentence fragments are grammatical errors. They occur when a writer punctuates a phrase or dependent clause as though it were a full sentence. Here are some examples of sentence fragments:

Fragment Errors

> By writing on the sidewalk in colored chalk and then hiring an airplane to write the message in the sky.

> Because the grand opening of the hotel coincided with the holiday parade and the community's main fundraising festival.

> Just when Marvin flummoxed the toss and flailed wildly at Herdie's aunt, who was then experiencing an intestinal expression.

None of the preceding examples can stand alone as full sentences. This is not because of the content, but because of the grammatical structure. None of them is an independent clause. But some writers venture into fragments intentionally. They deliberately craft fragments because breaking the conventions calls readers out of a comfortable intellectual pattern. Notice the (italicized) stylistic fragments in the following passages. They are technically incorrect. But the writers decided to use the unconventional to help create vitality and intensity.

Stylistic Fragments

> At some point in its life cycle, business must conserve. *Like a lion or a bear. Like any organism.*

Sooner, rather than later, evaluating performance will not be the enterprise of faculty. It'll be the work of outside corporations. Profit hounds. Performance peddlers.

When everything seems broken. When nothing seems fixable. When persistent crisis looms. These are the conditions that make political parties comfortable. Then, they can further etch their agendas into the masses by detailing the wrongs of the other party.

Deliberately Break a Rule!

Grammar is a set of conventions—a code agreed upon and supported by institutions within a culture. But all codes are toyed with. People who know the codes of a culture intentionally tamper for one of several reasons: They want to explore the limits of language and not simply use it; they want to assert some sense of individuality, something beyond their complicity in rules; they want readers to share in a brief moment of nonconformity.

Believe it or not, academia is a perfect place for intellectual rule breaking. In fact, many would argue that the job of academia is to make certain that students know the rules so well that they can break them with grace and purpose. Playing with the conventions of language helps us understand what's possible, intellectually speaking. Keep in mind that rule breaking should not be a mere game of self-indulgence. It should increase the vitality of the text and the readers' understanding of your ideas.

QUESTIONS FOR VITALIZING YOUR WRITING

Even for the most attentive readers, lifeless, wordy, and monotone language is easy to ignore. But vibrant and lively language draws in readers. It calls them away from the other thoughts and issues vying for their attention. Once you have developed a focused draft, apply the following questions to create more lively sentences:

Controlling Pace

- Where can I increase the pace of the sentences? Where should readers move along more quickly? (For these passages, apply any of the following strategies: turn clauses to phrases, turn phrases to words, combine sentences, subordinate less important ideas, avoid unnecessary interruption, avoid over-embedding, avoid pileups, and avoid vague pronouns.)

- Where can I slow down the pace? Where should readers experience more immersion in the ideas? For these passages, try to combine sentences and experiment with length.

Cleaning the Language

- What passages contain unnecessary phrases and terms?

- What passages draw unnecessary attention to the writer (*I*), the reader (*you*), or the essay/project itself?

- What overused terms (clichés) could be substituted with more precise or descriptive words?

- What obvious statements and wordy phrases could be omitted?

Getting Specific

- What nouns could be made more specific? (Scan for broad and unhelpful terms such as *people, technology, society, things, today, children, men, women, adults, students,* and so on.)

- What verbs could be more active? (Scan for linking verbs such as *is, am, are, was, were, be,* or *being.*)

Experimenting with Patterns

- Where might a series of phrases or clauses help to intensify an idea?

- How could a repeating pattern (in a concluding or introductory paragraph, for instance) intensify the reading experience?

- Where might I try an absolute phrase or stylistic fragment?

Index

H

Hasty generalizations, 261
"'Have It Your Way': Consumerism
   Invades Education"
   (Benlow), 275–278, 290,
   528, 535, 548
Hawes, David, "Dog-Tied," 536
Heidecker, Cassie, "The Real,
   the Bad, and the Ugly,"
   133–137, 142–143, 145,
   147–149, 534–535, 539
"Hi, I'm a Digital Junkie, and I
   Suffer from Infomania"
   (Zomorodi), 367–369, 521
"Hive Talkin'" (Scollon), 240–244
Hollingsworth, Rebecca, "An
   Imperfect Reality," 190,
   197–200, 213, 216–218,
   522, 524, 556–557
Home, as point of contact
   for argumentative essays,
      246–247
   for essays analyzing concepts,
      139
Horton, Susan R., 123
"How I Lost the Junior Miss
   Pageant" (Bosley), 10–11,
   31–35, 46–48, 52, 520–
   521, 532, 540
Hudgens, Laura Hanby, "Your Kids
   Bored at School? Tell Them
   to Get Over It," 370–372,
   544
Humor
   subtext in, 175
   in voice, 550
Huxley, Aldous, *Brave New World*,
   223
Hyperbole
   definition of, 537
   in establishment of voice, 537

I

I (pronoun)
   avoiding unnecessary attention
      to, 561–562
   using, in establishment of voice,
      533–535
Ideas
   organization of (*See*
      Organization of ideas)
   sources of, 4–5, 7
   subordinate vs. main, 556
Illustration, definition of, 19
Images
   elements of, 208–210

   in essays explaining
      relationships, 91
   in observing essays, 121
   in photo essays, 362–363
   in remembering essays, 44
Images and videos, essays analyzing,
   188–221
   analysis in, 206–215
   point of contact in, 205–206
   reflection on, 220
   research for, 218–219
   revision of, 219–220
   rhetorical tools in, 217–219
   sample, 191–204
   thesis statements in, 215–217
Imperative mood, 546–547
"An Imperfect Reality"
   (Hollingsworth), 190,
   197–200, 213, 216–218,
   522, 524, 556–557
Implicit thesis statements, 49
"Important and Flawed" (Abdul-
   Jabbar), 305–309, 326
Indicative mood, 546–547
Informal evaluations, 299
Informative texts, 170
Intellectual agility, 8
Intellectual bridges
   between paragraphs, 522–523
   in radical thinking essays,
      419–420
Intended audience, 174
Intent, of authors, 185
Internal dialogues, 296
Internet. *See* Online sources;
   Websites
Interruption, avoiding unnecessary,
   557
Intertextuality
   definition of, 174, 213
   in images and videos, 213
   in written texts, 174–175
Interviews
   in APA style documentation,
      503
   conducting, 430–432
   integrating into writing,
      431–432
   in MLA style documentation,
      488
In-text citations
   in APA style, 496–498
   in MLA style, 477–479
Introductions, organization of ideas
   in, 519–522
Invention
   definition of, 13
   fear of ongoing, 357–358

   questions in, 5–6
   in rhetoric, 7
   writing in, 4–5, 7
Invention Questions
   for argumentative essays, 247,
      249
   for essays analyzing concepts,
      141
   for essays analyzing images and
      videos, 210, 213, 214
   for essays explaining
      relationships, 78–79
   for essays proposing solutions,
      380
   for essays searching for causes,
      353
   for evaluative essays, 319–320,
      326–327
   how to use, 13, 16
   introduction to, 5–6
   for observing essays, 112,
      114–115
   in radical thinking essays, 412
   for remembering essays, 44, 46
   for responses to arguments,
      286, 288
   for textual analysis, 176
Invention Workshops
   on argumentative essays, 248–
      249, 259
   on essays analyzing concepts,
      142, 148
   on essays analyzing images and
      videos, 214–215
   on essays explaining
      relationships, 81–82
   on essays proposing solutions,
      382–383
   on essays searching for causes,
      353–354, 360
   on evaluative essays, 322–323,
      328
   how to use, 13–15
   on observing essays, 115
   on remembering essays, 47
   on responses to arguments, 289
   videos of, 57
Invisible Man (Ellison), 299
"Is Google Making Us Stupid?"
   (Carr), 335–342, 359, 521,
   528

J

Journals
   in APA style documentation,
      500, 502
   vs. magazines, 443, 516

Reflection (*Continued*)
on radical thinking essays, 424
on remembering essays, 56–57
on responses to arguments, 296
on textual analysis, 185–186
Relational clusters, 78
Relationships, essays explaining,
    58–91
analysis in, 78–82
point of contact in, 76–78
public resonance in, 82–83
reflection on, 90
revision of, 88–90
rhetorical tools in, 86–88
sample, 61–75
thesis statements in, 84–86
Relevance, of sources, 455, 460
Reliability, of sources, 455–456,
    461
Remembering essays, 24–57
analysis in, 43, 44–47
delivery in, 43–44
learning from, 25–26
literacy narratives as, 43–44
point of contact in, 41–44
public resonance in, 43, 48
reflection on, 56–57
revision of, 44, 54–56
rhetorical tools in, 51–53
sample, 27–40
thesis statements in, 43, 49–51
Repetition, of clause or phrase
    patterns, 567–568
Research, 20–21. *See also* Outside
    sources
for argumentative essays, 251,
    264
for essays analyzing images and
    videos, 218–219
for essays proposing solutions,
    380–381
for essays searching for causes,
    355
for evaluative essays, 323
field/primary, 432
vs. mesearch, 421–422
for radical thinking essays,
    421–422, 424
for responses to arguments, 289,
    295–296
steps of, 20–21
Resonance. *See* Public Resonance
Responding to arguments. *See*
    Argument(s), responses to
Revelatory thesis statements,
    17–18
in argumentative essays,
    252–253

in remembering essays,
    49–50
"Reverence for Food" (Schofield),
    525
Revision, 19–20. *See also* Thesis
    statement revision
of argumentative essays,
    263–264
of essays analyzing concepts,
    149–150
of essays analyzing images and
    videos, 219–220
of essays explaining
    relationships, 88–90
of essays proposing solutions,
    387–388
of essays searching for causes,
    360–361
of evaluative essays, 328–329
of observing essays, 119–121
of radical thinking essays,
    422–424
of remembering essays, 44,
    54–56
of responses to arguments,
    294–296
of textual analysis, 186–187
Rhetoric
in ancient Greece, 7
definition of, 7
reading to learn about, 8–12
Rhetorical analysis
definition of, 389
of essays proposing solutions,
    389
Rhetorical tools
in advertisements, 190
analyzing, 171–173
in argumentative essays,
    172–173, 254–262
definition of, 9, 18
in essays analyzing concepts,
    146–149
in essays analyzing images and
    videos, 217–219
in essays explaining
    relationships, 86–88
in essays proposing solutions,
    384–386
in essays searching for causes,
    358–360
in evaluative essays, 325–327
how to use sections on, 13,
    18–19
in observing essays, 117–119
in radical thinking essays,
    418–421
reading to learn about, 9–12

in remembering essays, 51–53
in responses to arguments,
    292–294
in textual analysis, 171–173,
    179–185
types of, 18–19
"Rise of the Image Culture"
    (Thoman), 190, 191–196,
    521–524, 558–559
Rogerian argument, 544–545
Rogers, Carl, 544
Rowling, J. K., 279–282

S

Sample essays, how to use, 12
Santayana, George, 25
Scenarios
in argumentative essays, 255
definition of, 19, 172, 255
in essays analyzing concepts,
    148
in introductions, 520
in textual analysis, 172
Schofield, Rachel, "Reverence for
    Food," 525
School, as point of contact
for argumentative essays, 245
for essays analyzing concepts,
    139
for essays proposing solutions,
    377–378
for essays searching for causes,
    351
for remembering essays, 42
Schwind-Pawlak, Jennifer, "The
    Thrill of Victory . . . The
    Agony of Parents," 36–40,
    52
Scollon, Teresa, "Hive Talkin',"
    240–244
Scope, of thesis statements, 252
Scott, Justin, 534–535
Searching for causes. *See* Causes,
    essays searching for
"Selling Manure" (Campbell),
    27–30
Sentences
combining, 555
length of, in vitality, 556–557
length of, in voice, 539–540
placement of quotations in,
    471–472
stylistic fragments of, 569–570
verb moods of, 546–547
vitality of (*See* Vitality)
Series, of words, 568
Shedroff, Nathan, 151